ASP.NET 2.0 Instant Results

Imar Spaanjaars, Paul Wilton, and Shawn Livermore

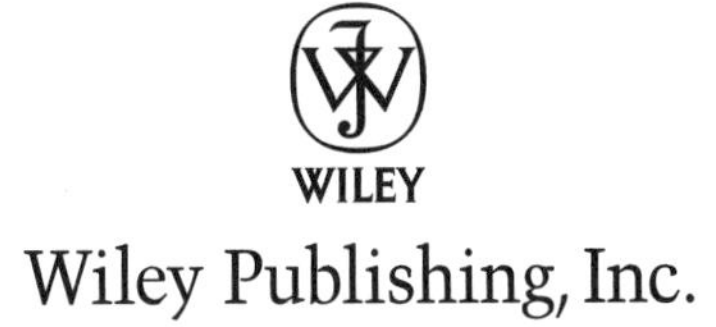

Wiley Publishing, Inc.

ASP.NET 2.0 Instant Results

Published by
Wiley Publishing, Inc.
10475 Crosspoint Boulevard
Indianapolis, IN 46256
www.wiley.com

Published simultaneously in Canada

ISBN-13: 978-0-471-74951-6
ISBN-10: 0-471-74951-6

Manufactured in the United States of America

10 9 8 7 6 5 4 3 2 1

1MA/QS/QT/QW/IN

For general information on our other products and services or to obtain technical support, please contact our Customer Care Department within the U.S. at (800) 762-2974, outside the U.S. at (317) 572-3993 or fax (317) 572-4002.

Wiley also publishes its books in a variety of electronic formats. Some content that appears in print may not be available in electronic books.

Library of Congress Catalog Number: 2006003345

Wiley also publishes its books in a variety of electronic formats. Some content that appears in print may not be available in electronic books.

About the Authors

Imar Spaanjaars graduated in Leisure Management from the Leisure Management School in the Netherlands, but quickly changed his career path into the Internet world. After working for a large corporation and doing some freelance work, he is now working for Design IT, an IT company in the Netherlands that specializes in Internet and Intranet applications built with Microsoft technologies like ASP.NET. As a software designer and lead developer, he's responsible for designing, building, and implementing medium- to large-scale e-commerce web sites and portals.

Before this book on ASP.NET 2.0, Imar wrote two books about Macromedia Dreamweaver, called *Beginning Dreamweaver MX* and *Beginning Dreamweaver MX 2004*, both published under the Wrox brand. Imar is also one of the top contributors to the Wrox Community Forums at `http://p2p.wrox.com` where he shares his knowledge with fellow programmers.

Imar lives in Utrecht, the Netherlands, together with his girlfriend Fleur. You can contact him through his web site at `http://imar.spaanjaars.com`.

Paul Wilton got an initial start as a Visual Basic applications programmer at the Ministry of Defense in the UK before finding himself pulled into the Net. Having joined an Internet development company, he spent three years helping create Internet solutions. He's now running his own company developing online holiday property reservation systems.

Paul's main skills are in developing web front ends using DHTML, JavaScript, and VBScript as well as back-end solutions with ASP, ASP.NET, Visual Basic, and SQL Server.

Shawn Livermore (MCAD, MCSD, PMP) [shawnlivermore.blogspot.com] has been architecting and developing Microsoft-based solutions for nearly a decade. Shawn consults as an architect for Fortune 500 clientele, leveraging time-proven methodologies and exceptional communications, within highly visible projects. His range of technical competence stretches across platforms, but specializes within Microsoft .NET development and server-based products such as Biztalk and SQL Server, among others. His experience implementing enterprise-level Microsoft solutions is extensive and has led to successful business ventures with numerous firms. Shawn lives in the Southern California area with his beautiful wife Shantell and amazing daughter Elexzandreia.

Credits

Senior Acquisitions Editor
Jim Minatel

Development Editor
Brian Herrmann

Technical Editors
Dan Maharry and Scott Spradlin

Production Editor
Felicia Robinson

Copy Editor
Kim Cofer

Editorial Manager
Mary Beth Wakefield

Production Manager
Tim Tate

Vice President and Executive Group Publisher
Richard Swadley

Vice President and Executive Publisher
Joseph B. Wikert

Project Coordinator
Michael Kruzil

Graphics and Production Specialists
Lauren Goddard
Brooke Graczyk
Denny Hager
Joyce Haughey
Barbara Moore
Alicia B. South

Quality Control Technicians
Jessica Kramer
Brian Walls

Media Development Project Supervisor
Shannon Walters

Media Development Specialist
Steven Kudirka

Proofreading and Indexing
TECHBOOKS Production Services

Imar Spaanjaars: To Fleur - The love of my life.

Shawn Livermore: This book is dedicated to my Lord Jesus, who has mastered all things, much less a simple piece of software.

Paul Wilton: With lots of love to my darling Beci, who now the book's finished will get to see me for more than 10 minutes a week.

Acknowledgments

Imar Spaanjaars

Writing a book like this one is definitely not a solo project. During development of this book I got a lot of support from many people who helped me to stay focused and get inspiration. I would like to give all of you that helped a big thanks! While I can't possibly thank all of you here personally, there are a few people I'd like to thank in particular.

First of all I'd like to thank the people at Wiley for working with me on this project, with Brian Herrmann in particular for his efforts during the editorial process.

I would also like to thank Anne Ward for helping me with the designs of some of the applications featured in this book.

A big thanks goes out to the people at Design IT for their participation in my "hallway usability tests" that I randomly brought up in the office. Thanks guys! It's always good to have a few extra sets of eyes.

My appreciation also goes out to my two good friends René and Joost for their friendship. Looking forward to spending more time with you again.

Last but certainly not least, I would like to thank my girlfriend Fleur for her support during this project. I know it wasn't always fun when I disappeared in my home office for hours, but you were a great supporter and motivator nonetheless.

Imar Spaanjaars contributed Chapters 5, 6, and 8–12 to this book.

Acknowledgments

Paul Wilton

I'd like to say a very big thank you to Brian Herrmann, who has been a great editor to work with and has done amazing work on the book. He manages to maintain professionalism and sense of humor even when faced with another of my "just a few more days and I'll get the chapter to you" e-mails!

Thanks also to Jim Minatel for making this book happen, and also his support in what has for me been a challenging and difficult year.

Many thanks to everyone who has supported and encouraged me over the many years of writing books. Your help will always be remembered.

Finally, pats and treats to my German Shepherd Katie, who does an excellent job warding off disturbances from door-to-door salespeople.

Paul Wilton contributed Chapter 1 to this book.

Shawn Livermore

I thank my gorgeous wife Shantell, who is a truly beautiful and caring person, and has always encouraged me to shoot higher. Your love has changed my life. Thanks for supporting me through the long hours and boring computer nerd conversations. I owe you a pair of Gucci shoes. And of course, to my daughter Elexzandreia, who is a gift from heaven. You have taught me so much about life and have made me want to be a better dad. I love you "134,000."

Shawn Livermore contributed the Introduction and Chapters 2–4 and 7 to this book.

Contents

Introduction

For all of the programmers out there who just love a good .NET book to get them up and running fast in a new technology, you are in luck. *ASP.NET 2.0 Instant Results* is the perfect fast-track book for the programmer or architect to pick up on the new features and tools available in the 2.0 version of ASP.NET. Sure, you could read a traditional book, and spend countless hours guessing what you really have to do in order to get the software to work properly—or you could simply use the materials in the following chapters to understand and test the example projects provided in a short amount of time.

Some of the compelling reasons to produce this book are tied to the incredible reviews about the 2.0 version of the .NET Framework, along with the development advancements seen within the Visual Studio 2005 environment. ASP.NET 2.0 is a hot technology, poised for rapid adoption and growth compared to the 1.1 version, thanks to some exciting features that focus on providing web developers with the tools they need for the majority of their development projects. These must-haves include the new login controls, which enable developers to quickly drag and drop a set of controls on the design surface, set a few properties, and have a near-instantaneous security system. Another new feature is the enhancements to the design-time user interfaces for binding data controls. A wizard-like aspect surrounds most of the controls, which are in fact very easy to operate. Other exciting controls exist, but they are not the end of the story. A vast amount of changes has been planted within ASP.NET 2.0, involving the architecture of sites, speed of page requests, management of stateful information, and efficiency of development overall. Sound too good to be true? Well, if you are taking on ASP.NET 2.0, your programming effort just got a whole lot easier.

Who This Book Is For

This book is ideal for any programmer with .NET experience to learn the new technology. Anyone who has experimented with .NET 1.1 or implemented full-scale solutions for their employers would be a perfect candidate to easily absorb all of the materials within this book. You should have some general understanding of how a basic database works, with experience in developing software to access a database object such as a stored procedure.

For a beginner, you may want to skip over to Chapter 7. This chapter is very lightweight in design, aimed at providing a simplistic approach to a very common web site style. That is, the family photo album web site. This chapter explains the basic concepts of sharing photos within a web site and adding and deleting photos. It would be a great way to catch the basic concepts early on, before diving into more complicated site designs and concepts within the book.

The best approach for advanced readers is to find a chapter that interests you, and skip right to it. No ground is lost by moving through this reference book of geniuses (shameless plug). It is meant to be a helpful guide and a reference quick-start for diving deep into working code, in an attempt to learn it rapidly. Each chapter is almost completely self-contained and is a completely different implementation of various overlapping features. Some chapters may repeat a concept for a redundant and thorough learning process, whereas others may divert from the consistent features and usages in order to provide a broad approach to the site's unique requirements. In some cases, where you require a full explanation of a topic that has previously been discussed, you'll find a reference to an earlier chapter that describes that topic in great detail.

What This Book Covers

The book contains a dozen projects you can use right off the disk with minimal setup needed. Each project has step-by-step instructions on installing the source code to your local machine. The goal of the chapter and accompanying project code is to enable you to understand and quickly modify the project to enhance its capabilities or to learn how to implement some of the features it uses within different situations. Through the repeated studying of simple project walkthroughs and hands-on experimentation, you learn more about the design and creation of full projects in the 2.0 version of ASP.NET. The book references some of the advancements since the older version 1.1, but not to any level of detail. Most of the logic and material is gauged toward explaining the deeper concepts within the 2.0 version in its entirety.

How This Book Is Structured

This book is designed in similar fashion to other Wrox Press Instant Results titles, in that it serves as more of a reference manual of usable and instructional source projects, as compared to a traditional end-to-end book. This is because most programmers do not need to absorb all of the available information on a particular subject in a traditional fashion. Many times, programmers are looking to find the answers within the code, and then read content or material on it as an afterthought. This book aims to satisfy this tendency, but not at the expense of providing quality information and useful instruction at the same time. Thus, the topics and concepts that must be learned are taught from basic to advanced forms, across all of the 12 projects, with overlapping tools and features to drive home the concepts.

The structure of each chapter follows the following general pattern:

- Overview—What does this project do?
- Design
- Code and code explanation
- Setting up the project

Each project is designed with reusable controls, class files, and/or modules. Classes and noteworthy project files are highlighted and analyzed with sufficient information in each chapter to make the research effort as easy as possible.

The chapters of the book, and consequently the source projects used within the book, are as follows:

- Chapter 1: The Online Diary and Organizer
- Chapter 2: Wrox File Share
- Chapter 3: Wrox Chat Server
- Chapter 4: Wrox Survey Engine
- Chapter 5: Wrox CMS
- Chapter 6: Wrox Blog
- Chapter 7: Wrox Photo Album
- Chapter 8: Customer Support Site

- Chapter 9: Wrox WebShop
- Chapter 10: Appointment Booking System
- Chapter 11: Greeting Cards
- Chapter 12: The Bug Base

The easier chapters to pick up and learn might include Chapters 4, 7, and 9, whereas Chapters 3, 10, and 12 all provide advanced topics you will be sure to learn from.

At the end of your studies, you will be able to create your own site from scratch, implementing security, a structured architecture, profiles, new and more efficient data-bound controls, object-based data binding, and many more features.

What You Need to Use This Book

The basic software needed to use this book includes Windows 2000 Professional or Windows XP Professional and an installation of Visual Web Developer Express Edition with SQL Server 2005 Express Edition. Visual Web Developer Express Edition is available from `http://msdn.microsoft.com/vstudio/express/vwd/`. As an alternative to Visual Web Developer Express Edition, you can use one of the full versions of Visual Studio 2005, including the Standard and Professional editions. It is understood with the development tools mentioned that the .NET Framework version 2.0 is required to run the project samples as well.

Source Code

As you work through the examples in this book, you may choose either to type in all the code manually or to use the source code files that accompany the book. All of the source code used in this book is available on the companion CD-ROM and for download at `www.wrox.com`. Once at the site, simply locate the book's title (either by using the Search box or by using one of the title lists) and click the Download Code link on the book's detail page to obtain all the source code for the book.

Because many books have similar titles, you may find it easiest to search by ISBN; this book's ISBN is 0-471-74951-6 (changing to 978-0-471-74951-6 as the new industry-wide 13-digit ISBN numbering system is phased in by January 2007).

Once you download the code, just decompress it with your favorite compression tool. Alternatively, you can go to the main Wrox code download page at `www.wrox.com/dynamic/books/download.aspx` to see the code available for this book and all other Wrox books.

Errata

We make every effort to ensure that there are no errors in the text or in the code. However, no one is perfect, and mistakes do occur. If you find an error in one of our books, like a spelling mistake or faulty piece of code, we would be very grateful for your feedback. By sending in errata you may save another reader hours of frustration and at the same time you will be helping us provide even higher quality information.

To find the errata page for this book, go to `www.wrox.com` and locate the title using the Search box or one of the title lists. Then, on the book details page, click the Book Errata link. On this page you can view all errata that has been submitted for this book and posted by Wrox editors. A complete book list including links to each book's errata is also available at `www.wrox.com/misc-pages/booklist.shtml`.

If you don't spot "your" error on the Book Errata page, go to `www.wrox.com/contact/techsupport.shtml` and complete the form there to send us the error you have found. We'll check the information and, if appropriate, post a message to the book's errata page and fix the problem in subsequent editions of the book.

p2p.wrox.com

For author and peer discussion, join the P2P forums at `p2p.wrox.com`. The forums are a Web-based system for you to post messages relating to Wrox books and related technologies and interact with other readers and technology users. The forums offer a subscription feature to e-mail you topics of interest of your choosing when new posts are made to the forums. Wrox authors, editors, other industry experts, and your fellow readers are present on these forums.

At `http://p2p.wrox.com` you will find a number of different forums that will help you not only as you read this book, but also as you develop your own applications. To join the forums, just follow these steps:

1. Go to `p2p.wrox.com` and click the Register Now link.
2. Read the terms of use and click Agree.
3. Complete the required information to join as well as any optional information you wish to provide and click Submit.
4. You will receive an e-mail with information describing how to verify your account and complete the joining process.

You can read messages in the forums without joining P2P but in order to post your own messages, you must join.

Once you join, you can post new messages and respond to messages other users post. You'll find this book's own forum under the Books category that is available from the homepage or by clicking View All Forums on the menu on the left. You can read messages at any time on the Web. If you would like to have new messages from a particular forum e-mailed to you, click the Subscribe to this Forum icon by the forum name in the forum listing.

For more information about how to use the Wrox P2P, be sure to read the P2P FAQs for answers to questions about how the forum software works as well as many common questions specific to P2P and Wrox books. To read the FAQs, click the FAQ link on any P2P page.

The Online Diary and Organizer

By the end of this chapter you'll have created an online diary, organizer, and contacts manager. So what exactly does the online diary and organizer do? Using a calendar-based interface it allows you to add, delete, and edit a diary entry for any day. It also allows you to create events: for example, to keep a note of your rich Uncle Bob's birthday — wouldn't want to forget that, would you? It's not just limited to birthdays, but any event: meetings, appointments, and so on.

The system has a basic username and password logon system, so that only you and no one else can view your own diary. This is what differentiates it from a blog. This system is a private diary and contacts manager — a place to put all those thoughts and comments you'd rather not have the world see. Unlike a blog, where you want the world to see it!

This whole project demonstrates the power of ASP.NET 2.0 and how easy it makes creating projects like this. Gone are the days of hundreds of lines of code to do security logons, create new users, and so on. This chapter employs the new security components of ASP.NET 2.0 to show just how easy it is to create fun, exciting, and useful projects.

The first section takes you through using the diary and its main screens. Then, the "Design of the Online Diary" section walks you through an overview of the system's design. After that you get into the nuts and bolts of the system and how it all hangs together. In the final section, you set up the diary.

Using the Online Diary

Each user has his or her own online diary; to access it requires logging on. Enter username `user5` with the password `123!abc` to log in as a test user. The log on screen is shown in Figure 1-1.

Although the screenshot may suggest lots of controls and lots of code to make the security function, in fact with the new security controls in ASP.NET 2.0 it's very easy and not much work at all.

If you have not registered, a link will take you to the Sign Up page, depicted in Figure 1-2.

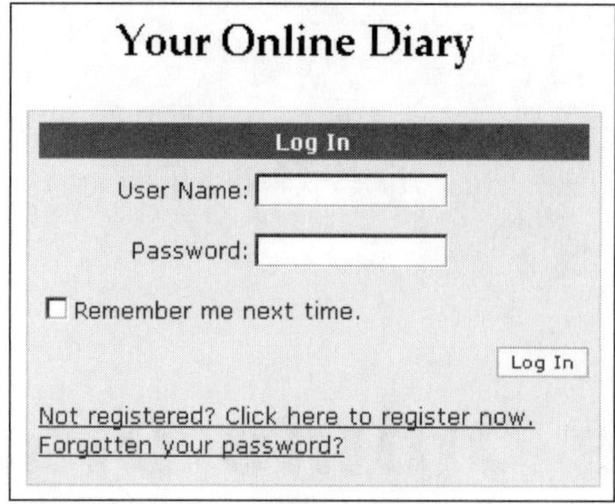

Figure 1-1

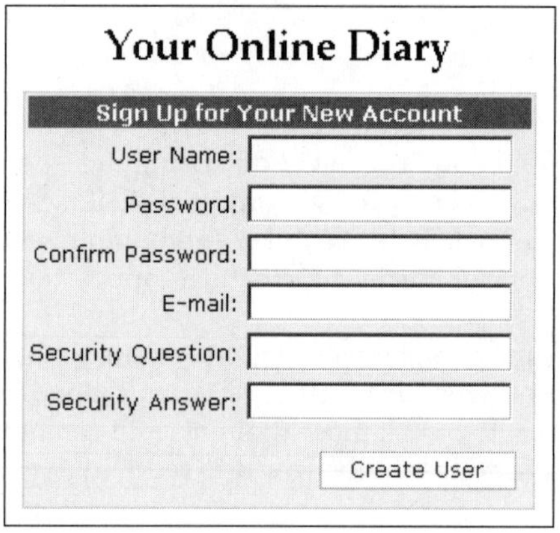

Figure 1-2

This shows another of the new security controls in ASP.NET 2.0; creating a registration process is now just a matter of adding a control to a form!

If you've forgotten your password, you can click the Forgotten Your Password? link, which directs you to the Password Reminder wizard pages (see Figure 1-3).

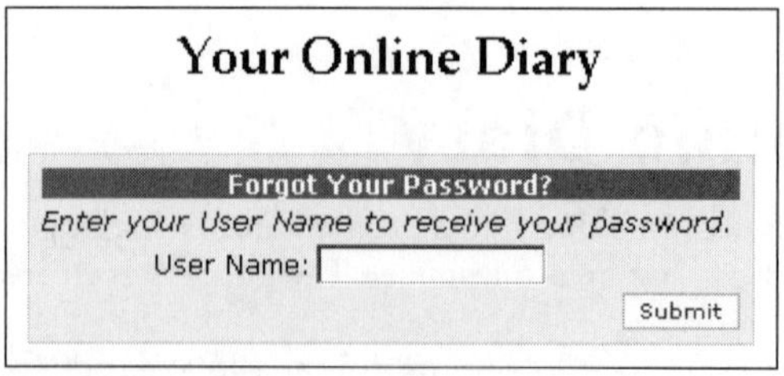

Figure 1-3

Having logged on, you arrive at the main diary page, as displayed in Figure 1-4.

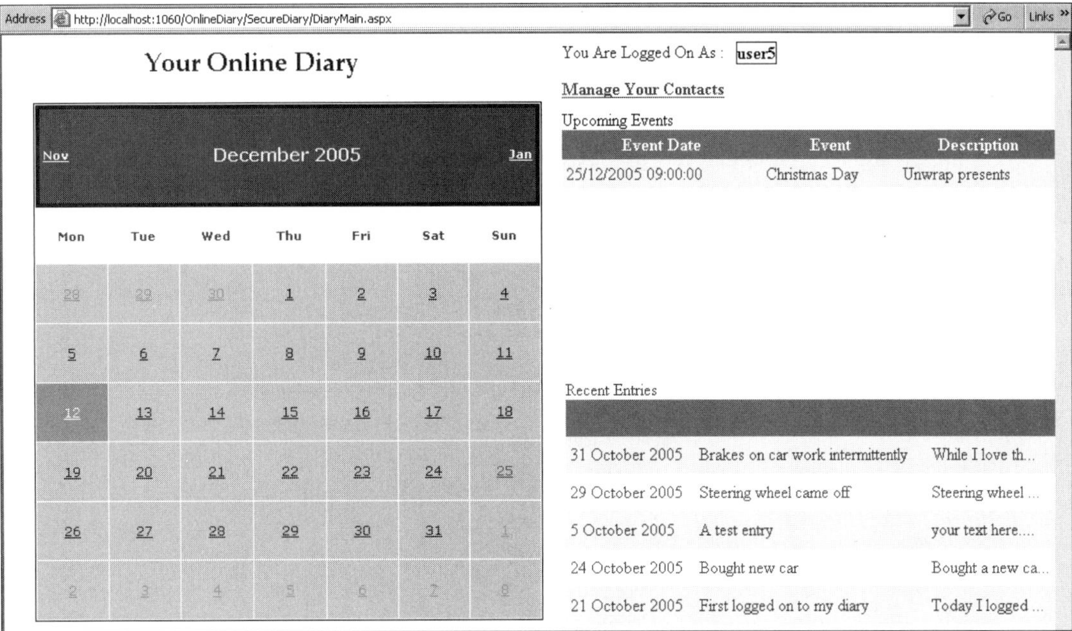

Figure 1-4

On this page you see a monthly calendar. Days with diary entries are marked with a blue background. Days with events are marked in red text. Notice also on the right that upcoming events are highlighted, as are recent diary entries.

Clicking on a day moves you through to the area where you can enter your diary entry for that day; and add, edit, and delete events (see Figure 1-5).

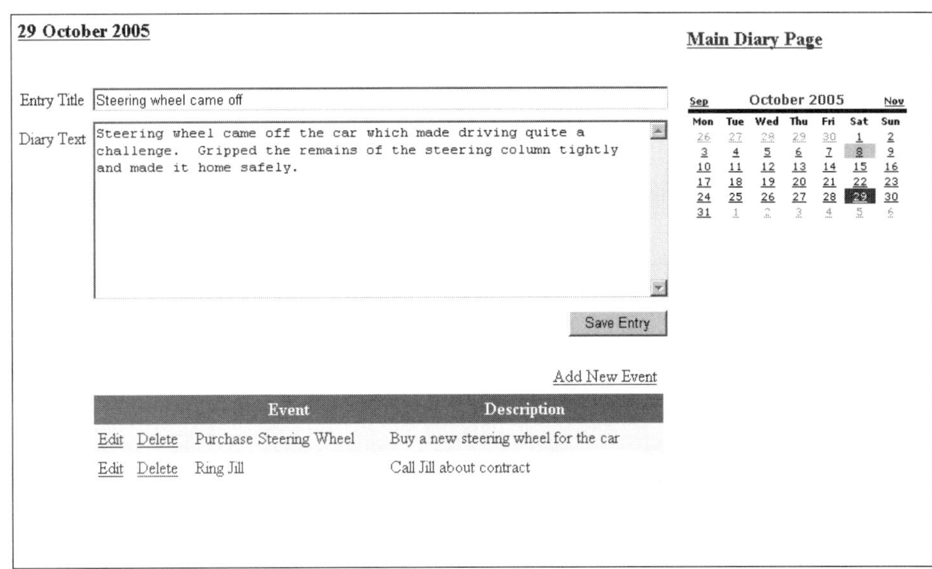

Figure 1-5

You can also navigate your diary from here via the small calendar to the right.

Adding a diary entry simply involves typing in the Entry Title and Diary Text boxes and clicking the Save Entry button.

Events happening on a particular day are listed in the Events table at the bottom-left of Figure 1-5. You can edit and delete events, or click the Add New Event link to add a new event. The Edit and Add event pages are almost identical in look. An example of the Edit Event page is shown in Figure 1-6.

22 October 2005

Edit Event

Event Name

Buy shopping

Event Description

Buy loaf of bread

Start Time

14 10

Event Duration (minutes)

30

Save Event

Figure 1-6

In the Edit Event page, you can set the event's name, include a brief description, what time the event starts, and how long it lasts.

Returning to the main diary page (refer to Figure 1-4) you'll see a Manage Your Contacts link, as shown in Figure 1-7.

Figure 1-7

Clicking that link takes you to the Contact Management page (see Figure 1-8).

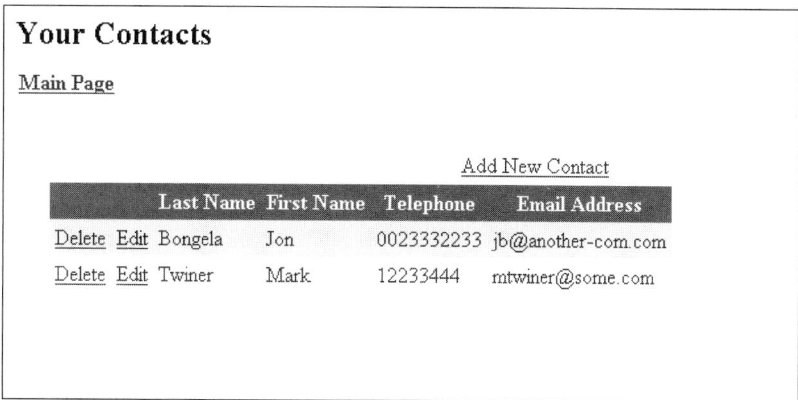

Figure 1-8

Here you see a list of your contacts, which you can edit and delete by clicking the appropriate link in the Contacts table. You can also add a new contact by clicking the Add New Contact link, which takes you to the New Contact page (no surprise there!), shown in Figure 1-9.

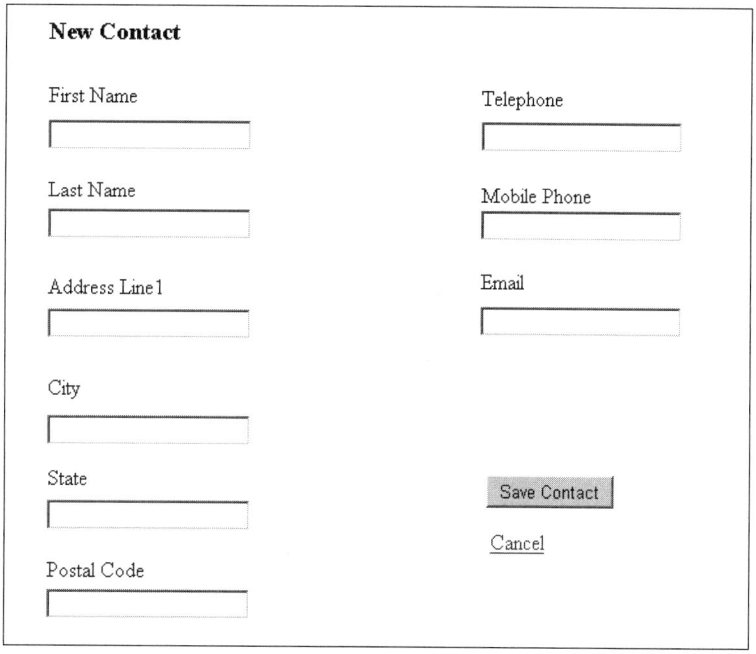

New Contact

First Name

Telephone

Last Name

Mobile Phone

Address Line1

Email

City

State

Save Contact

Cancel

Postal Code

Figure 1-9

Currently the contacts functionality is fairly simple, with such things as linking events and contacts and automatically e-mailing contacts to remind them of an event.

So you've seen what the Online Diary does, now you can look at how it does it! The next section describes the overall design and how the system hangs together. You get a high-level tour of the database setup and each of the classes the system uses.

Design of the Online Diary

The diary system is split into the common three-layer architecture. All data and direct data modifying code are in the data layer, a combination of database tables and stored procedures. The data access layer is examined next.

Above the data access layer is the business layer providing all the rules and intelligence of the system. The business layer has been coded as seven classes, which you tour through shortly.

Finally, the bit the user sees is the presentation layer, consisting of a number of .aspx files that utilize the business and data access layers to create the diary's interface. This layer is discussed in the last part of this section.

The Data Access Layer

The Online Diary uses a SQL Server 2005 Express database. However, there's no reason why this couldn't be changed to work with other databases. If the database supports stored procedures, then in theory all that's needed is a change of connection string and creation of stored procedures matching those in the current SQL Server database. If the database doesn't support stored procedures—for example, MS Access—changes to class code would be necessary but not difficult.

Figure 1-10 shows the tables in the Online Diary database (DiaryDB).

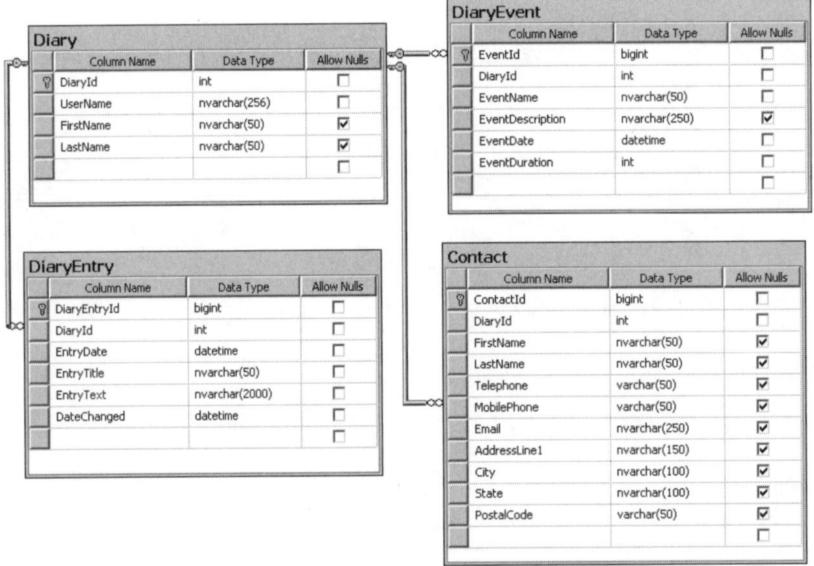

Figure 1-10

The default database created using the new membership features of ASP.NET 2.0 is also used. The database is a SQL Server Express database and not modified from the one created by Visual Studio Express. However, to link the log on and the diary details, the UserName field in the DiaryDB database takes its value originally from the membership database. You go through this in more detail shortly. Membership details are contained in the ASPNETDB database that Visual Web Developer Express creates for you. Although it contains quite a few tables, you never access them via the code in this project. It's accessed exclusively by the new `Login` controls — it does all the hard work behind the scenes!

This project only makes use of the aspnet_Users table, shown in Figure 1-11, to provide log on security checking and provide a username for the main DiaryDB. You may well want to extend the membership database to include extra functionality such as personalizing the user experience or providing different levels of membership (admin, user, operator), among other things.

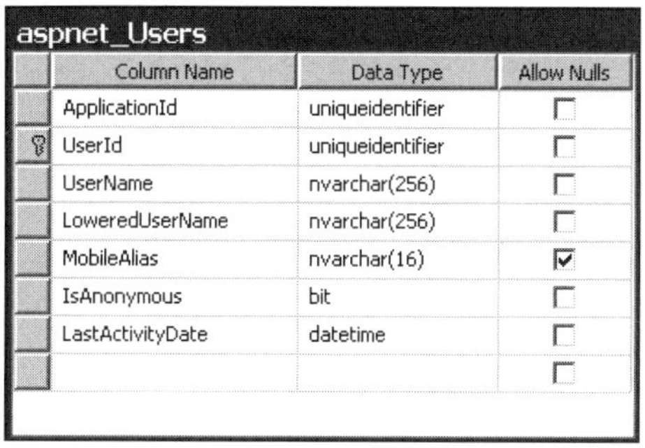

aspnet_Users

Column Name	Data Type	Allow Nulls
ApplicationId	uniqueidentifier	☐
UserId	uniqueidentifier	☐
UserName	nvarchar(256)	☐
LoweredUserName	nvarchar(256)	☐
MobileAlias	nvarchar(16)	☑
IsAnonymous	bit	☐
LastActivityDate	datetime	☐
		☐

Figure 1-11

The tables of the main Online Diary database and their roles are listed in the following table:

Table Name	Description
Diary	Contains details of all Online Diary users, their DiaryId, and names.
DiaryEntry	Contains all the diary entries for all diary users.
DiaryEvent	Contains all the diary events for all diary users.
Contact	Holds the details of all contacts for the diaries.

The key that links all of the tables together is the DiaryId field. It's the primary key field in the Diary table and a foreign key field in all the other tables. Why not use the UserName field? Basically speed — it's easier and therefore faster for the database to do joins and searches on an integer field than it is on character-based fields.

All access to the database is via a stored procedure. The naming convention is simply as follows:

```
ActionThingThisActionRelatesTo
```

Consider this very simple stored procedure:

```
DeleteContact
```

Rather unsurprisingly, `DeleteContact` deletes a contact from the database. The naming convention means the purpose of each stored procedure doesn't need a lot of explanation. As the code is discussed, you look at the stored procedures in more detail where necessary.

The Business Layer

The business layer is organized into seven classes. The four main classes are as follows:

- `OnlineDiary`
- `DiaryEntry`
- `DiaryEvent`
- `Contact`

These classes do most of the work of temporarily holding diary-related data and retrieving and storing it in the database. There are also three collection classes. The first order of business is the `OnlineDiary` class.

The OnlineDiary Class

This class contains only two shared public methods, detailed in the following table:

Method	Return Type	Description
`InsertDiary(ByVal UserName As String, ByVal FirstName As String, ByVal LastName As String)`	None	Inserts a new diary user into the OnlineDiary database.
`GetDiaryIdFromUserName(ByVal UserName As String)`	Integer	Looks up the UserName in the database and returns the associated DiaryId.

The purpose of the `OnlineDiary` class is simply to provide a couple of handy shared methods relating to an online diary as a whole. It could also be used to expand the diary system and add new functionality that relates to the overall diary system, rather than a specific part such as contacts.

The Contact Class

The `Contact` class objectifies a single contact—a person or thing for which you want to store contact information. It encapsulates everything to do with contacts, including the storing and retrieving of contact information in the database.

It has two constructors, outlined in the following table:

Constructor	Description
`New(ByVal Diaryid as Integer)`	Creates a new `Contact` object with all properties set to their default values.
`New(ByVal ContactId As Long)`	Creates a new `Contact` object with its properties retrieved from the database using the argument `ContactId`.

Having created a `Contact` object, saving it involves simply calling the `Save()` method. The class will work out whether it's a new contact that needs to be inserted into the database, or an existing one that needs to be updated. In addition to the `Save()` method, the `Contacts` class contains two `Delete()` methods, as well as two `GetContacts()` methods, all of which are outlined in the following table:

Method	Return Type	Description
`Save()`	None	Saves a fully populated `Contact` object. If it's a new contact, `Save()` calls `InsertNewContact` sub, and the details are inserted into the database. The new ContactId is returned from the database and entered into `mContactId`. If the contact already exists in the database, `Save()` calls `UpdateContact`, which updates the database values with those in the `Contact` object.
`DeleteContact()`	None	Deletes from the database the `Contact` object with ContactId equal to `mContactId` of the object. `Contact` object's values are re-initialized to their defaults.
`DeleteContact(ByVal ContactId As Long)`	None	Shared method that deletes the `Contact` object from the database with a ContactId value equal to the `ContactId` argument of the method.
`GetContactsByFirstLetter(ByVal DiaryId As Integer,Optional ByVal FirstLetterOfSurname As Char)`	`SqlDataReader`	Shared method that returns a `SqlDataReader`object populated with a list of contacts whose surname's first letter matches the `FirstLetterOfSurname` argument.This argument is optional; if left off, all `Contact` objects regardless of surname's first letter are included in the DataSet's rows.

Table continued on following page

Method	Return Type	Description
`GetContactsByFirstLetterAsCollection(ByVal DiaryId As Integer, Optional ByVal FirstLetterOfSurname As Char)`	`SqlDataReader`	Shared method that returns a `ContactCollection` object populated with `Contact` objects whose surname's first letter matches the `FirstLetterOfSurname` argument. This argument is optional; if left off, all `Contact` objects regardless of surname's first letter are included in the DataSet's rows.

Finally, the `Contact` class contains the following properties:

Property	Type	Description
`ContactId`	`Long`	Each contact is represented by a unique ID. The ID is autogenerated by the Contact table in the database whenever a new contact is inserted.
`FirstName`	`String`	Contact's first name.
`LastName`	`String`	Contact's surname.
`Email`	`String`	Contact's e-mail address.
`Telephone`	`String`	Contact's telephone number.
`MobilePhone`	`String`	Contact's mobile phone number.
`AddressLine1`	`String`	Contact's house name and street address.
`City`	`String`	Contact's city of residence.
`State`	`String`	Contact's state.
`PostalCode`	`String`	Contact's zip or postal code.

The ContactCollection Class

The `ContactCollection` class inherits from the `System.Collections.CollectionBase` class. The `ContactCollection` class's purpose is simply to store a collection of `Contact` objects. This class gets extensive use in the next chapter, when you create a contacts organizer.

The `ContactCollection` class has only one property:

Property	Type	Description
`Item(ByVal Index As Integer)`	`Integer`	Returns the `Contact` object stored at the position in index in the collection.

The `ContactCollection` class's public methods are as follows:

Method	Return Type	Description
`Add(ByVal NewContact As Contact)`	None	Adds a `Contact` object to the collection held by the `ContactCollection` object.
`Add(ByVal ContactId As Long)`	None	Creates a new `Contact` object. `ContactId` is passed to the `Contact` object's constructor to ensure it's populated with the contact's details from the database. The new `Contact` object is then added to the collection maintained by the `ContactCollection` object.
`Remove(ByVal Index as Integer)`	None	Removes the `Contact` object from the collection at the specified index.

That deals with the `Contact` classes; now take a look at the two classes dealing with diary entries.

The DiaryEntry Class

The `DiaryEntry` class objectifies a single entry in a diary. It encapsulates everything to do with diary entries, including creating, updating, and retrieving diary entry data. It handles all the database access for diary entries.

It has three constructors, outlined in the following table:

Constructor	Description
`New(ByVal DiaryId as Integer)`	Creates a new `DiaryEntry` object with all properties set to their default values.
`New(ByVal DiaryEntryId As Long)`	Creates a new `DiaryEntry` object with its properties retrieved from the database using the argument `DiaryEntryId`.
`New(ByVal DiaryId AS Integer, ByVal EntryDate As Date)`	Creates a new `DiaryEntry` object with its properties retrieved from the database using the arguments `DiaryId` and `EntryDate`.

Having created a `DiaryEntry` object, saving it involves simply calling the `Save()` method. As with the `Save()` method of the `Contacts` class, the `DiaryEntry` class will work out whether it's a new diary entry that needs to be inserted into the database, or an existing entry that needs to be updated. As well as enabling retrieval of one diary entry's details, the `DiaryEntry` class provides additional methods for getting details of a number of diary entries as either a collection or as a DataSet by returning a `sqlDataReader` object. The methods of this class are explained in the following table:

Method	Return Type	Description
`Save()`	None	Saves a fully populated `DiaryEntry` object. If it's a new entry, `Save()` calls `InsertNewDiaryEntry` sub and the details are inserted in to the database. The new `DiaryEntryId` is returned from the database and entered in to `mDiaryEntryId`. If the entry already exists in the database, `Save()` calls `UpdateContact`, which updates the database values with those in the `DiaryEntry` object.
`GetDaysInMonthWithEntries(ByVal DiaryId As Integer, ByVal Month As Integer, ByVal Year As Integer)`	Boolean Array	Shared method that returns a Boolean array detailing which days have a diary entry associated with them. The array index matches with the day of the month (1 is the first of the month, 2 the second, and so on).
`GetDiaryEntriesByDate(ByVal DiaryId As Integer, ByVal FromDate As Date, ByVal ToDate As Date)`	`SqlDataReader`	Shared method that returns a `SQLDataReader` object populated with rows from the database detailing diary entries between the `FromDate` and `ToDate` arguments.

Method	Return Type	Description
`GetDiaryEntriesByDateAsCollection(ByVal DiaryId As Integer, ByVal FromDate As Date, ByVal ToDate As Date)`	`DiaryEntryCollection`	Creates a new `DiaryEntry Collection` object and populates it with `DiaryEntry` objects whose `EntryDate` is between the `FromDate` and `ToDate` arguments.
`GetDiaryEntriesRecentlyChanged(ByVal DiaryId As Integer)`	`SqlDataReader`	Returns a `SqlDataReader` containing a DataSet of diary entries recently created.

In addition to the constructors and methods, the `DiaryEntry` class contains the following properties:

Property	Type	Description
`EntryTitle`	`String`	Title for the day's diary entry.
`EntryText`	`String`	Text of the day's diary entry.
`EntryDate`	`Date`	Date the entry was posted.

The other class dealing with diary entries is the `DiaryEntryCollection` class, which is explained next.

The DiaryEntryCollection Class

The `DiaryEntryCollection` class inherits from the `System.Collections.CollectionBase` class. Its purpose is simply to store a collection of `DiaryEntry` objects.

This class contains only one property, described in the following table:

Property	Type	Description
`Item(ByVal Index As Integer)`	`Integer`	Returns the `DiaryEntry` object stored at the specified position in index in the collection.

Along with the `Item()` property, the `DiaryEntryCollection` class has three public methods:

Method	Return Type	Description
`Add(ByVal New DiaryEntry As DiaryEntry)`	None	Adds a `DiaryEntry` object to the collection held by the `DiaryEntryCollection` object.
`Add(ByVal DiaryEntryId As Long)`	None	Creates a new `DiaryEntry` object. `DiaryEntryId` is passed to the `DiaryEntry` object's constructor to ensure it's populated with the diary entry's details from the database. The new `DiaryEntry` object is then added to the collection maintained by the `DiaryEntryCollection` object.
`Remove(ByVal Index as Integer)`	None	Removes the `DiaryEntry` object from the collection at the specified index.

So far the classes dealing with contacts and diary entries have been discussed. The next section discusses the diary events.

The DiaryEvent Class

The `DiaryEvent` class objectifies a single entry in a diary. It encapsulates everything to do with diary entries, including creating, updating, and retrieving diary events data. It handles all the database access for diary events.

The `DiaryEvent` class has three constructors, outlined as follows:

Constructor	Description
`New(ByVal Diaryid as Integer)`	Creates a new `DiaryEvent` object with all properties set to their default values.
`New(ByVal EntryId As Long)`	Creates a new `DiaryEvent` object with its properties retrieved from the database using the argument `EventId`.
`New(ByVal DiaryId AS Integer, ByVal EventDate As Date)`	Creates a new `DiaryEvent` object with its properties retrieved from the database using a combination of the arguments `DiaryId` and `EventDate`.

Having created a `DiaryEvent` object, saving it involves simply calling the `Save()` method. The class will work out whether it's a new diary event to insert into the database, or an existing one in need of updating. The `DiaryEvent` class also has two `Delete()` methods. One is a shared method and therefore doesn't require a `DiaryEvent` to be created, and requires an `EventId` parameter. It's used by some of the built-in data access components provided with ASP.NET 2.0. The second is an object method that deletes the event referenced by the current `DiaryEvent` object. As well as enabling the details of one diary entry to be retrieved, the `DiaryEvent` class provides additional methods for getting details of a number of diary events as either a collection or as a DataSet by returning a `SqlDataReader` object.

The following table explains these methods in detail:

Method	Return Type	Description
`Save()`	None	Saves a fully populated `DiaryEvent` object. If it's a new entry, `Save()` calls `InsertNew DiaryEvent` sub and the details are inserted into the database. The new `EventId` is returned from the database and entered in to `mEventId`. If the entry already exists in the database, `Save()` calls `UpdateDiaryEvent`, which updates the database values with those in the `DiaryEvent` object.
`GetDaysInMonthWithEvents(ByVal DiaryId As Integer, ByVal Month As Integer, ByVal Year As Integer)`	Boolean Array	Shared method that returns a Boolean array detailing which days have events associated with them. The array index matches with the day of the month (1 is the first of the month, 2 the second, and so on).
`GetDiaryEventsByDate(ByVal DiaryId As Integer, ByVal FromDate As Date, ByVal ToDate As Date)`	`SqlDataReader`	Shared method that returns a `SqlDataReader` object populated with rows from the database detailing diary events between the `FromDate` and `ToDate` arguments.
`GetDiaryEventsByDateAsCollection(ByVal DiaryId As Integer, ByVal FromDate As Date, ByVal ToDate As Date)`	`DiaryEventCollection`	Creates a new `Diary EventCollection` object and populates it with `DiaryEvent` objects whose `EntryDate` is between the `FromDate` and `ToDate` arguments.

Table continued on following page

Method	Return Type	Description
`DeleteEvent()`	None	Deletes from the database the event with `EventId` equal to `mEventId` of the object. The `DiaryEvent` object's values are re-initialized to their defaults.
`DeleteEvent(ByVal EventId As Long)`	None	Shared method that deletes the event from the database with an `EventId` value equal to the `EventId` argument of the method.

In addition to the constructors and public methods, the `DiaryEvent` class has these four properties:

Property	Type	Description
`EventDescription`	String	Description of the event.
`EventName`	String	Short name for the event.
`EventDate`	Date	Date the event starts.
`EventDuration`	Integer	Length of time in minutes that the event lasts.

One more class to go. The next section looks at the diary collection handling class: `DiaryEventCollection`.

The DiaryEventCollection Class

The `DiaryEventCollection` class inherits from the `System.Collections.CollectionBase` class. Its purpose is simply to store a collection of `DiaryEvent` objects. The class employs the following methods:

Method	Return Type	Description
`Add(ByVal NewDiaryEvent As DiaryEvent)`	None	Adds a `DiaryEvent` object to the collection held by the `DiaryEventCollection` object.
`Add(ByVal DiaryEventId As Long)`	None	Creates a new `DiaryEvent` object. `DiaryEventId` is passed to the `DiaryEvent` object's constructor to ensure it's populated with the event's details from the database. The new `DiaryEvent` object is then added to the collection maintained by the `DiaryEventCollection` object.
`Remove(ByVal Index As Integer)`	None	Removes the `DiaryEvent` object from the collection at the specified index.

This class contains only one property:

Property	Type	Description
`Item(ByVal Index As Integer)`	Integer	Returns the `DiaryEvent` object stored at the position in index in the collection.

That completes an overview of all the classes and their design, methods, and properties. The next section takes a more in-depth look at the code and the .aspx pages dealing with presentation.

Code and Code Explanation

This section digs into each of the important pages and shows you how they interact with each other, as well as how they use the classes in the business layer. This section doesn't cover every single line of every page, but rather it takes a general overview of how the application works and dives a bit deeper where necessary.

Discussion of the project is approached in a functionality-based way. Instead of discussing a specific page and what it does, the following sections discuss a process — such as registration — and how it's achieved.

It begins with an overview of the files and file structure.

File Structure

An overview of the file structure is shown in Figure 1-12.

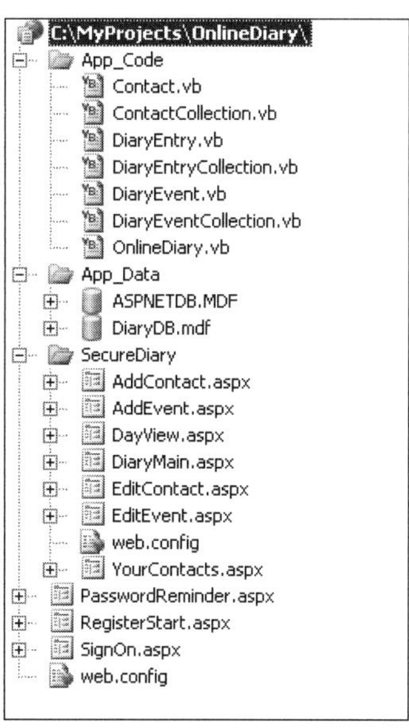

Figure 1-12

Each of the seven class files is stored in the App_Code directory (at the top of the figure). The App_Data directory contains the two databases: the login database (ASPNETDB.MDF) and the Online Diary database (DiaryDB.mdf). Pages that require you to log in before viewing are stored separately in the SecureDiary directory. Finally, the root directory contains login pages, registration pages, and password reminder pages; basically anything that requires you to be logged in to view.

Registration, Logging On, and Security

The Online Diary application uses the new `Login` controls to provide the diary's user handing features, including new user registration, log in, and password reminder.

The `Login` controls are a real time saver, allowing a lot of sophisticated functionality to be added with just a little work and hardly any code! ASP.NET 2.0 has seven new security or login controls:

- `Login`: Enables users to log in and verifies username and password.
- `LoginView`: Enables the display of different templates depending on whether a user is logged in and also his or her role membership.
- `PasswordRecovery`: Provides password reminder functionality for users who forget their password.
- `LoginStatus`: Displays whether a user is logged in or out.
- `LoginName`: Displays currently logged-in username.
- `CreateUserWizard`: Creates a new user wizard — registration of a new user in simple steps.
- `ChangePassword`: Enables users to change their password.

The Online Diary project, however, use only the `Login`, `LoginName`, `CreateUserWizard`, and `ChangePassword` controls.

Logging On

The SignOn.aspx page contains a `Login` control. The user database is created using the web site administration tools. This goes through the steps needed one by one, and once it's finished a new database called ASPNETDB.MDF appears in the App_Data directory of the diary project.

The markup for the `Login` control is shown here:

```
<asp:Login ID="Login1" runat="server" BackColor="#F7F6F3" BorderColor="#E6E2D8"
BorderPadding="4"
                        BorderStyle="Solid" BorderWidth="1px" CreateUserText="Not
registered?  Click here to register now."
                        CreateUserUrl="~/RegisterStart.aspx"
DestinationPageUrl="~/SecureDiary/DiaryMain.aspx" Font-Names="Verdana"
                        Font-Size="0.8em" ForeColor="#333333" Height="197px"
PasswordRecoveryText="Forgotten your password?"
                        PasswordRecoveryUrl="~/PasswordReminder.aspx" Style="z-
index: 100; left: 78px;
                        position: absolute; top: 55px" Width="315px">
                        <LoginButtonStyle BackColor="#FFFBFF" BorderColor="#CCCCCC"
BorderStyle="Solid" BorderWidth="1px"
```

```
                            Font-Names="Verdana" Font-Size="0.8em"
ForeColor="#284775" />
                        <TextBoxStyle Font-Size="0.8em" />
                        <TitleTextStyle BackColor="#5D7B9D" Font-Bold="True" Font-
Size="0.9em" ForeColor="White" />
                        <InstructionTextStyle Font-Italic="True" ForeColor="Black"
/>

                    </asp:Login>
```

Important attributes to note are `DestinationPageUrl`, which determines where the user is navigated to if he or she enters a valid username and password. In the Online Diary project it's the Diarymain.aspx page, the center of the Online Diary's interface.

To enable new users to register, the `CreateUserText` has been set to a friendly "register here" message; the URL for registering is specified in `CreateUserUrl`.

Finally, just in case the user has already registered but forgotten his or her password, the `PasswordRecoveryText` attribute displays a "Forgotten your password?" message and `PasswordRecoveryUrl` sets the URL the users are navigated to if they need to find out their password.

The only code you need to write is in the `Login` control's `LoggedIn` event, which fires if the user successfully enters a username and password:

```
    Protected Sub Login1_LoggedIn(ByVal sender As Object, ByVal e As
System.EventArgs) Handles Login1.LoggedIn
        Dim DiaryId As Integer = GetDiaryIdFromUserName(Login1.UserName)
        Session("DiaryId") = DiaryId
    End Sub
```

This uses the supplied username to look up the user's `DiaryId` in the Online Diary database. This is then stored in the session variable.

The SignOn.aspx page also allows new users to register.

New User Registration

The RegisterStart.aspx. page deals with the registration of a new user. As with SignOn.aspx, this page also uses one of the new `Login` controls, this time the `CreateUserWizard` control. The markup for the `CreateUserWizard` control is shown in the following code:

```
        <asp:CreateUserWizard ID="CreateUserWizard1" runat="server"
BackColor="#F7F6F3" BorderColor="#E6E2D8"
            BorderStyle="Solid" BorderWidth="1px" Font-Names="Verdana" Font-
Size="0.8em"
            Style="z-index: 100; left: 66px; position: absolute; top: 43px"
Height="164px" Width="300px" FinishDestinationPageUrl="~/SignOn.aspx">
            <SideBarStyle BackColor="#5D7B9D" BorderWidth="0px" Font-Size="0.9em"
VerticalAlign="Top" />
            <SideBarButtonStyle BorderWidth="0px" Font-Names="Verdana"
ForeColor="White" />
```

```
            <NavigationButtonStyle BackColor="#FFFBFF" BorderColor="#CCCCCC"
BorderStyle="Solid"
                BorderWidth="1px" Font-Names="Verdana" ForeColor="#284775" />
            <HeaderStyle BackColor="#5D7B9D" BorderStyle="Solid" Font-Bold="True"
Font-Size="0.9em"
                ForeColor="White" HorizontalAlign="Left" />
            <CreateUserButtonStyle BackColor="#FFFBFF" BorderColor="#CCCCCC"
BorderStyle="Solid"
                BorderWidth="1px" Font-Names="Verdana" ForeColor="#284775" />
            <ContinueButtonStyle BackColor="#FFFBFF" BorderColor="#CCCCCC"
BorderStyle="Solid"
                BorderWidth="1px" Font-Names="Verdana" ForeColor="#284775" />
            <StepStyle BorderWidth="0px" />
            <TitleTextStyle BackColor="#5D7B9D" Font-Bold="True" ForeColor="White"
/>
            <WizardSteps>
                <asp:CreateUserWizardStep runat="server">
                </asp:CreateUserWizardStep>
                <asp:WizardStep ID="personalDetailsStep" runat="server" Title="User
Details">
                        <table border="0" style="font-size: 100%; font-family:
Verdana; z-index: 100; left: 0px; position: absolute; top: 0px;">
                          <tr>
                            <td align="center" colspan="2" style="font-weight:
bold; color: white; background-color: #5d7b9d">
                              Your Personal Details</td>
                          </tr>
                          <tr>
                            <td align="right" style="height: 26px">
                              <label for="UserName">
                                Your First Name:</label></td>
                            <td style="width: 179px; height: 26px">
                              <asp:TextBox ID="firstNameTextBox"
runat="server" CausesValidation="True"></asp:TextBox> 
                            </td>
                          </tr>
                          <tr>
                            <td align="right">
                              <label for="Password">
                                Your Last Name:</label></td>
                            <td style="width: 179px">
                              <asp:TextBox ID="lastNameTextBox"
runat="server" CausesValidation="True"></asp:TextBox> 
                            </td>
                          </tr>
                          <tr>
                            <td align="center" colspan="2" style="height:
18px">
                               </td>
                          </tr>
                          <tr>
                            <td align="center" colspan="2" style="color: red">
                               </td>
                          </tr>
```

```
                        </table>
                    </asp:WizardStep>
                    <asp:CompleteWizardStep runat="server">
                        <ContentTemplate>
                            <table border="0" style="font-size: 100%; width: 383px;
font-family: Verdana; height: 164px">
                                <tr>
                                    <td align="center" colspan="2" style="font-weight:
bold; color: white; background-color: #5d7b9d">
                                        Complete</td>
                                </tr>
                                <tr>
                                    <td>
                                        Your account has been successfully
created.</td>
                                </tr>
                                <tr>
                                    <td align="right" colspan="2">
                                        <asp:Button ID="ContinueButton" runat="server"
BackColor="#FFFBFF" BorderColor="#CCCCCC"
                                            BorderStyle="Solid" BorderWidth="1px"
CausesValidation="False" CommandName="Continue"
                                            Font-Names="Verdana" ForeColor="#284775"
Text="Continue" ValidationGroup="CreateUserWizard1" />
                                    </td>
                                </tr>
                            </table>
                        </ContentTemplate>
                    </asp:CompleteWizardStep>
                </WizardSteps>
            </asp:CreateUserWizard>
```

Most of the markup and attributes relate to style settings. However, one essential attribute is the `FinishDestinationPageUrl`. This is where the user is taken once the registration process is completed; in the Online Diary it's the SignOn.aspx page.

You've probably noticed a number of `WizardStep` tags in the markup, such as this one:

```
<asp:WizardStep ID="personalDetailsStep" runat="server" Title="User Details">
```

The `CreateUserWizard` works on a step-by-step basis. There must be least one step that allows the user to choose a username and password and various security questions (see Figure 1-13).

This step and its style can be modified, but Figure 1-13 shows its default value. The control takes care of inserting the new user data into the user database.

A second step, shown in Figure 1-14, is displayed after the user is created.

Figure 1-13

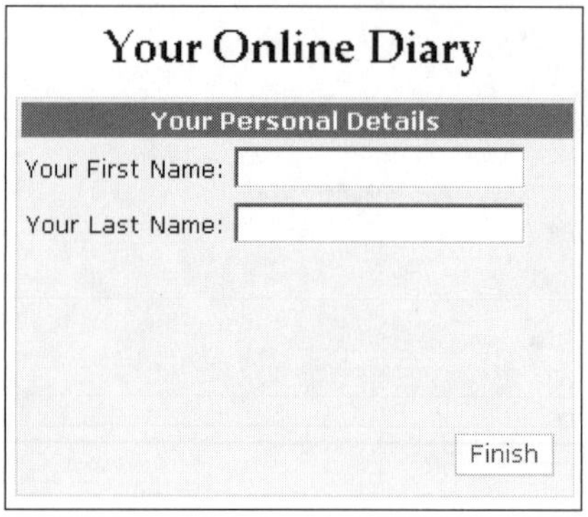

Figure 1-14

This screen asks users for their first name and last name. This time it's up to you to store the data somewhere, and you do that in the `CreateUserWizard` control's `FinishButtonClick` event:

```
    Protected Sub CreateUserWizard1_FinishButtonClick(ByVal sender As Object, ByVal
e As System.Web.UI.WebControls.WizardNavigationEventArgs) Handles
CreateUserWizard1.FinishButtonClick
        Dim myTextBox As TextBox
        Dim UserName, FirstName, LastName
        myTextBox = CreateUserWizard1.FindControl("firstNameTextBox")
        FirstName = myTextBox.Text
        myTextBox = CreateUserWizard1.FindControl("lastNameTextBox")
        LastName = myTextBox.Text
        UserName = CreateUserWizard1.UserName
        OnlineDiary.InsertDiary(UserName, FirstName, LastName)
    End Sub
```

This step creates a new diary for users and stores their first and last names. The `UserName` comes from the `CreateUserWizard` control's `UserName` property, and then uses the shared method `InsertDiary()` to insert the new user in the Online Diary's database.

Being human, sometimes people forget their passwords. Fortunately, ASP.NET 2.0 comes with the capability to refresh overloaded memories.

Password Reminder

Again with virtually no code, you can create a fully functional password reminder feature for the Online Diary, this time courtesy of the `PasswordRecovery` control. Virtually all of its settings are at the default values or simply related to style. Even better, there's just one line of code and that's in the `SendingMail` event:

```
Protected Sub PasswordRecovery1_SendingMail(ByVal sender As Object, ByVal e As
System.Web.UI.WebControls.MailMessageEventArgs) Handles
PasswordRecovery1.SendingMail
        returnToLogOnHyperLink.Visible = True
    End Sub
```

The `SendingMail` event fires when the user presses the Send Email button and simply displays the Return to Main Page link, rather than leaving the user guessing as to where to go next.

The main work involved is configuring the SMTP server settings that'll be used to actually send the password reminder e-mail. Visual Web Developer doesn't come with an SMTP server. However, if you are using Windows XP or 2000, all you need to do to install one is go to the Start➪Settings➪Control Panel➪Add or Remove Programs. From there, select Add/Remove Windows Components. Select the Internet Information Server (IIS) option and click Details at the bottom-right of the dialog. In the resulting dialog box, you'll see a list. Check the box next to SMTP Service and click OK. Then click Next to install an SMTP service.

Once the SMTP service is installed, add the following shaded code between the `<configuration>` tags in the Web.config file:

```
<configuration xmlns="http://schemas.microsoft.com/.NetConfiguration/v2.0">
 <connectionStrings>
  <add name="DiaryDBConnectionString" connectionString="Data
Source=.\SQLEXPRESS;AttachDbFilename=|DataDirectory|\DiaryDB.mdf;Integrated
Security=True;User Instance=True"
   providerName="System.Data.SqlClient" />
 </connectionStrings>
  <system.web>
    <roleManager enabled="true" />
  <authentication mode="Forms"/>
         <compilation debug="true"/></system.web>
 <system.net>
  <mailSettings>
   <smtp from="system@diary-system.com">
    <network host="localhost" password="" userName="" />
   </smtp>
  </mailSettings>
 </system.net>
</configuration>
```

Viewing the Online Calendar

The DiaryMain.aspx page is the central hub of the application. It displays a calendar of the current month, showing which days have events or diary entries associated with them. It also displays a list of upcoming events and diary entries for the current month.

To display when a day has events or a diary entry, the `OnDayRender` event of the `Calendar` control is used:

```
    Protected Sub Calendar1_OnDayRender(ByVal sender As Object, ByVal e As
System.Web.UI.WebControls.DayRenderEventArgs) Handles Calendar1.DayRender
        If Not e.Day.IsOtherMonth Then
            If entryArrayOfDays Is Nothing Then
                entryArrayOfDays = GetDaysInMonthWithEntries(Session("DiaryId"),
e.Day.Date.Month, e.Day.Date.Year)
            End If

            If eventArrayOfDays Is Nothing Then
                eventArrayOfDays = GetDaysInMonthWithEvents(Session("DiaryId"),
e.Day.Date.Month, e.Day.Date.Year)
            End If

            If entryArrayOfDays(CInt(e.Day.DayNumberText)) Then
                e.Cell.BackColor = Drawing.Color.Blue
            End If

            If eventArrayOfDays(CInt(e.Day.DayNumberText)) Then
                e.Cell.ForeColor = Drawing.Color.Red
            End If

        End If
    End Sub
```

The first `If` block in the preceding event code deals with ensuring `entryArrayOfDays` and `eventArrayOfDays` are populated with details of which days have an associated event or diary entry. They are both Boolean arrays; if a day has an event or entry, the array element for that day contains `True`. Arrays are populated by the `DiaryEnty` and `DiaryEvent` classes' shared functions `GetDaysInMonthWithEntries()` and `GetDaysInMonthWithEvents()`.

In the second `If` block of the event the code checks to see whether the day of the month being rendered has a diary event or diary entry. If there's an event, the day's text is set to red. If there's a diary entry the day's background is rendered in blue.

As well as a `Calendar` control, the main page also has two `GridView` controls (discussed a bit later). The upper one displays upcoming events; the lower one displays recent diary entries. Both `GridView` controls get their data from an `ObjectDataSource` control, new to ASP.NET 2.0. In the past, data source controls have interacted directly with the database. They are nice and easy to use — put on one a page, set a few properties, drop in a few data-aware controls, and away you go. However, that's not actually good coding practice. Splitting up the data access, business, and presentation layers is generally considered good practice, but means leaving behind nice and easy-to-use data source controls.

However, the new ObjectDataSource lets you have the best of both: easy-to-use data controls and use of classes to separate business, data, and presentation layers. Instead of connecting directly to a database, the `ObjectDataSource` takes its data from one of the classes. `diaryEntriesObjectDataSource` on DiaryMain.aspx, for example, takes its data from the `GetDiaryEntriesRecentlyChanged()` method of the `DiaryEntry` class, whose markup is shown here:

```
        <asp:ObjectDataSource ID="diaryEntriesObjectDataSource" runat="server"
SelectMethod="GetDiaryEntriesRecentlyChanged"
            TypeName="DiaryEntry">
            <SelectParameters>
                <asp:SessionParameter DefaultValue="-1" Name="DiaryId"
SessionField="DiaryId" Type="Int32" />
            </SelectParameters>
        </asp:ObjectDataSource>
```

The `TypeName` attribute specifies the class name to use, and the `SelectMethod` attribute specifies which method of that class will provide the data. `GetDiaryEntriesRecentlyChanged()` is a shared method, shown here:

```
    Public Shared Function GetDiaryEntriesRecentlyChanged(ByVal DiaryId As Integer)
As SqlDataReader
        Dim diaryDBConn As New SqlConnection(conString)
        Dim sqlString As String = "GetRecentDiaryEntries"
        Dim sqlCmd As New SqlCommand(sqlString, diaryDBConn)
        sqlCmd.CommandType = CommandType.StoredProcedure

        sqlCmd.Parameters.AddWithValue("@DiaryId", DiaryId)

        diaryDBConn.Open()
        Dim entrySQLDR As SqlDataReader =
sqlCmd.ExecuteReader(CommandBehavior.CloseConnection)
        sqlCmd = Nothing
        Return entrySQLDR
    End Function
```

The method returns a `SqlDataReader` object populated with the data the `ObjectDataSource` control will use.

Actually displaying the data is then just a matter of pointing a data-aware control at the `ObjectDataSource`:

```
            <asp:GridView ID="recentEntriesGridView" runat="server"
AutoGenerateColumns="False"
                Caption="Recent Entries" CaptionAlign="Left" CellPadding="4"
DataSourceID="diaryEntriesObjectDataSource"
                ForeColor="#333333" GridLines="None" Style="z-index: 105; left:
535px; position: absolute;
                top: 321px" Width="476px" Height="208px">
                <FooterStyle BackColor="#5D7B9D" Font-Bold="True" ForeColor="White"
/>
                <RowStyle BackColor="#F7F6F3" ForeColor="#333333" />
                <Columns>
                    <asp:BoundField DataField="EntryDate" />
                    <asp:BoundField DataField="EntryTitle" />
```

```
                    <asp:BoundField DataField="EntryText" />
                </Columns>
                <PagerStyle BackColor="#284775" ForeColor="White"
HorizontalAlign="Center" />
                <SelectedRowStyle BackColor="#E2DED6" Font-Bold="True"
ForeColor="#333333" />
                <HeaderStyle BackColor="#5D7B9D" Font-Bold="True" ForeColor="White"
/>
                <EditRowStyle BackColor="#999999" />
                <AlternatingRowStyle BackColor="White" ForeColor="#284775" />
            </asp:GridView>
```

In the `GridView` control's markup, the `DataSourceID` attribute specifies the source of the data, which is the `ObjectDataSource` control. In addition, the markup specifies which columns to display by setting `AutoGenerateColumns` to `False`. A final step is to create a list of columns:

```
                <Columns>
                    <asp:BoundField DataField="EntryDate" />
                    <asp:BoundField DataField="EntryTitle" />
                    <asp:BoundField DataField="EntryText" />
                </Columns>
```

As well as enabling the display of data, the `ObjectDataSource` control can also update, insert, and delete records from a database, as demonstrated shortly.

Creating, Editing, and Viewing a Diary Entry

The DayView.aspx page allows for diary editing. This page contains a simple form allowing you to enter title and diary entry details. It also displays any existing diary entry.

All of the hard work is done by use of the `DiaryEntry` class. Its `Page_Load` event creates a new `DiaryEntry` class, passing its constructor the current user's `DiaryId` and also the date the page refers to:

```
    Protected Sub Page_Load(ByVal sender As Object, ByVal e As System.EventArgs)
Handles Me.Load
        mDiaryEntry = New DiaryEntry(CInt(Session("DiaryId")),
CDate(dayShownLabel.Text))
        changeDayCalendar.SelectedDate = CDate(dayShownLabel.Text)
        changeDayCalendar.VisibleDate = changeDayCalendar.SelectedDate
        If Not IsPostBack Then
            entryTextTextBox.Text = mDiaryEntry.EntryText
            entryTitleTextBox.Text = mDiaryEntry.EntryTitle
        End If
    End Sub
```

mDiaryEntry is a global variable used to hold the DiaryEntry object relating to the day being edited.

The constructor, shown in the following code, does all the hard work of actually getting the data:

```
    Public Sub New(ByVal DiaryId As Integer, ByVal EntryDate As Date)
        mDiaryId = DiaryId
        If mDiaryId > 0 Then
            Try

                Dim diaryDBConn As New SqlConnection(conString)
                Dim sqlString As String = "GetDiaryEntryByDate"
                Dim sqlCmd As New SqlCommand(sqlString, diaryDBConn)
                sqlCmd.CommandType = CommandType.StoredProcedure

                sqlCmd.Parameters.AddWithValue("@DiaryId", mDiaryId)
                sqlCmd.Parameters.AddWithValue("@EntryFromDate", EntryDate)
                sqlCmd.Parameters.AddWithValue("@EntryToDate", EntryDate)


                diaryDBConn.Open()
                Dim diaryEntrySQLDR As SqlDataReader =
sqlCmd.ExecuteReader(CommandBehavior.CloseConnection)
                sqlCmd = Nothing
                If diaryEntrySQLDR.Read() Then
                    mDiaryEntryId = CLng(diaryEntrySQLDR("DiaryEntryId"))
                    mEntryDate = CDate(diaryEntrySQLDR("EntryDate"))
                    mEntryTitle = diaryEntrySQLDR("EntryTitle").ToString
                    mEntryText = diaryEntrySQLDR("EntryText").ToString
                Else
                    mDiaryEntryId = -1
                    mEntryDate = EntryDate
                End If

                diaryEntrySQLDR.Close()
                diaryEntrySQLDR = Nothing
                diaryDBConn.Close()
                diaryDBConn = Nothing

            Catch ex As Exception
                mDiaryEntryId = -1
            End Try

        End If
    End Sub
```

The GetDiaryEntryByDate stored procedure is called to get the data. If there isn't an existing entry for that day, mDiaryEntryId is set to -1 and all the other properties are left at their default values. Otherwise they are populated with the data from the database.

When the diary title or entry boxes are changed, `mDiaryEntry` is updated:

```
    Protected Sub entryTitleTextBox_TextChanged(ByVal sender As Object, ByVal e As
System.EventArgs) Handles entryTitleTextBox.TextChanged
        mDiaryEntry.EntryTitle = entryTitleTextBox.Text
    End Sub

    Protected Sub entryTextTextBox_TextChanged(ByVal sender As Object, ByVal e As
System.EventArgs) Handles entryTextTextBox.TextChanged
        mDiaryEntry.EntryText = entryTextTextBox.Text
    End Sub
```

Saving changes occurs when you click the Save button:

```
    Protected Sub saveDiaryEntryButton_Click(ByVal sender As Object, ByVal e As
System.EventArgs) Handles saveDiaryEntryButton.Click
        mDiaryEntry.Save()
    End Sub
```

All that's involved is calling the `Save()` method of the `DiaryEntry` object:

```
    Public Sub Save()
        If mDiaryEntryId = -1 Then
            InsertNewDiaryEntry()
        Else
            UpdateDiaryEntry()
        End If
    End Sub
```

Based on whether or not `mDiaryEntryId` is `-1`, the method either inserts a new entry into the database or updates an existing one. The private method `InsertNewDiaryEntry()` inserts a new diary entry:

```
    Private Sub InsertNewDiaryEntry()
        If mDiaryId <> -1 Then
            Dim diaryDBConn As New SqlConnection(conString)
            Dim sqlString As String = "InsertDiaryEntry"
            Dim sqlCmd As New SqlCommand(sqlString, diaryDBConn)
            sqlCmd.CommandType = CommandType.StoredProcedure

            sqlCmd.Parameters.AddWithValue("@DiaryId", mDiaryId)
            sqlCmd.Parameters.AddWithValue("@EntryDate", mEntryDate)
            sqlCmd.Parameters.AddWithValue("@EntryTitle", mEntryTitle)
            sqlCmd.Parameters.AddWithValue("@EntryText", mEntryText)
            sqlCmd.Parameters.Add("@NewDiaryEntryId", SqlDbType.BigInt)
            sqlCmd.Parameters("@NewDiaryEntryId").Direction =
ParameterDirection.ReturnValue

            diaryDBConn.Open()
            sqlCmd.ExecuteNonQuery()
            mDiaryEntryId = CLng(sqlCmd.Parameters("@NewDiaryEntryId").Value())

            diaryDBConn.Close()
            sqlCmd = Nothing
```

```
            diaryDBConn = Nothing
        End If
    End Sub
```

The private method `UpdateDiaryEntry()` updates it:

```
    Private Sub UpdateDiaryEntry()
        If mDiaryEntryId <> -1 Then
            Dim diaryDBConn As New SqlConnection(conString)
            Dim sqlString As String = "UpdateDiaryEntry"
            Dim sqlCmd As New SqlCommand(sqlString, diaryDBConn)
            sqlCmd.CommandType = CommandType.StoredProcedure

            sqlCmd.Parameters.AddWithValue("@DiaryEntryId", mDiaryEntryId)
            sqlCmd.Parameters.AddWithValue("@EntryDate", mEntryDate)
            sqlCmd.Parameters.AddWithValue("@EntryTitle", mEntryTitle)
            sqlCmd.Parameters.AddWithValue("@EntryText", mEntryText)

            diaryDBConn.Open()
            sqlCmd.ExecuteNonQuery()
            diaryDBConn.Close()
            sqlCmd = Nothing
            diaryDBConn = Nothing
        End If
    End Sub
```

Moving on, the next section discusses aspects of the code dealing with editing, viewing, and deleting events.

Creating, Editing, and Viewing Diary Events

Events are created by clicking the Add New Event link on the DayView.aspx page. This takes you to a simple form on the AddEvent.aspx page. When the Save button is clicked, the button's `click` event creates a new `DiaryEvent` object, populates its properties from the form, and then calls its `Save()` method. The code flow is much the same as for the `DiaryEvent` object's `Save()` method. Where the functionality is similar or the same, the names of methods on different objects have been kept the same. It reduces confusion and makes your life easier.

All events relating to a particular day are shown on the DayView.aspx page. An `ObjectDataSource` control on the DayView.aspx page draws its data from the `DiaryEvent` object's `GetDiaryEventsByDate()` shared method. The markup for the `ObjectDataSource` control is shown here:

```
        <asp:ObjectDataSource ID="eventsObjectDataSource" runat="server"
SelectMethod="GetDiaryEventsByDate"
            TypeName="DiaryEvent" DeleteMethod="DeleteEvent">
            <SelectParameters>
                <asp:SessionParameter DefaultValue="-1" Name="DiaryId"
SessionField="DiaryId" Type="Int32" />
                <asp:ControlParameter ControlID="dayShownLabel" DefaultValue=""
Name="FromDate" PropertyName="Text"
                    Type="DateTime" />
                <asp:ControlParameter ControlID="dayShownLabel" DefaultValue=""
Name="ToDate" PropertyName="Text"
```

```
                        Type="DateTime" />
                    <asp:Parameter DefaultValue="0" Name="MaxRows" Type="Int32" />
                </SelectParameters>
                <DeleteParameters>
                    <asp:Parameter Name="EventId" Type="Int64" />
                </DeleteParameters>
            </asp:ObjectDataSource>
```

Notice that the `SelectParameters` and the `DeleteParameters` are set to specify the data passed to the `GetDiaryEventsByDate()` method used to pull back the data, and the `DeleteEvent()` method is used to delete diary events.

A `GridView` control is hooked to the `ObjectDataSource` in the code above:

```
            <asp:GridView ID="eventsGridView" runat="server"
AutoGenerateColumns="False" CellPadding="4"
                DataSourceID="eventsObjectDataSource" ForeColor="#333333"
GridLines="None" Height="1px"
                PageSize="5" Style="z-index: 108; left: 78px; position: absolute; top:
357px"
                Width="542px" DataKeyNames="EventId">
                <FooterStyle BackColor="#5D7B9D" Font-Bold="True" ForeColor="White" />
                <RowStyle BackColor="#F7F6F3" ForeColor="#333333" />
                <Columns>
                    <asp:HyperLinkField DataNavigateUrlFields="EventId" Text="Edit"
DataNavigateUrlFormatString="~/SecureDiary/EditEvent.aspx?EventId={0}" />
                    <asp:CommandField ShowDeleteButton="True" />
                    <asp:BoundField DataField="EventName" HeaderText="Event" />
                    <asp:BoundField DataField="EventDescription"
HeaderText="Description" />
                </Columns>
                <PagerStyle BackColor="#284775" ForeColor="White"
HorizontalAlign="Center" />
                <SelectedRowStyle BackColor="#E2DED6" Font-Bold="True"
ForeColor="#333333" />
                <HeaderStyle BackColor="#5D7B9D" Font-Bold="True" ForeColor="White" />
                <EditRowStyle BackColor="#999999" />
                <AlternatingRowStyle BackColor="White" ForeColor="#284775" />
            </asp:GridView>
```

Again, the `AutoGenerateColumns` parameter is set to `False`, and the columns are specified as follows:

```
                <Columns>
                    <asp:HyperLinkField DataNavigateUrlFields="EventId" Text="Edit"
DataNavigateUrlFormatString="~/SecureDiary/EditEvent.aspx?EventId={0}" />
                    <asp:CommandField ShowDeleteButton="True" />
                    <asp:BoundField DataField="EventName" HeaderText="Event" />
                    <asp:BoundField DataField="EventDescription"
HeaderText="Description" />
                </Columns>
```

Notice the hyperlink and field that when clicked will take the user to the EditEvent.aspx page, and the URL contains data passed to the `EventId` in the URL by way of the `EventId` querystring parameter. It's set to be `{0}`, which at run time will be substituted by the value of the first column for each row in the DataSet.

In addition, the code specifies a Delete button on each row in the grid:

```
<asp:CommandField ShowDeleteButton="True" />
```

When you click the Delete button, the `GridView` control asks the `ObjectDataSource` control to call the specified delete method of the data providing class. In this case it's the `DeleteEvent()` method of the `DiaryEvent` class. The `DataKeyNames` attribute in the `GridView` control's markup specifies the primary key field that needs to be used to delete the row.

Returning to editing the event: When you click the Edit link you are taken to the EditEvent.aspx page. The clicked Edit link's `EventId` is passed as a URL parameter. The EditEvent.aspx page is virtually identical to the AddEvent.aspx page discussed previously. The main difference is when the page initializes. The `Page_Init` event handler is shown in the following code, and it's here that the event details are entered into the form:

```
    Protected Sub Page_Init(ByVal sender As Object, ByVal e As System.EventArgs)
Handles Me.Init

        Dim EventBeingEdited As New
DiaryEvent(CLng(Request.QueryString("EventId")))
        eventNameTextBox.Text = EventBeingEdited.EventName
        eventDescriptionTextBox.Text = EventBeingEdited.EventDescription
        dayShownLabel.Text = EventBeingEdited.EventDate.Day & " " &
MonthName(EventBeingEdited.EventDate.Month) & " " & EventBeingEdited.EventDate.Year


        Dim NewListItem As ListItem, HourCount, MinuteCount

        For HourCount = 0 To 23
            If HourCount < 10 Then
                NewListItem = New ListItem("0" & HourCount, HourCount.ToString)
            Else
                NewListItem = New ListItem(HourCount.ToString, HourCount.ToString)
            End If
            If EventBeingEdited.EventDate.Hour = HourCount Then
                NewListItem.Selected = True
            End If
            StartHourDropDownList.Items.Add(NewListItem)
        Next

        For MinuteCount = 0 To 59
            If MinuteCount < 10 Then
                NewListItem = New ListItem("0" & MinuteCount.ToString,
MinuteCount.ToString)
            Else
                NewListItem = New ListItem(MinuteCount.ToString,
MinuteCount.ToString)
            End If
            If EventBeingEdited.EventDate.Minute = MinuteCount Then
                NewListItem.Selected = True
            End If
            StartMinuteDropDownList.Items.Add(NewListItem)
        Next
        Dim itemToSelect As ListItem
```

```
        itemToSelect =
eventDurationDropDownList.Items.FindByValue(EventBeingEdited.EventDuration.ToString
())
        itemToSelect.Selected = True

        EventBeingEdited = Nothing
    End Sub
```

The `EventId` is extracted from the URL parameters and used to create a new `DiaryEvent` object. Populating the event text boxes is easy enough, but the details of time and duration of the event involve populating the Hour and Minute drop-down boxes and ensuring the correct value is selected. This is achieved by looping through hours from 0 to 23 and then minutes from 0 to 59. If the hour to be added to the list is the same as the hour about to be added to the list box, make sure it's the default selected one. The same goes for the minute list box population.

Managing Contacts

Managing contacts is the last aspect of the Online Diary you'll examine, and uses many of the same principles as the other sections. YourContacts.aspx is the central contact management page. Here a list of current contacts is displayed, and the option to add, edit, and delete contacts is possible.

All contacts are displayed using a `DataObjectSource` and a `GridView` control; the principles being identical to the displaying, deleting, and editing of the diary events. This time the `Contact` class is used for editing and display contact details, but otherwise the code is very similar to the events code.

The main page for displaying contacts is YourContacts.aspx, which contains a `GridView` control in which all current contacts are listed:

```
        <asp:GridView ID="GridView1" runat="server" AutoGenerateColumns="False"
CellPadding="4"
            DataSourceID="ObjectDataSource1" ForeColor="#333333" GridLines="None"
Style="z-index: 101;
            left: 36px; position: absolute; top: 137px" DataKeyNames="ContactId">
            <FooterStyle BackColor="#5D7B9D" Font-Bold="True" ForeColor="White" />
            <Columns>
                <asp:CommandField ShowDeleteButton="True" />
                <asp:HyperLinkField DataNavigateUrlFields="ContactId"
DataNavigateUrlFormatString="~/SecureDiary/EditContact.aspx?ContactId={0}"
                    Text="Edit" />
                <asp:BoundField DataField="LastName" HeaderText="Last Name" />
                <asp:BoundField DataField="FirstName" HeaderText="First Name" />
                <asp:BoundField DataField="Telephone" HeaderText="Telephone" />
                <asp:BoundField DataField="Email" HeaderText="Email Address" />
            </Columns>
            <RowStyle BackColor="#F7F6F3" ForeColor="#333333" />
            <EditRowStyle BackColor="#999999" />
            <SelectedRowStyle BackColor="#E2DED6" Font-Bold="True"
ForeColor="#333333" />
            <PagerStyle BackColor="#284775" ForeColor="White"
HorizontalAlign="Center" />
            <HeaderStyle BackColor="#5D7B9D" Font-Bold="True" ForeColor="White" />
            <AlternatingRowStyle BackColor="White" ForeColor="#284775" />
        </asp:GridView>
```

It gets its data from the `ObjectDataSource` control `ObjectDataSource1`, which in turn connects to the `Contact` class's `GetContactByFirstLetter()` shared method:

```
        <asp:ObjectDataSource ID="ObjectDataSource1" runat="server"
SelectMethod="GetContactsByFirstLetter"
            TypeName="Contact" DeleteMethod="DeleteContact">
            <SelectParameters>
                <asp:SessionParameter DefaultValue="6" Name="DiaryId"
SessionField="DiaryId" Type="Int32" />
                <asp:Parameter Name="FirstLetterOfSurname" Type="Char" />
            </SelectParameters>
            <DeleteParameters>
                <asp:ControlParameter ControlID="GridView1" Name="ContactId"
PropertyName="SelectedValue"
                    Type="Int64" />
            </DeleteParameters>
        </asp:ObjectDataSource>
```

The `ObjectDataSource` control's `DeleteMethod` parameter is also hooked to the `Contact` class's `DeleteContact`. The `GridView` control has been set to show a link to delete each contact, and it's this method that does the actual deleting:

```
    Public Shared Sub DeleteContact(ByVal ContactId As Long)
        Dim diaryDBConn As New SqlConnection(conString)
        Dim sqlString As String = "DeleteContact"
        Dim sqlCmd As New SqlCommand(sqlString, diaryDBConn)
        sqlCmd.CommandType = CommandType.StoredProcedure

        sqlCmd.Parameters.AddWithValue("@ContactId", ContactId)
        diaryDBConn.Open()
        sqlCmd.ExecuteNonQuery()
        diaryDBConn.Close()
        sqlCmd = Nothing
        diaryDBConn = Nothing
    End Sub
```

The `GridView` also includes an Edit link, which when clicked navigates the user to the EditContact.aspx page:

```
                <asp:HyperLinkField DataNavigateUrlFields="ContactId"
DataNavigateUrlFormatString="~/SecureDiary/EditContact.aspx?ContactId={0}"
                    Text="Edit" />
```

The corresponding `ContactId` is passed in the URL as URL data.

Adding a new user involves clicking the Add Contact link on the YourContacts.aspx page. This takes you to a basic form for adding contact information such as name, e-mail, phone number, and so on. This page and the EditContact.aspx page are identical in operation except for one important detail: The EditContact.aspx page retrieves the details of the contact to be edited using the `Contact` class. This happens in the `Page_Load` event:

```
    Protected Sub Page_Load(ByVal sender As Object, ByVal e As System.EventArgs)
Handles Me.Load

        If IsPostBack Then
            Dim currentContact As New
Contact(CLng(Request.QueryString("ContactId")))
            currentContact.FirstName = firstNameTextBox.Text
            currentContact.LastName = lastNameTextBox.Text
            currentContact.AddressLine1 = addressLine1TextBox.Text
            currentContact.City = cityTextBox.Text
            currentContact.PostalCode = postalCodeTextBox.Text
            currentContact.State = stateTextBox.Text
            currentContact.Telephone = telephoneTextBox.Text
            currentContact.MobilePhone = mobilePhoneTextBox.Text
            currentContact.Email = emailTextBox.Text
            currentContact.SaveContact()
            currentContact = Nothing
            Response.Redirect("YourContacts.aspx")
        Else
            Dim currentContact As New
Contact(CLng(Request.QueryString("ContactId")))
            firstNameTextBox.Text = currentContact.FirstName
            lastNameTextBox.Text = currentContact.LastName
            addressLine1TextBox.Text = currentContact.AddressLine1
            cityTextBox.Text = currentContact.City
            postalCodeTextBox.Text = currentContact.PostalCode
            stateTextBox.Text = currentContact.State
            telephoneTextBox.Text = currentContact.Telephone
            mobilePhoneTextBox.Text = currentContact.MobilePhone
            emailTextBox.Text = currentContact.Email
            currentContact = Nothing
        End If
    End Sub
```

The `If` statement determines whether this is a postback (the form has been submitted to itself) or whether the page has just been loaded. If it's a postback, you need to save the data and then move back to the main contacts section. If it's a new page load, it's necessary to create a new `Contact` object, and use the data from that to populate the form fields with the contact information.

The AddContact.aspx page is identical except there's no need to populate with existing contact data, because a new contact has no prior data!

Setting up the Online Diary

One of the great things about ASP.NET 2.0 is how easy it is to set up web applications created on one machine onto another. To install the application on your PC, simply copy the entire directory and files from the accompanying CD-ROM (or download it from `www.wrox.com`) onto a directory on your PC (for example, `C:\Websites`). In VWD, all you have to do is choose File⇨Open Web Site and browse to the folder where you copied the files. Then press F5 to run it.

Alternatively, if you have IIS installed make the `OnlineDiary` directory you copied over a virtual directory and then simply browse to SignOn.aspx.

To find out how to modify the Online Diary application, visit `www.wrox.com` and download this chapter's code, or you can grab it from the companion CD-ROM in the back of the book.

Summary

In this chapter you've seen how to create a fully functioning diary and contacts management system, all with only a little code thanks to ASP.NET 2.0's new controls and functionality. The new security controls in particular help save a lot of time and coding. In this chapter they've been used to create users and login control. However, they can also help provide a lot more functionality like creating different types of user roles, which then allows you to specify what users can and cannot do based on their role. Or you can let users determine the look and feel of their pages using their account details and ASP.NET 2.0's new login and role controls.

Another great control you discovered in this chapter is the `ObjectDataSource` control. In the past data source controls have made life nice and easy. But they were quick and dirty, which meant poor code design, and you had to wave goodbye to a three-tier architecture. Now with the `ObjectDataSource` control you can have quick and dirty and three-tier architecture — great news for creating easily maintainable, well-designed projects.

In the next chapter you will be creating a file sharing project and learning some more about ASP.NET 2.0's great new features.

Wrox File Share

If you have ever tried to send a large e-mail attachment and failed, you're not alone. The idea that you can attach a file or document to an e-mail message and send it over the Internet is a revolutionary concept in the history of computer technology. But not so fast! In order to send a document over the Internet, your Internet connection has to be fast enough to upload the file. In addition, the file has to be small enough to pass through the Internet connection before a timeout event occurs. If an Internet service provider decides that there is a limit on the size of files that can be transferred over the connection they provide, your e-mail capabilities may be greatly hindered. Furthermore, e-mail attachments can take up space on the server where they reside, and must be treated carefully. Some of the popular e-mail providers have to balance millions of e-mail users, and must create file storage policies that are fair and reasonable. Most of the time, there are limits to the size of e-mail attachments allowed to be sent through the e-mail server. Some providers allow for e-mail attachments up to 10MB; other providers allow for files even larger. This phenomenon has caused problems over the years because users are not able to send large files to their coworkers and friends over an Internet connection. What's a user to do?

A solution to the conundrum of sending large e-mail attachments is to use a go-between web site — commonly known as a file share — that acts as an online file repository. The web site can send out a notification as to the file being sent to the server and provide a clickable link for the user to click and prompt to download the file. In this way, you're not actually sending an e-mail message, but rather uploading a file tool web site for propagation. This solution has been copied many times over by many different web sites. This chapter, then, uses the file share as an opportunity to demonstrate some of the new and powerful features in ASP.NET 2.0.

The essential features of the Wrox File Share include the following:

- The capability to upload a file to the web site, specifying which e-mail address to send the file to via an e-mail hyperlink for downloading the file.
- Sending an e-mail automatically to the recipient, with the custom message and hyperlink to the download file.
- The option to change the text content of the automatically sent e-mail, using specific variables for the values of the sender, recipient, hyperlink, and a custom message to the recipient.

- The capability to specify SMTP server information and e-mail account information as a configuration entry rather than a hard-coded value.
- The capability to change the look and feel of the entire web site by simply modifying one entry in a configuration file.

This chapter also analyzes the various components that make up the web site, including the specific controls that ship with the ASP.NET 2.0 development environments. These controls include the following:

- `Login` control
- `PasswordRecovery` control
- `LoginStatus` control
- `Menu` control
- `SiteMapDataSource` control
- Themes
- `FileUpload` control

The section "File Share Design" explores the design of the application in great detail. This includes the essential elements of involvement with regard to the technology and structure of the web site, as well as the various classes involved, a detailed look at all of the members of each class, and an explanation regarding the database tables and their relationships and values.

The section titled "Code and Code Explanation" focuses on the code of each class or module of importance. Some areas of focus include the WebForms used to upload files to the system, inserting data into the database tables.

The final section reviews how to extract and customize the Wrox File Share in a development environment, and how to install it to production.

Using the Wrox File Share

Using the Wrox File Share is extremely easy and naturally intuitive. The web site has only a few functional areas, because its purpose in life is simply to upload files and send e-mails.

If the Wrox File Share web site has been successfully installed (refer to the section "Setting up the Project" later in this chapter), you can browse to view the site by going to `http://localhost/fileshare`. The screen shown in Figure 2-1 appears.

At the top of the menu are several links to choose from:

- Home
- About
- Contact Us
- Admin

Figure 2-1

On the homepage, a total of three steps are required to send a large file to the site. The steps are to capture the recipient's e-mail address, the actual file, a comment or message to the recipient, and, optionally, the e-mail address of the sender. Once these fields have been completed, clicking the Send button performs the upload and sends the e-mail.

An example of an e-mail sent to a recipient is shown in Figure 2-2.

This e-mail contains a hyperlink that streams via HTTP the file originally sent to the recipient.

Upon clicking the hyperlink, the dialog box depicted in Figure 2-3 appears.

Clicking Save opens the window's Save As dialog box, prompting you to select a location and filename. This completes the task of sending a very large file to an e-mail recipient through a file share.

When you click the Admin link in the main menu, you are brought to the login screen if you have not already logged in to the web site and created a session. This page contains a `Login` control and a `passwordRecovery` control for you to use. Enter in `Admin` for the username and `password#` for the password, then click the Log In button.

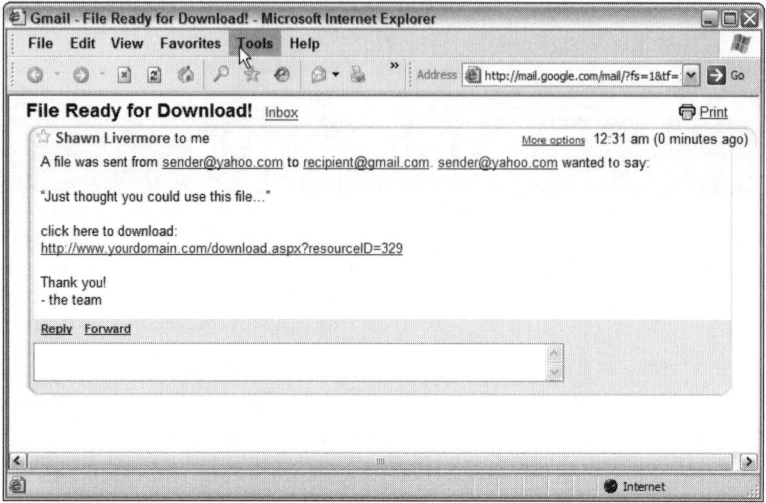

Figure 2-2

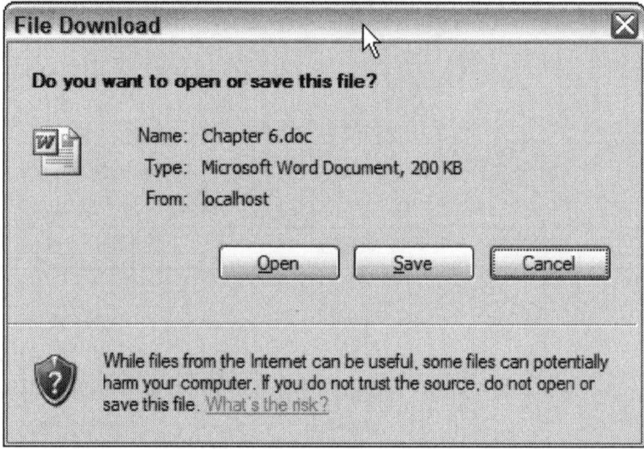

Figure 2-3

Once you log in to the site, you are brought to the administration section landing page, displayed in Figure 2-4.

This interface provides a way to customize the e-mails being sent out to file download recipients. The variables in use are the hyperlink, message, sender's e-mail, and recipient's e-mail. These variables are replaced as text in the body of the e-mail message, providing a customized e-mail experience.

This chapter covers the essential areas of the development that comprise the application. It walks through the class files in detail, explaining the methods and properties they expose. In addition, you will gain insight into the database, data model, and database objects.

The next section addresses the design of the Wrox File Share application, walking through the classes and database objects.

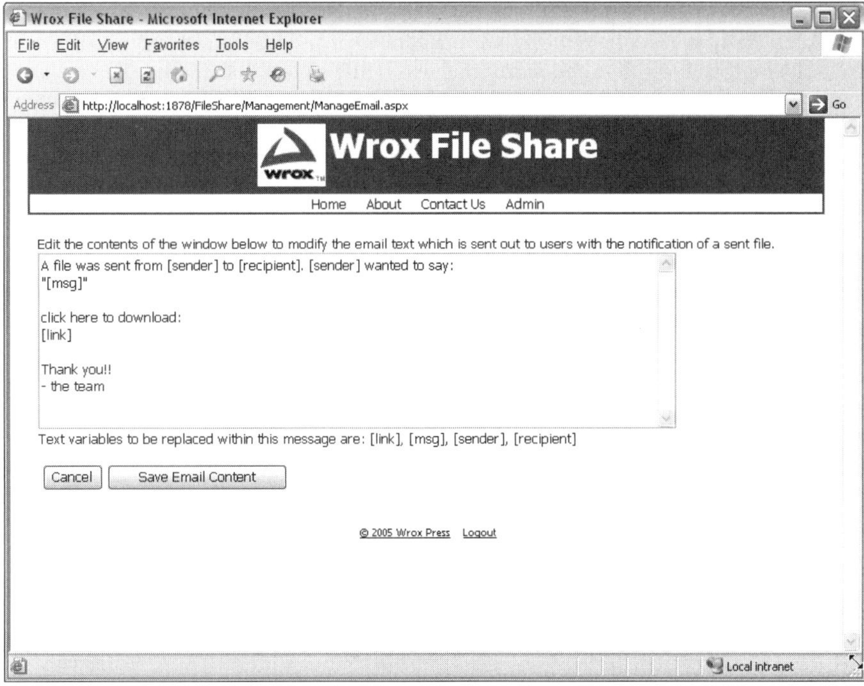

Figure 2-4

Wrox File Share Design

The Wrox File Share design is based on a few abstractions, including the following:

- The file saved to the server is considered as a `Resource` class.
- The methods used to save and get e-mail content are stored within the `EmailContent` class.
- For each business class object there is a data class object that retrieves data from the database or performs inserts into the database.
- The design provides visibility to the existence of business and data layers for the logical separation to occur.

In the sections that follow, you learn how to upload files and send e-mails; discern the Wrox File Share's structure; and understand the data model and database objects, site themes, and the security model. You also learn about the classes involved and their scope of impact within the web site's architecture.

Uploading Files

The `FileUpload` control is used to upload a file to the server. It displays a simple `TextBox` control next to a Browse button, which together allow users to select a file from their local machine to upload to the server. The `fileupload1` instance of the `FileUpload` control exposes properties such as `filename` or filebytes, which prior to ASP.NET 2.0 were very difficult to expose. Also, the FileUpload control does not automatically save a file to the server once the user chooses it and submits the form that contains the control. The logic in the submitted form must explicitly save the specified file to disk. This code to save the file simply called the SaveAs method, which saves the file to a stated path on the local server file system.

Sending E-Mails

To send e-mails in ASP.NET 2.0, there are numerous areas to consider in the planning and development process. The first area to be certain of is the use of a valid SMTP mail server, with a valid e-mail account. The e-mail account to be used must allow permissions to relay mail.

The classes provided by ASP.NET 2.0 are maintained out of the System.Net.Mail class, providing the essential properties and contents of a mail message. The SmtpClient subclass sends the e-mail to the SMTP server that you designate.

The Web.config file provides the e-mail settings necessary for the configuration of the SMTP server. These settings are as follows:

- EmailFrom
- EmailSubject
- SmtpServer
- MailUser
- MailPassword
- MailPort
- EmailFormatSelected

These are accessed from the Utilities class, formulating the contents of a struct variable. This struct variable is declared toward the top of the Utilities class, displayed here:

```
''' <summary>
''' MailSettings is a struct used to define the mail server information
''' </summary>
Public Structure MailSettings
    Public MailServer As String
    Public MailPort As Integer
    Public MailFrom As String
    Public MailUser As String
    Public MailPassword As String
End Structure
```

The actual sending of the e-mail is performed in the Utilities class, within the following function:

```
''' <summary>
''' SendEmail is used to send an email, with the established settings
''' </summary>
Public Shared Sub SendEmail(ByVal MsgTo As String, ByVal MsgFrom As String, _
```

```
        ByVal MsgSubject As String, ByVal MsgText As String)

        Dim SmtpSettings As MailSettings
        SmtpSettings = GetSmtpSettings()
        Dim SmptCl As New SmtpClient(SmtpSettings.MailServer, _
            SmtpSettings.MailPort)
        SmptCl.Credentials = GetCredentials(SmtpSettings)
        Dim MailMsg As New MailMessage(MsgFrom, MsgTo)
        MailMsg.Subject = MsgSubject
        MailMsg.Body = MsgText

        SmptCl.Send(MailMsg)
    End Sub
```

This concludes the design and usage of the e-mail classes built into ASP.NET 2.0, and how the Wrox File Share implements the e-mail functionality.

Structure of the Site

The ASP.NET 2.0 web site file structure has been standardized a bit since its predecessor versions. These standardizations have to do with the naming conventions given to the folders within the site. The sections of the project are listed in the following table:

Section	Description
App_Code	Houses the business layer class (resource.vb) and the data layer class (resourceDB.vb).
App_Data	The standard .NET folder for database files.
App_Themes	The themes folder, containing two themes for use within the site.
ContentFiles	The standard ASPX WebForm files for displaying content.
Controls	Stores all user controls.
FileStorage	The folder for storing uploaded files to be e-mailed to a recipient.
Images	Stores images for the header or any other pages.
Management	Stores the secured administrative WebForm pages.
[miscellaneous files]	These include the login page, config file, sitemap file, and master page file at the root of the site.

One of the essential pieces of the Wrox File Share web site is the database. This database is made up of a SQL Server 2005 Express file, which contains a full representation of the database objects within it. The next section highlights the areas of focus within the database file, namely the stored procedures and tables.

Data Model and Database Objects

The data model is very simple in nature; it only needs to store three basic data elements:

- Email
- Resource
- Contact

Each resource contains references to the Email contact table, with the e-mail addresses of the contacts that have sent and received the e-mails from files uploaded to the system. Figure 2-5 displays the diagram of the database tables involved.

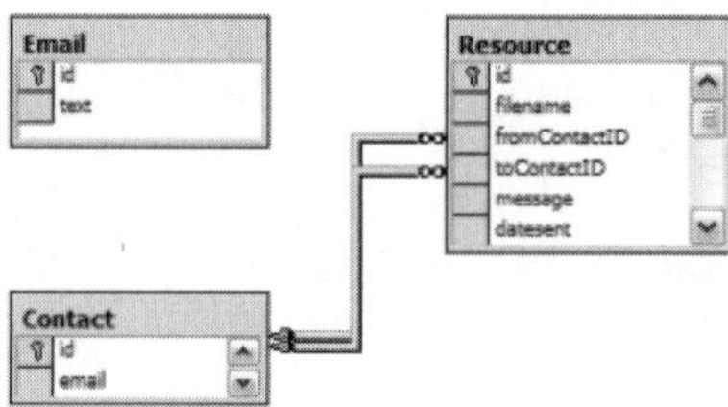

Figure 2-5

Following is a detailed view of each of the three tables.

The Email Table

Field Name	Data Type	Description
id	`Int`	The unique identifier for this record.
text	`varchar(MAX)`	The actual e-mail content stored as text, which the user can edit in the administrative section of the web site.

The Contact Table

Field Name	Data Type	Description
id	`Int`	The unique identifier for this record.
email	`Varchar(200)`	The e-mail address of the contact.

The Resource Table

Field Name	Data Type	Description
id	Int	The unique identifier for this record.
filename	varchar(300)	The question ID to which this response applies.
fromContactID	Int	The ID of the contact record that sent the file.
toContactID	Int	The ID of the contact record that received the file.
message	Varchar(1000)	The message that the sender provided with the file being uploaded.
datesent	Datetime	The datetime stamp at the time the file is uploaded.

In addition to these three tables, a number of stored procedures are in use. They follow a consistent naming pattern with the other chapters, as shown here:

- `sprocTableNameSelectList`
- `sprocTableNameSelectSingleItem`
- `sprocTableNameInsertUpdateItem`

In such fashion, the following stored procedures are used in the application:

- `sprocEmailInsertUpdateItem`
- `sprocEmailSelectSingleItem`
- `sprocResourceInsertUpdateItem`
- `sprocResourceSelectSingleItem`

The naming convention allows you to easily and quickly find the stored procedures that apply to a specific table, and whether they are selects, inserts, updates, or deletes.

There are a few stored procedures that you need to walk through. The first stored procedure, `sprocResourceSelectSingleItem`, is a basic `SELECT` statement based on the `ID` parameter, which selects a single resource record from the database and returns it to the caller:

```
ALTER PROCEDURE dbo.sprocResourceSelectSingleItem
    /*    '=============================================================
    '   NAME:                   sprocResourceSelectSingleItem
    '   DATE CREATED:           October 19, 2005
    '   CREATED BY:             Shawn Livermore (shawnlivermore.blogspot.com)
    '   CREATED FOR:            ASP.NET 2.0 - Instant Results
    '   FUNCTION:               Gets a specific resource from the DB
    '=============================================================
```

```
*/
(@id int)

as

select * from Resource where id = @id
```

The preceding stored procedure is called from the ResourceDB.vb data layer, in the `GetResourceFileName` function.

In similar fashion, the next stored procedure, `sprocEmailSelectSingleItem`, is used to select a single record from the Email table. There is no `ID` parameter in this one, because it assumes you will be storing only one record in this table for now. If you choose to add different e-mail versions or types in the system at a later time, this is the place to manage that information:

```
ALTER PROCEDURE dbo.sprocEmailSelectSingleItem
    /*   '=================================================================
    '    NAME:                   sprocEmailSelectSingleItem
    '    DATE CREATED:           October 19, 2005
    '    CREATED BY:             Shawn Livermore (shawnlivermore.blogspot.com)
    '    CREATED FOR:            ASP.NET 2.0 - Instant Results
    '    FUNCTION:               Gets the html and text message body from the DB
    '=================================================================
*/

as

select top 1 * from Email
```

Moving into the other two stored procedures, the level of complexity increases slightly. The following is the next stored procedure, `sprocEmailInsertUpdateItem`, which is used to update the e-mail text in the Email table's one record. It accepts one parameter, `@text`, which is simply the text content of the template e-mail that is used to send e-mails to recipients:

```
ALTER PROCEDURE dbo.sprocEmailInsertUpdateItem
/*    '=================================================================
    '    NAME:                   sprocEmailInsertUpdateItem
    '    DATE CREATED:           October 21, 2005
    '    CREATED BY:             Shawn Livermore (shawnlivermore.blogspot.com)
    '    CREATED FOR:            ASP.NET 2.0 - Instant Results
    '    FUNCTION:               Inserts or Updates the email content to the DB
    '=================================================================
*/
 (@text varchar(MAX))

AS

  UPDATE
   Email
    SET
      [text] = @text
```

The final stored procedure, `sprocResourceInsertUpdateItem`, is by far the most complex one, but not to worry. The basic idea of it is actually quite simple:

```
ALTER PROCEDURE dbo.sprocResourceInsertUpdateItem
/*    '===============================================================
    '   NAME:                   sprocResourceInsertUpdateItem
    '   DATE CREATED:           October 19, 2005
    '   CREATED BY:             Shawn Livermore (shawnlivermore.blogspot.com)
    '   CREATED FOR:            ASP.NET 2.0 - Instant Results
    '   FUNCTION:               Inserts or Updates a resource into the DB
    '===============================================================
*/
(@id int,
 @filename varchar(300),
 @fromContactEmail varchar(300),
 @toContactEmail varchar(300),
 @message varchar(1000))

AS

DECLARE @returnValue int
Declare @fromContactID int
Declare @toContactID int

/*
----------- fromContactID --------------
*/
--insert the contact records if they do not already exist...
if((select count(*) from contact where email = @fromContactEmail)=0)
   begin
      insert into contact (email) values (@fromContactEmail)
      SET @fromContactID = SCOPE_IDENTITY() --extract the contact id from the
insert
   end
else
   begin
      --extract the contact id from the insert
      SET @fromContactID = (select id from contact where email = @fromContactEmail)
   end

/*
----------- toContactID --------------
*/
if((select count(*) from contact where email = @toContactEmail)=0)
   begin
      insert into contact (email) values (@toContactEmail)
      SET @toContactID = SCOPE_IDENTITY() --extract the contact id from the insert
   end
else
   begin
      --extract the contact id from the insert
      SET @toContactID = (select id from contact where email = @toContactEmail)
   end

-- Insert a new resource record
```

```
IF (@id IS NULL)
BEGIN
  INSERT INTO
    Resource
    (
      filename,
      fromContactID,
      toContactID,
      message
    )
    VALUES
    (
      @filename,
      @fromContactID,
      @toContactID,
      @message
    )
    SET @returnValue = SCOPE_IDENTITY()
END
ELSE
BEGIN

  UPDATE
    Resource
    SET
      filename = @filename,
      fromContactID = @fromContactID,
      toContactID = @toContactID,
      message = @message
    WHERE
      Id = @id
    SET @returnValue = @id
END

   select @returnValue
```

This procedure is used to insert the resource information into the database, add new contacts to the Contact table, and resources to the Resource table. It uses the *upsert* methodology, wherein it will provide an update if the record already exists, or an insert if it does not.

`sprocResourceInsertUpdateItem` follows these specific steps:

1. Checks to see if the e-mail address of the sender (`@fromContactEmail`) is not already in the system:

```
/*
----------- fromContactID --------------
*/
--insert the contact records if they do not already exist...
if((select count(*) from contact where email = @fromContactEmail)=0)
```

2. If not, the stored procedure adds the e-mail address as new contact record, extracting the unique ID value to set the the `@fromContactID` locally declared variable for later insertion into the Resource table. If the record does exist, it performs a `select` statement to populate `@fromContactID`:

```
    begin
       insert into contact (email)
       values (@fromContactEmail)
       SET @fromContactID = SCOPE_IDENTITY()
       --we extracted the contact id from the insert
    end
 else
    begin
       --extract the contact id from the insert
       SET @fromContactID =
          (select id from contact
           where email = @fromContactEmail)
    end
```

* The next section of the stored procedure does the exact same thing, except this time it is with the `@toContactEmail` parameter, populating the `@toContactID` variable.

3. After you have valid `ContactIDs`, you can focus on the insertion of the resource record into the database. The following section is used to insert a new resource record into the Resource table, returning the new ID of the resource into the `@resourceID` variable:

```
-- Insert a new resource record
IF (@id IS NULL)
BEGIN
  INSERT INTO
    Resource
    (
      filename,
      fromContactID,
      toContactID,
      message
    )
    VALUES
    (
      @filename,
      @fromContactID,
      @toContactID,
      @message
    )
    SET @returnValue = SCOPE_IDENTITY()
END
```

4. The following `else` statement immediately follows this `if` clause, with the case in which the `@id` parameter is not null. This would be the case if the application passed an ID to the stored procedure, indicating that a resource record already existed, and the stored procedure is expected to perform an update, instead of an insert:

```
ELSE
BEGIN

  UPDATE
    Resource
    SET
      filename = @filename,
      fromContactID = @fromContactID,
```

```
          toContactID = @toContactID,
          message = @message
        WHERE
          Id = @id
        SET @returnValue = @id
    END

       select @returnValue
```

- The preceding code performs the `UPDATE` query, and returns the resulting `@resourceID` variable. Once the `@resourceID` variable is sent back to the caller (the data layer), the process for inserting a resource into the system is complete.

These are the stored procedures used within the Wrox File Share, and are entirely common for this type of application.

Themes and Skins

The Wrox File Share project provides a simple way to apply themes and skins to each page of the site, without modifying any HTML markup sections on any page (even the master page is safe from special control-based HTML markup). You can apply a theme to the entire web site by modifying the Web.config file to point to the name of your theme (assuming the theme exists in your project under the app_themes folder). This is carried out within each ASP.NET form by using the following code in each of the form's pre-initialization events:

```
        ''' <summary>
        ''' this preinit event fires to initialize the page. It allows for the
        ''' theme and title to be set for this page, which actually pulls from
        ''' the web.config setting via the shared Config class's exposed properties.
        ''' </summary>
        Protected Sub Page_PreInit(ByVal sender As Object, ByVal e As System.EventArgs)
    Handles Me.PreInit
            Page.Theme = Config.CurrentTheme
            Page.Title = Config.PageTitle
        End Sub
```

This basically accesses the `config` class's properties (pulled from the Web.config file), and sets the page's theme member to be the current theme value. In this way, you can maintain a consistent experience throughout the web site, with only one change needed to the Web.config to change the look and feel of the entire user experience! You are probably glad to hear that—I know I am. The exact place where you would change the theme for the site is in the `appSettings` section of the Web.config, as displayed here:

```
    <!--
        <add key="CurrentTheme" value="CleanBlue" />
    -->
        <add key="CurrentTheme" value="CleanRed" />
```

This code displays one of the theme entries as commented out, and one of them as active. Simply swap the two values to change the theme.

Security Model

The Wrox File Share uses ASP.NET 2.0 Forms Authentication with a SQL Server Security Provider. The initial designation to use this provider from within the ASP.NET Security Administration tool generates a new security database, which is included in the project and used to house all of the user account information and security settings. This security model implements Forms Authentication intrinsically within the various new ASP.NET 2.0 security controls, such as those used to log in, display login status, and recover your password. Fortunately, the heavy lifting is already done here (if there is any!), and a standard security starting point created for you. Using the ASP.NET Security Administration tool allows for further customization and changes to your settings as you see fit, but is not necessary to run the project properly with the basic Admin user.

The security model mentioned is utilized and referenced in several areas of the application. One such area is in reference to the Management folder of the site. The security model allows you to log in to the web site and become an authenticated user. The login.aspx form is loaded automatically whenever you try to access any of the ASPX files in the Management folder without first being unauthenticated. This is a clear glimpse at the new ASP.NET 2.0 security model implemented via the Role and Membership Providers. The configuration is such that the only provision to implement such security is an instance of the ASP.NET `Login` control:

```
<asp:Login ID="Login1" runat="server" />
```

As a practical use, this provides a clear example of a secure web site folder and the use of role-based access to pages within that folder via the ASP.NET 2.0 Configuration Tool. This tool is essentially used simply for security-rights management. The ASP.NET 2.0 Configuration Tool can be accessed within Visual Studio by choosing Website⇨ASP.NET Configuration from the main menu. Once the tool fully loads you'll see a Security tab. Clicking the Security tab allows you to modify the settings of any folder within your site to allow or restrict access based on roles that you can define and assign users to. The output of this effort generates the Web.config file that lies within the folder that you specified to restrict access to. An example of this Web.config file output is shown here:

```
<?xml version="1.0" encoding="utf-8"?>
<configuration xmlns="http://schemas.microsoft.com/.NetConfiguration/v2.0">
    <system.web>
        <authorization>
            <allow roles="Admin" />
            <deny users="?" />
        </authorization>
    </system.web>
</configuration>
```

This configuration file uses two main entries as the meat of the security settings. These are essentially XML statements that define the security rights for that folder, hierarchically within the web site, overriding the web site's root Web.config, as well as the machine.config on the server. In this file, the `<deny users="?" />` phrase means that the folder should deny any unauthenticated users, denoted by the question mark. Next, the `<allow roles="Admin"` entry represents the capability of the folder to allow access to `Admin` role.

Only one account is created for use within the Wrox File Share, and one role that the account is assigned to. These are as follows:

Username	Password	Account Description
Administrator	password#	This user is assigned to the Administrator role.

The following role is already in the security database and referenced within the application:

Role	Role Description
Administrator	This role has the ability to login to the administrative area, editing the contents of the e-mail text.

You can control access to form elements, functions, and file folders using the security roles implemented via the ASP.NET Configuration Tool, through your own scripted logic in VB.NET. This basic use of the ASP.NET 2.0 security model performs the bare minimum in application security.

Next, you have a chance to dive into the classes of the application, learning all about the layered approach to the flow of information within the site.

Classes Involved

The Wrox File Share contains some essential classes that represent the business and data layers of the application. In these basic class structures, you will find the basic methods and properties that provide the bulk of the features in the application.

The EmailContent Class

The `EmailContent` class (see Figure 2-6) is essentially the class that allows for the saving and retrieving of e-mail content text to and from the database.

Figure 2-6

The `EmailContent` class's methods are outlined in the following table:

Method	Return Type	Description
`SaveEmailContent()`	n/a	Saves the e-mail content, via the `EmailContentDB` class.
`GetEmailContent()`	String	Retrieves the e-mail from the database, via the `EmailContentDB` class.

The Resource Class

The `Resource` class (see Figure 2-7) is used to perform the bulk of the object provisioning for the business layer of the application. Its methods are accessible as public and shared for ease of use within the various forms and controls of the application. This means that you do not have to instantiate an instance of the `Resource` class in order call its methods. Instead, simply use the syntax of `Resource.MethodName()` in any VB.NET WebForm or control of the application to execute the function.

Figure 2-7

The following table displays the accessible members of the `Resource` class:

Method	Return Type	Description
`GetEmailBody()`	String	Returns the HTML body of the e-mail message to be sent out.
`GetResourceFileName()`	String	Returns the filename of the class by sending in the resource ID.
`SaveResource()`	Integer	Saves the new resource (file) to the database, passing in the sender information, receiver information, a message, and the filename.

The Config Class

The `Config` class, shown in Figure 2-8, is used as the configuration manager of the application. It is essentially the main access point for all configuration settings that any of the application tiers may require access to.

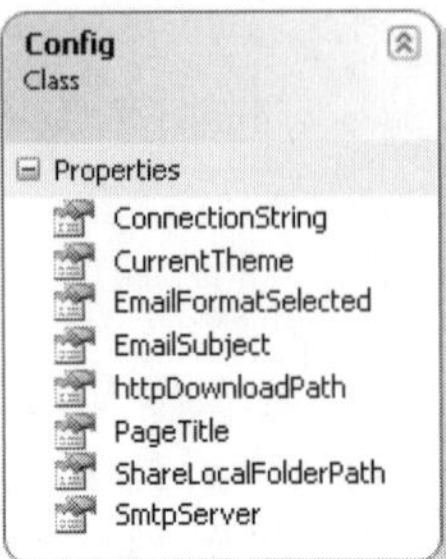

Figure 2-8

The following table displays the accessible members of the `Config` class:

Property	Return Type	Description
`ConnectionString()`	String	The connection string property that pulls from Web.config.
`CurrentTheme()`	String	The current theme of the web site as defined in the Web.config file.
`EmailFormatSelected()`	String	The extendable format variable for the type of e-mail format to be used. Text is the only value in use so far, but HTML may be desired.
`EmailSubject()`	String	The e-mail subject line for all outgoing e-mails notifying users that they have been sent a file to download.
`httpDownloadPath()`	String	The configuration entry determining the `httpDownloadPath http://localhost/FileShare/`, which is set at the Web.config.
`PageTitle()`	String	The HTML title value that each page displays, from the Web.config file.
`ShareLocalFolderPath()`	String	The local folder file path for all files to be uploaded onto the server from the Web.config file.
`SmtpServer()`	String	The configuration entry determining the SMTP server name and address.

The Utilities Class

The `Utilities` class is used to house the e-mail sending functionality of the Wrox File Share application (see Figure 2-9).

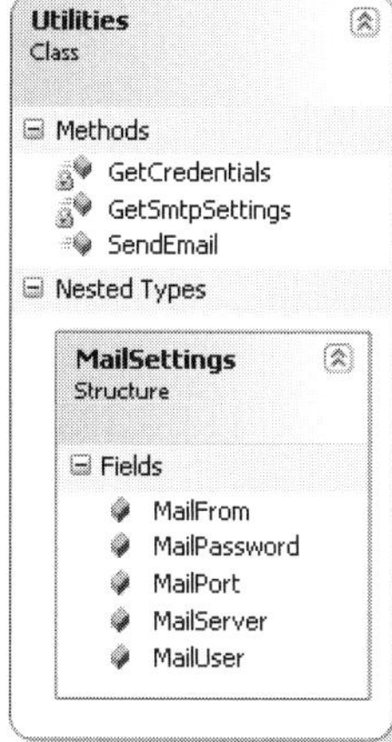

Figure 2-9

The following table displays the accessible members of the `Utilities` class:

Property	Return Type	Description
`GetCredentials()`	`System.Net .NetworkCredential`	Creates and returns a `System.Net .NetworkCredential` class object reference with the applicable config values.
`GetSmtpSettings()`	`MailSettings` (struct)	Used to retrieve the Web.config file values and set them to the struct instance properties.
`SendEmail()`	n/a	Used to send an e-mail, with the established settings.

Now you have seen the classes involved, and their applicable method calls. The next section, "Code and Code Explanation," dives deep into the development and walks you through all of the essential pieces of code you need to understand.

Code and Code Explanation

This section explains each of the essential code files in the Wrox File Share project. You look in detail at the files in the each of the different folders and learn how they interact and are used across the project.

Root Files

The root of the Wrox File Share contains several important files, including the main ASPX shell-pages, and the configuration and formatting pages.

Web.config

The Web.config stores vital configuration entries used within the application. One entry, named as the `SqlServerConnectionString`, controls the connection to the SQL Server 2005 Express database file FileShareDB.mdf, as shown here:

```
<connectionStrings>
      <add name="ConnectionString" connectionString="Data
Source=(local)\SqlExpress;AttachDbFilename=|DataDirectory|\FileShareDB.mdf;Integrat
ed Security=True;User Instance=True" providerName="System.Data.SqlClient"/>
   </connectionStrings>
```

Web.config also contains information managing the SMTP e-mail settings for sending out e-mails:

```
<configuration xmlns="http://schemas.microsoft.com/.NetConfiguration/v2.0">
   <appSettings>
      <add key="EmailFrom" value="admin@wroxfileshare.com"/>
    <add key="EmailSubject" value="File Ready for Download!"/>
    <add key="SmtpServer" value="127.0.0.1"/>
    <add key="MailUser" value="myalias"/>
    <add key="MailPassword" value="mypassword"/>
    <add key="MailPort" value="25"/>
    <add key="EmailFormatSelected" value="Text"/>
    <add key="PageTitle" value="Wrox File Sharing Website"/>
    <add key="ShareLocalFolderPath"
value="C:\inetpub\wwwroot\FileShare\FileStorage\"/>
    <add key="httpDownloadPath" value="http://localhost/FileShare/"/>
    <!--
    <add key="CurrentTheme" value="CleanBlue" />
    -->
      <add key="CurrentTheme" value="CleanRed"/>
   </appSettings>
```

These SMTP configuration entries are where you can specify the mail server settings that your application will use to send out e-mails to the specified recipients. The Web.config file is also used to provide easy modification to the themes in use for the entire site. More information on this is located in the design portion of this chapter, in the section "Themes and Skins."

config.vb

The `Config` class is used as an available business object for values and settings through visibility of some static members. Its members are listed as properties in order to abstract the location in which these values are stored. All of the values for the properties are stored in the Web.config file, with this `Config` class to retrieve them when they are needed:

```
Imports Microsoft.VisualBasic

Public Class Config
    ''' <summary>
```

```
    ''' The connection string property that pulls from the web.config
    ''' </summary>
    Public Shared ReadOnly Property ConnectionString() As String
        Get
            Return
ConfigurationManager.ConnectionStrings("ConnectionString").ConnectionString
        End Get
    End Property
    ''' <summary>
    ''' The current theme of the website as defined in the web.config file
    ''' </summary>
    Public Shared ReadOnly Property CurrentTheme() As String
        Get
            Return ConfigurationManager.AppSettings("CurrentTheme").ToString()
        End Get
    End Property
    ''' <summary>
    ''' The HTML title value that each page displays, as defined here from the
web.config file
    ''' </summary>
    Public Shared ReadOnly Property PageTitle() As String
        Get
            Return ConfigurationManager.AppSettings("PageTitle").ToString()
        End Get
    End Property
    ''' <summary>
    ''' The Local Folder File-Path for all files to be uploaded to on the server
    '''  as defined here from the web.config file
    ''' </summary>
    Public Shared ReadOnly Property ShareLocalFolderPath() As String
        Get
            Return
ConfigurationManager.AppSettings("ShareLocalFolderPath").ToString()
        End Get
    End Property
    ''' <summary>
    ''' The email subject line for all outgoing emails notifying users that they
have been sent a file to download...
    ''' </summary>
    Public Shared ReadOnly Property EmailSubject() As String
        Get
            Return ConfigurationManager.AppSettings("EmailSubject").ToString()
        End Get
    End Property
    ''' <summary>
    ''' The configuration entry determining whether the email body is in HTML or
plain text...
    ''' </summary>
    Public Shared ReadOnly Property EmailFormatSelected() As String
        Get
            Return
ConfigurationManager.AppSettings("EmailFormatSelected").ToString()
        End Get
    End Property
    ''' <summary>
```

```
    ''' The configuration entry determining the SMTP Server Name / Address ...
    ''' </summary>
    Public Shared ReadOnly Property SmtpServer() As String
        Get
            Return ConfigurationManager.AppSettings("SmtpServer").ToString()
        End Get
    End Property
    ''' <summary>
    ''' The configuration entry determining the httpDownloadPath...
    ''' the default local value is : "http://localhost/FileShare/" which is set at
the web.config
    ''' </summary>
    Public Shared ReadOnly Property httpDownloadPath() As String
        Get
            Return ConfigurationManager.AppSettings("httpDownloadPath").ToString()
        End Get
    End Property

End Class
```

As the `Config` class displays, the properties are marked as `Public Shared ReadOnly`, which allows them to be accessed from anywhere in the project by the config-dot notation. An example of this would be `config.ConnectionString()`. This would return the connection string from the `Config` class, without instantiating a `Config` class object first.

Resource.vb

The `Resource` class is used to retrieve and save the resource information being sent up to the web site. The class acts as a business layer and provides a level of abstraction between the requests for database records and the user interface.

By using `#Region` tags in the Resource.vb class file, the Visual Studio IDE allows the page to be grouped into organized sections. Sections that are commonly used to group the code in this way include Variables, Constructors, Methods, and Properties. This does not impact the .NET assemblies in any way, but is simply a great way to maintain organized logic. Figure 2-10 is a visual display of the regionalized code as it is displayed within the Visual Studio IDE.

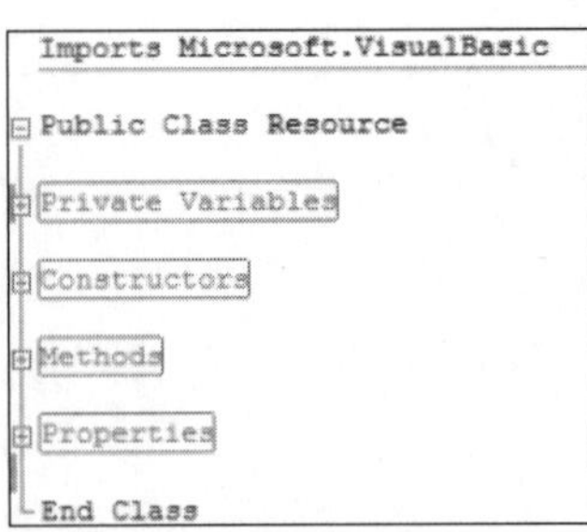

Figure 2-10

One of the more important method calls of the resource is the `SaveResource` method. The code for this is as follows:

```
    ''' <summary>
    ''' Saves the <see cref="Resource" /> by sending in the resource fields
    ''' </summary>
    ''' <param name="filename">The filename of the Resource.</param>
    ''' <param name="fromContactEmail">The email of the sender </param>
    ''' <param name="message">The message of the Resource.</param>
    ''' <param name="toContactEmail">The email of the recipient</param>
    ''' <param name="ID">The optional param: the id of the Resource.</param>
    Public Shared Function SaveResource(ByVal filename As String, ByVal
fromContactEmail As String, ByVal toContactEmail As String, ByVal message As
String) As Integer
        Return ResourceDB.SaveResource(filename, fromContactEmail, toContactEmail,
message)
    End Function
```

This method provides the means by which to hand off a `Resource` class object to the data tier for processing. It accepts five parameters:

- `filename`
- `fromContactEmail`
- `message`
- `toContactEmail`
- `ID`

These parameters represent the entire view of the `resource` class as it exists in the system.

resourceDB.vb

The `resourceDB` class is essentially the data layer for the application. It provides method calls to retrieve information from the database and insert or update data within the database as well. This class serves as the only file or object that will have access to the database files. In this way, you can isolate data-specific operations outside of the business logic layer. In so doing, you can see that it protects a developer from writing duplicate data access code and lends itself well to the function of maintaining organized and structured data access logic. This also supports the application being logically separated into tiers, or layers, with the deliberate feasibility of migrating and expanding the application onto separate servers at any point in time.

In line with the documented function call from the `Resource` class, the `resourceDB` class contains a `Save` method, as displayed here:

```
''' <summary>
    ''' Saves the <see cref="Resource" /> to the database
    ''' </summary>
    ''' <param name="filename">The filename of the Resource.</param>
    ''' <param name="fromContactEmail">The email of the sender</param>
    ''' <param name="message">The message of the Resource.</param>
    ''' <param name="toContactEmail">The email of recipient.</param>
    ''' <param name="ID">The optional param: the id of the Resource.</param>
    Public Shared Function SaveResource(ByVal filename As String, ByVal
fromContactEmail As String, ByVal toContactEmail As String, ByVal message As
String, Optional ByVal ID As Integer = Nothing) As Integer
```

```
        Using mConnection As New SqlConnection(Config.ConnectionString)

            Dim mResourceID As Integer

            'Create a command object
            Dim mCommand As SqlCommand = New
SqlCommand("sprocResourceInsertUpdateItem", mConnection)

            'set it to the type of 'stored procedure'
            mCommand.CommandType = CommandType.StoredProcedure

            'add in the parameters: the surveyID,
            'the question text, and the possible choices (A,B,C,or D)
            If ID > 0 Then
                mCommand.Parameters.AddWithValue("@id", ID)
            Else
                mCommand.Parameters.AddWithValue("@id", DBNull.Value)
            End If
            mCommand.Parameters.AddWithValue("@filename", filename)
            mCommand.Parameters.AddWithValue("@fromContactEmail", fromContactEmail)
            mCommand.Parameters.AddWithValue("@toContactEmail", toContactEmail)
            mCommand.Parameters.AddWithValue("@message", message)

            'open the connection and execute the stored procedure
            mConnection.Open()
            mResourceID = mCommand.ExecuteScalar()
            mConnection.Close()

            Return mResourceID

        End Using

    End Function
```

Another method of interest is the `GetEmailBody()` method, returning a string variable of the body of the e-mail template used for sending out e-mails to the recipient of the file share sender. The following is an excerpt of this method:

```
    ''' <summary>
    ''' Returns the HTML body of the email message to be sent out
    ''' </summary>
    ''' <param name="msg">The additional message provided by
    ''' the user to be within the body of the email.</param>
    Public Shared Function GetEmailBody(ByVal msg As String, _
        ByVal id As Integer, ByVal SenderEmail As String, _
        ByVal RecipientEmail As String) As String
        Dim emailBody As String = ""
        Try
            Using mConnection As New SqlConnection(Config.ConnectionString)

                Dim mLink As String
                mLink = Config.httpDownloadPath & "Download.aspx?resourceID="

                Dim mCommand As SqlCommand = New _
                    SqlCommand("sprocEmailSelectSingleItem", mConnection)
```

```
                mCommand.CommandType = CommandType.StoredProcedure
                mConnection.Open()
                Using mDataReader As SqlDataReader = _
                  mCommand.ExecuteReader(CommandBehavior.CloseConnection)
                  If mDataReader.Read() Then
                    'get the email body template content from the email table
                    emailBody = mDataReader.GetString( _
                        mDataReader.GetOrdinal(Config.EmailFormatSelected))
                    'replace the custom msg area with the message from the sender
                    emailBody = emailBody.Replace("[msg]", msg)
                    emailBody = emailBody.Replace("[link]", mLink & id.ToString())
                    emailBody = emailBody.Replace("[sender]", SenderEmail)
                    emailBody = emailBody.Replace("[recipient]", RecipientEmail)

                  End If
                  mDataReader.Close()
                End Using
            End Using
        Catch ex As Exception
            'By calling the "Throw" statement, you are raising the error to
            'the global.asax file, which will use the default error handling
            'page to process/display the custom error to the user
            Throw
        End Try
        Return emailBody
End Function
```

The preceding page logic performs the following steps:

1. Creates a new `SqlCommand` object, passing in the stored procedure name and the connection:

```
Using mConnection As New SqlConnection(Config.ConnectionString)
```

2. Creates a local variable used to concatenate the real hyperlink based on the configuration-driven design:

```
Dim mLink As String
mLink = Config.httpDownloadPath & "Download.aspx?resourceID="
```

3. Sets the `CommandType` to be `StoredProcedure`, and provides the name of `sprocEmailSelectSingleItem`:

```
Dim mCommand As SqlCommand = New SqlCommand("sprocEmailSelectSingleItem",
mConnection)
mCommand.CommandType = CommandType.StoredProcedure
```

4. Creates a new `SqlDataReader`:

```
Using mDataReader As SqlDataReader = _
mCommand.ExecuteReader(CommandBehavior.CloseConnection)
```

5. Calls the command's `Execute` method. This executes the `sprocEmailSelectSingleItem` stored procedure and returns the result as a string value in a one-record row:

```
mCommand.ExecuteReader(CommandBehavior.CloseConnection)
```

6. Assigns the ordinal value of data within the `DataReader` to a string variable, `emailBody`:

```
If mDataReader.Read() Then
     'get the email body template content from the email table
     emailBody = mDataReader.GetString( _
       mDataReader.GetOrdinal(Config.EmailFormatSelected))
```

7. Replaces the values of the dynamic variables for the text message from the sender, the URL for the hyperlink used to download the file, the e-mail address of the sender, and the e-mail address of the recipient:

```
'replace the custom msg area with the message from the sender
emailBody = emailBody.Replace("[msg]", msg)
emailBody = emailBody.Replace("[link]", mLink & id.ToString())
emailBody = emailBody.Replace("[sender]", SenderEmail)
emailBody = emailBody.Replace("[recipient]", RecipientEmail)
```

8. Returns the string value to the caller:

```
Return emailBody
```

This provides the desired abstracted functionality to retrieve the e-mail message body from the database, and return this text content to caller.

WebForms

The WebForms are standard ASPX pages that contain the client-side graphical user interface of the application. A few WebForms are of particular importance within the project, as noted in the following sections.

Default.aspx

The Default.aspx file is of course used as the first page that loads when the site is accessed. Within this page are the controls used to capture the essential file information for the uploading of the file into the system.

Several specific functions from this page should be mentioned. The first one is a common event with logic that is somewhat redundant throughout the application's ASPX pages. This is the page `initialize` event, displayed here:

```
    ''' <summary>
    ''' this preinit event fires to initialize the page. It allows
    ''' for the theme and title to be set for this page, which
    ''' actually pulls from the web.config setting via the shared
    ''' Config class's exposed properties.
    ''' </summary>
    Protected Sub Page_PreInit(ByVal sender As Object, ByVal e As System.EventArgs)
Handles Me.PreInit
        Page.Theme = Config.CurrentTheme
        Page.Title = Config.PageTitle
    End Sub
```

The `Page.Theme` is the `theme` property of the `Page` reference. By setting this `theme` property to the `Config` class's exposed `CurrentTheme` value, you are assigning a theme at run time. This model of assignment is ideal, because each page can dynamically utilize the theme that is controlled via the Web.config file, without requiring any other file changes.

The other area of special interest is the `btnSend` button's `Click` event handler. This provides the uploading and saving of the information, and sends out an e-mail to the recipient.

Specifically, three processes provide the sending or capturing of the file. They are as follows:

- Text data inserted into the database about the file.
- The actual file uploaded to the storage folder on the server.
- An e-mail sent to the recipient with notification of the file being ready to download.

The code for the `Click` event is as follows:

```
Protected Sub btnSend_Click(ByVal sender As Object, ByVal e As System.EventArgs)
Handles btnSend.Click
        If FileUpload1.FileName <> "" Then
            'upload the file to the server...
            FileUpload1.SaveAs(Config.ShareLocalFolderPath _
                + FileUpload1.FileName)
            'save the info to the database...
            Dim ResourceID As Integer = Resource.SaveResource( _
                FileUpload1.FileName, txtSenderEmail.Text, _
                txtRecipientEmail.Text, txtMessage.Text)
            'get the body of the email message...
            Dim emailBody As String = Resource.GetEmailBody( _
                txtMessage.Text, ResourceID, txtSenderEmail.Text, _
                txtRecipientEmail.Text)
            'send an email to the recipient...
            Utilities.SendEmail(txtRecipientEmail.Text, _
                txtSenderEmail.Text, Config.EmailSubject, emailBody)
            Server.Transfer("UploadComplete.aspx", True)
        End If
    End Sub
```

This event performs the most essential portion of logic within the application by far, and is the crux of the programming effort to host a file share application of this kind. The event is so critical because it performs the specific upload, save, and e-mail functionality that the application is known for. If you want to add additional features to the application in a big way, you will probably want to start here and work your way into the deeper layers of the application.

Login.aspx

The Login page contains a `Login` control and a `PasswordRecovery` control. The Login page is located at the root of the web site and does not use a master page. The `Login` controls contain HTML markup (shown in the following code) that defines the specific values for the destination page and text values of the controls.

```
    <fieldset style="height: 128px; width: 270px;">
    <asp:Login ID="Login1" runat="server" DestinationPageUrl=
"~/Management/ManageEmail.aspx">
```

```
        </asp:Login>
        </fieldset>
        <br />
        <br />
        <fieldset style="height: 118px; width: 270px;">
        <asp:PasswordRecovery ID="PasswordRecovery1" runat="server">
        </asp:PasswordRecovery>
        </fieldset>
```

The preceding HTML markup contains the control definitions for the `Login` and `PasswordRecovery` controls and their properties.

Download.aspx

The Download.aspx WebForm is used to provide access to the files stored within the web site, without forcing the user to view a web page filled with advertisements.

The `Page_Load` event of the page is as follows:

```
    ''' <summary>
    ''' this load event fires to process the display of
    ''' the download dialogue for the file
    ''' </summary>
    Protected Sub Page_Load(ByVal sender As Object, ByVal e As System.EventArgs)
Handles Me.Load
        DisplayDownloadDialog(Config.ShareLocalFolderPath & _
            Resource.GetResourceFileName(Request.QueryString("resourceID")))
    End Sub
```

This event calls the `DisplayDownloadDialog` function, passing in the `Config.ShareLocalFolder Path` and a querystring variable, `resourceID`. The `Config.ShareLocalFolderPath` is the property exposed by the `Config` class that refers to the local file share on the web site. This allows for a direct output of the file object programmatically, because it is a local pointer to the file on the server. The `resourceID` querystring variable is the ID of the resource record the page will be referencing as it attempts to return a downloadable file to the client. Each file on the Wrox File Share has an ID number, known as the `resourceID`. It is this number that allows you to query the database and extract the name of the file to be downloaded.

The following is the `DisplayDownloadDialog` function from the download.aspx.cs WebForm code-behind page:

```
Sub DisplayDownloadDialog(ByVal PathVirtual As String)
        Dim strPhysicalPath As String
        Dim objFileInfo As System.IO.FileInfo
        Try
            'strPhysicalPath = Server.MapPath(PathVirtual)
            strPhysicalPath = PathVirtual
            'exit if file does not exist
            If Not System.IO.File.Exists(strPhysicalPath) Then
                Exit Sub
            End If
            objFileInfo = New System.IO.FileInfo(strPhysicalPath)
            Response.Clear()
```

```
            'Add Headers to enable dialog display
            Response.AddHeader("Content-Disposition", _
                "attachment; filename=" & objFileInfo.Name)
            Response.AddHeader("Content-Length", objFileInfo.Length.ToString())
            Response.ContentType = "application/octet-stream"
            Response.WriteFile(objFileInfo.FullName)
        Catch ex As Exception
            'By calling the "Throw" statement, you are raising the error to
            'the global.asax file, which will use the default error handling
            'page to process/display the custom error to the user
            Throw
        Finally
            Response.End()
        End Try
    End Sub
```

This excerpt provides a file in the form of an Open or Save dialog box, as noted in the previous section, "Using the Wrox File Share."

Instead of a typical web page displaying advertisements, the Wrox File Share provides a directly streamed file to HTTP caller from the click of a hyperlink. The response of the page is cleared, headers are added to it, and the file object is written to it before it is returned to the caller. This allows the page to return a file, a fast and clean approach to downloading the file.

The Download page is extensible in that the application could be easily modified so that another page would be loaded first, with a link to the download.aspx page, passing in a `resourceID` querystring variable. As such, the file could be re-downloaded or downloaded in a safer fashion, using a clickable button or button-link to initiate the request. This is more commonly used across the board, because many download pages are riddled with advertisements and problematic page elements that seem to be the cause for failed download attempts.

User Controls

Some specific user controls in the site assist with the navigation and content display for multiple pages. Because web user controls promote a practice of creating and using reusable code, they were made to be applicable within multiple pages of the site, depending on the nature of the controls.

header.ascx

The `header` user control is used to provide the top area of each page with meaningful content. If anything needs to reside at or near the top of a web page, you would want to add it to the `header` control so it will be visible through all of the pages.

The following code represents entire header.ascx source:

```
<%@ Control Language="VB" AutoEventWireup="false" CodeFile="header.ascx.vb"
Inherits="Controls_header" %>
<div style="text-align: center">
    <table><tr>
```

```
            <td><img src="../Images/headerlogo.gif" /></td>
            <td><h1><% Response.Write(Page.Title) %></h1>
            </td>
        </tr></table>
    </div>
```

Notice that the `<%Response.Write(Page.Title)%>` tags are used to write back to the response stream a title of the web site on the top of each page, which originated from the Web.config file.

footer.ascx

The `footer` user control is used as the bottom section of the site, for each page that uses the master page. That is, the `footer` control, among others, is a referenced control within the master page. In this way, it is propagated to all pages in the same exact manner.

The content of the `footer` control is displayed here:

```
<%@ Control Language="VB" AutoEventWireup="false" CodeFile="footer.ascx.vb"
Inherits="Controls_footer" %>
<a href="http://wrox.com" target="_blank">&copy; 2005 Wrox Press</a>   
<asp:LoginStatus ID="LoginStatus1" runat="server"
LogoutAction="RedirectToLoginPage"
    LogoutPageUrl="~/Login.aspx" />
```

This excerpt includes a reference to a `LoginStatus` control, brand new in the ASP.NET 2.0 controlset. The new control displays a changing link-button for providing log-in and log-out functionality. When users are *logged in* to the site, the `LoginStatus` control displays a Logout link-button. Clicking the Logout link-button logs users out of the site, and directs them to the Login page. When users are *logged out* of the site, the `LoginStatus` control displays a Login link-button. Clicking the Login link-button directs them to the Login page, where they are able to log in.

navigation.ascx

The `navigation` user control is used to provide the reusable menu on each page of the site. The `Menu` control itself is a brand new ASP.NET 2.0 control that binds to a `SiteMapDataSource` control, also new in version 2.0 of the .NET Framework. The `SiteMapDataSource` control is used to bind to an XML file, wherein the site files are listed as entries in the XML file.

The following excerpt is the HTML markup of the `navigation` control:

```
<%@ Control Language="VB" AutoEventWireup="false" CodeFile="navigation.ascx.vb"
Inherits="Controls_navigation" %>
<asp:Menu ID="Menu1" runat="server" DataSourceID="SiteMapDataSource1"
Orientation="Horizontal"
    StaticDisplayLevels="2"></asp:Menu>
<asp:SiteMapDataSource  ID="SiteMapDataSource1" runat="server" />
```

The XML file of the `SiteMapDataSource` control is displayed here:

```
<?xml version="1.0" encoding="utf-8" ?>
<siteMap xmlns="http://schemas.microsoft.com/AspNet/SiteMap-File-1.0" >
  <siteMapNode url="ContentFiles/default.aspx" title="Home">
```

```
      <siteMapNode url="ContentFiles/about.aspx" title="About" />
      <siteMapNode url="ContentFiles/contact.aspx" title="Contact Us" />
      <siteMapNode url="Management/ManageEmail.aspx" title="Admin" />
    </siteMapNode>
  </siteMap>
```

To add a page to the menu of the web site, you must simply copy and paste (with the necessary modifications) an entry of the Web.sitemap file. In this way, the master page (which contains the only reference to the `navigation` control) provides visibility to the menu of the site on each page.

The next section explains in detail how to install and configure the source files of the web site and how to deploy the site to a server in a production environment.

Setting up the Project

The time has come to learn how to install this Wrox File Share and see for yourself how quickly you can be up and running with a working resource application. You can install the web site either as a hosted web site application or as a source codebase for editing in Visual Studio 2005 or VWD.

Because the application involves sending e-mails, the configuration of a usable e-mail account is imperative for the project to run properly. Many mail providers do not openly provide SMTP relay to their user accounts, and some careful use of the mail server security protocols may be necessary. This sample application assumes you have access to a mail server with relay permissions granted for a valid user account.

Hosted Web Site Installation

This section assumes that the .NET Framework 2.0 is already installed. If you want to install the Wrox File Share as a hosted web site on a computer or server, without customizations or enhancements at all, follow these steps:

1. Open the folder Chapter 02 – Wrox File Share\Installation Files\ from the CD-ROM that came with this book and double-click the setup.exe file.
2. This process installs the files properly for hosting the web site locally to `C:\wwwRoot\FileShare` as a file-based web site application. Click Next to install the application, and close the installation program when it completes.
3. Browse to your local web site (for example, `http://localhost/FileShare`). The Wrox File Share application should appear. To test the Administration section, click the Admin link and log in with a username of `Admin` and a password of `password#`.
4. Finally, if you need to expose the site to the outside world, be sure to configure the public IP address to the IIS web site application. The details of this IIS configuration and its implications are outside the scope of this book, but the Wrox File Share is easily configurable as a public web site with a brief tutorial on web site hosting.

Local Developer Installation

This section assumes that the .NET Framework 2.0 is already installed, along with either Visual Studio 2005 or VWD. If you would like to open the project in Visual Studio or VWD, perform the following steps:

1. Create a new web site in Visual Web Developer or Visual Studio 2005.
2. Open the folder Chapter 02 – Wrox File Share Installer\ from the CD-ROM that came with this book and extract the contents of the file FileShareSource.zip to a folder on your hard drive.
3. Open a Windows Explorer and browse to the folder that contains the unpacked files. Next, arrange both Visual Web Developer and the Windows Explorer in such a way that both are visible at the same time.
4. In the Windows Explorer, select all the folders and files within the codebase and drag them from the explorer window into VWD's Solution Explorer. If you're prompted to overwrite files, select Yes. You should end up with a Solution Explorer that contains all of the necessary files for the project to run properly.
5. In the `appSettings` section of the Web.config file, modify the various mail server settings' values to reflect the SMTP relay e-mail account information to be used for sending e-mails. Also, the `PageTitle` property is changeable here, which applies to the window title bar of each page in the site:

```
<appSettings>
      <add key="EmailFrom" value="admin@wroxfileshare.com"/>
    <add key="EmailSubject" value="File Ready for Download!"/>
    <add key="SmtpServer" value="127.0.0.1"/>
    <add key="MailUser" value="myalias"/>
    <add key="MailPassword" value="mypassword"/>
    <add key="MailPort" value="25"/>
    <add key="EmailFormatSelected" value="Text"/>
    <add key="PageTitle" value="Wrox File Sharing Website"/>
    <add key="ShareLocalFolderPath" value=
"C:\inetpub\wwwroot\FileShare\FileStorage\"/>
    <add key="httpDownloadPath" value="http://localhost/FileShare/"/>
    <!--
    <add key="CurrentTheme" value="CleanBlue" />
    -->
      <add key="CurrentTheme" value="CleanRed"/>
   </appSettings>
```

6. Press F5 to run the application in the development environment. The most engaging portion of effort in this process will probably be the use and configuration of the mail server account within the Web.config file.

For some insight on how you can modify your project in order to take advantage of some of the possible uses of the Wrox File Share, head to `www.wrox.com` and find this book's download page.

Summary

This chapter reviewed some of new controls within the ASP.NET 2.0 Framework, such as the `Login`, `LoginStatus`, `PasswordRecovery`, `SiteMap`, `SiteMapDataSource`, master pages, and `Menu` controls. The flow of the chapter was centered around a simple application design, using business layer classes, data layer classes, and a basic database structure. You learned how each of these new controls can save development time and effort in great proportions.

The Wrox File Share design provided a glimpse at the class files in use, their properties, their methods, and the general purposes of each. It also gave visibility to the stored procedures, table designs, relationships, and generalized data entities.

The chapter finished by showing you how to extract and customize the Wrox File Share in a development environment, and how to install it to production.

Wrox Chat Server

A web-based chat application can be a very useful component to your online presence. It is a great way for customers and support representatives to communicate and achieve instantaneous results. Questions can be answered within seconds, whereas e-mail and phone calls have delays that seem to drag the online experience to a grueling halt. Customers can simply type their question along with their order number into the browser window and receive the status of their order almost instantly from the customer support representative on the other side of the world. In other cases, chat applications allow companies to provide cost-effective support regardless of the language barriers that may normally exist between the two people communicating. Certainly, chat applications have had a tremendous impact on the way information is exchanged over the Web. For these reasons and more, many businesses add chat pages to their sites so they can provide instant access to their helpful customer support services. But this simple web site addition can end up becoming a larger effort than it initially appears. What's the big deal, you ask? It's just a little chat page! How hard can it be? Well, numerous ways exist to implement a chat application for an organization, and tons of implications may follow. For example, a chat application could require customizations, such as the following:

- The capability to store chat messages within a database for reporting purposes.
- A provision to logically group the chat rooms for special needs that web users may find helpful.
- A way to identify common chat words and phrases that users are chatting about, which may lead to finding commonalities in the user community that provide insight to their interest or concerns.
- A way to change the server name and settings of the chat system, allowing for maintenance to server configurations or infrastructure.
- A means by which to share chat messages coming in to the web site among many customer support personnel.
- Automated chat responses for commonly asked questions. These may include detecting a series of words or phrases that combine to form phrases that can be catalogued, and responses can be sent back in a form of artificial dialogue that might help people find what they are looking for.

Considering the possibilities, you must take a broad approach to implementing a chat section of a web site for any sort of successful online presence. The basic technology infrastructure needs to focus on the chat mechanisms specifically, because they are the crux of the application and seem to be the differentiator between applications on the market. That is, some chat applications are slower than others, and some are limited to being executed at the desktop level.

The time and energy it takes to create such an application, and the reusable nature of the application itself, make it a perfect candidate to include in this Instant Results book, which provides the basic foundational templates for implementing similar solutions on your own.

The essential features of the Wrox Chat Server include the following:

- The capability to enter only your e-mail address and be able to start chatting immediately, without waiting for any sort of applet or heavy application to load.
- The display of each chat room is grouped by category, allowing for an organized approach to the available chat categories within your application.
- The display of each chat room is accompanied by a number of current chat room members, allowing web browsers to see which chat rooms are currently being accessed.
- The use of asynchronous callbacks, a new feature in ASP.NET 2.0, which allow for easy implementation of Ajax methods and technologies (providing behind-the-scenes `xmlHttp` posts with JavaScript and responding to the posts via events on the server, all without refreshing the page).
- The capability to specify the number of hours for which each chat session maintains its messages on the server.
- The capability to change the look and feel the entire web site by simply modifying one entry in a configuration file.

These features comprise the bulk of this Wrox Chat Server application — it is fairly straightforward in its use of generalized chat application concepts, but actually implements some very exciting and complicated technologies. So get ready to learn about a few of the greatest web-based features with the all-new ASP.NET 2.0 release!

This chapter analyzes the various components that make up the web site, including the specific controls that ship with the ASP.NET 2.0 development environments. These controls include the following:

- `Menu` control
- `SiteMapDataSource` control
- Themes
- Master Pages
- Callbacks

The section, "Wrox Chat Server Design," digs into the physical design of the project in great detail. This includes the core pieces of technology and outlines the file structure of the site. It also looks at the various classes involved, the members of each class, and walks you through the database tables and their relationships.

The section titled "Code and Code Explanation" focuses on the design of each class, exposing their methods and properties.

The final section, "Setting up the Project," reviews how to load up the Wrox Chat Server in a development environment, and how to customize it to meet your needs.

Using the Wrox Chat Server

Using the Wrox Chat Server is completely intuitive. The application has been designed to be the most simplistic approach possible to conducting a chat over the Internet. All you need to do is wrapped up in three simple steps:

1. Enter your e-mail address and click Continue.
2. Select a chat room.
3. Type a message in the chat window and press Enter to send.

So, cut the chatter and get to business! If you have installed the chat source code to your local machine, (refer to the section "Setting up the Project" later in this chapter), you can browse to view the site by going to `http://localhost/ChatServer`. The screen shown in Figure 3-1 appears.

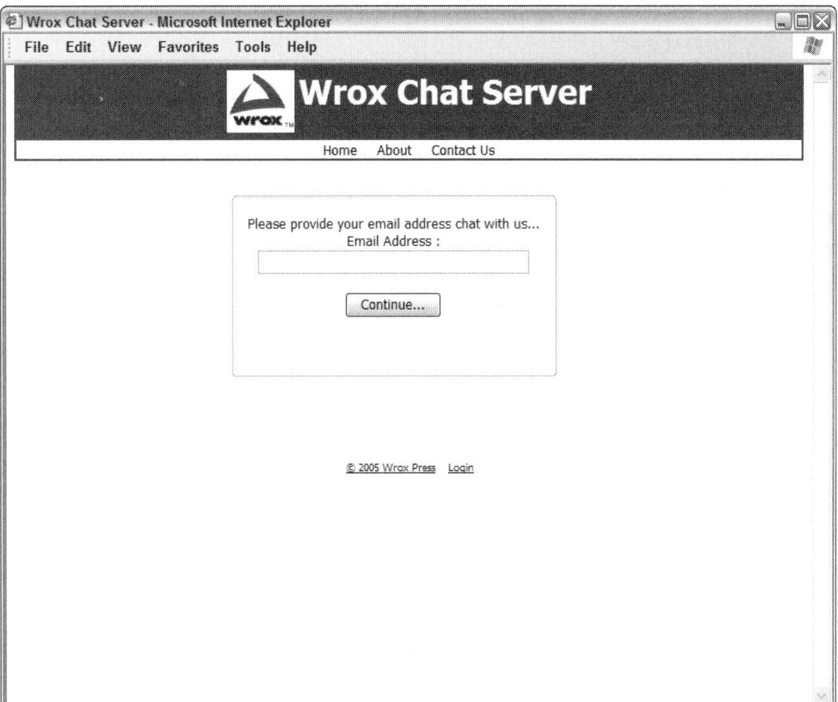

Figure 3-1

At the top of the menu are three links to choose from:

- Home
- About
- Contact Us

On the homepage, you will see a text box used to capture your e-mail address. Once you enter your e-mail address here, click Continue to proceed. This simply opens up a session variable for your e-mail address, and uses it for the extent of your session within the site. The next screen you are brought to is the chat room selection page (see Figure 3-2), where you will see a list of all the chat rooms available, separated by categories.

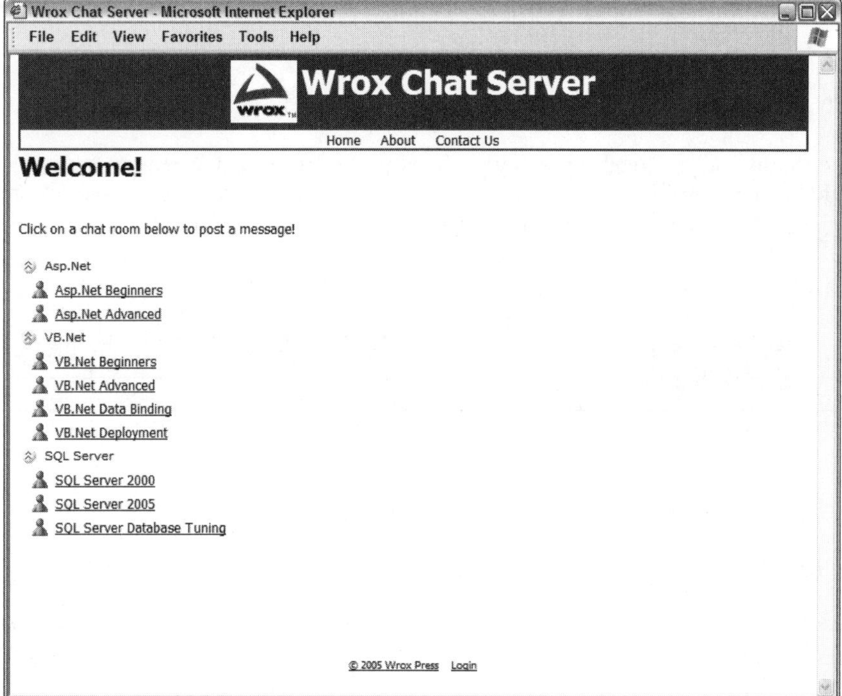

Figure 3-2

From the interface in Figure 3-2, you can select the chat room by simply clicking its name. You are then brought to the actual chat room, like the one in Figure 3-3, where you are able to enter any text you like into the window.

Figure 3-3 displays the basic chat room interface, with the title of VB.Net Data Binding. It is here that the actual chat interactions will take place.

This chapter covers the essential areas of the development that comprise the application. It walks you through the core class files in detail, outlining their behavior. In addition, you also gain insight into the database, data model, and database objects.

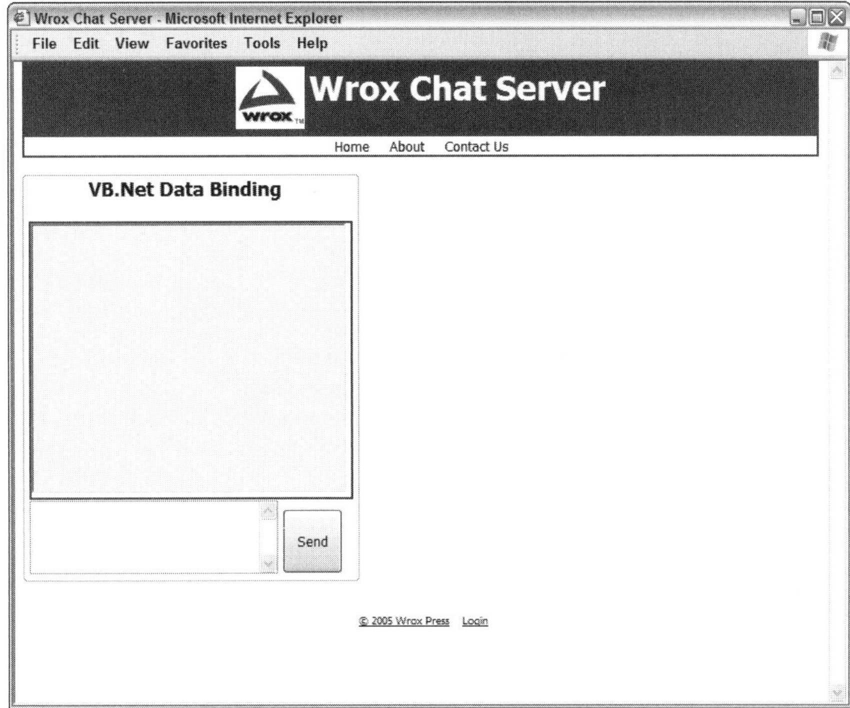

Figure 3-3

The next section addresses the physical design of the application, covering the client, business, and data layers.

Wrox Chat Server Design

In this section you explore the entire design of the Wrox Chat Server, learning how to initiate callbacks, discerning the site's structure and data model, understanding the themes and skins employed, and finally, absorbing all the classes involved.

Sending Messages Using Callbacks

Callbacks are brand new to the .NET Framework 2.0. They basically allow local browser scripts to make asynchronous calls to remote servers without the need to refresh the page. This technology provides a highly responsive user interface over the Internet, and has been much-needed for many years. Raw data can be sent and received in separate memory spaces without ever refreshing the user's browser window. This concept is similar to recent technologies that have been masterfully implemented in various online solutions using technologies such as Ajax or Remote Scripting. Although these methods and techniques provide dramatically greater levels of performance within most web interfaces, the actual code to implement such solutions is slightly complicated in nature. Callbacks provide an alternative to the complex implementations of hand-written JavaScript and `xmlHTTP` post logic.

The flow of events when executing a callback is outlined here:

1. The `GetCallbackEventReference` method obtains the name of your client-side JavaScript function that is identified as the initiator of the callback. This occurs because your page implemented the `ICallbackEventHandler` interface. By implementing the interface, the webform automatically adds client-side JavaScript functions for you.
2. The JavaScript that was intrinsically registered at the client contains an extra layer, called the *Callback Manager*, which is a set of JavaScripts used to launch and receive `xmlHTTP` posts between the browser and the web server. This Callback Manager intercepts the request that is to be sent to the server as a callback, and creates the actual request mechanism itself as a value-added feature. The Callback Manager sends off the asynchronous `xmlHTTP` post to the server at this point.
3. Once the Callback Manager has sent the post off to the server, the server receives the request and invokes the `ICallbackEventHandler.RaiseCallbackEvent()` method, which is where your custom logic can reside, before the server processes the call and returns any sort of response to the caller. Arguments can be accepted in this event as parameters, often used to look up data from a database or process information.
4. The server returns the call over the Internet to the Callback Manager, notifying the client that the request has been received and sent back. String values can be sent back as return values of the call, which are then handed off to the original caller in step 5.
5. Finally, the Callback Manager notifies the JavaScript calling method that the callback has been completed, and passes back any string values the server may have provided. This allows for additional local client-side scripting such as the updating of the user interface.

You must take several required actions in order to use callbacks within ASP.NET 2.0 pages:

- Implement the `ICallbackEventHandler` interface.
- Create custom JavaScript methods.
- Provide logic in two server-side events.
- Register a specific client-side script.

The detailed steps needed to actually create a callback in a new web application are as follows.

1. To create a callback from a WebForm, you first need to decide on the WebForm you want to use. As a reference for troubleshooting, the ChatWindow.aspx page in the ContentFiles folder is where the sample project implements the callback methods. Start by opening the code-behind file you want to process callbacks from, and implement the System.Web.UI.ICallbackEventHandler interface:

```
Implements System.Web.UI.ICallbackEventHandler
```

2. This automatically creates an event handler called `RaiseCallbackEvent()` and a method called `GetCallbackResult()`.

    - The actual code generated for these two items is as follows:

```
Public Sub RaiseCallbackEvent(ByVal eventArgument As String) Implements _
System.Web.UI.ICallbackEventHandler.RaiseCallbackEvent
```

```
End Sub

Public Function GetCallbackResult() As String Implements _
System.Web.UI.ICallbackEventHandler.GetCallbackResult
End Function
```

- The `RaiseCallbackEvent()` accepts the call from the client, allowing the server to process business logic as needed, and the `GetCallbackResult()` function sends a response back to the client, allowing the client to display the update in the browser via JavaScript (keep reading, it will make sense in a moment).

3. Next, provide the client-side script, which provides the Callback Manager script's entry point and exit point as embedded JavaScript functions on the client side. This script's functions are named `CallServer` and `ReceiveServerData`:

```
Sub Page_Load(ByVal sender As Object, ByVal e As System.EventArgs) Handles Me.Load
        Dim cm As ClientScriptManager = Page.ClientScript
        Dim cbReference As String
        cbReference = cm.GetCallbackEventReference(Me, "arg", _
            "ReceiveServerData", "")
        Dim callbackScript As String = ""
        callbackScript &= "function CallServer(arg, context)" & _
            "{" & cbReference & "; }"
        cm.RegisterClientScriptBlock(Me.GetType(), "CallServer", _
            callbackScript, True)
End Sub
```

4. Add a standard HTML text box to the HTML markup on the form. This will be named `txtMessage`. This provides the mechanism of input from the user to the server:

```
<input id="txtMessage" style="width: 218px; height: 55px" type="text" />
```

5. Then, with the following code, add a browser-side button that contains a special `onclick` event call to the Callback Manager entry point (for which you embedded the name of `CallServer` in step 3). This `onclick` event accepts an argument of the `txtMessage` control's `text` value. This is how the local client-side scripting captures the user input and sends it off to the server:

```
<input type="button" value="Send"
onclick="CallServer(document.getElementById('txtMessage').value, null)"
style="width: 57px; height: 60px" id="Button1"/><br />
```

6. Add a JavaScript routine called `ReceiveServerData()` to the HTML markup on the form. This routine accepts the arguments of `arg` and `context`. Don't worry about `context`, but `arg` provides the response of data back from the server, once it is done processing the call. This is the actual implementation of the Callback Manager's exit point. Any code can go here, but it is the Wrox Chat Server's primary way of updating the user as the result of the behind-the-scenes callback event. In this case, an HTML element's contents are updated with a string value from the server:

```
<script type="text/javascript">
function ReceiveServerData(arg, context)
{
    //send txt to a different html control, or process the info via javascript...
    var obj = document.getElementById("MyOtherHTMLcontrol");
```

```
        obj.innerHTML += arg;
    }
    </script>
```

Now you have a working callback routine. The client has the necessary JavaScript routines, and the server provides the necessary references to the Callback Manager classes and events. Not bad for 10 minutes of work and a little bit of elbow grease!

Structure of the Site

The sections of the web site project are listed in the following table:

Section	Description
App_Code	The folder that houses the business layer class (chatroom.vb) and the data layer class (chatroomDB.vb).
App_Data	The standard .NET folder for database files.
App_Themes	The themes folder, containing two themes for use with the site.
ContentFiles	The standard ASPX WebForm files for displaying content.
Controls	Stores all user controls.
Images	Stores images for the header or any other pages.
[miscellaneous files]	These include the Web.config file, sitemap file, and Master Page file at the root of the site.

Data Model

The data model is very simple in nature; it needs to store only four basic data elements:

- Chat Room Categories
- Chat Rooms
- Messages
- Users

Each chat room is classified under a single chat room category. There is no limit to the number of chat rooms and categories you can create, although it must be done manually at the database level for now. Each message is posted under exactly one chat room and is tracked by the user ID who sent it. All messages for all chat rooms are stored on the server, but only the chat messages for the last hour are sent back to the users. You can change the number of hours to keep messages active in the Web.config file of the site.

The diagram of the database tables involved is displayed in Figure 3-4.

A detailed view of each of the four tables is given in the following sections.

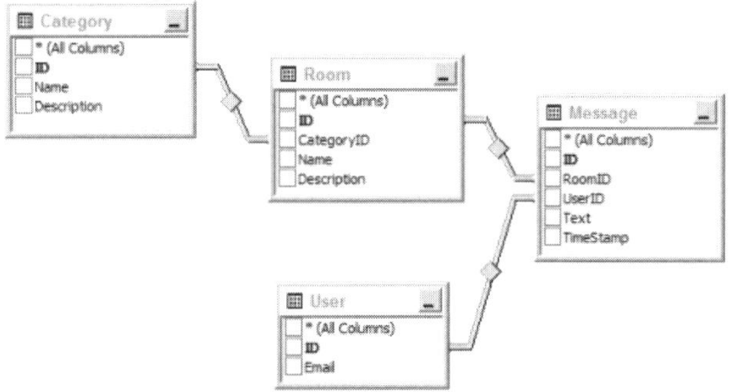

Figure 3-4

The Category Table

The Category table stores all of the categories to which each chat room is assigned. It contains three fields, defined as follows:

Field Name	Data Type	Description
ID	`Int`	The unique identifier for this record.
Name	`varchar(MAX)`	The name of the category that the user sees when viewing all of the chat rooms by category in the tree view of the homepage.
Description	`varchar(MAX)`	The textual description of the category, which can be displayed at will within the application.

The next table houses the data for the chat rooms themselves.

The Room Table

The Room table is essentially a basic entity containing what you would need to describe a chat room; that is, the category of the room, a name for the room, and a textual description.

Field Name	Data Type	Description
ID	`Int`	The unique identifier for this record.
CategoryID	`Int`	The foreign key that identifies under which category this chat room is classified.
Name	`varchar(MAX)`	The name of the chat room.
Description	`varchar(MAX)`	The textual description of the chat room, which can be displayed at will within the application.

Now that you have an idea of where the categories and chat rooms fit into the data model, you will be able to understand where and how the actual messages are stored and used within the same model.

The Message Table

The Message table contains the text messages for each and every chat room by all of the users. Although all of the visible messages provided to the chat users are filtered to show only the messages sent within a certain number of hours, all of the messages are maintained here until a database administrator determines it is time to delete or archive the data. Following are the columns for this Message table, and their respective type and description information:

Field Name	Data Type	Description
ID	`Int`	The unique identifier for this record.
RoomID	`Int`	The foreign key that identifies to which chat room this message is posted.
UserID	`Int`	The foreign key that identifies which user posted this message.
Text	`varchar(MAX)`	The actual chatted message text.
Timestamp	`Datetime`	The automatically generated date and time of the message as it was entered into the database.

The messages have a foreign key of the UserID, which is a reference to the User table, explained next.

The User Table

The User table provides specific information about the chat users, allowing their presence and usage to be customized, secured, tracked, and reported on. The following is a depiction of the columns within the User table:

Field Name	Data Type	Description
ID	`Int`	The unique identifier for this record.
Email	`varchar(MAX)`	The e-mail address of the user.

The data model seems to meet the essential element needs, and provides a level of simplistic design you would hope for.

Next, you dive into the visual customization techniques with the use of themes and skins.

Themes and Skins

The project provides a simple way to apply themes and skins to each page of the site, without modifying any HTML markup sections on any page (even the master page is safe from special control-based HTML markup). You can apply a theme to the entire web site by modifying the Web.config file to point to the name of your theme (assuming the theme exists in your project under the App_Themes folder). This is carried out within each ASP.NET form by using the following code in each of the form's pre-initialization events:

```
    ''' <summary>
    ''' this preinit event fires to initialize the page. It allows for the
    ''' theme and title to be set for this page, which actually pulls from
    ''' the web.config setting via the shared Config class's exposed properties.
    ''' </summary>
    Protected Sub Page_PreInit(ByVal sender As Object, ByVal e As System.EventArgs)
Handles Me.PreInit
        Page.Theme = Config.CurrentTheme
        Page.Title = Config.PageTitle
    End Sub
```

This basically accesses the `config` class's properties (pulled from the Web.config file), and sets the page's theme member to be the current theme value. In this way, you can maintain a consistent experience throughout the web site, with only one change needed to Web.config in order to change the look and feel of the entire user experience! You are probably glad to hear that—I know I am. The exact place where you would change the theme for the site is in the `appSettings` section of Web.config, as displayed here:

```
<!--
    <add key="CurrentTheme" value="CleanBlue" />
-->
    <add key="CurrentTheme" value="CleanRed" />
```

This code displays one of the theme entries as commented out, and one of them as active. Simply swap the two values in order to make the change.

Classes Involved

The Wrox Chat Server contains some essential classes that represent the business and data layers of the application. In these basic class structures, you will find methods and properties that provide the bulk of the features in the application.

The ChatRoom Class

The `ChatRoom` class (see Figure 3-5) is essentially the class that allows for the actual saving and retrieving of the chat room's textual messages to and from the database. The `ChatRoom` class is used to perform the bulk of the object and contextual user interface provisioning as a business layer for the application. Its methods are accessible as public and shared for ease of use within the various forms and controls of the application. This means that you do not have to instantiate an instance of the resource class in order to call its methods. Instead, simply use the syntax of `ChatRoom.MethodName()` in any VB.NET WebForm or control of the application to execute the function.

The `ChatRoom` class's methods are detailed in the following table:

Method	Return Type	Description
`SaveMessage()`	n/a	Saves the chat message, passing it off to the `ChatRoomDB` class.

Table continued on following page

Method	Return Type	Description
`GetMessagesForChatRoom()`	String	Retrieves the chat room's HTML string from the database, via the `ChatRoomDB` class.
`GetChatRoomList()`	String	Retrieves an HTML string listing of chat rooms, grouped by category as an HTML string from the database, via the `ChatRoomDB` class.

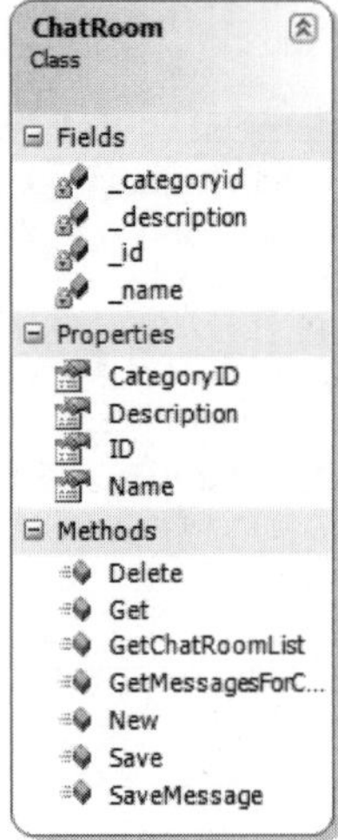

Figure 3-5

This `ChatRoom` class acts as the business layer, providing an interface to the data access layer, the `ChatRoomDB` class.

The ChatRoomDB Class

The `ChatRoomDB` class (see Figure 3-6) acts as a data layer for the application, because it is the sole entity responsible for selecting data from or inserting data into the database. This is a typical way of consolidating commonly used data execution logic into a single managed class.

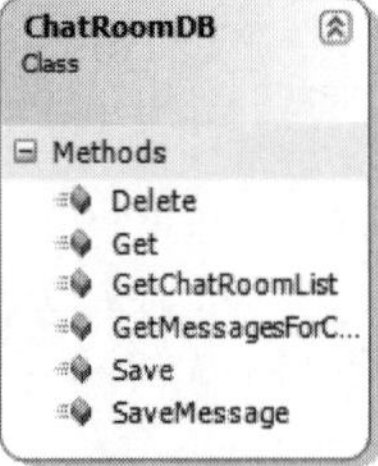

Figure 3-6

The following table displays the accessible members of the `ChatRoomDB` class:

Method	Return Type	Description
`SaveMessage()`	n/a	Saves the chat message into the database.
`GetMessagesForChatRoom()`	String	Retrieves the chat room's HTML string of messages out of the database.
`GetChatRoomList()`	String	Retrieves an HTML string listing of chat rooms, grouped by category as an HTML string from the database.

This wraps up the essential classes of the application. The next class stores references to the configuration variables of the application, which are stored in the Web.config file.

The Config Class

The `Config` class, depicted in Figure 3-7, is used as the configuration manager of the application. It is essentially the main access point for all configuration settings that any of the application tiers may require access to.

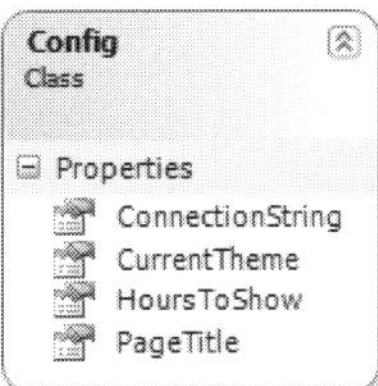

Figure 3-7

The following table displays the accessible members of the `Config` class:

Property	Return Type	Description
`ConnectionString()`	String	The connection string property that pulls from Web.config.
`CurrentTheme()`	String	The current theme of the web site as defined in the Web.config file.
`PageTitle()`	String	The HTML title value that each page displays, as defined here from the Web.config file.
`HoursToShow()`	Integer	The number of hours for the recent chat room messages to keep showing.

Now you have seen the classes involved and their applicable method calls. The next section walks you through each of the code sections of interest.

Code and Code Explanation

This section explains each of the essential code files in the Wrox Chat Server project. It looks in detail at the files in the each of the different folders and explains how they interact and are used across the project.

Root Files

The root of the Wrox Chat Server contains several important files, including the main ASPX shell-pages, and the configuration and formatting pages.

Web.config

The Web.config stores vital configuration entries used within the application. One entry, named the `SqlServerConnectionString`, controls the connection to the SQL Server 2005 Express database file ChatServerDB.mdf, as seen here:

```
<connectionStrings>
    <add name="ConnectionString"
         connectionString="Data Source=(local)\SqlExpress;AttachDbFilename=
|DataDirectory|\ChatServerDB.mdf;Integrated Security=True;User Instance=True"
providerName="System.Data.SqlClient"/>
  </connectionStrings>
```

It also contains the other entries for showing chat messages, the page title, and the currently used theme, as displayed here:

```
<appSettings>
    <add key="HoursToShow" value="1"/>
    <add key="PageTitle" value="Wrox Chat Server"/>
    <!--
    <add key="CurrentTheme" value="CleanBlue" />
    -->
    <add key="CurrentTheme" value="CleanRed"/>
  </appSettings>
```

This is where the easy modification can take place for changing which theme is used for each page of the site. You can find more information on this in the "Themes and Skins" section earlier in the chapter.

Config.vb

The `Config` class is used as an available business object for values and settings through visibility of some static members. Its members are listed as properties in order to abstract the location in which these values are stored. All of the values for the properties are stored in the Web.config file, with this `Config` class retrieving them when they are needed:

```
Imports Microsoft.VisualBasic

Public Class Config
    ''' <summary>
    ''' The connection string property that pulls from the web.config
    ''' </summary>
    Public Shared ReadOnly Property ConnectionString() As String
        Get
```

```
            Return ConfigurationManager.ConnectionStrings( _
                "ConnectionString").ConnectionString
        End Get
    End Property
    ''' <summary>
    ''' The current theme of the website as defined in the web.config
    ''' </summary>
    Public Shared ReadOnly Property CurrentTheme() As String
        Get
            Return ConfigurationManager.AppSettings("CurrentTheme").ToString()
        End Get
    End Property
    ''' <summary>
    ''' The HTML title value that each page displays, as defined
    ''' here from the web.config file
    ''' </summary>
    Public Shared ReadOnly Property PageTitle() As String
        Get
            Return ConfigurationManager.AppSettings("PageTitle").ToString()
        End Get
    End Property

    ''' <summary>
    ''' The number of hours back in time from the current time
    ''' that each chat room displays, as defined here from the
    ''' web.config file
    ''' </summary>
    Public Shared ReadOnly Property HoursToShow() As String
        Get
            Return ConfigurationManager.AppSettings("HoursToShow").ToString()
        End Get
    End Property
End Class
```

As the `Config` class displays, the properties are marked as `Public Shared ReadOnly`, which allows them to be accessed from anywhere in the project by the config-dot notation. An example of this would be `config.ConnectionString()`. This would return the connection string from the `Config` class, without instantiating a `Config` class object first.

ChatRoom.vb

The `ChatRoom` class is used to retrieve and save the chat messages being passed between the web site and the client browsers. The class acts as a business layer and provides a level of abstraction between the requests for database records and the user interface.

One of the more important method calls of the resource is the `SaveResource` method. The code for this is as follows:

```
    ''' <summary>
    ''' Saves a Message to the ChatRoom in the database
    ''' </summary>
    Public Shared Function SaveMessage(ByVal ChatRoomID As Integer, _
        ByVal Text As String, ByVal Email As String) As Boolean
        Return ChatRoomDB.SaveMessage(ChatRoomID, Text, Email)
    End Function
```

It accepts the following three parameters:

- ChatRoomID
- Text
- Email

These represent the necessary pieces of information to save the message into the database. The SaveResource method provides the means by which to hand off a Resource class object to the data tier for processing. Thus, the ChatRoomDB.SaveMessage call is made to pass on the heavy lifting to the data layer (the ChatRoomDB class).

ChatRoomDB.vb

The ChatRoomDB class is essentially the data layer for the application. It provides method calls to retrieve information from the database and insert or update data within the database. This class serves as the only file or object that will have access to the database files. In so doing, you can isolate data-specific operations outside of the business logic layer. This technique protects a developer from writing duplicate data access code and helps to maintain organized and structured data access logic. This also supports the application from being logically separated into tiers, or layers, with the deliberate feasibility of migrating and expanding the application onto separate servers at any point in time.

The ChatRoomDB class contains a SaveMessage() method, as displayed here:

```
''' <summary>
''' Saves a Message to the ChatRoom in the database
''' </summary>
Public Shared Function SaveMessage(ByVal ChatRoomID As Integer, _
    ByVal Text As String, ByVal Email As String) As Boolean

    Using mConnection As New SqlConnection(Config.ConnectionString)
        'Create a command object
        Dim mCommand As SqlCommand = New SqlCommand( _
            "sprocMessageInsertUpdateItem", mConnection)
        'set it to the type of 'stored procedure'
        mCommand.CommandType = CommandType.StoredProcedure
        'parameters: the ChatRoomID, the Message text, and the UserID
        mCommand.Parameters.AddWithValue("@roomID", ChatRoomID)
        mCommand.Parameters.AddWithValue("@Email", Email)
        mCommand.Parameters.AddWithValue("@text", Text)
        'open the connection and execute the stored procedure
        mConnection.Open()
        Dim result As Integer = mCommand.ExecuteNonQuery()
        'close the connection and dispose of the command
        mConnection.Close()
        mCommand.Dispose()
        Return True
    End Using
End Function
```

Another method of interest is the GetChatRoomList() method, returning a DataSet containing the chat rooms entered into the database, along with their assigned categories.

The following is a copy of the entire contents of the `GetChatRoomList()` method:

```
''' <summary>
''' Retrieves a DataSet of ChatRooms from the database
''' </summary>
Public Shared Function GetChatRoomList() As DataSet
    Dim dsChatRooms As DataSet = New DataSet()
    Try
        Using mConnection As New SqlConnection(Config.ConnectionString)

            Dim mCommand As SqlCommand = New SqlCommand( _
                "sprocChatRoomSelectList", mConnection)
            mCommand.CommandType = CommandType.StoredProcedure
            Dim myDataAdapter As SqlDataAdapter = New SqlDataAdapter()
            myDataAdapter.SelectCommand = mCommand
            myDataAdapter.Fill(dsChatRooms)
            mConnection.Close()
            Return dsChatRooms
        End Using
    Catch ex As Exception
        'When we call the "Throw" statement, we are raising the error
        'to the global.asax file, which will use the default error
        'handling page to process/display the custom error to the user
        Throw
    End Try
End Function
```

The preceding logic performs the following steps:

1. Creates a new `SqlCommand` object, passing in the stored procedure name and the connection:

```
        Using mConnection As New SqlConnection(Config.ConnectionString)
```

2. Sets the `CommandType` to be `StoredProcedure`, and provides the name of `sprocChatRoomSelectList`:

```
            Dim mCommand As SqlCommand = New SqlCommand( _
                "sprocChatRoomSelectList", mConnection)
            mCommand.CommandType = CommandType.StoredProcedure
```

3. Creates a new `DataAdapter`, and assigns its `SelectCommand` property to the `mCommand` ADO.NET command object reference. The `DataAdapter` calls the `Fill` method, which assigns the data to the passed-in `dsChatRooms` DataSet variable:

```
            Dim myDataAdapter As SqlDataAdapter = New SqlDataAdapter()
            myDataAdapter.SelectCommand = mCommand
            myDataAdapter.Fill(dsChatRooms)
```

4. Closes the connection, and returns the DataSet to the calling function:

```
            mConnection.Close()
            Return dsChatRooms
```

Now that you have had a glimpse at how the business and data layers are structured, the next section looks at the client layer (WebForms), and what the real deal is with callbacks in the graphical user interface execution logic.

WebForms

WebForms are standard ASPX pages that contain the client-side and very visible portion of the application. A few WebForms are of particular importance within the project, as noted in the subsequent sections.

SignIn.aspx

The SignIn.aspx file is the first page that loads when the site is accessed. Within this page is the `TextBox` control used to capture the e-mail address of the user before he or she continues any further in the application. The e-mail address is needed to reference the person who sent the chat messages to the server, assigning a UserID to the e-mail address upon the user's first message to any of the chat rooms.

Several specific functions from this page are important to mention. The first one is a common event with logic that is somewhat redundant throughout the application's ASPX pages. This is the page pre-initialization event, as shown here:

```
    ''' <summary>
    ''' this preinit event fires to initialize the page. It allows
    ''' for the theme and title to be set for this page, which
    ''' actually pulls from the web.config setting via the shared
    ''' Config class's exposed properties.
    ''' </summary>
    Protected Sub Page_PreInit(ByVal sender As Object, ByVal e As System.EventArgs)
Handles Me.PreInit
        Page.Theme = Config.CurrentTheme
        Page.Title = Config.PageTitle
    End Sub
```

The `Page.Theme` is the theme property of the `Page` reference. By setting this `Theme` property to the `Config` class's exposed `CurrentTheme` value, you are assigning a theme at run time. This model of assignment is ideal, because each page can dynamically utilize the theme that is controlled via the Web.config file without requiring any other file changes.

Default.aspx

The obvious area of special interest is the page's instance of the `TreeView` control. The control, new in the ASP.NET 2.0 control library, has been completely rewritten from the ground up for the 2.0 version, and boy does it show! It is especially easy to use and very intuitive. Although you can bind a `TreeView` control to a `SiteMapDataSource` control and an `XmlDataSource` control, this instance of the `TreeView` control does not do either. Instead, it is dynamically loaded on the first loading of the page, from the DataSet returned by the business layer.

The following steps include references to code found within the Default.aspx.vb code-behind file, and walk you through the loading of the `TreeView` control's nodes and subnodes with the appropriate category data and chat room data:

1. First, iterate through the chat room DataSet's rows using the For-Next syntax:

```
            For Each drChatRoom In dtChatRoom.Rows
```

2. Next, set the variables:

```
            Dim CategoryId As Integer = _
                dtChatRoom.Rows(currentRow).Item("CatID").ToString()
            Dim CategoryName As String = _
                dtChatRoom.Rows(currentRow).Item("CatName").ToString()
            Dim RoomId As Integer = _
                dtChatRoom.Rows(currentRow).Item("RoomID").ToString()
            Dim RoomName As String = _
                dtChatRoom.Rows(currentRow).Item("RoomName").ToString()
```

3. Then, the Load event checks for new `CategoryId` values, adding nodes at this time for all of the categories before even thinking about adding subnodes (that comes in a minute):

```
            If CategoryId <> lastCategoryID Then
                TreeView1.Nodes.Add(New TreeNode(CategoryName, CategoryId))
            End If
```

4. Then, increment the `currentRow` counter and set the `lastCategoryID` variable to be the value of the current `CategoryId` variable from the existing loop. This is a sort of *flag* or temporary variable used to determine when the category column changes between records:

```
            currentRow = currentRow + 1
            lastCategoryID = CategoryId
```

5. Iterate to the next record:

```
        Next
        currentRow = 0
```

6. Now that you have all of the main categories in the `TreeView`, iterate through each of the nodes:

```
        For Each mNode As TreeNode In TreeView1.Nodes
```

7. Now, you need to obtain a row-level set of records for each of the nodes. Because each node has a value, and each of the values is a `CategoryId`, you can find the exact rows you need from the datatable by using the `Select` method of the datatable object. The following gets a datatable with rows that are under each node's category:

```
            For Each drChatRoom In dtChatRoom.Select("CatID=" & mNode.Value)
                If Not drChatRoom.IsNull(0) Then
                    Dim RoomId As Integer = _
                        drChatRoom.Item("RoomID").ToString()
                    Dim RoomName As String = _
                        drChatRoom.Item("RoomName").ToString()
                    'add the chat room node under that category
```

8. Finally, add the new node, for that `ChatRoom` specifically:

```
                    mNode.ChildNodes.Add(New _
                        TreeNode("<a href='chatroom.aspx?chatRoomID=" _
                         & RoomId.ToString() & "'>" & RoomName & "</a>",
RoomId))
                End If
            Next
        Next
```

Once the `TreeView` control on the default page is populated with the chat room records in the database, you can click one of the nodes representing a chat room. These nodes are actually hyperlinks, directing the browser to the ChatRoom.aspx page, explained in the following section.

ChatRoom.aspx

The ChatRoom.aspx WebForm is used to house the chat *sending* functionality of the application. Its goal and purpose are to provide a one-way channel of asynchronous communication to a web site database, within a specific chat room. This is performed via the technology of the new ASP.NET 2.0 `Callback` method. A look at providing web-based callbacks is explained in detail within the "Wrox Chat Server Design" section earlier in this chapter. The ChatRoom WebForm implements a `Callback` method to send data to the server, but purposely ignores the response from the server coming back.

Several methods are located within this ASPX file, as well as its code-behind .vb file. These areas are broken down in the following table:

Method	Location	Description
`Page_Load()`	Chatroom.aspx.vb	Registers an embedded script for the use of the Callback Manager middle layer, which provides the necessary JavaScript on the client.
`MyClickEventHandler()`	Chatroom.aspx	Calls the built-in Callback Manager's entry point, which is the `CallServer()` method from the button's `Click` event. This `CallServer()` method is embedded from the code-behind file when it registers the client scripts on the `Page_Load` event.
`RaiseCallbackEvent()`	Chatroom.aspx.vb	Captures the call from the client and processes it on the server, saving the message to the chat room (saves it to the database).

These methods provide a send-receive event pair, which makes up the main idea of the callback. Data is captured within the ASPX file (via the `MyClickEventHandler` event) and sent off to the .vb code-behind file (to the `RaiseCallbackEvent` event). From there it is saved to the database. No response data is actually sent back to the client in this case, although it may be the case in a typical round-trip callback implementation. In such a case, the other methods on the server and client are used, as they are in the ChatWindow.aspx and its code-behind file, ChatWindow.aspx.vb.

The `RaiseCallbackEvent` contents are shown in the following code. Notice the call to the `ChatRoom.SaveMessage` function, and how it accepts the `ChatRoomID`, the text of the message (`eventArgument`), and the user's e-mail address:

```
''' <summary>
''' the RaiseCallbackEvent captures the content from the
''' chat message from the window...
''' </summary>
```

```
    Public Sub RaiseCallbackEvent(ByVal eventArgument As String) _
        Implements System.Web.UI.ICallbackEventHandler.RaiseCallbackEvent

        If eventArgument.Length > 0 Then
            ChatRoom.SaveMessage(Request.QueryString("chatRoomID"), _
                eventArgument, Session("Email"))
        End If
    End Sub
```

The button and text area in the WebForm are used to process the user input and send it into the entry point for the asynchronous call, through the local custom JavaScript method, entitled `MyClickEventHandler()`. The `MyClickEventHandler()` JavaScript event also performs an important role in making this callback work. From here, the text is processed into the locally registered client callback proxy script. It is the first step to making the server call from a browser script. The following code is the contents of the event. The `CallServer` method is easy to spot, passing in the `txtMessage` value as a parameter:

```
function MyClickEventHandler()
{
    //call the built-in function 'callserver()' on the click event
    //this CallServer method is embedded from the codebehind file, as
    //it registers the client script on the load event...
    CallServer(document.getElementById('txtMessage').value, null);
    //clear the message box for the user
    document.getElementById('txtMessage').value = '';
}
```

The `load` event of the page does something very important for using callbacks. It registers the `ReceiveServerData` event and the `CallServer` event on the client. These are the main entry and exit points of the Callback Manager layer, which provides the implementation of the asynchronous `xmlHttp` posts to the server. Even though this WebForm used only the `CallServer` event in this case, the `ReceiveServerData` event is registered on the client because it is useful for future troubleshooting and enhancements to the circular page event cycle. Thus, the chat message is sent up to the server with no response back to the client, because it doesn't necessarily need any response.

> **This WebForm uses half of the available ASP.NET 2.0 `Callback` method. That is, it sends the callback data asynchronously, but does not need to capture anything from the callback response. The other file, ChatWindow.aspx, does just the opposite.**

The following is the `Page_Load` event. Notice the registration of the two methods:

```
    ''' <summary>
    ''' the Page_Load event will allow for the necessary callback script to be
    ''' embedded into the browser's javascript
    ''' </summary>
    Sub Page_Load(ByVal sender As Object, ByVal e As System.EventArgs) Handles
Me.Load
        Dim cm As ClientScriptManager = Page.ClientScript
        Dim cbReference As String
        cbReference = cm.GetCallbackEventReference(Me, "arg", _
```

```
            "ReceiveServerData", "")
        Dim callbackScript As String = ""
        callbackScript &= "function CallServer(arg, context)" & _
            "{" & cbReference & "; }"
        cm.RegisterClientScriptBlock(Me.GetType(), "CallServer", _
            callbackScript, True)
        'retrieve an instance of a chat room class by passing in the
        'chat room id as a parameter to the 'get' method
        Dim mChatRoom As ChatRoom = ChatRoom.Get( _
            Request.QueryString("ChatRoomId"))
        'set the text of the label to the chat room name property
        Label1.Text = mChatRoom.Name
    End Sub
```

In addition to the registration of the two items above, some specific HTML and ASP.NET controls play a critical role in implementing this callback function. The following represents the main HTML content of the ChatRoom.aspx WebForm:

```
        <iframe src="ChatWindow.aspx?ChatRoomID=<%=Request.Querystring
("ChatRoomId") %>"
         class="ChatWindow" scrolling="no">
        </iframe>
       <textarea onkeypress="return EnterKeyCheck(event);" id="txtMessage"
        rows="4" style="width: 231px"></textarea>
       <input type="button" value="Send" onclick="Javascript:MyClickEventHandler()"
        style="width: 57px; height: 60px" id="Button1"/><br />
```

The `iframe` HTML tag is used to insert the view into another WebForm, ChatWindow.aspx, which acts as the chat window the user reads messages from. This is because the actual receiving of messages from the server is quite tricky, but is solved by yet another instance of the use of callbacks.

Now the ChatRoom.aspx WebForm has served its purpose in life. Keep reading, and you will see how the ChatWindow WebForm fits into this experience.

ChatWindow.aspx

The ChatWindow.aspx WebForm uses a completely separate callback implementation to *display* the messages of all users within this chat room. It is not used to accept any user-chatted messages; however, it does accept the `ChatRoomID` parameter for which it will retrieve records.

Several methods are located within this ASPX file, as well as its code-behind .vb file. These areas are broken down in the following table:

Method	Location	Description
`Page_Load()`	ChatWindow.aspx.vb	Registers an embedded script for the use of the Callback Manager middle layer, which provides the necessary JavaScript on the client.

Method	Location	Description
`ReceiveServerData()`	ChatWindow.aspx	Calls the built-in Callback Manager's exit point, which is the `ReceiveServerData()` method. This method is embedded from the code-behind file when it registers the client scripts on the `Page_Load` event. This JavaScript method contains custom logic that displays the result of the callback to the user.
`GetCallbackResult()`	ChatWindow.aspx.vb	Prepares the return string value to be sent back to the client. This string value is in this case an HTML string full of message data for a particular chat room.

These methods provide a send-receive event pair that makes up the main idea of the callback. Data is accepted within the ChatWindow.aspx file (via the `QueryString` variable) and sent off to the .vb code-behind file (to the `GetCallbackResult` event). From there it is used to query the database and find all of the messages for that `ChatRoomID`. The records are prepared as an HTML string and sent back to the client. This process is invoked via the use of a JavaScript timer event, which sends callback requests at intervals of a second or more. Each callback request that is sent will engage an asynchronous call to the server for the retrieval of more message data.

The following code shows the `GetCallbackResult` contents. Notice the call to the `GetMessagesForChatRoom` function, and how it accepts the `ChatRoomID` as a parameter to retrieving the messages from the database. Then, observe as it iterates through the DataSet and generates an HTML string within the local `Message` variable. The `Message` variable is eventually returned to the caller as a string value:

```
''' <summary>
''' the GetCallbackResult function returns the html string
''' as a response back to the browser
''' </summary>
Public Function GetCallbackResult() As String Implements _
    System.Web.UI.ICallbackEventHandler.GetCallbackResult

    Dim Message As String
    Dim ds As DataSet = ChatRoom.GetMessagesForChatRoom( _
        Request.QueryString("chatRoomID"))
    For i As Integer = 0 To ds.Tables(0).Rows.Count - 1
        Message += "<b>" & ds.Tables(0).Rows(i)("Email").ToString() & _
            "</b> said: " & ds.Tables(0).Rows(i)("Text").ToString() & "<BR>"
    Next
    'send back to the form...
    Return Message & "<a name='bottom'></a><BR>"
End Function
```

The receiving of data within the browser's JavaScript is a critical part of the work and allows you to update the browser with the result of the callback. Take a look at the `ReceiveServerData` method, as the `divChatWindow` is assigned the text value of the callback results:

```
function ReceiveServerData(arg, context)
{
    //send the value to the html control...
    var obj = document.getElementById("divChatWindow");
    obj.innerHTML = arg;
    location.href = "#bottom";
}
```

The `load` event of the page does something very important for using callbacks. It registers the `ReceiveServerData` event and the `CallServer` event on the client. These are the main entry and exit points of the Callback Manager layer, which provides the implementation of the asynchronous `xmlHttp` posts to the server. In this case (different from the ChatRoom.aspx WebForm previously mentioned), the application needs both calls for it to provide the messages from the database for a particular chat room. The following code displays the `Page_Load` event. Notice the registration of the two methods:

```
    Sub Page_Load(ByVal sender As Object, ByVal e As System.EventArgs) Handles
Me.Load
        Dim cm As ClientScriptManager = Page.ClientScript
        Dim cbReference As String
        cbReference = cm.GetCallbackEventReference(Me, "arg", _
            "ReceiveServerData", "")
        Dim callbackScript As String = ""
        callbackScript &= "function CallServer(arg, context)" & _
            "{" & cbReference & "; }"
        cm.RegisterClientScriptBlock(Me.GetType(), "CallServer", _
            callbackScript, True)
    End Sub
```

You should now understand the basic usage of each intrinsic and available area of the new ASP.NET 2.0 callback feature, how it works, and what the required code configurations are.

> **This WebForm uses the entire callback process. That is, it sends the callback data asynchronously and captures HTML in a string variable from the server's callback response.**

Thus, the `ChatRoomID` is received by the server, passed in as a parameter to a stored procedure call, and data is returned via the asynchronous `xmlHttp` post. This data being returned is then displayed to the user in the browser window via the local JavaScript `receive` method.

Phew! You made it. Pat yourself on the back as you skim through the user controls section ahead.

User Controls

Some specific user controls in the site assist with the navigation and content display for multiple pages. Because web user controls promote a practice of creating and using reusable code, they were made to be applicable within multiple pages of the site, depending on the nature of the controls.

header.ascx

The `header` user control is used to provide the top area of each page with meaningful content. If anything needs to reside at or near the top of a web page, you should add it to the `header` control so it is visible through all of the pages.

The following code represents entire header.ascx source:

```
<%@ Control Language="VB" AutoEventWireup="false" CodeFile="header.ascx.vb"
Inherits="Controls_header" %>
<div style="text-align: center">
    <table><tr>
        <td><img src="../Images/headerlogo.gif" /></td>
        <td><h1><% Response.Write(Page.Title) %></h1>
        </td>
    </tr></table>
</div>
```

Notice that the `<%Response.Write(Page.Title)%>` tags are used to write back to the response stream a title of the web site on the top of each page, which originated from the Web.config file.

footer.ascx

The `footer` user control is used as the bottom section of the site, for each page that uses the master page. That is, the `footer` control, among others, is a referenced control within the master page. In this way, it is propagated to all pages in the same exact manner.

The content of the `footer` control is displayed here:

```
<%@ Control Language="VB" AutoEventWireup="false" CodeFile="footer.ascx.vb"
Inherits="Controls_footer" %>
<a href="http://wrox.com" target="_blank">&copy; 2005 Wrox Press</a>   
<a href="SignIn.aspx" target="_self">Login</a>
```

This excerpt includes a few hyperlinks. One is for the Wrox Press web site, and the other is a link to the Login page for the chat application.

navigation.ascx

The `navigation` user control is used to provide the reusable menu on each page in the site. The `Menu` itself is a brand new ASP.NET 2.0 control that binds to a `SiteMapDataSource` control, also new in the 2.0 version of the .NET Framework. The `SiteMapDataSource` control is used to bind to an XML file, wherein the site files are listed as entries in the XML file. This is where you can change the data that feeds the menu of the site.

The following excerpt is the HTML markup of the `navigation` control:

```
<%@ Control Language="VB" AutoEventWireup="false" CodeFile="navigation.ascx.vb"
Inherits="Controls_navigation" %>
<asp:Menu ID="Menu1" runat="server" DataSourceID="SiteMapDataSource1"
Orientation="Horizontal"
    StaticDisplayLevels="2"></asp:Menu>
<asp:SiteMapDataSource  ID="SiteMapDataSource1" runat="server" />
```

The XML file of the `SiteMapDataSource` control is shown here:

```
<?xml version="1.0" encoding="utf-8" ?>
<siteMap xmlns="http://schemas.microsoft.com/AspNet/SiteMap-File-1.0" >
  <siteMapNode url="ContentFiles/default.aspx" title="Home">
    <siteMapNode url="ContentFiles/about.aspx" title="About" />
    <siteMapNode url="ContentFiles/contact.aspx" title="Contact Us" />
  </siteMapNode>
</siteMap>
```

To add a page to the menu of the web site, you must simply copy and paste (with the necessary modifications) an entry of the preceding XML file. In this way, the master page (which contains the only reference to the `navigation` control) provides visibility to the menu of the site on each page.

The next section explains in detail how to install and configure the source files of the Wrox Chat Server and how to deploy the site to a server in a production environment.

Setting up the Project

The time has come to learn how to install the Wrox Chat Server and see for yourself how quickly you can be up and running with a working resource application. You can install the web site either as a hosted web site application or as a source codebase for editing in Visual Studio 2005 or VWD.

Hosted Web Site Installation

If you want to install the Wrox Chat Server as a hosted web site on a computer or server without customizations or enhancements at all, follow these steps (assuming the .NET Framework 2.0 is already installed):

1. Open the folder Chapter 03 – Wrox Chat Server from the CD-ROM that came with this book and double-click the setup.exe file.
2. This process installs the files properly for hosting the web site locally to `C:\inetpub\wwwRoot\ChatServer` as a file-based web site application. Click Next to install the application, and close the installation program when it completes.
3. Then, browse to your local web site (for example, `http://localhost/ChatServer`). The Wrox Chat Server application should appear.
4. Finally, if you need to expose the site to the outside world, be sure to configure the public IP address to the IIS web site application. The details of this IIS configuration and its implications are outside the scope of this book, but the Wrox Chat Server is easily configurable as a public web site with a brief tutorial on web site hosting.

Local Developer Installation

If you would like to open the project in Visual Studio or Visual Web Developer, perform the following steps (assuming the .NET Framework 2.0 is installed, along with either Visual Studio 2005 or VWD):

1. Create a brand new web site in Visual Web Developer or Visual Studio 2005.
2. Open the folder Chapter 03 – Wrox Chat Server from the CD-ROM that came with this book and extract the contents of the file ChatServerSource.zip to a folder on your hard drive.
3. Open a Windows Explorer and browse to the folder that contains the unpacked files. Next, arrange Visual Web Developer and the Windows Explorer in such a way that both are visible at the same time.
4. In the Windows Explorer, select all of the folders and files within the codebase and drag them from the explorer window into the Solution Explorer in Visual Web Developer. If you're prompted to overwrite files, select Yes. You should end up with a Solution Explorer that contains all of the necessary files for the project to run properly.
5. Press F5 to run the application in the development environment.

For some insight on how you can modify your project in order to take advantage of some of the possible uses of the Wrox Chat Server, find this book's download page at `www.wrox.com`.

Summary

This chapter reviewed some of new controls within the ASP.NET 2.0 Framework, such as the `Callback` method, `SiteMap` control, the `SiteMapDataSource`, the use of Master Pages, and the databound `Menu` control. The flow of the chapter was centered around a standard approach to application design, using business layer classes, data layer classes, and a basic database structure. You learned how each of these new controls can save development time and effort in great proportions.

The "Wrox Chat Server Design" section provided a glimpse at the technology behind the Callback feature, because it shines in version 2.0 of the .NET Framework as one of the much-needed features for developers to use. The section also touched on class files in use, their properties, their methods, and the general purposes of each. It also gave visibility to the database tables, their relationships, and general entities displayed as classes.

The chapter finished with the necessary additions to provide a basic enhancement to the system, allowing for the chat system to automatically respond to user messages during off-hours.

Wrox Survey Engine

If you have ever taken an online survey before, you might have found that it is often very interesting to see the results and nod your head in agreement. Surveys can produce a sense of intrigue to the viewer, because they are aimed at gathering and compiling information about public opinion. The political scene is constantly speculating based on the polls and surveys conducted for a given set of people. Company changes and truckloads of monetary investments are made at the helm of an informative survey. You also may have noticed that surveys are often intentionally aimed and phrased to make sense to the average user. In fact, surveys are one of the proven best ways of extracting information from web users of the general public. Online surveys are found all over the Internet and have been a source of valuable data for companies of various sizes. The user is prompted with very simple and easy-to-understand questions that offer enticing answers from a list of multiple choices. Results from the survey questions are compiled immediately and available to management personnel for many times what proves to be important decisions for the company or department. It makes perfect sense, then, to implement surveys in order to ascertain the true state of a group or market sector.

The Survey Engine is an interesting application. It is easily reproducible in various environments with any number of multiple-choice questions. Once a survey has been conducted, the information gathered should be available to view in an organized and legible format. Reports can be run on survey results to demonstrate the responses of the majority.

The Wrox Survey Engine is a great example project that you can learn from in your valiant effort of tackling ASP.NET 2.0. This survey management web site provides the ability for an admin user to create surveys and monitor their results through the use of a user-friendly interface.

The Wrox Survey Engine provides a list of useful features, including the following:

- Create a survey on the fly.
- View survey responses with percentages.
- Embed surveys into an existing web site.

These features comprise the core functionality of the web site, with room for plenty of enhancements and modifications.

This chapter demonstrates how easy it is to implement some of the newer controls and techniques available in ASP.NET 2.0. Some of these new areas include the `ObjectDataSource` control, enhanced SQL Server `DataSource` control, ASP.NET Web Security Interface, the application of themes at the Web .config file level, the new navigation controls, the login and password retrieval controls, and the use of master pages within a solution.

In the section "Wrox Survey Engine Design" you explore the design of the application in great detail. This includes the database file structures, class designs, a basic inheritance model, and the loosely coupled application architecture.

The section titled "Code and Code Explanation" performs a methodical examination of the code, breaking down the important modules and functions and explaining their role from the GUI to the database and back. In addition, it reviews the logic within the classes involved, and some possible modifications you can make to the project with specific instructions.

The final section, "Setting up the Project," reviews how to extract and customize the Survey Engine in a development environment and how to install it to production.

But first things first: a review of the basics of using the Survey Engine.

Using the Wrox Survey Engine

Using the Wrox Survey Engine is a remarkably simple task. It is essentially a web site that has been developed to be the starting point for a company or an individual to easily and quickly create online surveys. Only a few pages are needed for an individual to complete a survey, because it is simply a list of multiple-choice questions with no right or wrong answers. This lends itself well to implementing a reusable component or module to generate a survey because every survey has questions and exactly four possible choices.

If the Wrox Survey Engine web site has been successfully installed (refer to the section "Setting up the Project" later in this chapter), you can browse to view the site by going to `http://localhost/surveyengine`. You'll see the screen shown in Figure 4-1.

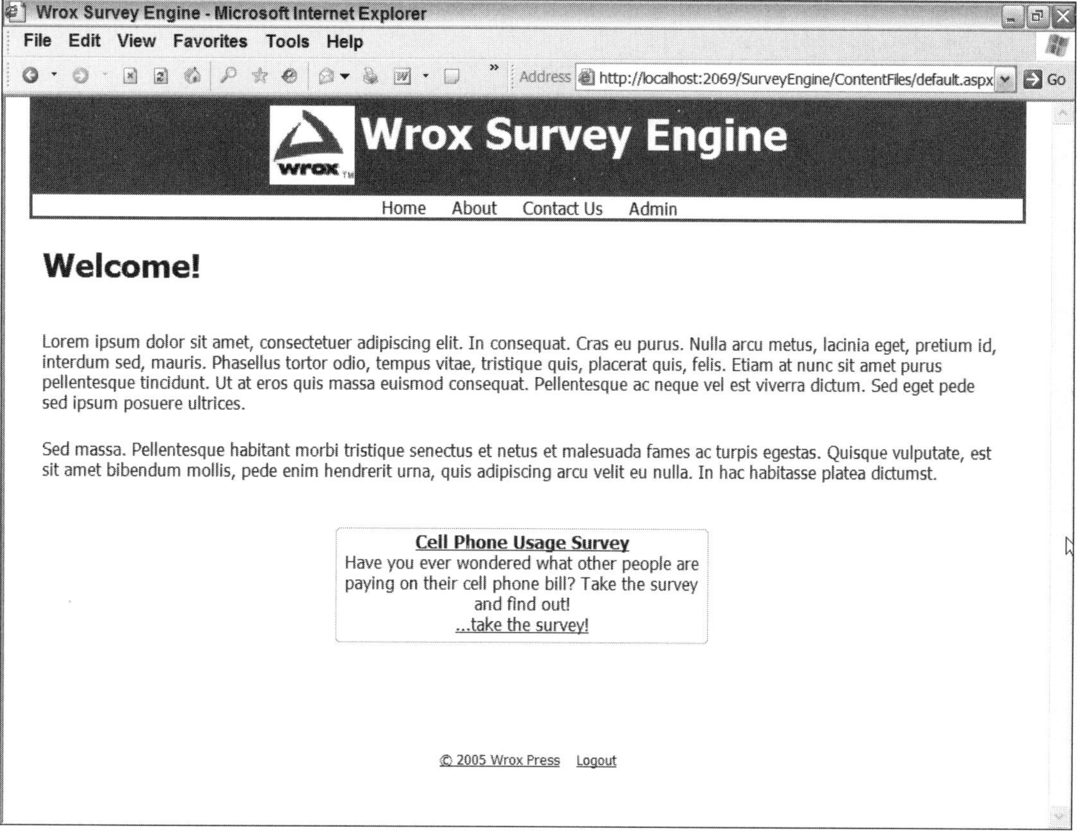

Figure 4-1

At the top of the homepage are several links to choose from:

- Home
- About
- Contact Us
- Admin

On the homepage, you will see a rounded box area toward the bottom of the page. This is essentially the hyperlink the user can click in order to take a survey. As you click the link, you are brought to the page used to present all of the survey questions at one time (see Figure 4-2).

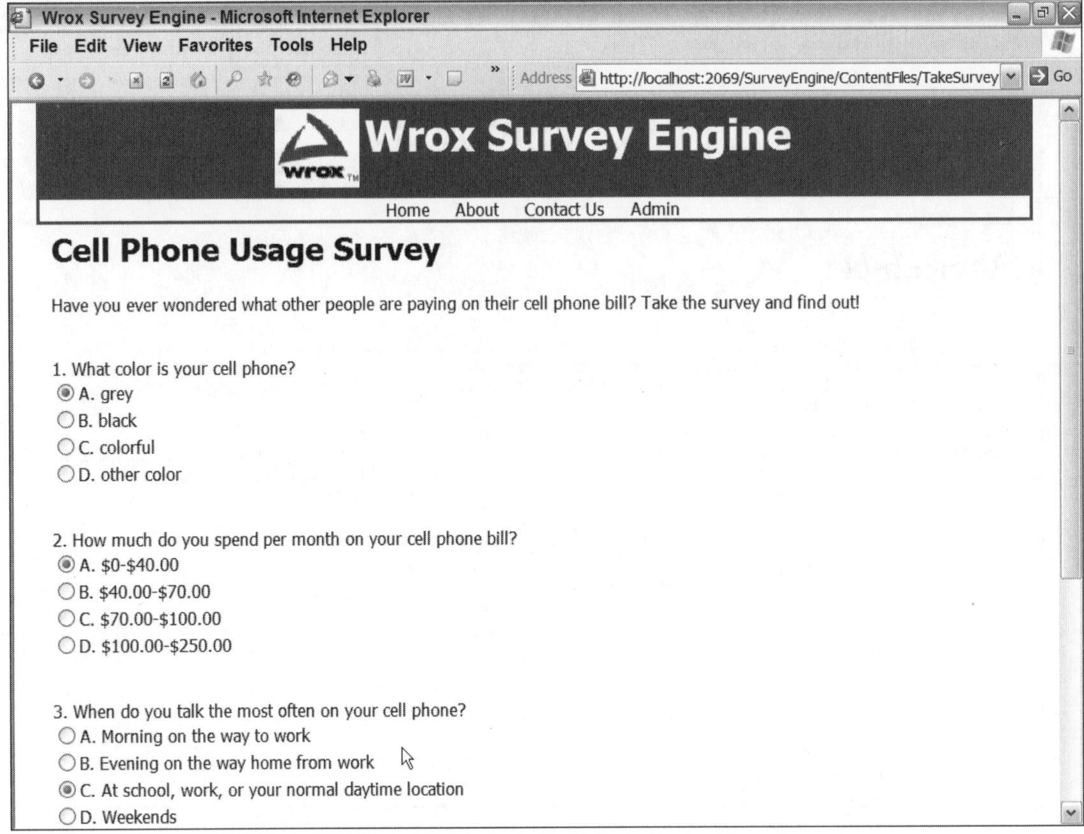

Figure 4-2

Multiple choices are given (A, B, C, D), from which users can pick to answer the survey questions. Once you select an answer for every question, you can click the View Results button to submit the form, at which point you'll see the screen depicted in Figure 4-3.

Now that the survey has been submitted, you will see the results for the survey so far. As more people complete surveys on the web site, the statistics will obviously change.

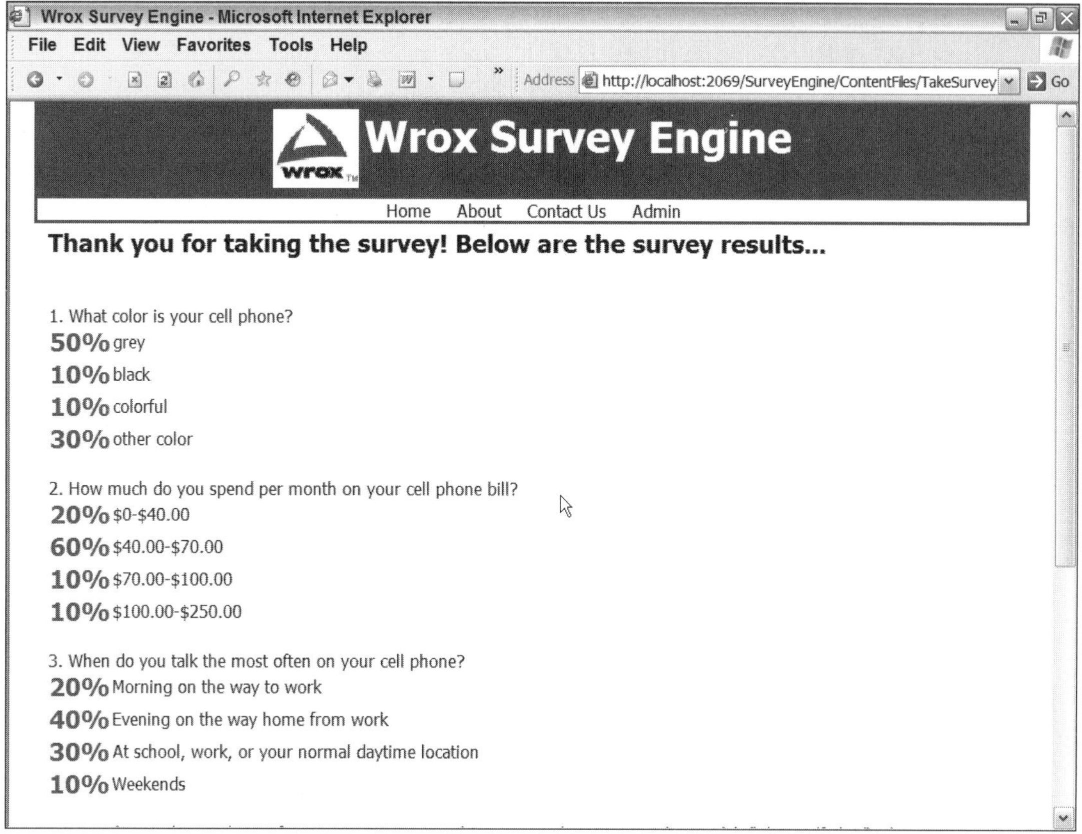

Figure 4-3

That actually concludes the main portion of content that the typical user would be exposed to. Behind the scenes, however, an administration section provides you with a great way to quickly and easily create surveys and view their responses.

When you click the Admin link in the main menu, you are brought to the login screen if you have not already logged into the web site and created a session. Figure 4-4 shows the login interface.

This page has a login feature and a password retrieval feature for you to use. Enter `Admin` for the username and `password#` for the password and click the Log In button.

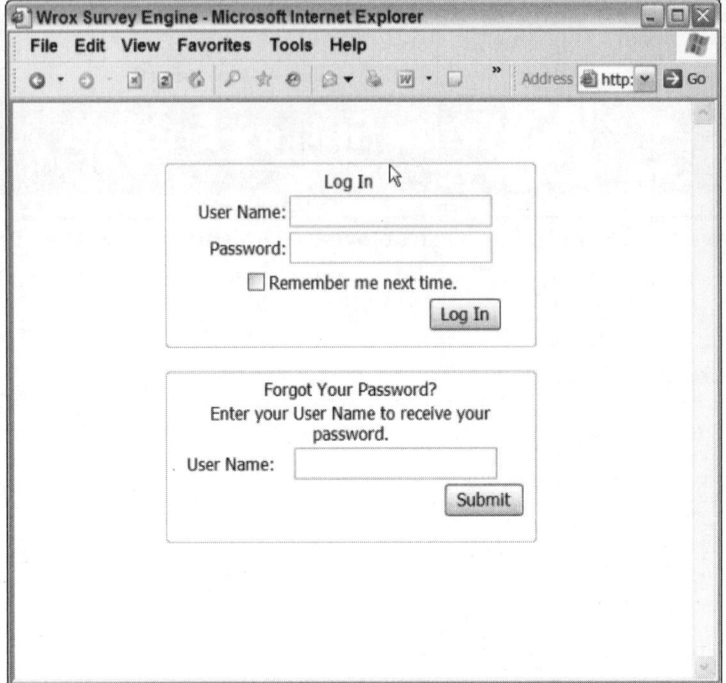

Figure 4-4

Once you log in to the site, you are brought to the Administrator landing page, displayed in Figure 4-5.

This Administrator page provides a grid of all of the surveys that exist in the system. Each survey in the grid has several features you can choose from in order to perform administrative functions, including the following:

- ❑ Create a new survey.
- ❑ Edit the questions or name of an existing survey.
- ❑ Add additional questions to an existing survey.
- ❑ View responses of a survey.
- ❑ Designate a specific survey to be the one that is displayed to the user.

By clicking any one of the hyperlinks in the grid, you navigate to the appropriate pages to complete the activity selected. These pages are described in the sections that follow.

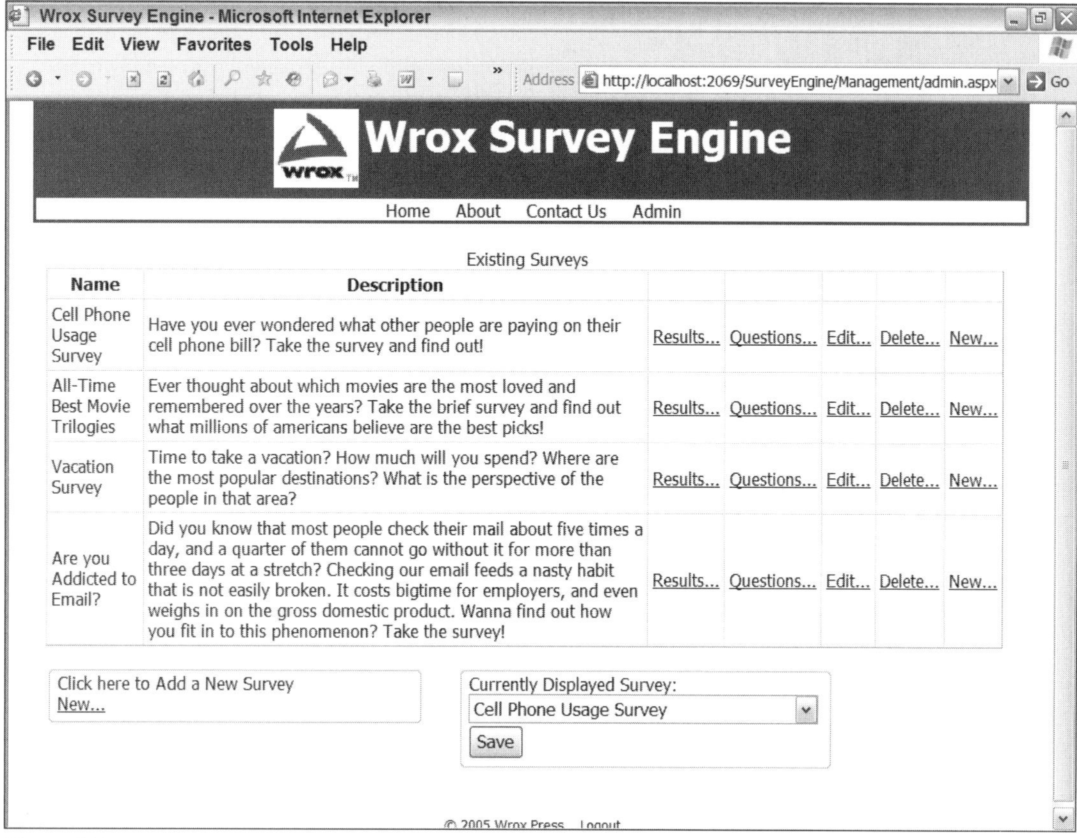

Figure 4-5

Adding a New Survey

One of the very first selections you may want to invoke could be the Add Survey Wizard, via the link that exists on the bottom-left of the page, or the New link in any of the rows of the data grid. Once clicked, the Add Survey Wizard appears and prompts you for specific information on the survey you are trying to add. Figure 4-6 depicts this process.

This figure illustrates the beginning of the wizard, with a Next button on the bottom right. This is a brand-new control to ASP.NET 2.0, and the next section, "Wrox Survey Engine Design," dives into its usage scenarios and details.

By clicking Next, you can enter a name for the new survey, as shown in Figure 4-7.

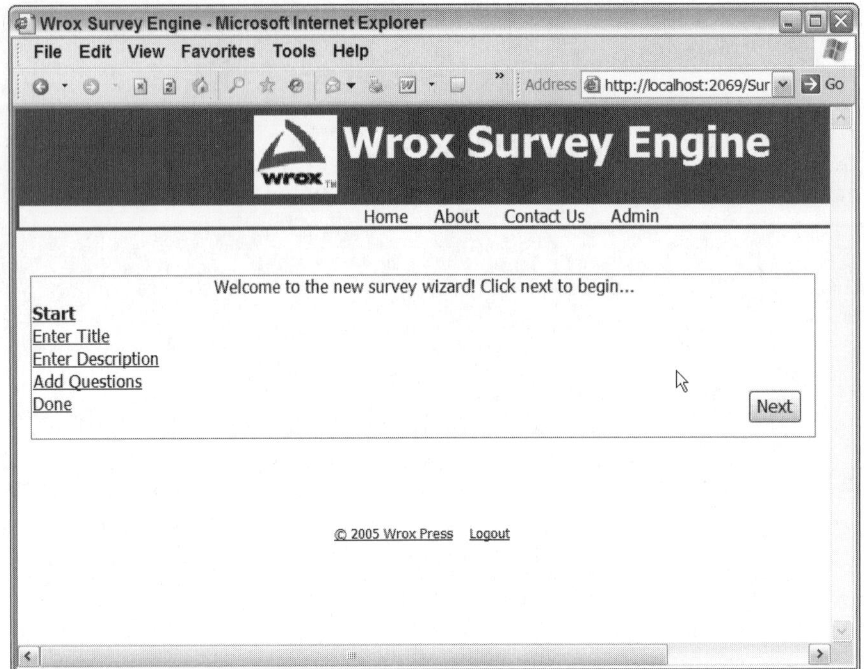

Figure 4-6

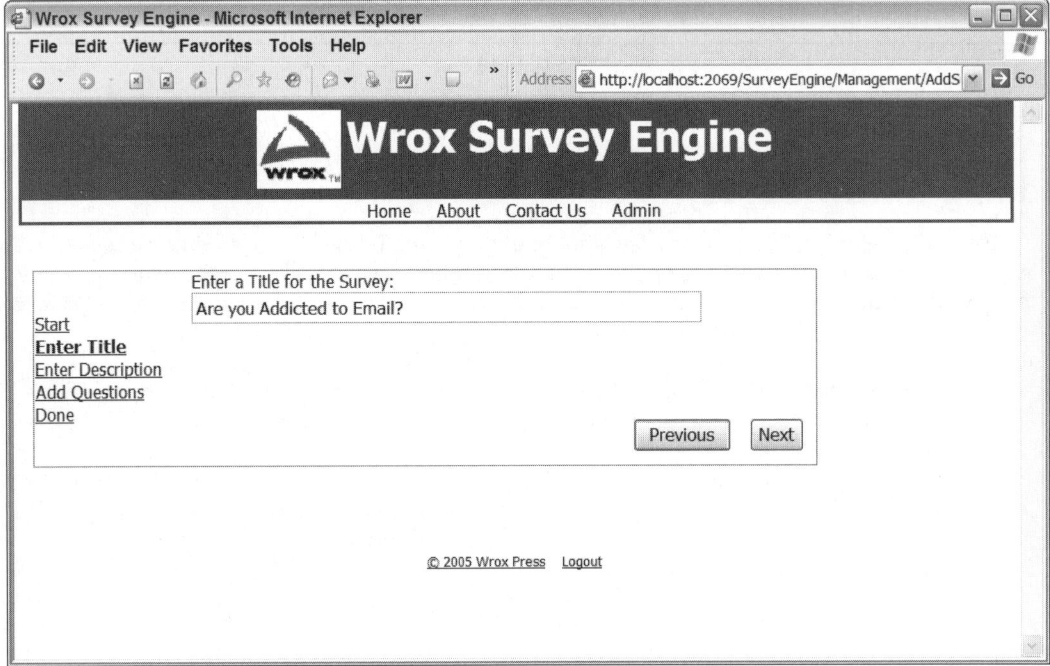

Figure 4-7

In the text box at the top of the screen, you can enter in a name for your new survey. This example new survey is titled "Are you Addicted to Email?" Once you enter the title of your choice, click Next to continue. You are brought to the screen in Figure 4-8, the next step in the wizard.

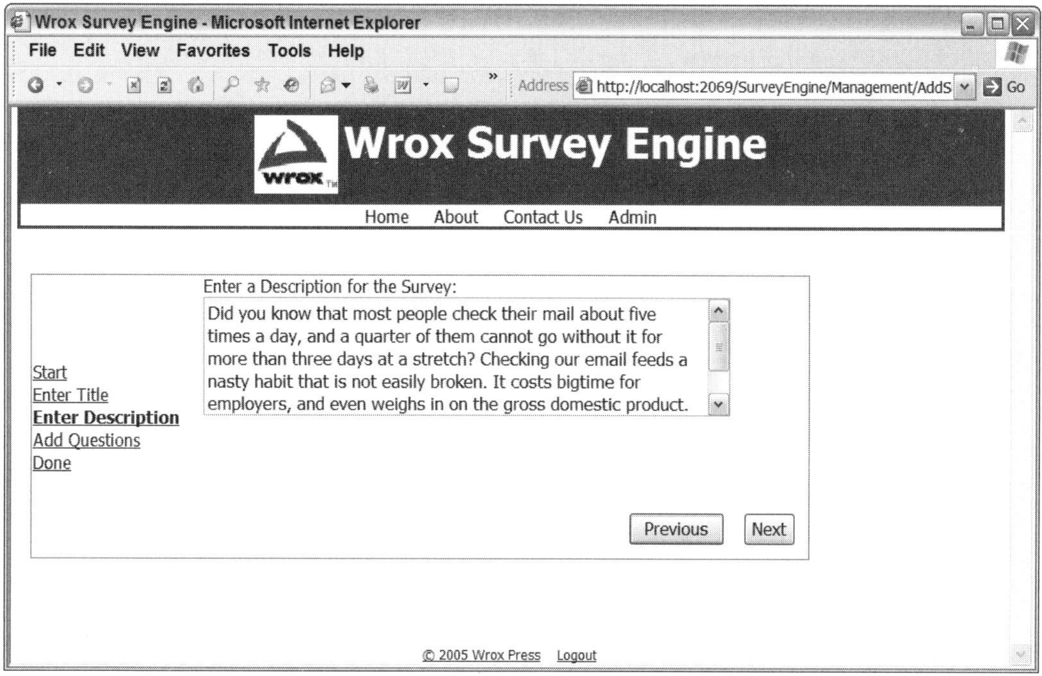

Figure 4-8

Figure 4-8 displays a multi-line text box used to store lengthy descriptions about the survey, which are displayed beneath the name of the survey to the user. Once the description has been entered, click Next to go to the Add Questions page, as displayed in Figure 4-9.

You can enter one question and its correlating answers at a time, clicking the Save Question button to save them to the database. After the questions have been entered, click Next, and know that the survey and its questions are now completely entered into the database. This final page of the New Survey is shown in Figure 4-10.

In addition to creating new surveys, you also have the ability to edit existing surveys.

Figure 4-9

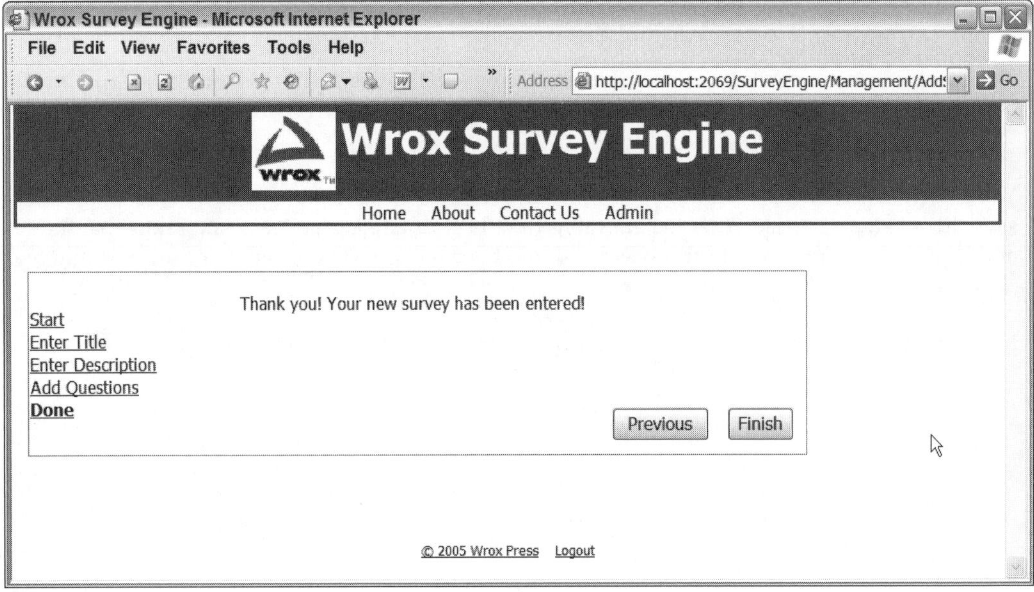

Figure 4-10

Editing an Existing Survey

If you want to edit an existing survey, you can do so by returning to the Administrator page by clicking the Admin link in the menu bar. Then, click one of the Questions survey row-links. This link loads a page used to manage the existing questions for an existing survey, depicted in Figure 4-11.

Figure 4-11 displays each of the questions within a given survey, with clickable hyperlinks in each row provided in order to add, edit, or delete questions for any survey.

So the basic usage of the Survey Engine is summarized as a way of creating and displaying a survey from the web site, and providing management tools to monitor and control the survey as it is responded to.

The next section provides insight to the technically challenging portions of the application and how they all fit together to form the solution. You learn how the classes are modeled and where the important design elements reside.

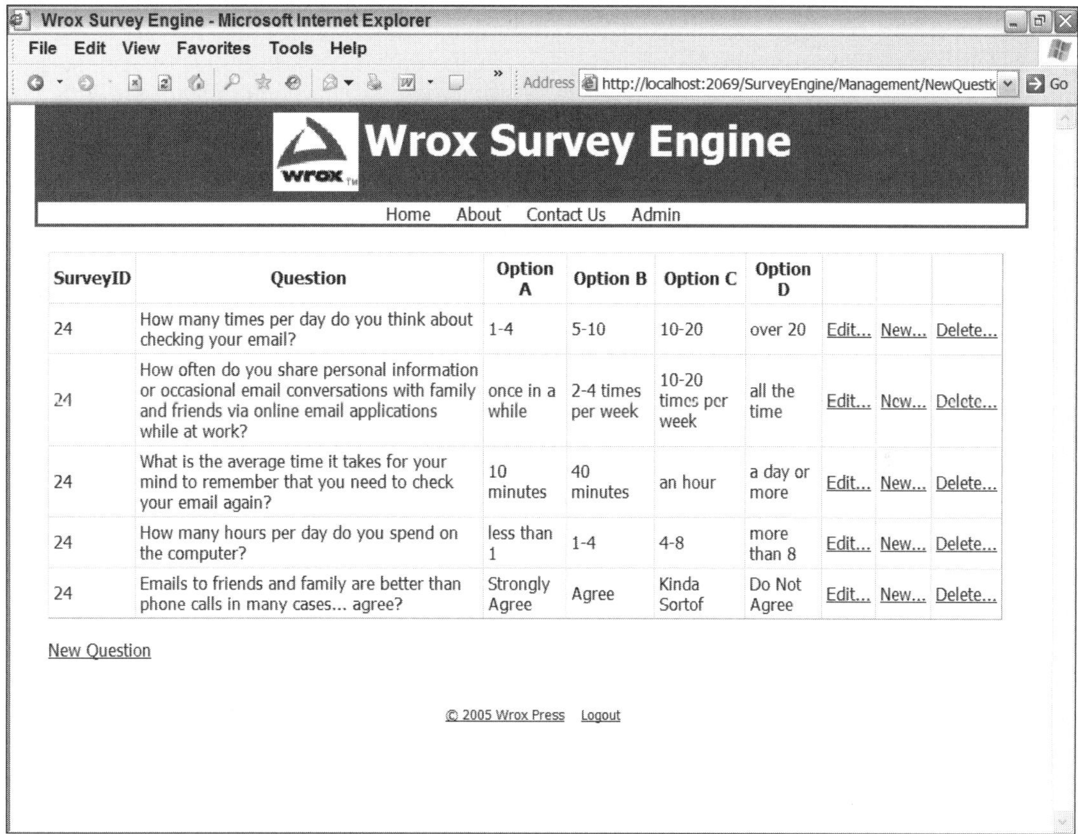

Figure 4-11

Wrox Survey Engine Design

This section provides a detailed look at the inner workings of the web site application, focusing on the classes involved and the integration of data-bound controls to their object connections and SQL Server data connections.

The design of the Wrox Survey Engine is an object-oriented and logically *tiered* approach, using a limited amount of logical abstraction between the client, business, and data layers of the application. This allows for a developer to conceptualize how the application could be separated into multiple projects, spanning servers and/or locations. This section also explains in detail the two approaches used to bind data to form elements: the SQL Server `DataSource` and the `ObjectDataSource` controls.

This topic, as well as other areas of the architecture, is expounded upon later within this section.

Object Binding and SQL Server Data Binding

In an effort to develop an application rapidly and efficiently, there is always a tradeoff for developers to consider. Some project planning and design sessions may point toward the use of faster and lightweight GUI controls to perform the bulk of the work for the developer, saving countless hours of effort. A specific example of lightweight GUI controls would be the `GridView` and `DataList` controls. These allow you to drag and drop controls to a WebForm, set some properties in Design View, and run the application. Without writing one line of VB .NET or C# code, you can configure a data source and data-bound control to render completely on the WebForm. The new ASP.NET 2.0 control creates the ADO.NET `Connection`, `Command`, `Dataset`, or `DataReader` objects for you, providing everything you need to bind to the data at run time. It also properly handles the events used for data binding on the page—something that ASP.NET 1.1 did not do for you (Phew! Thank goodness!). These are in fact a great set of features to take advantage of. But even so, many programmers will read through this book to learn the more extensive and far-reaching features of ASP.NET 2.0, moving on as programmers in the new and improved .NET universe, and rightly so. But for those who are interested in larger-scale deployments with ASP.NET 2.0, it is a worthwhile effort to identify the reasons why the tradeoffs of using more scalable architectures, and what you are losing or gaining with each methodology in ASP.NET 2.0 specifically. The scalability of an architecture has a lot to do with the load it can carry in cases where a large volume of data is involved, or a heavy amount of processing is required. It also refers to the level of control that exists in throttling or directing the processing, traffic, or data appropriately. ASP.NET 2.0 handles such cases with several intrinsic benefits that set it apart as a world class platform for development.

Truly decoupled architectures in the industry are more often seen in larger corporate application development cycles and are usually designed as more generic and pattern-based. The decoupled approach tends to isolate user, business, and data layers of an application into specific sections, allowing each to function independently. This is the nature of distributed development, and has evolved into what is sometimes referred to as *composite applications*. The distributed design would tend to only provide database execution logic within a layer of code (classes) that are specifically positioned and designed to make such data calls. Only those classes are able to extract and handle data out of the database, acting as a go-between for the other application modules or classes. As such, the use of business objects (such as the `Survey` class) would allow a request for data to go out to other classes as a data layer (for example, the `SurveyDB` class), returning data back to the client and binding to the data grid, list box, and so on. This approach is generally acceptable for most applications.

In this area of object and data binding, you will notice in this Wrox Survey Engine application we make use of the built-in ASP.NET `ObjectDataSource` controls to bind data from business objects to GUI (graphical user interface) controls. This in many ways mimics a decoupled, object-based approach that has been held as a best practice in recent years, but by itself may not provide all of the custom and robust features that a corporate project's requirements or design may mandate. Some class objects need to be serialized and transferred through an Internet connection between tiers, in order to allow for the separate server environments. Other class objects or modules are pooled and managed closely using process instrumentation (WMI) or ASP.NET performance monitors (PerfMon). These additional object-level requirements can be met using the `ObjectDataSource` controls, but it may require additional development and is worthy of mentioning in the course of this book.

In addition to the `ObjectDataSource` controls, the Wrox Survey Engine also uses the SQL Server `DataSource` controls to extract data from the SQL Server Express 2005 database files and bind it to the GUI controls. Contrary to this line of thinking, the `SqlDataSource` controls are typically designed as a quick and dirty way to select records from a database and bind them to a form. This process actually includes the SQL statements in the markup of your ASPX files. In direct opposition to a safer and more distributed approach of the decoupled tiers, this poses a risk to the application and management thereof. As more users access such pages, more database connections may be created (depending on the connection strings used), thereby increasing the number of pooled or non-pooled connections to the database on the server. This can ultimately cause a loss of scalability, and speed, and if not used carefully could pose a risk to sites with heavy traffic. The use of the `SqlDataSource` controls also requires updates to the source ASPX files of your site whenever database changes are made that affect your queries or stored procedures. This is not ideal for an application to maintain a predictable and manageable state. But as stated in other chapters, and expounded herein, such risks are overlooked, instead providing a meaningful experience with both the `ObjectDataSource` and the `SqlDataSource` controls.

Structure of the Site

The site has been structured in an organized fashion, with files contained within folders that make sense for maintaining the code in the most efficient manner. The Controls folder houses all of the user controls, and the ContentFiles folder contains the main ASPX WebForm files of the web site.

The different folder sections of the web application are listed in the following table:

Folder	Description
App_Code	Houses the business layer class (survey.vb) and the data layer class (surveyDB.vb).
App_Data	The standard .NET folder for database files.
App_Themes	The themes folder, containing two themes for use with the site.
ContentFiles	The standard ASPX WebForm files for displaying content.
Controls	Stores all user controls.
Images	Stores images for the header or any other pages.
Management	Stores the secured administrative WebForm pages.
Miscellaneous files	These include the Login page, the Web.config file, the sitemap file, and the master page file at the root of the site.

Figure 4-12 is a developer's view of the project's folders and files from within the Solution Explorer.

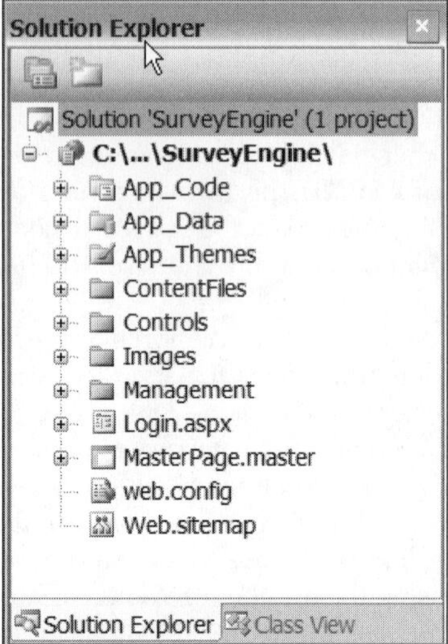

Figure 4-12

The next section explains the main database entities involved and how the various survey concepts are implemented within the database.

Data Model and Database Objects

The data model is very simple in nature, being comprised of essentially three basic data elements:

- Surveys
- Questions
- Responses

Each survey has questions, for which you or any web user can provide their own selections, which generates the response values. As such, Figure 4-13 displays a diagram of the database tables involved.

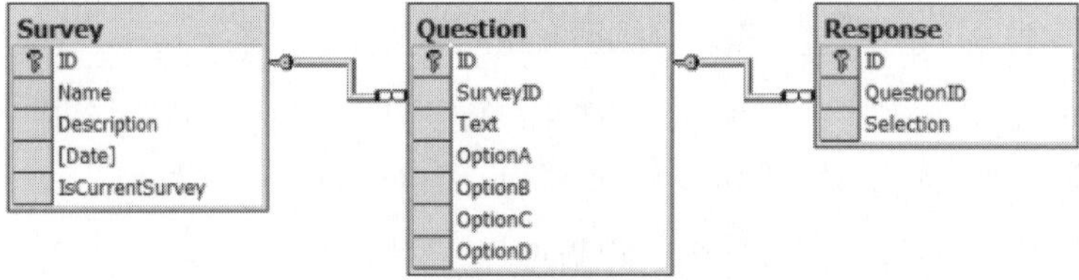

Figure 4-13

Detailed explanations of each of the three tables appear in the subsequent sections.

The following table describes the contents of the Question table:

Field Name	Data Type	Description
ID	`Int`	The unique identifier for this record.
SurveyID	`Int`	The survey to which this question belongs.
Text	`varchar(1000)`	The actual question text.
OptionA	`varchar(1000)`	The first of four choices.
OptionB	`varchar(1000)`	The second of four choices.
OptionC	`varchar(1000)`	The third of four choices.
OptionD	`varchar(1000)`	The fourth of four choices.

The next table outlines the Survey table:

Field Name	Data Type	Description
ID	`Int`	The unique identifier for this record.
Name	`varchar(200)`	The name given to the survey.
Description	`varchar(1000)`	The text description given to the survey.
Date	`Datetime`	The date and time stamp at the time that the survey was created.
IsCurrentSurvey	`Char(1)`	The 0 or 1 value indicating that the survey is the one used within the web site as the currently displayed survey. 1 represents that the record is the current survey, and 0 signifies the record is not the current survey.

The following table details the contents of the Response table:

Field Name	Data Type	Description
ID	`Int`	The unique identifier for this record.
QuestionID	`Int`	The question ID to which this response applies.
Selection	`Char(1)`	The A, B, C, or D value corresponding to the user's selection for the question being responded to.

In addition to these three tables, a number of stored procedures are in use. They follow a consistent naming pattern with the other chapters, as shown here:

- sproc*TableName*SelectList
- sproc*TableName*SelectSingleItem
- sproc*TableName*InsertUpdateItem

In such fashion, the following stored procedures are used in the application:

- `sprocQuestionDeleteSingleItem`
- `sprocQuestionInsertUpdateItem`
- `sprocQuestionSelectList`
- `sprocResponseInsertItem`
- `sprocSurveyInsertUpdateItem`
- `sprocSurveySaveSingleItemAsCurrent`
- `sprocSurveySelectList`
- `sprocSurveySelectSingleItem`
- `sprocSurveySelectSingleItemWhereCurrent`

As you can see, the naming convention allows you to easily and quickly find the stored procedures that apply to a specific table, and whether they are selects, inserts, updates, or deletes.

Several noteworthy stored procedures should be reviewed. The first procedure selects a single survey record from the database to display in the `CurrentSurvey` user control on the Default.aspx homepage:

```
ALTER PROCEDURE dbo.sprocSurveySelectSingleItemWhereCurrent
/*'=============================================================
  '   NAME:                sprocSurveySelectSingleItemWhereCurrent
  '   DATE CREATED:        October 5, 2005
  '   CREATED BY:          Shawn Livermore (shawnlivermore.blogspot.com)
  '   CREATED FOR:         ASP.NET 2.0 - Instant Results
  '   FUNCTION:            Returns the 'current' survey from the database.
  '=============================================================
*/
as

select top 1 * from Survey where iscurrentsurvey = 1
```

As you can see, the level of complexity within these stored procedures is down to a minimum in this project. The simple table structure of the application is partly the reason for the ease of use and low level of design complexity.

The next procedure is used to select out all of the questions for a given survey ID:

```
ALTER PROCEDURE dbo.sprocQuestionSelectList
/*'=============================================================
  '   NAME:                sprocQuestionSelectList
  '   DATE CREATED:        October 5, 2005
  '   CREATED BY:          Shawn Livermore (shawnlivermore.blogspot.com)
```

```
  '   CREATED FOR:        ASP.NET 2.0 - Instant Results
  '   FUNCTION:           retrieves all questions and options for a
  '                       specific survey from the database.
  '==============================================================
*/
(@id int)

as

SELECT Question.SurveyID, Question.Text, Question.OptionB, Question.OptionA,
Question.OptionD, Question.OptionC, Question.ID
FROM  Survey INNER JOIN Question ON Survey.ID = Question.SurveyID
WHERE (Survey.ID = @id)
```

These are the basic stored procedures used as examples, but entirely common for these types of applications.

In addition to stored procedures and tables, the Wrox Survey Engine also employs the use of views to provide visibility to somewhat complex queries used to display the percentage results of a survey's questions. These views are as follows:

- `viewAnswerPercentByQuestion`
- `viewAnswerSumByQuestion`
- `viewNumberResponsesBySurvey`
- `viewQuestionCountBySurvey`
- `viewResponseCountBySurvey`

These are used in conjunction with one another as dependencies, where one view uses or points to the fields of another view. The end result of the views is the `viewAnswerPercentByQuestion`, which is used by the SurveyResults user control.

Themes and Skins

The project provides a simple way in which to apply themes and skins to each page of the site, without modifying any HTML markup sections on any page (even the master page is safe from special control-based HTML markup). You can apply a theme to the entire web site by modifying the Web.config file to point to the name of your theme (assuming the theme exists in your project under the App_Themes folder). This is carried out within each ASP.NET form by using the following code in each of the form's pre-initialization events:

```
    Protected Sub Page_PreInit(ByVal sender As Object, ByVal e As System.EventArgs)
Handles Me.PreInit
        'this preinit event fires to initialize the page
        'it allows for the theme and title to be set for this page,
        'which actually pulls from the web.config setting
        'via the shared Config class's exposed properties.
        Page.Theme = Config.CurrentTheme
        Page.Title = Config.PageTitle
    End Sub
```

This code accesses the `config` class's properties (pulled from the Web.config file), and sets the page's theme member to be the current theme value. In this way, you can maintain a consistent experience throughout the web site, with only one change needed to the Web.config in order to change the look and feel of the entire user experience! You are probably glad to hear that — I know I am. The exact place where you would change the theme for the site is in the `appSettings` section of the Web.config, as displayed here:

```
<!--
    <add key="CurrentTheme" value="CleanBlue" />
-->
    <add key="CurrentTheme" value="CleanRed" />
```

This code displays one of the theme entries as commented out, and one of them as active. Simply swap the two values in order to make the change.

Security Model

The project uses ASP.NET 2.0 Forms Authentication with a SQL Server Security Provider. The initial designation to use this provider from within the ASP.NET Security Administration tool generates a new security database, which is included in the project and used to house all of the user account information and security settings. This security model implements Forms Authentication intrinsically within the various new ASP.NET 2.0 security controls, such as those used to log in, display login status, recover your password, change your password, and create a new user.

The security model mentioned is utilized and referenced in several areas of the application. One such area is in reference to the Management folder of the site. The security model allows you to log in to the web site, and become an authenticated user. The login.aspx form is loaded automatically whenever you try to access any of the ASPX files in the Management folder without first being unauthenticated. This is a clear glimpse at the new ASP.NET 2.0 security model implemented via the Role and Membership Providers. The configuration is such that the only provision to implement such security is an instance of the ASP.NET `Login` control, such as the following example:

```
<asp:Login ID="Login1" runat="server" />
```

As a practical use, this provides a clear example of a secure web site folder and the use of role-based access to pages within that folder via the ASP.NET 2.0 Configuration Tool. This tool is essentially used simply for security-rights management. The ASP.NET 2.0 Configuration Tool can be accessed within Visual Studio by clicking Website⇨ASP.Net Configuration from the menu. Once the tool fully loads you'll see a Security tab. Clicking the Security tab enables you to modify the settings of any folder within your site to allow or restrict access based on roles that you can define and assign users to. The output of this effort generates the Web.config file that lies within the folder that you specified to restrict access to. The following is an example of this Web.config file output:

```
<?xml version="1.0" encoding="utf-8"?>
<configuration xmlns="http://schemas.microsoft.com/.NetConfiguration/v2.0">
    <system.web>
        <authorization>
            <deny users="?" />
            <allow roles="Admin" />
            <allow roles="SuperAdmin" />
```

```
        </authorization>
    </system.web>
</configuration>
```

This configuration file uses three main entries as the meat of the security settings. These are essentially a series of statements in XML format that define the security rights for that folder, hierarchically within the web site, overriding the web site's root Web.config, as well as the machine.config on the server. In this file, the `<deny users="?" />` phrase means that the folder should deny any unauthenticated users, denoted by the question mark. Next, the `<allow roles="Admin" />` and the `<allow roles="SuperAdmin" />` entries both represent the ability of the folder to allow access to Admin or Superadmin roles.

Two accounts are created for use within the Survey Engine, and two different roles that those accounts are assigned to, respectively. These are as follows:

Username	Password	Account Description
Admin	password#	This user is assigned to the Administrator role.
SuperAdmin	password#	This user is assigned to the Super Administrator role.

The following two roles are already in the security database and referenced within the application for certain areas of interest to remain very secure:

Role	Role Description
Administrator	This role has the ability to add, edit, and delete surveys and their questions.
Super Administrator	This role has the same privileges as the Administrator role, but also can delete surveys and/or their individual questions from the system.

Thus, you can control access to form elements and folders alike, using the ASP.NET Configuration Tool, or your own scripted logic in VB .NET.

Classes Involved

Only a few basic classes are in use for the Wrox Survey Engine, but they are intelligent classes that are designed to work in an object-friendly fashion. That is, in a typical object-oriented environment, the class structures would seem to fare well as compared to other object structures.

The SurveyBase Class

The `SurveyBase` class (see Figure 4-14) is essentially the inheritable base class to which every survey refers. It allows the derived `Survey` class objects to provide exposure to the `Save` and `New` methods for consistent and convenient class management.

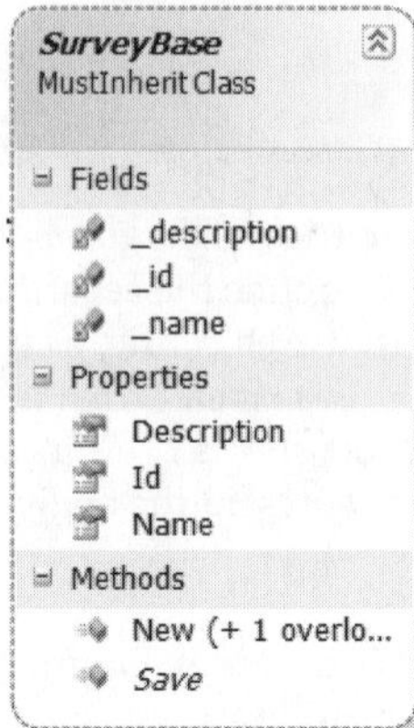

Figure 4-14

The following table describes the methods available to the `SurveyBase` class:

Method	Return Type	Description
`New()`	n/a	The constructor for the `SurveyBase` class
`Save()`	`Int`	The `save` method used to save the derived survey class object

The `Survey` class follows the `SurveyBase` class, because it is a class that inherits from the `SurveyBase` class. This provides access to shared methods and functionality within the `SurveyBase` class.

The Survey Class

The `Survey` class (see Figure 4-15) is used to perform the bulk of the object provisioning for the business layer of the application. Its methods are accessible as public and shared for ease of use within the various forms and controls of the application. This means that you do not have to instantiate an instance of the `Survey` class in order to call its methods. Instead, simply use the syntax of `Survey.MethodName()` in any VB .NET WebForm or control of the application to execute the function.

The following table displays the accessible members of the `Survey` class:

Method	Return Type	Description
`Delete`	n/a	Deletes a survey from the database by calling `Delete()` in the `SurveyDB` class.
`DeleteQuestion`	n/a	Deletes a question from the database by calling `DeleteQuestion()` in the `SurveyDB` class.
`Get`	Survey Class Object	Retrieves a survey from the database by calling `Get()` in the `SurveyDB` class.
`GetCurrentSurvey`	DataSet	Returns the current survey from the database.

Method	Return Type	Description
`GetQuestionIDs`	Collection	Gets a set of question IDs for a given survey.
`GetQuestions`	DataSet	Gets a set of questions and their multiple choices for a given survey.
`GetSurveyList`	DataSet	Returns a list with surveys in the specified category from the database.
`New`	n/a	Provides potential functionality to process actions and information on the create event for the object.
`Save`	Integer	Saves a survey in the database by calling `Save()` in the `SurveyDB` class. Because this class inherits the `SurveyBase` class, the `Save` method is overrideable and the `Me` keyword is utilized.
`SaveQuestion`	Boolean	Saves a set of questions for a survey.
`SaveResponses`	Boolean	Saves a set of answers to questions for a given survey.
`SaveSurvey`	n/a	Saves a survey to the database.
`SaveSurveyAsCurrent`	n/a	Saves a survey as the current survey.

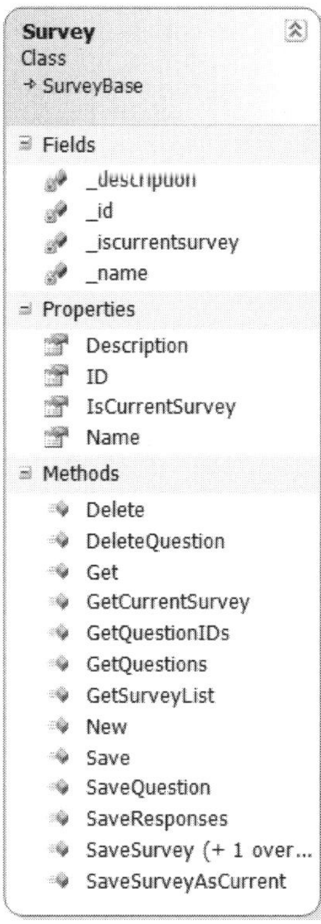

Figure 4-15

The next class represents the callable data-related methods of the application.

The SurveyDB Class

The `SurveyDB` class (see Figure 4-16) is used to as the data layer of the application. It is essentially the main go-between for all method calls from the business tier that require access to the database. No other class or code section of the application makes data-related executions except for this `SurveyDB` class.

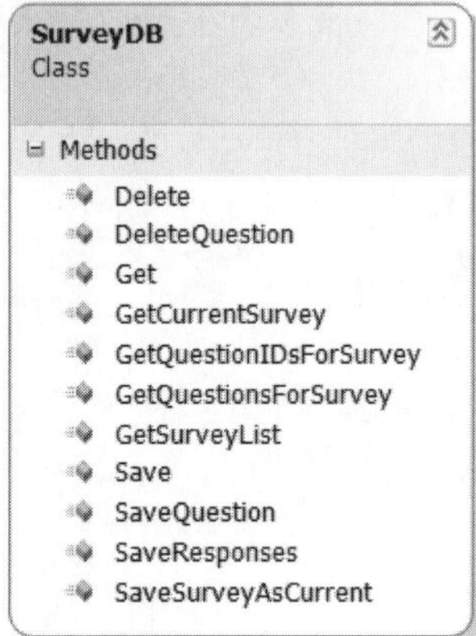

Figure 4-16

The following table displays the accessible members of the `SurveyDB` class:

Method	Return Type	Description
`Delete`	n/a	Deletes a survey from the database.
`DeleteQuestion`	n/a	Deletes a question from the database.
`Get`	Survey	Returns in instance of the class by sending in the survey ID.
`GetCurrentSurvey`	DataSet	Retrieves the current survey from the database.
`GetQuestionIDsForSurvey`	Collection	Retrieves a collection of survey question IDs from the database.
`GetQuestionsForSurvey`	DataSet	Retrieves a DataSet of survey questions from the database.
`GetSurveyList`	DataSet	Retrieves a DataSet of surveys from the database.
`Save`	Integer	Saves a survey to the database.

Method	Return Type	Description
`SaveQuestion`	Boolean	Saves a question to the survey in the database.
`SaveResponses`	Boolean	Saves a response to the question in the survey.
`SaveSurveyAsCurrent`	n/a	Makes a specified survey the current one within the database.

The next class portrays the configuration class that has been commonly used in this book.

The Config Class

The `Config` class, depicted in Figure 4-17, is used as the configuration manager of the application. It is essentially the main access point for all configuration settings that any of the application tiers may require access to. No other class or code section of the application makes configuration-related calls except for this `Config` class.

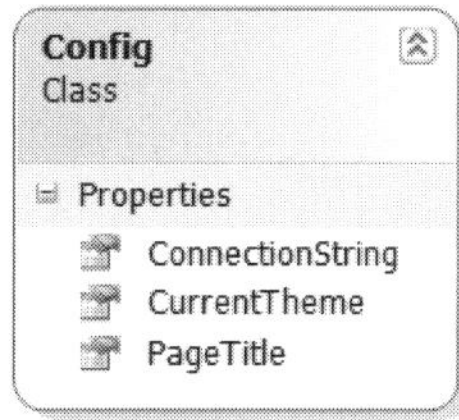

Figure 4-17

The following table displays the accessible members of the `Config` class:

Property	Return Type	Description
`ConnectionString`	String	The connection string property that pulls from Web.config.
`CurrentTheme`	String	The current theme of the web site as defined in the Web.config file.
`PageTitle`	String	The HTML title value that each page displays, as defined here from the Web.config file.

So you have a good idea at this point about what classes are involved in the application, and how those classes may be used. The next section explains the detailed business logic within the application and the processes or workflow that they accommodate.

Code and Code Explanation

This section explains each of the essential code files in the Wrox Survey Engine project. You look in detail at the files in the each of the different folders and learn how they interact and are used across the project.

Root Files

The root of the Wrox Survey Engine contains several important files, including the main ASPX shell-pages, and the configuration and formatting pages.

Web.config

The Web.config stores vital configuration entries used within the application. One entry, named the `SqlServerConnectionString`, controls the connection to the database, as shown here:

```
<connectionStrings>
<add name="ConnectionString" connectionString="Data
Source=(local)\SqlExpress;AttachDbFilename=|DataDirectory|\SurveyDB.mdf;Integrated
Security=True;User Instance=True" providerName="System.Data.SqlClient"/>
 </connectionStrings>
```

The `SqlServerConnectionString` also contains information managing the SMTP e-mail settings for sending out e-mails:

```
<appSettings>
    <add key="EmailFrom" value="admin@mysurveyengine.com" />
    <add key="EmailTo" value="admin@mysurveyengine.Com" />
```

The Web.config is also used to provide easy modification to the themes in use for the entire site. You can find more information on this in the "Themes and Skins" section earlier in the chapter.

Survey.vb

The `Survey` class is one of the most important areas of the Survey Engine application. The class contains methods and properties that allow for the storage of survey-related information and logic to implement updates to that information within the data access layer. Some of the methods provide access to the general information for surveys, whereas others provide the capability to obtain a full dataset of all surveys. In addition, the `GetQuestions` method returns all of the questions for any given survey.

This `Survey.vb` class can also be bound to an `ObjectDataSource` control within the user interface, thereby providing a business layer for the application. Its methods are listed as public and shared to provide a more rapid development model without being required to instantiate an instance of the `Survey` class in order to call its methods or access its members.

By using `#Region` tags in the Survey.vb class file, the Visual Studio IDE allows the page to be grouped into organized sections. Sections that are commonly used to group the code in this way include Variables, Constructors, Methods, and Properties. This does not impact the .NET assemblies in any way, but is simply a great way to maintain organized logic. Figure 4-18 is a visual display of the regionalized code as it is displayed within the Visual Studio IDE.

```
Imports System.Data

''' <summary>
''' The Survey class provides access to the information
''' within a survey, such as its questions or title
''' </summary>
Public Class Survey
    Inherits SurveyBase

Private Variables

Constructor(s)

Public Methods

Public Properties

End Class
```

Figure 4-18

One of the more important method calls of the survey is the `SaveSurvey` method. The code for this is as follows:

```
Public Shared Sub SaveSurvey(ByVal Name As String, ByVal Description As String,
ByVal ID As Integer)

        Dim mSurvey As New Survey
        mSurvey.ID = ID
        mSurvey.Name = Name
        mSurvey.Description = Description
        SurveyDB.Save(mSurvey)

End Sub
```

This method provides the means by which to hand off a `Survey` class object to the data tier for processing.

Config.vb

The `Config` class is used as an available object with three static members. Its members are listed as properties in order to abstract the location in which these values are stored. Currently, the three properties are `ConnectionString`, `CurrentTheme`, and `PageTitle`. The values for the three properties are stored in the Web.config file, with a `Config` class to retrieve them when they are needed:

```
Imports Microsoft.VisualBasic

Public Class Config
    ''' <summary>
    ''' The connection string property that pulls from the web.config
    ''' </summary>
    Public Shared ReadOnly Property ConnectionString() As String
        Get
            Return ConfigurationManager.ConnectionStrings("ConnectionString")
.ConnectionString
        End Get
```

```
    End Property
    ''' <summary>
    ''' The current theme of the website as defined in the web.config file
    ''' </summary>
    Public Shared ReadOnly Property CurrentTheme() As String
        Get
            Return ConfigurationManager.AppSettings("CurrentTheme").ToString()
        End Get
    End Property
    ''' <summary>
    ''' The HTML title value that each page displays, as defined here from the
web.config file
    ''' </summary>
    Public Shared ReadOnly Property PageTitle() As String
        Get
            Return ConfigurationManager.AppSettings("PageTitle").ToString()
        End Get
    End Property
End Class
```

As the preceding `Config` class displays, the properties `ConnectionString`, `CurrentTheme`, and `PageTitle` are marked as `Public Shared ReadOnly`, which allows them to be accessed from anywhere in the project by the config-dot notation. An example of this would be `config.ConnectionString()`. This would return the connection string from the `Config` class, without instantiating a `Config` class object first.

SurveyDB.vb

This class is essentially the data layer for the application. It provides method calls in order to retrieve information from the database and insert or update data within the database as well. This class serves as the only file or object that will have access to the database files. In this way, you isolate data-specific operations outside of the business logic layer. In so doing, you can see that it protects a developer from writing duplicate data access code because it is organized in nature and located in the same place. This also allows for the application to be logically separated into tiers, or layers, with the deliberate feasibility of migrating and expanding the application onto separate servers at any point in time.

In line with the documented function call from the `Survey` class, the `surveyDB` class contains a `Save` method, as displayed here:

```
Public Shared Function Save(ByVal mSurvey As Survey) As Integer

        Using mConnection As New SqlConnection(Config.ConnectionString)

            Dim mNewSurveyID As Integer
            Dim mCommand As SqlCommand = New
SqlCommand("sprocSurveyInsertUpdateItem", mConnection)
            mCommand.CommandType = CommandType.StoredProcedure
            If mSurvey.ID > 0 Then
                mCommand.Parameters.AddWithValue("@id", mSurvey.ID)
            Else
                mCommand.Parameters.AddWithValue("@id", DBNull.Value)
            End If
            mCommand.Parameters.AddWithValue("@name", mSurvey.Name)
```

```
            mCommand.Parameters.AddWithValue("@description", mSurvey.Description)
            If mSurvey.IsCurrentSurvey = False Then
                mCommand.Parameters.AddWithValue("@iscurrentsurvey", 0)
            Else
                mCommand.Parameters.AddWithValue("@iscurrentsurvey", 1)
            End If

            mConnection.Open()
            mNewSurveyID = mCommand.ExecuteScalar()
            mConnection.Close()

            Return mNewSurveyID

        End Using
    End Function
```

This accepts a parameter of the type `survey` and accesses the members to save values into the database.

Another method of interest is the `GetCurrentSurvey()` method, returning a DataSet of the currently selected survey in the system. The following is a code excerpt for this method:

```
   ''' <summary>
    ''' Retrieves the 'current' survey from the database
    ''' </summary>
    Public Shared Function GetCurrentSurvey() As DataSet
        Dim dsSurveys As DataSet = New DataSet()
        Try
            Using mConnection As New SqlConnection(Config.ConnectionString)

                Dim mCommand As SqlCommand = New SqlCommand
("sprocSurveySelectSingleItemWhereCurrent", mConnection)
                mCommand.CommandType = CommandType.StoredProcedure
                Dim myDataAdapter As SqlDataAdapter = New SqlDataAdapter()
                myDataAdapter.SelectCommand = mCommand
                myDataAdapter.Fill(dsSurveys)
                mConnection.Close()
                Return dsSurveys
            End Using
        Catch ex As Exception
            'When you call the "Throw" statement, you are raising the error to the
global.asax file, which will use the default error handling page to process/display
the custom error to the user
            Throw
        End Try
    End Function
```

The preceding page logic performs the following steps:

1. Creates a new `SqlCommand` object, passing in the stored procedure name and the connection.
2. Sets the command type to be stored procedure.
3. Creates a new DataAdapter.
4. Assigns the SelectCommand of the DataAdapter to the newly created command.

5. Calls the data adapter's `Fill` method, passing in the DataSet to be filled with data.
6. Closes the connection.
7. Returns the DataSet to the caller.

It is worth mentioning that the `CurrentSurvey` web user control is the way that you currently display a survey to the user. By extending the application, you could offer a list of surveys to choose from, and provide dynamic page logic to pull the right survey for the user to complete.

WebForms

The WebForms are standard ASPX pages that contain the client-side graphical user interface of the application. A few WebForms are of particular importance within the project, as noted in the following sections.

Default.aspx

The Default.aspx file is of course used as the first page that loads when the site is accessed. Within this page is an instance of the user control `currentsurvey.ascx`, which provides visibility to the title and description of the survey that is marked as current in the database. In this way, the web site viewers will be able to see a survey they can click to complete and view the results.

Login.aspx

The Login page contains a `Login` control and a `PasswordRecovery` control. As mentioned in other chapters, these are brand new to the .NET environment. This Login.aspx WebForm is located at the root of the site and is not using a master page. The login controls contain HTML markup that defines the specific values for the destination page and text values of the controls:

```
    <fieldset style="height: 128px; width: 270px;">
    <asp:Login ID="Login1" runat="server" DestinationPageUrl= "~/Management/
Admin.aspx">
    </asp:Login>
    </fieldset>

    <fieldset style="height: 118px; width: 270px;">
    <asp:PasswordRecovery ID="PasswordRecovery1" runat="server">
    </asp:PasswordRecovery>
    </fieldset>
```

This HTML markup contains the control definitions for the `Login` and `PasswordRecovery` controls and their properties.

TakeSurvey.aspx

The TakeSurvey.aspx WebForm is used to provide a survey from the database to complete with inserts into the response table. The basic controls on the WebForm are an `ObjectDataSource` control, `SqlDataSource` control, `DataList` control, and a set of fields within the `DataList` control that are bound to the object properties. The following excerpt is the defined values of an `ObjectDataSource` control as it is used to bind to values from the `SelectMethod` of its designated `Survey` business object. The `GetQuestions` method is used to retrieve the survey table records in the form of a DataSet, for this `ObjectDataSource` control to bind to:

```
<asp:ObjectDataSource ID="odsSurveyQuestions" runat="server"
SelectMethod="GetQuestions" TypeName="Survey">
        <SelectParameters>
   <asp:QueryStringParameter Name="id" QueryStringField="surveyID" Type="Int32" />
        </SelectParameters>
</asp:ObjectDataSource>
```

Just below this section in the form is the `DataList` control that this `ObjectDataSource` control binds to. The fields and settings of this control exist solely within the HTML markup, as displayed here:

```
<asp:DataList ID="DataList1" runat="server" DataSourceID="odsSurveyQuestions">
  <ItemTemplate>
    <%=GetQuestionNum()%>. <%#Server.HtmlEncode(Eval("Text").ToString())%>
      <br />
       <input name="Q<%#Eval("ID")%>" type="radio" value="A">A.
            <%#Server.HtmlEncode(Eval("OptionA").ToString())%></option><br />
       <input name="Q<%#Eval("ID")%>" type="radio" value="B">B.
            <%#Server.HtmlEncode(Eval("OptionB").ToString())%></option><br />
       <input name="Q<%#Eval("ID")%>" type="radio" value="C">C.
            <%#Server.HtmlEncode(Eval("OptionC").ToString())%></option><br />
       <input name="Q<%#Eval("ID")%>" type="radio" value="D">D.
            <%#Server.HtmlEncode(Eval("OptionD").ToString())%></option><br />
      <br /><br />
  </ItemTemplate>
</asp:DataList>
```

This code specifies the object properties that the `DataList` binds to by the use of the `<%#Eval("ID")%>` tags. This provides the connectivity and bindings to the object properties for the repeating data values in the `DataList` control.

User Controls

Some specific user controls in the site assist with the navigation and content display for multiple pages. Because web user controls promote a practice of creating and using reusable code, they were made to be applicable within multiple pages of the site, depending on the nature of the controls.

header.ascx

The `header` user control is used to provide the top area of each page with meaningful content. If anything needs to reside at or near the top of a web page, you would add it to the `header` control so it would be visible through all of the pages.

The following code represents entire header.ascx source:

```
  <%@ Control Language="VB" AutoEventWireup="false" CodeFile="header.ascx.vb"
Inherits="Controls_header" %>
<div style="text-align: center">
    <table><tr>
        <td><img src="../Images/headerlogo.gif" /></td>
        <td><h1><% Response.Write(Page.Title) %></h1>
        </td>
    </tr></table>
</div>
```

Notice that the `<%Response.Write(Page.Title)%>` tags are used to write back to the response stream a title of the web site on the top of each page, which originated from the Web.config file.

footer.ascx

The `footer` user control is used as the bottom section of the site, for each page that uses the master page. That is, the `footer` control, among others, is a referenced control within the master page. In this way, it is propagated to all pages in the same exact manner.

The content of the `footer` control is displayed here:

```
<%@ Control Language="VB" AutoEventWireup="false" CodeFile="footer.ascx.vb"
Inherits="Controls_footer" %>
<a href="http://wrox.com" target="_blank">&copy; 2005 Wrox Press</a>   
<asp:LoginStatus ID="LoginStatus1" runat="server"
LogoutAction="RedirectToLoginPage"
    LogoutPageUrl="~/Login.aspx" />
```

This excerpt includes a reference to a `LoginStatus` control, brand new in the ASP.NET 2.0 control set. The new control displays a changing link-button for providing login and logout functionality. When the user is logged in to the site, the `LoginStatus` control displays a Logout link-button. Clicking the Logout link-button logs users out of the site, and directs them to the Login page. When the user is logged out of the site, the `LoginStatus` control displays a Login link-button. Clicking the Login link-button directs users to the Login page, where they are able to log in.

navigation.ascx

The `navigation` user control is used to provide the reusable menu that each page includes within itself in structure of the site. The menu itself is a brand new ASP.NET 2.0 control that binds to a `SiteMapDataSource` control, also new in version 2.0 of the .NET Framework. The `SiteMapDataSource` control is used to bind to an XML file, wherein the site files are listed as entries in the XML file.

The following excerpt is the HTML markup of the `navigation` control:

```
<%@ Control Language="VB" AutoEventWireup="false" CodeFile="navigation.ascx.vb"
Inherits="Controls_Navigation" %>
<asp:Menu ID="Menu1" runat="server" DataSourceID="SiteMapDataSource1"
Orientation="Horizontal"
    StaticDisplayLevels="2"></asp:Menu>
<asp:SiteMapDataSource ID="SiteMapDataSource1" runat="server" />
```

The XML file of the `SiteMapDataSource` control is displayed here:

```
<?xml version="1.0" encoding="utf-8" ?>
<siteMap xmlns="http://schemas.microsoft.com/AspNet/SiteMap-File-1.0" >
    <siteMapNode url="ContentFiles/default.aspx" title="Home"  description="">
      <siteMapNode url="ContentFiles/about.aspx" title="About"  description="" />
      <siteMapNode url="ContentFiles/contact.aspx" title="Contact Us"
description="" />
      <siteMapNode url="Management/admin.aspx" title="Admin"  description="" />
    </siteMapNode>
</siteMap>
```

To add a page to the menu of the web site, you must simply copy and paste (with the necessary modifications) an entry of the preceding XML file. In this way, the master page (which contains the only reference to the `navigation` control) provides visibility to the menu of the site on each page.

surveyresults.ascx

The SurveyResults control displays the results of the survey that is specified via the surveyed QueryString value. It is referenced within the SurveyResults.aspx WebForm page in the ContentFiles folder, and the MgtSurveyResults.aspx page in the Management folder. The SurveyResults control provides visibility to the percentage results of each of the survey questions of the specified survey.

The following HTML markup is from the SurveyResults.aspx page, displaying a `SqlDataSource` control. Note the use of the QueryString surveyID as an entry in the `<SelectParameters>` section of the file:

```
        <asp:SqlDataSource ID="SqlSurveyResults" runat="server" ConnectionString=
"<%$ ConnectionStrings:ConnectionString %>" SelectCommand="SELECT * FROM
[viewAnswerPercentByQuestion] WHERE ([SurveyID] = @SurveyID)">
          <SelectParameters>
              <asp:QueryStringParameter Name="SurveyID" QueryStringField="surveyID"
Type="Int32" />
          </SelectParameters>
      </asp:SqlDataSource>
```

The next section of the file contains the data-bound `DataList` control, with all the applicable data-bound fields listed within server-side tags, as shown here:

```
<asp:DataList ID="DataList1" runat="server" DataSourceID="SqlSurveyResults">
    <ItemTemplate>
        <%=GetQuestionNum()%>. <%#Server.HtmlEncode(Eval("Text").ToString())%>
       <table border="0" cellpadding="1" cellspacing="0">
        <tr><td>
           <span class="Pct"><%#Server.HtmlEncode(Eval("PctA").ToString())%>%
</span>
        </td><td>
           <%#Server.HtmlEncode(Eval("OptionA").ToString())%>
       </td></tr><tr><td>
           <span class="Pct"><%#Server.HtmlEncode(Eval("PctB").ToString())%>%
</span>
        </td><td>
                <%#Server.HtmlEncode(Eval("OptionB").ToString())%>
       </td></tr><tr><td>
           <span class="Pct"><%#Server.HtmlEncode(Eval("PctC").ToString())%>%
</span>
        </td><td>
                <%#Server.HtmlEncode(Eval("OptionC").ToString())%>
       </td></tr><tr><td>
           <span class="Pct"><%#Server.HtmlEncode(Eval("PctD").ToString())%>%
</span>
        </td><td>
                <%#Server.HtmlEncode(Eval("OptionD").ToString())%>
       </td></tr></table>
         <br />
    </ItemTemplate>
</asp:DataList>
```

The preceding HTML markup provides data-bound controls that show you which fields are being displayed to the browser, all within a set of HTML tables and fields.

currentsurvey.ascx

The CurrentSurvey web user control is used to provide the name and description of the survey listed in the Survey table with the field `IsCurrentSurvey` field set to 1, rather than 0. The 1 value indicates that this record represents the current or selected survey to be displayed to the user at run time. That is, in a typical web site, only one survey could be exposed to the users of the site at a time. In such a case, the administrator may want to select one at a time by allowing one of the surveys to have a current value.

The top portion of the CurrentSurvey control is as follows:

```
  <%@ Control Language="VB" AutoEventWireup="false" CodeFile="currentsurvey
.ascx.vb" Inherits="Controls_currentsurvey" %>

<asp:ObjectDataSource ID="odsCurrentSurvey" runat="server"
    SelectMethod="GetCurrentSurvey" TypeName="Survey"></asp:ObjectDataSource>
```

Notice in this excerpt the use of `ObjectDataSource` control with a `SelectMethod` of `GetCurrentSurvey` for the retrieval of the one record in the Survey table with an `IsCurrentSurvey` value of 1. The next section of the `currentsurvey` control, shown in the following code, displays the use of the `DataList` control as it binds to the `ObjectDataSource` control's properties, providing the name and description of the current survey in the database:

```
<asp:DataList ID="DataList1" runat="server" DataSourceID="odsCurrentSurvey">
   <ItemTemplate>
          <fieldset class="CurrentSurveySection">
          <b><a href="TakeSurvey.aspx?surveyID=<%# Eval("ID") %>">
          <%#Server.HtmlEncode(Eval("Name").ToString())%></a></b><br />
          <%#Server.HtmlEncode(Eval("Description").ToString())%> <br />
          <a href="TakeSurvey.aspx?surveyID=<%# Eval("ID") %>">...take the
survey!</a>
          </fieldset>
   </ItemTemplate>
</asp:DataList>
```

As mentioned earlier in this chapter, there are other ways of displaying surveys, but this provides an easy means by which to present one survey at a time to the user through a small area of HTML real estate. A web site could squeeze this user control into just about any section of a site, so it lends itself well to the design.

The next section explains in detail how to install and configure the source files of the web site and how to deploy the site to a server in a production environment.

Setting up the Project

The time has come to learn how to install this Wrox Survey Engine and see for yourself how quickly you can be up and running with a working survey application. The two ways you can install the web site are as a hosted web site application and as a source codebase for editing in Visual Studio 2005 or VWD.

Hosted Web Site Installation

If you want to install the Wrox Survey Engine as a hosted web site on a computer or server, without customizations or enhancements at all, follow these steps (which assume you have already installed the .NET Framework 2.0):

1. Open the folder Chapter 04 – Wrox Survey Engine\Installation Files\ from the CD-ROM that came with this book and double-click the setup.exe file.
2. This process installs the files properly for hosting the web site locally to `C:\wwwRoot\SurveyEngine` as a file-based web site application. Click Next to install the application, and close the installation program when it completes.
3. Then, browse to your local web site (for example, `http://localhost/SurveyEngine`). The Wrox Survey Engine application should appear. To test the administration section, click the Admin link and log in with a username of `SuperAdmin` and a password of `password#`.
4. Finally, if you need to expose the site to the outside world, be sure to configure the public IP address to the IIS web site application. The details of this IIS configuration and its implications are outside the scope of this book, but the Wrox Survey Engine is easily configurable as a public web site with a brief tutorial on web site hosting.

Local Developer Installation

If you would like to open the project in Visual Studio or VWD, perform the following steps (assuming the .NET Framework 2.0 is installed, along with either Visual Studio or VWD):

1. Create a new web site in Visual Web Developer or Visual Studio 2005.
2. Open the folder Chapter 04 – Wrox Survey Engine Installer\ from the CD-ROM that came with this book and extract the contents of the file PhotoAlbumSource.zip to a folder on your hard drive.
3. Open a Windows Explorer and browse to the folder that contains the unpacked files. Next, arrange both Visual Web Developer and the Windows Explorer in such a way that both are visible at the same time.
4. In the Windows Explorer, select all of the folders and files within the codebase and drag the selected folders and files from the explorer window into the Solution Explorer in Visual Web Developer. If you're prompted if to overwrite files, click Yes. You should end up with a Solution Explorer that contains all of the necessary files for the project to run properly.
5. In the Web.config file, modify the `EmailTo` and `EmailFrom` values in the `appSettings` section (see the following code) to reflect the administration e-mail accounts to be used for sending and receiving e-mail, should you decide to use this feature. Also, the `PageTitle` property is changeable here, which applies to the window title bar of each page in the site.

```
<appSettings>
   <add key="EmailFrom" value="admin@mysurveyengine.com" />
   <add key="EmailTo" value="admin@mysurveyengine.Com" />
   <add key="PageTitle" value="Wrox Survey Engine" />
```

6. Also in the Web.config file, you can modify the `smtp` value in the `mailSettings` section (see following code) to reflect the e-mail SMTP outbound mail server name to be used for sending and receiving e-mail, should you decide to use this feature.

```
<system.net>
    <mailSettings>
      <smtp deliveryMethod="Network">
        <network host="smtp.YourMailServerName.com" port="25" />
      </smtp>
    </mailSettings>
  </system.net>
  <system.web>
```

7. Right-click the Default.aspx WebForm in the ContentFiles folder and select the Set as Start Page option. Press F5 to run the application in the development environment.

Now that you've set up the project, head to `www.wrox.com`, find this book's download page, and check out some possible modifications to the Wrox Survey Engine.

Summary

In this chapter you learned about some of the more exciting controls and tools in the ASP.NET 2.0 framework, such as the `Login`, `LoginStatus`, `PasswordRetrieval`, `SiteMap`, master pages, `SqlDataSource`, `ObjectDataSource`, `SiteMapDataSource`, `GridView`, `DataList`, and `Menu` controls. The flow of the chapter was visually rich, providing plenty of examples for you to absorb the logical flow of the application. You learned how each of these new and exciting features provides the rapid development everyone has been waiting for in Visual Studio.

The focus of the chapter was the understanding of how surveys are completed and retrieved, with some emphasis on the layered application approach. Some expanded and informative areas of the reading were related to the `ObjectDataSource` control versus the `SqlDataSource` control. The benefits and risks were outlined for both, and an argument was formed in favor of the `ObjectDataSource` control.

Wrox CMS

Many of today's web sites are database-driven, which means they get their content from a database and not from static HTML files alone. Although this gives you great possibilities in the content you can present, it also brings a problem in updating that content. With static HTML sites you can design and create your files offline, and when you're ready you simply use FTP or other network communication tools to get your files to the production server. However, with a site based on a database, this won't work. Because the site must remain up and running, you often cannot simply overwrite the old database with new information. Also, because the site may be collecting run-time information (such as page views, user logins, and so forth) you could lose that information when you upload a new database with fresh content.

The most common way to solve this problem is to use an online *Content Management System* (CMS). Such a system allows you to log in to your site, and then manage the content right on the location where it's stored and used: the web server.

In this chapter you learn how to build a generic CMS that allows you to manage content and the categories that this content is stored in. You can use the web site and CMS to publish information for a wide variety of scenarios. You can use it to publish information about your local soccer club, your company's press releases, or any other topic you want to share with the world. The demo web site presented in this chapter uses the CMS to manage information about programming-related topics, including ASP.NET 2.0 and Visual Web Developer. The chapter begins with a quick tour of the web site and the CMS section. You see how to create new categories that will appear as menu items in the web site and how to enter the actual content in the database.

The section "Design of the Wrox CMS" explains how the CMS is designed, and what pages and classes are involved, and the section "Code and Code Explanation" takes a thorough look at the files and code in the site and explains how it all works.

Using the Wrox CMS

The site demonstrated in this chapter has two important sections: the public front end and the (protected) content management system. The public front end displays what are called *content items* in this chapter; a collection of news, articles, and frequently asked questions. These content items can be managed with the content management system that is part of the web site. This chapter focuses mainly on the latter section, but it also shows you how the information from the CMS is displayed on the public side.

Viewing Content on the Site

If the Wrox CMS web site has been installed successfully (refer to the section "Setting up the Wrox CMS" later in this chapter for more details) you can view the site by browsing to `http://localhost/Cms`. You'll see the screen shown in Figure 5-1.

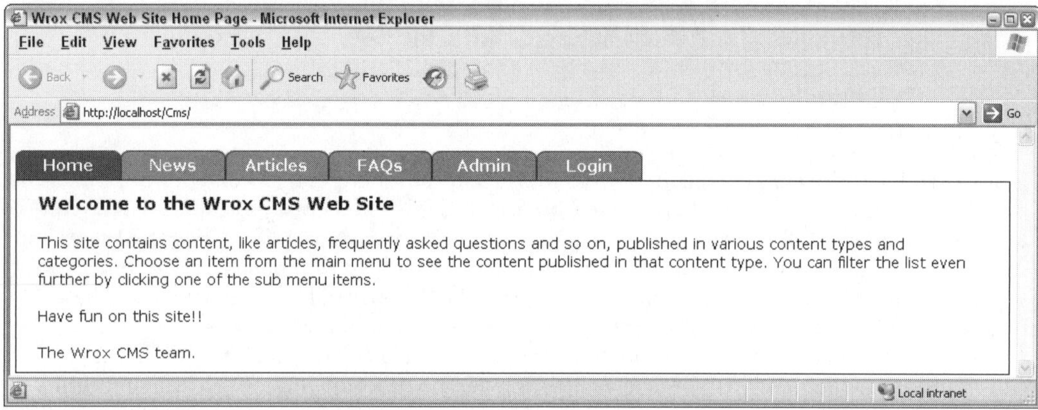

Figure 5-1

The main menu, with the big tabs at the top of the screen, contains both static and dynamic menu items. The Home, Admin, and Login items are fixed elements. The Home button always brings you back to the homepage and the Login button allows you to log in. The Admin button provides access to the Content Management System, referred to as the Management section in this chapter. The other three, referred to as *content types*, come from the database. Once you click a content type, such as Articles, you see a sub-menu appear, as depicted in Figure 5-2.

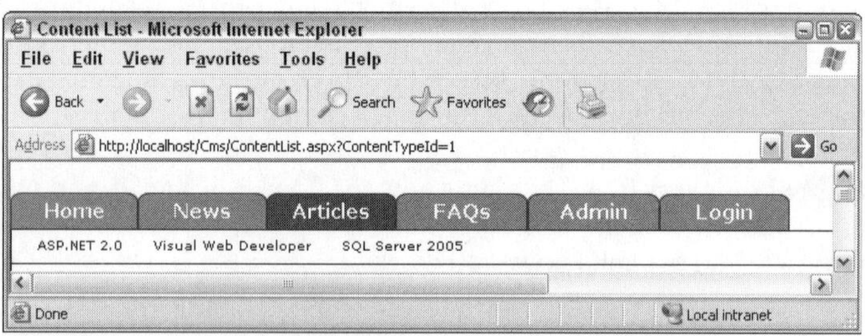

Figure 5-2

The sub-menu displays the *categories* that are available within the chosen content type. When you click a sub-menu, such as Visual Web Developer, you see a list with *content items* (see Figure 5-3) that are assigned to that category.

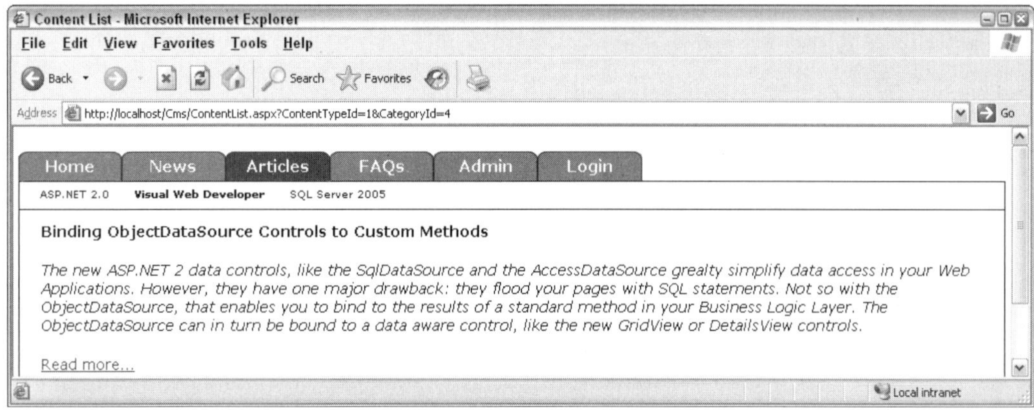

Figure 5-3

When you click the "Read more" link below one of the content items, a detail page appears that shows you the full version of the content item.

Managing Content with the CMS

To manage the content in the system and the various content types and categories, you need to log in first. If you installed the application using the supplied installer or through the manual process — as described in the section "Setting up the Wrox CMS" later in the chapter — you can log in with a username of `Administrator` and the password `Admin123#` (note that the password is case-sensitive).

Once you're logged in, you see the CMS main menu appear with links to manage content types, categories, and content. Managing content types and categories is pretty straightforward. You can create new and update existing items. You can also reassign a category to a different content type by editing the category and choosing a new content type from the drop-down.

You can manage the content of the site by clicking the Manage Content item on the left menu that you can see in Figure 5-4. You then get a list with all the available content, filtered by the content type. To choose a different type, select the item from the drop-down list. To change a content item, click the Edit button in the list. If you click the Create New button you're taken to the AddEditContent.aspx page (shown in Figure 5-4) that is used to add new and change existing content items.

In addition to the Title, Intro Text, and Full Text of the content item, you can also specify the content type and the category. As soon as you choose a new content type, the page refreshes and the category drop-down is updated to display the categories that belong to the chosen content type. An HTML editor called the FCKeditor was used for the Intro Text and Full Text fields. Use of this editor is explained later in the chapter.

If you leave the Visible checkbox unchecked, the item will no longer show up on the web site. It won't be deleted from the database, however, so you can always reactivate the item later.

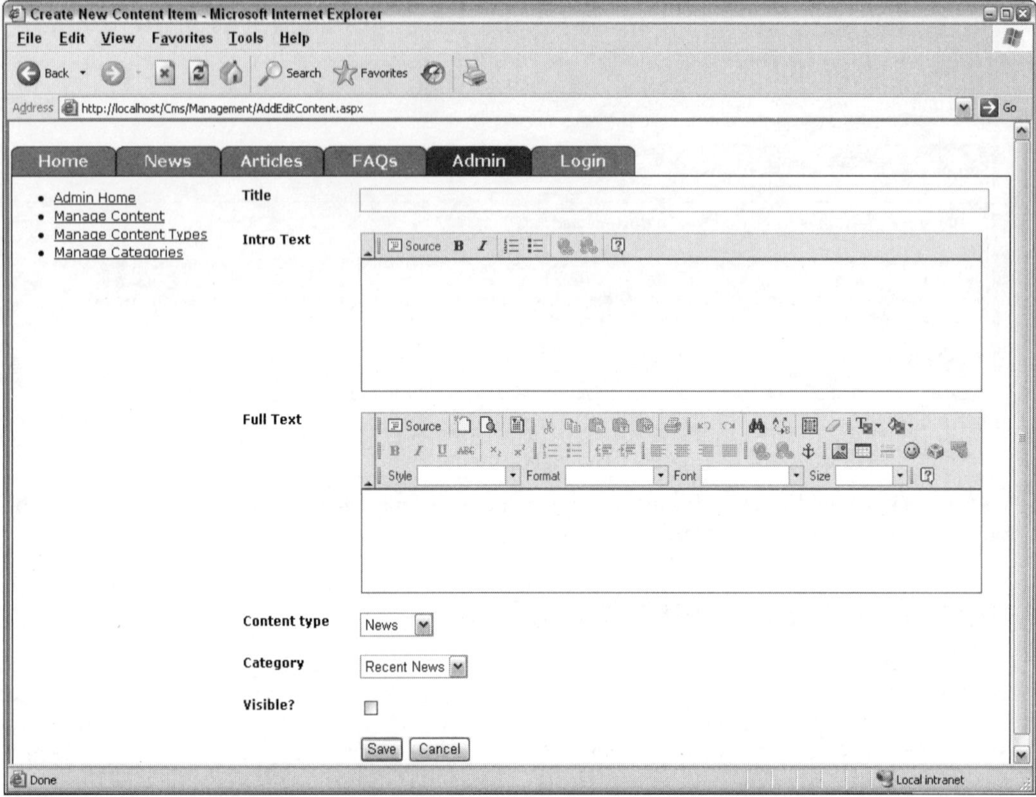

Figure 5-4

Managing the content and various categories in this web-based CMS is pretty easy to do. Fortunately, the design and implementation of the CMS are pretty straightforward as well. In the next section you learn about the design of the application. The section describes the business layer and data access classes and shows you the design of the database and the stored procedures used to get data in and out of the database.

Design of the Wrox CMS

Most of the pages in the Wrox CMS rely on `SqlDataSource` controls to get the data in and out of the database. These new data source controls, in combination with the `GridView` and `FormView`, allow you to create database-driven pages in no time, with very little to no code at all. However, these controls suffer from a few problems. First of all, they are best suited for rather simple scenarios. For example, the page in the Management section that allows you to create or change categories is well suited for the `SqlDataSource` in combination with a `GridView` (for the list of categories) and a `FormView` (to insert new items) because the underlying data structure is quite simple. However, with more complex pages, like the AddEditContent.aspx page that has two drop-downs that are bound to each other, things become a bit more difficult. To make the `SqlDataSource` and `FormView` controls work in these scenarios you have to jump through all kinds of hoops, resulting in bloated markup and far from straightforward code in the code-behind of your pages.

The second problem with the `SqlDataSource` controls is the fact that they usually embed SQL statements directly in the markup of your pages. This breaks about every rule of good multi-tiered design because this forces you to update possibly many pages in your site whenever you make even a little change to the structure of your database.

Despite these disadvantages, using the `SqlDataSource` control can be a great way to rapidly develop relatively small web sites that require little to no changes in the database structure. To show you how they work and how to use them, they are used for most of the data access in the Wrox CMS. The only exception is the AddEditContent.aspx page. Instead of working with a `SqlDataSource` control, the Wrox CMS uses a few custom classes and methods to get information from and in the database.

To minimize the impact of the SQL statements all over the page, stored procedures are used in all of the `SqlDataSource` controls in the Wrox CMS. Instead of storing the entire `INSERT` or `UPDATE` statement in the ASPX portion of the page, you now only store the name of a procedure in the database. Whenever a change is made to either the database structure or the queries, all that needs to be updated are a few stored procedures.

In later chapters — including Chapter 9 and Chapter 12 — you use `ObjectDataSource` controls to enforce a three-tiered architecture.

The decision to use the `SqlDataSource` controls in your pages results in very slim business and data access layers. The next section discusses the only class in the business layer. The section following that describes the database and the classes in the data access layer.

The Business Layer

As stated earlier, no `SqlDataSource` controls are used to create and update content items in the Content table. The two drop-downs with the content types and categories that are related to each other result in bloated code that is very hard to understand and maintain. Instead, a simple, straightforward class — called `Content` — was designed that represents a content item in the database. The class exposes a number of properties like its `Title`, `IntroText`, and its `CategoryId` and has two methods to get the content item in and out of the database. You can find the definition of the `Content` class in the file Content.vb in the App_Code\BusinessLogic folder of the web site. Figure 5-5 shows the design of the `Content` class.

Figure 5-5

The following table lists each of the seven public properties the class exposes:

Property	Data Type	Description
`BodyText`	`String`	The `BodyText` property holds the full text for the content item and is displayed on the detail page only.
`CategoryId`	`Integer`	Indicates to which category the content item belongs.
`ContentTypeId`	`Integer`	Indicates to which content type the content item belongs.
`Id`	`Integer`	This is the unique ID of the content item and is assigned by the database automatically whenever a new item is inserted.
`IntroText`	`String`	This property contains the introduction text for the content item. This intro text is displayed, possibly with a different formatting, on the content list page and at the top of the content detail page.
`Title`	`String`	This is the title of the content item as it appears on the content list and detail pages.
`Visible`	`Boolean`	Determines whether the item is visible in the public area of the web site.

In addition to these seven properties, the `Content` class has a total of four methods: the two constructors, a `Save` method, and a `GetItem` method, each of which is discussed in the following table:

Method	Return Type	Description
`Public Sub New()`	n/a	The default constructor for the `Content` class. Initializes a new instance with all of its properties set to their default values.
`Public Sub New (ByVal id As Integer)`	n/a	This overloaded constructor initializes a new instance of the `Content` class with all of its properties set to their default values except for the `Id` that is filled with the ID passed to constructor. This overload is used to re-create existing items when updating them in the management section.
`Public Sub Save()`	n/a	Saves a new or an existing content item in the database by calling the `Save` method in the `ContentDB` class, which is discussed later.
`Public Shared Function GetItem (ByVal id As Integer) As Content`	An instance of the `Content` class or `Nothing` when the item could not be found.	Gets an existing content item from the database by calling `GetItem` in the `ContentDB` class.

The Data Access Layer

Because most of the pages in the site use `SqlDataSource` controls for their data access, you need only one class in the data access layer: the `ContentDB` class, shown in Figure 5-6, which is responsible for retrieving and saving a single content item from the database.

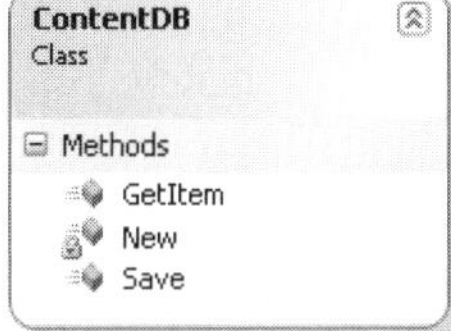

Figure 5-6

Because the `ContentDB` class exposes only shared members, it has no public constructor. It also has no public properties, but it does have two public methods, outlined in the following table:

Method	Return Type	Description
`Public Shared Sub Save (ByVal contentItem As Content)`	n/a	Saves a new or an existing content item in the database.
`Public Shared Function GetItem (ByVal id As Integer) As Content`	An instance of the `Content` class or `Nothing` when the item could not be found.	Gets an existing content item from the database.

In addition to this single class, the data access layer contains the database that is discussed next.

The Data Model

The database for the Wrox CMS has three tables and a number of stored procedures that are responsible for getting the data in and out of those tables. Figure 5-7 shows the three tables and their relations to each other.

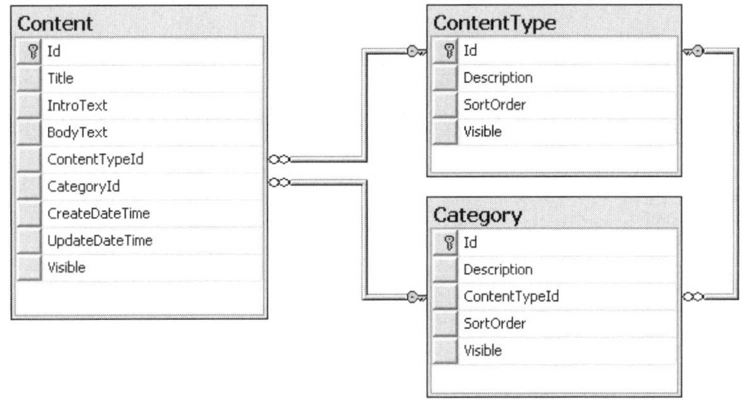

Figure 5-7

The Content table is the main entity in the database, because it stores the content that is displayed on the web site. The following table lists all of the Content table's columns and their usage:

Column Name	Data Type	Description
Id	`int`	The unique ID of each content item. This ID is generated automatically by the database each time a new record is inserted.
Title	`nvarchar(100)`	The title of the content item. The title is displayed on the content list and detail pages.
IntroText	`nvarchar(MAX)`	Used to store the introduction text of the content item that is displayed on the content list page and above the full text on the details page.
BodyText	`nvarchar(MAX)`	The full text for the article, not including the introduction text. This text is displayed on the content detail page, right below the intro text.
ContentTypeId	`int`	The type of content to which this item belongs.
CategoryId	`int`	The ID of the category to which the item belongs.
CreateDateTime	`datetime`	The date and the time the item was inserted.
UpdateDateTime	`datetime`	The date and the time the item was last updated.
Visible	`bit`	Indicates whether the item is visible in the public section of the site.

Each content item is linked to the ContentType table with its ContentTypeId. This relation allows you to find a list of all content items within a certain content type without specifying a category first. In addition to its internal ID and its Description, the ContentType table also has SortOrder and Visible columns. The SortOrder column allows you to control the order of the items in the main menu, and the Visible column allows you to hide the entire content item from the menu.

A content item is also linked to a category in the Category table by its CategoryId. The Category table is similar to the ContentType table, but it has an additional ContentTypeId that enables you to link categories to content types.

To simplify the maintenance of the site, the SQL statements have been moved to separate stored procedures. That means you won't find a single `SELECT` or `UPDATE` or other SQL statement anywhere in the code. If you want to see or change the stored procedures in the database, look under the Stored Procedures node of the database on the Database Explorer (which you can open with Ctrl+Alt+s) in Visual Web Developer. Each of the relevant stored procedures is discussed as part of the page or pages that use them later in this chapter.

Helper Class

The final class located in the special App_Code folder is the `AppConfiguration` class. This class belongs more to the web site than to the business or data access layer, so it has been put in the App_Code folder directly. This isn't a requirement, so you could move it to one of the existing folders, or create an entirely new folder such as Configuration or Helpers and place it there. The class is called `AppConfiguration` and not `Configuration`, for example, to avoid a naming conflict with the existing ASP.NET `System.Configuration` namespace. The `AppConfiguration` class exposes a single shared property called `ConnectionString`, which is essentially a wrapper around the `ConnectionString` held in the Web.config file. The pages in the site that use `SqlDataSource` controls use their own binding syntax to get their `ConnectionString` property from the Web.config directly. However, the two methods in the data access layer use the `AppConfiguration` class to retrieve information about the connection. Instead of writing code that directly accesses the Web.config file, these methods can now access this property. You see this property in use in the next section when the code in the business, data access, and presentation layers is discussed.

Code and Code Explanation

This section walks you through each of the important pages in the Wrox CMS web site. It starts off by looking at a few files located in the root of the site that are used by the other pages. Then you see in great detail the files in the Management folder that allow you to manage the content in the database.

Finally, this section closes with an examination of the two files that are responsible for displaying the content in the public section of the site.

Root Files

The root of the CMS web site contains two master files, a config file, a login page, the default page, and two files that are used to display the content in the database. This section discusses all of these files, except for the last two, which are dealt with after the Management folder has been discussed.

Web.config

This global configuration file contains one `appSetting` key and one `connectionString`. The `appSetting` key is used by the FCKeditor, the inline HTML editor discussed later. The connection string is used by the various pages and data access classes in the application.

Under the `<system.web>` node, you'll find two configuration sections that configure the `Membership` and `Role` providers. The CMS uses these providers to enable users of the CMS to log in to access the protected Management folder and its contents. Because the site uses a custom database, and not the default aspnetdb.mdf as defined in the machine.config that applies to the entire server, you need to configure the application to use the custom database instead. Both the `<membership>` and the `<roleManager>` nodes are very similar to the ones you find in machine.config. In fact, the only changes made to the settings copied from the global machine.config are the `name` and `connectionStringName` attributes of the `<providers>` node that instructs ASP.NET to use the custom connection string and database instead:

```
<providers>
  <add
    name="SqlProvider"
    type="System.Web.Security.SqlRoleProvider"
    connectionStringName="Cms" />
</providers>
```

Right under the provider settings, you'll find these settings:

```
<authentication mode="Forms">
  <forms loginUrl="~/Login.aspx" />
</authentication>

<authorization>
  <allow users="*"/>
</authorization>

<pages theme="Cms">
```

The first element, `<authentication>`, tells .NET to use Forms Authentication. Whenever you're trying to request a protected page as an anonymous user, you're taken to the Login.aspx page located in the root of the site that allows you to log on. The second node, `<authorization>`, allows access to all pages in the site to all users. The Management folder is blocked for users that are not in the Administrator role with a `<location>` tag that you see next.

The `<pages>` node tells ASP.NET to use the theme defined in the App_Themes folder. The site features a very simple theme, with a single .skin file that defines the looks of `GridView` controls used in the site. The GridView.skin file contains a few style definitions with `CssClass` attributes that point to classes defined in the Styles.css file in the CSS folder.

The final section in the Web.config file you need to look at is the `<location>` tag at the bottom of the file:

```
<location path="Management">
  <system.web>
    <authorization>
      <allow roles="Administrator" />
      <deny users="*"/>
    </authorization>
  </system.web>
</location>
```

This code instructs ASP.NET to block access to all users that are not in the Administrator role. When you try to access one of those pages in that folder, you're taken to Login.aspx instead.

The remainder of the elements in the Web.config file is placed there by Visual Web Developer when you create a new ASP.NET 2.0 web site.

SiteMaster.master and AdminMaster.master

These two master files determine the look and feel of all the pages in the site. The SiteMaster.master file is used for the public pages in the site, whereas AdminMaster.master defines the look for the pages in the Management folder. The two files have a lot in common; the only difference is that inside the AdminMaster.master file there is a new HTML table and a user control that displays the sub-menu for the Management section. Although ASP.NET 2.0 allows you to use nested master files, the CMS web site doesn't use that feature. With a nested template, you lose design-time capabilities in Visual Web Developer, which can be a real productivity killer because you'll need to hand-code the pages yourself. So, instead SiteMaster.master was created first and then its contents were copied to the AdminMaster.master file.

In addition to some regular HTML tags, the SiteMaster.master contains a user control called `SiteMenu` that displays the main and sub-menus. The `SiteMenu` control that you find in the Controls folder contains two `Repeater` controls for the two menus. Each menu item in the main and sub-menus links to the ContentList page and passes it the ID of the selected content type and, if present, of the category through the query string. This allows that page, and any user controls in it, to see which content type and category is currently being displayed. The `SiteMenu` control also contains two `SqlDataSource` controls that get their data from stored procedures in the database. Take a look at the data source for the sub-menu that displays the categories to see how this works:

```
<asp:SqlDataSource ID="sdsSubMenu" runat="server"
    ConnectionString="<%$ ConnectionStrings:Cms %>"
ProviderName="System.Data.SqlClient" SelectCommand="sprocCategorySelectlist"
    SelectCommandType="StoredProcedure"
>
   ... Select Parameter is shown later
</asp:SqlDataSource>
```

The markup for this control contains a few important bits of information. First of all, there is the `ConnectionString` attribute. To assign the proper connection string at run time, a new form of data binding is used. The new `<%$ %>` expression syntax is used to bind attributes to connection strings, resources, and application settings in the Web.config file. In this case, a connection string with the name `Cms` is retrieved from the application's configuration file.

The next important pieces are the `SelectCommand` and `SelectCommandType` attributes. These tell the .NET Framework to run the stored procedure called `sprocCategorySelectlist` in the database defined by the connection string.

The stored procedure is pretty straightforward: it requests all the categories that belong to a certain content type:

```
CREATE PROCEDURE sprocCategorySelectlist

@contentTypeId int

AS

  SELECT
      Category.Id,
      Category.Description,
      Category.ContentTypeId,
      ContentType.Description AS ContentTypeDescription,
      Category.SortOrder
  FROM
    Category INNER JOIN
    ContentType ON Category.ContentTypeId = ContentType.Id
  WHERE
    (Category.ContentTypeId = @contentTypeId)
    AND Category.Visible = 1
  ORDER BY
    SortOrder
RETURN
```

In addition to the fields of the Category table, the description of the content type is retrieved as well, aliased as `ContentTypeDescription`. This description is used in the Management section of the site, to show the name of the content type that the category belongs to. The stored procedure expects the ID of the content type as a parameter. In the code for the `SqlDataSource` that parameter is set up as follows:

```
<SelectParameters>
  <asp:QueryStringParameter Name="contentTypeId"
      QueryStringField="ContentTypeId" Type="Int32" />
</SelectParameters>
```

With this code, a single `Parameter` object is defined that gets its value from a `QueryStringField` called `ContentTypeId`. When the `SqlDataSource` is about to retrieve the data from the database, it gets the value from the query string and then stores it in this parameter so it gets passed to the stored procedure.

By using the query string as a parameter, the `SqlDataSource` control will always retrieve the categories that belong to the currently requested content type.

The other data source control, which gets the items for the main menu, works the same way. However, because this control always needs to return all content types, it does not have any select parameters.

When you view a page that is using the `SiteMenu` control, you'll see something like Figure 5-8.

Figure 5-8

All the menu items between Home and Admin come from the ContentType table, whereas the sub-menus come from the Categories table. You can also see that in the link for the sub-menu both the `ContentTypeId` and the `CategoryId` are passed to the ContentList page. The final thing you should notice in Figure 5-8 is that one main menu and one sub-menu (Articles and Visual Web Developer) appear as selected by using a different color or font type. This is done by some code in the `Load` event in the code-behind file of the user control.

When the two `Repeater` controls for the menus get their data from the `SqlDataSource` controls they fire their `ItemDataBound` event for each item added to the repeater. This event is a great place to preselect the menu items because you have access to both the query string holding the ID of the chosen content type and category and to the item that is about to be displayed. The following code shows how a sub-menu gets a bold typeface when it is selected:

```
Protected Sub repSubMenu_ItemDataBound(ByVal sender As Object, _
      ByVal e As System.Web.UI.WebControls.RepeaterItemEventArgs) _
      Handles repSubMenu.ItemDataBound

  If e.Item.ItemType = ListItemType.Item Or _
      e.Item.ItemType = ListItemType.AlternatingItem Then

    Dim myDataRowView As DataRowView = DirectCast(e.Item.DataItem, DataRowView)

    If Convert.ToInt32(myDataRowView("Id")) = _
        Convert.ToInt32(Request.QueryString.Get("CategoryId")) Then
      Dim lnkSubmenu As HyperLink = _
          DirectCast(e.Item.FindControl("lnkSubmenu"), HyperLink)
      lnkSubmenu.CssClass = "Selected"
    End If
  End If
End Sub
```

This code examines the `ItemType` of the item that is currently being data-bound. When an `Item` or `Alternating` item is created, the code retrieves the item's `DataItem`, which in this case holds a `DataRowView`. Then `DirectCast` is used to cast the generic `DataItem` object to a `DataRowView`. Using `DirectCast` is very similar to `CType` but it performs a bit faster. The downside of `DirectCast` is that it can only cast objects of exactly the same type. You can't use it to cast an object to another type higher or deeper in the inheritance hierarchy. In this case, however, that is no problem because the `DataItem` *is* a `DataRowView` so you can safely use `DirectCast`.

Once you have the `DataRowView` object, you can retrieve its ID column that holds the ID for the category you're adding to the `Repeater`. If the ID of that category matches the ID of the category you're currently displaying (determined by looking at the `CategoryId` query string), the code gets a reference to the hyperlink in the menu called `lnkSubmenu`, again using `DirectCast`. And finally, the hyperlink's `CssClass` is set to `Selected`. The behavior for the `Selected` class (a bold font in this case) is defined in the Core.css file:

```
#SubMenu a.Selected
{
  font-weight: bold;
}
```

This code applies a bold font to all `<a>` tags that fall within the `#SubMenu` div tag and that have a `Selected` class applied which happens to be the selected sub-menu item.

The menu items Home, Admin, and Login are not database-driven, so you cannot preselect them in an `ItemDataBound` event. Instead, in `Page_Load` of the `SiteMenu` control you examine the `AppRelativeCurrentExecutionFilePath` property of the `HttpRequest` class. By using string comparing you can see if you need to preselect one of the static menu items:

```
If Request.AppRelativeCurrentExecutionFilePath.ToLower() = "~/default.aspx" Then
    liHome.Attributes("class") = "Selected"
End If
```

This code applies the class `Selected` to the static Home menu item when the currently requested page is ~/default.aspx, which is the homepage for the CMS web site. The same principle is applied to preselect the other two menu items.

Login.aspx

This page allows you to log in to the site and is shown automatically whenever you try to access one of the pages in the Management folder as an unauthenticated user. The page takes full advantage of the ASP.NET 2.0 security framework offered by the Membership and Role providers. All that this page requires is one simple `<asp:Login>` control like this:

```
<asp:Login ID="Login1" runat="server" />
```

Although the control doesn't look too good with only this markup, it is still fully functional. The purposes of this CMS don't require any visual customization, but if you want you can apply a host of behavior and appearance changes to the control through the Visual Web Developer IDE.

The final two pages located in the root, ContentList.aspx and ContentDetail.aspx, are discussed after the Management folder that's coming up next.

The Management Folder

All the files in the Management folder are used for maintaining the content types, categories, and the actual content that gets displayed in the public area of the web site. The folder contains five pages: the default homepage of the management section, one page to manage content types, one to manage categories, and two pages to manage the content items. The homepage does nothing more than display simple static text and the Admin menu. The other pages are much more interesting so they are explained in more detail. Because managing content types is very similar to managing categories, the ContentType page is skipped in favor of the Categories page, because that's the more comprehensive of the two. All of the concepts used in the Categories page are used in the ContentType page as well.

Managing Categories

As you have seen before, the categories are displayed as text menu items whenever you choose a specific content type. Each category is tied to a specific content type by its `ContentTypeId`. To control the order in which the items appear on the sub-menu, a Category also has a SortOrder column.

To allow you to manage existing categories and create new ones all in the same page, Categories.aspx is divided in two sections using `<asp:Panel>` controls. The first panel, called `pnlList`, holds a `GridView` that displays the existing categories. A drop-down above the `GridView` allows you to filter categories that belong to a specific content type. The second panel, `pnlNew`, is used to insert new categories. The panel holds a `FormView` control that is bound to a `SqlDataSource` to handle the insertion in the database. At any time, only one of the two views is visible to make it easier to focus on the task at hand. You get a deeper look at the `pnlList` panel first, and then you see how you can insert new categories with the controls in the second panel.

Besides a few static controls for informational and error messages, `pnlList` holds two important controls: a drop-down called `lstContentTypes` and a `GridView` called `gvCategories`. The drop-down control lists the available content types in the site. The `GridView`, in turn, displays the categories that belong to the content type selected in the drop-down control.

When the page loads, the drop-down gets its data from a `SqlDataSource` called `sdsContentTypes`. Both the drop-down and the data source have very simple markup:

```
<asp:DropDownList ID="lstContentTypes" runat="server"
       DataSourceID="sdsContentTypes"
       DataTextField="Description" DataValueField="Id" AutoPostBack="true">
</asp:DropDownList>
```

The `DataSourceID` of the control is set to the `SqlDataSource` so the control knows where to get its data. The `DataTextField` and `DataValueField` are then set to the two columns that are available in the DataSet that is returned by the `SqlDataSource`. `AutoPostBack` is set to `True` to ensure that the page will reload whenever you choose a new content type from the drop-down list.

The `SqlDataSource` gets its data by calling a stored procedure called `sprocContentTypeSelectList`. This is done with the following markup:

```
<asp:SqlDataSource ID="sdsContentTypes" runat="server"
    ConnectionString="<%$ ConnectionStrings:Cms %>"
    SelectCommand="sprocContentTypeSelectList"
    SelectCommandType="StoredProcedure">
</asp:SqlDataSource>
```

This markup is very similar to the code you saw earlier used to retrieve the menu items from the database. The stored procedure used by the data source is very simple; all that it does is request a list with the available content types:

```
CREATE PROCEDURE sprocContentTypeSelectList

AS

SELECT
  Id, Description, SortOrder
FROM
  ContentType
WHERE
  Visible = 1
ORDER BY
  SortOrder
```

With the drop-down list in place, the next thing to look at is the `GridView`. Just as with the drop-down, the `GridView` is bound to a `SqlDataSource` by setting its `DataSourceID` property:

```
<asp:GridView ID="gvCategories" runat="server" AutoGenerateColumns="False"
      DataKeyNames="Id" DataSourceID="sdsCategories" AllowPaging="True"
      AllowSorting="True">
    ... control's inner content goes here
</asp:GridView>
```

The `DataKeyNames` property is set to `Id`, which is the ID of the category in the database to tell the `GridView` what the primary key of table is. In addition, `AllowPaging` and `AllowSorting` are set to `True`. This way, the data in the `GridView` gets easier to manage because you can now sort specific columns and see the data displayed in smaller pages instead of having to scroll through a long list with items.

To understand what data needs to be displayed in the `GridView`, take a look at the page as it is displayed in the Management section (see Figure 5-9).

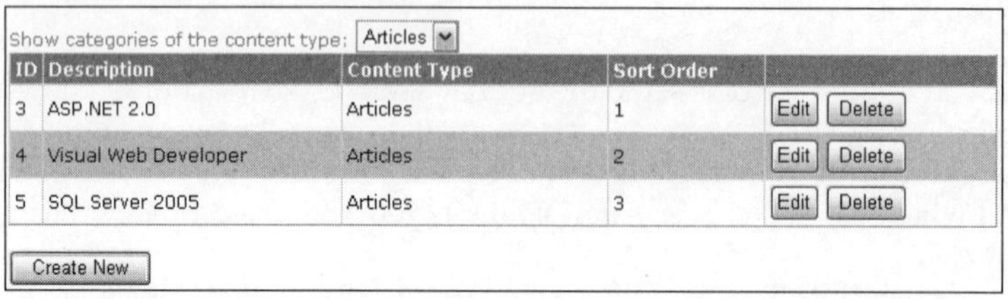

Show categories of the content type: Articles

ID	Description	Content Type	Sort Order	
3	ASP.NET 2.0	Articles	1	Edit Delete
4	Visual Web Developer	Articles	2	Edit Delete
5	SQL Server 2005	Articles	3	Edit Delete

Create New

Figure 5-9

Above the `GridView` you see the drop-down discussed earlier. In the `GridView` you see columns that display the category's ID, its own description, the description of the content type it belongs to, the sort order, and two buttons to edit and delete the categories. When you click the Edit button, the `GridView` jumps in edit mode and displays editable controls for the description, content type, and sort order, as shown in Figure 5-10.

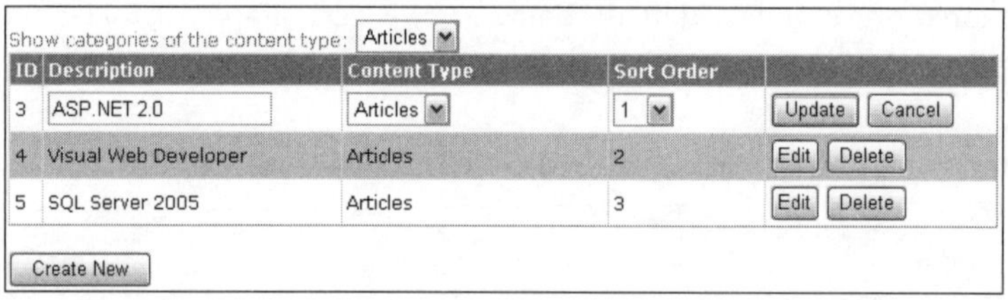

Show categories of the content type: Articles

ID	Description	Content Type	Sort Order	
3	ASP.NET 2.0	Articles	1	Update Cancel
4	Visual Web Developer	Articles	2	Edit Delete
5	SQL Server 2005	Articles	3	Edit Delete

Create New

Figure 5-10

To display the items in both read-only and edit mode, the `GridView` contains a mix of `BoundField`, `TemplateField`, and `CommandField` controls. It's a bit too much code to repeat all of it here, but a few of them are examined in more detail. First, take a look at the ID column:

```
<asp:BoundField DataField="Id" HeaderText="ID"
     ReadOnly="True" SortExpression="Id" />
```

The field is bound to the Id column in the database by setting the `DataField` attribute. The `ReadOnly` attribute is set to `True` to ensure the column is not editable when the `GridView` is in edit mode. Because the database automatically assigns new IDs to the category, there is no point in allowing the user to change the value. By setting `SortExpression` to `Id` you accomplish two things. First, the `HeaderText` for the column changes from a simple label to a clickable hyperlink. Secondly, when the column is clicked, the data is sorted on the column specified by the `SortExpression` attribute.

For the description column a `TemplateField` is used that displays a simple label in read-only mode and a text box when the item is edited. To ensure that the field is not left empty, the text box is hooked up to a `RequiredFieldValidator` control.

The column for the content type is a bit more complex, because it displays a drop-down control in edit mode. Fortunately, the code you require for such a column is still pretty easy:

```
<asp:TemplateField HeaderText="Content Type">
  <ItemTemplate>
    <asp:Label ID="Label1" runat="server"
         Text='<%# Bind("ContentTypeDescription") %>'>
    </asp:Label>
  </ItemTemplate>
  <EditItemTemplate>
    <asp:DropDownList ID="DropDownList1" runat="server"
           DataSourceID="sdsContentTypes" DataTextField="Description"
           DataValueField="Id" SelectedValue='<%# Bind("ContentTypeId") %>'>
    </asp:DropDownList>
  </EditItemTemplate>
  <ItemStyle Width="175px" />
</asp:TemplateField>
```

Just as with the Description, a `TemplateField` control is used. In read-only mode (defined by the `ItemTemplate`) a `Label` is displayed with its text bound to the `ContentTypeDescription` column that is retrieved from the database.

The `EditItemTemplate` holds a single `<asp:DropDownList>` with its `DataSourceID` set to `sdsContentTypes`. This is the same `SqlDataSource` that is used to display the drop-down at the top of the page. To preselect the right item in the list when the `GridView` is put in edit mode, and to get the right value back when the item is saved in the database, the `SelectedValue` of the control is set to `<%# Bind("ContentTypeId") %>`.

The `<ItemStyle>` element defined in the `TemplateField` is used to set the width of the column in read-only and edit mode.

The SortOrder column is similar to the ContentType column. The only difference is that this column doesn't use a separate data source to get its data; the items in the drop-down list are hard-coded in the page.

The final column you need to look at is the column with the Edit and Delete buttons. Again, the markup for the column is remarkably simple:

```
<asp:CommandField ShowDeleteButton="True"
     ShowEditButton="True" ButtonType="Button" >
  <ItemStyle Width="150px" />
</asp:CommandField>
```

The `CommandField` control has a `ShowDeleteButton` and a `ShowEditButton` property, both of which are set to `True`. When you click the Edit button, the control switches to edit mode, the Delete button disappears temporarily, and the Edit button is replaced with an Update and a Cancel button. When you make a change in the data and then click the Update button, the `GridView` triggers the `UpdateCommand` of the `SqlDataSource` it is bound to. When you click the Delete button, it triggers the `DeleteCommand` on the associated data source. To see how that works, it's time to look at the code for the `SqlDataSource` control that is used by the `GridView`:

```
<asp:SqlDataSource ID="sdsCategories" runat="server"
    ConnectionString="<%$ ConnectionStrings:Cms %>"
    DeleteCommand="sprocCategoryDeleteSingleItem"
```

```
    DeleteCommandType="StoredProcedure"
    InsertCommand="sprocCategoryInsertUpdateSingleItem"
    InsertCommandType="StoredProcedure"
    SelectCommand="sprocCategorySelectlist"
    SelectCommandType="StoredProcedure"
    UpdateCommand="sprocCategoryInsertUpdateSingleItem"
    UpdateCommandType="StoredProcedure"
  ... Parameters are defined here
</asp:SqlDataSource>
```

In addition to the familiar connection string, the `SqlDataSource` has a number of `Command` and `CommandType` attributes defined. For each of the four main data actions — selecting, inserting, updating, and deleting — the control has a command that points to an associated stored procedure. For each of these commands, the `CommandType` has been set to `StoredProcedure`.

Within the `SqlDataSource` tags, the parameters for the stored procedure are defined. The `<SelectParameters>` element defines the parameters passed to the `Select` stored procedure to select a list of categories. As you recall, this list is filtered on the content type specified by the drop-down list at the top of the page:

```
<SelectParameters>
  <asp:ControlParameter ControlID="lstContentTypes"
    Name="contentTypeId" PropertyName="SelectedValue"
    Type="Int32" DefaultValue="-1" />
</SelectParameters>
```

The only parameter is one of type `ControlParameter` that looks at the `lstContentTypes` drop-down. When the data source is about to get the data from the database, it looks at that control, gets its `SelectedValue`, and then passes that to the stored procedure.

To allow updating of data, the data source also has `UpdateParameters` defined:

```
<UpdateParameters>
  <asp:Parameter Name="returnValue" Type="Int32" Direction="ReturnValue" />
  <asp:Parameter Name="id" Type="Int32" />
  <asp:Parameter Name="description" Type="String" />
  <asp:Parameter Name="contentTypeId" Type="Int32" />
  <asp:Parameter Name="sortOrder" Type="Int32" />
</UpdateParameters>
```

For each of the parameters of the stored procedure, one `Parameter` object is defined. Note that there is no need to tie these parameters to controls. Instead, the `GridView` uses `Bind` to bind its controls to the parameters of the data source by their name. So, the `Bind` expression for the ContentType drop-down in the edit template binds directly to this parameter by its name.

Note the additional `returnValue` parameter that is used to get the return value from the stored procedure. When you use the Configure Data Source command from the Smart Tasks panel for the data source, you don't get a chance to add this parameter. However, you can either type the parameter directly in Source View, or click the ellipses (see Figure 5-11) after the UpdateQuery (or other queries) on the Properties Grid for the data source control in Design View.

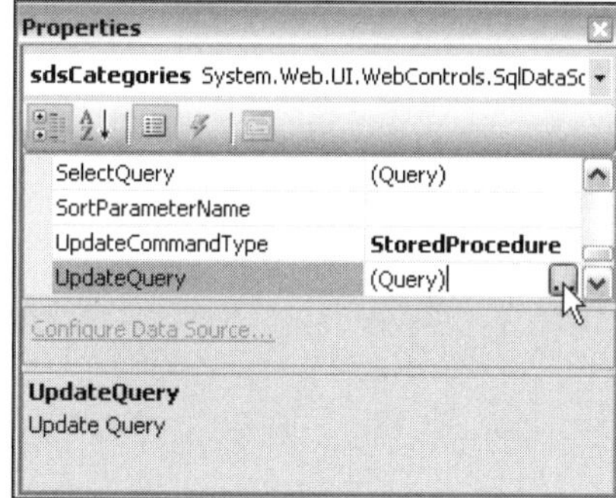

Figure 5-11

This brings up the Command and Parameter Editor shown in Figure 5-12 that allows you to reorder, delete, and create new or change existing parameters. To change the Direction for a parameter, you need to click the Show Advanced Properties link and then choose an option from the Direction drop-down.

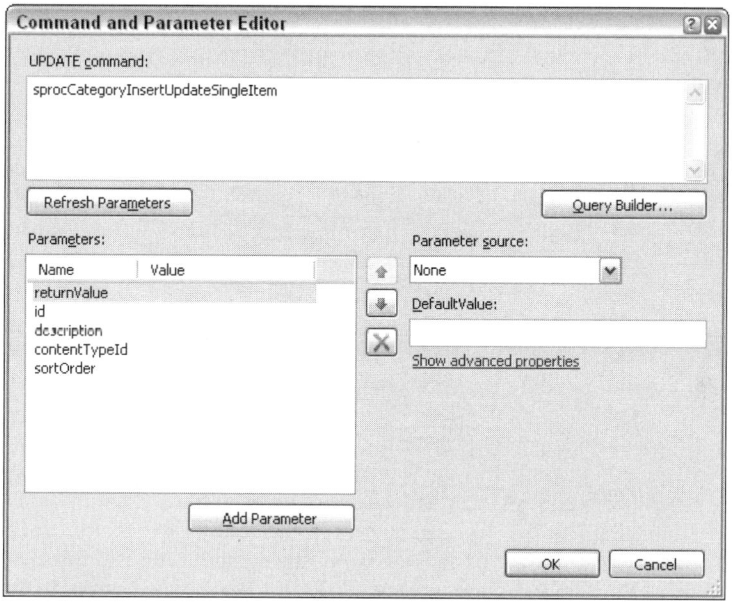

Figure 5-12

With the `GridView` and its fields collection bound to the data source control, which in turn is bound to stored procedures in the database, you have everything in place to allow updating and deletion of data. There are, however, two other things you need to examine. The first thing is how to handle duplicate records. The other is how to insert new categories. Take a look at solving the duplicates problem first.

Each category within a specific content type must have a unique description because it doesn't make sense to have two menu items with the same name. The stored procedure that inserts and updates categories handles this by finding out if there is already a category with the same name before the insert or update takes place:

```
IF NOT EXISTS (SELECT Id FROM Category
        WHERE Description = @description AND ContentTypeId = @contentTypeId)
BEGIN
    -- Insert the item here
END
ELSE
BEGIN
    SET @returnValue = -1  -- record already exists
END
```

Only when the `IF NOT EXISTS` check returns `True` is the new item inserted. Otherwise, the stored procedure returns `-1` to the `SqlDataSource` through its `returnValue` parameter you saw earlier. In the code-behind for the Categories page, that return value is examined. If it's not `-1`, the insert or update succeeded. Otherwise, an error message is displayed to the user, indicating the database action didn't succeed. The place where the parameter is examined is inside the `Inserted` and `Updated` events of the data source:

```
Protected Sub sdsCategories_AfterInsertOrUpdate(ByVal sender As Object, _
    ByVal e As System.Web.UI.WebControls.SqlDataSourceStatusEventArgs) _
    Handles sdsCategories.Inserted, sdsCategories.Updated

  Dim id As Integer = Convert.ToInt32(e.Command.Parameters("@returnValue").Value)
  If id = -1 Then
    lblErrorMessage.Text = "There is already a category with this description." & _
         "Your changes have not been applied.<br />"
    lblErrorMessage.Visible = True
  End If
End Sub
```

Note the comma-separated list of the `Handles` clause; this allows you to hook up one event handler to multiple events of the same or different controls.

Because the `GridView` does not support inserting data, a `FormView` control is used to allow the user to insert a new category. Very similar to the way the `GridView` is set up, the `FormView` contains an `InsertItemTemplate` with controls that expose their values to the `SqlDataSource` control to allow the insert to happen. The `InsertItemTemplate` contains a text box for the Description, a `RequiredFieldValidator`, and two drop-downs for the content type and the sort order columns. To view the `FormView` so you can insert a new item, click the Create New button on the Categories page. This fires the `btnNew_Click` method in the code-behind that hides the List panel and then shows the New panel, allowing you to insert the new category.

Just like the `GridView`, the `FormView` is bound to the `sdsCategories` data source, this time using its `InsertCommand` to send the details the user entered to the stored procedure that eventually inserts the new category. When you click the Insert button, the values you entered in the `FormView` are sent to the `SqlDataSource`, which forwards them to the database. Just as with the `GridView`, the `sdsCategories_AfterInsertOrUpdate` method is used to determine whether a duplicate category has been inserted.

Now that you're able to define the appearance of the site by managing the items in the main and sub-menu, it's time to look at how you can create the actual content for the site. The next section looks at the ContentList.aspx and AddEditContent.aspx pages that allow you to manage content items.

Managing Content

When you click the Manage Content button in the Admin menu, you're taken to ContentList.aspx that displays a list with the available content items in the database. To make it easy to distinguish between active and deleted content, the page has a drop-down with an Active and Deleted item. Whenever you choose a new item from that drop-down the page is refreshed and displays a list with either previously deleted or active content items. The page also contains a `SqlDataSource` with its `Select` and `Delete` commands set to stored procedures in the database to allow you to get a list of content items, or to delete a single item.

The `GridView` that is used on this page has some similarities with the one used to display the categories. Two important differences exist, though, which are examined now. First of all, the `GridView` is not editable, so you'll see no `TemplateFields` with an `EditItemTemplate`.

The other difference is the way in which the buttons to delete and edit existing items are set up. With the categories page you used a single `CommandField` with `ShowDeleteButton` and `ShowEditButton` both set to `True`. For the content page, however, each button has its own column:

```
<asp:ButtonField ButtonType="Button" CommandName="Edit"
       HeaderText="Edit" Text="Edit">
  <ItemStyle Width="100px" />
</asp:ButtonField>
<asp:CommandField ButtonType="Button" ShowDeleteButton="True">
  <ItemStyle Width="100px" />
</asp:CommandField>
```

The Delete button is still generated by a `CommandField` with `ShowDeleteButton` set to `True`. When you click the Delete button, the `GridView` triggers the `DeleteCommand` on the associated `SqlDataSource` control to delete the item from the database. This works exactly the same as deleting categories.

When you start editing a content item, things behave a bit differently, though. Because a content item requires some fields other than the default single-line text boxes or even a few drop-down controls you can add in the `EditItemTemplate` of the `GridView`, it's not really an option to edit a content item inline in the grid. Instead, when you click the Edit button, the `GridView` control's `RowCommand` is triggered and you're taken to a separate page, AddEditContent.aspx, that allows you to enter content using complex controls. You'll see that page later. The code that sends you to this page looks like this:

```
Protected Sub gvContent_RowCommand(ByVal sender As Object, _
    ByVal e As System.Web.UI.WebControls.GridViewCommandEventArgs) _
    Handles gvContent.RowCommand
  Select Case e.CommandName.ToLower()
    Case "edit"
      Dim recordIndex As Integer
      Dim recordId As Integer
      recordIndex = Convert.ToInt32(e.CommandArgument)
      recordId = Convert.ToInt32(gvContent.DataKeys(recordIndex).Value)
      Response.Redirect("AddEditContent.aspx?Id=" & recordId.ToString())
  End Select
End Sub
```

The ButtonField for the Edit button you saw earlier has its CommandName set to Edit. Inside the RowCommand event, this command name is made available through the CommandName property of the GridViewCommandEventArgs passed to the method. When the command name matches Edit, you know the Edit button has been clicked. You can then use the CommandArgument to find the zero-based index of the clicked row in the grid. So, when you click the third item, the CommandArgument will have a value of 2. You can then use this index to ask the GridView for the DataKey that belongs to the clicked item. The DataKeys collection of the GridView returns the primary key of a content item in the database, which is exactly what you need because AddEditContent.aspx expects that ID in case you're editing a content item. Finally, when you have the key, you can construct a URL with the ID appended to the query string and send the user to that page.

Earlier you learned that the FormView is a great control that allows you to enter data into the database with little to no code. However, its usage is often limited to simpler data access scenarios like the Categories page in the Management folder. One of the biggest drawbacks of the control is the fact that you need to define separate templates for insertion and for updating data. With complex, multi-control data pages, setting up such a form can become tedious and error-prone.

To avoid these problems, a different approach was taken with the AddEditContent page. Instead of relying exclusively on built-in controls to get data from and in the database, a single Content class was created that represents a content item in the database. Additionally, the ContentDB class was designed, which is responsible for communicating with the database. Inside the page, you use these classes to get a content item from the database, and then use regular controls like text boxes and drop-downs in the page directly. To see how this all works, look at the markup of the AddEditContent.aspx page.

At the bottom of the page, you see two SqlDataSource controls that are used to display the available content types and categories in a drop-down. The data source for the categories, called sdsCategories, is tied to the content types drop-down with a single SelectParameter. This ensures that whenever you choose a new content type from the drop-down, the page will refresh and show an updated list with categories for that content type. The two drop-down controls are exactly the same as the others you have seen so far. They have their DataSourceID set to the relevant SqlDataSource control, and their DataTextField and DataValueField properties point to the columns held in the DataSet returned by the data sources. So far, there is nothing new in the page. But how do the other controls in the page get their values? To understand how that works, open up the code-behind for AddEditContent.aspx and look at the Page_Load event:

```
Protected Sub Page_Load(ByVal sender As Object, _
    ByVal e As System.EventArgs) Handles Me.Load
  If Request.QueryString.Get("Id") IsNot Nothing Then
    contentId = Convert.ToInt32(Request.QueryString.Get("Id"))
  End If
  If Not Page.IsPostBack And contentId > 0 Then
    Dim myContentItem As Content = Content.GetItem(contentId)
    If myContentItem IsNot Nothing Then
      Me.Title = "Edit " & myContentItem.Title
      txtTitle.Text = myContentItem.Title
      txtIntroText.Value = myContentItem.IntroText
      txtBodyText.Value = myContentItem.BodyText
      chkVisible.Checked = myContentItem.Visible

      lstContentTypes.DataBind()
```

```
        lstContentTypes.SelectedValue = myContentItem.ContentTypeId.ToString()

        lstCategories.DataBind()
        lstCategories.SelectedValue = myContentItem.CategoryId.ToString()
      End If
    End If

  End Sub
```

Inside this method, the code tries to retrieve the requested `contentId` from the query string if it has been provided. If there is no query string it means a new item should be inserted, so the next `If` block won't run. If there is a query string, however, a few actions are carried out. First of all, a call is made to the `GetItem` method of the `Content` class. This method expects the ID of the content item in the database, and then returns a strongly typed `Content` item. You look at the `Content` object and its associated `ContentDB` class in full detail after finishing the discussion of the `Page_Load` method. Once you have a valid `Content` object, you can use its public properties like `Title`, `IntroText`, and `BodyText` to set the initial values of the controls and the title of the page. The `txtIntroText` and `txtBodyText` controls are in fact complex HTML editors powered by the FCKeditor. Again, this is examined in full detail a little later.

Unlike the text controls such as the Title text box, the drop-down controls require a bit more thought. The Categories drop-down is bound to the Content Type drop-down so it always displays categories from the currently selected content type. This means that you should fill and preselect the content type list before you can work with the categories. The code in the `Page_Load` method does exactly that:

```
        lstContentTypes.DataBind()
        lstContentTypes.SelectedValue = myContentItem.ContentTypeId.ToString()
```

First, a call is made to the `DataBind` method of the `lstContentTypes` control. This in turn triggers its associated `SqlDataSource` control that gets the items from the database, which are then added as `<asp:ListItem>` controls to the drop-down. The second line of code then sets the `SelectedValue` of the control equal to the `ContentType` of the content item.

The next two lines then get the items for the second drop-down that displays the available categories:

```
        lstCategories.DataBind()
        lstCategories.SelectedValue = myContentItem.CategoryId.ToString()
```

When the call to `DataBind` of the categories drop-down is made, its related `SqlDataSource` is triggered. As stated previously, this control has a single `SelectParameter` that looks at the selected value of the Content Type drop-down. Because just before the call to `DataBind`, you have set that `SelectedValue`, the data source will now get the right categories belonging to the selected content type. When the items have been added to the drop-down list, the last line sets its `SelectedValue` to the one retrieved from the `CategoryId` of the `Content` object, just as with the content type.

Now that you know how the data from the `Content` object is displayed in the various controls, you may be wondering how the content item is created in the first place. As you saw in the section "Design of the Wrox CMS" earlier in this chapter, the `Content` class has a number of public properties and a shared method called `GetItem` that accepts the ID of a content item and returns an instance of the `Content` class. All the `GetItem` method in the business layer does is delegate its responsibility to a method with the same name in the `ContentDB` class:

```
Public Shared Function GetItem(ByVal id As Integer) As Content
  Return ContentDB.GetItem(id)
End Function
```

This `GetItem` method in the `ContentDB` class in turn gets the item from the database and returns it to the calling code:

```
Public Shared Function GetItem(ByVal id As Integer) As Content
  Dim theContentItem As Content = Nothing
  Using myConnection As New SqlConnection(AppConfiguration.ConnectionString)
    Dim myCommand As SqlCommand = New SqlCommand _
        ("sprocContentSelectSingleItem", myConnection)

    myCommand.CommandType = CommandType.StoredProcedure
    myCommand.Parameters.AddWithValue("@id", id)
    myConnection.Open()

    Using myReader As SqlDataReader = _
          myCommand.ExecuteReader(CommandBehavior.CloseConnection)
      If myReader.Read Then
        theContentItem = New Content(myReader.GetInt32(myReader.GetOrdinal("Id")))
        theContentItem.Title = myReader.GetString(myReader.GetOrdinal("Title"))
        theContentItem.IntroText = _
             myReader.GetString(myReader.GetOrdinal("IntroText"))
        theContentItem.BodyText = _
             myReader.GetString(myReader.GetOrdinal("BodyText"))
        theContentItem.ContentTypeId = _
             myReader.GetInt32(myReader.GetOrdinal("ContentTypeId"))
        theContentItem.CategoryId = _
             myReader.GetInt32(myReader.GetOrdinal("CategoryId"))
        theContentItem.Visible = _
             myReader.GetBoolean(myReader.GetOrdinal("Visible"))
      End If
      myReader.Close()
    End Using
  End Using
  Return theContentItem
End Function
```

The code starts off by declaring a new variable of type `Content` and setting it to `Nothing`. If the item cannot be found in the database, this value will be returned from the method, so the calling ASPX page can take that into account.

Next, an instance of a `SqlConnection` and a `SqlCommand` are created. The new `Using` statement ensures the connection object is disposed of automatically when the block of code has finished. The name of the stored procedure you want to execute is passed to the constructor of the `Command` object, together with the connection. The `CommandType` of the `Command` object is set to `StoredProcedure` and a single parameter that holds the ID of the content item in the database is created.

Then the connection is opened and the command's `ExecuteReader` method is fired, resulting in a `SqlDataReader`. If the `Read()` method returns `True`, it means a record has been found, so you can instantiate a new `Content` object and set each of its public properties retrieved from the `SqlDataReader`. Notice the use of the `GetOrdinal` methods. By design the `Get*` methods, like `GetInt32` and `GetString` of the `SqlDataReader`, accept only a zero-based integer with the index of the requested column. This means that to get at the Title of the content item, you'd need to use something like `myReader.GetString(1)`. This results in quite unreadable code, because you'll quickly forget which column has what index number. Fortunately, the `SqlDataReader` also has a `GetOrdinal` method that accepts a column's name and returns its ordinal position in the result set. This makes the previous bit of code much easier to read and maintain: `myReader.GetString(myReader.GetOrdinal("Title"))`. Using the `GetOrdinal` method may cause a tiny bit of overhead, but compared to the benefits of better code, this is a cheap price to pay.

Once all the public properties of the content item have been set, the `SqlDataReader` is closed and the content item is returned to the calling code.

Undoubtedly you have noticed the fancy HTML editor used in the AddEditContent.aspx page. This editor is not a part of the .NET Framework, nor is it an integral part of ASP.NET. Instead, the editor, called FCKeditor, is developed by a group of people lead by Frederico Caldeira Knabben (hence the FCK in FCKeditor) and made available to the public as an open source project. You can find the latest version of the editor at `www.fckeditor.com`. Because the (easy) installation process for the editor is explained in the section "Setting up the Wrox CMS," this section focuses exclusively on how to use it.

Using the FCKeditor is about as simple as installing it. For ASP.NET pages, the creators of the editor developed a separate .NET assembly (a .dll file) that must be placed in the Bin folder of the application. You can use that same DLL to customize the toolbox of Visual Web Developer, so you can drag instances of the editor from your toolbox onto the page. To customize the toolbox, open up the toolbox (Ctrl+Alt+x), right-click it, and select Choose Items. In the dialog that follows, click Browse and then select the file FredCK.FCKeditorV2.dll located in the Bin folder of your application (located at `C:\Inetpub\wwwroot\Cms\Bin` after a default installation of the Wrox CMS). The editor will end up as an item called FCKeditor with the default gear icon on the toolbox. Now whenever you need an HTML editor, drag an instance of it on your page instead of a standard text box.

The editor is very easy to work with, both from an end-user's and a programmer's point of view. Just like a regular .NET control it exposes properties such as width and height. However, when working with the editor, you'll find a few differences that are worth discussing. First of all the editor doesn't have a `Text` property like a default text box does, but has a `Value` property instead. For all practical purposes, these properties can be treated the same in that the `Value` allows you to set and get the HTML-formatted text from the control.

Another important thing to notice is the way the editor works with validator controls. By default, the ASP.NET validators are triggered when the associated form control loses focus; for example, when you tab away or click a Submit button. However, with the FCKeditor this seems to happen too late. The editor works by copying the formatted HTML from the editor to a hidden form field, which in turn is validated. This copying also takes place when the editor loses focus, but after the controls have been validated. For your end-user, this results in a message that the field used for the editor is required when in fact it already has a valid value. The quickest way to fix that is to simply press Submit again. Obviously, this is not a good solution for a real-world application. The next best thing is to disable client-side validation in pages that use the editor. That technique was applied to the AddEditContent.aspx page by simply setting the `CausesValidation` attribute of the Save button to `False`. Making this change won't prevent validation from occurring. Back at the server, each of the controls is still checked for their values; the validation just doesn't fire at the client anymore.

Notice the use of a property called ToolbarSet to give the control for the IntroText a different set of buttons than the one for the BodyText. The configuration for the FCKeditor, stored in the file FCKeditor\fckconfig.js, allows you to define various toolbar sets and refer to them by name. The Default toolbar set contains all of the available buttons, whereas WroxCms and Basic use a limited set. To create a new toolbar set, make a copy of Default, and then remove whatever button you don't need.

Because the FCKeditor controls can contain HTML tags and possibly JavaScript, the ASP.NET framework by default blocks these values and instead throws an HttpRequestValidationException exception with a message like "A potentially dangerous Request.Form value was detected." To prevent that error from occurring, the ValidateRequest is set to False in the page directive for the AddEditContent.aspx page.

The final part of the AddEditContent.aspx page you need to look at is saving an item in the database. When you fill in all the required fields in the page, possibly formatting the IntroText and BodyText parts of the item using the FCKeditor, and press the Save button, the following code in the Click event handler of the Save button fires:

```
Protected Sub btnSave_Click(ByVal sender As Object, ByVal e As System.EventArgs) _
   Handles btnSave.Click
  Page.Validate()
  If Page.IsValid Then
    Dim myContentItem As Content
    If Request.QueryString.Get("Id") IsNot String.Empty Then
      myContentItem = New Content(Convert.ToInt32(Request.QueryString.Get("Id")))
    Else
      myContentItem = New Content()
    End If
    myContentItem.Title = txtTitle.Text
    myContentItem.IntroText = txtIntroText.Value
    myContentItem.BodyText = txtBodyText.Value
    myContentItem.Visible = chkVisible.Checked
    myContentItem.ContentTypeId = Convert.ToInt32(lstContentTypes.SelectedValue)
    myContentItem.CategoryId = Convert.ToInt32(lstCategories.SelectedValue)
    myContentItem.Save()
    Response.Redirect("ContentList.aspx")
  End If
End Sub
```

First Page.Validate() is called to see if each of the controls in the page has a valid value. If the page is valid, you can create a new instance of a Content item instance. This can happen in two different ways, depending on whether you're currently editing an existing item or creating a brand new one. In the class design for the Content class, the ID of the Content class is read-only to prevent calling code from changing it during the object's lifetime. That's why an overloaded constructor of the Content class is called, which receives the ID of the content item in case you're updating an existing item. Otherwise, when you're creating a new content item, the code simply calls the default constructor to get a new Content instance.

The code then assigns each of the public properties of the Content class a value by retrieving them from the relevant controls. Notice again the use of the .Value instead of .Text to get the values of the two FCKeditors. Once all properties have been set, call the Save method on the Content class. Similar to the GetItem method, this method simply calls the Save method in the ContentDB class and passes itself to it using the keyword Me:

```
Public Sub Save()
  ContentDB.Save(Me)
End Sub
```

Just like the `GetItem` method you saw earlier, `Save` sets up a `SqlConnection` and a `SqlCommand`. It then assigns the `Command` object the relevant parameters whose values it derives from the `Content` item passed to the method. In the end, `ExecuteNonQuery` is used to send the command to the database:

```
If contentItem.Id > 0 Then
  myCommand.Parameters.AddWithValue("@id", contentItem.Id)
End If

myCommand.Parameters.AddWithValue("@title", contentItem.Title)
myCommand.Parameters.AddWithValue("@introText", contentItem.IntroText)
myCommand.Parameters.AddWithValue("@bodyText", contentItem.BodyText)
myCommand.Parameters.AddWithValue("@contentTypeId", contentItem.ContentTypeId)
myCommand.Parameters.AddWithValue("@categoryId", contentItem.CategoryId)
myCommand.Parameters.AddWithValue("@visible", contentItem.Visible)

myConnection.Open()
myCommand.ExecuteNonQuery()
myConnection.Close()
```

When this method is finished, control is returned to the calling ASPX page, which simply redirects the user back to the ContentList page where the content item is now visible.

If you have some previous experience with programming you may recognize some problems with the data access code you just saw. First of all, there is no error handling. Instead of using a `Try/Catch` block the code is simply executed, letting any error bubble up to the final ASPX page. This isn't considered good programming practice, as it's very hard to see where, when, and how the errors in your site occur. In the next chapter you see a neat way to catch any error that occurs at run time and use it to construct a detailed error e-mail that can be sent to the site's administrator or a developer.

The second thing you may have noticed is that the code you saw is strongly tied to SQL Server. Although developing for a single database type is quick and easy, it may not always be a good solution. In the next chapter you learn how to write data access code that works with SQL Server and Microsoft Access without any modifications.

Inserting new content or managing existing items is the final step in the Content Management process. All that's left now is to look at how to present the content in the front end of the site. With the more advanced technologies of inserting, updating, and deleting content behind you, displaying content is now a piece of cake.

Displaying Content on the Web Site

The display of the content in the public area of the site is handled by two pages: ContentList.aspx and ContentDetail.aspx. The first is responsible for displaying a list of content items published in the requested content type and category. It displays a short version of each content item in a `DataList` control that holds `HyperLink` controls that take you to the detail page. This detail page then shows the full details of the content item.

The ContentList.aspx page contains a single `SqlDataSource` control with two select parameters: one for the content type and one for the category. Both these parameters are retrieved from the query string, when available:

```
<asp:SqlDataSource ID="sdsContentList" runat="server"
      ConnectionString="<%$ ConnectionStrings:Cms %>"
      SelectCommand="sprocContentSelectListByContentTypeAndCategoryId"
      SelectCommandType="StoredProcedure"
      CancelSelectOnNullParameter="False">
  <SelectParameters>
    <asp:QueryStringParameter Name="contentTypeId"
            QueryStringField="ContentTypeId" Type="Int32" />
    <asp:QueryStringParameter Name="categoryId"
            QueryStringField="CategoryId" Type="Int32" DefaultValue="" />
  </SelectParameters>
</asp:SqlDataSource>
```

When this data source is about to get the data from the database, it gets the values for the content type and the category from the query string first and assigns them to the parameters. Notice the use of the `CancelSelectOnNullParameter` attribute on the `SqlDataSource` control. The default of this parameter is `True`, which means the control won't get data from the database if any of the parameters contains a null value. In this situation, this is not what you want. When one of the content types is clicked, and no category has been selected yet, you want to display all the content items that belong to the chosen content type, regardless of their category. The stored procedure in the database returns all the items for a certain content type when the `CategoryId` parameter is `null` so you must ensure that the code still accesses the procedure even if there is no query string for the category. You accomplish this by setting `CancelSelectOnNullParameter` to `False`.

The `SqlDataSource` that gets the content items from the database is used by a `DataList` in the page. It has a simple `ItemTemplate` that displays the item's Title, IntroText, and a "Read more" link:

```
<asp:DataList ID="dlContent" runat="server" DataKeyField="Id"
            DataSourceID="sdsContentList">
  <ItemTemplate>
    <h2 class="ItemTitle"><asp:Literal ID="lblTitle"
          runat="server" Text='<%# Bind("Title") %>'></asp:Literal></h2>
    <div class="IntroText">
      <asp:Literal ID="lblIntroText" runat="server"
          Text='<%# Eval("IntroText") %>'></asp:Literal></div><br />
    <asp:HyperLink ID="hyperReadMore" runat="server"
        NavigateUrl='<%# "~/ContentDetail.aspx?Id=" &
        Eval("Id") & "&ContentTypeId=" & Eval("ContentTypeId")& "&CategoryId=" &
        Eval("CategoryId") %>' Text="Read more..."></asp:HyperLink><br /><br />
  </ItemTemplate>
  <SeparatorTemplate>
    <hr />
  </SeparatorTemplate>
</asp:DataList>
```

Each content item in the list is separated from the previous using an `<hr />` tag in the `<SeparatorTemplate>`. The contents of this separator can be fully customized. You could put anything you want between two items, including images, banners, or plain HTML.

Notice the use of `Eval` instead of `Bind` to bind the data to the controls in the template. Because you need to display read-only data, there is no need to set up two-way data-binding, and you can use the faster `Eval` method.

If you request the list page in the browser and then click a main menu, you'll see a list with content items appear. The "Read more" link below each item takes you to the ContentDetails page. This page holds three `<asp:Literal>` controls that display the relevant content from the database:

```
<h1 class="ItemTitle"><asp:Literal ID="litTitle" runat="server"></asp:Literal></h1>
<div class="IntroText"><asp:Literal ID="litIntrotext"
        runat="server"></asp:Literal></div>
<div class="BodyText"><asp:Literal ID="litBodyText"
        runat="server"></asp:Literal></div>
```

The `Literal` controls are wrapped inside `<h1>` and `<div>` elements so it's easy to apply a CSS class that changes their formatting at run time. The Styles.css file has an `ItemTitle` class that gives the text a large and bold font, whereas the `IntroText` class changes the text to an italic font. You can use any CSS you see fit to format the text by changing the classes defined in the Styles.css file in the CSS folder.

The three `Literal` controls get their value from an instance of the `Content` class using the same `GetItem` method you saw earlier. When the details page loads, the following code is executed in its `Page_Load` event:

```
Protected Sub Page_Load(ByVal sender As Object, ByVal e As System.EventArgs) _
     Handles Me.Load
  If Request.QueryString.Get("Id") IsNot Nothing Then
    contentId = Convert.ToInt32(Request.QueryString.Get("Id"))
    Dim contentItem As Content = Content.GetItem(contentId)
    If contentItem IsNot Nothing Then
      Me.Title = contentItem.Title
      litTitle.Text = contentItem.Title
      litIntrotext.Text = contentItem.IntroText
      litBodyText.Text = contentItem.BodyText
    End If
  End If
End Sub
```

Similar to the AddEditContent.aspx page, this code gets a new instance of the `Content` class by calling `GetItem` and passing it the ID of the content item retrieved from the query string. If the method returns a `Content` instance, the page's `Title` and the `Text` property of the three `Literal` controls are filled with the `Title`, `IntroText`, and `BodyText` properties. The `Literal` controls can also hold HTML that comes from the FCKeditor used to format the content item in the management section.

The Wrox CMS is only the beginning of the things you can do with fully database-driven web sites. Both the presentation and the functionality of the site are pretty simple at this point, to allow you to focus on important concepts and technologies without being caught up by complex design and formatting markup. But it's easy to come up with a list of new features and enhancements to the Wrox CMS that make it even more useful than it already is.

For examples of possible modifications to the Wrox CMS, look at the companion CD-ROM or go to `www.wrox.com` and find this book's download page.

Setting up the Wrox CMS

You can set up the Wrox CMS in two ways: by using the supplied installer or by manually setting up the site with the code that comes with this book.

You can use the installer when you have IIS running on your machine and want to use it for the Wrox CMS. Running the installer creates a virtual directory called Cms under your default web site. The folder that is created during setup contains the full source of the application and all other files required to run the application, including the database.

Alternatively, you can choose to unpack the source from the CD-ROM or code download to a folder of your choice. This gives you a bit more choice with regard to where the files are placed, but you'll have to set up IIS manually, or browse to the site from within Visual Web Developer.

For both installation methods it's assumed that the .NET 2.0 Framework, which is an installation requirement for Visual Web Developer, has already been installed. It's also assumed that you have installed SQL Server 2005 Express Edition with an instance name of SqlExpress. If you chose a different instance name, make sure you use that name in the connection string for the Wrox CMS in the Web.config file.

Using the Installer

To install the Wrox CMS, open the folder Chapter 05 - Wrox CMS\Installer and double-click setup.exe. This starts the installer. By default the web site will be installed as a virtual directory called CMS under the default web site. You should leave all values in the setup dialog to their defaults and click Next until the installer has finished. Once the site is installed, refer to the section "Changing IIS Settings" later in the chapter for further installation instructions.

Manual Installation

You can also manually install the Wrox CMS by extracting the files from the accompanying CD-ROM or code download to your local hard drive. To install manually, locate the folder Chapter 05 - Wrox CMS and then open the Source folder. In that folder you'll find a zip file called Chapter 05 - Wrox CMS.zip. Extract the contents of the zip file to a location on your hard drive, for example `C:\Inetpub\wwwroot\`. Make sure you extract the files with the option Use Folder Names or something similar to maintain the original folder structure. You should end up with a folder like `C:\Inetpub\wwwroot\Cms` that in turn contains a number of files and other folders. The remainder of this section assumes you extracted the CMS to `C:\Inetpub\wwwroot\Cms`.

Changing IIS Settings

Regardless of the installation method you chose, you might need to configure IIS to work properly with your site. If you have previous versions of the .NET Framework on your machine, IIS will be configured to use that version of the framework, and not version 2.0. Follow these steps to configure IIS:

1. Click Start➪Run, type `inetmgr` in the dialog box, and press Enter.
2. Expand the tree on the left until you see your server. Right-click it and choose Properties.

3. Click the ASP.NET tab.
4. From the ASP.NET version drop-down, choose 2.0.50727 and click OK.

You may need to restart IIS for the changes to take effect.

Changing Security Settings

The final configuration change you need to make is to enable Write permissions on the UserFiles folder that is used by the FCKeditor and the App_Data folder where the database is stored. You'll need to give permissions to the account that the web site runs under. On Windows XP this is the ASPNET account, and on Windows Server 2003 the account is called Network Service. If you're running the site on the built-in development web server from within Visual Web Developer, the account used is the one you use to log on to your machine.

In all cases, follow these steps to set the permissions:

1. Open a Windows Explorer and locate the UserFiles folder in your CMS web site. If the folder isn't there, create it first.
2. Right-click the UserFiles folder, choose Properties, and click the Security tab. If you don't see the Security tab, choose Tools➪Folder Options in Windows Explorer, open the View tab, scroll all the way down to the bottom of the Advanced settings list, and uncheck Use Simple File Sharing, as shown in Figure 5-13.

   Click OK to dismiss the Folder Options dialog.

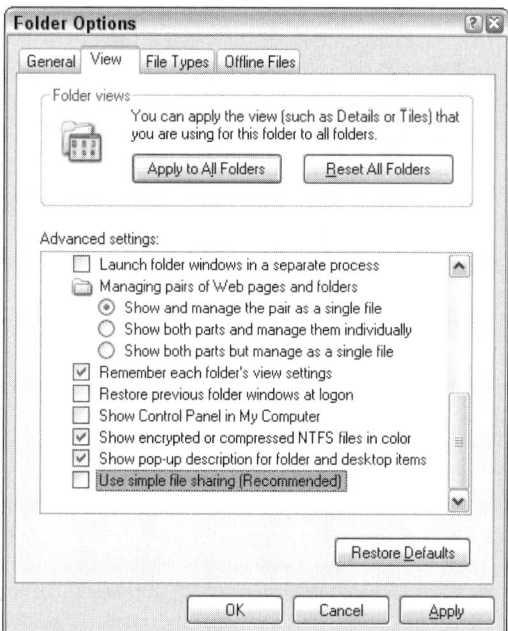

Figure 5-13

3. Back on the Security tab for the UserFiles folder, click the Add button, type the name of the account that requires the permissions, and click OK.

4. Next, make sure the account you just added has at least Read and Modify permissions in the Permissions For list, as shown in Figure 5-14.

Figure 5-14

5. Finally, click OK to apply the changes.

6. Repeat the first five steps, but this time configure the settings for the App_Data folder that holds the CMS database.

Testing Out the Site

With the configured database and file system, you're now ready to launch the application. Back in Visual Web Developer, press Ctrl+F5 to open up Wrox CMS. To manage the categories and the content in the Management section of the site, click the Admin tab. Because the Management folder is protected with a setting in the Web.config file, you'll need to log in first. If you used the installer to set up the Wrox CMS, you can log in with a username of `Administrator` and a password of `Admin123#`. If you can't access the Management section, make sure you created the Administrator role. Also make sure you assigned the account you created to that role.

The first time the page loads, it might take a while before you see the CMS homepage appear. The connection string in the Web.config file instructs SQL Server Express to attach the CMS database automatically, which takes some time. If you get a time-out error, refresh your browser to try again.

If after waiting a long time you get a "The page cannot be displayed" error instead of the CMS homepage, close your browser and go back to Visual Web Developer. Choose Website⇨Start Options and then make sure the NTLM authentication checkbox is unchecked. Then press Ctrl+F5 again to open the web site.

Summary

In this chapter you learned how to design, build, and use a content management system. With this content management system, you have easy access to the content you publish, allowing you to add and update content online.

The chapter started with a tour of the web site and the CMS. You saw how the site uses content types and categories that are displayed as main and sub-menu items. You also saw how the site displays these content items, and how you can change these items using the CMS.

In the section "Design of the Wrox CMS" you saw how the site is organized by looking at the individual files in the web site and the classes in the business and data access layer. That section also explained the design of the database for the web site.

You then got a good look at the inner workings of the pages and classes that make up the CMS. You learned how to use `SqlDataSource` controls to get data in and out of the database. You also learned how to create a custom class that can access the database, to avoid some of the problems that the `SqlDataSource` controls have. Besides the individual pages, user controls, and classes that make up the site, you also saw how to embed the FCKeditor in your application, to allow your end-users to format their content using a fancy HTML editor.

At the end of the chapter you saw two different ways to install the Wrox CMS. The automated installer gives you a quick and easy way to get the CMS up and running with little effort. The manual process in turn gives you finer control over how and where the application is installed.

Wrox Blog

Undoubtedly, blogging — a contraction of web and logging — is the most popular Internet application of the past few years. Relatively new to the Internet world, blogging has now reached millions of web users, turning them into mini-publishers of news, diaries, and biographies.

Blogging applications come in all sorts and sizes. There are subscription-based blog sites from commercial companies, where you need to sign up for an account. Once you have an account, you can sign in to the company's web site to manage your blog. People who want to read your blog should come to that same site. Other companies provide blogging services that allow you to manage your blog entries on their site, and make them available publicly (for example, on your own site) through XML and Web Services. Yet other organizations have developed ready-made blogging applications that you can install on your own server. Some of them come as free or open source packages, of which probably the most well known is Community Server (`www.communityserver.org`), which is also the driving force behind the forums on Microsoft's community site, `www.asp.net`.

Despite the many advantages these ready-made applications have, they all share one disadvantage: They are often hard to incorporate into your web site, especially when you don't control your own server but use a shared hosting service instead.

The Wrox Blog application presented in this chapter is really easy to integrate in an existing web application. This is accomplished by a few design decisions.

First of all, the Blog application does not contain normal ASPX WebForms; it consists solely of user controls. This makes it easy to embed the Blog application in existing pages, simply by dragging a few controls onto your page.

Secondly, the Blog application is designed to work with both a Microsoft Access database and with SQL Server 2005. This can be very useful if you have a host that hasn't upgraded to SQL Server 2005 yet, or if you have to pay for the additional SQL Server services. Switching the application over from SQL Server to Access or vice versa is as simple as changing two settings in the Web.config file. This means you could even switch without taking the site offline.

The first section in this chapter shows you how to use the Blog application. You see how the user controls are incorporated in standard ASPX pages, enabling you to view and manage your blog.

The section "Design of the Wrox Blog" describes the design principles behind the Wrox Blog application. You see the classes involved, and how they interact together. You also see the design of the SQL Server and Microsoft Access databases.

The section that follows, "Code and Code Explanation," gives you a good look at the classes, pages, and the code-behind files that make up the Wrox Blog application.

In "Setting up the Wrox Blog" you get a thorough explanation of setting up the Wrox Blog. You see how to run the supplied installer to create a full web site that uses the Blog application. You also learn how to incorporate the Blog application in an existing web site. But, first things first: learning how to use the Wrox Blog.

Using the Blog

Using the Wrox Blog web site is very easy. If you know how to use a word processor, you should have no problems creating content for your blog site. When you have installed the Wrox Blog (see the section "Setting up the Wrox Blog" near the end of this chapter for details) you can browse to the site by going to `http://localhost/Blog`. The start page shown in Figure 6-1 appears.

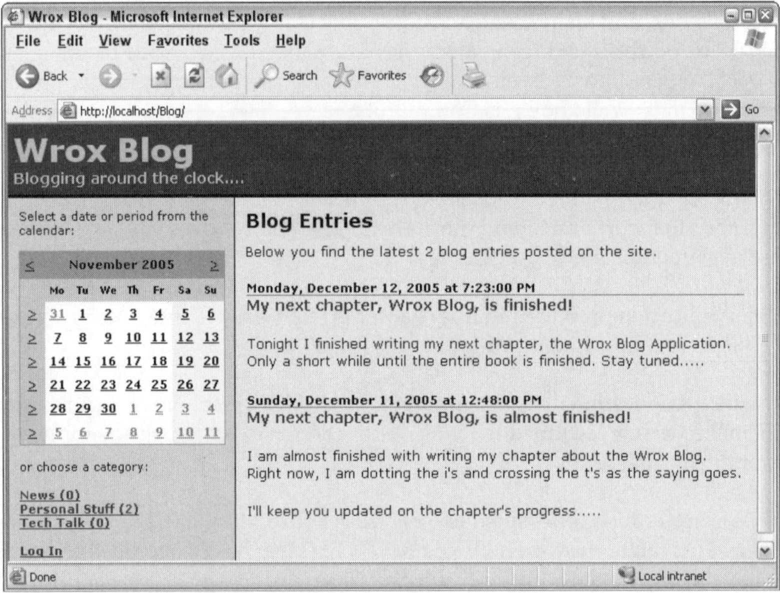

Figure 6-1

This page contains two user controls; one for the left-hand bar with the calendar and the category list and one for the items in the list on the right, referred to as *blog entries* or *blog posts*. The left-hand bar displays a calendar and a list with the categories available in the system. The number between the parentheses indicates how many blog posts have been published in that category. Both the calendar and the category list are used to filter the list with blog entries you see in the right-hand pane. When the page first loads, that pane displays the latest 15 blog entries in the system (or fewer when there aren't that many entries in the database). When you click a date in the calendar, the list on the right updates itself to display the blog entries for that date. You can also click the greater than symbol (>) on the left of the calendar to see entries posted during an entire week. If you click one of the categories, you'll see all the entries posted in that category.

To manage blog entries on the web site, you need to log in first. Once you're authenticated, you'll see a Create New Entry button appear at the bottom of the page, as shown in Figure 6-2.

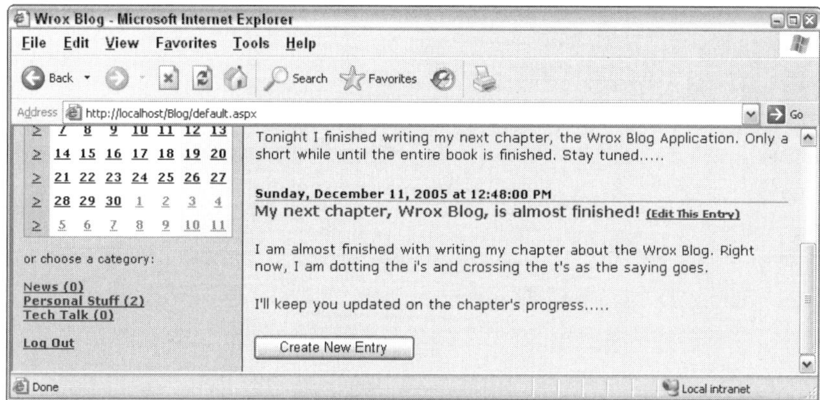

Figure 6-2

If you click that button, the page refreshes and shows a screen (see Figure 6-3) where you can enter a new blog entry.

Here you can enter a title, the post's body text, and the category in which you want to publish the item. The calendar's selected date defaults to today's date, but to allow you to predate your blog entries you can select a different date from the calendar.

Once you click the Save button, the entry appears on the web site and can be viewed by selecting the appropriate category or date on which the item was published.

If you're logged in, you also see an Edit This Entry link after each blog entry's title. Clicking this link brings up a similar edit screen with all the details already filled in, so you can easily change the entry.

Now that you know how to use the Wrox Blog application, it's time to take a look at its design. In the next section you see how the Wrox Blog application is designed, what classes are involved, and how the code is able to operate with different kinds of databases.

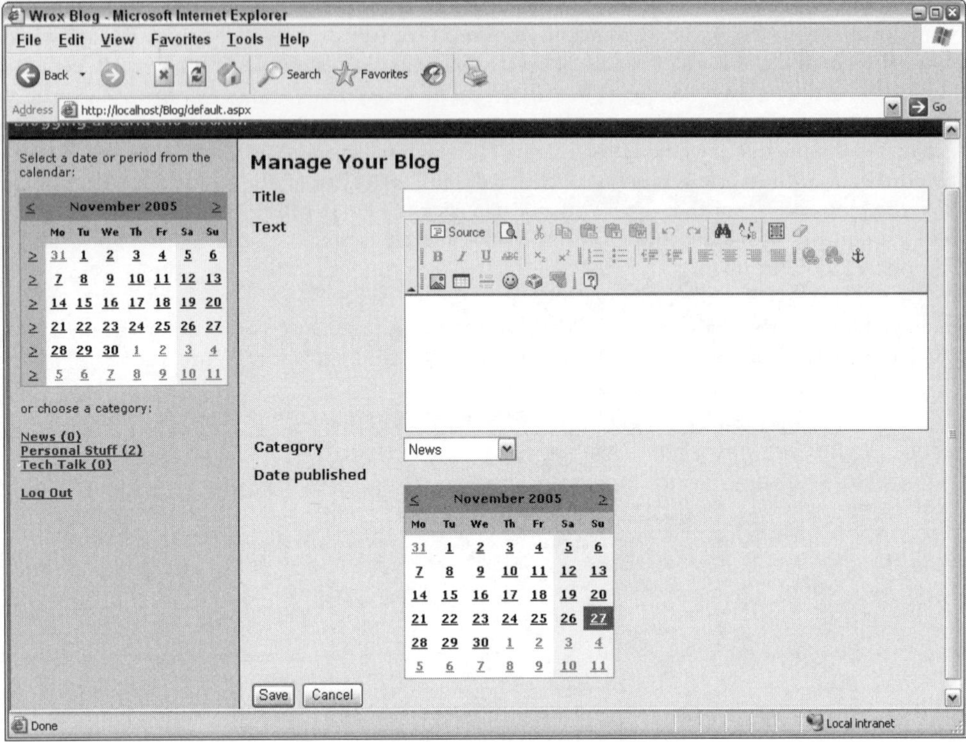

Figure 6-3

Design of the Wrox Blog

The Wrox Blog is designed as a three-tier application, meaning the application consists of a presentation layer, a business layer, and a data access layer. The presentation layer consists of two ASP.NET user controls that are discussed later in the chapter. Both the business and the data access layers contain custom classes defined in the files in the special App_Code folder in the root of the web site. You find the files related to the business layer in the subfolder called BusinessLogic, and the data access layer is placed in the DataAccess folder. This distinction isn't really necessary, because the ASP.NET run time compiles each file it finds in the App_Code folder or any of its subfolders automatically. However, placing the files in separate folders makes it easier to see to what layer each file and class belongs. The files in the folder are named after the classes they contain, so you'll find the class `BlogManager` in the file BlogManager.vb, and so on.

The Business Layer

The business layer of the Wrox Blog is built around two important entities: the `BlogEntry` and the `BlogManager` classes. The `BlogEntry` class represents a blog entry that is stored in the database and can be viewed on the web site, and the `BlogManager` class is responsible for getting the blog entries in and out of the database. In addition to these two important classes, you'll also find a `UserManager` class in the BusinessLayer folder. This class is used to allow users to log in and retrieve information about the roles they are assigned to when you're using an Access database. ASP.NET 2.0 provides a very convenient platform that handles user authentication and role management for you. However, this framework works only with SQL Server and not with a Microsoft Access database. To still allow you to log in to the site when you're using an Access database, the `UserManager` class provides the necessary methods.

To see what these classes can do, each of them is discussed in the following sections.

The BlogEntry Class

The `BlogEntry` class is used to represent a blog post that gets stored in the database and that can be viewed on the web site. All the interaction with a `BlogEntry` instance is done by the `BlogManager`. Therefore, the `BlogEntry` class, depicted in Figure 6-4, has only public properties and no methods (other than its two constructors).

Figure 6-4

The following table lists all of the public properties of the `BlogEntry` class:

Property	Data Type	Description
`Body`	String	This property holds the text for the blog entry.
`CategoryId`	Integer	This indicates to which category the blog entry belongs.
`DatePublished`	DateTime	This property holds the date and time the blog entry was published.
`Id`	Integer	This is the unique ID of the blog entry and is assigned by the database automatically whenever a new item is created.
`Title`	String	This is the title of the blog entry as it appears on the `BlogEntries` user control.

In addition to these five properties, the `BlogEntry` class has two constructors. The first, a parameterless default constructor, is used to create an entirely new `BlogEntry` instance. The second, an overloaded version that accepts a `BlogEntry` instance's ID as an `Integer`, is used when an existing `BlogEntry` is re-created when it's being edited. The ID passed to the constructor is stored in the private field`_Id` and is made available through the public and read-only property `Id`. You see both constructors at work later when the code is discussed in more detail.

Because the `BlogEntry` class is used only to hold data and cannot perform any operations, another class is needed that can work with instances of the `BlogEntry`. That class is the `BlogManager`.

The BlogManager Class

Quite the opposite of the `BlogEntry` class, the `BlogManager` class (see Figure 6-5) has only shared methods and no properties. It also has one private constructor to prevent calling code from creating instances of the `BlogManager` class.

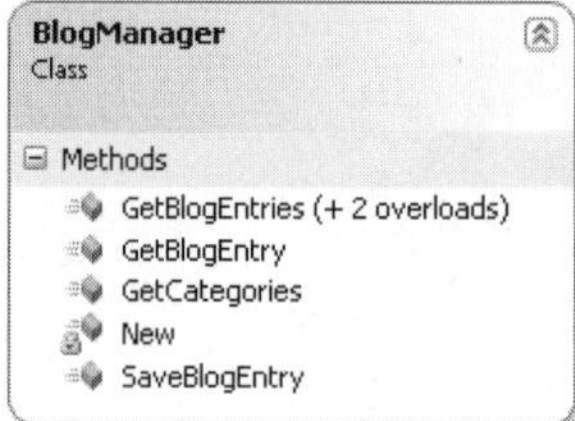

Figure 6-5

As you can see by the method names in Figure 6-5, the `BlogManager` class is not only responsible for working with blog entries, but is also capable of retrieving a list of categories. In larger applications it would be a wise design decision to introduce separate `Category` and `CategoryManager` classes, but in a relatively small application like the Wrox Blog it's perfectly acceptable to designate one class for multiple tasks.

These methods need some explanation, so the following table describes all of them in more detail:

Method	Return Type	Description
`Public Shared Function GetBlogEntries () As DataSet`	DataSet	This method returns the latest 15 blog entries from the database by calling into the `BlogManagerDB` class.
`Public Shared Function GetBlogEntries (ByVal categoryId As Integer) As DataSet`	DataSet	Returns all blog entries in the specified category from the database by calling into the `BlogManagerDB` class.
`Public Shared Function GetBlogEntries (ByVal startDate As DateTime, ByVal endDate As DateTime) As DataSet`	DataSet	Returns all blog entries in the specified period from the database by calling into the `BlogManagerDB` class. If `startDate` and `endDate` are the same, blog entries are returned for a single day.

Method	Return Type	Description
`Public Shared Function GetBlogEntry (ByVal blogEntryId As Integer) As BlogEntry`	BlogEntry	This method retrieves a single `BlogEntry` instance from the database based on the `blogEntryId` passed to this method. It does this by calling `GetBlogEntry` in the `BlogManagerDB` class. Because this method is only used when editing blog entries, the code checks if the current user is a member of the Administrator group and throws an exception if this isn't the case.
`Public Shared Function GetCategories () As DataSet`	DataSet	Returns the available categories as a DataSet.
`Public Shared Sub SaveBlogEntry (ByVal myBlogEntry As BlogEntry)`	n/a	This method saves a blog entry in the database. This can be a completely new or an updated blog entry. Just as with `GetBlogEntry`, this method checks the access rights of the current user.

In Figure 6-5 you see the method `GetBlogEntries` with (+ 2 overloads) behind its name. In the table describing the methods, you see `GetBlogEntries` listed three times. Although the name of these three methods is the same, their argument lists differ. There is a version without arguments, one that accepts the ID of the category, and one that accepts a start and end date. To avoid cluttering up the class diagram, these methods have been grouped together under one method name in Figure 6-5. To help you see the method has overloads, (+ 2 overloads) is put behind the method name.

The class diagram in Figure 6-5 also shows a `New` method with a little lock icon in front of it. This is the constructor for the `BlogManager` class. Because this class exposes only shared methods (that operate on the class itself, rather than on an instance of the class) the constructor has been hidden by marking it as private. This makes it impossible for calling code to create new instances of the `BlogManager` class. All classes in the App_Code folder for the Wrox Blog except the `BlogEntry` class follow this pattern and thus have a private constructor.

The final class in the BusinessLayer folder is the `UserManager` class, which is discussed next.

The UserManager Class

The ASP.NET 2.0 Framework provides very powerful yet easy-to-use features to manage authentication and role membership. These features are referred to as the Membership and Role providers. By simply activating these features in your application's configuration, the application is able to allow users to log in and grant them different rights depending on the roles they are assigned to. These providers have one great shortcoming: They work only with SQL Server and not with another database such as Microsoft Access. The provider model allows developers to override the behavior of the default providers, so it is possible to write your own providers that work with an Access database instead of with SQL Server. Because of the large amount of functionality and methods these providers offer, writing your own provider can easily be the subject of an entire chapter or book. Because the Wrox Blog doesn't need all this functionality, it contains a simple alternative in the form of the `UserManager` class. This class has a single method called `GetUserRoles` (see Figure 6-6) that retrieves the roles for a user.

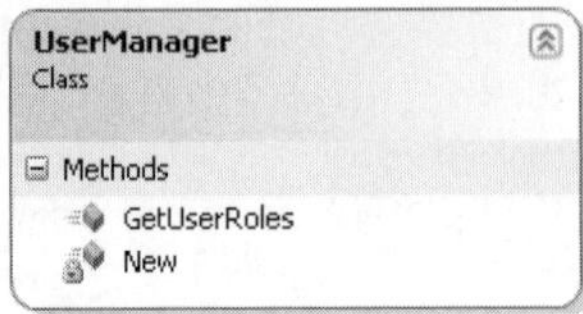

Figure 6-6

The `GetUserRoles` method accepts the username and a hash of the user's password and returns a list with the roles the user has been assigned to (that is, if the user was found in the database, of course). These roles are then used by the application to determine the access rights for the user. This method is used in the Login page that is discussed later.

For the `BlogManager` and the `UserManager` classes in the business layer, you'll find a database counterpart that ends with DB inside the DataAccess folder. These classes carry out database interaction and are discussed next.

The Data Access Layer

One of the main design goals for the Wrox Blog was database independence. Because it's likely you use this application with a remote host, you can't know in advance whether that hosts supports SQL Server 2005 or just Microsoft Access. So, the code should work with SQL Server and with a Microsoft Access database without any modification. When you look at the three classes present in the data access layer, you won't be able to see that these can work with multiple databases at the same time. Instead, these classes expose a single interface with methods that can work with different kinds of databases. This is made possible by a concept called *factories*, something you see more about when the code is discussed later. To understand how this all works, and why this is so great, you need to look a bit at the history of ASP and ADO.

When the .NET Framework version 1.0 was released, one area that caused a lot of confusion among developers was the way databases were accessed. In classic ASP—or to be more exact, with classic ADO—you had a single object model that could work with a wide variety of databases. Simply by passing a proper connection string to a `Connection` object you could talk to SQL Server, Access, Oracle, and other databases. Recordsets retrieved through that connection always worked the same, and exposed the same set of methods. However, with .NET, things changed drastically. Instead of a generic `Connection` or `Recordset` object, developers were faced with objects bound to specific providers. For example, for the SQL Server provider, you have a `SqlConnection` and a `SqlDataReader`; for the OleDb provider there is an `OleDbConnection` and an `OleDbDataReader`; and so on. The only exception is the DataSet that, instead of being tied to a specific data provider, is hosted in the general System.Data namespace. Though these strongly typed objects brought great performance and a rich feature set targeted at the specific provider, developers wanting to target both SQL Server and Oracle or any other database at the same time were faced with a huge challenge. To work around this problem, a few methods are available.

First, there is the abstract base class model. In this model, a designer creates an abstract base class (a class that must be inherited and cannot be instantiated directly) or an interface that supplies the signature of each of the necessary methods, like `GetBlogEntry` and `GetCategoriesList`. Then for each required database provider a child class is created that inherits from this base class or implements the appropriate interface. This concrete child class then implements each of the methods defined in the contract of the base class or interface. At run time, the proper child class is instantiated and the appropriate methods are called. This solution results in good performance because each of the child classes uses the most appropriate data providers, so the SQL Server implementation of the child class can benefit from the optimizations found in the SQL Server provider, for example. The downside of this solution is the amount of code required. For each new database provider, an entirely new child class needs to be created and maintained.

Another solution to write database-independent code is to write against the generic interfaces of each of the important data access objects. Each of the main ADO.NET objects, like a `Connection`, a `DataReader`, and so on, implements a specific interface. The `SqlConnection` implements `IdbConnection`, an `OleDbDataReader` implements `IdataReader`, and so on. With this solution, you have to create a method that returns the proper object type, based on the provider you want to use. This method could look similar to this:

```
Public Function GetConnection() As IDbConnection
  Select Case GetProviderFromConfiguration()
    Case "System.Data.SqlClient"
      Return New SqlConnection()
    Case "System.Data.OleDb"
      Return New OleDbConnection()
  End Select
End Function
```

This method looks up the requested provider from the application's configuration file, for example, and returns the appropriate connection type. The biggest downside of this method is that you use the generic interface shared by all providers. This means you can, by default, only use the common denominator shared by all providers. It also means that you should modify this code whenever a new provider is added to the application.

Along come .NET 2.0 and ADO.NET 2.0 with a *factories pattern* that solves many of these problems. In a factory pattern, a class is responsible for creating instances of other classes. In the Wrox Blog, the `DbProviderFactories` class from the `System.Data.Common` namespace is used. This class is able to create instances of other classes that are used to interact with databases. In terms of design, the ADO.NET factories pattern looks a lot like the generic interface solution you just saw. However, implementing it is now a lot more straightforward. You see the code to actually implement this later in the section "Writing Provider-Independent Code."

Even though .NET 2.0 fixes many of the problems related to object instantiation, some impacting differences between each data provider still exist that make it difficult to write data provider-independent code. These differences include the use of built-in functions, the capabilities of stored procedures, and the way parameters are passed to stored procedures. Not all of these problems can be fixed completely, but with some careful planning and some smart helper code it is possible to work around most of these limitations. Later in this chapter, when the inner workings of the code are discussed in the data access layer, you see the code responsible for these workarounds.

Now that you have some background on the design goals and decisions made for the data access layer of the Wrox Blog, take a look at the actual classes defined in this layer. Because the `BlogEntry` class in the business layer does not have its own behavior, you'll see no `BlogEntryDB` class in the data access layer. Instead, all interaction with the database to get information about blog entries and to save them is carried out by the `BlogManagerDB` class.

The BlogManagerDB Class

The `BlogManagerDB` class has the exact same methods as the `BlogManager` class. However, the `BlogManagerDB` class is responsible for actually getting the requested data from and into the database. The `BlogManagerDB` class does not only work with blog items or lists of entries; it's also responsible for getting a list with the available blog categories from the database.

Figure 6-7 lists the four methods and the private constructor defined in this class.

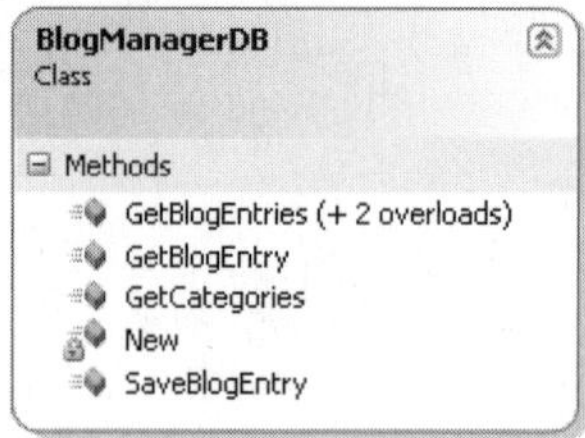

Figure 6-7

Each of these methods and their overloads, except the constructor, are discussed in the following table:

Method	Return Type	Description
`Public Shared Function GetBlogEntries () As DataSet`	DataSet	This method returns the latest 15 blog entries from the database, again by calling a stored procedure or query.
`Public Shared Function GetBlogEntries (ByVal categoryId As Integer) As DataSet`	DataSet	Returns all blog entries in the specified category from the database.
`Public Shared Function GetBlogEntries (ByVal startDate As DateTime, ByVal endDate As DateTime) As DataSet`	DataSet	Returns all blog entries in the specified period from the database. If `startDate` and `endDate` are the same, entries are returned for a single day.
`Public Shared Function GetBlogEntry (ByVal blogEntryId As Integer) As BlogEntry`	BlogEntry	This method retrieves a single `BlogEntry` instance from the database based on the `blogEntryId` passed to this method. It does this by calling a stored procedure (or query) in the database. The procedures used in the data access layer are discussed later.

Method	Return Type	Description
`Public Shared Function GetCategories () As DataSet`	DataSet	Returns the available categories as a DataSet.
`Public Shared Sub SaveBlogEntry (ByVal myBlogEntry As BlogEntry)`	n/a	This method saves a blog entry in the database. This can be a completely new or an updated blog item.

To simplify the data access code so it can work with multiple databases, there is also a `DalHelpers` class (see Figure 6-8) that serves as a helpers class for the data access layer (DAL). This class has a single method called `ReturnCommandParamName`.

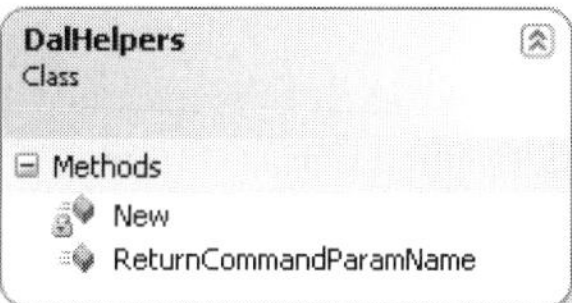

Figure 6-8

The `ReturnCommandParamName` method accepts the name of a parameter that must be passed to a stored procedure (in SQL Server) or a query (in Microsoft Access) and returns the correctly formatted parameter name. For SQL Server this is the name prefixed with an at symbol (@), whereas for Access this is a single question mark symbol (?) without the initial name. You see later why and how this code is used.

The UserManagerDB Class

Just as the `UserManager` class in the business layer, the `UserManagerDB` class has a single method called `GetUserRoles`, as shown in Figure 6-9.

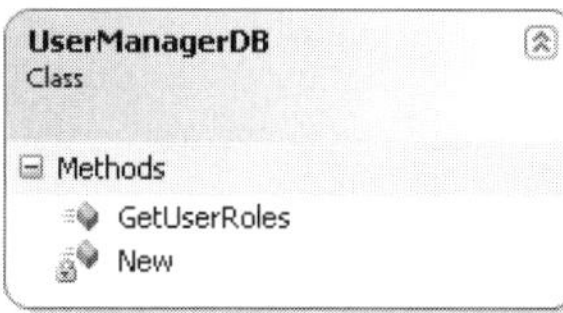

Figure 6-9

To simplify the code to log in a user, the traditional `LoginUser` and `GetRoles` methods have been combined into one method. The `GetUserRoles` method functions as a `LoginUser` method in that it accepts the user's name and a hashed password. It then returns the roles for the user as an ArrayList if the user is found in the database, or `Nothing` otherwise.

The Data Model

Because the Wrox Blog can work with SQL Server and a Microsoft Access database, you'll find both these databases in the App_Data folder if you installed the application with the supplied installer. It should come as no surprise that both databases have a similar data model. Figure 6-10 shows the database model for SQL Server 2005 as it looks in Visual Web Developer.

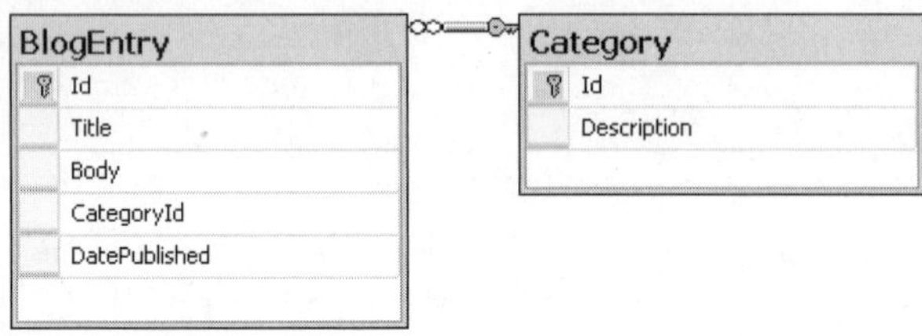

Figure 6-10

The BlogEntry table contains five columns, each of which is described in the following sections. Note that the table lists both the data type for each column in SQL Server and in Microsoft Access.

The BlogEntry Table

The BlogEntry table stores the blog entries for the entire application. It should come as no surprise that this table has five columns that exactly map to each of the five public properties of the `BlogEntry` class. These five columns are discussed in the following table.

Column Name	Data Type SQL Server	Data Type Microsoft Access	Description
Id	`int (Identity)`	`AutoNumber`	The unique ID of each blog entry. This ID is generated automatically by the database each time a new record is inserted.
Title	`nvarchar(200)`	`Text (200)`	The title of the blog item. The title is displayed in the BlogEntries list.
Body	`nvarchar(MAX)`	`Memo`	Used to store the body text of the blog entry.
CategoryId	`int`	`Number`	The ID of the category to which the item belongs.
DatePublished	`datetime`	`Date/Time`	Stores the date and time the blog item was published.

Each record in the BlogEntry table is linked to a specific category in the Category table through its CategoryId column.

The Category Table

The Category table is a simple lookup table that holds an ID and a description for each category.

Column Name	Data Type SQL Server	Data Type Microsoft Access	Description
Id	`int(Identity)`	`AutoNumber`	The unique ID of each category. This ID is generated automatically by the database each time a new record is inserted.
Description	`nvarchar(100)`	`Text (100)`	The description of the category as it is displayed in the `BlogEntries-Filter` user control on the site.

The code in the business and data access layers is only used to insert and update blog items and to retrieve a read-only list of categories. If you want to manage the categories in the database with a web interface, you need to implement some CMS functionality, similar to that presented in Chapter 5.

Stored Procedures and Queries

To make the data access layer easier to write and maintain, it does not contain direct SQL statements. Instead, the code calls stored procedures (when SQL Server is used) or queries (in Microsoft Access) to get the data from and into the database. To a large extent, stored procedures and queries can perform the same actions. In the case of the Wrox Blog, they are used to select single and lists of records from the BlogEntry and Category tables, and to insert and update records in the BlogEntry table. You need to be aware of a few differences between the two types when you try to write provider-independent code. Take a look at the following snippet, which shows the stored procedure required to insert a new item in the BlogEntry table in SQL Server:

```
CREATE PROCEDURE sprocBlogEntryInsertSingleItem

@title nvarchar(200),
@body nvarchar(MAX),
@categoryId int,
@datePublished datetime

AS

  INSERT INTO
    BlogEntry
    (
      Title, Body, CategoryId, DatePublished
    )
    VALUES
    (
      @title, @body, @categoryId, @datePublished
    )
```

The same code in an Access query looks like this:

```
INSERT INTO
  BlogEntry (Title, Body, CategoryId, DatePublished)
  VALUES (?, ?, ?, ?);
```

As you can see, for a stored procedure you need to declare each parameter and its type explicitly. In an Access query, all you need to do is supply a question mark at the places where you want to insert a parameter. Sometimes when you save a query in Microsoft Access, it adds square brackets around the question mark parameter placeholders, causing the application to break. When this happens, remove the brackets and save the query again.

In addition to the name, the order in which parameters are sent to the database is important as well. SQL Server uses named parameters, so it doesn't care in which order the parameters are added. However, since Access has no way to figure out to which parameter you are referring because they all have the same name (only a question mark), you must pass the parameters in the order that the query expects them. In the preceding example, you'd need to pass the `Title` first, then the `Body`, the `CategoryId`, and finally the `DatePublished`.

In addition to these two tables that are present in both databases, the Microsoft Access database also has three tables to store users, roles, and the roles to which the users are assigned. The names of these tables match those in the SQL Server database that are created by the .NET 2.0 Framework.

Helper Classes

The final class that is hosted in the special App_Code folder is called `AppConfiguration` (see Figure 6-11). It has three read-only and shared properties called `ConnectionStringSettings`, `EmailFrom`, and `EmailTo`.

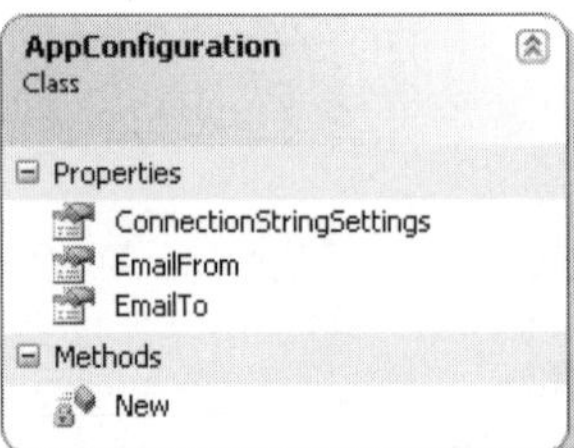

Figure 6-11

The `ConnectionStringSettings` property provides access to the active connection used in the application. This property plays a vital role in accessing different types of databases and is examined in great depth in the next section.

The other `EmailFrom` and `EmailTo` properties are used for sending e-mails with error information. You see where they are used exactly later in this chapter.

Code and Code Explanation

In this section you learn how all the different parts of the Wrox Blog, including the user controls `Blog Entries` and `BlogEntriesFilter` and the code in the App_Code folder, work and interact together. This section begins with some important files that are used by the entire application and then discusses the Controls folder that contains the user controls.

Root Files

Before dissecting the user controls and their code-behind that make up the largest part of the Wrox Blog, you should first look at the few files that are located in the root of the site. These files play an important role in authenticating a user. As stated previously, the ASP.NET run time takes care of user authentication and role membership when a SQL Server database is used. To accommodate for Microsoft Access as well, you need to write some custom code that authenticates a user and stores the roles the user is assigned to in a cookie so the roles are available to other pages throughout the lifetime of the user's session. Even though this authentication solution requires some custom code, you can still make use of the many available .NET classes.

Web.config

Just as with other ASP.NET applications, the Web.config file in the Wrox Blog is used for settings that apply to the entire application. In the Wrox Blog, this file contains a few important settings. At the top of that file, you'll find an `<appSettings>` key called `DefaultConnectionString`. The value of this key contains the name of one of the two connection strings defined in the same file. Both settings are used in the data access layer and are discussed later. The `EmailFrom` and `EmailTo` keys are used when sending error messages, described near the end of the chapter. Similar to the previous chapter, the `FCKeditor:UserFilesPath` key holds the path to the folder where files uploaded with the FCKeditor are stored.

Further down in the Web.config file, you also see two nodes called `<membership>` and `<roleManager>`. These nodes set up the membership and role providers for use with SQL Server, similar to those you saw in the previous chapter. On the `roleManager` node you see an important attribute called `enabled`. When this attribute is set to `true`, the Wrox Blog assumes that the ASP.NET authentication scheme is used, and will not attempt to authenticate the user manually but instead use the SQL Server database for authentication. When the attribute is `false`, the code in the Login.aspx page overrides the default login behavior and fires the custom code to authenticate the user against the Microsoft Access database.

Login.aspx

The markup of this file contains a small bit of HTML and a single `Login` control. Normally, this control takes care of authenticating a user against a SQL Server database using the built-in providers. However, in the `Authenticate` event of this control you'll see some code that overrides this behavior when the role manager is not enabled and fires when the user tries to log in. To ensure the custom code in the `Authenticate` event runs only when the Access database is in use, the following code in the `Page_Load` event dynamically hooks up the `Authenticate` event to the `Login1_Authenticate` method:

```
Protected Sub Page_Load(ByVal sender As Object, ByVal e As System.EventArgs) _
        Handles Me.Load
  If Page.IsPostBack AndAlso Roles.Enabled = False Then
    AddHandler Login1.Authenticate, AddressOf Login1_Authenticate
  End If
End Sub
```

When Roles are enabled for the application, the code in the `If` block won't run, allowing ASP.NET to fire its own code to authenticate a user against a SQL Server database. If Roles are disabled, this code causes the `Authenticate` event to fire the code defined in the `Login1_Authenticate` event handler.

The code inside that event handler retrieves the roles for the current user and stores them in an encrypted cookie. On subsequent requests to pages in the site, these roles are retrieved from the cookie again and assigned to the current user. This way, you have to access the database for role information only once, which greatly enhances the performance of your site. The code responsible for retrieving and storing the roles looks like this:

```
If Roles.Enabled = False Then

  Dim userName As String = Login1.UserName
  Dim passwordHash As String = _
          FormsAuthentication.HashPasswordForStoringInConfigFile( _
          Login1.Password, "MD5")

  Dim userRoles As ArrayList = UserManager.GetUserRoles(userName, passwordHash)
  ' The rest of the code is shown later
```

First, the code checks to see if roles are enabled for this application. This is controlled by the `Enabled` attribute on the `roleManager` element in the Web.config file. When this attribute is `False`, it is assumed that not SQL Server but a Microsoft Access database is used and that the custom authentication code should fire.

The username and password are retrieved from the standard `Login` control. This is a good example of mixing the available ASP.NET 2.0 functionality with custom code. Instead of writing a login page from scratch, you simply drop a `Login` control on your page, and overwrite the `Authenticate` event, while you still have access to the control's `UserName` and `Password` properties.

Passwords are not stored as plain text in the database; instead, only a hash of the password is saved. To compare that hash to the password the user entered, that password must be hashed as well using `FormsAuthentication.HashPasswordForStoringInConfigFile`. To create a hash for a password when you want to create a new user in the database, you can use that same method.

The username and password are then sent to the `GetUserRoles` method in the `UserManager` class. This method in turn sends them to the `GetUserRoles` method in the `UserManagerDB` class that tries to retrieve the roles for the user from the database. When the user is found and has roles assigned, those roles are returned as an `ArrayList`; otherwise the method returns `Nothing`. You see exactly how this method accesses the database in the section "Writing Provider-Independent Code" later in the chapter. The query that's responsible for retrieving the roles looks like this:

```
SELECT
  aspnet_Roles.Description
FROM
```

```
    aspnet_Users INNER JOIN (aspnet_Roles INNER JOIN aspnet_UsersInRoles ON
    aspnet_Roles.Id=aspnet_UsersInRoles.RoleId) ON
    aspnet_Users.Id=aspnet_UsersInRoles.UserId
  WHERE
    aspnet_Users.UserName=? And aspnet_Users.PasswordHash=?;
```

This query links the Users, Roles, and UsersInRoles tables together and returns the description of each role the user is assigned to. It uses a `WHERE` clause to filter the list to only the specified user and password hash. If the username or password is incorrect, no records are returned; otherwise a list with one or more role names is returned from the query.

Remember, you'll find this query only in the Access database. For SQL Server, the ASP.NET run time takes care of user authentication and role membership.

The `GetUserRoles` method in the `UserManagerDB` class passes the results up to the `UserManager` class, which returns the results to the calling code in the Login page where the remainder of the `Authenticate` event fires:

```
    If userRoles IsNot Nothing Then
      Dim userData As String = String.Empty
      For Each myRole As String In userRoles
        userData &= myRole & ","
      Next
      userData = userData.TrimEnd(","c)

      Dim ticket As New FormsAuthenticationTicket( _
        2, _
        userName, _
        System.DateTime.Now, _
        System.DateTime.Now.AddMinutes(30), _
        Login1.RememberMeSet, _
        userData, _
        FormsAuthentication.FormsCookiePath)

      Dim encTicket As String = FormsAuthentication.Encrypt(ticket)

      Response.Cookies.Add(New HttpCookie( _
              FormsAuthentication.FormsCookieName, encTicket))

      Response.Redirect(FormsAuthentication.GetRedirectUrl(userName, True))
    Else
      e.Authenticated = False
    End If
  End If
```

If the `GetUserRoles` method did not return `Nothing` (which means the user was found and had roles assigned) the `ArrayList` is used to build up a comma-separated list of roles. This list is then added to the `userData` field of a `FormsAuthenticationTicket`, a class that is used to create a wrapper around critical information for authentication that can be stored in a cookie. Its constructor expects a version number, the name of the user, the start and expiration date of the authentication period, a Boolean to indicate whether to create a persistent cookie, and the path to which the cookie should apply.

As the second-to-last parameter, the constructor also expects a `userData` parameter. In this parameter you can store user-related data that is saved with the cookie and can be retrieved on subsequent requests. In the preceding code, the comma-separated list of role names is stored in the cookie. These role names are retrieved later inside the Global.asax files and assigned to the user again.

When the ticket has been constructed, it's encrypted with the `Encrypt` method of the `Forms Authentication` class and stored in a cookie. At the end of the code, the user is redirected to the page he initially requested, or to the default homepage using `GetRedirectUrl`.

If authentication failed because the username or password were incorrect or the user did not have any roles assigned, the `Authenticated` property of the `AuthenticateEventArgs` parameter is set to `False`. This ensures that the `Login` control displays an error message to the user, saying that the login attempt failed.

Global.asax

The Global.asax file is responsible for retrieving the roles from the cookie that has been created by the Login page. Inside the Global file, you can write code for the `Application_AuthenticateRequest` event that is triggered for *each* request to the site. It fires before any code in the page itself runs, so it's a perfect location to retrieve the roles from the cookie and assign them to the user:

```
Sub Application_AuthenticateRequest(ByVal sender As Object, ByVal e As EventArgs)
  If User IsNot Nothing AndAlso User.Identity.IsAuthenticated Then
    If System.Web.Security.Roles.Enabled = False Then
      Dim id As FormsIdentity = CType(User.Identity, FormsIdentity)
      Dim ticket As FormsAuthenticationTicket = id.Ticket

      Dim roleAsString As String = ticket.UserData
      Dim roles() As String = roleAsString.Split(New Char() {","})
      Context.User = New GenericPrincipal(Context.User.Identity, roles)
    End If
  End If
End Sub
```

The code first checks if the `User` object exists and is authenticated. It also checks if the role manager is enabled, because when it is, ASP.NET takes care of role management and this custom code doesn't need to run.

If all these conditions are met, the `FormsAuthenticationTicket` is retrieved from the current user's `Identity`. ASP.NET handles all the steps required to create this identity and to retrieve and decrypt the cookie. Once the ticket is stored in a local variable, the comma-separated string with the role names can be retrieved from the `UserData` property. This string is then converted to an array using the `Split` method and assigned to the user for the current request by creating a new `GenericPrincipal` and passing the array of roles to its constructor.

Once the code in this event has finished, you can check whether a user is in a specific role with the following code:

```
If Context.User.IsInRole("Administrator") Then
  ' Run code for an Administrator
End If
```

The Global.asax file contains another method called `Application_Error` that is used to send application errors by e-mail. This method is discussed a bit later, but first you need to look at how you can write provider-independent code.

Writing Provider-Independent Code

In the discussion of the Login page you saw the `GetUserRoles` method in the `UserManagerDB` class. The discussion of how the database is accessed was skipped, so you could focus on the authentication mechanism instead. However, now is the time to look at that method in great detail because the concepts used in this method are used in all the data access code. The following code block lists the entire `GetUserRoles` function, which is then discussed line by line:

```
Public Shared Function GetUserRoles( _
    ByVal userName As String, ByVal passwordHash As String _
    ) As ArrayList

  Dim myFactory As DbProviderFactory = _
         DbProviderFactories.GetFactory( _
         AppConfiguration.ConnectionStringSettings.ProviderName)

  Dim myConnection As DbConnection = myFactory.CreateConnection

  myConnection.ConnectionString = _
         AppConfiguration.ConnectionStringSettings.ConnectionString
  myConnection.Open()

  Dim myCommand As DbCommand = myConnection.CreateCommand()

  myCommand.CommandText = "sprocUserGetRoles"
  myCommand.CommandType = CommandType.StoredProcedure

  Dim param As DbParameter
  param = myCommand.CreateParameter()
  param.ParameterName = DalHelpers.ReturnCommandParamName("userName")
  param.DbType = DbType.String
  param.Value = userName
  myCommand.Parameters.Add(param)

  param = myCommand.CreateParameter()
  param.ParameterName = DalHelpers.ReturnCommandParamName("passwordHash")
  param.DbType = DbType.String
  param.Value = passwordHash
  myCommand.Parameters.Add(param)

  Dim arrRoles As ArrayList = Nothing

  Dim myDataReader As DbDataReader = myCommand.ExecuteReader( _
        CommandBehavior.CloseConnection)
  If myDataReader.HasRows Then
    arrRoles = New ArrayList()
    Do While myDataReader.Read()
```

```
        arrRoles.Add(myDataReader.GetString( _
              myDataReader.GetOrdinal("Description")))
      Loop
    End If

    Return arrRoles
  End Function
```

Right below the function header, you see code that creates a variable of type `DbProviderFactory` that gets a value by calling `GetFactory` on the `DbProviderFactories` class. You can see this `DbProviderFactory` as a class this is capable of creating different instances of database-related objects like connections and commands. To tell it what kind of object you want to create (such as a `SqlConnection` or an `OleDb Connection`) you need to pass it a `ProviderName`. If you're targeting SQL Server, you should pass it `System.Data.SqlClient`, and for an Access database you should pass `System.Data.OleDb`.

When you think about how you want to pass the right `ProviderName` to this method, your first idea might be to store it in the Web.config with a key like `DefaultProvider`. Then you can use `ConfigurationManager.AppSettings.Get("DefaultProvider")` to get the provider name from the Web.config file and pass it to the constructor of the factory. Although this would certainly work, ASP.NET 2.0 offers a much more elegant solution to the problem. This is where the `ConnectionStringSettings` property in the custom `AppConfiguration` class comes in. In .NET 1.x the only way to store a connection string was to add it to the general `<appSettings>` section in the Web.config. ASP.NET 2.0, however, has a new `<connectionStrings>` element available in the Web.config file that allows you to get strongly typed information about the chosen connection. Take a look at the `ConnectionStringSettings` property to see how this works:

```
Public Shared ReadOnly Property ConnectionStringSettings() As _
        ConnectionStringSettings
  Get
    Dim connectionStringKey As String = _
        ConfigurationManager.AppSettings.Get("DefaultConnectionString")
    Return ConfigurationManager.ConnectionStrings(connectionStringKey)
  End Get
End Property
```

This code first retrieves the default connection string key from the database. This is a custom key defined in the Web.config file that can hold either `SqlServerConnectionString` (for the SQL Server connection) or `AccessConnectionString` (for the Access database connection). This key is then used to retrieve the connection string *settings* that belong to that key. The `ConnectionStringSettings` class exposes both the `ConnectionString` and the `ProviderName`, provided that you supplied that name on the connection string in the Web.config file. Both connection strings in the Web.config file have that name set. Here's how the connection string for SQL Server with the `providerName` attribute looks:

```
<add name="SqlServerConnectionString" connectionString="server=(local)\SqlExpress;
        AttachDbFileName=|DataDirectory|Blog.mdf;Integrated Security=true;
        User Instance=true" providerName="System.Data.SqlClient"
/>
```

If you look at the code that instantiates the factory, you'll see how it all fits together:

```
Dim myFactory As DbProviderFactory = _
  DbProviderFactories.GetFactory( _
  AppConfiguration.ConnectionStringSettings.ProviderName)
```

Imagine that in the Web.config file the `DefaultConnectionString` key is set to `SqlServerConnectionString`. Then the `ConnectionStringSettings` property of the `AppConfiguration` class returns a reference to the connection with the name `SqlServerConnectionString` in the Web.config file. This connection in turn has a `providerName` of `System.Data.SqlClient`. Passing this provider name to the `GetFactory` method tells it you want it to instantiate objects that are part of the SQL Server provider, like the `SqlConnection` and `SqlCommand` objects.

Note that you cannot pass arbitrary provider names to the factory. Each data provider that is present on your system should register itself in the machine.config file for your server. Only those providers that are registered can be created by the factory.

Once the factory has been created, creating an instance of a provider object is as simple as calling a method:

```
Dim myConnection As DbConnection = myFactory.CreateConnection()

myConnection.ConnectionString = _
    AppConfiguration.ConnectionStringSettings.ConnectionString
myConnection.Open()
```

This code uses `CreateConnection` to create a connection object. If the `DefaultConnectionString` is set to `SqlServerConnectionString`, the variable `myConnection` now holds a `SqlConnection`. If the application was configured to use the Access database instead, the connection would be of type `OleDbConnection`.

Once the connection is created, it's opened with the connection string that is also retrieved from the `ConnectionStringSettings` property.

```
Dim myCommand As DbCommand = myConnection.CreateCommand()

myCommand.CommandText = "sprocUserGetRoles"
myCommand.CommandType = CommandType.StoredProcedure
```

The next step is to create a command object and assign it a `CommandText` and a `CommandType`. This is similar to data access code you saw in previous chapters.

To pass both the username and password to the query, two parameter objects are created with the `CreateParameter` method:

```
Dim param As DbParameter
Param = myCommand.CreateParameter()
param.ParameterName = DalHelpers.ReturnCommandParamName("userName")
param.DbType = DbType.String
param.Value = userName
myCommand.Parameters.Add(param)
```

Again, this code is very similar to code you saw before. What is different, though, is the way the parameter name is set up. You'll recall from earlier in the chapter that SQL Server uses an at symbol (@) in front of the parameter name, whereas Access doesn't use the name at all but only uses a question mark. The `ReturnCommandParamName` method in the `DalHelpers` class takes care of that:

```
Public Shared Function ReturnCommandParamName( _
    ByVal paramName As String) As String
  Dim returnValue As String = String.Empty
  Select Case AppConfiguration.ConnectionStringSettings.ProviderName.ToLower()
    Case "system.data.sqlclient"
      returnValue = "@" & paramName
    Case "system.data.oledb"
      returnValue = "?"
    Case Else
      Throw New NotSupportedException("The provider " & _
          AppConfiguration.ConnectionStringSettings.ProviderName & _
          " is not supported")
  End Select
  Return returnValue
End Function
```

This method simply looks at the current provider name and formats the parameter accordingly. Given the example of the `userName` parameter, this function returns `@userName` for SQL Server and only `?` for an OleDb connection. When an unknown provider is encountered, an error is thrown.

The remainder of `GetUserRoles` opens a `DataReader` to see if the query returned any roles and then adds them to an `ArrayList`, which is returned at the end of the function.

Once you understand how the `GetUserRoles` method works, you'll have no trouble understanding all the other methods in the data access layer. All those methods use the same principle to instantiate connection, command, and datareader objects. The only differences you'll see in those methods are related to what the method must do. Some of these differences are discussed in the next section, which deals with the two user controls that make up the Wrox Blog application.

The Controls Folder

To make it easy to plug the Wrox Blog into an existing application, the presentation layer of the application consists of only user controls. The code download for this application comes with a Login.aspx page and a Default.aspx as well, but those are only used to demonstrate how the blog is incorporated in an existing site. If you want to use the blog application in your site, all you need is the two user controls from the Controls folder, the code in the App_Code folder, and some helper assets—such as the Css and FCKeditor folders—and some settings from the Web.config file. Refer to the section "Setting up the Wrox Blog" later in the chapter to find out more about installing the blog application.

The Controls folder contains two user controls called BlogEntriesFilter.ascx and BlogEntries.ascx. The first control allows a user to select specific entries using the calendar or the category list. The other control presents the selected blog items and allows you to edit them. Because the filter criteria selected in the `BlogEntriesFilter` control are used to determine the items displayed in the `BlogEntries`, the filter control is discussed first.

BlogEntriesFilter.ascx

The only purpose of the `BlogEntriesFilter` user control is to allow users to select a period of time (either a single date or an entire week) or a category for which they want to see blog entries. Once the criteria are known, the user control adds those criteria to the query string and reloads the current page. The `BlogEntries` control then looks at these parameters and loads the correct list of blog entries.

The user has two options to select the criteria. At the top of the BlogEntriesFilter control you find an <asp:Calendar> control that allows you to select a single date or an entire week. The latter is made possible by setting the control's SelectionMode property to DayWeek. This draws a greater-than symbol in front of each week's row.

When a new date or week has been chosen, the calendar fires its SelectionChanged event that then executes the following code:

```
If calBlogEntries.SelectedDates.Count > 0 Then
  Dim startDate As DateTime = calBlogEntries.SelectedDates(0)
  Dim endDate As DateTime = _
       calBlogEntries.SelectedDates(calBlogEntries.SelectedDates.Count - 1)

  Dim queryString As String = String.Empty

  If Request.QueryString.Count > 0 Then
    queryString = Server.UrlDecode(Request.QueryString.ToString())
    If Request.QueryString.Get("startDate") IsNot Nothing Then
      queryString = queryString.Replace("startDate=" & _
            Request.QueryString.Get("startDate"), "startDate=" & _
            startDate.ToShortDateString())
    Else
      queryString &= "&startDate=" & startDate.ToShortDateString()
    End If
    If Request.QueryString.Get("endDate") IsNot Nothing Then
      queryString = queryString.Replace("endDate=" & _
            Request.QueryString.Get("endDate"), "endDate=" & _
            endDate.ToShortDateString())
    Else
      queryString &= "&endDate=" & endDate.ToShortDateString()
    End If
  Else
    queryString = String.Format("startDate={0}&endDate={1}", _
          startDate.ToShortDateString(), endDate.ToShortDateString())
  End If

  Response.Redirect(Request.CurrentExecutionFilePath & "?" & queryString)
End If
```

This code first ensures that at least one date is selected on the calendar. It then creates two variables called startDate and endDate, both of which are retrieved by looking at the SelectedDates property. This property exposes the selected dates as an array of DateTime objects in sorted order. To get at the last element in the array, the end date selected on the calendar, SelectedDates.Count -1, is used.

The remainder of the code in this method is responsible for assigning the startDate and endDate to a variable called queryString. Because the user control BlogEntriesFilter can be used in pages that use their own query string parameters, you can't just replace the entire query string with the start and end dates. Instead, this code first assigns the entire query string to the queryString variable. Then when there is already a start date variable present (possibly from an earlier selection on the calendar), its value is replaced with the newly selected date. If the query string variable wasn't present, it is added to the queryString variable instead. To see how this works, take a look at the following two examples.

First, imagine the current query string is something like this:

```
id=123&someVariable=456
```

The code then sees that there is already a query string but it doesn't contain a start date. This means the `startDate` parameter is added so the `queryString` variable ends up like this:

```
id=123&someVariable=456&startDate=12/12/2005
```

Now imagine that this page is loaded again so it now contains the start date. When the user selects a different date, such as 12/5/2005, the code in `SelectionChanged` sees there is already a `startDate` present so instead of appending it to `queryString`, it replaces its value, like this:

```
id=123&user=456&startDate=12/5/2005
```

This ensures that any existing `queryString` variable remains intact while the `startDate` variable simply has its value updated with the new date.

The same process is used to get the value of the `endDate` into the `queryString` variable. Once the entire query string has been set up, the page is reloaded by redirecting to `Request.CurrentExecution FilePath`, which returns the name of the current page, and appends the `queryString` variable to it.

The other method that allows users to choose the blog entries they want to see is with the list of categories in the `BlogEntriesFilter` control. This list, implemented as a simple `<asp:Repeater>` control, displays the available categories that are linked to the current page with the ID of the category in the query string. That `Repeater` control has a `HeaderTemplate` and a `FooterTemplate` that start and close a simple HTML `<ul>` tag. The `ItemTemplate` then defines a `<li>` item for each category like this:

```
<li><asp:HyperLink ID="hyperCategory" runat="server"
    NavigateUrl='<%#GetNavigateUrl(Eval("Id")) %>'
    Text='<%#Eval("Description") & " (" & Eval("NumberOfBlogEntries") & ")" %>' />
</li>
```

Inside the `Page_Load` method this `Repeater` control gets its data by calling `GetCategories()` in the `BlogManager` class like this:

```
repCategories.DataSource = BlogManager.GetCategories()
repCategories.DataBind()
```

The `BlogManager` class then delegates its responsibility to the `BlogManagerDB` class to get the categories from the database. That method calls the stored procedure or query called `sprocCategorySelectList` with code very similar to the code you saw for `GetUserRoles` earlier in this chapter.

Once the data gets bound to the control with `DataBind()`, the `GetNavigateUrl` method is called for each item. This method is defined in the code-behind for the `BlogEntriesFilter` control and works pretty much the same as the `SelectionChanged` code for the Calendar in that it tries to find a CategoryId in the query string and then tries to replace its value. If the variable is not found, the value for CategoryId is appended to the `queryString` variable in exactly the same way as is done with the `startDate` and `endDate` variables. What's different, though, is that this code also *removes* any date variables from the query string. The `BlogEntries` user control you see later looks at the date variables first. When they are present, it uses those to get the requested blog entries. This means that if you want to displays entries from a certain category, you have to remove all traces of the date variables from the query string.

The final thing you need to look at in the BlogEntriesFilter list is the code for Page_Load. This code first tries to retrieve the start date and end date from the query string. If they are there, a loop is set up that preselects the dates between the start date and the end date:

```
While endDate >= startDate
  calBlogEntries.SelectedDates.Add(startDate)
  startDate = startDate.AddDays(1)
End While
```

While endDate is still larger than startDate, the date held in startDate is selected on the calendar. The variable startDate is then increased by one day and the loop continues. This makes all dates between the start and end date appear as selected on the calendar, so it's easy for users to see which date or period they selected.

With the filter control set up, it's time to look at the BlogEntries user control that is responsible for displaying the selected blog entries.

BlogEntries.ascx

This user control is used for two distinct tasks: It can display a list with blog items for the requested category or period and it allows an administrator to add new or edit existing entries. To provide a clean interface to the end-user of the application, the page is split up using two <asp:Panel> controls. The first displays the list of blog posts; the other provides a form where an administrator can create new or edit existing posts. At any given time, only one of the two panels is visible.

Showing Blog Entries

The first panel, called pnlBlogEntries, displays a label telling the user how many blog entries were found. It also has a DataList control that displays all the blog entries returned from the database:

```
<asp:DataList ID="dlBlogEntries" runat="server" Width="100%">
  <ItemTemplate>
    <div class="ItemHeading"><h3>
      <%#Convert.ToDateTime(Eval("DatePublished")).ToLongDateString() + " at " +
           Convert.ToDateTime(Eval("DatePublished")).ToLongTimeString()%>
    </h3></div>
    <h2><%#Eval("Title")%>
      <asp:LinkButton id="lnkEdit" runat="server" CommandName="Edit"
        Text="(Edit This Entry)" CssClass="EditLink"
        CommandArgument='<%#Eval("Id")%>' Visible='<%#CanEdit()%>'>
     </asp:LinkButton></h2>
    <div class="BlogEntryText"><asp:Literal ID="litBodyText" runat="server"
            Text='<%#Eval("Body") %>'></asp:Literal></div>
  </ItemTemplate>
</asp:DataList>
```

This template displays a small <h3> tag with the date and time the entry was posted. This is followed by an <h2> tag that displays the title of the blog item. After the title an Edit This Entry link is displayed. The visibility of that link is determined by the property CanEdit that you'll find in the code-behind for the user control. This property returns True when the user has been assigned to the Administrator role or False otherwise. You should also notice the CommandArgument property of the Edit link. This is used later in the editing process to determine which entry must be edited.

The DataList control gets its data from the LoadData method in the user control. This method looks at the query string to see which entries to load. The blog entries can be retrieved from the database in three ways: either by a start and end date, a category ID, or with no filter criteria at all. The code first tries to find out if there is a query string called StartDate. If there is, both the startDate and endDate variables get a value and the overloaded version of GetBlogEntries that accepts two dates is called.

If there is no StartDate query string but there is one for the CategoryID, another overloaded version of GetBlogEntries is called that gets passed the ID of the chosen category. Finally, if there is no query string at all, the parameterless version of GetBlogEntries is called that retrieves the latest 15 blog entries from the database.

The three overloaded versions of GetBlogEntries share a lot of code, so you'll see the one that accepts two dates only. The code starts off with creating a DbProviderFactory, a connection, and a command object in exactly the same way as in the GetUserRoles method you saw earlier. Once those objects are created, two parameters are created for the start and the end date, using ReturnCommandParamName to get the proper parameter names.

A little trick was deployed for the endDate parameter. As you recall, the end date is ultimately retrieved from the calendar when the user selects a new date or period. This date does not contain a time part so when a new DateTime object is created from the query string value, its time part defaults to 12 midnight. However, the stored procedure that gets the blog entries from the database, called sprocBlogEntry SelectListByDate, uses BETWEEN to select the right BlogEntry records like this:

```
-- SELECT list and FROM clause go here

WHERE
  (BlogEntry.DatePublished BETWEEN @startDate AND @endDate)
```

Now, imagine that startDate is 12/12/2005 and endDate is 12/18/2005. Because the endDate defaulted to 12 midnight, this query does not return blog entries that have been created on December the 18*after* midnight. To make sure that entries are retrieved that have been created somewhere during the day, one day is added to the endDate parameter like this:

```
        param.Value = endDate.AddDays(1)
```

This ensures that all blog posts with a creation date less than December 19th at midnight are returned, which includes all entries created on the 18th.

Once the parameters have been set up correctly, a new DataAdapter is created with the CreateData Adapter method. This adapter then fills a DataSet, which is returned to the calling code like this:

```
      Dim myDataAdapter As DbDataAdapter = myFactory.CreateDataAdapter()
      myDataAdapter.SelectCommand = myCommand
      myDataAdapter.Fill(myDataSet)
      myConnection.Close()
      Return myDataSet
```

The two other overloaded versions of GetBlogEntries that retrieve blog posts for a specific category or the latest 15 posts work pretty much the same way. The biggest differences are the parameters that are set up and the name of the stored procedure that gets the data from the database.

The DataSet returned from `GetBlogEntries` is ultimately assigned to the `DataSource` property of the `DataList` control in the `BlogEntries` user control that is then responsible for displaying all the selected blog posts on the web page.

Depending on the type of filter chosen, the `LoadData` method sets up the text for the `lblResults` label. When a period of time was chosen, the label displays something like, "Below you find blog entries posted between 12/12/2005 and 12/18/2005." When a category was selected in the `BlogEntriesFilter`, the label displays the name of the chosen category by looking at the Description column of the first record returned from the database:

```
lblResults.Text = "Below you find blog entries posted in the category " & _
          myDataSet.Tables(0).Rows(0)("Description").ToString() & "."
```

When no filter has been chosen, and the blog list just displays the most recent entries, the label is filled as follows:

```
lblResults.Text = "Below you find the latest " & myDataSet.Tables(0).Rows.Count & _
         " blog entries posted on the site."
```

This concludes the discussion of displaying blog posts with the user control. The final part you need to look at is managing blog posts as an administrator.

Managing Blog Entries

If you are a member of the Administrator role you have two ways to manage blog entries. The first is with the Create New Entry button that allows you to create a new blog entry. The other way is with the Edit This Entry link that appears after each published entry. Both the Create New Entry button and the Edit link become visible automatically when you're logged in as an Administrator.

In both scenarios editing is done in the panel `pnlAddEditBlogEntry` that is hidden until you click the New button or the Edit link. This panel contains a few controls that allow you to enter details about an entry, such as its title, the body text, a category, and the publication date. This form looks very similar to the one you used in the previous chapter to manage content in the Wrox CMS. It also features the FCKeditor to allow you to enter rich content for the body text of the entry.

If you click the Create New Entry button, the following code in the code-behind fires:

```
Protected Sub btnCreateNewBlogEntry_Click(ByVal sender As Object, _
          ByVal e As System.EventArgs) Handles btnCreateNewBlogEntry.Click
  pnlAddEditBlogEntry.Visible = True
  pnlBlogEntries.Visible = False
  txtTitle.Text = ""
  txtBody.Value = ""
  lstCategory.SelectedIndex = -1
  calDatePublished.SelectedDate = DateTime.Now.Date
  ViewState("EditingId") = Nothing
End Sub
```

This code hides the List panel and shows the Edit panel. It also clears the form controls that may still have a value from a previous edit action. To make it easier for a user to post a new blog entry, the `SelectedDate` on the calendar is set to today's date. Of course you can still choose a different date if you want.

The drop-down for the categories deserves a close examination:

```
<asp:DropDownList ID="lstCategory" runat="server"
       DataSourceID="ObjectDataSource1" DataTextField="Description"
       DataValueField="Id">
</asp:DropDownList>
```

To get a list with categories, the drop-down has its `DataSourceID` set to an `ObjectDataSource` control defined at the end of the page. An `ObjectDataSource` works similarly to a `SqlDataSource` control you saw in earlier chapters in that it can retrieve data from a data source that can be used by a control like the drop-down list. It's different in that it doesn't access a database directly, but instead calls a method in the business layer of the site. If you look at the definition for the `ObjectDataSource` control you can see how this works:

```
<asp:ObjectDataSource ID="ObjectDataSource1" runat="server"
       SelectMethod="GetCategories" TypeName="BlogManager">
</asp:ObjectDataSource>
```

The `TypeName` in the tag points to the `BlogManager` class defined in the business layer of the Wrox Blog. The `SelectMethod` then points to the method in that class that must be invoked to get the requested data. Because the `GetCategories` is defined as `Shared` in the code, the `ObjectDataSource` doesn't require an instance of the `BlogManager`. However, if the method hadn't been marked `Shared`, the .NET 2.0 Framework would automatically try to instantiate an instance of the `BlogManager` before it calls the `GetCategories` method. `ObjectDataSource` controls are a great way to enforce a three-tier architecture for your application, because they remove the need for the `SqlDataSource` controls that clutter up your pages with SQL statements. You can read more about the `ObjectDataSource` controls in Chapter 12.

When editing a blog entry, the `Visibility` property of the two panels is changed as well. However, when the Edit button is clicked, the form's controls should be prepopulated with information from the BlogEntry. Because the Edit link is contained in the `DataList` control, you can't directly write an event handler for it like you did with the `btnCreateNewBlogEntry` button. You saw earlier that the Edit link had a `CommandName` and a `CommandArgument` set up inside the `ItemTemplate` for the `DataList`. These properties are used in the `EditCommand` event for the `DataList` that fires when the Edit button is clicked:

```
Protected Sub dlBlogEntries_EditCommand(ByVal source As Object, _
          ByVal e As System.Web.UI.WebControls.DataListCommandEventArgs) _
          Handles dlBlogEntries.EditCommand
  Dim id As Integer = Convert.ToInt32(e.CommandArgument)
  Dim myBlogEntry As BlogEntry = BlogManager.GetBlogEntry(id)
  If myBlogEntry IsNot Nothing Then

    ' Fill the form fields; this is shown later.

  End If
End Sub
```

This code retrieves the ID of the selected blog entry from the `CommandArgument` of the Edit link. With this ID the proper `BlogEntry` record is retrieved from the database by calling `GetBlogEntry`. Because the `GetBlogEntry` method can be used only by an administrator, the code in the business layer checks role membership:

```
Public Shared Function GetBlogEntry(ByVal blogEntryId As Integer) As BlogEntry
  If HttpContext.Current.User.IsInRole("Administrator") Then
    Return BlogManagerDB.GetBlogEntry(blogEntryId)
  Else
    Throw New NotSupportedException("Calling GetBlogEntry is not allowed when " & _
        "you're not a member of the Administrator group.")
  End If
End Function
```

When the user is not an administrator, an error is thrown. Otherwise, `GetBlogEntry` in the `BlogManagerDB` class is called. By now, the code in this method should look familiar. Connection and command objects are created by calling the appropriate factory methods. Then the name of the stored procedure or query is set and a parameter for the ID of the blog entry is created, again using `ReturnCommandParamName` to get the right name, depending on the current connection type.

Finally, a `DataReader` is opened and a new blog item is created and filled when the item was found in the database:

```
    Using myReader As DbDataReader = _
          myCommand.ExecuteReader(CommandBehavior.CloseConnection)
      If myReader.Read() Then
        myBlogEntry = New BlogEntry(myReader.GetInt32(myReader.GetOrdinal("Id")))
        myBlogEntry.Title = myReader.GetString(myReader.GetOrdinal("Title"))
        myBlogEntry.Body = myReader.GetString(myReader.GetOrdinal("Body"))
        myBlogEntry.CategoryId = myReader.GetInt32(myReader.GetOrdinal("CategoryId"))
        myBlogEntry.DatePublished = _
                  myReader.GetDateTime(myReader.GetOrdinal("DatePublished"))
      End If
      myReader.Close()
    End Using
  End Using
  Return myBlogEntry
```

The code in the `EditCommand` handler checks if the `BlogEntry` instance returned from `GetBlogEntry` is not `Nothing`. If it isn't, the blog entry's ID is stored in `ViewState` so it's available later when the item is saved. Then the controls on the form are filled with the public properties from the blog entry:

```
ViewState("EditingId") = id
pnlAddEditBlogEntry.Visible = True
pnlBlogEntries.Visible = False
txtTitle.Text = myBlogEntry.Title
txtBody.Value = myBlogEntry.Body
If lstCategory.Items.FindByValue(myBlogEntry.CategoryId.ToString()) _
       IsNot Nothing Then
  lstCategory.Items.FindByValue( _
       myBlogEntry.CategoryId.ToString()).Selected = True
End If
calDatePublished.SelectedDate = myBlogEntry.DatePublished.Date
```

Because it is possible that a category has been removed from the database, and is no longer present in the drop-down list, `FindByValue` is used to find out if it is possible to preselect the right category. When the item is not found, the drop-down simply preselects the first item in the list.

Whether you are creating a new or updating an existing BlogEntry object, the final step in the process is saving it. This is done with the Save button at the end of the form that triggers the following code:

```
Protected Sub btnSave_Click(ByVal sender As Object, _
      ByVal e As System.EventArgs) Handles btnSave.Click
  Page.Validate()

  If calDatePublished.SelectedDate <> DateTime.MinValue Then
    If Page.IsValid Then
      Dim myBlogEntry As BlogEntry
      If ViewState("EditingId") IsNot Nothing Then
        myBlogEntry = New BlogEntry(Convert.ToInt32(ViewState("EditingId")))
      Else
        myBlogEntry = New BlogEntry
      End If
      myBlogEntry.Title = txtTitle.Text
      myBlogEntry.Body = txtBody.Value
      myBlogEntry.CategoryId = Convert.ToInt32(lstCategory.SelectedValue)
      myBlogEntry.DatePublished = calDatePublished.SelectedDate

      BlogManager.SaveBlogEntry(myBlogEntry)
```

The ID of the BlogEntry class has been made read-only to avoid calling code from changing it during the object's lifetime. However, when an item is being edited, the ID must be made available in the BlogEntry object somehow, so SaveBlogEntry knows which item to update in the database. This is why the BlogEntry class has two constructors. The parameterless version is used to create a new object without its ID set. The second, overloaded constructor accepts the ID of the blog entry in the database, which is then stored in the private_Id field. The value of this field can later be retrieved through the public (and read-only) Id property, as you see in the code for the SaveBlogEntry method.

The SaveBlogEntry method in the BlogManager class performs the same security check as the GetBlog Entry method you saw earlier. If the user is an administrator, the BlogEntry instance is forwarded to SaveBlogEntry in the BlogManagerDB class that saves the entry in the database. Once again, this data access method sets up a connection object by calling the appropriate method on the DbProviderFactory class. Then a command object is created and its CommandText is set:

```
If myBlogEntry.Id = -1 Then ' Insert a new item
  myCommand.CommandText = "sprocBlogEntryInsertSingleItem"
Else
  myCommand.CommandText = "sprocBlogEntryUpdateSingleItem"
End If
```

Earlier you saw that when you're editing a blog entry, its ID is retrieved from ViewState and passed to the overloaded constructor of the BlogEntry class. In the SaveBlogEntry this ID is used to determine which stored procedure or query to call. If the ID is still -1, a new blog entry is created, so the CommandText is set to sprocBlogEntryInsertSingleItem. If there is an existing ID, sprocBlogEntryUpdateSingleItem is used instead.

The SQL Server stored procedures and Microsoft Access queries look pretty similar. The following snippet shows the Access query to update an existing blog item:

```
UPDATE
  BlogEntry
SET
  Title = ?, Body = ?, CategoryId = ?, DatePublished = ?
WHERE
  Id = ?;
```

The stored procedure for SQL Server contains the following code:

```
@id int,
@title nvarchar(200),
@body nvarchar(MAX),
@categoryId int,
@datePublished datetime

AS

  UPDATE
    BlogEntry
  SET
    Title = @title,
    Body = @body,
    CategoryId = @categoryId,
    DatePublished = @datePublished
  WHERE
    Id = @id
```

Except for the way the parameters are named, these procedures are identical. These different parameter names are once again taken care of by the `ReturnCommandParamName`.

Because the parameters have no name in an Access database, it's important they are added in the right order. The `Id` parameter is used in the `WHERE` clause at the end of the `UPDATE` statement, so its parameter must be added last as well.

Once all the parameters have been set up correctly, the database is updated by calling `ExecuteNonQuery()` on the `Command` object.

When the code in the `SaveBlogEntry` methods has finished, control is returned to the `BlogEntries` control that then executes `EndEditing()` so the list with blog entries is refreshed:

```
    myBlogEntry.DatePublished = calDatePublished.SelectedDate

    BlogManager.SaveBlogEntry(myBlogEntry)
    EndEditing()
  End If
```

`EndEditing()` hides the Edit panel and shows the List panel again. It then calls `LoadData()` to ensure the blog list displays up-to-date information.

With the `SaveBlogEntry` method you have come to the end of the `BlogEntries` control. With the code you have seen you can now create new blog items and manage existing ones. You can also list the blog items in the `BlogEntries` control using the filters from the `BlogEntriesFilter` control.

Structured Error Handling and Logging

Chapter 5 told you that this chapter would cover a way to handle errors in ASP.NET applications. However, so far you haven't seen any code that puts that into practice. Yet the Wrox Blog does deploy a nice way of catching and logging errors. At the same time, end-users are shielded from nasty error messages and instead get a friendly page stating that somehow an error occurred. "How does this work?" you may ask. To understand how this error-handling mechanism works, you need to look at two important areas: configuration and handling and logging errors.

Configuration

First, there is an important setting in the Web.config file called `<customErrors>`. When you add a new Web.config file to your application, this element is commented out so it doesn't do anything. However, in the Wrox Blog, the comment tags are removed and the element is changed so it now looks like this:

```
<customErrors mode="On" defaultRedirect="Error.aspx">
  <error statusCode="404" redirect="Error.aspx"/>
  <error statusCode="500" redirect="Error.aspx"/>
</customErrors>
```

Now whenever an error occurs, ASP.NET looks at this element to see how to handle it. The `defaultRedirect` is the page in your site you want to redirect the user to whenever an error occurs that isn't handled. On this page, you can display a message telling users that the server encountered an error, that you are aware of it, and you are busy fixing it while they are reading that message.

You also see different `<error>` nodes for each type of error. You can use these settings to redirect to different pages for different errors. For example, when a page cannot be found, the web server throws a 404 error. You can then set up an `<error>` node with a `statusCode` of `404` that redirects to PageNot Found.aspx where you can tell the users the page could not be found and offer them a way to search the site, for example. You could do the same with 500 errors (server errors) and redirect to another page instead. Any error code not specifically set by an `<error>` element is sent to the page specified in `defaultRedirect`. In the case Wrox Blog application, the different error codes all point to the same file.

Sending your users to a friendly error page is only one piece of the puzzle. All it does is shield the user from ugly-looking error messages. However, with only these settings, you'll never be aware the errors occurred in the first place, so you can't fix them. This is where the Global.asax file comes into play again.

Handling and Logging Errors

Whenever an unhandled exception in your site occurs — for instance, because the database is down, a user entered bad data in the system, or because a requested page could not be found or processed — two things happen. One of the things the ASP.NET run time does is redirect the user to the specified error page as you saw in the previous section. However, before it does that, it fires the `Application_Error` event that you can handle in the Global.asax file. Inside that event you can get access to the error that occurred with `Server.GetLastError()`. Once you have a reference to that error, you can build up a message with the error details and send it to yourself by e-mail. This is exactly what is being done in the Global.asax for the Wrox Blog:

```
Sub Application_Error(ByVal sender As Object, ByVal e As EventArgs)
  Dim sendMailOnErrors As Boolean = True
  If sendMailOnErrors Then
```

```
    Dim subject As String = "Error in page " & Request.Url.ToString()
    Dim errorMessage As StringBuilder = New StringBuilder
    Dim myException As Exception = HttpContext.Current.Server.GetLastError()

    If myException IsNot Nothing Then
      Do While myException IsNot Nothing
        errorMessage.Append("<strong>Message</strong><br />" & _
            myException.Message & "<br /><br />")
        errorMessage.Append("<strong>Source</strong><br />" & _
            myException.Source & "<br /><br />")
        errorMessage.Append("<strong>Target site</strong><br />" & _
            myException.TargetSite.ToString() & "<br /><br />")
        errorMessage.Append("<strong>Stack trace</strong><br />" & _
            myException.StackTrace & "<br /><br />")
        errorMessage.Append("<strong>ToString()</strong><br />" & _
            myException.ToString() & "<br /><br />")
        myException = myException.InnerException
      Loop
    Else
      errorMessage.Append("No exception information available.")
    End If

    Dim mySmtpClient As SmtpClient = New SmtpClient()
    Dim myMessage As MailMessage = New MailMessage( _
        AppConfiguration.EmailFrom, AppConfiguration.EmailTo, subject, _
        errorMessage.ToString().Replace(ControlChars.CrLf, "<br />"))
    myMessage.IsBodyHtml = True

    mySmtpClient.Send(myMessage)
  End If
End Sub
```

This code starts off by declaring a variable that determines whether or not error messages should be sent by e-mail. You can use this variable to quickly turn off error handling when you're developing new things. You could also move it to a key in the Web.config file and create an entry in the `AppConfiguration` class for it.

The error (the exception in .NET terminology) is retrieved with `HttpContext.Current.Server.GetLastError()`. There is one thing you should be aware of when you call this method. Whenever an exception occurs in your site somewhere, ASP.NET wraps that exception inside a general `HttpUnhandledException`. By default, this exception doesn't provide you with much detail. However, the original exception (such as a `NullReferenceException`, an `ArgumentException`, or any of the other exception types) is available in the `InnerException` of the error returned from `GetLastError()`. The loop in the code gets the exception's `InnerException` as long as there is one; this way, you can get detailed information not only about the generic outer exception, but also about each inner exception it contains.

If you're not interested in the hierarchy that leads to the innermost exception, you can use `GetBaseException()` to get the exception that is the root cause of the problem, like this:

```
Dim myException As Exception = _
       HttpContext.Current.Server.GetLastError().GetBaseException()
```

All the error information from the exceptions is appended to a `StringBuilder` using the `.Append()` method. At the end, that error message is added as the body of the e-mail message using its `ToString()`

method. Notice the use of `AppConfiguration.EmailFrom` and `AppConfiguration.EmailTo` to get the e-mail address from the Web.config file through the `AppConfiguration` class.

Finally, the mail message is sent using `mySmtpClient.Send(myMessage)`. This method uses the SMTP server defined in the `<mailSettings>` element in the Web.config file:

```
<system.net>
  <mailSettings>
    <smtp deliveryMethod="Network">
      <network host="smtp.YourProvider.Com" port="25" />
    </smtp>
  </mailSettings>
</system.net>
```

If you can't get the error handling to work, check that you defined a valid SMTP server in the configuration file. Also, make sure that `EmailFrom` and `EmailTo` defined in the same file contain valid e-mail addresses.

You can expand the code in `Application_Error` so it sends you even more useful information. To diagnose complicated errors it can be useful to have an overview of information like the user's cookies, session variables, and various server settings found in `Request.ServerVariables`. With these additions, you can make the error message even more usable.

With this code setup, you get an e-mail with detailed error information whenever an error occurs on the server. This should enable you react quickly and efficiently, fixing possible bugs before they get worse and trouble many users.

This also concludes the detailed discussion of the Wrox Blog, its design, and its code. In the next section you learn how to install the Wrox Blog and embed it in your own site.

Setting up the Wrox Blog

You can choose to install the Wrox Blog application manually or by using the installer application supplied on this book's CD-ROM. The installer not only installs the necessary files for the Wrox Blog, but also creates a sample web site that uses the user controls of the Wrox Blog. Running the installer creates a virtual directory under IIS called Blog. The folder that is created by the installer contains the full source for the Wrox Blog.

Alternatively, you can choose to unpack the supplied zip file to a folder on your machine. This gives you a bit more choice with regard to where the files are placed, but you'll have to add the necessary files to an existing or new web site manually.

For both installation methods it's assumed that the .NET 2.0 Framework, which is an installation requirement for Visual Web Developer, has already been installed. It's also assumed that you have installed SQL Server 2005 Express Edition with an instance name of `SqlExpress`. If you chose a different instance name, make sure you use that name in the connection string for the Wrox Blog in the Web.config file.

Using the Installer

To install the Wrox Blog follow these steps:

1. Open the folder Chapter 06 - Wrox Blog\Installer from the CD-ROM that came with this book and double-click setup.exe to start up the installer.
2. In the Setup wizard, accept all the defaults by clicking Next until the application has been installed completely. Click Close to close the installer.
3. Next, open up the Web.config file in the Blog's folder (by default, located at `C:\Inetpub\wwwroot\Blog`) and verify that the two connection strings for the Access database and SQL Server are correct. For the Access database, verify that the path to the .MDB file is correct. For SQL Server, ensure that the name of the SQL Server instance is correct.
4. Set the `DefaultConnectionString` key to the connection you want to use. When you set it to `AccessConnectionString`, make sure you set the `enabled` attribute of the `<roleManager>` element to `False`. When you use a SQL Server connection, set that same attribute to `True`.
5. Now browse to `http://localhost/Blog`. The Wrox Blog application should appear. Click the Login link and log in with a username of `Administrator` and a password of `Admin123#`.

Manual Installation

If you want to add the Blog application to a new or an existing application, you shouldn't use the supplied installer; you'll have to follow these steps instead:

1. Start by creating a brand new web site in Visual Web Developer.
2. Open the folder Chapter 06 - Wrox Blog\Source from the CD-ROM that comes with this book and extract the contents of the file Chapter 06 - Wrox Blog.zip to a folder on your hard drive.
3. Open aWindows Explorer and browse to the folder that contains the unpacked files. Next, arrange both Visual Web Developer and the Windows Explorer in such a way that both are visible at the same time.
4. In the Windows Explorer, select the folders App_Code, App_Data, Bin, Controls, Css, and FCKeditor, as well as the files ErrorPage.aspx, ErrorPage.aspx.vb, Web.config, and Global.asax. Then drag the selected folders and files from the explorer window onto the project in the Solution Explorer in Visual Web Developer. When prompted if you want to overwrite any of the files, click Yes. You should end up with a Solution Explorer that looks like Figure 6-12.

Figure 6-12

5. Open the file Default.aspx and create a skeleton for your page that can hold the `BlogEntries Filter` and `BlogEntries` controls. You can use tables or any other HTML tag to control the page layout.

6. Next, switch to Design View for the page, and from the Controls folder on the Solution Explorer, drag the BlogEntriesFilter.ascx on the design surface at the location where you want the control to appear. Repeat this step for the BlogEntries.ascx control. You should end up with markup similar to this:

```
<table>
<tr>
  <td>
    <Wrox:BlogEntriesFilter ID="BlogEntriesFilter1" runat="server" />
  </td>
  <td>
    <Wrox:BlogEntries ID="BlogEntries1" runat="server" />
  </td>
</tr>
</table>
```

7. Open the Web.config file and locate the `<connectionStrings>` element. Make sure that the connections for SQL Server and the Access database are set up correctly. If necessary, change the path to the Access database and the name of your SQL Server instance. Also check that the `Default ConnectionString` setting points to the database you want to use. Finally, when you're using SQL Server, make sure you set the `enabled` attribute of the `<roleManager>` to `True`. When you use an Access database, set the `enabled` attribute to `False`.

8. You can now open the page in the browser by pressing F5 in Visual Web Developer. If everything went as planned, you should now see the `BlogEntriesFilter` control and the list with blog entries appear.

Note that you cannot edit blog entries at this stage because you have no way of authenticating the user. If you want to use the supplied Microsoft Access database, you can simply copy the page Login.aspx (and its code-behind file) from the supplied code file into your new web project and request it in the browser. You can then log in with the account `Administrator` with the password `Admin123#`.

If you're using a SQL Server database, you can configure the application so it supports the Membership and Role providers. To do that, choose Website⇨ASP.NET Configuration from the main menu in Visual Web Developer. Then click the Security tab in the browser window that opened and create a new security role called Administrator. Next, create a new account and assign it to the role you just created.

If you need more information about how the Web Site Administration Tool works, click the "How do I use this tool?" link in the upper-right corner of the screen.

Once the application is configured correctly, create a new file and call it Login.aspx. From the Toolbox, drag a `Login` control on the page. Alternatively, you can use the Login.aspx file from the code that comes with this book and modify it to suit your needs. If you're using SQL Server and you get an error stating that `sprocUserGetRoles` could not be found, make sure you have set the `enabled` attribute of the `<roleManager>` to `True` in the Web.config file.

Now that you've set up the Wrox Blog successfully, browse to this book's download page at `www.wrox.com` and check out how you can modify your blog.

Summary

In this chapter you saw how to create and use a blogging application that can easily be incorporated in an existing web site. You saw how to use the blog application from an end-user's point of view.

You learned how the Wrox Blog application is designed and what classes it contains. You also read about the challenges developers face when writing database-independent code and the possible solutions to overcome these problems.

In the code explanation section you learned how to write code that can work with a SQL Server and an Access database at the same time. Using the new factories pattern of the .NET 2.0 Framework enables you to greatly decrease the complexity of writing code that can be run against multiple databases. In this section you also saw how the classes and pages that make up the Wrox Blog application work internally, and how they communicate with each other.

Wrox Photo Album

In recent years, the phenomenon of photo album web sites has provided viewers access to digital images that capture the essence of an amateur or professional photographer's work. From personal family pictures to highly specialized artistic imaging, the Web is a great way to share photography from any source to the known digital world. A popular approach to sharing pictures over the Internet is to use an online photo album or catalogue of sorts. In this way, pictures can be logically grouped into collections and include contextual information for a viewer to properly observe the photograph in all its glory.

Although they usually serve the same overall purpose, photo album web sites exist in all sorts of styles and flavors. From thumbnail generators to photograph-editing batched systems, these image manipulation applications provide a wide array of features. However different and extensive they may be, they all usually provide a list of essential features, including the following:

- View thumbnails of digital photos in a grid-like fashion
- Click a single photo to view a larger or full-size version.
- Upload a new digital picture file.
- Enter a name and/or description for the picture.
- Classify the picture as a specific category or type.
- Edit an existing picture's contextual information.
- Delete an existing picture.

These features alone would substantiate a useful web site package that any reasonable web developer would consider as a valid third-party software purchase. However, it is often difficult to modify such software applications or tools, because they often lock the developer into the standardized views and limit control over the display and position of the images on the web page. From the format of the font to the size of the thumbnails, there are usually undesirable constraints to customizing the web site design and implementation, unless the programmer has access to the source code files where the changes can occur. These considerations would point to the selection of an open source codebase to develop an online photo album, allowing for a maximum amount of customization with a nominal amount of time and effort.

The Wrox Photo Album is a great sample project that allows for easy customizations to be made on the display and functionality of a photo album web site. It implements not only the new development approaches to security and data, but also the desirable features that the user would expect for a better-than-average online photo album.

This chapter takes a practical approach to understanding some of the newer concepts now available in ASP.NET 2.0 by analyzing the implemented features within the Wrox Photo Album. Some of the new features you tackle include data binding, themes, security, page markup, and navigation.

In the section "Wrox Photo Album Design," you explore the design of the application in great detail. This includes the structure of the web site, the pages and user controls, the database and data model used, file management, and image storage considerations.

The section titled "Code and Code Explanation" performs a thorough and complete examination of the areas of development necessary for storing and displaying photo albums online in the most effective fashion. It reviews the classes involved, as well as the specific areas of focus in which a developer could modify the application to his or her specific needs.

The final section reviews how to extract and customize the photo album in a development environment, and how to install it to production. First things first, though: You need to know how to use the photo album before you can modify or enhance it.

Using the Wrox Photo Album

Using the Wrox Photo Album is actually quite simple. If you have ever used a photo album or similar sort of digital image application in the past, you'd agree that the features and functionality of this photo album exist in similar fashion. Many of the common features shared across different picture viewing applications exist in the Wrox Photo Album as you would expect, in a predictable fashion.

If the Wrox Photo Album web site has been successfully installed (refer to the section "Setting up the Project" later in this chapter), you can browse to view the site by going to `http://localhost/photoalbum`. The screen displayed in Figure 7-1 appears.

At the top of the menu are several links to choose from:

- Photo Albums
- About Me
- Contact Me
- Site Map
- Admin

These are considered the main menu items of the web site and can be edited within the site's XML site map navigation file. The next section discusses the editing process in greater detail.

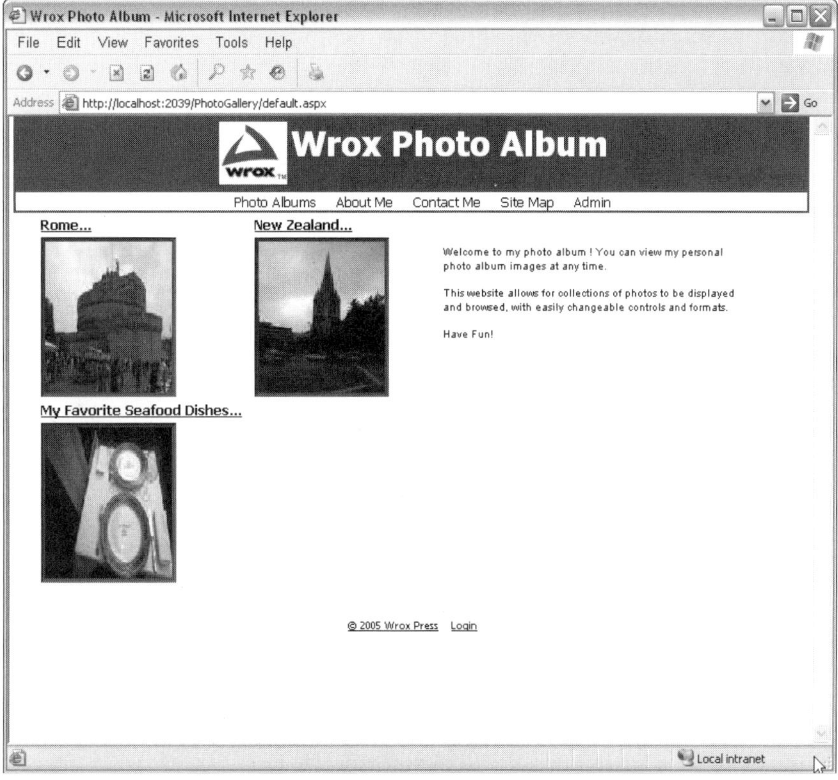

Figure 7-1

Clicking one of the main collection images — the images directly beneath the main menu items — loads up the collection contents page, which consists of a grid of images, displayed in Figure 7-2.

Further clicking on any of these images loads the photo detail page, as shown in Figure 7-3.

The look and feel of the web site is managed by the use of ASP.NET 2.0 feature *themes*. Themes are essentially sets of user interface management files, which allow the entire application's look and feel to be easily modified at the change of a single configuration entry. You learn more about themes and skins in the design section to follow.

The homepage is basically a photo selection page (see Figure 7-2) where you will see a list of large thumbnail images displayed for each collection. These images are simply the first photo from each of the collections arbitrarily selected in order to graphically represent the collection. The page contains a user control for the bulk of the image display screens of the application. The groups of digital images are called *collections*, and the images are referred to as *photos*. Each collection can have any number of photos. Collections also have a name and a description. Each photo can have a name, description, and a collection to which it belongs. You can click one of the collection thumbnails to display the contents of the collection, which are the photos themselves. Once the actual photos of a collection are displayed, you can click an individual photo in order to view its full and unaltered state.

By clicking the About Me link, you'll see there is a placeholder for the artist or photographer to identify themselves pictorially. In similar fashion, the Contact Me page has the same placeholder.

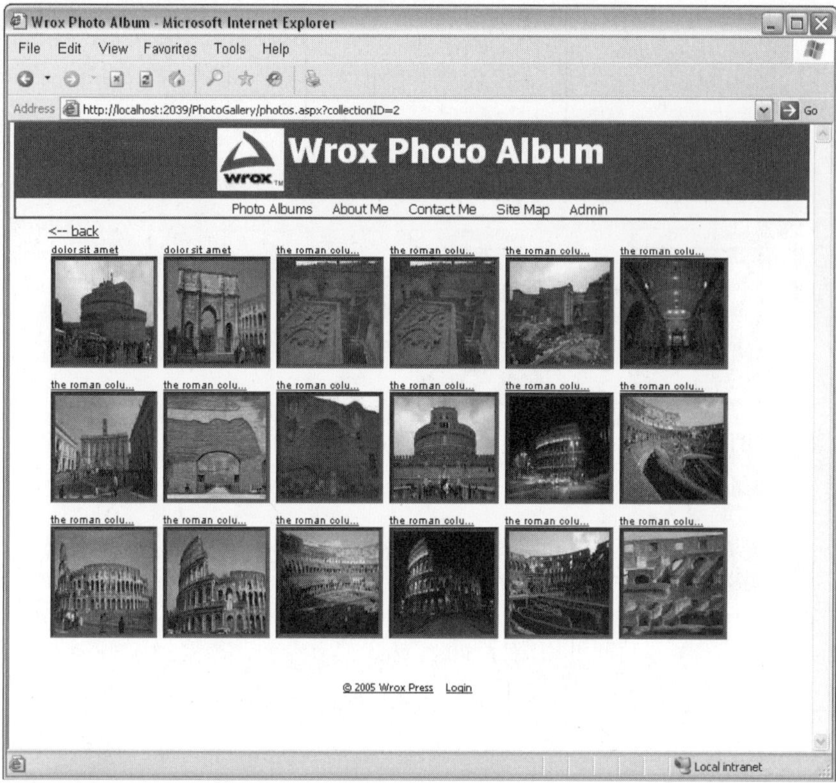

Figure 7-2

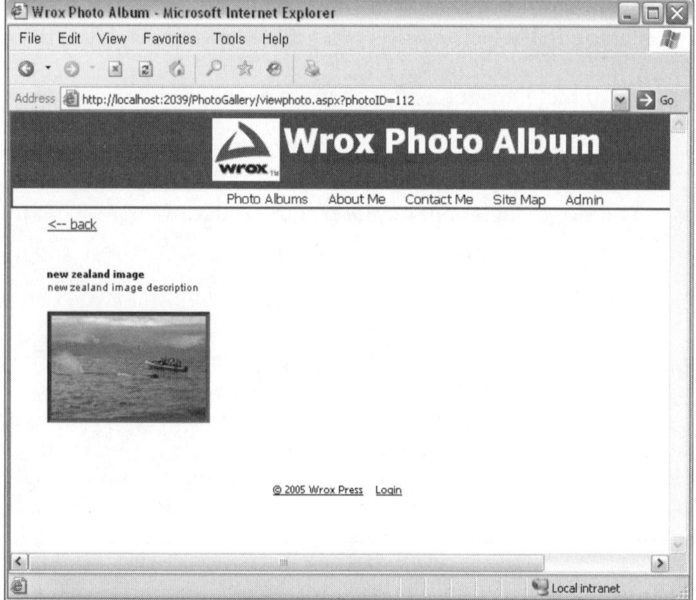

Figure 7-3

Figure 7-4 depicts the simple Contact Me page, with a placeholder for the web site owner's picture.

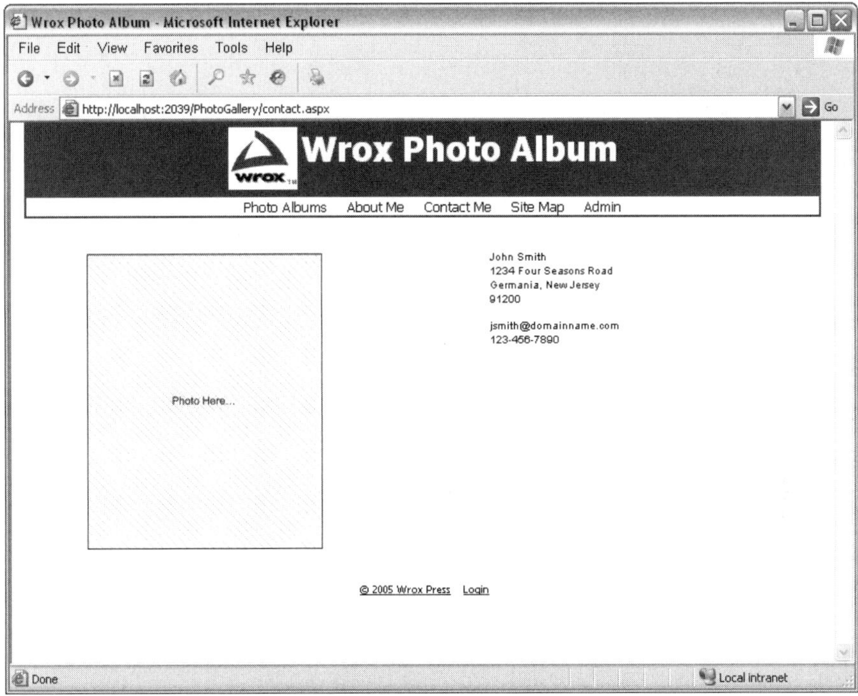

Figure 7-4

The site map page contains a data-bound `TreeView` control, which contains links to each page on the web site, just like the main menu at the top of the screen.

When you click Admin from the main menu, you enter into the secure administrator section of the web site. You're greeted with a `Login` control to authenticate your user credentials in the system. If you're not sure what your password is you can click the Password Recovery hyperlink at the bottom of the `Login` control. Once you're logged into the system, you will see the main menu for the administrator area, shown in Figure 7-5.

Figure 7-5 shows the main menu administration page, with a `GridView` control displaying all of the collections in the system by default. From this page, you're greeted with a list of the existing collections the system contained in a `GridView` control. This grid contains collections of photos that you can add or delete at will. On the right-hand side of the grid, you see clickable hyperlinks for editing or deleting a collection. You also see a hyperlink for editing the photos contained within a collection.

Clicking the Edit Photos link loads the page displaying the photos within that collection in an editable grid (see Figure 7-6). This grid has all you will need to manage the existing photos in the system.

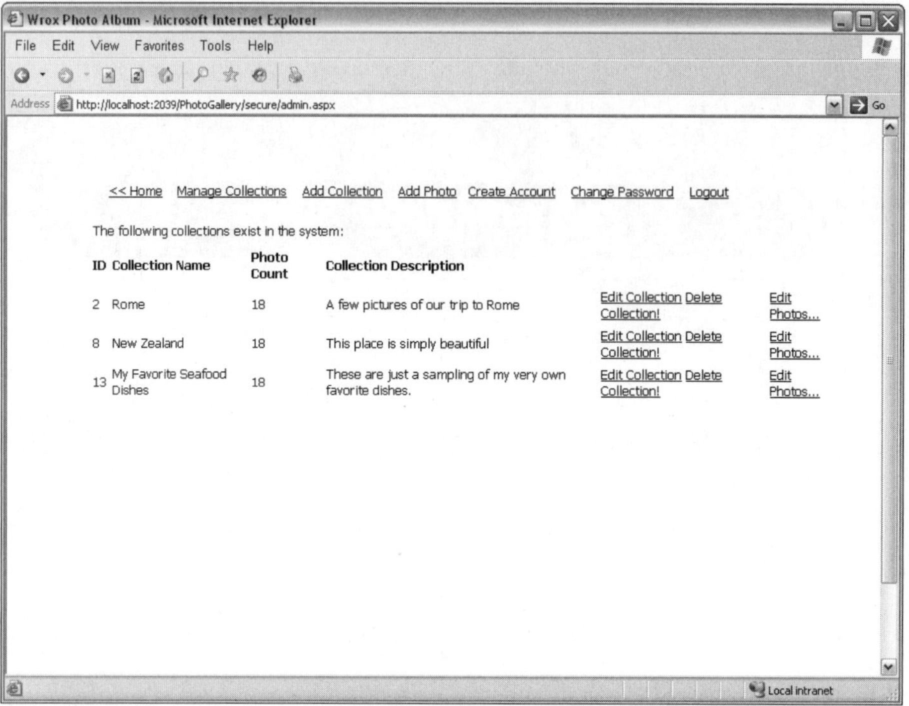

Figure 7-5

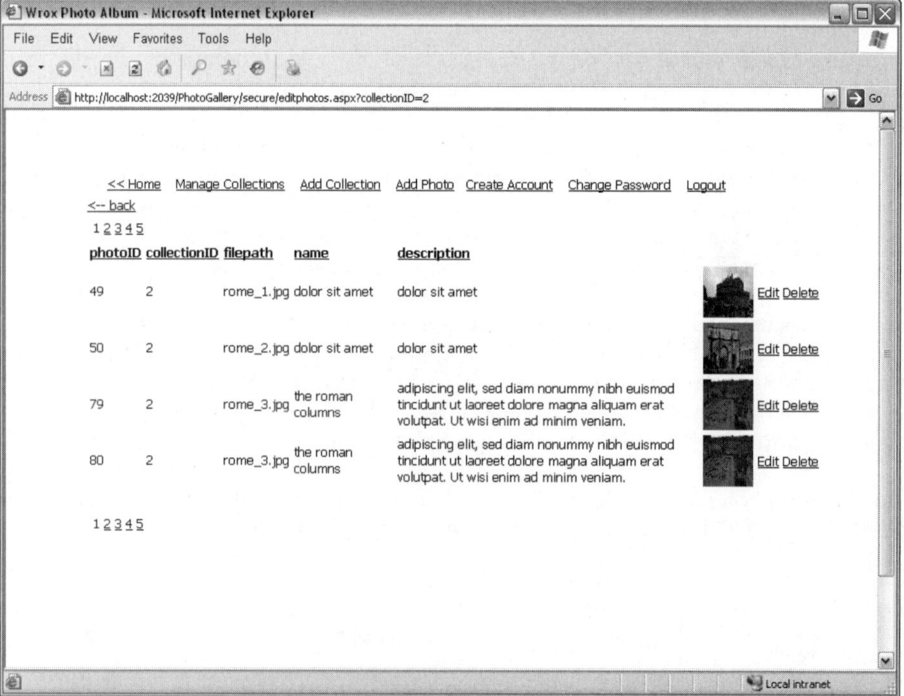

Figure 7-6

From the main menu of the Admin section you can also click the Add Collection link. Clicking this link loads the page displayed in Figure 7-7.

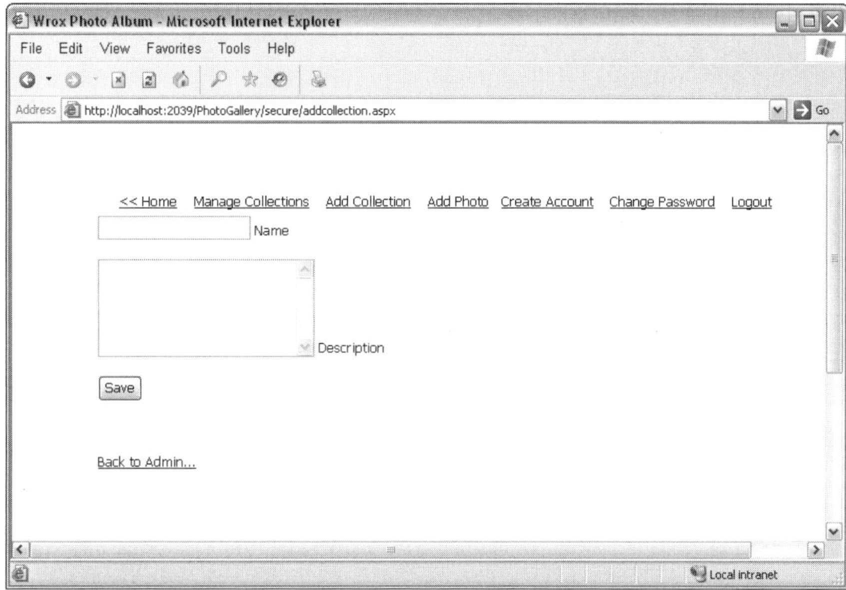

Figure 7-7

Figure 7-7 shows the simple add-collection interface, which allows you to add a new collection to the database, stating its name and description. To add a photo to any collection in the system, click the Add Photo link at the top of the administration area. From this page, you can select the photo on your local machine, enter a name for the photo, select a collection from the drop-down, and enter any descriptive information about the image in the description field. Clicking the Upload button saves the image and textual fields to the server where it is catalogued and viewable immediately.

After walking through the useful features of the Wrox Photo Album, you will be pleased to know there is an insightful design involved in the project. The next section describes the design in detail.

Wrox Photo Album Design

The design of the Wrox Photo Album includes considerations for how the various pieces fit together, and the structure of the site in general. It also explains the way in which images are managed within the system, and how the images are bound to controls on the WebForms.

How It All Fits Together

The design chosen for the Wrox Photo Album has several distinct characteristics and takes into consideration some very specific complexities of displaying and managing images online. These include the following:

- Storing images (database versus file system)
- Displaying images (data-bound controls versus custom queries)
- Structure of the site
- Themes and skins
- Design of the data model
- Security model

The design decisions implemented within the Wrox Photo Album are not by any means locked in place. They can be changed in various capacities in the areas of the security model chosen, data tables used, file structures, and data binding as a whole. In short, nearly all of the application can easily be restructured to accommodate your unique design decisions.

Storing Images

Two popular methods of storing and rendering images for a web site exist: Either store the images as binary data within a database, or store them within a file folder on the web server as an alternative. Storing the image in the database as binary data is not necessarily the best way to manage images over the Internet. Studies have been performed that measure the quality and resolution of a JPEG image that is created from a database and converted from binary data to a streamed image and sent to a browser. Results have shown *in some cases* that for some reason the images that stream to the browser are of the lower quality in comparison with images that are stored in a file folder on the web server and sent over a normal HTTP protocol response. In addition, storing images outside of the database can arguably provide a greater amount of flexibility in the movement and control over storage and volume issues. This is especially true if your Wrox Photo Album becomes large and unmanageable. That is, if you will be storing thousands of images in the SQL Server Express 2005 database, there may be a performance hit to text-based SQL queries on the database. As more and more queries run against your application, and the size of the data begins to increase due to image volume, you may experience some level of performance degradation. As an alternative to storing images in the database, storing them in a traditional web-based file folder will ensure maximum control over your image content, while maintaining near-zero latency in your database queries.

Displaying Images

In the classic ASP (ASP 3.0) world, in order to display thumbnails of images any grid-like fashion, a developer would have to create some fairly intelligent dynamic execution logic. With the advent of ASP.NET data-bound controls, however, images can be rendered in a grid within what is known as `Repeater` controls. The `DataList` control, which is one of the many repeater-like controls available, allows developers to create a set of HTML that can be easily repeated every time a new record is processed through the control.

Following is an excerpt of the `DataList` control HTML markup in the Wrox Photo Album photo display grid:

```
<asp:DataList ID="DataList1" runat="Server"  dataSourceID="SqlDataSource1"
    repeatColumns="6"  repeatdirection="Horizontal" borderwidth="0px"
cellpadding="3">
    <ItemStyle cssClass="item" />
    <ItemTemplate>
```

```
        <table align=left border="0" cellpadding="0" cellspacing="0">
            <tr>

                <td></td>
                <td nowrap width="100" valign="top">
                <a class="photoname" href="viewphoto.aspx?photoID=<%# Eval("photoID")
%>">
                <%#GetName(Server.HtmlEncode(Eval("Name").ToString()))%>
                </a>
                </td>
            <td></td>
            </tr>
            <tr>
                <td></td>
                <td>
                    <a href='viewphoto.aspx?photoID=<%# Eval("photoID") %>' >
                        <img class="viewphoto" src="upload/<%# Eval("filepath") %>"
                        height="95" width="95" alt='<%# Eval("description") %>' />
                    </a>
                </td>
                <td></td>
            </tr>
        </table>
        </ItemTemplate>
</asp:DataList>
```

As displayed in the preceding HTML tags, the `DataList` control allows for the HTML to be repeated with the specific image filename replaced each time the HTML section is rendered. The `<%# Eval("fieldname") %>` fields are where the data fields will be replaced with the data rows from the database. The table structure within the `DataList` control provides a formatted display of information for each photo record. The section titled "Code and Code Explanation" reviews this in detail.

Site Structure

The site is composed of numerous separate files being referenced in an intelligent and systematic way, adhering to popular practices of using user controls, WebForms, class files, master pages, and code-behind files. The user controls are the commonly used ASP.NET files that represent the actual code and processing of the ASP.NET WebForms. Each ASP.NET WebForm contains a single user control to contain the business logic of the page. The class files are used to represent the photo and collection objects as they are passed into the system from other WebForm pages. The master pages are used to provide consistent aesthetics and structure to each page, showing the menu and title area for the page.

The sections of the project are listed in the following table:

Section	Description
App_Code	The object classes and helper classes such as those used for data access calls.
App_Data	The actual SQL Server Express .mdf data file.
App_Themes	The location of the contents of two themes to use.
Images	Any images not associated to a particular theme.

Table continued on following page

Section	Description
Secure	Administrator area, locked down with controlled access by the ASPNET security database and ASP.NET built-in security protocol to the administrator role and the super-administrator role.
Upload	The folder where images are uploaded and stored.
Controls	The location for all user controls, to which most WebForm pages point.
Webforms	The .aspx files in the root of the web site folder structure.
Configuration Files	The Map.sitemap and Web.config files used to store the navigation and configuration settings for the web site.

Figure 7-8 shows a developer's view of the project's folders and files from within the Solution Explorer.

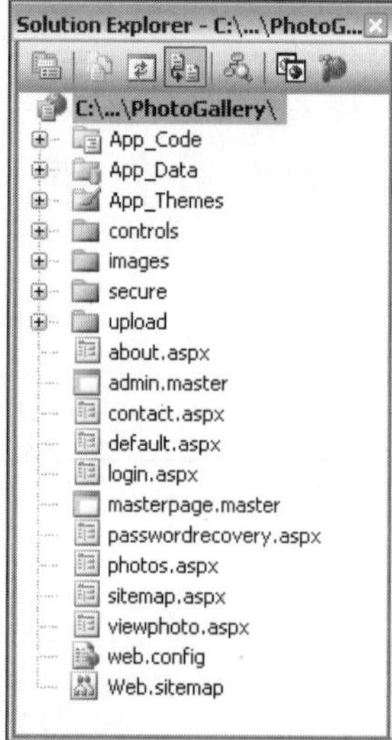

Figure 7-8

Themes and Skins

The Wrox Photo Album look and feel is managed by the use of themes and skins in the folder App_Themes in the root of the application. A *skin* allows you to define the visual styles that can be applied to any controls. A *theme*, however, is a collection or grouping of skins and applies to the ASP.NET page itself. By using these two techniques in conjunction, the entire site's look and feel can be configured and managed from a configuration file or application setting. Specifically, the actual theme that the application is currently using can be found in the `appSettings` section of the Web.config file, as displayed here:

```
<appSettings>

    <add key="CurrentTheme" value="openbook" />

   <!--  Commented Lines Here...

    <add key="CurrentTheme" value="ultraclean" />
    -->

  </appSettings>
```

The Wrox Photo Album is configured with two themes:

- The OpenBook theme
- The UltraClean theme

Each theme can be used by simply changing the entry within the Web.config file as documented in the preceding code. The actual entries for each of these are displayed in the text that follows and are mutually exclusive in nature. That is, only one `appSettings CurrentTheme` entry is allowed to exist at a time. The other setting must be commented out or deleted.

You could leave the OpenBook theme in place with the following entry in the Web.config file:

```
<appSettings>
  <add key="CurrentTheme" value="openbook" />
</appSettings>
```

Or instead, you could use the following entry for the UltraClean theme:

```
<appSettings>
  <add key="CurrentTheme" value="ultraclean" />
</appSettings>
```

The OpenBook theme uses a much more elegant font style, and a beautiful background image of an open book. Figure 7-1 at the beginning of the chapter shows what the OpenBook theme looks like in your browser.

The UltraClean theme (see Figure 7-9) uses a standard Arial font style, with hardly any other formatting or background colors and images. This is provided purposefully, because many developers would naturally like to make changes to an existing skin in order to customize it to their liking.

Thus, themes allow you to make changes to the visual elements of the site as a whole. But if you want to make granular changes to individual controls, you would have to modify the skin files within the theme folders, respectively. The skin files represent how the ASP.NET controls are to be formatted, including the application of CSS style sheets and specific server-side HTML markup tags.

Figure 7-9

Data Model

The data model is simplistic by design and by purpose. Only two tables are used in the site: Photo and Collection. The model is displayed in Figure 7-10.

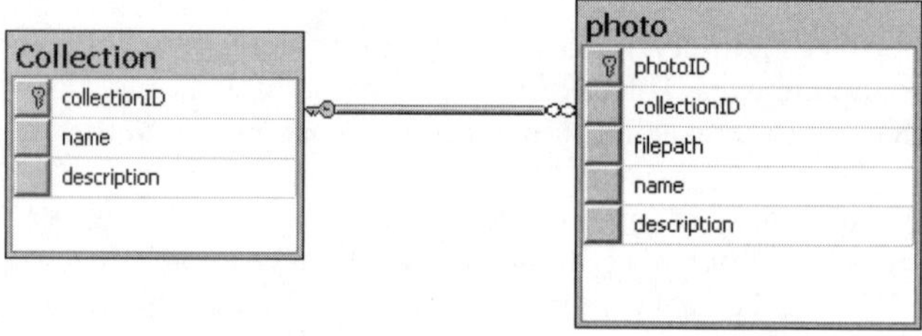

Figure 7-10

The following tables depict the specific fields of each of the database tables in use:

The Photo Table

Field Name	Data Type	Description
photoID	`Int`	The unique identifier for this record.
collectionID	`Int`	The foreign key collection ID within the system.
filepath	`Varchar`	The file path of the photo file in the web server's folder path.
name	`Varchar`	The name of the photo.
description	`Varchar`	The detailed description of the photo.

The Collection Table

Field Name	Data Type	Description
collectionID	`Int`	The unique identifier for this record.
name	`Varchar`	The name of the collection.
description	`Varchar`	A description of the collection.

The next section walks you through the security model and its implied mechanisms within the application.

Security Model

You need some level of security to protect your precious photos from the untrusted user out in cyberspace. The Wrox Photo Album provides a basic security model using Forms Authentication and a SQL Server Express Data Provider. This SQL Server Express provider generates a new security database when implemented, which is included in the project and used to house all of the user account information and security settings. This security model implements Forms Authentication intrinsically within the various security controls, such as those used to login, display login status, recover your password, change your password, and create a new user.

Two accounts are created for use within the photo album, and two different roles that those accounts are assigned to, respectively. These are outlined in the following table:

Username	Password	Account Description
Admin	password#	This user is assigned to the Administrator role.
SuperAdmin	password#	This user is assigned to the Super Administrator role.

In successive fashion, the following table details the list of roles created in the system, and what permissions those roles have:

Role	Role Description
Administrator	This role has the ability to add photos and photo collections to the system, but does not have any edit or delete permissions.
Super Administrator	This role has the ability to add, edit, and delete both photos and collections.

Aside from these design considerations, the Wrox Photo Album has been designed in accordance with the ASP.NET 2.0 features that you'd expect. Nothing is earth-shattering or groundbreaking in nature, just typical, and the new .NET 2.0 tools, including the navigation controls, master pages, `GridView` control, file upload control, and others.

Classes Involved

The following sections outline the classes involved in the system from a design perspective.

The Photo Class

The `Photo` class is used to represent an instance of the photo in the application logic. Figure 7-11 is a graphical representation of the `Photo` class in the system, showing its fields, properties, and methods separately.

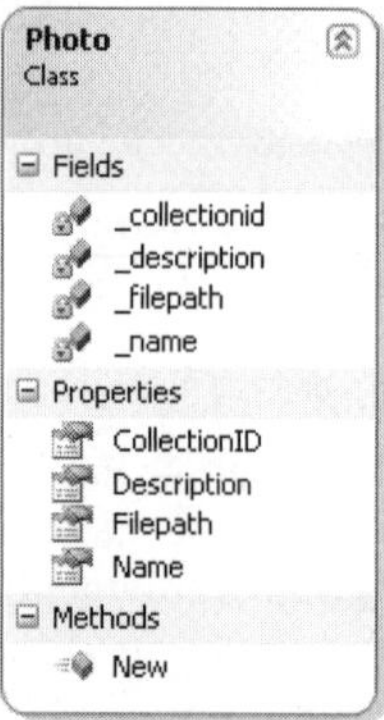

Figure 7-11

The `Photo` class is used to represent a `Photo` object as it is passed into the business object layer for entry into the system. The following table lists the properties of the `Photo` class:

Property	Return Type	Description
`CollectionID`	Integer	The specific parent collection to which the photo belongs.
`Description`	String	The description entered for the photo.
`FilePath`	String	The image's filename as it exists in the filesystem of the server for storage.
`Name`	String	The name of the photo.

The next class is where the photo items are managed and contained within.

The PhotoCollection Class

The `PhotoCollection` class, shown in Figure 7-12, outlines the basic composition of the class, with its fields, properties, and events.

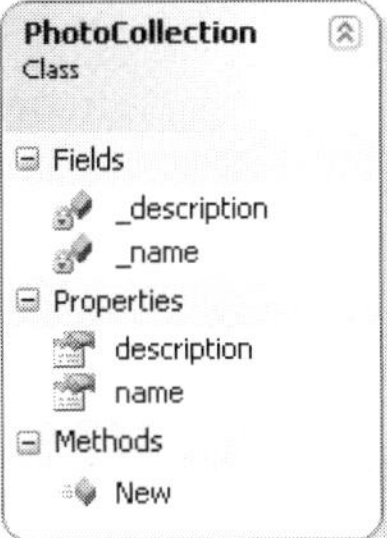

Figure 7-12

The `PhotoCollection` class is used to represent a `PhotoCollection` object as it is passed into the business object layer for entry into the system. The following table lists the properties of the `PhotoCollection` class:

Property	Return Type	Description
`Description`	String	The text description provided for the collection.
`Name`	String	The name entered for the collection.

The next class ties in how the business classes you have already studied will interact with the database.

The PhotoDB Class

The data access layer is managed and provided via this `PhotoDB` class (see Figure 7-13), because it provides a window to the data and data objects.

Figure 7-13

The data access strategy is to maintain a lightweight set of database command logic that provides data management capabilities to the presentation layer. The `DataAccessLayer` class is primarily used to insert new photos and collections into the database. The basis of this class is essentially to separate the implementation of the data access activities from the presentation layer of the application as much as possible. By using class object references as parameters to method calls within this business layer, you can potentially save time in customizations, because you need only to manage the class definition and class references in a few places to provide additional fields or functionality.

The data access layer contains the following properties and methods:

Property or Method	Return Type	Description
`ConnectionString`	String	This property is the textual connection string from the Web.config file's connection string entry.
`GetFirstImage`	String	This function accepts a `collectionID` as a parameter, and returns a string image path for the single photo that was selected from the database to represent that collection.
`InsertCollection`	Boolean	This function accepts a `photocollection` object as its only parameter, and adds it as a collection into the database.
`InsertPhoto`	Boolean	This function accepts a `photo` object as its only parameter, and adds the photo to the database.

The `InsertPhoto` function is possibly the most important area of the class, and is listed here:

```
    Public Shared Function InsertPhoto(ByVal p As Photo) As Boolean
          Try
              'Declare the objects for data access
              Dim conn As New SqlConnection()
              Dim cmd As New SqlCommand()
              'set the connection string
              conn.ConnectionString = DataAccessLayer.ConnectionString
              cmd.Connection = conn
              conn.Open()
              cmd.CommandType = CommandType.StoredProcedure
              cmd.CommandText = "add_photo"
              ' Create a SqlParameter for each parameter in the stored proc.
              Dim idParam As New SqlParameter("@path", p.Filepath)
              Dim cParam As New SqlParameter("@collectionID", p.CollectionID)
              Dim nameParam As New SqlParameter("@name", p.Name)
              Dim descParam As New SqlParameter("@desc", p.Description)
              'add each parameter to the command object
              cmd.Parameters.Add(cParam)
              cmd.Parameters.Add(idParam)
              cmd.Parameters.Add(nameParam)
              cmd.Parameters.Add(descParam)
              cmd.ExecuteNonQuery()

              Return True

          Catch ex As Exception
              Throw (ex)
          End Try
      End Function
```

This excerpt provides insight to the basic data insertion operation that the `DataAccessLayer` class provides. `Dim conn As New SqlConnection()` provides a reference to a new connection. This connection will be set to be the SQL Server Express 2005 PhotoDB.mdf database as per the Web.config setting, with the following line of code:

```
conn.ConnectionString = DataAccessLayer.ConnectionString
```

Next, the function opens the connection and begins to set the properties of the `SqlCommand` object. The command is stated to be a stored procedure with the name of `add_photo`. This stored procedure accepts four parameters, and is shown here:

```
ALTER PROCEDURE dbo.add_photo
(
 @collectionID int,
 @path varchar(300),
 @name varchar(300),
 @desc varchar(300)
)
AS

insert into photo (collectionID, filepath, [name], description) values
(@collectionID, @path, @name, @desc)

   RETURN
```

In order to call the stored procedure from the ADO.NET `SqlCommand` object, you need to add `SqlParameter` objects to it. The following code creates the four parameter object variables, assigns values to them, and adds them into the command parameters collection:

```
            ' Create a SqlParameter for each parameter in the stored proc.
            Dim idParam As New SqlParameter("@path", p.Filepath)
            Dim cParam As New SqlParameter("@collectionID", p.CollectionID)
            Dim nameParam As New SqlParameter("@name", p.Name)
            Dim descParam As New SqlParameter("@desc", p.Description)
            'add each parameter to the command object
            cmd.Parameters.Add(cParam)
            cmd.Parameters.Add(idParam)
            cmd.Parameters.Add(nameParam)
            cmd.Parameters.Add(descParam)
```

Now you just need to execute the stored procedure, which inserts a record into the photo database table. The `cmd.ExecuteNonQuery()` statement provides just that.

The next section walks you through each code file with a detailed explanation on the background and/or purpose of the modules.

Code and Code Explanation

This section explains each of the essential code files in the Wrox Photo Album project. You look in detail at the files in each of the different folders and learn how they interact and are used across the project.

Root Files

The root of the Wrox Photo Album contains several important files, including the main ASPX shell-pages, and the configuration and formatting pages. Most of the business logic is hidden from these pages and contained in the reusable web user controls held in the Usercontrols folder.

Web.config

The Web.config stores vital configuration entries used within the application. One entry, named the `SqlServerConnectionString`, controls the connection to the database, as shown here:

```
<connectionStrings>
    <add name="SqlServerConnectionString"
connectionString="server=(local)\SqlExpress;AttachDbFileName=|DataDirectory|PhotoDB
.mdf;Integrated Security=true;User Instance=true"
providerName="System.Data.SqlClient" />
  </connectionStrings>
```

It also contains information managing the SMTP e-mail settings for sending out e-mails:

```
<appSettings>
    <add key="EmailFrom" value="admin@myphotoalbum.com" />
    <add key="EmailTo" value="admin@myphotoalbum.Com" />
</appSettings>
```

In order to access these entries, such as in the `DataAccessLayer` class, use the following code:

```
Public Class DataAccessLayer
    Public Shared ReadOnly Property ConnectionString() As String
        Get
            Return
ConfigurationManager.ConnectionStrings("SqlServerConnectionString").ConnectionString
        End Get
    End Property
```

This is simply referencing the Web.config file to extract the values from the textual data and place them into the class variable references.

In the next section you get a look at the use of the various master pages in use.

Masterpage.master and Admin.master

The master pages are used to maintain a consistent view of the pages with different formats for each. The Masterpage.master is the master page for the public pages on the site, which all users see when viewing the web site. The master page contains several important controls that are used across the public pages of the site. These include a `SiteMapDataSource`, `Menu`, `SiteMapPath`, and a `ContentPlaceHolder` control.

The Admin.master is a different master page that is used only for the pages contained within the Secure folder. These are considered to be the administrative pages, and are accessible only once the user logs in to the system.

Web.sitemap

This XML file is simply a hierarchical list of `siteMapNode` elements that allow a web site to abstract its links of pages into a separate area for shared consumption. The contents of the file are as follows:

```
<?xml version="1.0" encoding="utf-8" ?>
<siteMap xmlns="http://schemas.microsoft.com/AspNet/SiteMap-File-1.0" >
  <siteMapNode url="#" title="" description="Welcome to PhotoShare!">
    <siteMapNode url="default.aspx" title="Photo Albums" />
    <siteMapNode url="about.aspx" title="About Me" />
    <siteMapNode url="contact.aspx" title="Contact Me" />
    <siteMapNode url="sitemap.aspx" title="Site Map" />
    <siteMapNode url="secure/admin.aspx" title="Admin" />
  </siteMapNode>
</siteMap>
```

The Web.sitemap file is used as a data source for the menu of the web site, which is contained within the master page. It's also used to feed the `TreeView` control in the sitemap.aspx page. In this way, if you need to add a page to the web site, it can be instantly positioned within all of the navigation controls by simply adding the entry to this file.

WebForms

The root of the Wrox Photo Album contains several important files, including the main ASPX pages, and the configuration and formatting pages. The following pages comprise the pages used when a general user visits the site.

Photos.aspx

This WebForm displays the photos from the web server in the form and appearance of a grid. This implements an ASP.NET 2.0 `DataList` control that renders an HTML `image` control across the page from left to right and from top to bottom. The `DataList` control has been called a *big brother* to the `Repeater` control. They are both essentially the same, except that the `DataList` control has a bit more value in having built-in templates and a more flexible layout.

The following code represents the data-bound `DataList` control:

```
<asp:DataList ID="DataList1" runat="Server"  dataSourceID="SqlDataSource1"
    repeatColumns="6"  repeatdirection="Horizontal" borderwidth="0px"
cellpadding="3">
    <ItemStyle cssClass="item" />
    <ItemTemplate>
    <table align=left border="0" cellpadding="0" cellspacing="0"
class="collection">
         <tr>
            <td></td>
            <td nowrap width="100" valign="top">
            <a class="photoname" href="viewphoto.aspx?photoID=<%# Eval("photoID")
%>">
            <%#GetName(Server.HtmlEncode(Eval("Name").ToString()))%>
            </a>
            </td>
```

```
            <td></td>
         </tr>
         <tr>
             <td></td>
             <td>
                 <a href='viewphoto.aspx?photoID=<%# Eval("photoID") %>' >
                     <img class="viewphoto" src="upload/<%# Eval("filepath") %>"
                     height="100" width="100" alt='<%# Eval("description") %>' />
                 </a>
             </td>
             <td></td>
         </tr>
     </table>
     </ItemTemplate>
</asp:DataList>
```

The data-binding settings of the preceding HTML markup, `dataSourceID="SqlDataSource1"`, point to the `SqlDataSource` control also contained within the page, and are listed here:

```
<asp:SqlDataSource ID="SqlDataSource1" runat="server" ConnectionString="<%$
ConnectionStrings:SqlServerConnectionString %>"
    SelectCommand="SELECT [photoID], [collectionID], [filepath], [name],
[description] FROM [photo] WHERE ([collectionID] = @collectionID)">
    <SelectParameters>
        <asp:QueryStringParameter Name="collectionID"
QueryStringField="collectionID" Type="Int32" />
    </SelectParameters>
</asp:SqlDataSource>
```

The `SqlDataSource` control accepts a querystring parameter, `collectionID`, which is passed in from the clicking of a collection image on the default.aspx page. From Design View, you can click the smart tag of a `DataSource` control and view the wizard for configuration and parameterization of the control at run time. This wizard provides the capability to view and select querystrings, cookies, posted forms, or session parameters to feed the dynamic SQL queries of the control.

Login.aspx

Figure 7-14 shows the `Login` control, new in ASP.NET 2.0.

The `Login` WebForm contains an ASP.NET `Login` control, which intrinsically accesses the SQL Server Express ASPNET database for authentication calls. As shown in the following code, there is very little HTML markup needed to implement this login functionality in the site:

```
<asp:Login ID="Login1" runat="server" PasswordRecoveryText="forgot password?"
PasswordRecoveryUrl="~/passwordrecovery.aspx"
DestinationPageUrl="~/secure/admin.aspx">
</asp:Login>
```

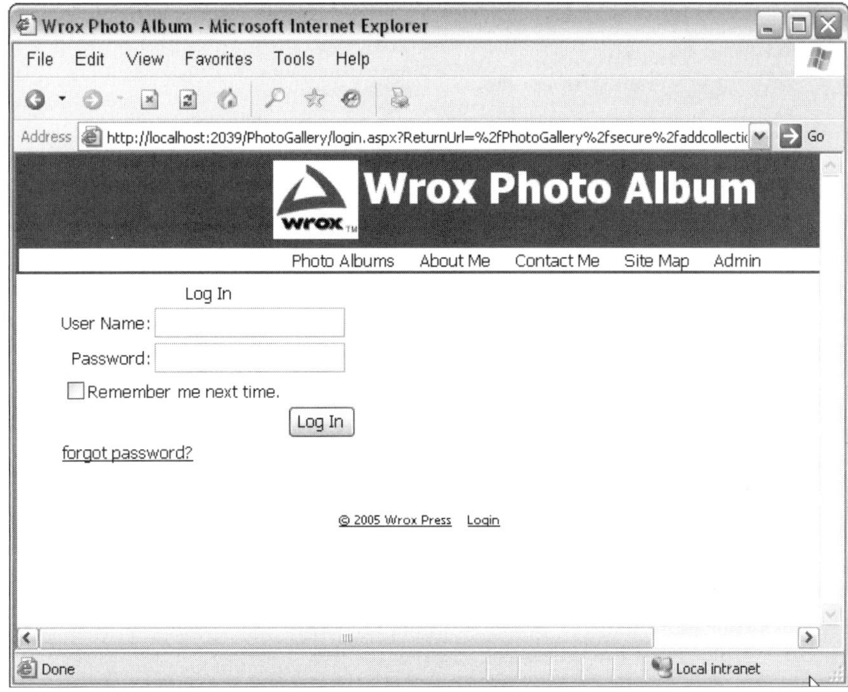

Figure 7-14

As you can see within the HTML markup of the page, just a few properties are set for the `Login` control that change the behavior of the control in the site. These are listed and explained in the following table:

Property	Description
`PasswordRecoveryText`	This is the text you see where the link exists for a user to recover his or her password by a potential secret question used when creating the account.
`PasswordRecoveryUrl`	This is the URL used for the password recovery URL, which points to a page with the password recovery control somewhere in it.
`DestinationPageUrl`	This is the URL to send the user to when the user successfully answers the secret question and is allowed to recover the password via an e-mail sent to him or her by the system.

This is just one example of how ASP.NET 2.0 provides robust functionality built into the security controls and usable right out of the box.

Admin.aspx

The Admin.aspx WebForm is essentially the landing page for the secure section of the site, seen immediately after logging in. This Admin page contains a `GridView` control, which is data-bound to the site's collection data, as displayed in Figure 7-15.

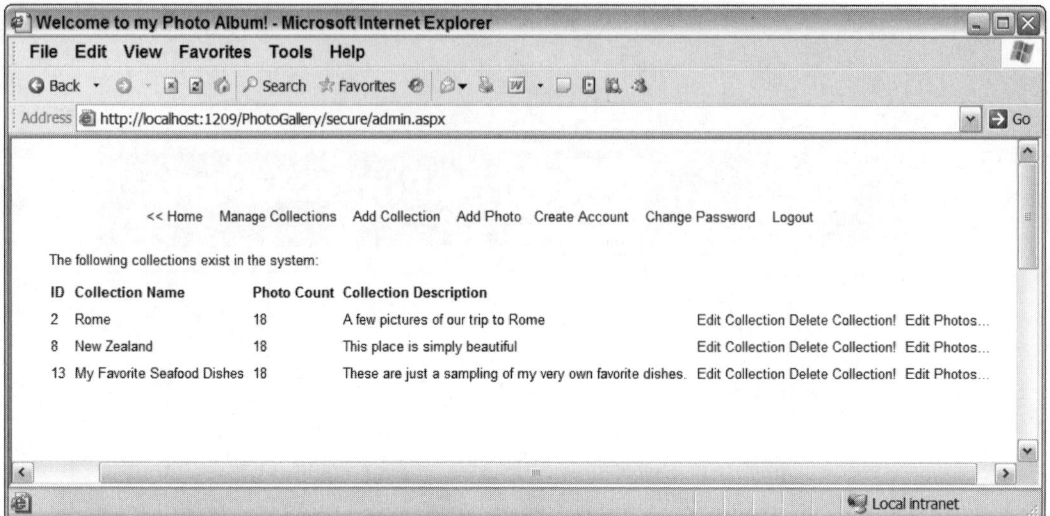

Figure 7-15

The `GridView` of collections allows a Super Administrator to edit or delete a collection by clicking the appropriate hyperlinks in the row of the collection grid view.

From the `Page_Load` event of this page, the user is authenticated to ensure he or she is a member of either an Administrator or a Super Administrator role within the security configuration. Either of these roles allows for access to the secure folder of the site. The Super Administrator role, however, is the only role that provides edit and delete functionality to the images and collections of the site. Thus, the `GridView` control is hidden for Administrator users, but visible for Super Administrator users.

This authentication logic is depicted in the following excerpt:

```
<%@ Control Language="VB" ClassName="admin" %>

<script runat="server">
    Protected Sub Page_Load(ByVal sender As Object, ByVal e As System.EventArgs)
        'we check for a super admin or admin...
        If Context.User.IsInRole("Administrator") Then
            grdCollectionManagement.Visible = False
        End If
        If Context.User.IsInRole("Super Administrator") Then
            grdCollectionManagement.Visible = True
        End If
    End Sub
</script>
```

The `GridView` is bound to the `SqlDataSource` control on the page, and the database actions that the grid provides are configured within the HTML markup of the `SqlDataSource`. The following code displays the `SelectCommand`, `UpdateCommand`, and `DeleteCommand` queries, as well as the parameters for each database command:

```
<asp:SqlDataSource ID="SqlDataSource1" runat="server" ConnectionString="<%$
ConnectionStrings:SqlServerConnectionString %>"
    SelectCommand="SELECT [collectionID] AS collectionID, [collection name] AS
collection_name, [description] AS description, [number of photos] AS
number_of_photos FROM [collection_count]" UpdateCommand="UPDATE Collection SET
description =@description, name =@collection_name where collectionID =
@collectionID" DeleteCommand="DELETE from Collection where collectionID =
@collectionID">
    <DeleteParameters>
        <asp:Parameter Name="CollectionID" />
    </DeleteParameters>
    <UpdateParameters>
        <asp:Parameter Name="description" />
        <asp:Parameter Name="collection_name" />
    </UpdateParameters>
</asp:SqlDataSource>
```

This `SqlDataSource` control acts as a responsive party for all data interactions for the `GridView`. Any edits, deletes, selects, and so on, must pass through this control before they can make their way to the database. Although this approach may not be suitable for large-scale enterprise application development, it suffices for the nature of this photo album application.

Editphotos.aspx

The Editphotos.aspx WebForm displays the photos from the web server in a `GridView` for the purpose of editing or deleting the photos. As with the collection `GridView` on the Admin page, the `GridView` control is bound to the `SqlDataSource` control on the page. The database actions that the grid provides are configured within the HTML markup of the `SqlDataSource`. The following code displays the `SelectCommand`, `UpdateCommand`, and `DeleteCommand` queries, as well as the parameters for each database command:

```
<asp:SqlDataSource ID="SqlDataSource1" runat="server" ConnectionString="<%$
ConnectionStrings:SqlServerConnectionString %>"
    SelectCommand="SELECT [photoID], [collectionID], [filepath], [name],
[description] FROM [photo] WHERE ([collectionID] = @collectionID)"
    UpdateCommand="UPDATE photo SET description = @description, name = @name,
filepath = @filepath, collectionID = @collectionID where photoID = @photoID"
DeleteCommand="DELETE From photo where photoID = @photoID">
    <SelectParameters>
        <asp:QueryStringParameter Name="collectionID"
QueryStringField="collectionID" Type="Int32" />
    </SelectParameters>
    <UpdateParameters>
        <asp:Parameter Name="collectionID" />
        <asp:Parameter Name="name" />
        <asp:Parameter Name="filepath" />
        <asp:Parameter Name="photoID" />
        <asp:Parameter Name="description" />
    </UpdateParameters>
    <DeleteParameters>
        <asp:Parameter Name="photoID" />
    </DeleteParameters>
</asp:SqlDataSource>
```

The actual implementation of the grid is shown in the following code, displaying bound field entries for the textual data, and an `ImageField` bound field for a thumbnail of the image:

```
<asp:GridView ID="GridView1" runat="server" AllowPaging="True" AllowSorting="True"
    AutoGenerateColumns="False" DataKeyNames="photoID"
DataSourceID="SqlDataSource1" CellPadding="2" CellSpacing="1" GridLines="None"
PageSize="4" ShowFooter="True">
    <PagerSettings Position="TopAndBottom" />
    <Columns >
        <asp:BoundField DataField="photoID" HeaderText="photoID"
InsertVisible="False" ReadOnly="True"
            SortExpression="photoID" />
        <asp:BoundField DataField="collectionID" HeaderText="collectionID"
SortExpression="collectionID" />
        <asp:BoundField DataField="filepath" HeaderText="filepath" ReadOnly="True"
SortExpression="filepath" />
        <asp:BoundField DataField="name" HeaderText="name" SortExpression="name" >
            <ItemStyle Width="100px" />
        </asp:BoundField>
        <asp:BoundField DataField="description" HeaderText="description"
SortExpression="description" >
            <ItemStyle Width="300px" />
        </asp:BoundField>
        <asp:ImageField DataImageUrlField="filepath"
DataImageUrlFormatString="~/upload/{0}" NullImageUrl="~/upload/{0}.jpg" >
            <ControlStyle Height="50px" Width="50px" />
        </asp:ImageField>
        <asp:CommandField ShowDeleteButton="True" ShowEditButton="True" />
    </Columns>
</asp:GridView>
```

The `GridView` allows for inline editing of data by clicking the Edit link within a row on the `GridView`. This automatically provisioned inline row editing is a new ASP.NET 2.0 feature, and saves the developer from creating complex and difficult routines for text boxes and editable areas within a grid.

Secure Area Files

The Secure folder of the Wrox Photo Album contains the administrator area files, including the pages that allow for adding, editing, and deleting photos and collections of photos. As with the public area of the site, most of the business logic is hidden from these pages, and contained in the reusable web user controls held in the Usercontrols folder. See the "User Controls" section for more detailed analysis of the logic contained within the user controls for this section.

The Secure folder is set to deny anonymous access within the ASPNET security database and prevents unauthorized access intrinsically. If a page is requested by the browser within this Secure folder, and the current user has not been authenticated (not logged in), the browser is directed to a login page as a preventative measure. If the user has logged into the application, the Secure folder's permissions would be satisfied, and the requested page would load normally.

User Controls

Some specific user controls in the site provide all of the navigation and content display for multiple pages. Because web user controls promote a practice of creating and using reusable code, they were made to be applicable within multiple pages of the site, depending on the nature of the controls.

header.ascx

The `header` user control is used to provide the top area of each page with meaningful content. If anything needs to reside at or near the top of a web page, you should add it to the `header` control so it is visible through all of the pages.

The following code represents entire header.ascx source:

```
<%@ Control Language="VB" AutoEventWireup="false" CodeFile="header.ascx.vb"
Inherits="Controls_header" %>
<div style="text-align: center">
    <table><tr>
        <td><img src="../Images/headerlogo.gif" /></td>
        <td><h1><% Response.Write(Page.Title) %></h1>
        </td>
    </tr></table>
</div>
```

Notice that the `<%Response.Write(Page.Title)%>` tags are used to write back to the response stream a title of the web site on the top of each page, which originated from the Web.config file.

footer.ascx

The `footer` user control is used as the bottom section of the site, for each page that uses the master page. That is, the `footer` control, among others, is a referenced control within the master page. In this way, it is propagated to all pages in the same exact manner.

The content of the `footer` control is as follows:

```
<%@ Control Language="VB" AutoEventWireup="false" CodeFile="footer.ascx.vb"
Inherits="Controls_footer" %>
<a href="http://wrox.com" target="_blank">&copy; 2005 Wrox Press</a>   
<a href="SignIn.aspx" target="_self">Login</a>
```

This excerpt includes a few hyperlinks. One is for the Wrox Press web site, and the other is a link to the Login page for the chat application.

navigation.ascx

The `navigation` user control is used to provide the reusable menu on each page in the site. The `Menu` itself is a brand-new ASP.NET 2.0 control that binds to a `SiteMapDataSource` control, also new in version 2.0 of the .NET Framework. The `SiteMapDataSource` control is used to bind to an XML file, wherein the site files are listed as entries in the XML file. This is where you can change the data that feeds the menu of the site.

The following excerpt is the HTML markup of the `navigation` control:

```
<%@ Control Language="VB" AutoEventWireup="false" CodeFile="navigation.ascx.vb"
Inherits="Controls_navigation" %>
<asp:Menu ID="Menu1" runat="server" DataSourceID="SiteMapDataSource1"
Orientation="Horizontal"
    StaticDisplayLevels="2"></asp:Menu>
<asp:SiteMapDataSource  ID="SiteMapDataSource1" runat="server" />
```

The XML file of the `SiteMapDataSource` control is shown here:

```
<?xml version="1.0" encoding="utf-8" ?>
<siteMap xmlns="http://schemas.microsoft.com/AspNet/SiteMap-File-1.0" >
  <siteMapNode url="#" title="" description="Welcome to PhotoShare!">
    <siteMapNode url="default.aspx" title="Photo Albums" />
    <siteMapNode url="about.aspx" title="About Me" />
    <siteMapNode url="contact.aspx" title="Contact Me" />
    <siteMapNode url="sitemap.aspx" title="Site Map" />
    <siteMapNode url="secure/admin.aspx" title="Admin" />
  </siteMapNode>
</siteMap>
```

To add a page to the menu of the web site, you must simply copy and paste (with the necessary modifications) an entry of the preceding XML file. In this way, the master page (which contains the only reference to the `navigation` control) provides visibility to the menu of the site on each page.

The next section explains in detail how to install and configure the source files of the Wrox Photo Album and how to deploy the site to a server in a production environment.

Setting up the Project

You can set up the Wrox Photo Album in two ways: hosted web site installation or local developer installation.

Hosted Web Site Installation

If you want to install the Wrox Photo Album as a hosted web site on a computer or server, without customizations or enhancements at all, follow these steps (assuming that the .NET Framework 2.0 is already installed):

1. Open the folder Chapter 06–Wrox Photo Album\Installation Files\ from the CD-ROM that came with this book and double-click the file setup.exe.
2. This process installs the files properly for hosting the web site locally to `C:\inetpub\wwwRoot\PhotoGallery` as a file-based web site application. Note, in the Setup wizard, one of the initial screens will require you to confirm the name of the virtual directory where your application will be installed to within IIS. This virtual directory name is important, because it will allow navigation from `localhost/your virtual directory name`. Try a name like PhotoGallery, which would then allow for browsing to `http://localhost/photogallery/`.

3. Click Next to install the application, and close the installation program when it completes.

4. Finally, browse to your local web site (in step 2, for example, `http://localhost/photogallery`). The Wrox Photo Album application should appear. To test the administration section, click the Admin link and log in with a username of `SuperAdmin` and a password of `password#`.

Local Developer Installation

If you would like to open the project in Visual Studio 2005 or Visual Web Developer, perform the following steps (assuming that the .NET Framework 2.0 is already installed, along with either Visual Studio 2005 or VWD):

1. Start by creating a brand-new web site in Visual Web Developer using Visual Basic .NET.

2. Open the folder Chapter 06–Wrox Photo Album Installer\ from the CD-ROM that came with this book and extract the contents of the file PhotoAlbumSource.zip to a folder on your hard drive.

3. Open a Windows Explorer and browse to the folder that contains the unpacked files.

4. Next, arrange both Visual Web Developer (VWD) and the Windows Explorer in such a way that both are visible at the same time.

5. In the Windows Explorer, select all of the folders and files within the codebase and drag the selected folders and files from the explorer window into the Solution Explorer in VWD. If you're prompted to overwrite files, select Yes. You should end up with a Solution Explorer that contains all of the necessary files for the project to run properly.

6. In the Web.config file, modify the `EmailTo` and `EmailFrom` values in the `appSettings` section to reflect the administration e-mail accounts to be used for sending and receiving e-mail, should you decide to use this feature (see the following code). Also, uncomment the entry you would like to use for the theme of the web site: either OpenBook or UltraClean. This can be changed back at any time, should you change your mind. These settings will require changing to your needed e-mail settings even if you performed the installation of the application via the install files.

```
<configuration xmlns="http://schemas.microsoft.com/.NetConfiguration/v2.0">
  <appSettings>
    <add key="EmailFrom" value="admin@myphotoalbum.com" />
    <add key="EmailTo" value="admin@myphotoalbum.Com" />
    <!--
    <add key="CurrentTheme" value="openbook" />
   -->
    <add key="CurrentTheme" value="ultraclean" />

  </appSettings>
```

7. In the Web.config file, modify the `smtp` value in the `mailSettings` section (as shown in the following code) to reflect the e-mail SMTP outbound mail server name to be used for sending and receiving e-mail, should you decide to use this feature:

```
  </connectionStrings>
  <system.net>
    <mailSettings>
      <smtp deliveryMethod="Network">
```

```
        <network host="smtp.YourMailServerName.com" port="25" />
      </smtp>
    </mailSettings>
  </system.net>
  <system.web>
```

8. Press F5 to run the application in the development environment.

If you want to see an example of how to extend the functionality of the Wrox Photo Album, head to www.wrox.com and find this book's download page.

Summary

In this chapter you learned about some of the more useful controls and tools in the ASP.NET 2.0 environment, such as themes, navigation controls, security controls, the SQL Server Express database tools, and the use of master pages in authoring a consistent web site look and feel. The reading was gauged to lead you to an understanding of how each of these new and exciting features provides the rapid development everyone's been waiting for in Visual Studio 2005.

In the code explanation section you studied the different techniques in handling images on a web server, in regards to storing and delivering images to a user. You also saw how the classes and pages that comprise the Wrox Photo Album work, and how they communicate with each other.

Customer Support Site

No matter how well your products might work, how stable the hardware you sell is, or how happy your customers are about your company and your products, your users are likely to have a need for more information about your products and services sooner or later. They may want to look up the specifications of a product, find the latest drivers to make the product work with a more recent version of their operation system, or find out handy tips about cleaning and maintaining it.

The Customer Support Site presented in this chapter is a web site that allows users to quickly find information about the products or services that your company might be selling. Although this chapter is based on a fictitious hardware-selling company called Wrox Hardware, the principles you learn in this chapter can be applied to many other sites that use a hierarchical content model.

Because this is a book about ASP.NET, this chapter focuses on a lot of the new features of ASP.NET 2.0. However, when Microsoft released the .NET Framework version 2.0 with ASP.NET 2.0, it not only released developer's tools like Visual Studio and Visual Web Developer Express Edition, it also released a new version of its relational database management system called SQL Server 2005. This new version of SQL Server tightly integrates with the .NET 2.0 Framework and Visual Web Developer and has a long list of new features and improvements. Because many web applications make use of a database, it's important to understand the capabilities of the database engine in use. Therefore, in this chapter you get a good look at one of the new features of SQL Server called *Common Table Expressions*. You see more of this when the data access layer and stored procedures are discussed.

Using the Customer Support Site

The Customer Support Site presented in this chapter is the support home for the fictitious hardware-selling company called Wrox Hardware. This company sells hardware from popular best-selling manufacturers such as BNH (Brand New Hardware), Eccentric Hardware Makers, and Rocks Hardware. To minimize the costs for the support department, most of the company's support system is web-based. With the Customer Support Site, users can browse the product catalog with the Product Locator to look for products and their specifications. This is useful if you want to find out if your brand-new hand-held scanner uses AAA or simple AA batteries, for example. The Product Locator uses drop-downs (see Figure 8-1) to allow users to drill down in a hierarchy of categories to locate the product they want to find out more about.

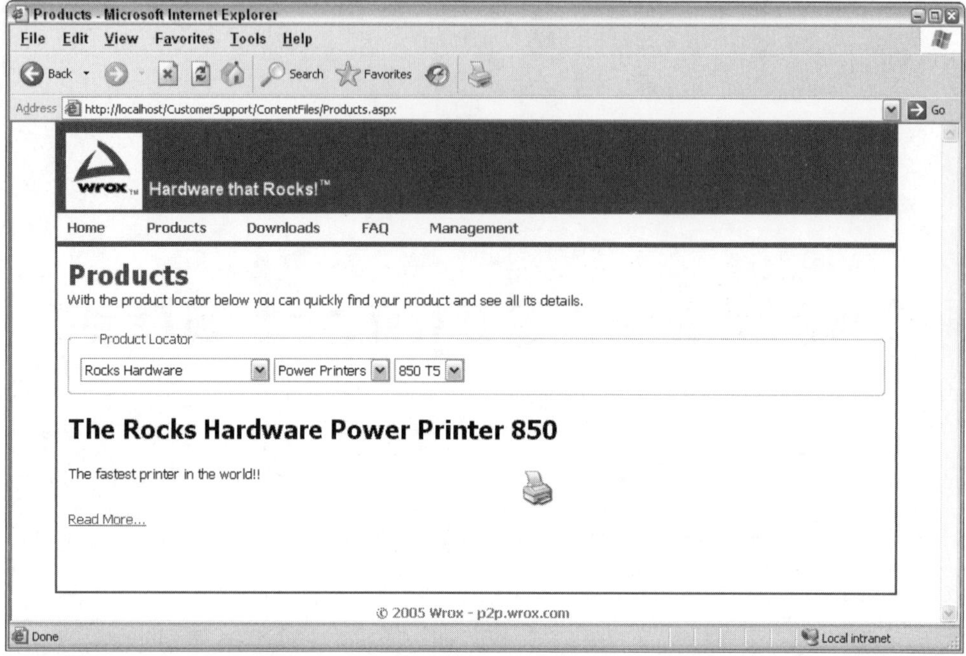

Figure 8-1

In addition to the Product Locator, the site also has a Downloads section. With a drill-down mechanism similar to the one in the Product Locator, users can quickly locate files related to their product. These downloads range from general files such as the warranty document for all BNH products to driver files for a specific product.

The third section of the public site, shown in Figure 8-2, is a searchable list of Frequently Asked Questions (FAQs). These questions are not categorized as the products and downloads are but they are searchable with a small search engine that supports Boolean logic, using `AND` and `OR` expressions.

The Customer Support Site also has a CMS that can be used by content managers to manage the products, downloads, and FAQs in the back-end database of the web site.

In the next section, you get a good look at the design of the Customer Support Site. You see the classes that make up the business and data access layer of the web site and you learn how the database and its stored procedures and user-defined functions are designed.

The section that follows digs much deeper into the site and shows you how each of the individual parts are developed and how they interact together.

Toward the end of the chapter, you see how to install the Customer Support Site on your own server using the supplied installer or by manually installing the necessary files.

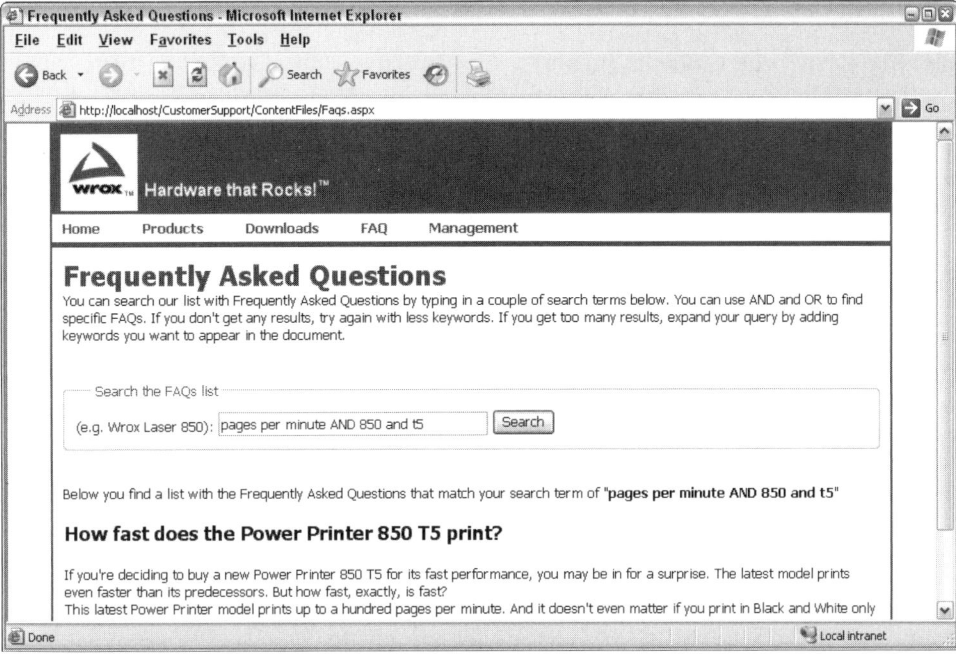

Figure 8-2

Design of the Customer Support Site

Just like many of the other applications in this book, the Customer Support Site is based on a three-tier architecture. The presentation layer consists of the ASPX pages and ASCX user controls located in the root and a few subfolders of the site.

Both the business layer and the data access layer are stored in the special App_Code folder. To make it easier to locate code in the right layer, the business code is stored in a subfolder called BusinessLogic, and the data access code is hosted in the DataAccess folder. Common configuration properties, used by the other layers, are stored in a file called AppConfiguration.vb directly in the App_Code folder.

Most of the data access is performed with <asp:ObjectDataSource> controls in the .aspx pages that talk to the classes (through their public methods) in the business layer, which in turn forwards the calls to methods in the data access layer. In other pages, such as the InsertUpdate pages in the Management section, the code in the code-behind file instantiates instances of the classes from the business layer directly, without an additional data source control.

The next section shows you each of the classes in the business layer and explains how and where they are used. In the section that follows, you discern the design of the data access layer and the database.

The Business Layer

The business layer of the Customer Support Site contains five classes, each of which is used to display categorized information on the web site. For each of the site's main sections, Products, Downloads, and FAQs, you'll find an associated class in the files named after the classes they contain. So, you'll find the `Product` class in the file Product.vb, and so on. In addition to these three classes are two others, called `Category` and `ContentBase`. The `Category` class is used to manage the available categories in the database and get information about them.

The `ContentBase` class is the parent class of `Product` and `Download`, and is discussed next.

The ContentBase Class

A Product and a Download have a lot in common. They both have a title and a description to display the item on the site. They also have an ID to uniquely identify each item. And finally, both are linked to a category in the database. When you start designing these classes, your first attempt may be to code the `Product` class and then duplicate the shared code in the `Download` class. However, this design has a few drawbacks. First, you need to copy and paste the code from the Product file into the Download file, which results in a lot of superfluous work. But more importantly, when you need to make changes to the code — for example, because you want to rename Category to CategoryId — you now have to make these changes at two locations!

To overcome this problem, the `ContentBase` class is introduced. This class exposes the properties and methods that the Product and Download (and future web content items) have in common. This class serves as a base class that other classes can inherit from. The child classes then automatically get all the public members from the base class. Figure 8-3 shows the `ContentBase` class and the two child classes that inherit from it.

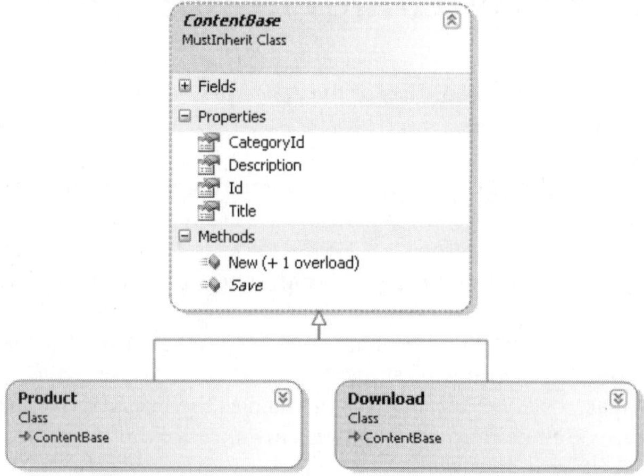

Figure 8-3

In addition to the inherited members, the child classes implement their own properties and methods. You see what those are later when the respective classes are discussed.

Right below the class name in Figure 8-3 you see `MustInherit Class`. This means that the `ContentBase` cannot be instantiated directly, but that you must create an instance from a child class that inherits from `ContentBase`. This is exactly what you want, because there is no point in having a plain `Content` object somewhere on the site. Only the child classes, like `Product` and `Download`, are useful to display on the web site.

The public properties of the `ContentBase` classes were discussed briefly earlier, but the following table lists them again, together with their data type and a description:

Property	Data Type	Description
CategoryId	`Integer`	The ID of the Category in the database to which the content item belongs. This ID holds only the ID of the deepest nested category in a hierarchy of categories. You see how this works later.
Description	`String`	The description, or body text, of the content item.
Id	`Integer`	The ID of the content item in the database.
Title	`String`	The title of the content item.

In addition to these properties, the `ContentBase` class defines one method called `Save`. The base class only defines the signature of the method and has been marked with the `MustOverride` keyword. This way, classes that inherit from `ContentBase` *must* implement the `Save` method. You see how this is done for the `Product` and `Download` classes later in the chapter.

The Product Class

The first class that inherits from `ContentBase` is the `Product` class. An instance of the `Product` class represents a real-world product that a customer may have bought in the Wrox Shop. On the Customer Support Site, the `Product` class is used to provide additional information about the product, like the product specifications.

In addition to the members inherited from `ContentBase`, this class has the members shown in Figure 8-4.

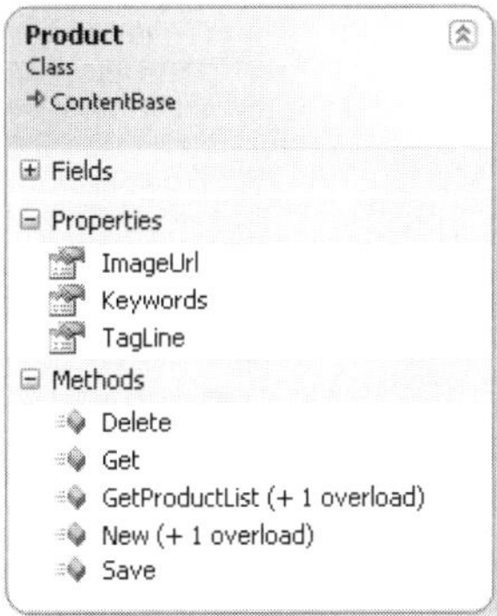

Figure 8-4

The Product class extends the ContentBase class with three properties, described in the following table:

Property	Data Type	Description
ImageUrl	String	A virtual path to an image that displays the product.
Keywords	String	A comma-separated list of keywords describing the product.
TagLine	String	A short and attractive description of the product.

The Product class also adds three methods (of which one is overloaded) and two overloaded constructors. Although you can't see it in Figure 8-4, the Save method is actually inherited from the ContentBase class, whereas the Get and Delete methods are specific to the Product class.

The following table lists the methods for the Product class. In addition to its two constructors (the New method), it also lists the Get, Save, and Delete methods, and two overloaded versions for GetProductList.

Method	Return Type	Description
Public Sub New ()	n/a	The default constructor of the Product class.
Public Sub New (ByVal id As Integer)	n/a	An overloaded constructor that accepts a product ID that is stored in a private variable. This overload is used when editing existing products.
Public Shared Function [Get] (ByVal id As Integer) As Product	Product	This method retrieves a single product from the database by calling a method with the same name in the ProductDB class.
Public Overrides Sub Save ()	n/a	Saves a product in the database by calling into the ProductDB class.
Public Shared Sub Delete (ByVal id As Integer)	n/a	Deletes a product from the database by calling into the ProductDB class.
Public Shared Function GetProductList () As DataSet	DataSet	Returns a list with all the available products in the database. This method is used exclusively in the Management section.
Public Shared Function GetProductList (ByVal categoryId As Integer) As DataSet	DataSet	Returns a list with products for the specified category.

Because just like the `Product` class the `Download` class inherits from `ContentBase`, it should come as no surprise that the `Download` class has some methods in common with the `Product` class. The similarities and differences of the `Download` class are discussed next.

The Download Class

The `Download` class represents files that customers can download from the Wrox Hardware Customer Support Site. The downloads on the site are categorized using a three-level category hierarchy so it's easy to find relevant download files. Just like the `Product` class, `Download` inherits from `ContentBase` and adds a few properties and methods of its own (see Figure 8-5).

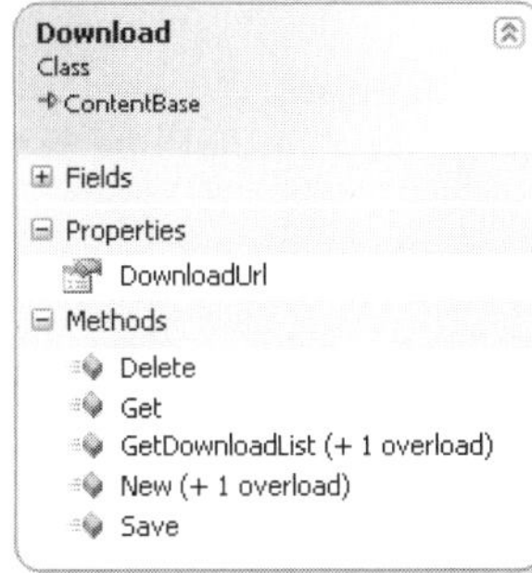

Figure 8-5

The `DownloadUrl` property is a string holding a virtual path to a file that can be downloaded by a customer in the front end of the site. A content manager can upload a file in the Management section and then its path is saved in this property.

Just like the `Product` class, the `Download` class has `Get`, `Save`, and `Delete` methods and two overloaded constructors that work pretty much the same. Refer to the section "The Product Class" for a description of these methods.

In addition to these methods, the `Download` class has a method called `GetDownloadList` that returns a list with downloads as a DataSet.

The Faq Class

The `Faq` class represents a frequently asked question that is displayed on the web site and is stored in the customer support database. Though at first anFAQ may seem to be a good candidate to inherit from `ContentBase` as well, this isn't the case. First of all, the FAQ doesn't have a CategoryId. Also, the FAQ doesn't have a title, but does have two `Question` properties and an `Answer` property. These differences make it hard (or at least very awkward) to have an FAQ inherit from `ContentBase`. Therefore, the `Faq` class is implemented as a stand-alone class with the members shown in Figure 8-6.

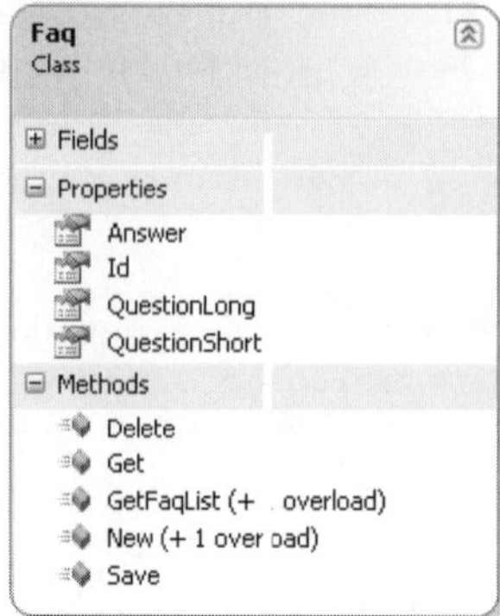

Figure 8-6

The following table describes each of the public properties of the `Faq` class:

Property	Data Type	Description
`Answer`	`String`	The answer to the question.
`QuestionLong`	`String`	A longer and more detailed version of the question.
`Id`	`Integer`	The ID of the content item in the database.
`QuestionShort`	`String`	A short summary of the question used in the list with Frequently Asked Questions.

Just like a `Product` and a `Download`, the `Faq` class has methods to get, save, and delete FAQs from the database. It also has two overloaded methods, outlined in the following table, to retrieve a list of FAQs from the database. One is used to get the questions based on a search term, and the other returns an unfiltered list of FAQs in the database.

Method	Return Type	Description
`Public Shared Function GetFaqList (ByVal searchTerm As String) As DataSet`	`DataSet`	Returns a list with FAQs based on `searchTerm`. This search term can holdsomething like "Printer AND 850 T5".
`Public Shared Function GetFaqList () As DataSet`	`DataSet`	Returns a list with all available FAQs. This method is used exclusively in the Management section.

Earlier you saw that the `ContentBase` class has a property `CategoryId` to link a content item to a category. To work with those categories, the `Category` class has been designed.

The Category Class

The `Category` class (see Figure 8-7) is used to retrieve and create categories in the database. These categories in turn are used to enable a user to quickly locate a product or download in the front end of the site.

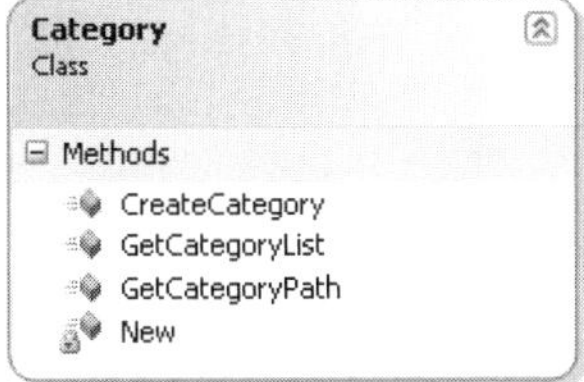

Figure 8-7

The `Category` class has no public or private properties and exposes only shared and public methods (other than its private constructor) to retrieve categories from the database and to create new categories. The following table lists all three methods and describes their purpose:

Method	Return Type	Description
`Public Shared Sub CreateCategory (ByVal description As String, ByVal parentCategoryId As Integer)`	n/a	Creates a new category in the database. The `parentCategoryId` passed to this method must contain the ID of an existing category in the database, or must be less than one to create a new root category.
`Public Shared Function GetCategoryPath (ByVal categoryId As Integer) As DataSet`	`DataSet`	Returns all the parent categories for a given child category. This is useful to determine all parent categories of a product or download as only the deepest child's `CategoryId` is saved.
`Public Shared Function GetCategoryList (ByVal parentCategoryId As Integer) As DataSet`	`DataSet`	Returns a list with categories as a DataSet with an ID and a Description column. When `parentCategoryId` is less than one, the root categories are returned. Otherwise, the child categories for the given parent category are returned.

Now that you have seen all the classes that make up the business layer, it's time to look at the classes and database tables that make up the data access layer.

The Data Access Layer

Because many of the classes in the business layer work with data that is stored in the database, it should come as no surprise that for most of those classes there is an associated class in the data access layer (in the DataAccess folder, which in turn is located in the special App_Code folder in the root of the site) with a name ending in DB. The only exception is the `ContentBase` class. Being the parent for the `Product` and

Download classes, the ContentBase class does not have implementation code that requires database access, so it also doesn't need a companion ContentBaseDB class. The other four classes that do access the database are described in the sections that follow.

The ProductDB Class

The ProductDB class implements the same four methods you saw earlier for the Product class. However, the methods in the ProductDB class, shown in Figure 8-8, perform the real work in getting the data in and out of the database. Notice there isn't an overloaded version of the GetProductList in this database class. The Product class does have two overloaded versions, but calls the same, single method in the ProductDB class.

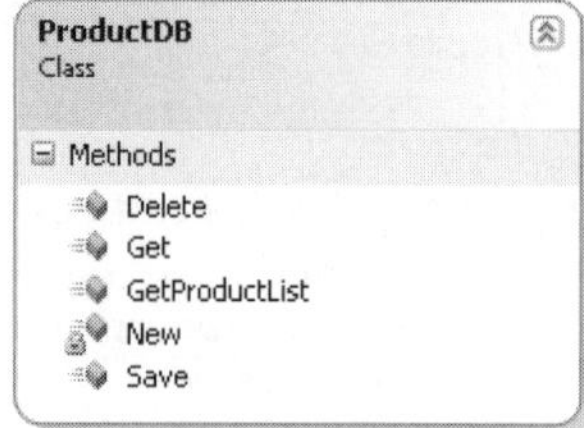

Figure 8-8

The methods listed in Figure 8-8 are discussed in the following table:

Method	Return Type	Description
`Public Shared Sub Delete (ByVal id As Integer)`	n/a	Deletes a product from the database.
`Public Shared Function [Get] (ByVal id As Integer) As Product`	Product	Retrieves a single product instance from the database. Returns Nothing when the requested product could not be located.
`Public Shared Function GetProductList (ByVal categoryId As Integer) As DataSet`	DataSet	Returns a list with products from the database. When CategoryId is -1, all products are returned.
`Public Shared Sub Save (ByVal the Product As Product)`	n/a	Saves the product in the database. This is the only instance method, because all the others are marked as Shared. This instance method saves the underlying values of the product in the database.

The DownloadDB class, which has a lot in common with the ProductDB class, is discussed next.

The DownloadDB Class

Just as the `Product` and `Download` classes are very similar, so are the `ProductDB` and `DownloadDB` classes. This means that this class implements similar `Get`, `Save`, `Delete`, and `GetDownloadList` methods, as illustrated in Figure 8-9.

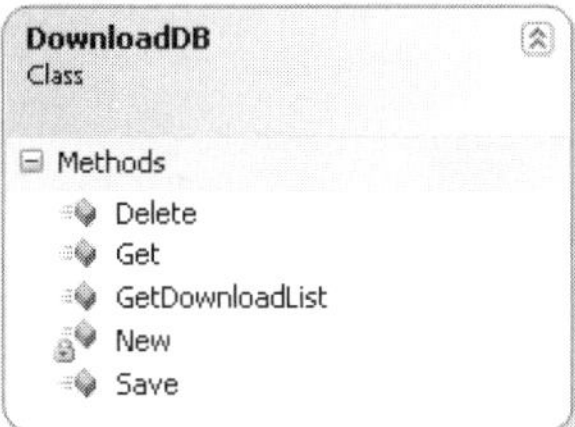

Figure 8-9

The behavior and description for most of these methods are identical to those of the `ProductDB` class. Refer to the table with methods for the `ProductDB` class for a description, replacing Product with Download in any of the names and descriptions you see. The only exception in the method names is `GetDownloadList`. Similar to `GetProductList`, this method returns a list with downloads as a DataSet.

The FaqDB class

Although the `Faq` class does not inherit from `ContentBase`, it does implement the same methods that the `Product` and `Download` classes have. Therefore, the `FaqDB` class (see Figure 8-10) implements the methods `Get`, `Save`, `Delete`, and `GetFaqList`.

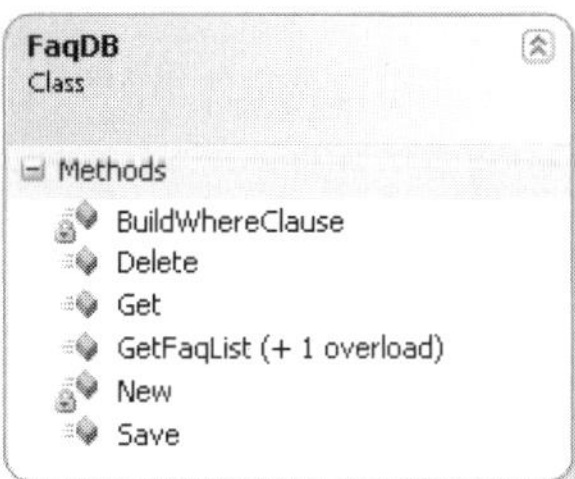

Figure 8-10

In addition to those familiar methods, the `FaqDB` class also has a `BuildWhereClause` method. This method, marked as `Private` in the code so it's not accessible from outside the `FaqDB` class, accepts a search term and returns a fully formatted `WHERE` clause that can be used in a stored procedure. Although this potentially opens up your code for SQL injection attacks, this method deploys some defensive code to avoid this security risk. You see how this works later.

The CategoryDB class

The final class in the data access layer you should look at is the `CategoryDB` class. Just as its counterpart in the business layer, this class implements the three methods depicted in Figure 8-11 for working with categories.

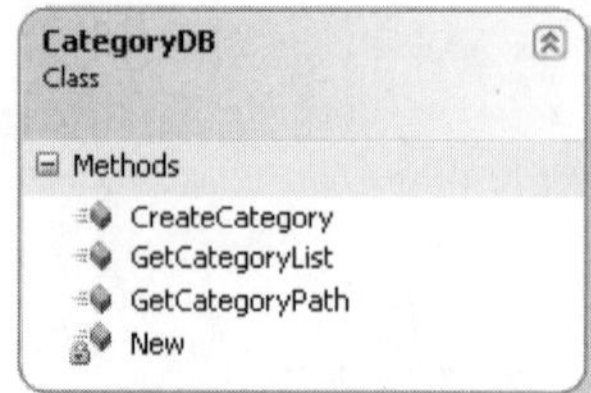

Figure 8-11

These methods are described in the following table:

Method	Return Type	Description
`Public Shared Sub CreateCategory (ByVal description As String, ByVal parentCategoryId As Integer)`	n/a	Creates a new category in the database. The `parentCategoryId` passed to this method must contain the ID of an existing category in the database, or must be less than one to create a new root category.
`Public Shared Function GetCategoryPath (ByVal categoryId As Integer) As DataSet`	`DataSet`	Returns all the parent categories for a given child category. This is useful to determine all parent categories of a product or download, because only the deepest child categoryId is saved.
`Public Shared Function GetCategoryList (ByVal parentCategoryId As Integer) As DataSet`	`DataSet`	Returns a list with categories as a DataSet with an ID and a Description column. When `parentCategoryId` is less than one, the root categories are returned. Otherwise, the child categories for the given parent category are returned.

In addition to the classes in the DataAccess folder, the data access layer also contains the actual database that consists of four database tables and a number of stored procedures.

The Data Model

The database for the Custom Support Site features four tables, 16 stored procedures, and two user-defined functions. Some of the tables in the database are related to each other, as shown in Figure 8-12.

Both the Product and the Download tables have a relation with the Category table through their CategoryId column. However, you should also note that the Category table has a relation with itself. The ParentCategoryId column is related to the Id column in the same table. This way, a category can be related to another category, called its *parent category*, therefore creating a hierarchy or tree structure of categories. To retrieve the hierarchical data from the database, the application makes use of Common Table Expressions, which are discussed later.

Although the names of the tables and their columns are pretty self-explanatory, the following tables list each of them and describe their purpose and data type.

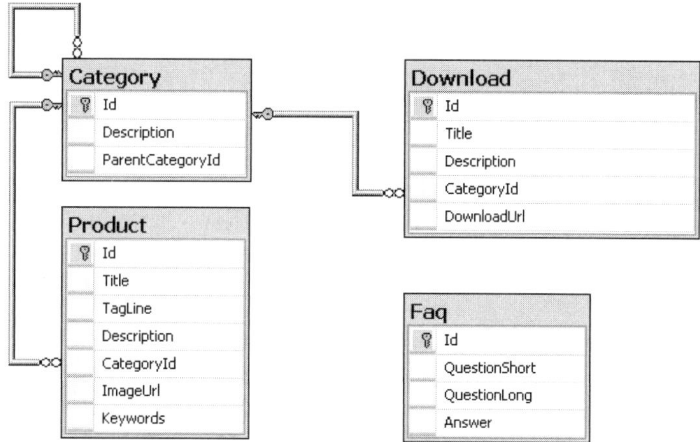

Figure 8-12

The Product Table

This table describes the contents of the Product table in the Customer Support Site database:

Column Name	Data Type	Description
Id	`int`	The unique ID of the product in the database. The ID is generated automatically whenever a new product is inserted.
Title	`nvarchar(100)`	The title of the product.
TagLine	`nvarchar(MAX)`	A longer title or a subtitle for the product that can also hold a short marketing message for the product.
Description	`nvarchar(MAX)`	The full product description, holding the product's specification, for example.
CategoryId	`int`	The ID of the category to which the product belongs.
ImageUrl	`nvarchar(255)`	The virtual path to an image showing the product.
Keywords	`nvarchar(200)`	Holds a comma-separated list with keywords applicable to the product.

The next table describes the five columns of the Download table in the database.

The Download Table

The Download and the Product tables have a lot in common. The columns that these tables share map exactly to the public properties of the parent `ContentBase` class that `Product` and `Download` inherit from.

Column Name	Data Type	Description
Id	`int`	The unique ID of the download in the database. The ID is generated automatically whenever a new download is inserted.
Title	`nvarchar(100)`	The title of the download, briefly describing the file that can be downloaded.
Description	`nvarchar(MAX)`	The full download description.
CategoryId	`int`	The ID of the category to which the download belongs.
DownloadUrl	`nvarchar(255)`	The virtual path to a downloadable file for this download.

It is possible to simulate inheritance in the database by creating a generic ContentBase table that stores information for both a product and a download. Then the other tables store their own data (such as ImageUrl for a product and DownloadUrl for the Download table) together with a foreign key pointing to the ContentBase table that holds the base data for the record like the Title and Description.

However, such a solution can result in a messy table structure pretty quickly. Also, the extra amount of work it takes to insert data in two tables and to keep those tables in sync makes this solution a less attractive alternative. Therefore, it was decided to duplicate the shared columns in both the Product and the Download tables.

The Faq Table

The Faq table stores the data for the Frequently Asked Questions and has the following four columns:

Column Name	Data Type	Description
Id	`int`	The unique ID of the FAQ in the database. The ID is generated automatically whenever a new FAQ is inserted.
QuestionShort	`nvarchar(200)`	A short version of the question of the FAQ.
QuestionLong	`nvarchar(MAX)`	A longer version of the question, possibly providing more background information about the question.
Answer	`nvarchar(MAX)`	The answer to the question.

Now, on to the final table in the Customer Support Site database: the Category table.

The Category Table

The Category table stores the categories used throughout the site. This table has a relation to itself through its ParentCategoryId column that is related to the Id column.

Column Name	Data Type	Description
Id	`int`	The unique ID of the category in the database. The ID is generated automatically whenever a new category is inserted.
Description	`nvarchar(100)`	The description of the category.
ParentCategoryId	`int`	The ID of the category that the current category relates to. When this column is `NULL` the category is a root category and has no parent of its own.

Stored Procedures and User-Defined Functions

The Customer Support Site interacts with the database exclusively with stored procedures. You'll find no SQL statements directly in the ASPX pages or their code-behind files. This way, the site is easier to maintain because if you need to make a change to the data structure, you need to make the change at exactly one place, the stored procedure, and not in all of the pages that are accessing the database.

To abstract some functionality even further, two user-defined functions (UDFs) were created. A UDF is essentially a reusable piece of T-SQL code that can be called by other code, including stored procedures, and that can return various types of data, including scalar values (such as a number or a piece of text) and entire tables. In the case of the Customer Support Site, the two UDFs return a custom table with an ID and a Description column holding categories from the Category table. You'll find the functions, called `fnSelectChildCategories` and `fnSelectParentCategories`, under the Functions node of the database on the Database Explorer in Visual Web Developer. The inner workings of these functions are discussed later.

Helper Classes

In addition to the code in the business and data access layers, the Customer Support Site makes use of one helper class called `AppConfiguration` that is saved in the App_Code folder directly.

The AppConfiguration Class

The `AppConfiguration` class provides configuration information to code in both the presentation and data access layers. It has three public and shared read-only properties that provide configuration information stored in the Web.config file (see Figure 8-13).

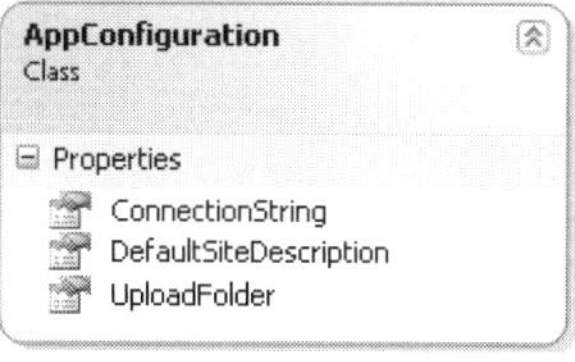

Figure 8-13

The `ConnectionString` property is used by the methods in the data access layer to connect to the database. The `DefaultSiteDescription` property is used to automatically inject a default description of the site in `<meta>` tags in the head of the page. You see how this is used when the master page file for the site is discussed.

The final property of this class is called `UploadFolder`. This property returns a virtual path to the folder that is used to save files that are uploaded in the Management section. To make maintenance simpler, the `UploadFolder` property uses the same key used by the FCKeditor. This means that files that are uploaded through the editor and through the file upload controls on the page end up in the same folder.

Code and Code Explanation

Before beginning discussion of the more advanced features of the Customer Support Site, such as the Product Locator and the Download List, you need to take a look at a few important files first. All of these files are located in the root of the web site.

Root Files

In the root of the web site you find five important files: two master pages with a .master extension, the Default.aspx page, the Global.asax file, and the Web.config file, which contains a few settings used by other pages, so this file is discussed first.

Web.config

Similar to other applications you have seen in this book, the Web.config file contains a few custom keys, the connection string for the application, and configuration information for the skin used in the site. The two custom keys under the `<appSettings>` node are used to set the path where images and other uploads are stored and to determine the default site description text.

Also inside Web.config, you'll find the `<pages>` node. This key sets the site theme to CustomerSupport, a custom theme stored inside the App_Themes folder. The theme has just a single file called GridView.skin that defines the look and feel of each `GridView` in the site.

All the other settings in Web.config should be familiar by now, so they aren't discussed in any more detail.

Global.asax

Just as in Chapter 6, the Global.asax contains code that can send e-mail whenever an error is raised in the site. The code is identical to that in Chapter 6 so refer to that chapter's "Code and Code Explanation" section in case you want to know how the code works.

Default.aspx

This is the homepage for the site and is based on the MainMaster master page (discussed next). The page just has some text welcoming the user. This page would be a good place to promote some of the new products that Wrox Hardware offers, or have a list with new additions to the site.

Master Pages

The Customer Support Site has two almost identical master pages: one for the public area of the site and one for the Management section. The biggest difference between the two is the user control of type ManagementMenu, which is called `ManagementMenu1` in the code. This menu holds the items for the administrative interface that is loaded by default in the Management master page. Another difference is the way metadata is added to the `<head>` section of the public master page automatically.

To see how this works, open up the file MainMaster.Master.vb in the root of the site, which is the code-behind file for the public master page. Refer to the section "Setting up the Customer Support Site" near the end of this chapter for instructions on installing the application so you get access to its code. You can choose either the automated or the manual installation process. With both methods, you'll end up with a folder that holds the files for the application, including the code-behind file MainMaster.Master.vb. In this code file, you see two properties called `Keywords` and `Description`. These properties can be accessed from code outside the `MainMaster` class because they are marked as `Public`. The `Page_Load` of the master page uses these properties to dynamically change some `<meta>` tags in the head of the page:

```
Protected Sub Page_Load(ByVal sender As Object, ByVal e As System.EventArgs) _
        Handles Me.Load
  Dim metaTag As HtmlMeta = New HtmlMeta()
  If Not Keywords Is String.Empty Then
    metaTag.Name = "keywords"
    metaTag.Content = Keywords
    Page.Header.Controls.Add(metaTag)
  End If

  metaTag = New HtmlMeta()
  metaTag.Name = "description"
  If Not Description = String.Empty Then
    metaTag.Content = Description
  Else
    metaTag.Content = AppConfiguration.DefaultSiteDescription
  End If
  Page.Header.Controls.Add(metaTag)
End Sub
```

This code first creates a new instance of `HtmlMeta`, a class designed specifically to represent metadata for your page. This class exposes a `Name` and a `Content` property that map directly to the `Name` and `Description` attributes you see in `<meta>` tags. The `keywords` meta tag is filled with the value from the public `Keywords` property defined in the same code-behind file, but only if it has a value. The `Description` tag employs a more sophisticated solution. The code first checks to see if the `Description` property has a value. If it does, that value is used. If the property hasn't been set, the default description is retrieved by calling `AppConfiguration.DefaultSiteDescription`, which in turn gets the requested value from the Web.config file.

When both the `Name` and `Content` properties have been set, the `HtmlMeta` tag object is added to the `Controls` collection of the `Header`, which is also a control itself. When the page is finally rendered, the `HtmlMeta` object renders itself as an HTML `<meta>` tag within the `<head>` section of the page. Given the previous example this results in HTML like this:

```
<head>
  <title>Welcome to the Wrox Hardware Support Site</title>
  <meta name="description" content="Wrox Hardware - The number one hardware
         shop in the world" />
</head>
```

Pages that use the master page can now access the public properties when the page loads. However, by default you cannot access these properties directly. The default `Master` property that a page exposes is of type `System.Web.UI.MasterPage`. This class does not have a `Keywords` property. To be able to access custom properties of a master page, you need to set the `MasterType` directive in the page where you want to access these properties. One page that implements this is the ProductDetails.aspx page located in the ContentFiles folder. This is the code that page has at the top of its markup file:

```
<%@ MasterType VirtualPath="~/MainMaster.Master" %>
```

With the `MasterType` set, the page can now access the `Keywords` property of the master page in its `Load` event:

```
Me.Master.Keywords = myProduct.Keywords
```

This simply accesses the public `Keywords` property of the master page. Because the `MasterType` has been set, Visual Web Developer is now aware of the additional methods and properties of the master page, so you get full IntelliSense.

With the `Keywords` property set on the master page, the `<meta>` tags are added to the page automatically when the page gets rendered.

The keywords itself are added to the Product in the page InsertUpdateProduct.aspx in the content management section of the site, which is discussed later in this chapter.

With this bit of code in the master file you have created a very flexible way to inject metadata in the head of the page. By default, the master page makes sure that each page has at least a description meta tag that gets its value from the Web.config file. However, pages that need to set a more detailed description or keywords can do so now, simply by accessing the public properties of the master page. It's also easy to expand the code in the master page so it adds other meta tags like copyright, author, and revisit-after.

Other Files and Folders

In addition to the files in the root, the Customer Support Site consists of a lot of other files and folders. A little later in this section you learn about the files in the ContentFiles folder because those make up most of the public interface of the web site. This section also briefly touches on some of the files in the Management folder that contains the content management system for the site.

That leaves you with a few files and folders that need a short explanation:

- **Bin:** This folder contains the DLL used by the FCKeditor in the Management section.
- **Controls:** This folder stores the user controls that are used throughout the site:
    - The ManagementMenu.ascx control is used in the Management folder and contains links to each of the four important management pages.

- Footer.ascx is used on every page and is therefore added to the MainMaster and ManagementMaster pages. It contains a copyright notice and a link to the web site, but of course you can change it to whatever you see fit.
- The Header.ascx control contains the logo. To make it easier for a user to browse to the homepage, the whole logo is clickable and links to the root of the site.
- The MainMenu.ascx control contains a simple unordered list with a few list items that make up the menu. A couple of CSS selectors in the style sheet then change the appearance of these list items so they look like a true menu.

- **Css:** The Css folder contains two CSS files: Core.css and Styles.css. Core.css contains all the main CSS elements that control the looks and positioning of the web site. Styles.css contains custom style classes that influence appearance of smaller elements, like buttons, and the headers and rows from items in a `GridView` control.
- **FCKeditor:** This folder contains the FCKeditor used in the Management section. Refer to Chapter 6 for more information about this editor.
- **Images:** Contains the images used in the design of the web site, such as the logo. Note that this is not the folder where uploaded images and files are stored.
- **UserFiles:** Used by the FCKeditor and the Management section to store uploaded images of products, downloads, and so on.

Now that you have seen most of the additional files in the web site, it's time to turn your attention to the actual pages that make up the Wrox Hardware support site. The next section starts off by discussing the Product Locator, which enables a user to find a product by choosing categories from a drop-down. The section that follows the Product Locator describes how the Downloads List works, which allows users to find downloadable files for their products. Finally, you see how the FAQ page works where users can search the list with frequently asked questions.

The Product Locator

Despite its fancy name, the Product Locator (located in ContentFiles/Products.aspx) is actually a pretty simple page. It has three drop-downs that allow a user to drill down in a list with categories. The first drop-down displays categories from level one, and the second drop-down then displays all categories of level two that are a child of the selected parent. This works the same for the third drop-down. To understand how this works, look at the markup for the Products page:

```
<asp:DropDownList ID="lstCategoryLevel1" runat="server"
        DataSourceID="odsCategoryLevel1" DataTextField="Description"
        DataValueField="Id" AutoPostBack="True" AppendDataBoundItems="True">
  <asp:ListItem Value="">Select a category</asp:ListItem>
</asp:DropDownList>
<asp:DropDownList ID="lstCategoryLevel2" runat="server"
        DataSourceID="odsCategoryLevel2" DataTextField="Description"
        DataValueField="Id" Visible="False" AutoPostBack="True" >
</asp:DropDownList>
<asp:DropDownList ID="lstCategoryLevel3" runat="server"
        DataSourceID="odsCategoryLevel3" DataTextField="Description"
        DataValueField="Id" Visible="False" AutoPostBack="True">
</asp:DropDownList>
```

In this code, some of the important properties are highlighted so they are easier to see. In the first drop-down, `AppendDataBoundItems` has been set to `True`, to ensure that any static item, like the "Select a category" item that is added in the markup of the page, is not replaced by the items from the database. In addition, `AutoPostBack` on all controls is set to `True` to ensure the page refreshes when the user chooses a new item from one of the drop-downs. Initially when the page loads, the second and third drop-downs are hidden by setting `Visible` to `False`. There is some code in the code-behind for the page that makes the drop-downs visible when appropriate. That code is examined a little later.

Another important property of the drop-downs is the `DataSourceID`. The first drop-down points to a `<asp:ObjectDataSource>` control called `odsCategoryLevel1`, the second to `odsCategoryLevel2`, and the third to `odsCategoryLevel3`. All three `ObjectDataSource` controls are using the same method and class name. The following snippet shows the markup for the first `ObjectDataSource`:

```
<asp:ObjectDataSource ID="odsCategoryLevel1" runat="server"
        SelectMethod="GetCategoryList" TypeName="Category">
  <SelectParameters>
    <asp:Parameter Name="parentCategoryId" Type="Int32" />
  </SelectParameters>
</asp:ObjectDataSource>
```

The new `<asp:ObjectDataSource>` controls are a great way to enforce good n-tier architecture in your site, resulting in scalable and maintainable web pages. By using an `ObjectDataSource` control, you don't clutter your pages with names of stored procedures or worse, entire SQL statements. Instead, you point the control to a class name and a `SelectMethod` in the business layer, and when the control is told to get its data, it calls the method you specified. In the preceding code example, this `ObjectDataSource` control calls the `GetCategoryList` method of the `Category` class in the file Category.vb. This method looks like this:

```
Public Shared Function GetCategoryList(ByVal parentCategoryId As Integer) _
        As DataSet
  Return CategoryDB.GetCategoryList(parentCategoryId)
End Function
```

What's important about this method is the `Shared` keyword. This means that the method runs on a *type* (the `Category` class in this example) rather than on an *instance* of that type. Because the method is shared, the `ObjectDataSource` doesn't need a reference to an instance of `Category` but can call the `GetCategoryList` method directly. If the method isn't marked as `Shared`, the `ObjectDataSource` automatically creates an instance of the `Category` class by calling its default parameterless constructor. If the method isn't marked as `Shared` and the class has no default parameterless constructor, the `ObjectDataSource` cannot create an instance of your class and call the method. However, you can still manually assign the `ObjectDataSource` an instance of your class in its `ObjectCreating` event. You see how this works in Chapter 12.

The `GetCategoryList` method simply forwards the call to a method with the same name in the `CategoryDB` class:

```
Public Shared Function GetCategoryList(ByVal parentCategoryId As Integer) _
          As DataSet
  Dim myDataSet As DataSet = New DataSet()
  Using myConnection As New SqlConnection(AppConfiguration.ConnectionString)
    Dim myCommand As SqlCommand = New SqlCommand( _
```

```
                "sprocCategorySelectList", myConnection)
      myCommand.CommandType = CommandType.StoredProcedure

      If parentCategoryId > 0 Then
        myCommand.Parameters.AddWithValue("@parentCategoryId", parentCategoryId)
      Else
        myCommand.Parameters.AddWithValue("@parentCategoryId", DBNull.Value)
      End If

      Dim myDataAdapter As SqlDataAdapter = New SqlDataAdapter()
      myDataAdapter.SelectCommand = myCommand
      myDataAdapter.Fill(myDataSet)
      myConnection.Close()
      Return myDataSet
    End Using
  End Function
```

This code looks very similar to the code you saw in previous chapters. The only thing that needs explaining is the code that assigns the parameter for the stored procedure with `AddWithValue`. When the `parent CategoryId` passed to this method is larger than zero, its value is sent to the stored procedure that in turn gets all the categories with a `parentCategoryId` of that value. When the value is less than one, the value of `DBNull` is passed to the procedure. In that case, the stored procedure returns all the categories that have `NULL` for their ParentCategoryId columns, which are all the root categories.

To see how this all fits together, taker another look at the Products page. The first drop-down is bound to `odsCategoryLevel1`, which has a `<SelectParameter>` with a name of `parentCategoryId` and a type of `Int32`. You can also see this parameter never gets a value in the code, so it defaults back to the intrinsic default value of an integer: zero. This is why the `ObjectDataSource` for the first drop-down returns all the root categories. The second and third data source controls have a `<SelectParameter>` that is bound to a drop-down like this:

```
<asp:ObjectDataSource ID="odsCategoryLevel2" runat="server"
                SelectMethod="GetCategoryList" TypeName="Category">
  <SelectParameters>
    <asp:ControlParameter ControlID="lstCategoryLevel1" Name="parentCategoryId"
                PropertyName="SelectedValue" Type="Int32" />
  </SelectParameters>
</asp:ObjectDataSource>
```

When this control is about to get the data, it gets the `SelectedValue` from the previous drop-down, which is the drop-down with the root categories. This ID is then stored in the `SelectParameter` of the `Object DataSource` control and eventually passed to `GetCategoryList`, which gets all the child categories for the selected parent category.

The same process is repeated for the third drop-down, but this time the `SelectedValue` from the second drop-down is retrieved and passed to `GetCategoryList` to get the categories at the third level.

The current implementation of the three linked drop-down controls requires a postback to the server each time a new category is chosen in one of the lists. To improve the page's load time and the user experience you could implement these linked lists using AJAX — a combination of JavaScript, XML, and server-side techniques — to get just the data for the related drop-downs. The beauty of this is that the entire page is not refreshed, but only the contents of the drop-down controls. This results in a flicker-free page and faster population of the drop-down controls. Get a copy of Wrox's *Professional Ajax* for more information about AJAX.

The final step in the Product Locator is retrieving the products that are related to the category chosen in the third drop-down. Once again, this is done with an `ObjectDataSource` control:

```
<asp:ObjectDataSource ID="odsProducts" runat="server"
            SelectMethod="GetProductList" TypeName="Product">
  <SelectParameters>
    <asp:ControlParameter ControlID="lstCategoryLevel3" Name="categoryId"
            PropertyName="SelectedValue" Type="Int32" />
  </SelectParameters>
</asp:ObjectDataSource>
```

This `ObjectDataSource` control has its `SelectMethod` set to a method in the `Product` class. This means when the control must get its data, it fires `GetProductList` in the `Product` class and sends it the `SelectedValue` of the third drop-down (`lstCategoryLevel3`). `GetProductList` in the `Product` class simply delegates its responsibility to `GetProductList` in the `ProductDB` class and passes it the `categoryId`.

That method is similar to the `GetCategoryList` method you saw before in that it fires a stored procedure and then returns the results as a DataSet.

The only difference is the way the `categoryId` is passed to the database:

```
If categoryId = -1 Then
  myCommand.Parameters.AddWithValue("@categoryId", DBNull.Value)
Else
  myCommand.Parameters.AddWithValue("@categoryId", categoryId)
End If
```

When `categoryId` is not `-1`, its value is sent to the stored procedure with the `AddWithValue` method. When it is `-1`, the value of `DBNull` is sent instead. This distinction is necessary because the `GetProduct List` is also used in the Management section of the site. The page that displays the products displays all of them regardless of the category. To that end, the `Product` class has an overloaded method that has no parameters and sends the value of `-1` to the method in the `ProductDB` class like this:

```
Public Shared Function GetProductList() As DataSet
  Return ProductDB.GetProductList(-1)
End Function
```

This value of `-1` passed to `GetProductList` eventually results in `DBNull.Value` being passed to the stored procedure. In that procedure, the following code is used in the `WHERE` clause to limit the list with products:

```
FROM
  PRODUCT
WHERE
  CategoryId = @categoryId
  OR @categoryId IS NULL
ORDER BY
  Title
```

When @categoryId has a value, the first line in the WHERE clause code returns all records with a Category Id equal to @categoryId. This makes sure the correct products are returned in the front end of the site when a valid child category has been chosen. The second line of the WHERE statement compares the *parameter* @categoryId against the value NULL. This is the case in the Management section where NULL is passed to the stored procedure. Now all products are returned, regardless of their CategoryId. This is a quick trick to distinguish between the front-end and the back-end functionality without the need for complex IF/THEN logic or multiple stored procedures.

The final step in the Product Locator is displaying the items returned from the database. The page has an <asp:DataList> control called dlProducts that is bound to the datasource odsProducts you saw earlier. This DataList has an <ItemTemplate> that displays the fields like the product's title, tag line, image, and a link to the ProductDetails.aspx page:

```
<asp:DataList ID="dlProducts" runat="server" DataKeyField="Id"
        DataSourceID="odsProducts" EnableViewState="False" >
  <ItemTemplate>
    <h2>
      <%# Eval("Title") %>
    </h2>
    <p class="Summary">
      <asp:Image ID="productImage" runat="server"
              ImageUrl='<%# Eval("ImageUrl") %>' ImageAlign="Right" />
      <%# Eval("TagLine") %>
    </p>
    <br />
    <asp:HyperLink ID="hyperReadMore" runat="server"
             NavigateUrl='<%# "ProductDetails.aspx?Id=" & Eval("Id") %>'
             Text="Read More..." />
  </ItemTemplate>
</asp:DataList>
```

The ProductDetails.aspx page uses Product.Get(productId) to get an instance of a product and displays its properties on the page. You see the product's keywords being added to a <meta> tag in the master page discussed previously. When you look at the Get method in the business layer folder, you'll notice the square brackets around the method's name:

```
Public Shared Function [Get](ByVal id As Integer) As Product
  Return ProductDB.Get(id)
End Function
```

Because Get is a reserved word in Visual Basic .NET, you have to surround the name with the brackets to tell the compiler to ignore the special meaning of the Get keyword. If you find this makes your code look awkward, simply rename the method to something like GetItem or GetProduct. All Get methods in the business and data access layer have the square brackets around their name.

Now that you have seen how the product locator works, it's time to look at a bit more advanced code in the Downloads page. That page uses the same concepts as the Product Locator, but it has a few twists that are worth looking at in more detail.

The Downloads List

At first glance, the Downloads.apsx file in the ContentFiles folder looks almost identical to the Product page. Though this is certainly true for the markup portion of the page, the code-behind for the page contains code that makes it behave entirely differently. This code is needed because the Downloads page displays downloadable files that are related to the currently chosen category at each level and all of its parent and child levels. With the Products page, you have to make a selection in all of the three drop-downs first because the `DataList` control used to display the products only retrieves products that are related to the final and deepest category you selected.

The Downloads page enables a content manager to link a certain downloadable file to only the main category, or to the second or third category. For example, the Warranty Card or Terms and Conditions document may apply to all products that Rocks Hardware creates so it's logical to bind those downloads to a category in the root only. When users then select Rocks Hardware from the drop-down they expect to see the card and terms appear. However, they also expect the drivers for the 850 T5 Printer and for the 3D Printer 740 to appear because ultimately, these drivers fall under the Rocks Hardware category as well. If they then select the category Power Printers, they'll expect that all downloads related to the other category, 3D Printers, will disappear. The Warranty Card and the drivers for the 850 T5 Printer should remain visible, because they still fall under the path of Rocks Hardware and Power Printers.

If you're confused by this, look at Figure 8-14, which displays the hierarchy of some of the categories in the database. The diagram focuses on the Rocks Hardware category, so it doesn't display the children for the other two categories.

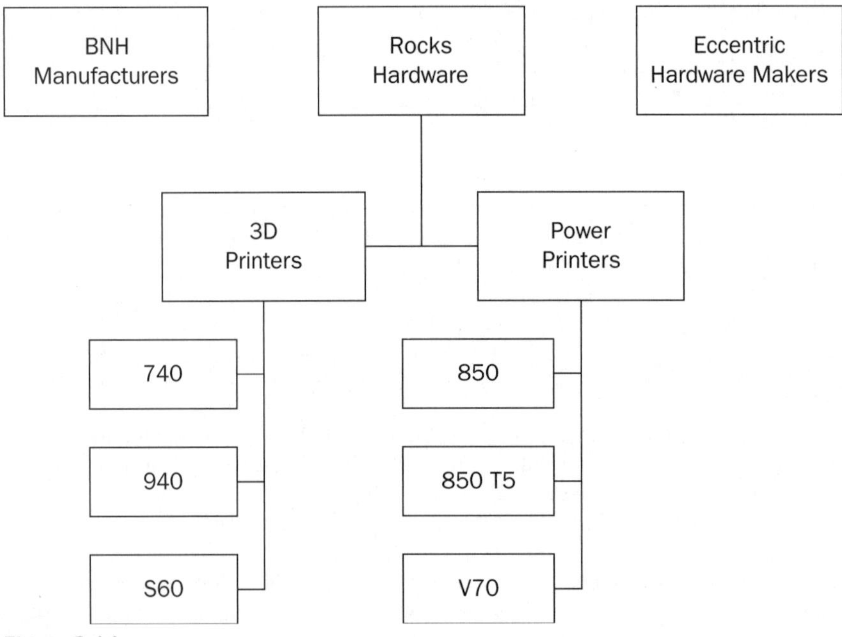

Figure 8-14

From this diagram you can see that Rocks Hardware has two child categories: 3D Printers and Power Printers. Each of these categories has three child records of its own. When you select Rocks Hardware as the first category, the Downloads list displays all records that are related to Rocks Hardware, including its children and their children. If you select the Power Printers from the second drop-down, you'll see records that belong to the root category Rocks Hardware (like the Warranty Card), the Power Printers, and all of its child categories. The list no longer displays records that are linked to the 3D Printers category. Finally, if you select the 850 T5 from the last drop-down, you'll see the downloads that are linked to that category directly, or to its parent or grandparent but no longer those related to the 850 or V70 category.

Hierarchical data selection as in the preceding example has always been difficult in SQL Server, until the release of SQL Server 2005, which introduces a concept called Common Table Expressions (CTE). A CTE is a temporary result with a name that can be used in other expressions and code. It's a bit like an in-memory table that you can link to other tables. The good thing about CTEs is that they support recursion, which allows you to perform very powerful queries with just a few lines of code.

To see CTEs at work, you need to take one step back and look at the source for the `ObjectDataSource` control in the Downloads page and see how it gets its data:

```
<asp:ObjectDataSource ID="odsDownloads" runat="server"
         SelectMethod="GetDownloadList" TypeName="Download">
  <SelectParameters>
    <asp:ControlParameter ControlID="lstCategoryLevel1" Name="categoryId"
           PropertyName="SelectedValue" Type="Int32" />
    <asp:Parameter Direction="InputOutput" Name="recordsAffected" Type="Int32" />
  </SelectParameters>
</asp:ObjectDataSource>
```

So far, not much is new. The data source control is linked to the `GetDownloadList` method in the `Download` class. You also see a `recordsAffected` parameter that returns the number of products returned from the database. You see where this is used later.

`GetDownloadList` gets its records from a method with the same name in the `DownloadDB` class, counts the number of records and assigns that to an output parameter, and then returns the DataSet like this:

```
Public Shared Function GetDownloadList(ByVal categoryId As Integer, _
             ByRef recordsAffected As Integer) As DataSet
  Dim dsDownloads As DataSet = DownloadDB.GetDownloadList(categoryId)
  recordsAffected = dsDownloads.Tables(0).Rows.Count
  Return dsDownloads
End Function
```

The `GetDownloadList` method in the `DownloadDB` class has code similar to the `GetProductList` method you saw earlier. It's the stored procedure that gets the requested downloads where things get interesting (and a bit more complicated). Take a look at the `SELECT` statement for that procedure:

```
SELECT TOP 100
  Id,
  Title,
  Description,
  CategoryId,
  DownloadUrl
FROM
  Download
WHERE
  CategoryId IN
  (
```

```
    SELECT DISTINCT Id FROM fnSelectChildCategories(@categoryId)
    UNION
    SELECT DISTINCT Id FROM fnSelectParentCategories(@categoryId)
  )
  OR @categoryId IS NULL
ORDER BY
  Title
```

The first part, the `SELECT` and the `FROM` clause, looks pretty normal, and so does the `ORDER BY` clause. It's the `WHERE` clause that looks odd. First of all, you see an `IN` statement. The `IN` statement in the T-SQL language is a convenient way to select multiple records; for example, by their ID. The following `SELECT` statement returns downloads in the categories with in ID of `3`, `7`, or `8`:

```
SELECT Id, Description FROM Download WHERE CategoryId IN (3, 7, 8)
```

The second part of the `WHERE` clause uses a `UNION` statement to combine the results of the two inner `SELECT` statements. Ignoring the actual implementation of the two `SELECT` statements for now, assume that the first `SELECT` returns something like `3, 7, 8` and the other `SELECT` returns `4, 7, 9`. The end result for the outer `WHERE` clause is then

```
WHERE CategoryId IN (3, 4, 7, 8, 9)
```

Notice that the duplicate values (`7`) have been removed automatically. If you don't want that to happen, use `UNION ALL` instead.

Now on to the hardest part: `fnSelectChildCategories` and `fnSelectParentCategories`. These two are user-defined functions (UDFs) that return a table to the calling code. They also accept a parameter of type `int`. These functions are capable of returning the parent IDs or the child IDs plus its own ID of a given category. So, given Figure 8-14, imagine you called `fnSelectParentCategories` with the ID of the category V70; you'll get the IDs of the categories V70, Power Printers, and Rocks Hardware. To see how this works, take a look at the `fnSelectParentCategories` function that returns a category's parents:

```
CREATE FUNCTION fnSelectParentCategories
(
  @categoryId int
)

RETURNS @theCategoryTable TABLE (Id int, Description nvarchar(100))

AS

BEGIN

WITH CategoriesCte(Id, Description, ParentCategoryId)
AS
(
  SELECT Id, Description, ParentCategoryId
  FROM Category
  WHERE Id = @categoryId

  UNION ALL

  SELECT C.Id, C.Description, C.ParentCategoryId
```

```
    FROM Category AS C
       JOIN CategoriesCte AS E
          ON C.Id = E.ParentCategoryId
   )

   INSERT INTO @theCategoryTable (Id, Description)
            SELECT Id, Description FROM CategoriesCte

   RETURN

   END
```

First, the function signature is defined, with the function's name and its input parameter called `@categoryId`. The `RETURNS` statement that follows tells calling code that this function returns a table object with an ID and a Description column. The table returned from this function can be used like any other normal table; you can select from it, join it with other tables, and so on.

The second part of the function might be new to you, so it's important to look at it closely. The `WITH` statement indicates the start of a Common Table Expression (CTE). This code example shows a recursive CTE, although it's also possible to use CTEs without recursion.

A *recursive* CTE consists of two parts: the *anchor member* and the *recursive member*. In the preceding code, the first `SELECT` statement is the anchor member. When the function is executed, this `SELECT` statement is fired first. Then for each record in the result set of that expression, the recursive member is triggered. Then for each record that the recursive member added to the result set, the recursive member is triggered again, until no more records are encountered.

Given the example of the V70 printer again, look at Figure 8-15, which displays the results from the CTE for the category V70.

Id	ParentCategoryId	Category	Member
67	64	V70	Anchor
64	55	Power Printers	Recursive
55	null	Rocks Hardware	Recursive

First recursion

Second recursion

Figure 8-15

When the anchor member's `SELECT` statement runs, it adds the first record to the result set with an ID of 67 and a ParentCategoryId of 64. The recursive member then runs, and selects the categories whose ID matches the ParentCategoryId of the V70 record. This is only one record, the one for the Power Printers, which has an ID of 64 and a ParentCategoryId of 55. This record is also added to the result set. The

SELECT statement is then repeated for the record that has just been added, and this time it selects the parent category for the Power Printers record, which results in the Rocks Hardware category being added to the result set.

The function fnSelectChildCategories, which selects a category's child records, works in pretty much the same way. However, because a parent category can have multiple child records that in turn can have even more child records, the result set that is returned is likely to be larger.

The stored procedure that selects the downloads from the database selects both the child records and the parent records using a UNION statement. This way, the full path of a category is returned, including its parent and grandparent, and all of its children and their children. If you only want to retrieve the child records for a category, remove the UNION statement and the line that selects from the fnSelect ParentCategories function from the stored procedure sprocDownloadSelectList.

Now that you have seen how the stored procedure sprocDownloadSelectList gets its records from the database, the next part you need to look at is how the Downloads page is able to figure out for which selected drop-down it should return records. Take another look at the ObjectDataSource that gets the downloads, but this time focus on the <SelectParameters> node that has a single <asp:ControlParameter>:

```
<asp:ObjectDataSource ID="odsDownloads" runat="server"
        SelectMethod="GetDownloadList" TypeName="Download">
  <SelectParameters>
    <asp:ControlParameter ControlID="lstCategoryLevel1" Name="categoryId"
          PropertyName="SelectedValue" Type="Int32" />
    <asp:Parameter Direction="InputOutput" Name="recordsAffected" Type="Int32" />
  </SelectParameters>
</asp:ObjectDataSource>
```

Initially, the ControlID of the ControlParameter is set to lstCategoryLevel1. This means that if you choose an item from the first drop-down, the page will refresh and you'll see the downloads that belong to that category and all of its child categories using the recursive CTE you just saw. However, when you then select a category from the second drop-down, the downloads list should display records that are connected to that category instead. The code in the code-behind for the page is responsible for that:

```
Protected Sub lstCategoryLevel2_SelectedIndexChanged(ByVal sender As Object, _
        ByVal e As System.EventArgs) Handles lstCategoryLevel2.SelectedIndexChanged
  If Not lstCategoryLevel2.SelectedValue = "" Then
    ' Enable the third drop-down
    lstCategoryLevel3.Visible = True
    ' Next, bind the odsDownloads to this drop-down.
    Dim myParam As ControlParameter = _
            CType(odsDownloads.SelectParameters(0), ControlParameter)
    myParam.ControlID = "lstCategoryLevel2"
    lstCategoryLevel3.DataBind()
  Else
    Dim myParam As ControlParameter = _
            CType(odsDownloads.SelectParameters(0), ControlParameter)
    myParam.ControlID = "lstCategoryLevel1"
    lstCategoryLevel3.Visible = False
  End If
End Sub
```

This code fires when you select a different option in the second drop-down. Inside the event handler for `SelectedIndexChanged` of that drop-down the `SelectedValue` is checked. If there is a value (which means a valid category was chosen), the `SelectParameter` you saw earlier for the `ObjectDataSource` is dynamically changed to the second drop-down:

```
Dim myParam As ControlParameter = _
                CType(odsDownloads.SelectParameters(0), ControlParameter)
    myParam.ControlID = "lstCategoryLevel2"
```

The first line of code gets a reference to the first `SelectParameter` of the data source control (the second parameter is an output parameter used to find out how many records were returned from the database). The `SelectParameters` collection returns a more generic `Parameter` object, so `CType` is used to cast it to the appropriate `ControlParameter` type. Once `myParam` contains a `ControlParameter`, you can access its `ControlID` property and assign it the ID of the second drop-down. This causes the `ObjectDataSource` to get the `SelectedValue` from that drop-down, which is then passed to its `SelectMethod`, the `Get DownloadList` method of the `Download` class. This in turns causes the `DataList` to display the downloadable files that are related to the chosen category.

This same principle is repeated for the third and first drop-down as well. This way, you can be sure that the `DataList` always displays records that are related to the category chosen in the last affected drop-down.

This code example shows that the code you define for controls in the page's markup is not set in stone. You can easily modify the controls at run time using code in various events and methods in the code-behind. This can be very useful if you want to change a page's behavior at run time.

The final part in the Downloads page you need to look at is the `Selected` event of the `odsDownloads` control. This event fires when the control is done retrieving data from its data source and is an ideal place to display a message to the user indicating if and how many records were returned from the database. The `GetDownloadList` method in the `Download` class has an output parameter (indicated by the keyword `ByRef`) that returns the number of affected records to the calling code. Inside the `Selected` event for the data source, this output parameter is retrieved from the `OutputParameters` collection of the `ObjectDataSourceStatusEventArgs` argument passed to the method:

```
Protected Sub odsDownloads_Selected(ByVal sender As Object, _
   ByVal e As System.Web.UI.WebControls.ObjectDataSourceStatusEventArgs) Handles _
      odsDownloads.Selected
    Dim recordsAffected As Integer = _
       Convert.ToInt32(e.OutputParameters.Item("recordsAffected"))
  ' The rest of the code is omitted
End Sub
```

The remainder of the code in the event handler is used to build up a message that is shown on the page to tell the user how many records were found.

This concludes the discussion of the Downloads page. With this page in place, users can browse the list of downloads, filtering the number of downloads to those they are most interested in.

Another feature of the site that allows the user to search for content is the Frequently Asked Questions page, which is discussed next.

Searching Frequently Asked Questions

The page with the frequently asked questions behaves differently from the pages you have seen so far. Instead of drilling down in the list of FAQs using drop-downs for the categories, the FAQs page allows a user to search the entire FAQs table with a Boolean query that supports `AND` and `OR` logic. So searching for `driver AND failure` brings up all frequently asked questions that contain the words driver and failure, whereas searching for `driver OR failure` brings up the FAQs that have at least one of those words in them.

The commercial versions of SQL Server 2005 support a concept called Full Text Indexing. This is a very smart search technology enabling you to ask much more sophisticated questions than simple Boolean queries. However, Full Text Indexing is not available in the Express Edition of SQL Server, so you'll have to pay for the full version if you want to use this feature. Search the SQL Server books online or search Microsoft's MSDN web site (`http://msdn.microsoft.com`) for the article "SQL Server 2005 Full-Text Search: Internals and Enhancements" for more information about Full Text Indexing.

The markup of the FAQs page is very simple. It contains some introduction text, a text box for the search term, a button to initiate the search action, and two placeholders that display a message to the user about the number of results found. It also contains a `DataList` control that displays the frequently asked questions and the answers. You might notice the absence of a data source control in the markup of the page. The page doesn't have one, and all data binding is done in the code-behind of the page, in the button's `Click` event:

```
Protected Sub btnSearch_Click(ByVal sender As Object, _
                ByVal e As System.EventArgs) Handles btnSearch.Click
    dlFaqs.DataSource = Faq.GetFaqList(txtSearchTerm.Text)
    dlFaqs.DataBind()

    If dlFaqs.Items.Count > 0 Then
      lblSearchedFor2.Text = txtSearchTerm.Text
      plcRecords.Visible = True
      plcNoRecords.Visible = False
    Else
      lblSearchedFor1.Text = txtSearchTerm.Text
      plcNoRecords.Visible = True
      plcRecords.Visible = False
    End If
End Sub
```

This code calls the `GetFaqList` method of the `Faq` class. That method, which is examined in a moment, returns a `DataSet` that is assigned to the `DataList` control's `DataSource` property. Because no `Object DataSource` controls are used that handle data binding automatically, you have to explicitly call `DataBind` on the `DataList`. This causes the `DataList` to be rendered, displaying the FAQs returned from the database. After `DataBind` has been called, you can check out the number of items currently being displayed by the `DataList`, by looking at the `Count` property of its `Items` collection. When `Count` is zero, the page shows the `<asp:PlaceHolder>` called `plcNoRecords` that holds a message telling the user no FAQs were found. To show the user what he searched for, the label `lblSearchedFor1` is updated with the search term.

Instead of binding the control directly in the code-behind using `dlFaqs.DataBind()`, you could also use one of the data source controls, like an `ObjectDataSource`. However, using such a control would have meant a lot more work implementing the required functionality on the page. First of all, you'd need to create an `<asp:Parameter>` to feed the search term to the control. You'd also need to find a way to stop the control from executing its `Select` operation when the page first loads. Finally, you'd need to write code in the event handler for its `Selected` event (which fires after the control has selected the data from the data source) to determine if any records have been returned from the data source so you can hide and display the appropriate panels. Using `DataBind` directly on the `DataList` control in the code-behind solves all these problems in one fell swoop. Chapter 12 shows you how to use an `ObjectDataSource` control's `Selected` event to get useful information about the data returned by the control after it has finished with its `Select` method.

When the `DataList` does contain records, the reverse action is performed. The `plcNoRecords` placeholder is hidden and `plcRecord` is shown instead.

As you might expect, `GetFaqList` of the `Faq` class simply calls the `GetFaqList` method in the `FaqDB` class to get the frequently asked questions from the database. This method is worth examining closely, because it is different from other data access code you have seen so far. All the stored procedures you have seen so far were self-contained. That is, they contained complete SQL statements that are optionally fed one or more parameters that control the `WHERE` clause. However, because a user can search the site with the aforementioned Boolean query syntax, a normal `WHERE` clause doesn't work. Instead the code in the `FaqDB` class builds up the `WHERE` clause dynamically, and passes it as a parameter to the stored procedure. That procedure then uses SQL Server's `EXEC` method to execute a dynamic SQL statement that includes the `WHERE` clause. To see how this works, the process is explained step by step. First, take a look at how the final SQL statement should end up. Assume a user searched for `driver AND failure` because she wanted to see all the FAQs that contain these terms. The `SELECT` statement for this search should end up like this:

```
SELECT
  Id,
  QuestionShort,
  QuestionLong,
  Answer
FROM
  Faq
WHERE
  (
    QuestionShort LIKE '%driver%' OR QuestionLong LIKE '%driver%'
               OR Answer LIKE '%driver%'
  )
  AND
  (
    QuestionShort LIKE '%failure%' OR QuestionLong LIKE '%failure%'
               OR Answer LIKE '%failure%'
  )
```

Because of the dynamic nature of the search term, you cannot simply replace `%driver%` and `%failure%` with two parameters to the stored procedure to make the query dynamic. What if the user searched for `driver AND failure AND Power Printer`? Instead of two parameters, you now need three. The answer to this problem is not to make the search terms dynamic, but the entire `WHERE` clause. This is done with the `BuildWhereClause` method that is called in the code for the `GetFaqList` method:

```
Private Shared Function BuildWhereClause(ByVal searchTerm As String) As String
  Dim simpleSearch As Boolean = True
  Dim whereClause As String = String.Empty

  searchTerm = searchTerm.Trim()
  searchTerm = searchTerm.Replace("'", "''")
  searchTerm = searchTerm.Replace("""", "")
  searchTerm = searchTerm.Replace("%", "")
  searchTerm = searchTerm.Replace("--", "")
  searchTerm = searchTerm.Replace(";", "")
  searchTerm = searchTerm.Replace("(", "")
  searchTerm = searchTerm.Replace(")", "")
  searchTerm = searchTerm.Replace("_", "")

  Dim testReplace As String = ""
  testReplace = searchTerm.ToUpper().Replace(" AND ", "")
  If testReplace <> searchTerm.ToUpper() Then
    simpleSearch = False
  End If

  testReplace = searchTerm.ToUpper().Replace(" OR ", "")
  If testReplace <> searchTerm.ToUpper() Then
    simpleSearch = False
  End If

  If simpleSearch = True Then
    searchTerm = searchTerm.Replace(" ", " AND ")
  End If

  Dim myAndSplits() As String = Regex.Split(searchTerm, " and ", _
             RegexOptions.IgnoreCase)

  For i As Integer = 0 To myAndSplits.Length - 1

    Dim myOrSplits() As String = Regex.Split(myAndSplits(i), " or ", _
        RegexOptions.IgnoreCase)
    whereClause += "("
    For j As Integer = 0 To myOrSplits.Length - 1
      whereClause += "(F.QuestionShort LIKE '%" & myOrSplits(j) & "%' OR _
          F.QuestionLong LIKE '%" & myOrSplits(j) & "%' OR F.Answer LIKE '%" & _
          myOrSplits(j) & "%')"

      If (j + 1) < myOrSplits.Length Then
        whereClause += " OR "
      End If
    Next

    whereClause += ") "

    If (i + 1) < myAndSplits.Length Then

      whereClause += " AND "
```

```
    End If

  Next
  Return whereClause
End Function
```

The code starts off with declaring two variables and a number of calls to the `Replace` method:

```
Dim simpleSearch As Boolean = True
Dim whereClause As String = String.Empty

searchTerm = searchTerm.Trim()
searchTerm = searchTerm.Replace("'", "''")
searchTerm = searchTerm.Replace("""", "")
searchTerm = searchTerm.Replace("%", "")
searchTerm = searchTerm.Replace("--", "")
searchTerm = searchTerm.Replace(";", "")
searchTerm = searchTerm.Replace("(", "")
searchTerm = searchTerm.Replace(")", "")
searchTerm = searchTerm.Replace("_", "")
```

The variable `simpleSearch` is used to determine whether the initial request contained an `AND` or an `OR` statement. The variable `whereClause` is used to hold the actual `WHERE` clause this method builds up. Then the `Replace` method is used several times to clean the SQL statement from unwanted characters. If you don't sanitize the code passed to the database like this, your database is open to *SQL injection*, a popular hacker's technique to gain unauthorized access to your database and system. Normally, the parameterized stored procedure code takes care of this, but with a dynamic SQL statement you have to do this yourself. In the current implementation, the cleaning code is embedded directly in the method's body, but if you intend to use this technique more often, it's a good idea to move it to a separate method. You can see that some important characters that have special meaning in T-SQL have been replaced. For example, the two dashes (--) are replaced with nothing. These two characters denote the start of a comment but are also used by hackers practicing SQL injection to stop the rest of a SQL statement from being executed. Also, the single quote (') is escaped with a double single quote, and a double quote (") in the search term is completely removed because they could be used to inject illegal string delimiters. The percentage sign (%) is removed to block users from searching with wild cards.

The next statements use the variable `testReplace` and the `Replace` method to find out if the initial search term contains the keywords `AND` or `OR`:

```
Dim testReplace As String = ""
testReplace = searchTerm.ToUpper().Replace(" AND ", "")
If testReplace <> searchTerm.ToUpper() Then
  simpleSearch = False
End If

testReplace = searchTerm.ToUpper().Replace(" OR ", "")
If testReplace <> searchTerm.ToUpper() Then
  simpleSearch = False
End If
If simpleSearch = True Then
  searchTerm = searchTerm.Replace(" ", " AND ")
End If
```

If one of these two keywords is present in the search term, it's assumed the user deliberately used Boolean logic in her search term. Otherwise, all spaces in the search term are replaced with AND. So, when the user searched for `driver OR failure`, the initial search term is not touched. If, however, the user searched for `driver failure` the initial statement is changed to `driver AND failure`.

The next block of code uses the `Regex` object's `Split` method to split the search term on the word AND, then loops through this array and looks at each individual element:

```
Dim myAndSplits() As String = Regex.Split(searchTerm, " and ", _
          RegexOptions.IgnoreCase)
For i As Integer = 0 To myAndSplits.Length - 1
```

The code then tries to split the element on the keyword `Or`. If this keyword is not present in the element, the `For j` loop runs exactly once and adds the element to the `WHERE` clause surrounded by parentheses. If the element does contain the keyword `Or`, the loop adds each individual item to the `WHERE` clause separated by the `Or` keyword:

```
  Dim myOrSplits() As String = Regex.Split(myAndSplits(i), " or ", _
       RegexOptions.IgnoreCase)
  whereClause += "("
  For j As Integer = 0 To myOrSplits.Length - 1
    whereClause += "(F.QuestionShort LIKE '%" & myOrSplits(j) & "%' OR _
         F.QuestionLong LIKE '%" & myOrSplits(j) & "%' OR F.Answer LIKE '%" & _
         myOrSplits(j) & "%')"

    If (j + 1) < myOrSplits.Length Then
      whereClause += " OR "
    End If
  Next

  whereClause += ") "

  If (i + 1) < myAndSplits.Length Then

    whereClause += " AND "
  End If

Next
Return whereClause
End Function
```

At the end of the function, the entire `WHERE` clause is returned from the function back to the calling code.

To see how the `WHERE` clause ends up, consider the following search term that a user might enter: `driver AND failure AND Power Printer OR 3D Printer`.

This search expression should return all the frequently asked questions with the words driver and failure and either Power Printer or 3D Printer. With this example, at the end of the `BuildWhereClause` function, the variable `whereClause` holds the following string:

```
(
 (
  F.QuestionShort LIKE '%driver%' OR F.QuestionLong LIKE '%driver%'
```

```
          OR F.Answer LIKE '%driver%'
    )
  )
  AND
  (
    (
      F.QuestionShort LIKE '%failure%' OR F.QuestionLong LIKE '%failure%'
          OR F.Answer LIKE '%failure%'
    )
  )
  AND
  (
    (
      F.QuestionShort LIKE '%Power Printer%' OR F.QuestionLong LIKE '%Power
          Printer%' OR F.Answer LIKE '%Power Printer%'
    )
    OR
    (
     F.QuestionShort LIKE '%3D Printer%' OR F.QuestionLong LIKE '%3D Printer%'
          OR F.Answer LIKE '%3D Printer%'
    )
  )
```

When executed by SQL Server, this WHERE clause returns all the frequently asked questions that match the user's search criteria. Because of the way the code is set up, it doesn't matter if the short question contains the word driver and the answer contains the word failure, or vice versa. In all cases, this code finds the records the user is looking for.

The WHERE clause is eventually passed to the database through a SQL parameter called @whereClause, where it is appended to a SQL statement and executed with the EXEC command:

```
CREATE PROCEDURE sprocFaqSelectListBySearchTerm

@whereClause nvarchar(1000)

AS

DECLARE @sqlStatement nvarchar(MAX)

SET @sqlStatement = '
  SELECT
    Id,
    QuestionShort,
    QuestionLong,
    Answer
  FROM
    Faq F
  WHERE ' + @whereClause
  + '
  ORDER BY
    Id DESC'

  EXEC(@sqlStatement)
```

The `EXEC` command returns the requested FAQ items, just like a regular `SELECT` statement would have done.

This concludes the discussion of the FAQs page and the entire public section of the Customer Support Site. With the pages in the public ContentFiles folder, users of the Customer Support Site can now easily locate products, downloads for the products they may have purchased, and browse through the collection of frequently asked questions.

The final part of the "Code and Code Explanation" section takes a quick look at the pages in the Management folder that contain the CMS for the Customer Support Site.

The Customer Support Site CMS

Most of the concepts used in the content management system of the support site have been discussed in previous chapters, most notably Chapter 6. However, a few things are worth discussing, so some of the highlights of these pages are briefly discussed in the sections that follow.

Categories.aspx

This page allows you to add new categories to the database. Using the now familiar drop-downs you can drill down in the hierarchy of categories and add a category at each of the three levels. An important thing to notice about this page is the way the validators are used. The page contains three text boxes that enable you to type a new category to be added to the database at each of the three available levels. Each text box also has an `<asp:RequiredFieldValidator>` control attached to it. Normally, with three validators, you need to fill all three text boxes before the page will validate. However, at any time, only one of the text boxes is required. To enable only one validator control at a time, each validator has a different `ValidationGroup` attribute. The following code snippet shows the code for the validator that checks the first text box:

```
<asp:RequiredFieldValidator ID="reqLevel1" ValidationGroup="Level1" runat="server"
    ControlToValidate="txtLevel1" Display="Dynamic"
    ErrorMessage="*" />
```

Controls that cause the validation to be triggered, like buttons, now also have a `ValidationGroup` attribute. This way, you can relate postback controls with a specific validation group like this:

```
<asp:Button ID="btnAddNewLevel1" runat="server" Text="Add New Level 1"
    ValidationGroup="Level1" />
```

When this button gets clicked, only the controls that share the same `ValidationGroup` are checked for valid values.

The List Pages

The pages that list the products, downloads, and FAQs are all very similar. They have a `GridView` that displays the items. An Edit and a Delete button allow you to change existing items and delete them. The `RowCommand` for each `GridView` looks at the `CommandName` of the `e` argument to determine the action that must be taken using a `Select Case` statement. Inside each of the `Case` blocks, the code converts the `CommandArgument` to an Integer and uses that to retrieve the grid's `DataKey`. You may be tempted to move this code to outside the `Select Case` statement so you only have to write it once. However, when you do so, you'll run into trouble when you try to sort the `GridView`. Although sorting is carried out by

ASP.NET automatically, it still fires the `RowCommand` when you click one of the column headers to sort the grid. When you do so, the `CommandArgument` of the `e` parameter contains the name of the column you're trying to sort on. Obviously, a column name cannot be converted to an Integer, so the code will crash.

The Create and Update Pages

For each of three content types — Downloads, FAQs, and Products — there is an InsertUpdate page that allows you to create new and change existing items. All three use the FCKeditor that you have seen in previous chapters. The code for the Download and Product pages uses the `GetCategoryPath` method of the `Category` class. This method returns the path of a category from a child to the parent record. This method is necessary because the content item in the database only stores the deepest child category. To be able to preselect the drop-downs of the parent levels, you need to know to which parents a category belongs. The stored procedure `sprocCategorySelectPath` once again uses Common Table Expressions in a similar way you have seen before.

With these pages and their code, you have come to the end of the "Code and Code Explanation" section. By now you should have learned enough to use and understand the inner workings of the Customer Support Site. In the next section, you see how to install the application on a web server.

Setting up the Customer Support Site

Just as with the most of the other chapters in this book, you can choose to install the Customer Support Site manually or by using the supplied installer. The installer ensures a quick and easy installation process, whereas the manual process gives you a bit more flexibility with regard to where the files are placed.

Using the Installer

To install the Customer Support Site so you can run it on your server, follow these steps:

1. Open the folder Chapter 08 - Customer Support\Installer from the CD-ROM that came with this book and double-click setup.exe to start up the installer.
2. In the Setup wizard, accept all the defaults by clicking Next until the application has been installed completely. Click Close to close the installer. The setup procedure has copied all the required files to a folder called CustomerSupport under your default web site.
3. Next, open up the Web.config file in the CustomerSupport folder (by default, located at `C:\Inetpub\wwwroot\CustomerSupport`) and locate the `<connectionStrings>` node. Check that the connection string points to your installation of SQL Server and modify the string if required.
4. Just like you did in Chapter 6, you'll need to configure the security permissions of the UserFiles folder, so the web site can save the files that are uploaded through the site and the FCKeditor. Refer to that chapter for detailed instructions.
5. Now browse to `http://localhost/CustomerSupport`. The Customer Support Site should appear and you can browse through the products, downloads, and FAQs lists.

Manual Installation

Although the installer is a very convenient way to set up the Customer Support Site, manual installation isn't much more difficult. To install the site manually, follow these steps:

1. Open the folder Chapter 08 - Customer Support\Source from the CD-ROM that came with this book.
2. Extract the contents of the file Chapter 08 - Customer Support.zip to a location on your hard drive; for example, `C:\Inetpub\wwwroot\`. Make sure you extract the files with the option Use Folder Names or something similar to maintain the original folder structure. The exact setting depends on the extraction utility you're using. You should end up with a folder like `C:\Inetpub\wwwroot\CustomerSupport` that in turn contains a number of files and other folders.
3. Start Visual Web Developer, choose File➪Open Web Site, and browse to the folder that was created in step 2. The site should open and display on the Solution Explorer window.
4. Next, open up the Web.config file from the Solution Explorer and locate the `<connectionStrings>` node. Check that the connection string points to your installation of SQL Server and modify the string if required. Save and close the file.
5. Just like you did in Chapter 6, you'll need to configure the security permissions of the UserFiles folder, so the web site can save the files that are uploaded through the site and the FCKeditor. Refer to that chapter for detailed instructions.
6. You can now browse to the site by pressing Ctrl+F5. Visual Web Developer will start its internal web server and then the site will be displayed in your default web browser.

Using the Customer Support Site

No matter which of the two installation methods you chose, you should now see the Customer Support Site in your browser. You can use the main menu items like Products and Downloads in the way described at the start of this chapter. You'll also see the Management menu item, which allows you to manage the content in the system.

To make it easier to explain how the Customer Support Site works, and make it easier for you to explore the Management section, there is no authentication mechanism in place on this web site. This means anyone accessing this web site has full access to the Management section. Naturally, this isn't something you want, so you should take some steps to protect that area of the site. The easiest way to do this is to configure the application for Membership and Role management by choosing Website➪ASP.NET Configuration in Visual Web Developer. This opens the Web Site Administration Tool in a browser window. Create at least one user and a ContentManagers role and assign the new user to this role. If you need more information about working with the Web Site Administration Tool, click the "How do I use this tool?" link in the upper-right corner of the window.

The next step is to add the following code to the end of your Web.config file, right after the closing tag of the `<system.web>` node:

```
</system.web>
<location path="Management">
  <system.web>
    <authorization>
```

```
      <allow roles="ContentManagers" />
      <deny users="*"/>
    </authorization>
  </system.web>
</location>
```

This blocks access to the Management folder to all users except those that are assigned to the ContentManagers role.

Another solution is to create an entirely new CMS site that connects to the Customer Support database. This way, you can fully separate the public front end from the protected back-end part of the web site.

If you go to `www.wrox.com` and find this book's download page, you'll discover ways to extend the Customer Support Site to make it even more useful than it already is. It suggests a couple of extensions and guides you through implementing one of those features.

Summary

In this chapter you were introduced to the Wrox Hardware Customer Support Site, a web site that allows users to find and retrieve information about the products that the Wrox Hardware company sells.

You first got a quick tour of browsing through the system from an end-user's point of view. You saw how to locate Products and Downloads, and how to search the list of Frequently Asked Questions.

Then you got an overview of the system's design. You saw that the application is separated in three different layers: one for the presentation, one for the business logic, and one for the data access code. You saw a list of all the classes involved and the methods they support. You also got an explanation of these methods and how the interact together.

In the "Code and Code Explanation" section you got a detailed look at the code inside all these classes and pages. You learned how to deploy `ObjectDataSource` controls to enforce good n-tier architecture in your application. Using these controls enables you to create well-designed and easy-to-maintain applications without cluttering up your pages with tons of SQL statements or stored procedure names. You also saw how to use the new Common Table Expressions feature in SQL Server, a powerful technique to create recursive code that enables you to retrieve complex, hierarchical data structures from the database.

At the end of the chapter you learned how to install the Customer Support Site with either the supplied installer or by a manual installation process, and got a few tips about securing the Management folder from unauthorized users.

9

Wrox WebShop

E-commerce is one of the largest driving forces behind the Internet. Even in the Internet's earliest days, many sites featured a shop where you could order products and have them shipped to your home. With the advent of server-side techniques, such as ASP and ASP.NET, it has been much easier and cheaper for smaller sites to offer their products and services online. Despite the large diversity in the goods these sites offer, they all have one thing in common. To allow customers to select the products they want to order, they all feature a product catalog and a shopping cart where products are stored during the shopping process. At checkout time, these products are taken from the cart and usually stored in a database so the order can be processed later. The Wrox WebShop is no exception; this chapter shows you how to create a web shop with a shopping cart in ASP.NET 2.0.

The chapter starts off with a quick tour of the WebShop from an end-user's point of view. It guides you through the process of browsing articles and adding them to a shopping cart, and shows you how the shopping cart is saved in the database as an order. Finally, this chapter also explains how you can manage the product catalog for the WebShop.

Once you have a basic understanding of the functionality in the WebShop you dig into its design, discovering the business and data access layer classes that make up the application.

The section "Code and Code Explanation" puts it all together and explains how the ASPX pages interact with the classes in the business layer.

If you want to set up the WebShop so you can follow along with the explanation, refer to the section "Setting up the WebShop" near the end of this chapter.

Using the WebShop

The user interface of the WebShop consists of two main parts: the public area and the protected Management section. The public site is where your visitors can view and order products, and the Management section allows you to manage the products in the catalog. The Management section is protected so only users in the Administrator group can access it.

The next section discusses the public interface of the WebShop, and demonstrates how you can browse the product catalog and order products. The section that follows briefly guides you through the Management section.

Navigating the WebShop

Because it's more interesting to focus on the functionality of the WebShop, rather than on its look and feel, the design of the shop is pretty simple and straightforward. If you open the homepage of the WebShop by browsing to `http://localhost/WebShop` (or another location you may have chosen during setup), you'll see the WebShop's homepage appear, as shown in Figure 9-1.

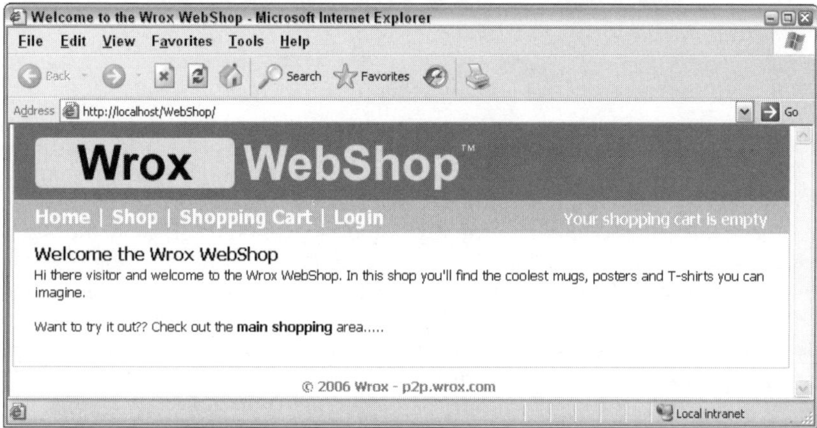

Figure 9-1

Besides the logo and the welcome text, you also see the main menu that appears on each page in the site. This main menu contains a few important navigation buttons. The Home button always brings you back to the homepage of the WebShop. The Shop button brings you to the main shopping area where you can browse the product catalog. With the Shopping Cart menu item you can view the contents of your shopping cart, if there is anything to show. The Login button allows you to log in manually. Usually, there is no need to use this button, because the WebShop shows the Login page automatically whenever you try to access a protected page. Once you're logged in, this button changes to Logout, allowing you sign out again.

If you click the Shop button you're taken to the Shop area (see Figure 9-2) where you can browse through the product catalog.

On the left you see the available product categories (Mugs, Posters, and T-Shirts), presented as a list of hyperlinks. When you click one of these links, the list of products on the right is updated and displays the products for that category. The categories and the products are all retrieved from the database — you see how that works in the "Code and Code Explanation" section later in this chapter.

To view the details of a product, you can click its image, heading, the little triangle, or the Read More link. The Product Details page appears where you can add the requested article to your shopping cart or return to the main shopping area. If you decide to purchase the item by clicking the Add to Cart button, you're taken to the Shopping Cart page, which is depicted in Figure 9-3.

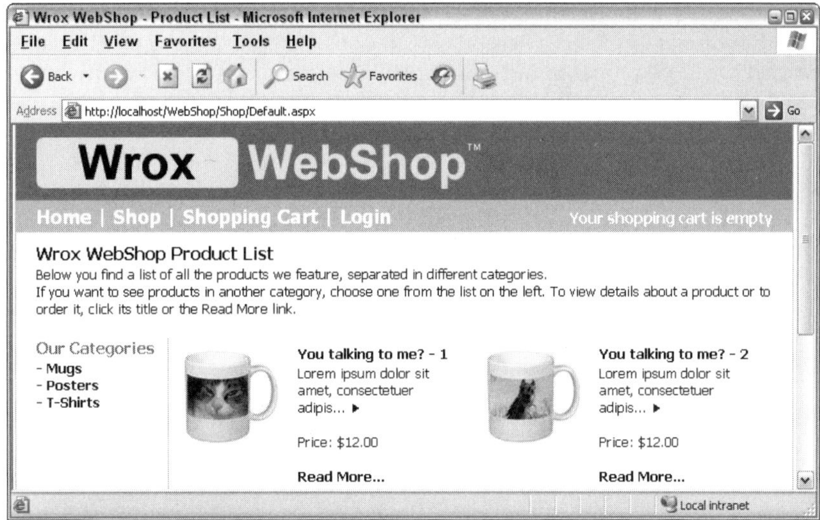

Figure 9-2

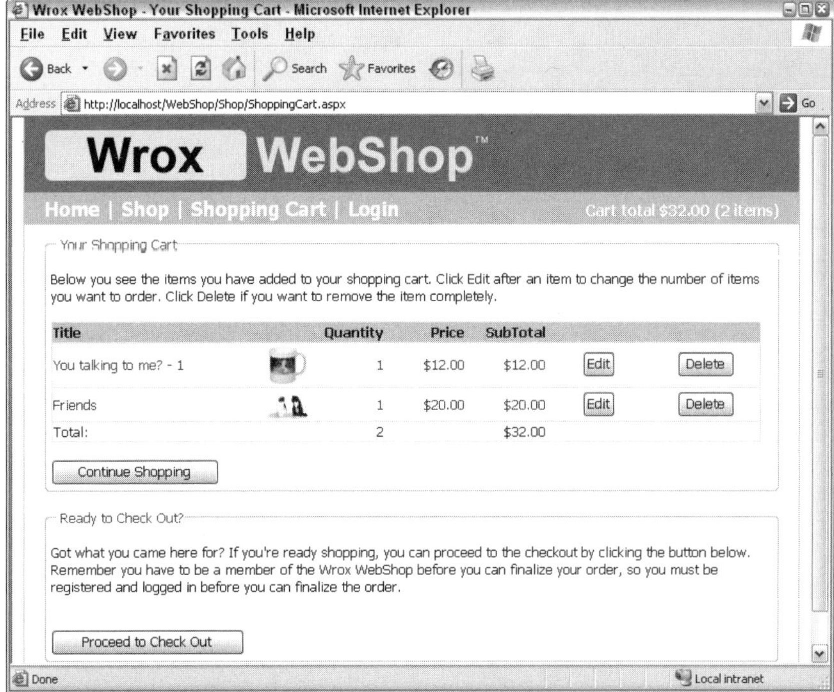

Figure 9-3

If you want to add more products to your cart, click the Continue Shopping button. Otherwise, make your move to the counter by clicking Proceed to Check Out. Because the checkout page is only accessible by authenticated users, you're taken to Login.aspx first if you're not logged in. If you're a new customer, you should sign up to get a new WebShop Customer account. If you made a purchase in the past, simply add your username and password to log in.

The Login page also allows you to retrieve a lost password that is sent to you by e-mail.

Once you successfully create an account and log in, you have to supply your name and shipping address, and then confirm your order. After reviewing the items in your shopping cart, click the Finalize Order button. This saves the order in the database and then redirects you to the Thank You page, where you get instructions about how to make the payment for the order. Further on in the chapter, when the code is discussed, you see a full flowchart of this process in Figure 9-13.

The Wrox WebShop does not have a connection with a payment provider to handle online payments. The diversity in payment providers makes it very hard to demonstrate a "one size fits all" solution here. Usually when you sign a contract with a payment provider, you get detailed documentation and sample code showing you how to access their services. The best place to integrate a payment provider in the WebShop is on the Check Out page. In the current WebShop, that page is responsible for finalizing the order. When connected to a payment service, you still save the order in the database, but mark it as "in progress." Then you redirect the user to the payment provider's web site to complete the purchase. You usually need to pass the order ID and the total order amount, and optionally the user's details. Once the user has either paid for or cancelled the order, the payment provider updates you on the result of the transaction. When the transaction has succeeded, you can update the order in the database and set it to Paid. Otherwise, you can cancel the order or remove it from your database altogether.

Maintaining the WebShop Product Catalog

The WebShop has a small maintenance section that allows you to create new products and delete existing ones. If you're logged in as an Administrator (you can use a username of `Administrator` and a password of `Admin123#`), you can click the Admin menu item to enter the maintenance section. In this section you can choose Add New Product to insert a new product (see Figure 9-4).

You need to provide a title, a description, a category, and a price for the product you want to add. To display the product on the product pages and in the shopping cart, you also need to provide an image for the product. From this image, three thumbnails are created automatically. You see how this works later in the chapter.

From the Product List page you can also delete products from the catalog. It's not possible to update existing products or to maintain categories. However, with the knowledge you gained in previous chapters, this will be easy to implement.

Now that you know how to use the WebShop as an end-user, it's time to look at its design.

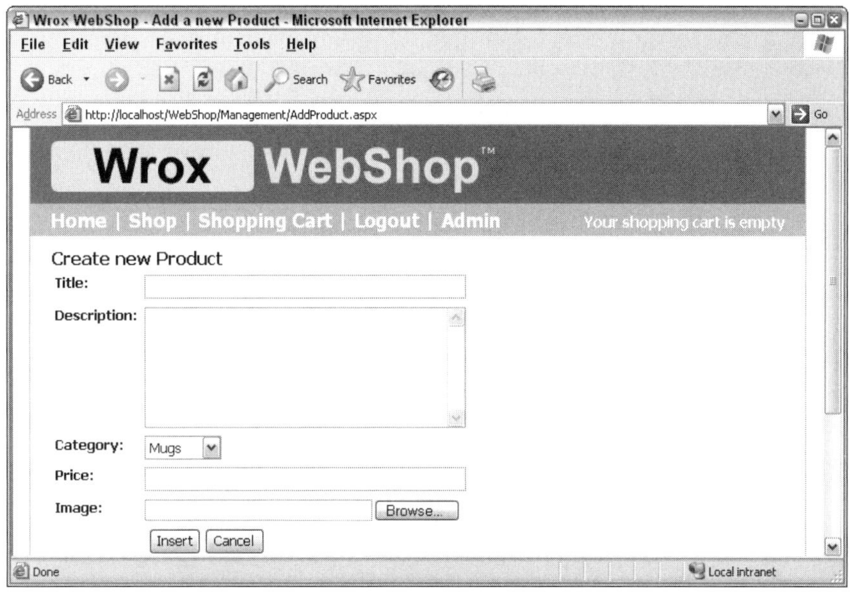

Figure 9-4

Design of the WebShop

To make the WebShop easy to maintain, it's based on a three-tier architecture where the ASPX pages are separated from the business layer and data access code. The code for the business layer is located in the BusinessLogic folder in the special App_Code folder, and the data access layer can be found in the DataAccess folder. The presentation layer, consisting of .aspx and .ascx files, is located in the root of the site and in a few subfolders that are listed later.

The Business Layer

The business layer consists of five classes that are stored in the BusinessLogic folder inside the App_Code folder in the root of the web site.

Because each file in the business layer contains only one class, the file is named after the class. So you'll find the `Product` class in the file Product.vb, and so on.

Product

The `Product` class (see Figure 9-5) represents the products that are displayed on the web site; it does not represent the actual ordered product customers can add to their shopping cart, although the two are closely related.

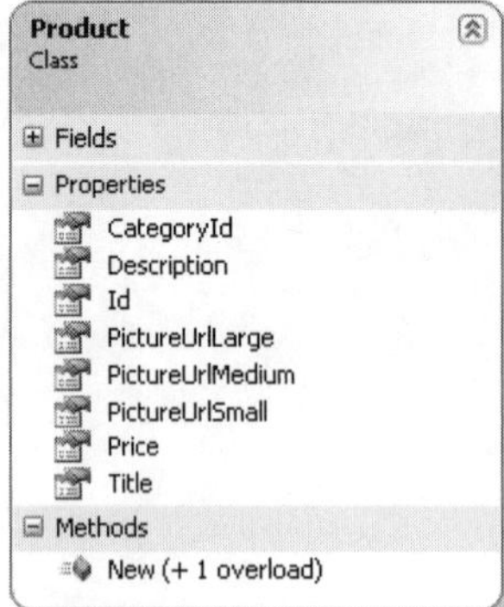

Figure 9-5

The `Product` class itself has no defined behavior. That is, it has only properties and no methods other than a default constructor. All interaction with products, such as getting a list of products or a product instance, is carried out by the `ShopManager` class, which is discussed later. In addition to Id, Price, and Description properties, the `Product` class also has multiple PictureURL properties that are used to display images of the product in the product catalog, the detail page, and the shopping cart. The following table lists each of the eight properties of the `Product` class and explains their usage:

Property	Type	Description
`CategoryId`	Integer	The database of the WebShop has a Category table to identify the various product categories. Each product is then linked to that table through its `CategoryId`.
`Description`	String	This is the full description of the product, allowing you to provide detailed information about it.
`Id`	Integer	This is the unique ID of the product in the database. The ID is assigned by the database automatically whenever a new product is inserted.
`PictureUrlLarge`	String	This property contains a virtual path to the large image of the product. This image is used on the detail page for each product.
`PictureUrlMedium`	String	This property contains a virtual path to a medium-sized thumbnail image of the product. This image is used on the product catalog with a list of products.
`PictureUrlSmall`	String	This property contains a virtual path to a small thumbnail image of the product. This small image is used in the shopping cart.
`Price`	Decimal	The price of the product.
`Title`	String	This is the title of the product used to identify the product in the catalog and in the shopping cart.

You should note that a product does not have properties like `Quantity` to indicate the number of items a user wants to order of a specific product. Whenever a user adds a product to the shopping cart, that product is wrapped inside an instance of the `OrderedProduct` class that does have these properties. The `OrderedProduct` class is discussed next.

OrderedProduct

In Figure 9-6, a diagram of the `OrderedProduct` class, you see a lot of properties that the `Product` class has as well. That's no surprise, because an `OrderedProduct` has a lot in common with a `Product`. To avoid duplication of functionality and copying information from a `Product` to an `OrderedProduct` whenever an item is added to the shopping cart, the `OrderedProduct` class has a private member of type `Product`. When a new instance of an `OrderedProduct` is created, an instance of the `Product` class is passed to its constructor, which is then stored in `_theProduct`. Properties such as `Description` and `PictureUrlSmall` then forward their calls to the inner `Product` to get at the actual values.

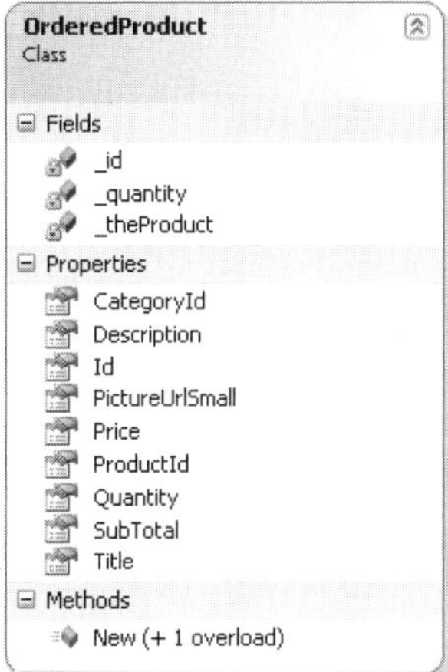

Figure 9-6

Besides the properties that delegate their responsibility to the inner `Product` object, the `OrderedProduct` class has the following additional properties:

Property	Type	Description
`Id`	Guid	A unique ID to identify each product in the shopping cart. This ID is generated whenever a new instance of `Ordered Product` is created, and is used when existing items are updated or removed from the cart.
`ProductId`	Integer	The ID of the underlying product.
`Quantity`	Integer	The number of items of the product that a user has ordered.
`SubTotal`	Decimal	Returns the read-only subtotal for the `OrderedProduct` items by multiplying their quantity and the price of the inner `Product`. This property is used in the shopping cart to display the subtotal for each item.

So far you have looked at classes that contain information, but cannot perform any actions. To do something useful with these classes you need some action classes that can operate on `Products` and `OrderedProducts`. Those classes are the `ShoppingCart` and the `ShopManager`, which are discussed next. Just as the `Product` and `OrderedProduct` classes, you'll find these two classes in the BusinessLogic folder in the App_Code folder.

ShoppingCart

The `ShoppingCart` class (see Figure 9-7) is, as its name implies, the central storage location for `OrderedProducts`. An instance of the `ShoppingCart` class is stored in a simple session variable and made accessible through a shared property on the `ShopManager` class. This way, all the pages and other classes in the site can access the cart.

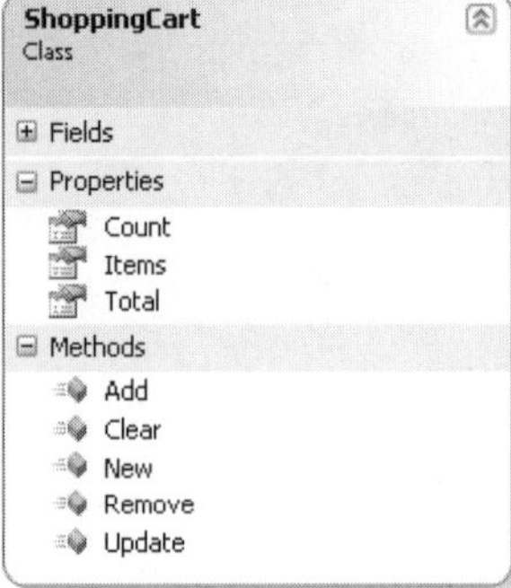

Figure 9-7

The `ShoppingCart` class contains a list with ordered products and a few methods to add, update, and remove those items. It also has properties to access the items in the shopping cart, get an item count, and get a total order amount for all the ordered products. Finally, it has a default, parameterless constructor to create new instances of type `ShoppingCart`.

The following table lists the properties of the `ShoppingCart` class:

Property	Type	Description
`Count`	Integer	Returns the total number of ordered items. It does this by looping through the `_items` collection, asking each `OrderedProduct` for its `Quantity`. This property is read-only.
`Items`	List (Of OrderedProduct)	Provides read-only access to the `_items` list. To add, update, or insert items in the list, the public methods of the `ShoppingCart` class must be used. This property is read-only.
`Total`	Decimal	Returns the total amount of money for the entire order. It does this by looping through the `_items` collection, asking each `OrderedProduct` for its `SubTotal`. This property is read-only.

To work with the items in the shopping cart the class exposes the following methods:

Method Name	Return Type	Description
`Public Sub Add (ByVal theProduct As Product)`	n/a	Adds a new `OrderedProduct` to the shopping cart. When the item is already present, its quantity is increased instead of adding a new instance to the cart. The product passed to this method is wrapped inside an `OrderedProduct` instance that in turn is added to the cart.
`Public Sub Clear ()`	n/a	Removes all items from the cart.
`Public Sub Remove (ByVal id As Guid)`	n/a	Removes an item from the cart based on its unique ID.
`Public Sub Update (ByVal newQuantity As Integer, ByVal id As Guid)`	n/a	Updates the quantity for an existing item in the cart based on its unique ID.

These four methods are never accessed by the ASPX pages in the presentation layer directly. The presentation layer should call one of the public methods on the `ShopManager` class that in turn call these methods on the `ShoppingCart` class.

ShopManager

The `ShopManager` class (see Figure 9-8) is the central entity in the application that deals with `Products` and `OrderedProducts`. It is used in two parts of the application: in the front end to provide access to the shopping cart and in the back end to allow an administrator to manage the products in the product catalog.

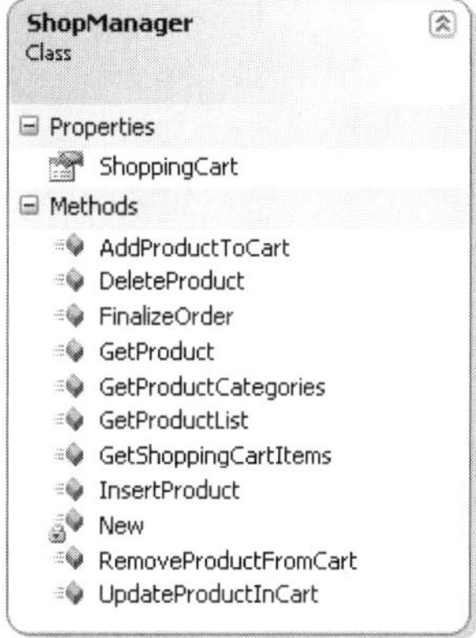

Figure 9-8

In addition to the `ShoppingCart` property, which is of type `ShoppingCart`, discussed earlier, the `ShopManager` has the following public methods:

Method Name	Return Type	Description
`Public Shared Sub AddProductToCart (ByVal theProduct As Product)`	n/a	Adds a new `OrderedProduct` to the shopping cart by calling the `Add` method of the `Shopping Cart` class.
`Public Shared Sub DeleteProduct (ByVal theProduct As Product)`	n/a	Deletes a product from the product catalog. This method is used in the maintenance section of the WebShop.
`Public Shared Function FinalizeOrder (ByVal theCustomer As Customer)`	Integer	Finalizes an order for a customer. This method calls the `FinalizeOrder` method in the data access layer to insert the order in the database and then returns the new order ID.
`Public Shared Function GetProduct (ByVal theProductId As Integer)`	Product	Returns a single instance of a product. This method is used in the Product Details page to display information about a specific product.
`Public Shared Function GetProduct Categories()`	DataSet	Returns a DataSet with the available product categories used in the catalog and the maintenance section.
`Public Shared Function GetProductList (ByVal theCategoryId As Integer)`	List (Of Product)	Returns a list with products in the specified category. Used to display products in the product catalog.
`Public Shared Function GetShoppingCartItems ()`	List (Of Ordered Product)	Returns a list with `OrderedProducts` from the `ShoppingCart` by accessing its `Items` property.
`Public Shared Sub InsertProduct (ByVal theProduct As Product)`	n/a	Inserts a new product in the product catalog. This method is used in the maintenance section of the WebShop.
`Public Shared Sub RemoveProductFromCart (ByVal id As Guid)`	n/a	Removes an `OrderedProduct` from the shopping cart by calling the `Remove` method of the `Shopping Cart` class.
`Public Shared Sub UpdateProductInCart (ByVal newQuantity As Integer, ByVal id As Guid)`	n/a	Updates an existing `OrderedProduct` in the shopping cart by calling the `Update` method of the `ShoppingCart` class.

Besides these methods, the `ShopManager` class has a single, hidden constructor. By hiding the constructor (using the access modifier `Private`) you can prevent calling code from creating useless instances of the `ShopManager` class. Because the class exposes only shared methods and properties, there is never the need for an instance of the `ShopManager`.

Obviously, a shop needs customers to stay in business and the Wrox WebShop is no exception. The next section shows you what the `Customer` class in the WebShop looks like.

Customer

The final class in the business layer you should look at is the `Customer` class. The WebShop uses the `Membership` provider and the `Profile` classes to store information about the user such as login name, password, and address details. Because all of this is handled by ASP.NET automatically, why do you need an additional `Customer` class?

The `Customer` class is used to reflect the user's details at the moment of a purchase in the WebShop. From a security standpoint it's a good practice to disallow users to change their details, such as the shipping address, *after* the purchase has been finalized. This way, for example, hackers cannot change the shipping address after the order has been paid and redirect the goods to their address instead of to the customer's.

Right before the order is finalized in the Check Out page the `Customer` class is filled with the user's details, which are retrieved from the Membership and Profile providers and then passed to the `FinalizeOrder` method in the `ShopManager` class. The details from the `Customer` class are inserted into the database together with the other order details. So, even if a customer changes the shipping address manually, the goods will still be delivered to the address that was supplied during the ordering process. If you want to allow customers to change their order details for an order that has already been finalized, you need to implement this functionality. To make this secure, you could allow them to temporarily update their details, but postpone applying the changes to the order until they have confirmed an e-mail, for example. This way, you can be sure that the original user has requested and approved the change.

The `Customer` class has only seven public properties and only one method, its constructor, as shown in Figure 9-9.

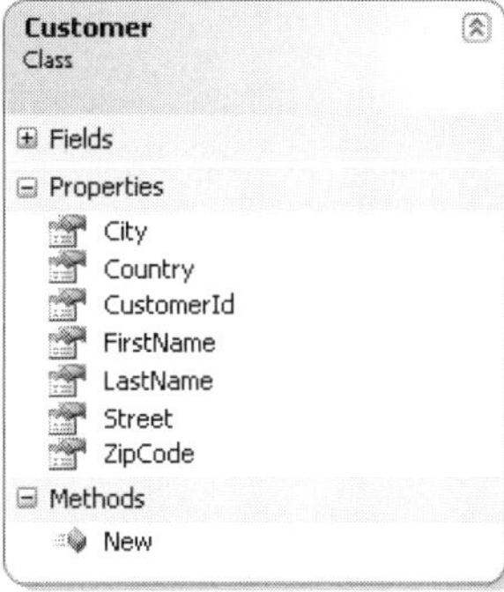

Figure 9-9

Most of the properties are pretty straightforward and don't need an additional explanation. The only exception is the `CustomerId` property. This ID, implemented as a Guid, is not generated by the `Customer` class itself, but is retrieved from the `ProviderUserKey` property of the `MembershipUser` class. This is the unique ID for each user in the application, automatically generated and stored by the ASP.NET Framework. Because the data stored by the `Membership` and `Profile` providers is in the same database used by the rest of the WebShop application, it makes sense to reuse this unique key so it's easy to retrieve related user details later based on this key.

All properties of the `Customer` class are read-only — to set their initial values, you need to pass them to the constructor of the class.

Out of the five classes in the business layer, only the `ShopManager` has methods that require data access to read from and write to the database. This data access is performed by the `ShopManagerDB` class, which is discussed in the next section.

The Data Access Layer

Two key elements make up the data access layer. First there is the database and its tables that store the data for the shop. The second part contains the methods in the `ShopManagerDB` class that uses stored procedures to get data in and out of the database. Because a fundamental knowledge of the database is important to understand how the data access methods work, the data model is discussed first, followed by the `ShopManagerDB` class.

The Data Model

For many of the operations that take place in the WebShop, a back-end database is used. This database, called WebShop.mdf and stored in the App_Data folder of the web site, stores data about products, orders, and categories. To understand how it all fits together, you should take a look at Figure 9-10, which shows the data model for the WebShop. It's quite a simple model, with only four tables.

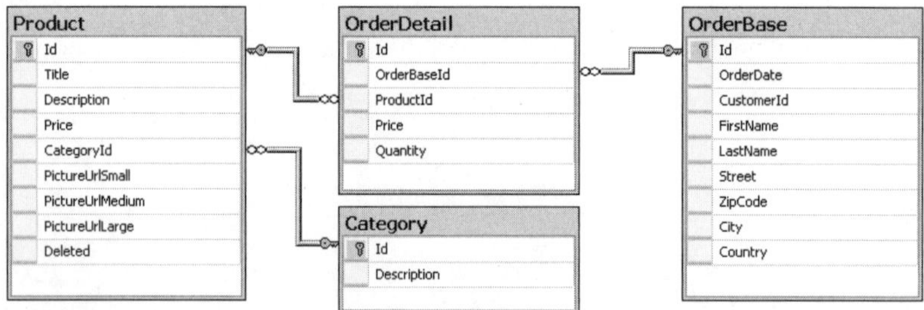

Figure 9-10

Figure 9-10 shows only the custom tables added for the WebShop; it does not list the tables that have been added by the Membership and Role providers. During run time, those tables are used by the ASP.NET Framework to authenticate users and determine their roles. They are not used for storing information about products, categories, or orders, other than the CustomerId in the OrderBase table that is used to determine what WebShop user placed the order. The following tables list each database table and their respective columns:

Product

Column Name	Data Type	Description
Id	`int`	The Unique ID of each product. This ID is generated automatically by the database each time a new product is inserted.
Title	`nvarchar(100)`	The title of the product. The title is displayed on the product list and details pages of the product catalog.
Description	`nvarchar(max)`	A longer description of the product. Although the `nvarchar(max)` data type, new in SQL Server 2005, allows you to store up to almost 2GB of information, the description is usually limited to a few K of text, describing the full product specs.
Price	`money`	The price of the product.
CategoryId	`int`	Each product is placed in a category that is displayed on the web site to allow for easy navigation of the product catalog. The names of the categories are stored in the Category table and the Product table stores only the primary key of that table as a foreign key.
PictureUrlSmall	`nvarchar(255)`	A small picture showing the product. This image is shown in the shopping cart.
PictureUrlMedium	`nvarchar(255)`	A medium-sized picture showing the product. This image is shown on the product list page.
PictureUrlLarge	`nvarchar(255)`	A larger picture showing the product. This image is shown on the product details page.
Deleted	`bit`	Indicates whether a product is still available on the web site. Because the product details are needed to display information about ordered products, a product can never be physically deleted from the database. Instead, it's marked as "deleted."

Each product is linked to a category that is stored in the Category table:

Category

Column Name	Data Type	Description
Id	`int`	The unique ID of each category. This ID is generated automatically by the database each time a new category is inserted.
Description	`nvarchar(100)`	The description of the category. The description of the category is used mainly in the navigation menu in the main shopping area to allow a user to select a category.

Once a customer has placed an order, the order data is stored in two tables—OrderBase and OrderDetails. The OrderBase table contains information that applies to the entire order, such as the order date and the customer that placed the order.

OrderBase

Column Name	Data Type	Description
Id	`int`	The unique ID of each order. This ID is generated automatically by the database each time a new order is inserted. The order ID is also communicated back to the customer as the order number.
OrderDate	`datetime`	The date and time the order was placed.
CustomerId	`uniqueidentifier`	The ID of the customer that placed the order. This is the primary key of the aspnet_Users table that has been added to the database to support the Role and Membership providers.
FirstName	`nvarchar(50)`	The first name of the customer.
LastName	`nvarchar(50)`	The last name of the customer.
Street	`nvarchar(100)`	The customer's shipping address.
ZipCode	`nvarchar(20)`	The zip code of the customer's address.
City	`nvarchar(100)`	The city of the customer's address.
Country	`nvarchar(50)`	The country of the customer's address.

The OrderDetail table stores information about each product a customer has ordered. This table is linked back to the OrderBase table with its OrderBaseId column.

OrderDetail

Column Name	Data Type	Description
Id	`int`	The unique ID of each order detail record. This ID is generated automatically by the database each time a new order detail is inserted.
OrderBaseId	`int`	The ID of the order to which this order detail belongs.
ProductId	`int`	The ID of the ordered product. This ID is used to link back to the product table to get information such as the title and the description.
Price	`money`	Because a product's price may change after it has been ordered, the price is stored with the order details. This ensures that the total price for an order doesn't change after it has been confirmed by a customer.
Quantity	`int`	The number of items of the product the customer has ordered.

The data in the database is not accessed by the code in the data access layer directly using inline SQL statements. Instead, for each relevant database action (insert, update, and so on), the database has a stored procedure that carries out the requested action. This makes it easier to reuse the SQL code in other parts of the application. It also makes it easier to make radical changes to the structure of the database; instead of examining many methods in the data access layer, all you need to do is change the stored procedures. The stored procedures for the WebShop are all pretty straightforward. Most of them do nothing but insert a single record, or retrieve one or more items.

ShopManagerDB

Because of the limited size of the WebShop application, all data access code is centralized in a single class, the `ShopManagerDB`. In larger applications it's a good idea to give most of the business classes their own counterpart in the business layer. That way it's easy to see how classes in both layers are related. For the WebShop that would likely result in numerous very small classes like the `ProductManagerDB`, `CategoryManagerDB`, `CustomerManagerDB`, and so on, each with only one or two methods. To keep things simple and straightforward, the WebShop uses the `ShopManager` class in the business layer and the `ShopManagerDB` class (Figure 9-11 shows its structure) in the data access layer. Just like a shop manager in the real world, these classes are responsible for showing the customers around (displaying products from the product catalog), stocking the shelves (maintaining the product catalog in the maintenance section), and completing the customer's order.

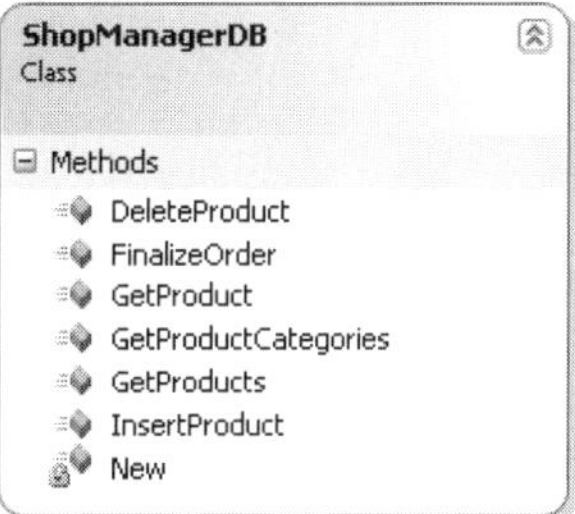

Figure 9-11

The `ShopManagerDB` class has only shared methods and no properties. Therefore, its constructor has been hidden by marking it as `Private`. This is indicated by the little lock icon you can see in Figure 9-11. The other methods in this class can be divided in two groups: methods that are used at the front end of the site to order products, and those that are used in the maintenance area to manage the products in the product catalog. The following table lists the six important methods of the `ShopManagerDB` class:

Method Name	Return Type	Description
`Public Shared Sub DeleteProduct (ByVal theProduct As Product)`	n/a	Marks a product as deleted by setting the Deleted column to 1 (true).

Table continued on following page

Method Name	Return Type	Description
`Public Shared Function FinalizeOrder (ByVal theShoppingCart As ShoppingCart, ByVal theCustomer As Customer)`	Integer	Inserts an order in the OrderBase table and adds an associated record for each ordered product in the OrderDetail table. It returns the new `orderId`.
`Public Shared Function GetProduct (ByVal productId As Integer)`	Product	Returns a single instance of a Product, indicated by the `productId` parameter. Returns Nothing when the product couldn't be found.
`Public Shared Function GetProductCategories ()`	DataSet	Returns a list with the available Categories as a DataSet with an ID and a Description column.
`Public Shared Function GetProducts (ByVal categoryId As Integer)`	List (Of Product)	Returns a strongly typed list of products. The `categoryId` parameter is used to limit the product list to products in one category.
`Public Shared Sub InsertProduct (ByVal theProduct As Product)`	n/a	Creates a new product in the Product table.

Helper Classes

The App_Code folder for the WebShop also contains two utility classes called `Helpers` and `AppConfiguration`. The `Helpers` class has one method called `ResizeImage`. This method takes a path to an image and a maximum and then resizes the image. The inner workings of this method are discussed in Chapter 11, which deals with manipulating images.

The `AppConfiguration` class has a single read-only and shared property called `ConnectionString` that reads the WebShop's connection string from the Web.config file and returns it to the calling code. This makes it very easy to change the connection string later; for example, when you switch from the development to the production environment. All you need to do is change the connection string in the Web.config file and the changes will be picked up by the ASP.NET run time automatically.

Another benefit of using a shared property like this is that you get IntelliSense on the `Helpers` class to help you remember the name of the connection. With this property, you don't have to remember the actual name of the key of the connection string or the code required to get the string from the Web.config file.

Now that you understand the design of the business and data access layers, it's time to turn your attention to the actual implementation. The following section explains most of the pages in the WebShop application and how they interact with the code in the business layer.

Code and Code Explanation

The files in the WebShop are logically grouped together in folders. The Css folder contains a single file called Core.css that contains the CSS used throughout the site. The Images folder contains the few images that are used throughout the site, such as the logo. Its subfolder Products contains the automatically generated thumbnails, three for each of the products.

In addition to these two folders the site contains three other important folders: Controls, Shop, and Management. The Controls folder contains three user controls that are used in various other pages in the site. The controls are explained as part of the pages that contain them in the next few sections. The Shop folder contains all the pages that make up the shopping section of the site, such as the Product Detail page and the Check Out page. These files are examined in great detail later. The Management folder contains the files that are required to maintain the products in the product catalog.

Root Files

A few files located in the root are also used by many other pages in the site, so it's important to look at them first.

Global.asax

The Global.asax for the WebShop contains code for one event only: `Application_Error`. In this event handler, which fires whenever an error occurs in the site, an e-mail is sent with the error details. Refer to Chapter 6 for an explanation of this code.

Web.config

As is common in any ASP.NET application, the WebShop has a Web.config file that contains settings that are critical to the application. This section shows you the most important keys only; many of the other settings in the file are placed there by default whenever you create a new web application in Visual Web Developer.

Under the `<appSettings>` node you find a single key/value pair called `MailFromAddress`. This key is used to set the From: address in e-mails that are sent by the application. This setting is used in the `PasswordRecovery` control in the Login page:

```
<appSettings>
  <add key="MailFromAddress" value="You@YourProvider.Com"/>
</appSettings>
```

Below the `<appSettings>` you find the `connectionStrings` node that has a single connection string defined called `WebShop`. The connection string uses the local SQL Express Edition of SQL Server and instructs it to automatically attach the WebShop.mdf file in the App_Data folder:

```
<connectionStrings>
  <add name="WebShop" connectionString="server=(local)\SqlExpress;
       AttachDbFileName=|DataDirectory|WebShop.mdf;Integrated Security=true;
       User Instance=true"/>
</connectionStrings>
```

The <profile> node sets up the Profile provider. Profiles are a great way to quickly save user-specific information such as name, addresses, and preferences. Storing and retrieving the information is transparently done by the ASP.NET Framework — no custom code is required. All you need to do is set up the <profile> node in the Web.config file. The <profile> element has a few sub-elements that require some explanation. Following is the entire <profile> element:

```
<profile>
  <providers>
    <clear />
      <add name="AspNetSqlProfileProvider"
             connectionStringName="WebShop"
             applicationName="/"
             type="System.Web.Profile.SqlProfileProvider, System.Web,
             Version=2.0.0.0, Culture=neutral, PublicKeyToken=b03f5f7f11d50a3a"
      />
  </providers>
  <properties>
    <add name="FirstName" />
    <add name="LastName" />
    <add name="ProfileCompleted" type="System.Boolean" />
    <group name="Address">
      <add name="Street" />
      <add name="ZipCode" />
      <add name="City" />
      <add name="Country" />
    </group>
  </properties>
</profile>
```

The <providers> element tells the ASP.NET run time what Profile provider to use. In the Machine.config file, the root of all configuration files on your server, there is already a default provider configured that uses a local connection string and a database called aspnetdb.mdf. Because the WebShop uses its own database, the <clear /> element is used to remove the inherited profile settings. The <add> element then adds a new provider that is very similar to the original one, except that the connectionStringName property now points to the WebShop database.

The <properties> node is where you add the actual <profile> properties you want to use. Properties come in two flavors: simple properties and grouped properties. An example of a simple property is the FirstName. Because no additional information is supplied, the type of the FirstName property defaults to a System.String, which is fine for a first name. The property ProfileCompleted is set to a Boolean by specifying type="System.Boolean" in the <add> element.

The Street, ZipCode, City, and Country properties are part of a properties group called Address. All these properties are of type String, because of the missing type attribute. Grouping properties is a very convenient way to provide a clean programming model to the developers using this profile. Figure 9-12 shows you how you can retrieve the ZipCode property from the Address group.

As you can see, the ZipCode property is now a property of the Address group, which in turn is a property of the Profile class. Behind the scenes, the information in the <properties> node is compiled into a class that is made available through the Profile class. This happens both at development time, so you get IntelliSense support, and at compile time, so the information is available at run time.

```
    If Not Page.IsPostBack Then
      If Profile.ProfileCompleted Then
        txtFirstName.Text = Profile.FirstName
        txtLastName.Text = Profile.LastName
        txtStreet.Text = Profile.Address.Street
        txtZipCode.Text = Profile.Address.
        txtCity.Text = Profile.Address.
        txtCountry.Text = Profile.Addre
        plcReturningUser.Visible = True
      Else
        plcNewUser.Visible = True
      End If
    End If
  End Sub
```


Figure 9-12

The <profiles> element has a few other settings that allow you to tweak the behavior of the profile feature. For example, the `allowAnonymous` attribute of a property controls whether the setting can be used by anonymous users, whereas the `automaticSaveEnabled` attribute of the <profile> element determines whether changes in the profile are saved automatically, or if you need to explicitly call the `Save` method. If you want to find out more about the Profiles feature of ASP.NET 2.0, pick up a copy of Wrox's *Professional ASP.NET 2.0.*

Next up in the Web.config are the settings for the Membership and Role providers. It's quite a bit of code and very similar to the code you have seen in previous chapters, so it's not repeated here but you're encouraged to take a look at it in the Web.config file. The most important elements are the <membership> and <roleManager>. They control the way users are authenticated in the site and to what roles they are assigned. The <roleManager> is used for only one role, the Administrator that needs to access the maintenance section.

At the bottom of the Web.config file you find two <location> nodes that override the authentication for the Management folder and the CheckOut.aspx page. Only users in the Administrator role can access the Management folder, whereas the Check Out page is blocked for all non-authenticated users.

MasterPage.master

The master page of the WebShop defines the general look and feel of all the pages in the site, as you saw in the introduction of this chapter. The master page contains a reference to the global CSS file called Core.css in the Css folder. It also includes a user control called `MainMenu` that you find in the Controls folder. This `MainMenu` control in turn contains a number of <a> tags that link to entry point pages of each main section. Some of the links are hidden from unauthenticated users by using a `LoginView` control. The display of the Login or Logout button and the Admin button is controlled as follows:

```
<asp:LoginView runat="server" ID="lv1">
  <AnonymousTemplate>
    <a href="~/Login.aspx" runat="Server">Login</a>
  </AnonymousTemplate>
  <LoggedInTemplate>
    <asp:LinkButton ID="lnkLogout" runat="server"
```

```
                OnClick="lnkLogout_Click">Logout</asp:LinkButton>
    </LoggedInTemplate>
    <RoleGroups>
      <asp:RoleGroup Roles="Administrator">
        <ContentTemplate>
          <asp:LinkButton ID="lnkLogout" runat="server"
               OnClick="lnkLogout_Click">Logout</asp:LinkButton>
          <span class="Separator">|</span>
          <a href="~/Management/" runat="Server">Admin</a>
        </ContentTemplate>
      </asp:RoleGroup>
    </RoleGroups>
  </asp:LoginView>
```

All anonymous users get to see the Login button defined in the `<AnonymousTemplate>` element. Authenticated users see the Logout button instead. Users that are in the Administrator role see the Logout button and the Admin button. The Logout link is repeated because the `<RoleGroups>` element takes precedence over the `<LoggedInTemplate>`. That is, you can't show content to a user from both the `<LoggedInTemplate>` and a `<ContentTemplate>` of a `<RoleGroup>` at the same time.

In addition to the `LoginView` control, you can also use a `LoginStatus` control for the Login and Logout links. This control displays either a Login or a Logout link, depending in the current status.

The final important piece of the master page is the `ContentPlaceHolder`. This defines the region that pages implementing the master page can override with their own custom content.

Default.aspx

Default.aspx is the homepage for the WebShop and contains only introduction text and a link to the product catalog.

Login.aspx

The Login.aspx page deals with anything related to a user logging in to the system. It contains three of the new ASP.NET 2.0 login controls, each placed in its own HTML `<fieldset>` control to provide some visual separation. The following table lists each of the controls and their usage:

Control Type	Description
`CreateUserWizard`	This control allows a user to sign up for an account at the WebShop. The control is used "out of the box" without any impacting changes.
`Login`	Allows an existing user to log in to the WebShop. Just as the `CreateUserWizard` control, there isn't much configured on this control except for some textual changes.
`PasswordRecovery`	Allows a user to get a new password by answering the secret question.

The PasswordRecovery control needs a bit more explanation. By default, the control retrieves a user's password based on his or her username. However, many users won't remember their username. They do, however, remember their e-mail address. That's why a little trick is deployed to get the user's name based on his or her e-mail address automatically. First the UserNameInstructionText and UserName LabelText attributes of the control are changed to instruct the user to type an e-mail address instead of a username. Then in the VerifyingUser method of the PasswordRecovery control the user's name is retrieved with the following code:

```
Protected Sub PasswordRecovery1_VerifyingUser(ByVal sender As Object, _
       ByVal e As System.Web.UI.WebControls.LoginCancelEventArgs) _
       Handles PasswordRecovery1.VerifyingUser
  PasswordRecovery1.UserName = _
           Membership.GetUserNameByEmail(PasswordRecovery1.UserName)
End Sub
```

This way, the user can supply an e-mail address, while under the hood the user's name is used to assign the new password.

UserDetails.aspx

The user details page allows a user to supply information such as a name and shipping address. The page contains six text boxes, one for each of the properties from the profile. At load time, the controls are filled with the user's details from the profile if the information is available. When the Save button is clicked, the values from the controls are saved in the profile. The page uses validation controls to make sure each field is filled in.

The Shop Folder

The Shop folder contains all files required for the front end of the shop, like the product catalog, the shopping cart, and the checkout page. Before each page in the front end is discussed, take a look at Figure 9-13, which shows a typical work flow a user follows while making purchases in the WebShop.

You enter the homepage of the site (1) and then proceed to the product catalog (2). When you see a product you want to purchase you can add it to the shopping cart (3). From there you can browse back to the product catalog and add more items. Once you're ready to make the purchase, you move on to the checkout page (4). To finalize the order, you need to log in (5). If you don't have an account yet, you should sign up for one first (6). After you log in, the system asks you for additional details like name and shipping address (7). Once all details have been filled in and validated, the order is finalized (8) and you get a confirmation message, showing the order details and order number (9).

The next section of this chapter digs deeper into each of the pages involved in this process.

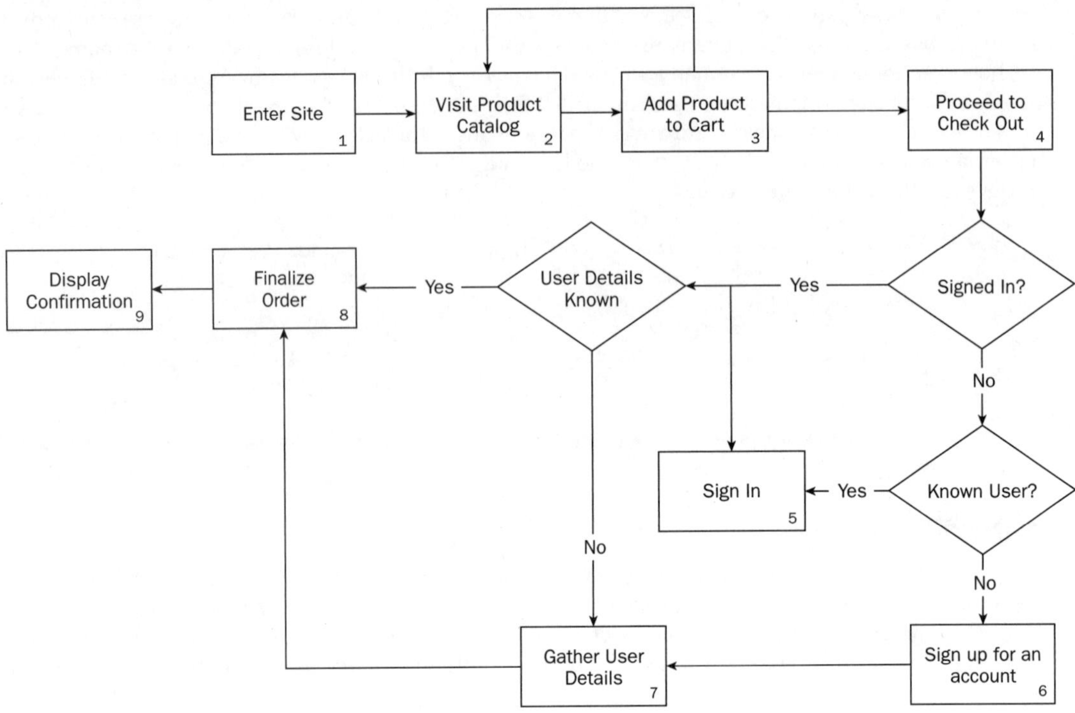

Figure 9-13

Displaying Products

When you click the Shop menu item on the homepage you're taken to Default.aspx in the shop folder (number 2 in Figure 9-13). This page is split into two parts using an HTML table. The left column contains an ASP.NET `Repeater` control that displays the available product categories. The categories are added to the `Repeater` through an `ObjectDataSource` control that gets the items as a DataSet from the `GetProductCategories` method in the `ShopManager` class. When you click one of the categories, the product list on the right is reloaded to show only the products that belong to that category.

The products are displayed using a `DataList` with its `RepeatColumns` set to `2`, so it displays two products next to each other. Right below the `DataList` are two `HyperLink` controls to move forward and backward in the list. The .aspx portion of this page doesn't feature much news so it isn't discussed any further. What's more interesting to look at is the code-behind for the file.

Because the `DataList` doesn't support paging out of the box, the page uses a custom paging solution with a `PagedDataSource`. The `PagedDataSource` control is the underlying mechanism for controls that support paging natively like the `GridView` and the `DetailsView`. In the `LoadData` method of the code-behind file a new `PagedDataSource` control is created, and then its `DataSource` is filled with the results of `ShopManager.GetProductList`. In addition to the data source you can set properties like `AllowPaging`, `PageSize`, and `CurrentPageIndex` the same way as you would for a `GridView`. The `CurrentPageIndex` is calculated by looking at a query string variable called `Page`. In the end, the `PagedDataSource` control is assigned to the `GridView`, which is then responsible for displaying the data held in the `PagedDataSource`.

The GetProductList method to fill the data source is simply a wrapper around the GetProducts method of the ShopManagerDB class. If scalability and performance is of the highest importance, you could use the method in the Business Layer class to cache the data in the ASP.NET cache. However, the current implementation always returns fresh data from the database. In Chapter 12 you learn how to cache data using the new SqlCacheDependency, which removes items from the cache whenever the underlying table in the database changes.

The GetProducts method in the ShopManagerDB class executes a stored procedure in the database to get a list of products for the requested category. That list is then returned to the calling code as a generic List with the new syntax (Of Product), which means a strongly typed list of individual products is returned. To see how that all works, take a look at the code for the method:

```
Public Shared Function GetProducts(ByVal categoryId As Integer) As List(Of Product)
  Dim productList As List(Of Product) = New List(Of Product)
  Try
    Using myConnection As New SqlConnection(AppConfiguration.ConnectionString)

      Dim myCommand As SqlCommand = New _
              SqlCommand("sprocProductSelectListByProductCategory", myConnection)
      myCommand.CommandType = CommandType.StoredProcedure
      myCommand.Parameters.AddWithValue("@categoryId", categoryId)

      Dim theProduct As Product 'Temp Product to add to our ProductList

      myConnection.Open()
      Using myReader As SqlDataReader = _
              myCommand.ExecuteReader(CommandBehavior.CloseConnection)
        While myReader.Read()
          theProduct = New Product( _
              myReader.GetInt32(myReader.GetOrdinal("Id")), _
              categoryId)
          theProduct.Title = myReader.GetString(myReader.GetOrdinal("Title"))
          ' Other properties are set here
          productList.Add(theProduct)
        End While
        myReader.Close()
      End Using
    End Using
  Catch ex As Exception
    Throw
  End Try
  Return productList
End Function
```

The method starts by declaring a string with the name of the stored procedure and a List of type Product. With the special syntax of Of Product, the variable productList is capable of performing all the actions defined in the List class (located in the System.Collections.Generic namespace), while at the same time it can only work with Product instances. This gives you a very flexible yet type safe way to work with collections of objects. Generics are a powerful but complex concept to understand. *Professional .NET 2.0 Generics* by Tod Golding provides you with all the information you need to know to successfully implement Generics in your code.

Next, a connection and a command object are constructed. The `categoryId` is passed up to the stored procedure so it only returns products that are in the requested category. If the stored procedure returns any results, the code inside the `While` loop creates a new instance of the `Product` class, sets its public variables, and then adds the product to the product list. In the end, the list of products, possibly holding zero, one, or many products, is passed back to the calling code.

You may have noticed the use of a `Try Catch` block to intercept any errors. Instead of logging the error to a log file, or dealing with it, it is simply passed up using the `Throw` keyword. Because there isn't much to be done about a SQL error, for example, inside this method, the error is passed up to the calling code. Eventually, the error will be caught by code in the Global.asax that was set up to handle these errors and log them. If you want to log errors at the place where they occur, you can create a custom method like `LogError` in the `Helpers` class that you call in each of the `Catch` clauses in addition to the `Throw` keyword. This method could accept an object of type `Exception`, which it then logs to the event log, a database, a text file, or an e-mail.

If you don't like this almost-empty `Catch` block, you can remove the `Try Catch` altogether. In that case, the error is passed up automatically. However, you then lose the ability to add a `Finally` block that you could use to clean up resources, such as open connections. That's why you'll see the `Try Catch` block with a `Throw` statement a lot in this and other chapters; that way, there's already a code template in place that you can extend later if required.

Instead of just `Throw`, other code examples you may have seen use `Throw Ex` to forward the caught exception to the next layer. However, this is not recommended. By using `Throw Ex`, you effectively destroy the call stack of the current execution. That way, final code that catches the exception (for example, the code in the Global.asax that sends error messages by e-mail) has no way to find out where the exception came from originally.

Adding a Product to the Cart

The `GridView` in the Product List page contains `HyperLink` controls that link to the ProductDetail.aspx where a user can view more information about a product and add it to the shopping cart (number 3 in Figure 9-13). The code in this page is very similar to that in the product list. But instead of a `GridView`, a `DetailsView` control is used that is bound to the return value of the `GetProduct` method using an `ObjectDataSource`. When the page loads, the `ObjectDataSource` calls into the business layer and gets a single product specified by the ID in the query string. This product is then presented on the page with the `DetailsView` control.

When a user clicks the Add to Cart button, a new instance of the product is created and added to the cart:

```
Dim productId As Integer
productId = Convert.ToInt32(Request.QueryString.Get("Id"))
Dim myProduct As Product = ShopManager.GetProduct(productId)
ShopManager.AddProductToCart(myProduct)
Response.Redirect("ShoppingCart.aspx")
```

The new instance of the product is created using the `GetProduct` method. This is the same method the `ObjectDataSource` control uses to display the product on the page. This instance is then passed to the `AddProductToCart` method that in turn calls the `Add` method of the `ShoppingCart`:

```
Public Shared Sub AddProductToCart(ByVal theProduct As Product)
  ShopManager.ShoppingCart.Add(theProduct)
End Sub
```

The user's shopping cart is made accessible by the `ShopManager` class with a shared property called `ShoppingCart`:

```
Public Shared ReadOnly Property ShoppingCart() As ShoppingCart
  Get
    If HttpContext.Current.Session("ShoppingCart") Is Nothing Then
      HttpContext.Current.Session("ShoppingCart") = New ShoppingCart()
    End If
    Return CType(HttpContext.Current.Session("ShoppingCart"), ShoppingCart)
  End Get
End Property
```

The first time this property is accessed, a new instance of the `ShoppingCart` is created, stored in a session variable, and then returned to the calling code. Subsequent calls to the property return the `ShoppingCart` from session state. This way the shopping cart is always available.

If there is already an `OrderedProduct` with the same ID in the shopping cart, its quantity is increased by one. Otherwise, a new instance of `OrderedProduct` is created. Its constructor expects an instance of `Product` that is stored in a private variable called `_theProduct` and the initial quantity, which is set to `1`. The ordered product is then added to the `_items` list that represents the user's shopping cart:

```
Public Sub Add(ByVal theProduct As Product)
  For Each existingProduct As OrderedProduct In _items
    If theProduct.Id = existingProduct.ProductId Then
      existingProduct.Quantity += 1
      Exit Sub
    End If
  Next
  Dim myOrderedProduct As OrderedProduct = New OrderedProduct(theProduct, 1)
  _items.Add(myOrderedProduct)
End Sub
```

The ShoppingCart.aspx Page

After the product has been added the user is taken to ShoppingCart.aspx, which displays the products. This page by itself doesn't do much. It has a few static text blocks that are displayed depending on whether the cart contains any items. The actual shopping cart is displayed by embedding a user control called `ShoppingCartView`:

```
<Wrox:ShoppingCartView ID="ShoppingCartView1" runat="server" />
```

The `ShoppingCartView` control, located in the Controls folder, contains a `GridView` that displays the products and an `ObjectDataSource` that's responsible for retrieving the items from the cart. To allow deleting and updating of products, the `ObjectDataSource` control sets up the appropriate methods and parameters for these actions:

```
<asp:ObjectDataSource ID="odsShoppingCart" runat="server"
  TypeName="ShopManager" DeleteMethod="RemoveProductFromCart"
  SelectMethod="GetShoppingCartItems" UpdateMethod="UpdateProductInCart">
  <UpdateParameters>
    <asp:Parameter Name="newQuantity" Type="Int32" />
  </UpdateParameters>
</asp:ObjectDataSource>
```

The SelectMethod, UpdateMethod, and DeleteMethod all call into the ShopManager class. The GetShoppingCartItems method simply returns the public Items list of the ShoppingCart. As you recall, this list is a strongly typed list of OrderedProduct items. This list is then bound to the GridView using a mix of BoundField, ImageField, and TemplateField columns when the page loads.

Changing Items in the Cart

The Quantity column is a bit more complicated than other columns like Price or Title. In edit mode, the GridView displays this column as a drop-down with the numbers 1 through 10 to allow a user to choose a new quantity:

```
<asp:DropDownList ID="lstQuantity" runat="server"
      SelectedValue='<%# Eval("Quantity") %>' AutoPostBack="True"
      OnSelectedIndexChanged="lstQuantity_SelectedIndexChanged">
  <asp:ListItem Value="1" Selected="True">1</asp:ListItem>
  ... Other items go here
</asp:DropDownList>
```

The SelectedValue for the drop-down list is bound to the Quantity property of the OrderedProduct with the Eval method. It also has its AutoPostBack property set to True to automatically post back when its selected value changes. When that happens, lstQuantity_SelectedIndexChanged is fired. This method then calls the UpdateRow method of the GridView. This in turn causes the ObjectDataSource to fire its Updating event, which fires right before it actually calls the Update method in the business layer. The Updating event is an excellent location to set the parameters that need to be passed to the UpdateProductInCart method. In the section about the design of the WebShop, you saw that the UpdateProductInCart method expects the ID of the OrderedProduct in the shopping cart and the new quantity. These values are passed through that method with the following code in the Updating event:

```
Protected Sub odsShoppingCart_Updating(ByVal sender As Object, _
          ByVal e As System.Web.UI.WebControls.ObjectDataSourceMethodEventArgs) _
          Handles odsShoppingCart.Updating
    e.InputParameters("Id") = _
          New Guid(GridView1.DataKeys(GridView1.EditIndex).Value.ToString())
    e.InputParameters("newQuantity") = Convert.ToInt32( _
          CType(GridView1.Rows(GridView1.EditIndex).FindControl("lstQuantity"), _
          DropDownList).SelectedValue)
End Sub
```

The GridView that uses the ObjectDataSource control (GridView1) has its DataKeys property set to Id, which uniquely identifies each OrderedProduct that is being displayed in the cart. The ObjectDataSource sees this relation and automatically sets up a parameter for this Id field. In the previous snippet, that Id parameter is then given a value with this code:

```
e.InputParameters("Id") = _
    New Guid(GridView1.DataKeys(GridView1.EditIndex).Value.ToString())
```

The item in the cart that is currently being edited is retrieved with GridView1.EditIndex. This index is then passed to the GridView control's DataKeys collection to get the unique Id for the OrderedProduct. This Id is then converted to a GUID and assigned to e.InputParameters("Id"), the first parameter that the UpdateProductInCart method of the ShopManager class expects.

The new ordered quantity is passed to that method in a similar way. Because the `GridView` knows nothing intrinsically about the `Quantity` of an `OrderedProduct`, an explicit parameter called `newQuantity` has been set up in the `<UpdateParameters>` node of the `ObjectDataSource` that you saw earlier. In the `Updating` event, this quantity is assigned a value with this code:

```
e.InputParameters("newQuantity") = Convert.ToInt32( _
      CType(GridView1.Rows(GridView1.EditIndex).FindControl("lstQuantity"), _
      DropDownList).SelectedValue)
```

Again, `GridView1.EditIndex` is used to get the ID of the item that is being edited. However, in this case not the `DataKeys` but the `Rows` collection is queried for an item with that ID. `Rows(GridView1.EditIndex)` returns a reference to the row in the cart that is being edited. Then the `FindControl` method is used to find a reference to the drop-down list with the new quantity. That quantity is converted to an `Integer` and finally passed to the `e.InputParameters("newQuantity")` parameter so it is eventually passed to `UpdateProductInCart` to update the ordered quantity for the `OrderedProduct` in the cart.

In addition to the Quantity column, the Edit column also deserves a closer examination. By default, when you add a `CommandField` with `ShowEditButton` set to `True`, you get a column that displays an Edit button. Once you click that Edit button, the selected row becomes editable and the Edit button is replaced with an Update and Cancel button.

For the shopping cart, the Update button is not desirable. The only item in each row that is editable is the Quantity drop-down. This drop-down posts back automatically and updates the cart. An additional Update button would confuse users. To remove the Update button, the `CommandField` is converted to a `TemplateField` using the `GridView` control's Fields dialog, shown in Figure 9-14.

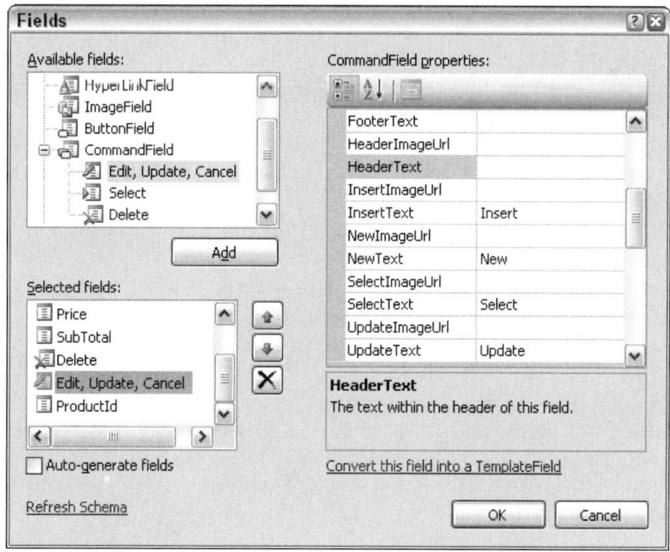

Figure 9-14

To get at this dialog, right-click the `GridView` and choose Show Smart Tag. On the resulting `GridView` tasks dialog, click Edit Columns. Then locate the column you want to convert to a template in the Selected Fields list, and click the blue link with the text "Convert this field into a TemplateField" at the bottom-right of the dialog. The column is then converted into an `<asp:TemplateField>` with an `<ItemTemplate>` and an `<EditItemTemplate>`.

Removing the highlighted code from the code generated by the conversion process removes the Update button from the column:

```
<asp:TemplateField ShowHeader="False">
  <ItemTemplate>
    <asp:Button ID="LinkButton1" runat="server" CausesValidation="False"
           CommandName="Edit" Text="Edit"></asp:Button>
  </ItemTemplate>
  <EditItemTemplate>
     <asp:LinkButton ID="LinkButton1" runat="server" CausesValidation="True"
           CommandName="Update" Text="Update"></asp:LinkButton> 
    <asp:Button ID="LinkButton2" runat="server" CausesValidation="False"
           CommandName="Cancel" Text="Cancel"></asp:Button>
  </EditItemTemplate>
  <ItemStyle Width="100px" HorizontalAlign="Center" />
</asp:TemplateField>
```

When you click the Edit button for a product in the cart, the `GridView` switches to edit mode and displays the `EditItemTemplate` for the quantity drop-down, as depicted in Figure 9-15.

Title		Quantity	Price	SubTotal	
Busy at Work - 1		1	$11.00	$11.00	Cancel
Total:		1		$11.00	

Figure 9-15

You can now choose a new quantity by using just the drop-down; there is no need for an additional Update button. If you change your mind, you can click the Cancel button to stop editing.

Deleting an item requires no additional code; when the Delete button is clicked, `RemoveProductFromCart` is called, which removes the ordered product from the shopping cart. However, to make the cart a bit more user-friendly, the Delete button was converted to a TemplateField as well, with the exact same method you just saw. With the Field converted to a TemplateField, it's easy to ask users for confirmation when they click the Delete button with the Button's `OnClientClick` event:

```
<ItemTemplate>
  <asp:Button ID="btnDelete" runat="server" CausesValidation="False"
  CommandName="Delete" Text="Delete" OnClientClick="return confirm('Are you sure
          you want to remove this product from your cart?');" />
</ItemTemplate>
```

When users click Cancel on the confirmation dialog, nothing happens. If they click OK, the page posts back to the server and the item is removed from the cart.

So far you have seen how the `ObjectDataSource` control is able to display, update, and delete items in the shopping cart. This solution, where the page posts back to itself, has one interesting challenge, though. The master page, on which the ShoppingCart.aspx page is based, has a `ShoppingCartTotal` control that displays the number of items in the cart and the total order amount. The label with the totals is filled in the `Load` event of the control. However, updating or removing the items from the cart happens *after* `Page_Load`. This means that the label with the totals has been set even before the cart is updated, causing the label to be out of sync with the actual shopping cart. To fix that problem, an event is implemented in the `ShoppingCartView` control that fires when the cart is updated. The following block of code shows you how the event is declared, and how it is used in the `RowUpdated` method for the `GridView`:

```
Public Event CartUpdated As EventHandler

Protected Sub GridView1_RowUpdated(ByVal sender As Object, _
    ByVal e As System.Web.UI.WebControls.GridViewUpdatedEventArgs) _
    Handles GridView1.RowUpdated

  RaiseEvent CartUpdated(sender, New System.EventArgs())
End Sub
```

The first line of this example sets up an `Event` that the control can raise when the shopping cart is updated. The next block shows the method `GridView1_RowUpdated`. This method fires whenever a row in the `GridView` is updated. This method uses `RaiseEvent` to raise the `CartUpdated` event. Calling code can subscribe to the event using the `Handles` syntax. This is done in the ShoppingCart.aspx page like this:

```
  Public Sub ShoppingCartView1_CartUpdated(ByVal Sender As Object, _
      ByVal e As EventArgs) Handles ShoppingCartView1.CartUpdated
    Response.Redirect("ShoppingCart.aspx")
  End Sub
```

This example simply redirects the user to ShoppingCart.aspx, which then loads the fresh order total from the cart into the `ShoppingCartTotal` control. As an alternative, you could create a method on the `ShoppingCartTotal` control that updates the label and then call that method instead.

Finalizing Orders

When you're happy with the products in your shopping cart, you can click the Proceed to Check Out button to go to CheckOut.aspx (number 4 in Figure 9-13). However, this page is protected to unauthenticated users with the follow settings in the Web.config file:

```
<location path="Shop/CheckOut.aspx">
  <system.web>
    <authorization>
      <deny users="?"/>
    </authorization>
  </system.web>
</location>
```

So instead of the Check Out page, you get the Login page. On this page, you can sign up for a new user account or log in if you already have a username and password. Refer to the section called "Root Files" earlier in this chapter to see how this page works.

Just like the Shopping Cart page, this Check Out page also contains a `ShoppingCartView` control to display the products in the cart. However, in `Page_Load` of the Check Out page, the `ReadOnly` property of the `ShoppingCartView` is set to `True`. When the `ShoppingCartView` control loads, it hides the columns that contain the Edit and Delete buttons, effectively blocking the user from making any more changes to the item in the cart:

```
If _isReadOnly Then
  GridView1.Columns(5).Visible = False
  GridView1.Columns(6).Visible = False
End If
```

If you click the Finalize Order button the following code checks if you have already completed your profile information:

```
If Profile.ProfileCompleted = True Then
 ... Shown later
Else
  Response.Redirect("~/UserDetails.aspx")
End If
```

When the Boolean value `ProfileCompleted` is `False`, you're taken to UserDetails.aspx. This page presents a series of text boxes where you can enter your first and last name and your address details. These details are then stored using the built-in `Profile` provider:

```
Page.Validate()
If Page.IsValid Then
  Profile.FirstName = txtFirstName.Text
  Profile.LastName = txtLastName.Text
  Profile.Address.Street = txtStreet.Text
  Profile.Address.ZipCode = txtZipCode.Text
  Profile.Address.City = txtCity.Text
  Profile.Address.Country = txtCountry.Text
  Profile.ProfileCompleted = True
  If ShopManager.ShoppingCart.Count > 0 Then
    Response.Redirect("~/Shop/CheckOut.aspx")
  Else
    Response.Redirect("~/")
  End If
End If
```

As you can see, the `Profile` feature makes it very easy to store user-specific data. All you need to do is assign the values from a control to the public profile property that's been set up in the Web.config file.

After you complete the profile, you are either taken back to CheckOut.aspx, where you can review the order and shipping details and then click the Finalize Order button, or you're taken back to the homepage. The code for the Finalize button retrieves the total order amount and then creates a new instance of a `Customer` object that it passes to the `FinalizeOrder` method of the `ShopManager` class. The total order amount must be retrieved here, because when `FinalizeOrder` has finished, the shopping cart is empty, and it no longer has a total order amount:

```
Try
  Dim orderAmount As Decimal = ShopManager.ShoppingCart.Total
  Dim theCustomer As Customer = _
```

```
        New Customer(CType(Membership.GetUser().ProviderUserKey, Guid), _
        Profile.FirstName, Profile.LastName, Profile.Address.Street, _
        Profile.Address.ZipCode, Profile.Address.City, Profile.Address.Country)
    Dim orderId As Integer = ShopManager.FinalizeOrder(theCustomer)
    Response.Redirect("ThankYou.aspx?OrderNumber=" & _
        orderId.ToString() & "&Total=" & orderAmount.ToString("c"))
    Catch ex As Exception
      lblFailure.Visible = True
      btnFinalize.Visible = False
  End Try
```

The customer details come from two different sources — the customer ID is taken from the MembershipUser class, which exposes a ProviderUserKey property that is unique for each user in the system. All the other properties come from the user's profile.

The FinalizeOrder method in the ShopManager class performs two actions. First it inserts the order and order details in the database by calling FinalizeOrder on the ShopManagerDB class. When the order has been saved successfully, the cart is then emptied to avoid the same order from being saved twice. The FinalizeOrder method in the ShopManagerDB class contains quite a bit of code, so the method is broken down in pieces and discussed line by line. The code begins by declaring a variable called myTransaction of type SqlClient.SqlTransaction:

```
Public Shared Function FinalizeOrder(ByVal theShoppingCart As ShoppingCart, _
        ByVal theCustomer As Customer) As Integer
  Dim myTransaction As SqlClient.SqlTransaction = Nothing
```

The order is saved partially in the OrderBase table and partially in the OrderDetail table. This is done with multiple INSERT statements. If any of the statements fails, you want to roll back the entire operation to avoid having incomplete orders in the database. It's the SqlTransaction object's responsibility to manage that process. All you need to do is wrap the code in a Try Catch block, assign the transaction object to each SqlCommand object you want to execute, and call Commit or Rollback, depending on the success of the operation. The SqlTransaction object is instantiated by calling the BeginTransaction method of a connection:

```
  Try
    Using myConnection As New SqlConnection(AppConfiguration.ConnectionString)
      myConnection.Open()

      myTransaction = myConnection.BeginTransaction
```

The next block of code sets up the first SqlCommand object that inserts the order's base data in the OrderBase table:

```
      Dim myCommand As SqlCommand = New SqlCommand( _
            "sprocOrderBaseInsertSingleItem", myConnection)
      myCommand.Transaction = myTransaction
      myCommand.CommandType = CommandType.StoredProcedure
```

With the SqlCommand object instantiated, it's time to pass the customer's details to the stored procedure using SqlParameters and execute it. The code for the stored procedure isn't shown here because it doesn't do anything special. All it does is insert a new record in the OrderBase table, returning its new

ID using the `Scope_Identity()` function of SQL Server. As of SQL Server 2000, `Scope_Identity()` is preferred over `@@IDENTITY` because the former returns the ID created in the current scope, like a stored procedure, whereas the latter could return an unrelated ID caused by a trigger on the table that you're inserting the record into.

The next step is to add the parameters to the `SqlCommand` object using the `AddWithValue` method:

```
myCommand.Parameters.AddWithValue("@CustomerId", theCustomer.CustomerId)
... Other parameters are added here
myCommand.Parameters.AddWithValue("@Country", theCustomer.Country)

Dim theReturnValue As SqlParameter = New SqlParameter()
theReturnValue.Direction = ParameterDirection.ReturnValue
myCommand.Parameters.Add(theReturnValue)

myCommand.ExecuteNonQuery()
```

The stored procedure returns the ID of the new record in the OrderBase table. That ID can be retrieved from the parameter `theReturnValue`. Because the return value is passed back as a generic object, it must be cast to an Integer using `Convert.ToInt32`:

```
Dim orderId As Integer = Convert.ToInt32(theReturnValue.Value)
```

The next block of code is responsible for inserting the order details and binding it to the OrderBase record that was created earlier. Another `SqlCommand` object is set up and assigned the transaction object that was created earlier (see the following code). This way this new command will participate in the same transaction:

```
Dim myCommand2 As SqlCommand = _
     New SqlCommand("sprocOrderDetailInsertSingleItem", myConnection)
myCommand2.Transaction = myTransaction
myCommand2.CommandType = CommandType.StoredProcedure
```

Just as with the first command, you need to pass parameters to the stored procedure. The code block that sets the parameters for the `myCommand` object used the convenient `AddWithValue` method that sets up the parameter automatically. However, in the case of the order details you cannot use that technique because you need to be able to use the parameters multiple times; once for each ordered product in the shopping cart. That's why you need to declare and instantiate each parameter explicitly:

```
Dim orderBaseIdParam As SqlParameter = _
   New SqlParameter("OrderBaseId", SqlDbType.Int)
myCommand2.Parameters.Add(orderBaseIdParam)

Dim productIdParam As SqlParameter = _
   New SqlParameter("productId", SqlDbType.Int)
myCommand2.Parameters.Add(productIdParam)

Dim priceParam As SqlParameter = _
    New SqlParameter("price", SqlDbType.Money)
myCommand2.Parameters.Add(priceParam)

Dim quantityParam As SqlParameter = _
    New SqlParameter("quantity", SqlDbType.Int)
myCommand2.Parameters.Add(quantityParam)
```

With the explicit parameters set up it's now very easy to reuse them in a loop and assign them a different value that is retrieved from the ordered product being added:

```
For Each myOrderedProduct As OrderedProduct In theShoppingCart.Items
  orderBaseIdParam.Value = orderId
  productIdParam.Value = myOrderedProduct.ProductId
  priceParam.Value = myOrderedProduct.Price
  quantityParam.Value = myOrderedProduct.Quantity
  myCommand2.ExecuteNonQuery()
Next
```

Just as the stored procedure that inserts the order base details, the stored procedure that inserts the order details is very simple as well. It simply inserts the product ID, the price, and the quantity of each item, and then relates the record to the OrderBase table by setting the OrderBaseId column. At this point, the entire order has been saved successfully so you call `Commit` to commit the transaction in the database and then return the new order ID to the calling code:

```
    myTransaction.Commit()
    Return orderId
  End Using
```

If an error occurred anywhere in this method, the code in the `Catch` block is executed. By calling `Rollback` on the transaction object you can let the database know that an error occurred and then it will undo any changes it has made so far. At the end, you call `Throw` to pass up the error in the call chain:

```
    Catch ex As Exception
      myTransaction.Rollback()
      ' Pass up the error
      Throw
    End Try
  End Sub
```

The order ID returned from the `FinalizeOrder` method in the data access layer is passed through the business layer to the Check Out page. That page passes it, together with the total order amount, to the Thank You page:

```
Response.Redirect("ThankYou.aspx?OrderNumber=" & _
    orderId.ToString() & "&Total=" & orderAmount.ToString("c"))
```

The Thank You page instructs the user to transfer the money to the Wrox WebShop account before the goods will be shipped. As a reference, the order number and total order amount are displayed. Passing the order amount in the query string sounds like a security risk, but in this case it isn't. The order has been completely finalized so there is no way to change it anymore. Also, the goods won't be shipped until the customer has paid the full amount into the shop's bank account.

This concludes the discussion of the front end of the web shop. With the finalization page, the whole ordering process is complete. Users can browse the product catalog, add items to their shopping cart, get a customer account and log in, and finalize their orders.

The Management Folder

The Management folder is used to allow an administrator of the site to make changes to the products in the catalog. You have already seen most of the concepts used in this mini content management system in Chapter 5. However, there may be one thing you're unfamiliar with. Whenever you create a new product and upload an image, three thumbnails are created automatically. In the classic ASP days, you'd need to buy a commercial third-party component or write some hefty C++ to resize images automatically. However, in the .NET era you need only a few lines of code. Take a look first at the code that fires whenever a new product is about to be inserted. You find the following code in the `FormView1_ItemInserting` method in the AddProduct.aspx.vb file:

```
' First. try to save the images
Dim theFileUpload As FileUpload = CType( _
      FormView1.FindControl("FileUpload1"), FileUpload)
If theFileUpload.HasFile Then
  Dim fileNameSmall As String = "~/Images/Products/" & Guid.NewGuid.ToString()
  Dim fileNameMedium As String = "~/Images/Products/" & Guid.NewGuid.ToString()
  Dim fileNameLarge As String = "~/Images/Products/" & Guid.NewGuid.ToString()

  Dim theExtension As String = Path.GetExtension(theFileUpload.FileName)

  fileNameSmall &= theExtension
  fileNameMedium &= theExtension
  fileNameLarge &= theExtension
  theFileUpload.SaveAs(Server.MapPath(fileNameLarge))

  ' Now resize the images
  Helpers.ResizeImage(Server.MapPath(fileNameLarge), _
          Server.MapPath(fileNameSmall), 40)
  Helpers.ResizeImage(Server.MapPath(fileNameLarge), _
          Server.MapPath(fileNameMedium), 100)
  Helpers.ResizeImage(Server.MapPath(fileNameLarge), _
          Server.MapPath(fileNameLarge), 250)
```

The code first checks if an image has been uploaded. If `HasFile` of the `Upload` control returns `True`, three filenames are generated, one for each thumb. The extension for the files is determined by using `Path.GetExtension` and passing it the name of the uploaded file.

The final block of code creates the three thumbs by calling `Helpers.ResizeImage` and passing it the name of the image to resize, the name the thumb should be saved to, and the maximum width or height for each image (40 for the thumb used in the shopping cart, 100 for the image in the product catalog, and 250 for the image on the detail page). You see the implementation for the `ResizeMethod` in Chapter 11, where it's discussed in full detail.

With this short description of the Management folder, you've come to the end of the "Code and Code Explanation" section. The next section describes the installation process of the WebShop application.

Setting up the WebShop

You can choose to install the WebShop manually or by using the supplied installer application (available on the companion CD-ROM and for download at `www.wrox.com`). You can use the installer when you have IIS running on your machine and want to use it for the WebShop. Running the installer creates a virtual directory under IIS. The folders it creates contain the full source.

Alternatively, you can choose to unpack the supplied zip file to a folder of your location. This gives you a bit more choice with regards to where the files are placed, but you'll have to set up IIS manually, or browse to the site from within Visual Web Developer.

For both installation methods it's assumed that the .NET Framework 2.0, which is an installation requirement for Visual Web Developer, has already been installed. It's also assumed that you have installed SQL Server 2005 Express edition with an instance name of SqlExpress. If you chose a different instance name, make sure you use that name in the connection string for the WebShop in the Web.config file.

Using the Installer

On the CD-ROM that comes with this book, locate the folder Chapter 09 - WebShop and then open the Installation folder. Inside that folder you'll find two files: setup.exe and WebShopInstaller.msi. Double-click setup.exe to start the installation. Keep clicking Next until the application is installed and then click Close to finish the installation wizard.

The WebShop is now ready to be run under IIS. However, before you can use it you may have to configure IIS to use the .NET Framework 2.0 version instead of version 1.x. Refer to the section "Changing IIS Settings" in Chapter 5 for information about changing this setting.

Manual Installation

Another way to set up the WebShop is by manually extracting the files from the accompanying zip file to your local hard drive. To install manually, locate the folder Chapter 09 - WebShop and then open the Source folder. In that folder you'll find a zip file called Chapter 09 - WebShop.zip. Extract the contents of the zip file to a location on your hard drive (for example, `C:\Websites`). Make sure you extract the files with the option Use Folder Names or something similar to maintain the original folder structure. You should end up with a folder like `C:\Websites\WebShop` that in turn contains a number of files and other folders. If you want to open the web site in Visual Web Developer, choose File➪Open Web Site, and browse to the folder where you extracted the files.

Modifying Security Settings

The maintenance section of the WebShop creates thumbnail images automatically for each product you add to the catalog. The account that your web site runs under needs permissions to write to that folder. To change the settings, open Windows Explorer and locate the Images folder inside the WebShop. The path should be something like `C:\Inetpub\wwwroot\WebShop\Images`, depending on where you installed the application. Inside the Images folder you'll find a Products folder. Right-click it, choose Properties, and then open the Security tab, which is depicted in Figure 9-16.

If you don't see a Security tab, open Windows Explorer, choose Tools➪Folder Options, and then click the View tab. At the bottom of the Advanced Settings list, make sure that Use Simple File Sharing (Recommended) is unchecked.

Figure 9-16

Click the Add button and add one of the accounts from the following table:

If You're Using	Running On	Add the Account
Windows 2000	IIS	ASPNET
Windows 2000	Built-in web server of Visual Web Developer	The account you use to log on to your machine.
Windows XP	IIS	ASPNET
Windows XP	Built-in server of Visual Web Developer	The account you use to log on to your machine.
Windows Server 2003	IIS	Network Service
Windows Server 2003	Built-in server of Visual Web Developer	The account you use to log on to your machine.

Once you add the account, make sure you give it at least Read and Write permissions.

Changing E-mail Settings

The WebShop uses e-mail functionality in a couple of places. Before you can use the functions that rely on e-mail, such as the password reminder and the order confirmation, you need to change a few settings. The first setting is at the top of the Web.config file in the root. Change the `MailFromAddress` element, used by the `PasswordRecovery` control in Login.aspx, to your own e-mail address. Then at the bottom of the Web.config file, change the settings in the `<smtp>` node.

The final change you need to make is in the file Global.asax, in the root of the site. In the `Application_Error` method, set `sendMailOnErrors` to `True` if you want to be notified of errors by e-mail. Near the end of the method, change the fake e-mail addresses in the line with `New MailMessage` to your own address.

Managing Products

You can manage the products in the product catalog by clicking the Login link on the main menu of the Wrox WebShop. You can log in with a username of `Administrator` and a password of `Admin123#` or the account you created yourself in the previous section. Once you're logged in, you'll see the Admin menu appear. If you click that menu item, you see two links that allow you to view the product list or to enter a new product.

For a walkthrough of possible extensions you can develop for the WebShop, the companion CD-ROM that comes with this book has an additional document with the details on implementing one of those extensions: sending an order confirmation to the customer by e-mail. The CD-ROM also features the complete source for this walkthrough. In addition, you can download the source from `www.wrox.com`.

Summary

The Wrox WebShop presented in this chapter features all the elements that you need for any serious e-commerce web shop: a product catalog, a shopping cart, and a mechanism to store the orders in a database.

The chapter started with a quick tour of the web site from an end-user's point of view. You also saw how to manage the product catalog in the protected Management section.

You then got a thorough look at the application's design. You saw the classes the make up the business and data access layers, and an explanation of each of the methods in these layers.

In addition to looking at the site from a customer's point of view, you learned about the site's classes, user controls, and pages. In particular, you learned how to do the following:

- Build a business and data access layer to retrieve information about products and categories.
- Develop a shopping cart that stores the `OrderedProducts` in session state so they are available throughout the lifetime of a user's session.

- Customize the GridView control and change its default behavior to streamline the user's browsing experience. By removing unneeded buttons, such as the Update button, the shopping cart becomes easier and more intuitive to use.
- Use the SqlTransaction object in data access code to ensure that multiple database actions either complete as a unit or are rolled back in case of a failure.
- Make use of the ASP.NET 20 Profile provider to store user details in the database. Instead of writing custom code to get this information in and out of a database, you can now simply add a few settings to the Web.config file, and these properties become available on the Profile class.

With the knowledge you gained in this chapter, you can now build full-featured e-commerce web sites that are easy to manage, extend, and maintain.

Appointment Booking System

No matter what business you're in or what organization you work for, a lot of day-to-day tasks involve appointments. Whether you run a hairdresser shop, hire out conference rooms or laptops, or you have a technical consultancy firm, you need a way to keep track of appointments that have been made. Quite often these kinds of appointments are made by phone, and then written down on sticky notes or saved in a calendar application like Microsoft Outlook or in a planning tool. Wouldn't it be great if you could remove all the hassle these phone calls bring and allow your customers to make the appointments online?

The Appointment Booking System presented in this chapter allows you to do just that. The application — which can be installed as part of your intranet or corporate web site — enables registered end-users to check availability and make direct appointments. To minimize abuse of the system, users have to sign up for an account and confirm their e-mail address before they can access the system's vital areas. Users from your organization have direct access to the appointments that have been made online.

The chapter has a strong focus on working with controls. You see how to use some of the less-known controls like the `Wizard` and the `MultiView`. You learn how to create reusable user controls with custom properties and methods. Finally, you see how to create instances of server controls on the fly using code in code-behind files to create output that cannot be achieved with the existing ASP.NET 2.0 server controls.

Using the Appointment Booking System

The Appointment Booking System consists of two parts: the public end-user section and the maintenance section. The public user section is where end-users can sign up for an account, check availability, and make appointments. To allow you to determine at run time what kind of appointments you want to book in the system, the system is built around a generic term called *Booking Objects*. A booking object is the person or object — such as a mechanic or a conference room — you can make an appointment with. Because this term doesn't make sense to an end-user, the application can be configured to display a user-friendly description, such as Mechanic, Hairdresser, or Conference Room, instead. This configuration can be done in the Web.config file for the application or through the administrative interface of the application. Because this configuration has an impact on the public interface, that section is discussed first. After that, you see how to use the Appointment Booking System from an end-user's point of view.

The remainder of this chapter uses conference rooms as the booking object so whenever you see Conference Room, think booking object and vice versa. However, because it's likely you'll use a different description for the booking object, your screens will be slightly different than the ones you see in this chapter.

Maintaining the Appointment Booking System

If the application is installed, you can browse to it by entering `http://localhost/Appointment Booking` in your browser (see "Setting up the Appointment Booking System" later in this chapter for more details about setting up the application). The screen shown in Figure 10-1 appears.

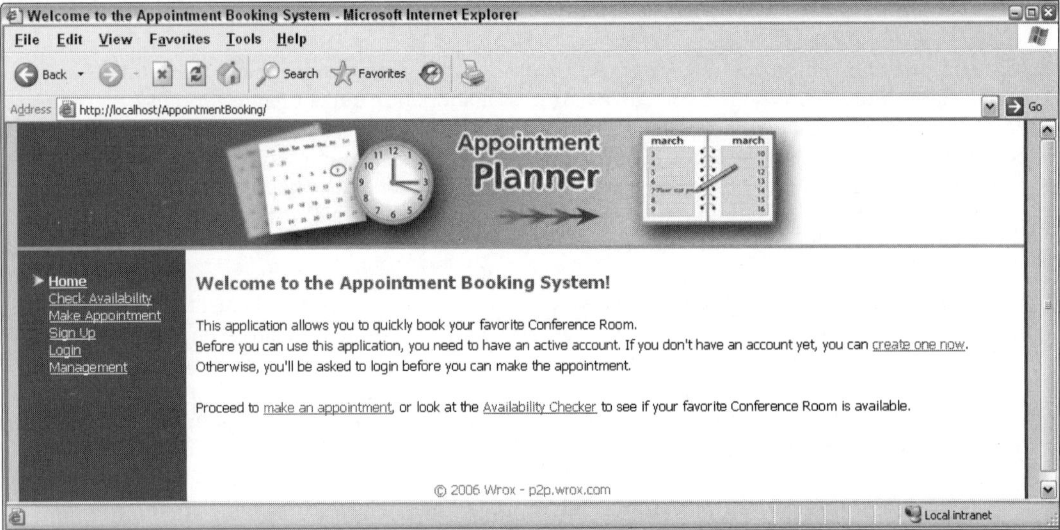

Figure 10-1

The first thing you'll need to do is change the user-friendly description of the booking object. To do this, click the Management link in the left menu. You'll be forced to log in first because the Management section is protected and can be accessed only by users in the Manager role. Type `Administrator` as the username and `Admin123#` as the password. Then click Application Settings in the Management menu (visible in Figure 10-2) that has appeared and provide a name for the singular form and for the plural form of your booking object.

So if you're using this application to make appointments for hairdressers, type in Hairdresser and Hairdressers. You can leave the Require Comments setting checked for now. This setting determines whether users have to enter a comment when they make an appointment. The Start Time and End Time settings determine the opening hours of your business. Changing these settings will impact the Appointment Wizard, the Availability Checker, and the management pages; all of which are shown later. Be aware that saving the settings forces an application restart as the new settings are written to the Web.config file.

With the user-friendly name set up, click the second link in the Management menu (visible in Figure 10-2), which should now display the name of the booking object you entered in the previous section. In addition to that link in the Management menu, the page title and the introduction text of the page now also show the user-friendly name you gave to the booking objects.

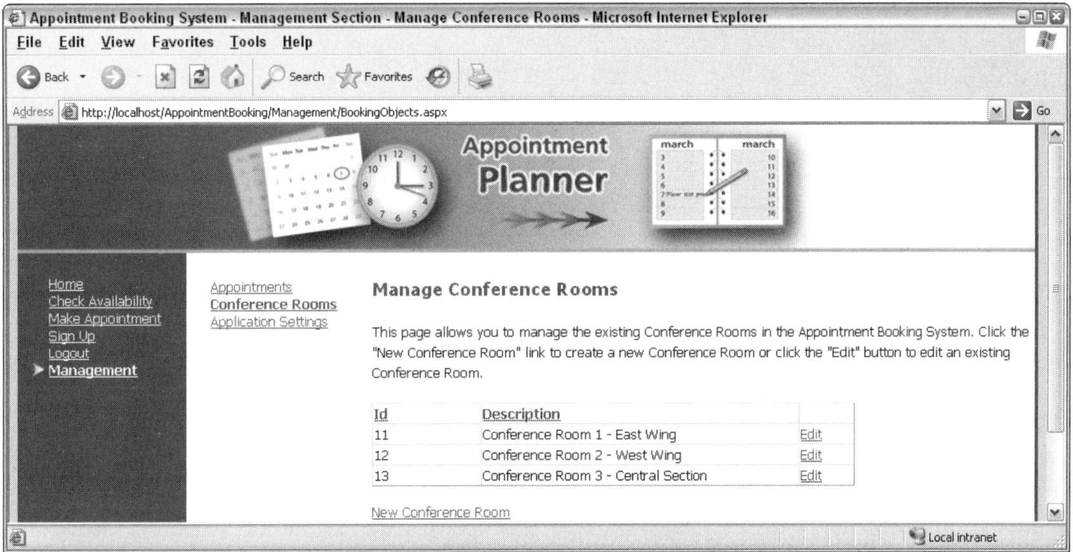

Figure 10-2

This page allows you to create new or change existing booking objects. The application comes with three pre-installed booking objects, but you can click the Edit link to change the description for each booking object. When you click Edit, the screen in Figure 10-3 appears.

Here you can give the booking object a title and determine between what times and on what days it's available for appointments. Once you're done, click the Update link and you're back at the page that lists the booking objects. Use the New link to create as many booking objects as your application requires. Note that in Figure 10-2 the link is called New Conference Room, but in your application it should show the name of your booking object.

Once you create the booking objects, the application is ready for use by end-users. You see how the public area of the web site works in the next section.

Figure 10-3

Making Appointments with the Appointment Booking System

To make the process of booking an appointment as simple as possible, the application features a wizard that guides the user through the process. Two menu items allow you to access this wizard. First, you can click the Check Availability link to see if your favorite booking object is available on a date and time of your choice. If it is, you can make an appointment by clicking an available timeslot. The alternative is through the Make Appointment menu option that allows you to make an appointment request directly. Both these menu items are blocked for unauthenticated users, so you'll need to create an account first.

Creating an Account

Before you can create an appointment, you need to have a valid account. You can create one on the Sign Up page available from the left menu. This page features a standard `CreateUserWizard` control that asks you for some information, such as your name and e-mail address. Once you have created an account, you'll receive an e-mail with a confirmation link that you'll need to click before your account is activated. This technique, called *double opt-in*, ensures that only users with a valid and confirmed e-mail address can use your application. You see later how this double opt-in technique works. Once your account is activated, you can login by clicking the Login link and then start using the Appointment Booking System.

The Availability Checker

When you click Check Availability in the main menu, you'll see a little calendar icon that allows you to select a date for which you want to see the availability. When you select a date, the page reloads and you see a screen similar to Figure 10-4.

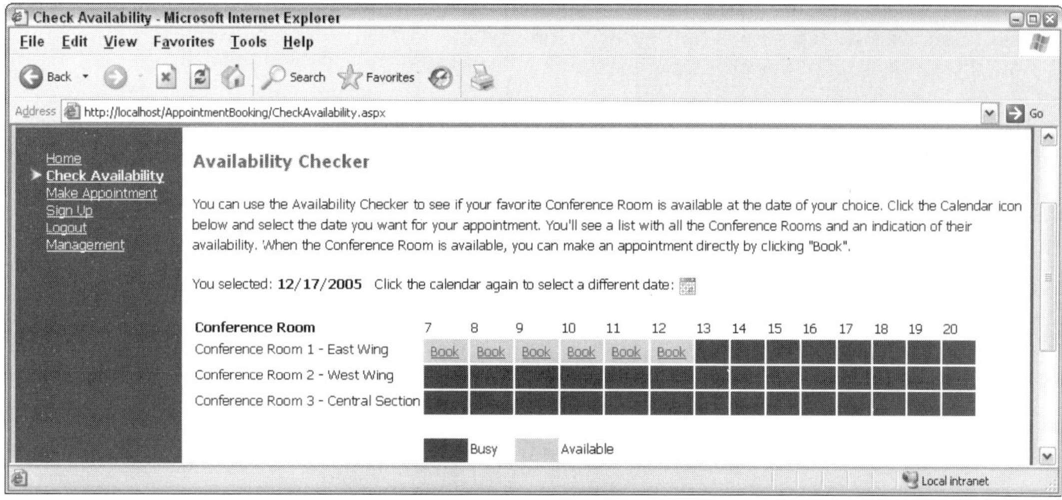

Figure 10-4

On this screen you see a grid that displays the booking objects. The first row in the grid is the header and displays the name of the booking object (Conference Room in this example) and the available hours, ranging from 7 a.m. until 8 p.m. You can also see that for this date, only Conference Room 1 is available, and only between 7 a.m. and 1 p.m. If you click Book for a free timeslot, you're taken to the appointment wizard that is discussed in the next section. You can click the calendar again to select a different date for which you want to see the availability.

The Appointment Wizard

If you click Make Appointment in the main menu, the Booking Object Selection Wizard, depicted in Figure 10-5, appears.

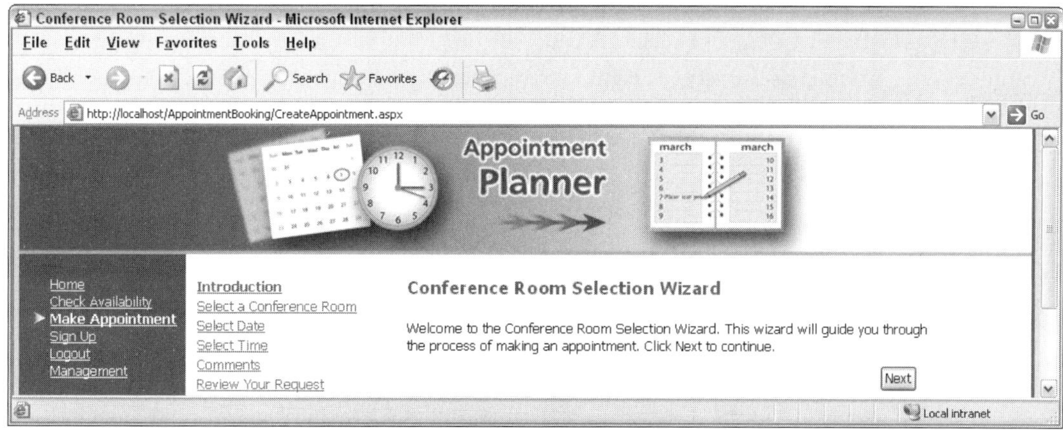

Figure 10-5

Notice that the text in the wizard menu and in the introduction text does not speak about general booking objects, but uses the term that's configured in the application, Conference Rooms in this case. You see how this works later in this chapter when the code is discussed.

The wizard is pretty straightforward and thus easy to use. Click Next to select an available booking object, then Next again to select a date, and then the time and duration. On the Comments page you can enter comments to go with the appointment. For example, you can enter special instructions for the lunch you'd like to have in the conference room. Finally, on the Review Your Request tab, you get a summary of the selections you made. When you click Finish, you get a screen that either confirms your appointment or explains to you that the requested booking object, date, and time are not available. In the latter case, you can restart the wizard and make a different selection, or go to the Availability Checker to find out when you can make an appointment.

Design of the Appointment Booking System

Similar to other applications you have seen in this book, the Appointment Booking System is built on a three-tier approach, which means it has a data access layer, a business layer, and a presentation layer. The data access layer is responsible for accessing the database and nothing else. The business layer is responsible for checking of business rules and serves as the bridge between the data access layer and the presentation layer. Finally, the presentation layer, which consists of .aspx and .ascx files, is responsible for the interaction with the user.

In this section, you see the design of the classes and methods in the data access and business layer. You'll find the code for the business layer in a subfolder called BusinessLogic inside the special App_Code folder in the root of the site. Similarly, you'll find the classes for data access in a folder called DataAccess.

The presentation layer is discussed in the section "Code and Code Explanation" later in the chapter.

The Business Layer

The application uses two main entities that each has its own class: `BookingObject` and `Appointment`. The `BookingObject` represents the real-life objects that you can make an appointment with, such as a conference room, whereas the Appointment represents the actual appointment made. To be able to work with instances of these classes, each class also has a `Manager` class that is capable of retrieving and saving the other classes by interacting with the data access layer.

The business layer also has an enumeration called `Weekdays` that represents the available days of the week.

In the sections that follow, each of these classes and the enumeration are discussed in more detail.

BookingObject

The `BookingObject` class (see Figure 10-6) exposes only public properties that are stored in so-called *backing variables* (the private fields prefixed with an underscore in the upper-half of Figure 10-6). Because all interaction with instances of the `BookingObject` class is done by the `BookingObjectManager` class, the `BookingObject` itself has no methods.

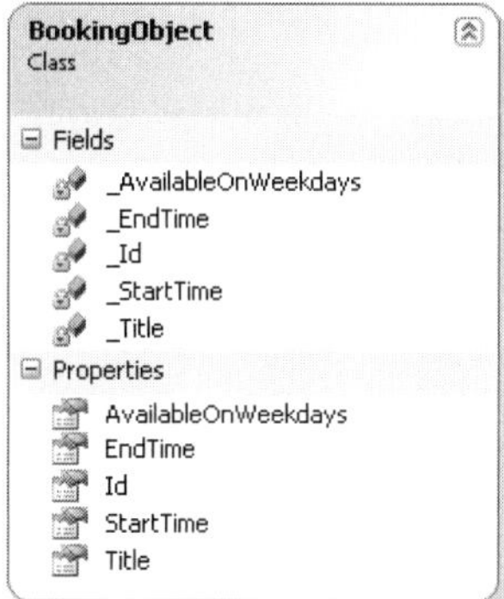

Figure 10-6

The following table describes the five public properties of the `BookingObject` class:

Property	Type	Description
`AvailableOnWeekDays`	`Weekdays`	This property is of type `Weekdays`, which is an enumeration. This property is used to store multiple days on which the booking object is available.
`EndTime`	`Integer`	The last hour that the booking object is available on a day. Because the application books appointments for a full hour, the maximum value for `EndTime` is 23, which means the booking object is available until midnight. (The last appointment then starts at 11 o'clock at night and lasts until midnight.)
`Id`	`Integer`	The unique ID of the `BookingObject` in the database.
`StartTime`	`Integer`	The first hour of the day that the booking object becomes available; for example, 9 for 9 a.m.
`Title`	`String`	The description for the `BookingObject`, such as Conference Room 1 — East Wing.

Next up is the `BookingObjectManager` class.

BookingObjectManager

This class is responsible for getting booking objects in and out of the database by interacting with the data access layer. It's also used to return a list with available working days from the data access layer through its `GetWorkingDays` method. The class has the methods shown in Figure 10-7.

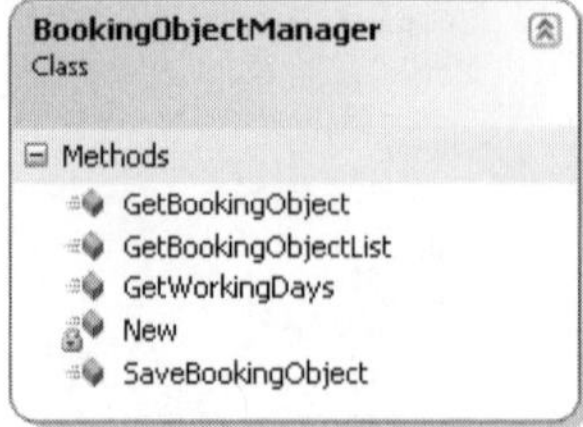

Figure 10-7

Because the class exposes shared methods exclusively, its constructor has been hidden by marking it as `Private`. This prevents calling code from instantiating the `BookingObjectManager` directly. Besides the constructor, the class exposes four shared and public methods that all call methods with the same name in the `BookingObjectManagerDB` class in the data access layer:

Method	Return Type	Description
`Public Shared Function GetBookingObject (ByVal id As Integer)`	`BookingObject`	Returns a single `BookingObject` instance by its ID.
`Public Shared Function GetBookingObjectList ()`	`DataSet`	Returns a list of available booking object records as a `DataSet`.
`Public Shared Function GetWorkingDays()`	`DataSet`	Returns a list with the available `Working Days`.
`Public Shared Sub SaveBookingObject (ByVal myBookingObject As BookingObject)`	n/a	Saves a new or an existing booking object in the database.

With the `BookingObject` and `BookingObjectManager` classes done, the next class is the `Appointment` class, which is used to make an actual appointment with a booking object.

Appointment

The `Appointment` class, shown in Figure 10-8, represents an appointment that has been made in the system. It exposes only public properties that are used to track when the appointment takes place, who made it, and for what booking object.

Figure 10-8

To help you understand what these properties are used for, the following table lists them all and describes their purpose:

Property	Type	Description
`BookingObjectId`	`Integer`	The ID of the booking object in the database that this appointment was booked against.
`Comments`	`String`	Stores the comment for an appointment. When a user makes an appointment, she has the opportunity to add a comment. Whether this comment is required depends on the application's settings.
`EndDate`	`DateTime`	The date and time the appointment ends.
`Id`	`Integer`	The unique ID of the appointment in the database.
`StartDate`	`DateTime`	The date and time the appointment starts.
`UserEmailAddress`	`String`	Holds the e-mail address of the user in the application and is retrieved through the Membership services in ASP.NET.
`UserName`	`String`	Holds the name of the user in the application and is retrieved through the Membership services in ASP.NET.

Similar to the BookingObject class, the Appointment class also has an accompanying Manager class, the AppointmentManager, discussed next.

AppointmentManager

The AppointmentManager class, depicted in Figure 10-9, has useful methods to get and create appointments. It can also determine whether a new appointment overlaps with an existing one, and it is capable of retrieving appointment information from the database to feed the Availability Checker.

Figure 10-9

Just as with the BookingObjectManager, the constructor for the AppointmentManager (the New method in Figure 10-9) has been hidden by marking it as Private. This prevents calling code from instantiating objects from this class. You never require an instance of these classes, because they expose shared methods that work only on a class and not on an instance of that class.

Besides the constructor, the AppointmentManager has five public and shared methods that all call methods with the same name in the AppointmentManagerDB class. These methods are discussed in the following table:

Method	Return Type	Description
Public Shared Function CheckAppointment (ByVal myAppointment As Appointment)	Boolean	Checks whether the requested appointment overlaps with an existing one. It returns True when the appointment passed in can be made, or False when it overlaps.
Public Shared Function CreateAppointment (ByVal myAppointment As Appointment)	Boolean	Creates an appointment in the database. It returns True when the appointment is successfully made, or False when it could not be booked.
Public Shared Function GetAppointment (ByVal id As Integer)	Appointment	Retrieves a single instance of an appointment from the database by its ID. This method is used in the reporting pages in the Management section of the site.
Public Shared Function GetAppointmentList (ByVal selectedDate As DateTime)	DataSet	Retrieves a list of all the appointments for a specific date from the database. This method is used in the reporting pages in the Management section of the site.

Method	Return Type	Description
`Public Shared Function GetTimeSheet (ByVal selectedDate As DateTime)`	`DataSet`	Returns a `DataSet` with two DataTables, holding booking objects and appointments. This `DataSet` is used generate the chart for the Availability Checker.

The final object in the business layer that you need to look at is not a class, but an enumeration. This enumeration, called `Weekdays`, is discussed next.

Weekdays

Although there is already good support for working with days of the week in .NET, the Appointment Booking System features a separate enumeration that lists all of the available weekdays. This enumeration allows you to store multiple selected weekdays in a single variable. The `BookingObject` uses this enumeration to indicate on which day the object can be booked. Instead of this enumeration, the `BookingObject` could expose seven Boolean properties, such as `AvailableOnMonday`, `AvailableOnTuesday`, and so forth, but that makes the class look a bit cluttered. Using this `Weekdays` enumeration, displayed in Figure 10-10, you can store the availability for multiple days in a single variable.

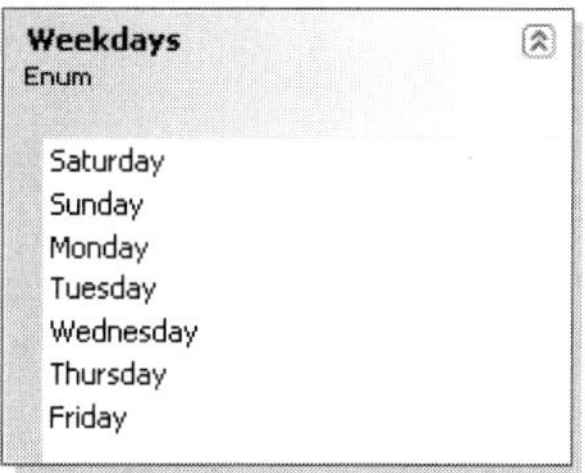

Figure 10-10

With this simple enumeration, you can store, for example, Friday and Wednesday in a variable of type `Weekdays` with the following code:

```
Dim myWeekdays As Weekdays = Weekdays.Wednesday Or Weekdays.Friday
```

Later, you can use similar code to determine whether a certain day has been stored in that variable:

```
If myWeekdays And Weekdays.Friday Then
  ' Friday was selected and stored in myWeekdays
Else
  ' Friday was NOT selected
End If
```

Because the Appointment Booking System is quite data-centric, it should come as no surprise it has its own database and data access layer. In the next section, the two classes in the data access layer are discussed. Once you understand how these classes work, you get a good look at the tables and stored procedures that make up the database.

The Data Access Layer

Because the BookingObject and Appointment classes have no behavior themselves but are managed by their respective Manager classes instead, they also have no companion class in the data access layer. The only classes that interact with the stored procedures in the database directly are the BookingObjectManagerDB and the AppointmentDB classes.

BookingObjectManagerDB

The BookingObjectManagerDB class (see Figure 10-11) exposes the exact same four public and shared methods and the private constructor as the BookingObjectManager class. Of course this isn't a coincidence, because each method in the business layer forwards the call to a method in the data access layer.

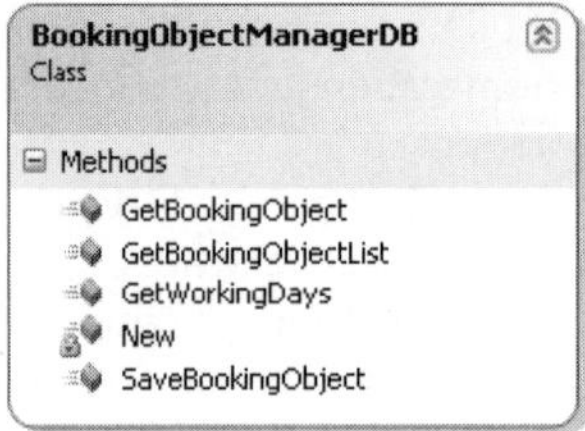

Figure 10-11

Because the methods are identical as those in the BookingObjectManager in terms of signature, return type, and functionality, they aren't described here again. Refer to the description of the BookingObject class earlier in this chapter for a full description of the four methods. The only difference between the methods in the business and data access layer is, of course, their implementation. The methods in the business layer forward their calls to methods in the data access layer. Those methods in turn perform the real work and communicate with the database. You see how this works in the section "Code and Code Explanation."

AppointmentManagerDB

The AppointmentManagerDB class (see Figure 10-12) is responsible for getting appointments, lists of appointments, and time sheet information from the database. It's also capable of checking and creating appointments.

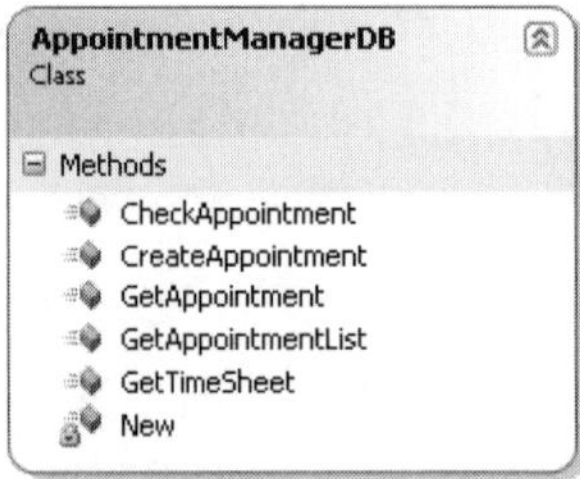

Figure 10-12

Each of the methods in this class has the same signature as those in the AppointmentManager class in the business layer, so refer to that section for more detail about their signatures and description.

In addition to these classes, the data access layer also consists of the database itself, including the stored procedures used to access the data. The following section describes the data model of the Appointment Booking System and describes each of the four tables.

The Data Model

The database for the Appointment Booking System contains three main tables and one junction table. Both the `BookingObject` and the `Appointment` classes you saw in the design of the business layer have their own table in the database.

There is also a table called WorkingDay that stores the available working days for the application. Don't confuse this table with the `Weekdays` enumeration. This enumeration always defines all seven days of the week, whereas the WorkingDay table stores only the actual days of the week that are appropriate for your booking objects. If your booking objects are available only during the week, you could remove Saturday and Sunday from this table.

The final table in the database is called BookingObjectWorkingDay. This junction table relates a certain booking object to one or more working days, as you can see in Figure 10-13. This allows you to have a different availability for different booking objects.

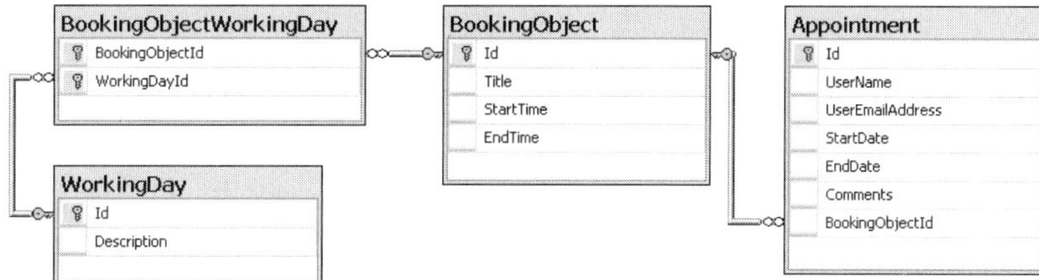

Figure 10-13

The BookingObject and Appointment tables require a bit more explanation, so they are described in more detail in the following two tables.

BookingObject

Column Name	Data Type	Description
Id	`int`	Stores the unique ID of each booking object.
Title	`nvarchar (100)`	Stores the title of a booking object such as Conference Room 6.
StartTime	`datetime`	Stores the first available time a booking object is available during the day. Although the column type is `datetime`, only the time portion of the `datetime` is used.
EndTime	`datetime`	Stores the last available time a booking object is available during the day. Although the column type is `datetime`, only the time portion of the `datetime` is used.

This BookingObject table is the data store for the BookingObject class. Four of the properties of that class have their own column in this table. The AvailableOnWeekdays property is not stored in that table, but in the junction table called BookingObjectWorkingDay.

Similar to this, the Appointment class has its own table, also called Appointment.

Appointment

Column Name	Data Type	Description
Id	int	Stores the unique ID of the appointment.
UserName	nvarchar (256)	Stores the name of the user that made the appointment.
UserEmailAddress	nvarchar (256)	Stores the e-mail address of the user that made the appointment.
StartDate	datetime	Stores the start date and time of the appointment.
EndDate	datetime	Stores the end date and time of the appointment.
Comments	nvarchar (max)	Stores the comments that a user may have added to the appointment request.
BookingObjectId	int	Stores the ID of the booking object that this appointment was booked against.

All of the interaction with the database is done through stored procedures. Some of the procedures are pretty straightforward and require no explanation. The others that are a bit more complex are discussed in detail when the inner workings of the Appointment Booking System are discussed.

Helper Classes

In addition to the classes and enumeration defined in the business and data access layer, the Appointment Booking System has two more classes: an AppConfiguration class that exposes configuration properties used throughout the application and a Helpers class that supplies a useful helper method.

AppConfiguration

The AppConfiguration class (see Figure 10-14) is essentially a wrapper around some of the configuration keys in the Web.config file. Although ASP.NET 2.0 provides a convenient way to bind keys from the Web.config file to controls in the markup of a page using the new expression syntax you see later, you still need to write some code to accomplish the same thing in code-behind files or in code in the App_Code folder. To avoid repeating this code many times over, the AppConfiguration class provides convenient access to the keys in the Web.config file through read-only and shared properties.

The BookingObjectNamePlural and BookingObjectNameSingular properties expose the user-friendly descriptions of the booking object. These properties are used to customize the user interface in the public and Management section of the web site.

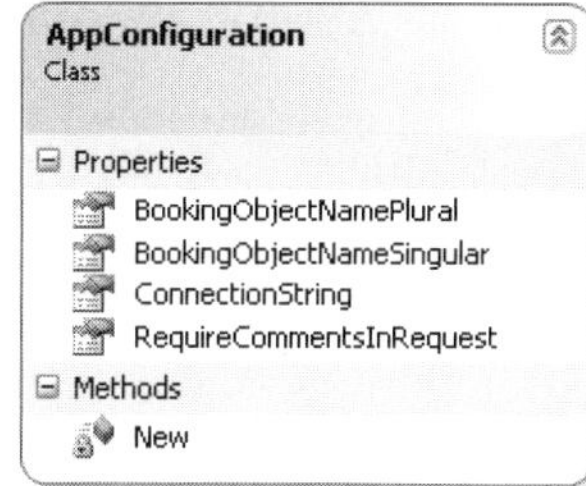

Figure 10-14

The `RequireCommentsInRequest` property determines whether a user has to enter a comment in the appointment wizard. You see how this works later.

The `ConnectionString` property is used by all methods in the two classes in the data access layer.

Helpers

The `Helpers` class, shown in Figure 10-15, provides one shared method — `GetCurrentServerRoot` — that returns the full root URL of the current application.

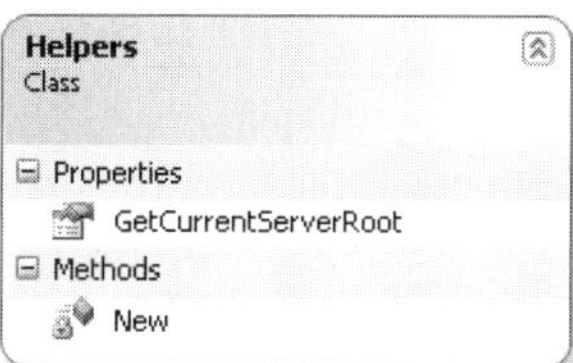

Figure 10-15

Instead of hard-coding the application URL, like `http://www.yoursite.com` somewhere in your code, this method determines the application's address at run time. It is used to customize the opt-in e-mail message in the Sign Up page that you see later.

Code and Code Explanation

Most of the pages in the root of the application and the Management folder are part of the public front end and Management sections of the site and are discussed in full detail later. There are, however, a few files and folders that you need to look at first.

Web.config

The Web.config file contains three `<appSettings>` keys and one connection string that map directly to the four properties of the `AppConfiguration` class you just saw. Most of the other settings in this file are either the default settings or have been discussed in previous chapters, so they aren't covered here anymore. The only exception are the three `<location>` nodes at the bottom of the file. These three nodes block access to the Management folder and the files CreateAppointment.aspx and CheckAvailability.aspx for unauthenticated users.

Global.asax

Just as in the previous three chapters, the Global.asax contains code that can send e-mail whenever an error is raised in the site. The code is identical to that in Chapter 6, so refer to that chapter if you want to know how the code works.

Default.aspx

This is the homepage for the Appointment Booking System and is based on the MasterPage.master page (discussed next).

Master Pages

The public section and the protected Management section each have their own master page. The difference between the public master (MasterPage.master) and the master page for the Management section (ManagementMaster.master) is the inclusion of the `ManagementMenu` user control in the latter.

Other Files and Folders

In addition to the files in the root, the Appointment Booking System uses other files and folders as well:

- **App_Themes:** The App_Themes folder contains a single .skin file that controls the looks of each `<asp:Calendar>` used in the web site. The `<pages>` node in the Web.config file instructs the application to apply this theme to each page in the site.
- **Controls:** This folder stores the user controls that are used throughout the site. The `MainMenu` and `ManagementMenu` controls are used to define the menus in the various pages in the site, similar to other applications in this book. The `HourPicker` and `TimeSheet` controls are very specific controls that are described in full later.
- **Css:** The Css folder contains two CSS files that control the general structure and look of the site (Core.css) and that influence more specific elements, such as the time sheet and error messages (Styles.css).
- **Images:** This folder contains the logo for the site, the calendar icon, and the arrow used in the main menu.
- **JavaScripts:** This folder contains a single file called ClientScripts.js that holds a JavaScript function used in multiple pages in the site.
- **StaticFiles:** The StaticFiles folder contains one HTML file with the contents for the opt-in e-mail. This file is used as a template for the body of the confirmation e-mail that users receive after they sign up for an account.

Now that you have seen the design of the application and database, it's time to look at the actual functionality of the site and the code that drives it. Instead of discussing the files in the application one by one, a more usage-oriented approach is taken. You see the typical workflows of the application and the files that are involved in the process.

The Availability Checker is discussed first, followed by the Appointment Wizard. You then see how the Sign Up page with its double opt-in feature works. Near the end of the chapter, you see some of the more complicated pages in the Management section.

The Availability Checker

As you saw in the section "Using the Appointment Booking System" at the beginning of this chapter, the Availability Checker displays a time sheet for all available booking objects for a specific date. The process for displaying the time sheet consists of the following steps:

1. Get the requested date from an `<asp:Calendar>` control on the page.
2. Get a list with available booking objects and appointments for the selected date from the database in a `DataSet`.
3. Build up the time sheet by adding a table row for each available booking object:
    - For each booking object in the `DataSet`, add an HTML row to the HTML table.
    - For each booking object being added to the table, get the appointments for the selected date from the database.
    - For each hour on the time sheet, see if the booking object is available on that hour. If the object is available, see if the hour conflicts with an existing appointment. If the hour doesn't conflict, add a link to allow a user to make an appointment.
4. Add a legend below the table, to visually differentiate the available and the unavailable hours.

The user interface for this functionality consists of two parts: the page CheckAvailability.aspx located in the root of the site and a user control called TimeSheet.ascx that you find in the Controls folder. Technically, the Time Sheet doesn't have to be a user control and could have been placed in the CheckAvailability.aspx directly. However, now that it is implemented as a user control, it's easy to reuse its functionality. For example, you could add another `TimeSheet` control on the homepage that shows the availability for today's date.

A huge improvement in working with user controls in Visual Web Developer is design-time support. When your user control has public properties, they show up automatically in the control's Property grid. Changes to public properties are now stored in the markup for the control automatically. Take a look at the `TimeSheet` control in the page to see how this works:

```
<Wrox:TimeSheet ID="TimeSheet1" runat="server"
     StartTime="<%$ AppSettings:FirstAvailableWorkingHour %>"
     EndTime="<%$ AppSettings:LastAvailableWorkingHour %>" />
```

In this case, both the `StartTime` and `EndTime` properties get their values from the Web.config file (you see later what these properties are used for). Now if you look at the Property grid for the control you'll see Figure 10-16.

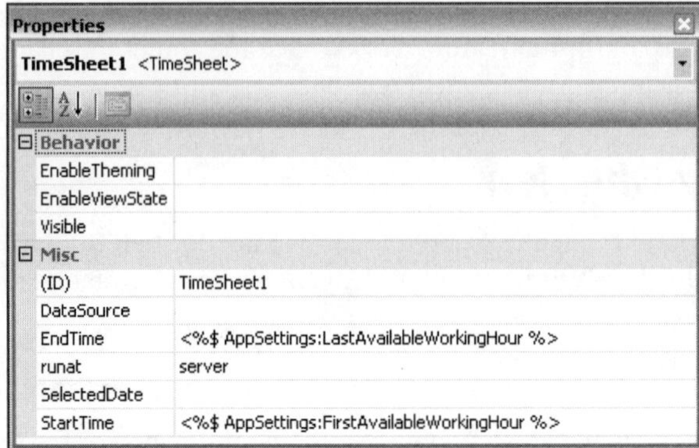

Figure 10-16

When you make a change to one of the properties, say you change `EndTime` to 23, the changes are automatically persisted in the control's markup:

```
<Wrox:TimeSheet ID="TimeSheet1" runat="server"
     StartTime="<%$ AppSettings:FirstAvailableWorkingHour %>"
     EndTime="23" />
```

Also, design-time rendering of user controls is now supported. Previous versions of Visual Studio just displayed a gray box instead of the actual control. Because the `TimeSheet` control is built up almost completely in the code-behind for the file at run time, you cannot benefit from this enhancement in the CheckAvailability.aspx.

In addition to the markup for the `TimeSheet` control, CheckAvailability.aspx contains a number of other controls, including a `Calendar` and a `Label` to allow a user to select a date for which they want to see the availability. The introduction text of the page also contains a number of `<asp:Literal>` controls that look like this:

```
<asp:Literal ID="Literal1" runat="server"
        Text="<%$ AppSettings:BookingObjectNameSingular %>"></asp:Literal>
```

The `Text` property of the `Literal` control is set using the new *declarative expression syntax* that allows you to bind properties to application settings, connection strings, and localization resources (used to create multi-lingual web sites). In this case, the `Text` property is directly bound to the `appSetting` key called `BookingObjectNameSingular`. At run time, the value for this key is retrieved from the Web.config file and added to the page. You see this expression syntax used in other pages where the friendly name of the booking object must be displayed.

Another important part of the Availability Checker page is the `Calendar` control. Whenever the user selects a new date on the calendar, the control fires its `SelectionChanged` event, which is handled in the code-behind for the page:

```
Protected Sub calAppointmentDate_SelectionChanged(ByVal sender As Object, _
        ByVal e As System.EventArgs) Handles calAppointmentDate.SelectionChanged
  If calAppointmentDate.SelectedDate.CompareTo(DateTime.Now.Date) < 0 Then
      valSelectedDate.IsValid = False
      divCalendar.Style.Item("display") = "block"
```

```
    Else
      divCalendar.Style.Item("display") = "none"
      lblSelectedDate.Visible = True
      lblSelectedDate.Text = "You selected: <strong>" & _
          calAppointmentDate.SelectedDate.ToShortDateString() & "</strong>"
      lblInstructions.Text = _
          "   Click the calendar again to select a different date:"
      LoadData()
    End If
  End Sub
```

This code first validates the selected date. If the new date is in the past, the `IsValid` property of the custom validator `valSelectedDate` is set to `False`. Otherwise, the label that displays the selected date is updated and the `LoadData` method is called.

The `LoadData` method retrieves time sheet information from the database by calling `AppointmentManager.GetTimeSheet` and passing it the selected date, as you can see in the following code block:

```
  Private Sub LoadData()
    If Not calAppointmentDate.SelectedDate = DateTime.MinValue Then
      TimeSheet1.DataSource = _
            AppointmentManager.GetTimeSheet(calAppointmentDate.SelectedDate)
      TimeSheet1.SelectedDate = calAppointmentDate.SelectedDate
      TimeSheet1.DataBind()
    End If
  End Sub
```

`GetTimeSheet` of the `AppointmentManager` class then forwards its call to the `AppointmentManagerDB` class, which retrieves the time sheet information from the database. Take a look at the code for this method to see how it works:

```
  Public Shared Function GetTimeSheet(ByVal selectedDate As DateTime) As DataSet
    Dim myDataSet As DataSet = New DataSet()

    Using myConnection As New SqlConnection(AppConfiguration.ConnectionString)
      Try
        Dim myCommand As SqlCommand = _
                New SqlCommand("sprocTimesheetSelectList", myConnection)
        myCommand.CommandType = CommandType.StoredProcedure

        myCommand.Parameters.AddWithValue("@selectedDate", selectedDate)

        Dim myDataAdapter As SqlDataAdapter = New SqlDataAdapter()
        myDataAdapter.SelectCommand = myCommand
        myDataAdapter.Fill(myDataSet)

        myDataSet.Tables(0).TableName = "BookingObject"
        myDataSet.Tables(1).TableName = "Appointment"

        myDataSet.Relations.Add("BookingObjectAppointment", _
            myDataSet.Tables("BookingObject").Columns("Id"), _
            myDataSet.Tables("Appointment").Columns("BookingObjectId"))

        Return myDataSet
```

```
      Catch ex As Exception
        Throw
      Finally
        myConnection.Close()
      End Try
    End Using
  End Function
```

Similar to other data access code you have seen in this book, this method creates a `SqlConnection` and a `SqlCommand` object to retrieve information from the database. What's different in this method is that the stored procedure `sprocTimesheetSelectList` does not return a single result set, but that it returns a result set for both the booking objects and the appointments:

```
CREATE PROCEDURE sprocTimesheetSelectList

@selectedDate datetime

AS

SELECT DISTINCT
  b.Id,
  b.Title,
  b.StartTime,
  b.EndTime,
  (
    SELECT COUNT(*) FROM BookingObjectWorkingDay WHERE BookingObjectId = b.Id
    AND BookingObjectWorkingDay.WorkingDayId = DATEPART(dw, @selectedDate)
  ) AS AvailableOnSelectedDay

FROM
  BookingObject b

SELECT
  BookingObjectId,
  StartDate,
  EndDate
FROM
  Appointment
WHERE
  CONVERT(varchar(8), StartDate, 112) = CONVERT(varchar(8), @selectedDate, 112)
  OR CONVERT(varchar(8), EndDate, 112) = CONVERT(varchar(8), @selectedDate, 112)
ORDER BY
  StartDate
```

As you can see, this procedure has two `SELECT` statements; the first returns a list with all the available booking objects and includes their ID, title, and the hours they are available. The inner `SELECT COUNT(*)` statement is used to determine whether the booking object is available on the requested weekday by looking at the junction table `BookingObjectWorkingDay`. It compares the weekday number (1 for Sunday, 2 for Monday, and so on) against a record in the junction table for each `BookingObject`. When the count returns `1`, the booking object is available on the requested date; `0` means the object is not available.

The second `SELECT` statement returns a list with all the current appointments for all booking objects on the requested date.

In the GetTimeSheet method, the two result sets that are returned from this stored procedure are added to a DataSet by calling Fill. This demonstrates that a DataSet can really be seen as an in-memory database. In many circumstances, a DataSet is used to hold just a single DataTable. However, in this code two DataTables are stored in the DataSet. By default, multiple tables in a DataSet get a sequential name, like Table2, Table3, and so forth. To be able to refer to the DataTables by name, they are renamed as soon as they have been added to the DataSet:

```
myDataSet.Tables(0).TableName = "BookingObject"
myDataSet.Tables(1).TableName = "Appointment"
```

The first DataTable (with an index of 0) holds the booking objects returned from the database, so it gets renamed to BookingObject. The second table is renamed to Appointment.

The final step in the GetTimeSheet method adds a DataRelation between these two tables. The appointments in the second DataTable have a BookingObjectId that points back to a BookingObject in the first DataTable. To relate these two result sets inside the DataSet, the following code is used:

```
myDataSet.Relations.Add("BookingObjectAppointment", _
      myDataSet.Tables("BookingObject").Columns("Id"), _
      myDataSet.Tables("Appointment").Columns("BookingObjectId"))
```

This DataRelation, called BookingObjectAppointment, allows you to retrieve all the child appointments for a certain booking object. The relation works very similarly to a traditional relation in a database in that it allows you to retrieve related records in a child table for a record in the parent table. You can get the rows in the child table by calling GetChildRows, which you see at work a little later.

At the end of this method, the DataSet is returned to the calling code in CheckAvailability.aspx, and then assigned to the DataSource property of the TimeSheet.ascx control:

```
TimeSheet1.DataSource = _
        AppointmentManager.GetTimeSheet(calAppointmentDate.SelectedDate)
TimeSheet1.SelectedDate = calAppointmentDate.SelectedDate
TimeSheet1.DataBind()
```

The DataBind method of the user control contains a lot of code, so not all of it is covered, but instead you'll see a few important sections. The method starts off with checking if the DataSource and the SelectedDate have been set. Both are critical properties for the TimeSheet control to operate correctly, so when one of the two is missing, an error is raised.

The code then declares two variables that can hold a DataRow (a row from a DataTable inside the DataSet): one to hold a BookingObject and one for an appointment. Two other variables are declared that can hold a TableRow and a TableCell (that represent the rows and cells of an HTML <table> in the browser).

Next, a new TableRow and a TableCell are created. The cell's Text property is set to the friendly name of the booking object with AppConfiguration.BookingObjectNameSingular. The cell is then added to the TableRow.

The number of hours that the TimeSheet control can display is configurable through two public properties on the control: StartTime and EndTime. For all the hours between these two values, a column is added to the HTML table with the following code:

```
For i As Integer = _StartTime To _EndTime
  myTableCell = New TableCell
  myTableCell.Text = i.ToString()
  myTableRow.Cells.Add(myTableCell)
Next
TimeSheetTable.Rows.Add(myTableRow)
```

So if the Appointment Booking System is set up to make appointments for conference rooms, and the `TimeSheet` user control must display the hours from 7 a.m. until 7 p.m., the first row in the table looks like Figure 10-17.

Conference Room	7	8	9	10	11	12	13	14	15	16	17	18	19

Figure 10-17

Both the friendly name of the booking object and the numbers serve as the column header for the rows that are about to be added.

The code continues with another loop, this time for each row in the `DataTable` called `BookingObject`:

```
For Each myBookingObjectRow In _DataSource.Tables("BookingObject").Rows
```

Inside this loop, a new `TableRow` is created that gets a cell with the name of the booking object:

```
myTableRow = New TableRow()
myTableCell = New TableCell()
myTableCell.Text = Convert.ToString(myBookingObjectRow("Title"))
myTableCell.Wrap = False
myTableRow.Cells.Add(myTableCell)
```

The next step is to create a table cell for each of the available hours on the `TimeSheet`. As with the column headers you just saw, this is done with a loop that runs from `_StartTime` till `_EndTime`. On each iteration of this loop, a new `TableCell` is created and added to the `TableRow`. A new `HyperLink` control is created and added to the `TableCell`:

```
Dim myHyperLink As New HyperLink()
myHyperLink.NavigateUrl = String.Format( _
    "~/CreateAppointment.aspx?" & _
     "BookingObjectId={0}&SelectedDate={1}&StartTime={2}", _
     Convert.ToString(myBookingObjectRow("Id")), _
     Server.UrlEncode(_SelectedDate.ToString()), i.ToString())
myHyperLink.Text = "Book"
myTableCell.Controls.Add(myHyperLink)
myTableCell.CssClass = "TimesheetCellFree"
```

This new `HyperLink` points to the CreateAppointment.aspx page and passes the selected date, the ID of the booking object, and the current hour to that page in the query string. The Appointment Wizard uses these query string variables to preselect the controls in the wizard, making it easier for the user to make an appointment for the requested booking object, date, and time.

Once the `TableCell` contains the hyperlink, the code checks whether the current hour (the hour being added to the `TimeSheet`) is actually available for new appointments. Four reasons exist for why the current hour could not be available for booking:

1. The booking object is not available on the day of the week that the time sheet is currently displaying.
2. The current hour is less than the starting hour of the booking object.
3. The current hour is greater than the end hour of the booking object.
4. There is already an appointment for the booking object that overlaps with the current hour.

The first three reasons are checked by a single `If` statement:

```
If i >= Convert.ToDateTime(myBookingObjectRow("StartTime")).Hour _
  And i <= Convert.ToDateTime(myBookingObjectRow("EndTime")).Hour _
  And Convert.ToInt32(myBookingObjectRow("AvailableOnSelectedDay")) > 0 Then
```

If all three of these conditions are not met, the code in the `Else` clause of this `If` statement removes the hyperlink from the `TableCell` and sets the cell's `CssClass` to `TimesheetCellBusy`:

```
Else
  myTableCell.CssClass = "TimesheetCellBusy"
  myTableCell.Controls.Clear()
  myTableCell.Text = " "
End If
```

If all three conditions are met, the code continues to query the appointments for the current booking object. It does this with the `GetChildRows` method of the `DataRow` with the booking object:

```
For Each myAppointmentRow In _
    myBookingObjectRow.GetChildRows("BookingObjectAppointment")
```

As the `relationName` argument for this method, the string `BookingObjectAppointment` is passed, which is the name of the relation that was set up in the `GetTimeSheet` method you saw earlier in this chapter. Through this relation, the `GetChildRows` method is able to correctly identify the appointment rows in the appointment `DataTable` that are related to the `BookingObject` row currently held in `myBookingObjectRow`. The method `GetChildRows` returns those rows as an array of `DataRows` so you can use `For Each` to loop through them:

```
For Each myAppointmentRow In _
    myBookingObjectRow.GetChildRows("BookingObjectAppointment")
  Dim currentDateAndTime As DateTime = _SelectedDate.Date.AddHours(i)
  Dim startDate As DateTime = Convert.ToDateTime(myAppointmentRow("StartDate"))
  Dim endDate As DateTime = Convert.ToDateTime(myAppointmentRow("EndDate"))

  If currentDateAndTime >= startDate And currentDateAndTime < endDate Then
    myTableCell.CssClass = "TimesheetCellBusy"
    myTableCell.Controls.Clear()
    myTableCell.Text = " "
    Exit For
  End If
Next
```

This code loops through all the appointments returned by `GetChildRows` and sees if they overlap with the current date and time that is added to the `TimeSheet`. If the appointment does overlap, the `HyperLink` control is removed from the `TableCell` and its `CssClass` is set to `TimesheetCellBusy`, making the cell unavailable.

The remainder of the `DataBind` method creates an empty `TableRow` and a `TableRow` that holds a legend with the colors and a label for available and unavailable hours. The code is pretty straightforward and has quite a lot of comments, so you should be able to figure out how it works.

To see how all the code for the `TimeSheet` control ends up in the browser, imagine that the system is used to book conference rooms. There are three conference rooms in the system. All three can be booked between 7 a.m. and 7 p.m. For the first booking room, there is already an appointment on November 14, from 2 p.m. until 4 p.m. If you request the time sheet with this setup, you see what appears in Figure 10-18.

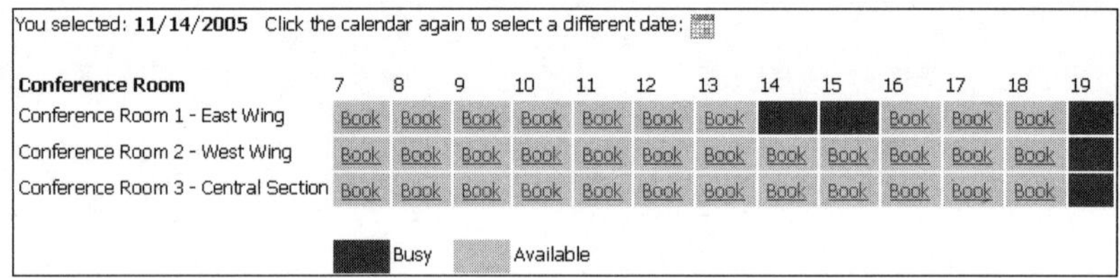

Figure 10-18

In the time sheet you can see that both booking objects can normally be booked from 7 a.m. until (and not including) 7 p.m. Because Conference Room 1–East Wing already has an appointment from 2 p.m. until 4 p.m., those two hours are marked as unavailable on the time sheet.

From this time sheet, users can click the Book link for a specific booking object and hour. This transfers them to CreateAppointment.aspx and passes along the selected date, hour, and ID of the booking object.

The page that allows users to create appointments is discussed next.

The Appointment Wizard

The CreateAppointment.aspx page contains a single `<asp:Wizard>` control and a `<asp:MultiView>` control. The `Wizard` control collects information from users about the appointment they want to book, and the `MultiView` is used to display information about the success or failure of this appointment request.

The `Wizard` control contains six wizard steps; one for each of the six Wizard menu items you saw at the beginning of this chapter when the functionality of the Appointment Wizard was discussed. The following table lists these steps and explains the data each step collects:

Step Title	Step Index	Description
Introduction	0	Displays a welcome message.
Select [Booking Object]	1	Displays a drop-down so the user can select a booking object. The title of the step is determined at run time with code in the `Page_Load` event.

Step Title	Step Index	Description
Select Date	2	Displays a calendar so the user can select a date for the appointment.
Select Time	3	Displays a drop-down with starting hours (with an `HourPicker` control that is explained later) and a drop-down for the duration of the appointment.
Comments	4	Displays a text area so the user can add comments to the appointment request.
Review Your Request	5	Displays a summary of all the data the user entered.

The `StepType` of the first and last step has been set to `Start` and `Finish`, respectively. The other four steps have their type set to `Step`. The `StepType` defines the buttons placed on the surface for each step. With a Start step, you only see a Next button; for the Finish type, you see a Previous and a Finish button; and for all the steps in between you see a Previous and a Next button, allowing you to move forward and backward through the wizard steps. If you want to block your users from going back to a previous step, you can set the `AllowReturn` property of the step to `False`. In the case of the Appointment Wizard, this is not necessary, because the user can follow an arbitrary path through each of the steps of the wizard.

When a user clicks the Next button on one of the steps, the current step is validated with code in the Wizard's `NextButtonClick` event:

```
Select Case e.CurrentStepIndex
  Case 1
    If Not ValidateStep(1) Then
      e.Cancel = True
    End If
  ' Other steps are validated here
End Select
```

This code checks that a booking object has been selected in the second wizard step (with an index of 1). If the validation fails, because a required field wasn't filled in, the `Cancel` argument of the `WizardNavigationEventArgs` argument is set to `True`. When this property is set to `True`, the wizard does not proceed to the next step, but stays on the current one instead so the user can fill in the required data.

The `ValidateStep` method itself uses a `Select Case` statement to determine which step needs to be validated. Inside the `Case` block for each step index, the required controls are validated, as you can see in the following code that checks the comments on step five (with an index of 4):

```
Case 4
  If AppConfiguration.RequireCommentsInRequest AndAlso _
        txtComments.Text.Length = 0 Then
  reqComments.IsValid = False
  wizAppointment.ActiveStepIndex = 4
  Return False
End If
```

When the configuration file dictates that a comment is required and the `txtComments` text box is still empty, the `RequiredFieldValidator` control's `IsValid` property is set to `False`. Then the `ActiveStepIndex` is set to `4`, to ensure that the user sees the error message and can fill in the required comment. At the end of the `If` block, the method returns `False` to signal calling code that validation failed. When validation succeeds, the method returns `True`.

This process is repeated for the other two steps (with the booking object and the date) to ensure they contain valid data.

Once all the data is filled in correctly, users are presented with the final step that displays all the data they entered. This is done in the `ActiveStepChanged` event when the `ActiveStepIndex` is `5` (the last step). Before the data is shown to the user, `ValidateAllSteps` is called to ensure that each of the previous steps is valid. Finally, when the user clicks the Finish button to finalize the appointment request, the following code runs:

```
Protected Sub wizAppointment_FinishButtonClick(ByVal sender As Object, _
        ByVal e As System.Web.UI.WebControls.WizardNavigationEventArgs) _
        Handles wizAppointment.FinishButtonClick
   Page.Validate()
    If Page.IsValid Then

      If ValidateAllSteps() Then
        wizAppointment.Visible = False

        Dim myAppointment As New Appointment()
        myAppointment.StartDate = _
            calStartDate.SelectedDate.AddHours(hpTime.SelectedHour)
        myAppointment.EndDate = _
            myAppointment.StartDate.AddHours(Convert.ToInt32( _
                lstDuration.SelectedValue))
        myAppointment.BookingObjectId = _
            Convert.ToInt32(lstBookingObject.SelectedValue)
        myAppointment.Comments = _
            Server.HtmlEncode(txtComments.Text)
        Dim myUser As MembershipUser = Membership.GetUser()
        myAppointment.UserName = myUser.UserName
        myAppointment.UserEmailAddress = myUser.Email

        If AppointmentManager.CheckAppointment(myAppointment) Then
          AppointmentManager.CreateAppointment(myAppointment)
          MultiView1.ActiveViewIndex = 0
        Else
          MultiView1.ActiveViewIndex = 1
        End If
      End If
    End If
End Sub
```

The code first validates the entire page by calling `Page.Validate()`. If the entire page is valid, it calls the custom `ValidateSteps` method again to ensure all steps contain valid data. Then a new `Appointment` object is instantiated and its public properties are filled with the values from the controls on the wizard and from the user's membership data. The code then calls `CheckAppointment` to see if the appointment can be made. The code for this method in the `AppointmentManagerDB` class is pretty straightforward, so it isn't shown it here. It's the stored procedure for this method that needs a close examination:

```
CREATE PROCEDURE sprocAppointmentCheckAvailability
@bookingObjectId int,
@startDate datetime,
@endDate datetime

AS

  SELECT COUNT(*)
  FROM
    BookingObject INNER JOIN
    BookingObjectWorkingDay ON BookingObject.Id =
BookingObjectWorkingDay.BookingObjectId INNER JOIN
    WorkingDay ON BookingObjectWorkingDay.WorkingDayId = WorkingDay.Id

  WHERE

    -- Check 1 - Select the correct BookingObject Id
    BookingObject.Id = @bookingObjectId

    -- Check 2 - Make sure the BookingObject is available on the
    -- start and the end date
    AND
    (
      DATEPART(dw, @startDate)IN (SELECT BookingObjectWorkingDay.WorkingDayId FROM
BookingObjectWorkingDay WHERE BookingObjectId = @bookingObjectId)
      AND
      DATEPART(dw, @endDate) IN (SELECT BookingObjectWorkingDay.WorkingDayId FROM
BookingObjectWorkingDay WHERE BookingObjectId = @bookingObjectId)
     )

    -- Check 3 - Make sure the appointment is between working
    -- hours for the BookingObject
    AND
    (
      (
        -- If the Appointment is on the same day, make sure the start and
        -- end time are between working hours
        CONVERT(varchar(8), @startDate, 112) = CONVERT(varchar(8), @endDate, 112)
        AND
        DATEPART(hh, @startDate) >= DATEPART(hh, BookingObject.StartTime)
        AND
        DATEPART(hh, @endDate) <= DATEPART(hh, BookingObject.EndTime)
      )
      OR
      (
        -- Else, the end date is on the next day. Make sure the
        -- booking object is available 24 hours a day
        CONVERT(varchar(8), @startDate, 112) < CONVERT(varchar(8), @endDate, 112)
        AND DATEPART(hh, StartTime) = 0
        AND DATEPART(hh, EndTime) = 23
      )
    )

    -- Check 4 - Make sure the BookingObject doesn't have an appointment yet
    AND (BookingObject.Id NOT IN (
```

```
        SELECT
          BookingObjectId
        FROM
          Appointment
        WHERE
          (@startDate >= StartDate AND @startDate < EndDate)
          OR (@endDate > StartDate AND @endDate <= EndDate)
      ))
```

The stored procedure returns a number indicating whether the appointment can be made on the requested date and time. When that number is 0, the appointment cannot be made. When the number is 1, it means the booking object is available on the requested date and time and does not have a conflicting appointment.

The `WHERE` clause of this procedure is where all the action is. Right after the `SELECT` statement, it uses four checks in the `WHERE` clause to determine whether or not the appointment can be made.

First, it filters out all booking objects except for the one with the ID that was passed in through the `@bookingObjectId` parameter.

It then ensures that the booking object is available on the date that was requested. Because an appointment could cross midnight into the next day, both the start date and end date are checked. It performs this check by seeing if the day of the week of the requested date is present in the BookingObjectWorkingDay table for the requested booking object.

The next check determines whether the booking object is available during the hours that the appointment should take place. If the appointment takes place on a single day, it means that its start and end time must be between the booking object's start and end hour.

When the appointment crosses midnight into the next day, the booking object has to be available 24 hours a day (that is, a start time of 0 and an end time of 23). Note that this is a limitation of the current Appointment Booking System. It does not allow for booking objects to be available for night shifts that start on one day and end on the next. This does not apply to appointments though; if a booking object is available 24 hours a day, you can make an appointment that ends on the next day.

The final check ensures that the booking object is not yet tied to another appointment by querying the Appointment table and checking the start and end date of the requested appointment against the existing appointments in the table.

When this complicated `WHERE` clause is carried out, it returns either 0 (not available) or 1 (available). This value is then converted to a Boolean at the end of the `CheckAppointment` method in the `AppointmentManagerDB` class:

```
Return Convert.ToInt32(myCommand.ExecuteScalar()) > 0
```

This value bubbles up all the way to the `FinishButtonClick` event in the CreateAppointment.aspx page, where it is used to determine whether the appointment can be saved in the database:

```
If AppointmentManager.CheckAppointment(myAppointment) Then
  AppointmentManager.CreateAppointment(myAppointment)
  MultiView1.ActiveViewIndex = 0
Else
  MultiView1.ActiveViewIndex = 1
End If
```

When `CheckAppointment` returns `True`, the appointment is saved in the database by the `CreateAppointment` method with code very similar to other insert code you have seen before. The only exception in this method is that `CheckAppointment` is called again, to ensure that no other appointments have been made since the check was carried out the last time.

If the appointment was saved correctly, the first view of the `MultiView` control is made visible. The `MultiView` is a simple control that allows you to selectively hide or show data based on certain criteria. In this case, View 1 (with an index of zero) is shown when the appointment was made successfully; otherwise View 2 is shown, which displays a message to the user saying that the appointment could not be made.

You may have noticed the user control called `HourPicker`. This is a custom user control saved in the Controls folder in the root of site. In the user interface, this control displays a drop-down list with a number of hours. To control the hours that appear in the list, the control has two public properties called `StartTime` and `EndTime`. Whenever you change the values of one of these properties, the control calls its internal `CreateListItems` method, which adds the required number of items to the drop-down list with the following code:

```
Private Sub CreateListItems()
  lstHour.Items.Clear()
  For i As Integer = StartTime To EndTime
    lstHour.Items.Add(New ListItem(i.ToString() & ":00", i.ToString()))
  Next
End Sub
```

First, `Items.Clear` is called to ensure the drop-down list contains no items. Then a loop is set up that adds the requested number of hours, using the `i` variable as the value for each `ListItem`, and then uses that same value followed by a colon and two zeros as the text for the item. To read from or set the selected item in the drop-down list, you can query its `SelectedHour` property, which returns the underlying value of the selected item:

```
Public Property SelectedHour() As Integer
  Get
    If lstHour.SelectedIndex >= 0 Then
      Return Convert.ToInt32(lstHour.SelectedValue)
    Else
      Return -1
    End If
  End Get
  Set(ByVal value As Integer)
    If lstHour.Items.FindByValue(value.ToString()) IsNot Nothing Then
      lstHour.Items.FindByValue(value.ToString()).Selected = True
    End If
  End Set
End Property
```

Although the `HourPicker` is a very simple control, it enables you to quickly show drop-down lists with hours on a page. The control is used in the public file CreateAppointment.aspx to allow a user to select a start time. It's also used in two files in the Management folder: Configuration.aspx and CreateUpdateBookingObject.aspx.

The Sign Up Page

To protect your appointment system from getting bogus appointments from malicious users, it's a good idea to block access to the Appointment Wizard to unauthenticated users. This means users need a valid account in your system before they can make an appointment. However, the default behavior for `CreateUserWizard` of the new ASP.NET 2.0 security framework allows a user to enter a fake e-mail address. As long as the user enters an address that *looks* like an e-mail address, the ASP.NET 2.0 framework will happily let the new user in. One way to overcome this problem is through a concept called *double opt-in*. With this technique, a user's account is not activated until he has confirmed his e-mail address. To do that, users sign up for an account on a web site. Then they receive an e-mail with instructions about activating their account. As long as the account is not activated, they are not allowed to log in. Once they activate their account, you know they entered a valid e-mail address because they were able to carry out the instructions they received on that very same e-mail address.

In traditional ASP and ASP.NET applications, creating such a double opt-in system meant quite a lot of work. However, with the new security controls in ASP.NET 2.0, this is now simpler than ever. You need to be aware of a few tricks to implement this system with the security controls. First of all, take a look at the `CreateUserWizard` control in the SignUp.aspx page:

```
<asp:CreateUserWizard ID="CreateUserWizard1" runat="server"
   DisableCreatedUser="True" CreateUserButtonText="Sign Up"
   LoginCreatedUser="False" CompleteSuccessText="Your account has been
       successfully created. You'll receive an e-mail with instructions about
       activating your account shortly.">
  <WizardSteps>
    <asp:CreateUserWizardStep runat="server" Title=""></asp:CreateUserWizardStep>
    <asp:CompleteWizardStep runat="server" Title=""></asp:CompleteWizardStep>
  </WizardSteps>
  <MailDefinition BodyFileName="~/StaticFiles/OptInEmail.html"
    From="Appointment Booking &lt;You@YourProvider.Com&gt;" IsBodyHtml="True"
       Subject="Please Confirm Your Account With the Appointment Booking System">
  </MailDefinition>
</asp:CreateUserWizard>
```

This code has a few important attributes. First, you should notice that `DisableCreatedUser` has been set to `True` and `LoginCreatedUser` has been set to `False`. This means that when the account is created, it is not activated yet, and the user is not logged on automatically.

The other important attribute is `BodyFileName` of the `MailDefinition` element. This property allows you to point to a text file that is used as a template for the body of the e-mail message that users receive after they sign up for an account. If you look at that file, you'll see some text mixed with placeholders marked by double hash marks (`##`). You'll also see a link back to the ConfirmAccount.aspx page that has a query string variable called `Id`. Users who receive the e-mail must click this link to activate their account.

This file is read by the `CreateUserWizard` control right before it fires its `SendingMail` event. Inside that event, the contents of that file are available through the `Message.Body` property of the `e` argument. Using some simple `Replace` methods, the placeholders are replaced with the user's data to customize the e-mail message:

```
e.Message.Body = e.Message.Body.Replace("##Id##", _
       Membership.GetUser(CreateUserWizard1.UserName).ProviderUserKey.ToString())
e.Message.Body = e.Message.Body.Replace("##UserName##", CreateUserWizard1.UserName)

Dim applicationFolder As String = _
       Request.ServerVariables.Get("SCRIPT_NAME").Substring(0, _
       Request.ServerVariables.Get("SCRIPT_NAME").LastIndexOf("/"))
e.Message.Body = e.Message.Body.Replace("##FullRootUrl##", _
       Helpers.GetCurrentServerRoot & applicationFolder)
```

This code replaces the placeholders in the message body with actual values. The ID in the query string back to the account confirmation page is filled with the unique ID of the user by calling the following:

```
Membership.GetUser(CreateUserWizard1.UserName).ProviderUserKey.ToString()
```

The same technique is deployed to add the user's `UserName` to the e-mail.

The second half of the code retrieves the name of the current server and application folder. It uses the `GetCurrentServerRoot` method defined in the `Helpers` class to retrieve information about the server's name or IP address and port number that is used. This is very useful during development because the path to the account confirmation page is not hard-coded in the application. On your development workstation, this path might be something similar to `http://localhost:2137/AppointmentBooking`, whereas on a production server it could return something like `http://www.YourDomain.com`. This ensures that the link in the e-mail always points back to the server from which the e-mail was requested.

After the final `Replace` method has been called, the mail body contains a link to the confirmation page that looks similar to this: `http://localhost:2137/AppointmentBooking/ConfirmAccount.aspx?Id=be2e8119-09ba-485e-8e09-d20218ef3f64`.

Once users click that link in the e-mail message, they are taken to the Account Confirmation page that activates the account with the following code in the `Page_Load` event:

```
Try
  Dim userId As Guid = New Guid(Request.QueryString.Get("Id"))

  Dim myUser As MembershipUser = Membership.GetUser(userId)
  If myUser IsNot Nothing Then
    myUser.IsApproved = True
    Membership.UpdateUser(myUser)
    plcSuccess.Visible = True
  Else
    lblErrorMessage.Visible = True
  End If
Catch ex As Exception
  lblErrorMessage.Visible = True
End Try
```

This code retrieves the unique user ID from the query string and creates a new Guid from it. This Guid is used to retrieve a user from the `Membership` provider. If the `MembershipUser` object does not equal `Nothing`, it means the user was found and the `IsApproved` field is set to `True`, the user account is updated, and a confirmation message is shown. In all other cases, an error message is displayed.

With the explanation of the double opt-in technique, you have come to the end of the explanation of the public area of the web site. What remains are a few pages in the Management section of the site.

The Management Section

Many of the concepts and techniques in the Management section shouldn't be new for you. For example, the page that lists the appointment details (AppointmentDetails.aspx) uses code you also saw in the Web Shop application in Chapter 9. Also, pages like BookingObjects.aspx (that lists the available booking objects) and CreateUpdateBookingObject.aspx contain a lot of familiar code. However, a few pages with a twist need to be discussed in more detail.

Saving Configuration Information

The first page worth looking at is the page that allows you to change the application's settings that are stored in the Web.config file. This page is called Configuration.aspx. If you look at the markup for the page, you won't notice many odd things. The page contains an HTML table with two text boxes, a checkbox, and two `HourPicker` controls that have their `Text`, `Checked`, or `SelectedHour` properties bound to a value in the Web.config file using the expression syntax you saw before:

```
<asp:TextBox ID="txtBookingObjectNamePlural" runat="server"
     Text="<%$ AppSettings:BookingObjectNamePlural %>"></asp:TextBox>
```

So far, not much is new. However, if you look at the code for the button that saves the settings, things turn out to be very different:

```
Dim myConfig As System.Configuration.Configuration = _
      WebConfigurationManager.OpenWebConfiguration("~/")

Dim myElement As KeyValueConfigurationElement = Nothing

myElement = myConfig.AppSettings.Settings("BookingObjectNameSingular")
If Not myElement Is Nothing Then
  myElement.Value = txtBookingObjectNameSingular.Text
End If

myElement = myConfig.AppSettings.Settings("BookingObjectNamePlural")
If Not myElement Is Nothing Then
  myElement.Value = txtBookingObjectNamePlural.Text
End If

myElement = myConfig.AppSettings.Settings("RequireCommentsInRequest")
If Not myElement Is Nothing Then
  myElement.Value = chkRequireCommentsInRequest.Checked.ToString()
End If

myElement = myConfig.AppSettings.Settings("FirstAvailableWorkingHour")
```

```
If Not myElement Is Nothing Then
  myElement.Value = hpStartTime.SelectedHour.ToString()
End If

myElement = myConfig.AppSettings.Settings("LastAvailableWorkingHour")
If Not myElement Is Nothing Then
  myElement.Value = hpEndTime.SelectedHour.ToString()
End If

Try
  myConfig.Save()
  Response.Redirect("Default.aspx")
Catch ex As Exception
  litErrorMessage.Visible = True
End Try
```

Unlike how it was in ASP.NET 1.x, writing to the Web.config file is now very easy. Three steps are involved: first, you need to get a reference to the current configuration using the `OpenWebConfiguration` method of the `WebConfigurationManager` class. As the argument for the method, `"~/"` is passed to indicate a virtual path to the root of the current site. This method has a few overloads allowing you to open other files at different locations as well.

Once `myConfig` holds a reference to the config file, you then use the `Settings` property of the `AppSettings` class to get a reference to a specific `<appSettings>` key defined in that Web.config file. To get that reference, all you need to do is pass the name of the key to the indexer of the `Settings` object. With this code example, all that is changed are a few values in the `<appSettings>` node, but the `Configuration` class allows you to change other sections as well. For example, to change the connection string for the web site, you can use this code:

```
myConfig.ConnectionStrings.ConnectionStrings("AppointmentBooking") _
      .ConnectionString =  New Connection String
```

Notice how the `ToString()` method is used for the `RequireCommentsInRequest`, `StartTime`, and `EndTime` properties. Because the `Value` of the `KeyValueConfigurationElement` class is a string (the Web.config file is just a text file so it can store only strings), you need to cast these Boolean and integer values to a proper string.

The third and final step in writing to the Web.config file is calling `Save()` on the `Configuration` element. Be aware that when you do that, the application will silently restart. This isn't a problem in the current Appointment Booking System because it doesn't use sessions. However, if you use this code in a web site that does use sessions, your users might lose valuable information when the application restarts. Just to be sure the administrator knows what he's doing, the application shows a warning when the page gets submitted. This warning is added in the `Page_Load` of the page:

```
If Not Page.IsPostBack Then
  btnSave.OnClientClick = "return confirm('Saving these settings " & _
    "might result in a loss of data for currently active users. Are you sure " & _
    "you want to continue?');"
End If
```

This adds a confirmation dialog to the Save button so you get a warning dialog, and a way to cancel the operation when you try to save the settings.

Although writing to the configuration file is now really easy in ASP.NET 2.0, you could still run into problems when you execute this code. If the Web.config file on disk is read-only or the current user's account doesn't have the necessary permissions, an error is raised. When that happens, the `Catch` block in the code displays a label with some troubleshooting tips.

Managing Booking Objects

Another page that you need to examine a little closer is CreateUpdateBookingObject.aspx. Most of the page contains code you're familiar with to insert or update a booking object, but there is one control you may not have seen before. At the end of the markup for the page, you'll see a `CheckBoxList` control:

```
<asp:CheckBoxList ID="chkLstWorkingdays" runat="server"
    DataSourceID="odsWorkingDays" DataTextField="Description" DataValueField="Id">
</asp:CheckBoxList>
```

This control works similarly to other list controls, such as the `<asp:DropDownList>`, but it displays checkboxes with a label that allows a user to select one or more items. The `DataSourceID` of the control is set to the `ObjectDataSource` control `odsWorkingDays`, which in turns gets a simple two-column DataSet with the working days and their IDs from the database by calling `GetWorkingDays` in the `BookingObjectManager` class.

When you're editing a `BookingObject`, the selected working days for that object need to be preselected. This is done with the code in `Page_Load` that also sets the other properties of the `BookingObject`:

```
chkLstWorkingdays.DataBind()
If Convert.ToBoolean(myBookingObject.AvailableOnWeekdays And Weekdays.Sunday) Then
    chkLstWorkingdays.Items.FindByValue("1").Selected = True
End If
' Other days are checked here
```

To make sure that the `CheckBoxList` is displaying all working days from the database, `DataBind()` is called first. Then the `AvailableOnWeekdays` property of the `BookingObject` is checked to see if it contains a selection for Sunday. This is done with the following statement:

```
myBookingObject.AvailableOnWeekdays And Weekdays.Sunday
```

If this returns `True`, it means that Sunday is a part of the `AvailableOnWeekdays` property and the code in the `If` block runs. That code simply searches the `Items` collection of the `CheckBoxList` for an item with a value of `1` (the ID for Sunday in the database) and then changes its `Selected` property to `True`. This process is repeated for all the seven days in the `Weekdays` enumeration.

This process is more or less reversed when the `BookingObject` is updated again in the `Click` event of the Update button:

```
For Each myItem As ListItem In chkLstWorkingdays.Items
  If myItem.Selected = True Then
    Select Case Convert.ToInt32(myItem.Value)
```

```
      Case 1 ' Sunday
        myBookingObject.AvailableOnWeekdays = _
           myBookingObject.AvailableOnWeekdays Or Weekdays.Sunday
       ' Other days are checked here
    End Select
  End If
Next
```

This code loops through all of the checkboxes in the `CheckBoxList` control. When the item is checked, its value is used in a `Select Case` statement. In this code, when the `Value` of the checkbox equals `1`, it means Sunday was selected and the value of Sunday is added to the `AvailableOnWeekdays` property of the `BookingObject`.

The code for the method `GetBookingObject` in the `BookingObjectManagerDB` class, responsible for getting a single `BookingObject` from the database, uses the same technique to fill the property.

The only section that treats the selected working days differently is the code in the method `SaveBookingObject` in the same `BookingObjectManagerDB`. Because SQL Server has no knowledge of the custom `Weekdays` enumeration, the stored procedure that inserts and updates a `BookingObject` has seven additional parameters; one for each of the available working days. The values of these parameters are used in the procedure `sprocBookingObjectInsertUpdateSingleItem` to create a relation between a `BookingObject` and a `WorkingDay` by adding a record in the BookingObjectWorkingDay table:

```
IF (@sunday = 1)
  INSERT INTO BookingObjectWorkingDay
    (BookingObjectId, WorkingDayId)
  VALUES (@id, 1)
```

When `@Sunday` equals `1`, it means Sunday was selected and a record is inserted in BookingObjectWorkingDay.

Viewing Appointments

The final page that needs to be discussed is the page that allows users to get a report on the appointments that have been made in the system. Right now, this page is accessible only by users in the Manager role, simply because the entire Management folder has been blocked for all users except managers. In a real-world scenario, it's probably wise to make a second group, such as Planning, that is allowed to view the reports without being able to make changes to the booking objects and the application settings. You can use the Web Site Administration Tool (choose Website⇨ASP.NET Configuration from the main menu in Visual Web Developer) to create the role and then add an additional `<location>` node to the Web.config file to open the Management folder for that group.

You can access the Appointments page by clicking Appointments in the Management menu. You then need to select a date from the calendar for which you want to see the appointments. You'll see a screen similar to the one in Figure 10-19.

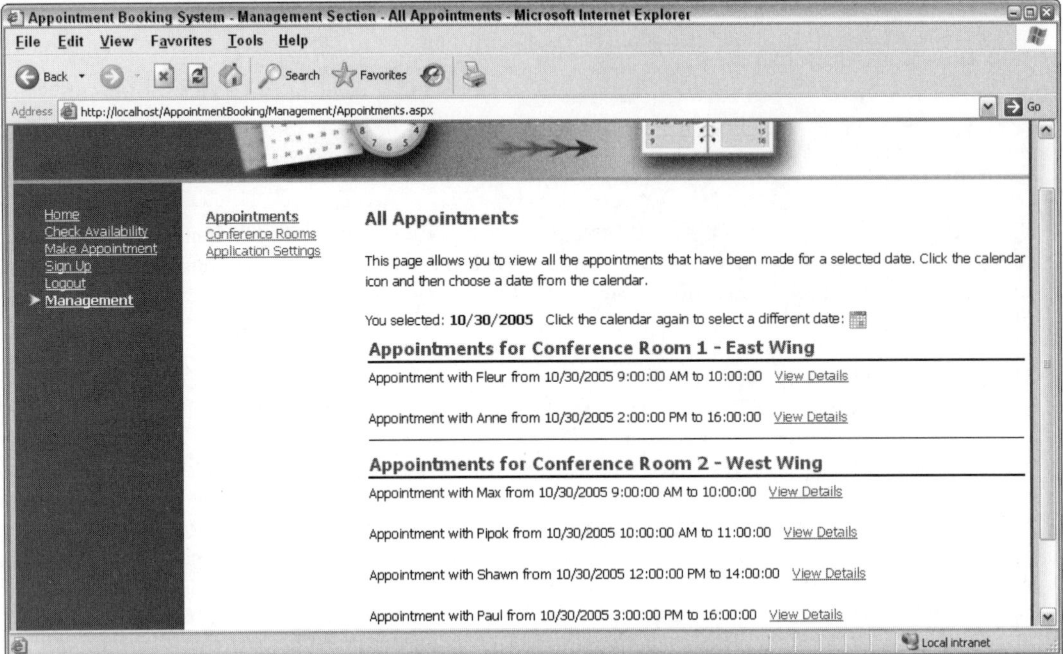

Figure 10-19

At first glance, you may not notice anything special about this page. All you see is a list with appointments, each one nicely placed under its parent booking object. However, if you look at the source for both the markup of the page and its code-behind, things are not as easy as they look. The markup for the page features a *nested Repeater*. A nested Repeater is a `Repeater` control that has been placed inside the `<ItemTemplate>` of another `Repeater`, referred to as the *outer Repeater*. Figure 10-20 shows three rows of an outer Repeater. The `<ItemTemplate>` for each row displays some text (indicated by the three thin lines) and the nested Repeater (the four stacked rectangles).

With a nested Repeater you can display hierarchical data that you cannot display with a single ASP.NET control. The Appointments page makes use of this technique to display the appointments (inside the nested Repeater) for each booking object (in the outer Repeater). The following code snippet shows a trimmed-down version of both `Repeater` controls:

```
<asp:Repeater ID="repBookingObjects" runat="server">
  <ItemTemplate>
    <h1>Appointments for <asp:Literal ID="litTitle" runat="Server"
                Text='<%# Container.DataItem("Title") %>' /></h1>
    <asp:Repeater ID="repAppointments" runat="server">
      <ItemTemplate>
          Appointment with <asp:Literal ID="litUserName" runat="server"
                Text='<%# Container.DataItem("UserName") %>' />
      </ItemTemplate>
    </asp:Repeater>
  </ItemTemplate>
</asp:Repeater>
```

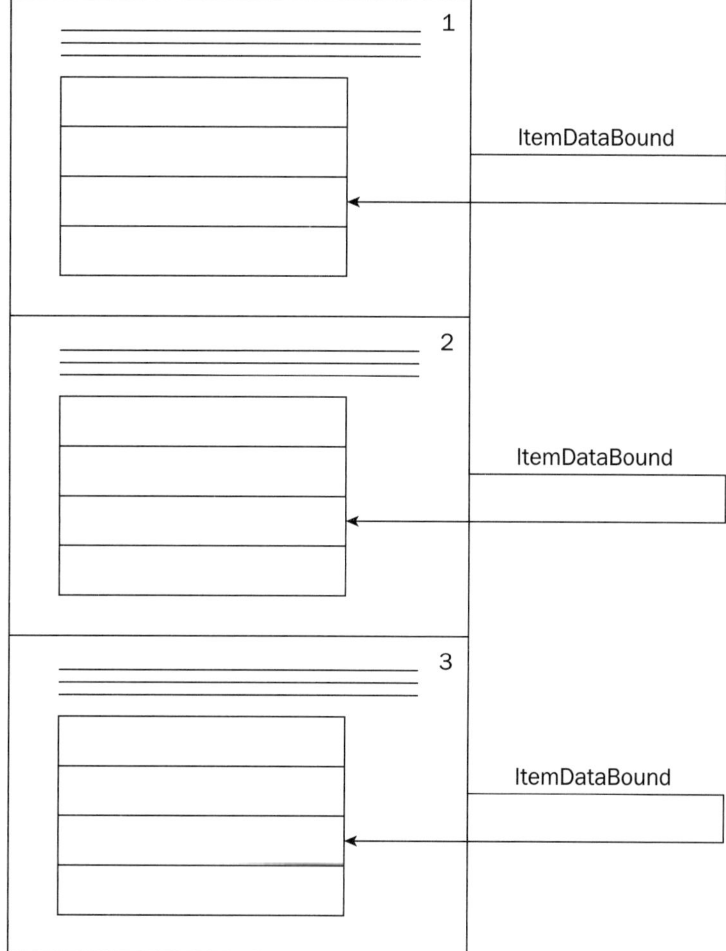

Figure 10-20

The outer Repeater, called `repBookingObjects`, has a single `<ItemTemplate>`. This template defines an `<h1>` tag that displays the booking object's title. You also see another `Repeater` that displays the appointments that belong to the booking object that is displayed in the `<ItemTemplate>`. To see how this control gets its data, you need to look at the `LoadData` method that is called whenever a user selects a date from the calendar that is placed on the page:

```
Private Sub LoadData()
  Dim dsAppointments As DataSet

  If Not calAppointmentDate.SelectedDate = DateTime.MinValue Then
    dsAppointments = _
            AppointmentManager.GetAppointmentList(calAppointmentDate.SelectedDate)

    repBookingObjects.DataSource = _
            dsAppointments.Tables("BookingObject").DefaultView
```

```
      repBookingObjects.DataBind()

      If repBookingObjects.Items.Count = 0 Then
        lblNoRecords.Visible = True
      End If
    End If
  End Sub
```

If the calendar called `calAppointmentDate` has a valid date, a call is made to `AppointmentManager .GetAppointmentList`, which returns a DataSet with two DataTables. Both the data access code for the `GetAppointmentList` method and the stored procedure follow a pattern similar to the code for the `TimeSheet` control, so it's not repeated here. What's important is that you recall that the DataSet holds two DataTables: one for the booking objects and one for the appointments. The two are related to each other with a `DataRelation`. It's this relation again that is used to display the child records in the nested Repeater.

The `DataSource` for the outer Repeater uses the first DataTable with the `BookingObjects`. When `DataBind` is called, the `Repeater` creates an item (based on the `<ItemTemplate>`) for each row (a `DataRowView` to be precise) in the DataTable's `DefaultView`. The `DefaultView` exposes the underlying data to the control, similar to a view in SQL Server. When the item is added to the `Repeater`, the control fires its `ItemDataBound` event. Inside that event, you can retrieve the appointments for the booking object that has just been added and add them to the nested Repeater:

```
Protected Sub repBookingObjects_ItemDataBound(ByVal sender As Object, _
       ByVal e As System.Web.UI.WebControls.RepeaterItemEventArgs) _
       Handles repBookingObjects.ItemDataBound

  Dim item As RepeaterItem = e.Item

  If item.ItemType = ListItemType.Item Or _
       item.ItemType = ListItemType.AlternatingItem Then
    Dim repAppointments As Repeater = item.FindControl("repAppointments")
    Dim myDataRowView As DataRowView = CType(item.DataItem, DataRowView)
    repAppointments.DataSource = _
        myDataRowView.CreateChildView("BookingObjectAppointment")
    repAppointments.DataBind()
  End If
End Sub
```

This code first checks whether `ItemDataBound` was called for an `Item` or an `AlternatingItem`. This is necessary because the same event is also called for other `ItemTypes`, such as the Header and the Footer. Then a reference to the nested Repeater is retrieved from the item object using `FindControl`, which is then stored in the variable `repAppointments`. The next line of code casts the `DataItem` (the underlying data used to build up the `Repeater` item) to a `DataRowView` because that is the actual object type of the `DataItem`. The `DataRowView` then has a convenient method called `CreateChildView` that accepts the name of a `DataRelation` as an argument. This method looks into the DataSet and retrieves all appointments that are related to the current booking object. The return value of this method can then be set as the `DataSource` for the nested Repeater. The final step is to call `DataBind`, which causes the nested Repeater to display all the appointments.

When you call `DataBind` on the nested Repeater it starts adding rows based on the data to which it is bound. For each row it adds, it also fires its own `ItemDataBound` event, allowing you to do the same trick over again. This way you can have multiple nested Repeaters to display detailed information.

In addition to the name of the user that made the appointment and the date and time, the nested Repeater also displays a link to AppointmentDetails.aspx for each appointment. This page displays the full details of the appointment, including the user's e-mail address and the comments. The code for this page uses the same techniques you have seen in other chapters, so it isn't repeated here.

With the Appointments page done, you have a complete working Appointment Booking System. You can set the name of your booking objects and manage the actual items in the Management section. Users can sign up for an account, then check the availability of your booking objects and make an appointment. Once the appointment has been made, you can access its details in the Management section again.

With the entire design and code implementation behind you, you hopefully can't wait to get the application installed and see for yourself how it works. The next section guides you through the process of setting up the application.

Setting up the Appointment Booking System

Because the Appointment Booking System has no dependencies other than the SQL Server database, setting it up is pretty easy. Once again, you can choose between an automated and a manual install. The automated installer process allows you to set up the application to run under IIS. This is useful if you want to deploy the system on your local intranet or Internet servers. If you want to look at the code in more detail and play around with it, you should choose the manual installation process.

Using the Installer

To install the Appointment Booking System with the supplied installer, open the folder Chapter 10 - Appointment Booking\Installer on the CD-ROM or from the code download and double-click setup.exe. Keep clicking Next until you get a confirmation that the application has been installed correctly and then click Close.

If you have a previous version of the .NET Framework installed on your machine, refer to Chapter 5 for instructions about configuring IIS to use version 2.0 of the framework.

Manual Installation

You can also manually install the Appointment Booking System so you can open the application with Visual Web Developer. To install manually, locate the folder Chapter 10 - Appointment Booking on the CD-ROM or in the code download and then open the Source folder. In that folder you'll find a zip file called Chapter 10 - Appointment Booking.zip. Extract the contents of this file to a location on your hard drive; for example, `C:\Inetpub\wwwroot\`. It's important that the files are extracted with the original folder structure. Depending on your extracting utility, this option is called something like Use Folder Names or Extract Pathnames. You should end up with a folder like `C:\Inetpub\wwwroot\Appointment Booking` that contains the files and other folders for the application.

Configuring the Application

No matter which installation method you chose, you may need to configure the Web.config so it uses your installation of SQL Server. Open Web.config, located in the root of your installation folder, and locate the `<connectionStrings>` node. The SQL server that is used in the connection string `AppointmentBooking` is called `(local)\SqlExpress`, which is the default instance name for a SQL Server Express installation. If you installed SQL Server with a different name or on a different server, be sure to adjust the connection string.

If you're using the full version of SQL Server, you can attach the supplied database as ASPNETDB through the SQL Server Management Studio application. Then you should modify the connection string again so it looks similar to this:

```
"Data Source=YourSqlServer;Initial Catalog=ASPNETDB;Integrated Security=SSPI;"
```

It's also important that you grant the necessary permissions to the ASP.NET worker process to access this database. On a default installation of ASP.NET, this account is called ASPNET on Windows 2000 and Windows XP, whereas it is called Network Service on Windows Server 2003. If you don't allow anonymous access to the web site, but use Windows Integrated Security instead, be sure to grant at least Read and Write permissions to the accounts (through group membership, for example) that need to access the Appointment Booking System.

Now that you know all about the Appointment Booking System, browse to this book's download page at `www.wrox.com` for a walkthrough of possible modifications to the system.

Summary

In this chapter you have seen how to design and create an online appointment booking system. You saw how the application can be configured dynamically to change the name of the so-called booking objects into a user-friendly description. Users of the application can sign up for an account, check availability of their favorite booking object, and make an appointment. Authorized users can manage the booking objects in the system and view the appointments that have been entered in the system.

You then got a good look at the design of the system. You saw the classes that make up the business and data access layer, and you saw the design of the database and its stored procedures.

The examination of the code showed you how it all fits together. You were introduced to the versatile `Wizard` control and saw how to dynamically create controls in the code-behind of a user control to create a unique user interface that cannot be created with the available ASP.NET server controls alone. You learned how to create stored procedures that return multiple result sets to create DataSets with related tables. You also saw how to bind these DataSets to a nested Repeater control.

Toward the end of the chapter the installation procedure for the Appointment Booking System was explained. The supplied installer allows you to deploy the application on a server with IIS installed, and the manual procedure allows you to examine and play with the code from within Visual Web Developer Express edition.

11

Greeting Cards

Most of the chapters in this book so far had a strong focus on many of the new and exciting ASP.NET 2.0 server controls. In addition to controls like the `Wizard`, the `MultiView`, and the new `Navigation` and `Login` controls, you also saw how to work with data-centric controls like the `SqlDataSource` and the `ObjectDataSource`.

Because these controls are so easy to use, allowing you to build applications in no time using drag-and-drop, you may almost forget that ASP.NET 2.0 largely depends on the underlying .NET 2.0 Framework. This framework not only enables ASP.NET pages, but it also allows you to create Windows Forms application, Windows services, command-line tools, and many other types of applications. In addition to direct support for these applications, the .NET Framework also has a lot of technologies that are not directly tied to one of the application types, but that can be used in those applications.

One of those enabling technologies is called GDI+, which stands for Graphics Device Interface. GDI+ and its predecessor GDI have been around for a long time in various flavors of Microsoft Windows and provide the OS with vector graphics, imaging, and typography capabilities. With the advent of the .NET Framework version 1.0, the capabilities of GDI+ became available as managed code within the .NET Framework. This makes it very easy to create complex drawings and images in .NET.

Although Visual Web Developer Express edition is limited in a number of ways compared to its bigger brothers Visual Studio Standard, Professional, and Team System editions, you still have full access to the entire feature set of the .NET Framework. This also means you have full access to the huge GDI+ library that is part of the .NET Framework.

In this chapter you see how to use some techniques for working with images that are used frequently in many ASP.NET web sites. You see how to handle and save an uploaded file, rotate or flip it, crop it, and add text to the image on the fly.

This chapter uses a Greeting Card application to showcase all these techniques. However, because of the design of the application, you should find it very easy to use and reuse existing parts of this application in one of your own that serves a completely different purpose.

To give you a feel for what can be accomplished with GDI+ in the .NET Framework, the next section guides you through creating your own greeting card. Once you've seen how to upload, alter, and e-mail an image, you see how the application is designed in the section "Design of the Greeting Cards Application." After the design, you get a good look at the actual implementation in the section "Code and Code Explanation." As usual, the chapter ends with instructions for installing the application.

Creating Your Own Greeting Card

If you've set up the application as per the instructions in the section "Setting up the Greeting Card Application" later in this chapter, you can start creating your own greeting card by browsing to `http://localhost/GreetingCards`. The Greeting Card application allows you to upload one of your favorite images. You can then customize it by cropping and rotating it and by adding text to it. The final stage of the application allows you to send the customized picture by e-mail.

The first screen you see welcomes you to the site and invites you to click Start to create your own personal greeting card. On the next screen, you see a file dialog that allows you to select an image you can upload to the server. You can choose an image type like JPG, GIF, or PNG. It doesn't really matter how large the image is because it's scaled to the maximum dimensions of 640×480 pixels automatically.

Once the image has been uploaded, the Rotate or Flip page appears, shown in Figure 11-1, with the scaled version of your image.

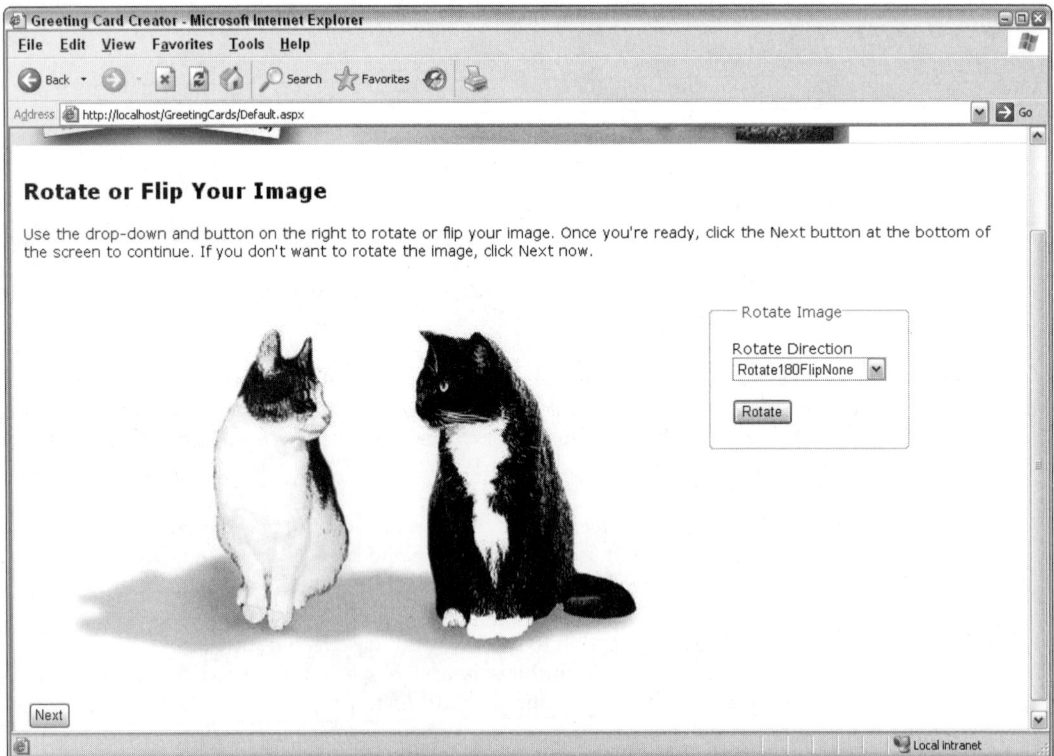

Figure 11-1

On this page, you can use the controls on the right to rotate or flip the image. You can use the drop-down to try out the various rotate and flip options. Once the image looks good, click the Next button. You are presented with the Crop Image screen (see Figure 11-2), which allows you to select a portion of the image.

If you want the entire image to be used in the greeting card, click Entire Image; otherwise use the two sets of four navigation buttons on the right to move the crop area (the black rectangle in Figure 11-2) over the image and to resize the area. You can use the pixels drop-down list in each of the fieldsets to control the number of pixels the crop area is moved or resized. Once you have positioned the crop area at the correct location, click Preview Image and the image is cropped to the part that falls within the selection area. If you're not satisfied with the results and want to make adjustments, click Undo and set a new crop area. Otherwise, click the Finalize Image button.

The next step is to add text to the image. Click the image at the location where you want the text to appear. Once you've clicked the image, the page refreshes and now shows a few controls visible in Figure 11-3 that allow you to enter text and determine that text's font, color, and size. Click Add Text to add the text on the image. If you want to move around the text on the image, simply click its new location (the location where you click determines the upper-left corner of an imaginary box around the text) and the text is moved to that spot.

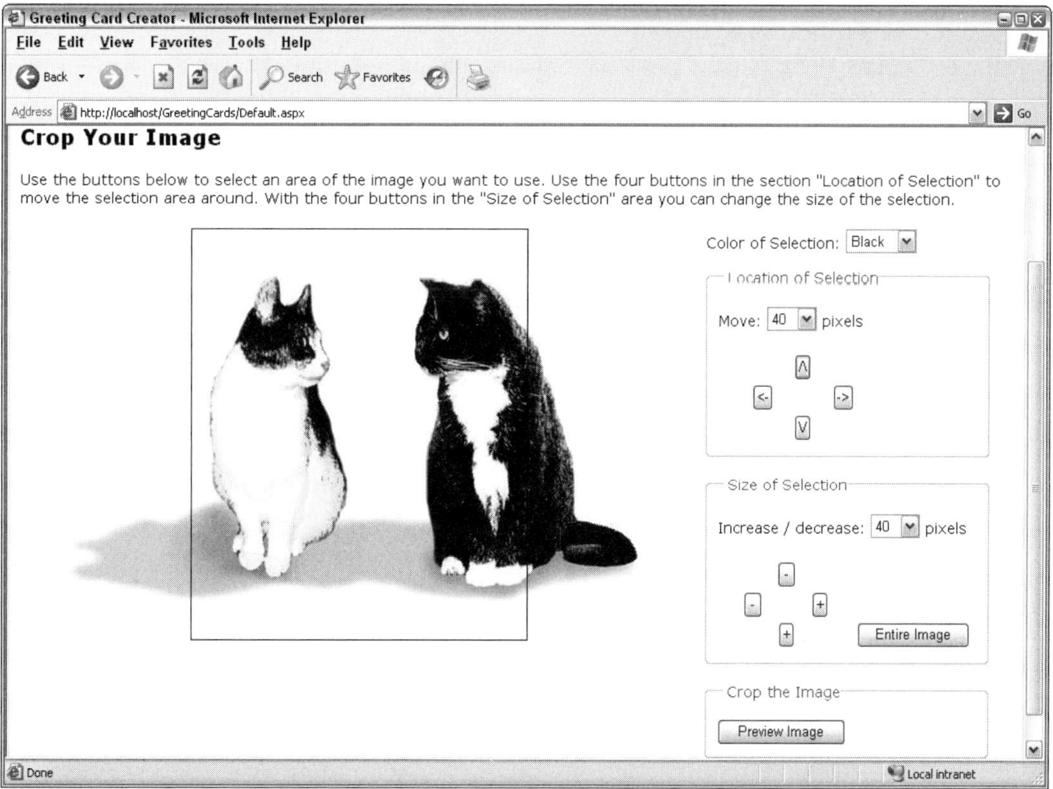

Figure 11-2

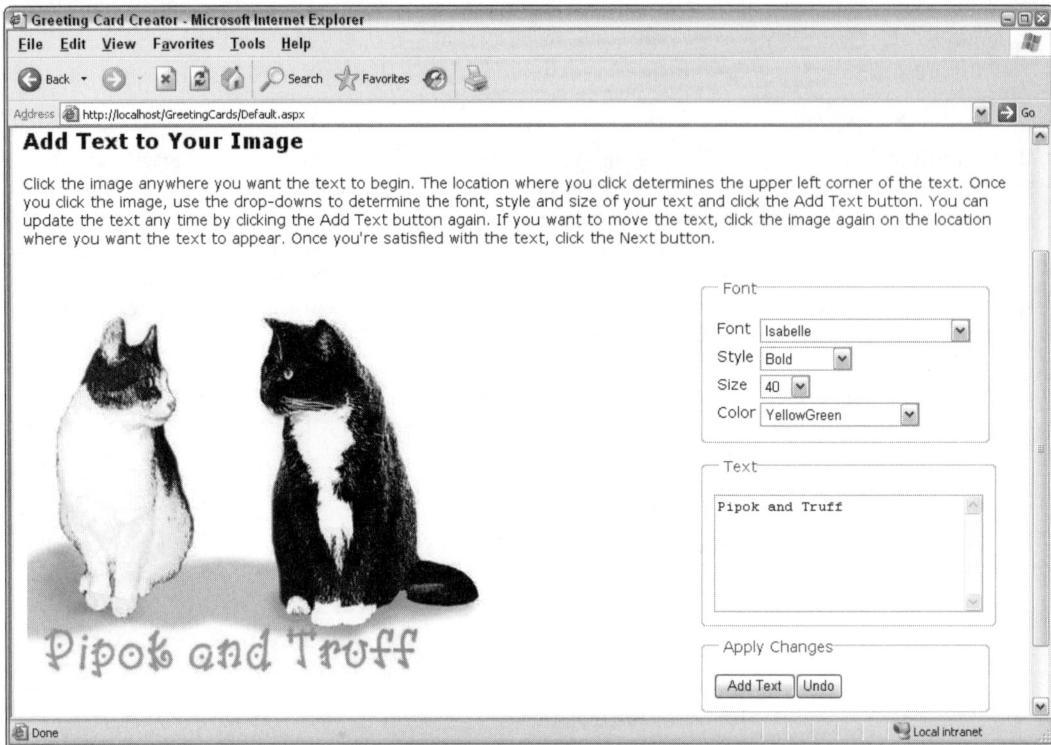

Figure 11-3

If the text doesn't fit, or its color doesn't look good on the background image, choose a new size, font, or color from the controls on the right side of the screen. Use the Add Text button again to update the image with the new font settings. If you want to start all over with the image from the previous step, click the Undo button.

If you're happy with the results, click Next once more to go to the Send Mail page. Here you can enter your name, an e-mail address of the person you want to send the greeting card to, and a personal message to accompany the card. After you click the Send Mail button, the image and the personal message are e-mailed to the address you provided. Depicted in Figure 11-4, the image shows up as an embedded image in the mail message in the recipient's e-mail program.

Now that you have seen the capabilities of the Greeting Card application, it's time to look at its design to see what classes, methods, and properties are behind this functionality.

In the next section you see the design of the application; you see the four classes in the special App_Code folder and their methods. Once you have a good understanding of the important elements of the application, you see the actual implementation in the section "Code and Code Explanation."

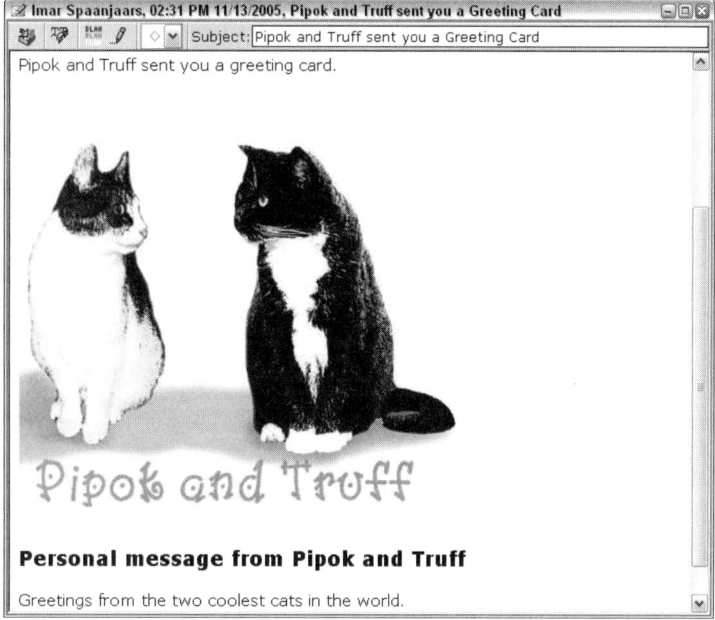

Figure 11-4

Design of the Greeting Cards Application

Unlike many of the applications you have seen in this book so far, the Greeting Cards application does not rely on or use a database. Although you could use a database to extend the application by storing user profiles or information about the cards that get sent, the current application does not need a reliable state storage. All the information the application needs is either saved as the actual image or stored in the page's ViewState. This also means the application is not built around a three-tier architecture. You won't find the familiar BusinessLogic and DataAccess folders in the App_Code folder of the site. Instead, you'll find a separate folder called Toolkit with two files, visible in Figure 11-5. This folder contains code for the functionality to upload and resize images.

The name Toolkit is not completely arbitrarily chosen. Just as a regular toolkit, it contains all kinds of useful tools that you can easily deploy in multiple applications. These tools (the methods in the classes in the Toolkit) can perform complex operations while hiding the details of the complexity completely from you. The Toolkit has been designed in such a way that it is very easy to reuse the same code in other applications. All you need to do is copy the Toolkit folder to the App_Code folder of another application and you're good to go.

If you own a copy of Visual Studio 2005 Standard, Professional, or Team System edition, you can even put this code into a Class Library project and compile it to a DLL file. You can then reference this DLL in your applications, including those you build with Visual Web Developer Express edition. A great advantage of a DLL file is that you're reusing binary code, not the actual source file. This means that if you enhance the Toolkit or fix a bug, you don't have to update all the individual files but only a single .DLL file instead.

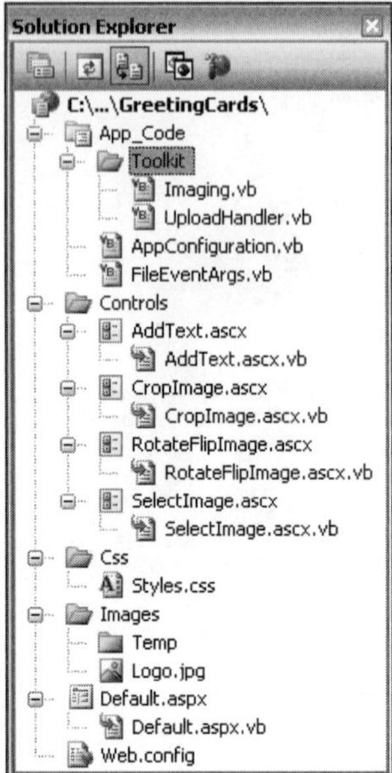

Figure 11-5

The other two files in the App_Code folder contain the application's configuration class (AppConfiguration .vb) and a class that derives from System.EventArgs, called `FileHandlingEventArgs`. Both these classes are discussed in detail later.

The classes that make up the Toolkit are discussed in the following section.

The Toolkit

If you look at the actions that the application is capable of performing, you'll notice two distinct areas. The first deals with uploading files from the client's computer to the web server. The behavior for this functionality has been put in the class `UploadHandler`. The second area deals with image processing; resizing, cropping, and so on. This is done by code in the `Imaging` class. To make these classes more accessible through IntelliSense and to avoid name collisions with existing classes with the same name, they have been put in the namespace Toolkit. You see more of this later.

The Imaging Class

The `Imaging` class is responsible for all the operations on images you saw at the beginning of this chapter, including resizing, rotating, flipping and cropping images, and adding text on top of an image. Figure 11-6 displays the class diagram with the methods of the `Imaging` class. When you take into account the overloaded versions of some methods, the `Imaging` class has 20 methods in total.

All of these methods are shared, which means they operate on the class rather than on an instance of that class. To stop calling code from creating useless instances of the `Imaging` class, its constructor (the `New` method) has been marked as Private. This is indicated by the little lock symbol in front of the `New` method in Figure 11-6.

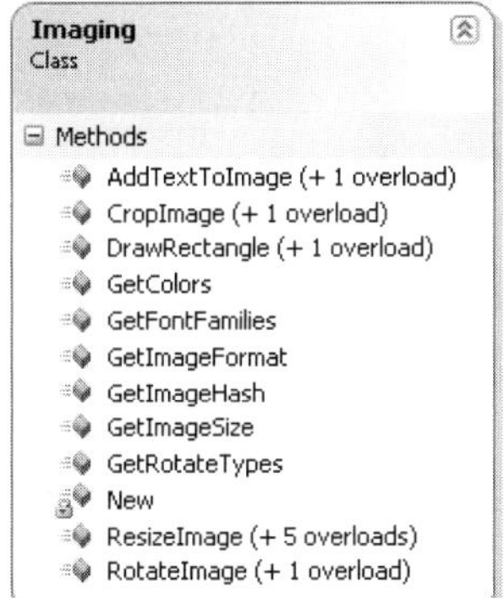

Figure 11-6

All of the other methods are listed in the following table. Because most of these methods have long argument lists, the table lists only the name of the method and not its arguments and their types. Refer to the section "Code and Code Explanation" later in this chapter for a description of these parameters, or look in the code for the `Imaging` class at the XML comments that are placed in front of each of the methods. These comments describe the purpose of each method and its parameters.

Method	Return Type	Description
`AddTextToImage`	n/a	This method is capable of adding text on top of an image at a specified location and in a specific font and color. This method has one additional overload.
`CropImage`	n/a	Crops an image passed to this method to a specified region. This method has one additional overload.
`DrawRectangle`	n/a	Draws a rectangle on top of an image. This method has one additional overload.
`GetColors`	`Color()`	Returns an array of `Color` objects. This method can return either all known colors, or return a list without the system colors such as `ActiveBorder` or `WindowText`.
`GetFontFamilies`	`FontFamily()`	Returns an array of `FontFamily` objects for the machine where this method is called.
`GetImageFormat`	`ImageFormat`	Returns the format of the image passed to this method, such as `ImageFormat.Jpeg`, `ImageFormat.Png`, and so on.
`GetImageHash`	`String`	Calculates the hash of an image. This method is useful for comparing two images. Because generating a hash always returns the same value for identical data, you can compare two images through code without looking at them.

Table continued on following page

Method	Return Type	Description
GetImageSize	Size	Returns the size of an image in pixels as a Size object.
GetRotateTypes	String()	Returns a list with the available rotating types as a String array. The array includes types like Rotate90FlipNone to indicate a rotation of 90 degrees clockwise.
ResizeImage	n/a	Resizes an image to the specified size or to a maximum height or width. This method has five additional overloads.
RotateImage	n/a	Rotates and flips an image in the specified direction. This method has one additional overload.

Not all of these methods are used in the Greeting Cards application. GetImageHash and GetImageFormat are not used at all, but because they could be very useful in other applications, they have been included in the Toolkit anyway. Refer to the accompanying code for more details on these methods.

Most of the overloads that work with an image expect the names of the source and target files as a string. For example, the signature for the CropImage looks like this:

```
Public Shared Sub CropImage(ByVal fileNameIn As String, ByVal fileNameOut As
          String, ByVal theRectangle As Rectangle)
```

The parameter fileNameIn determines the source file, and fileNameOut defines the file the cropped image should be saved to. To make it easier for you to overwrite an existing file without specifying the same name of the file twice in your code, these methods have an overload that has almost the same signature but without the fileNameOut parameter. Internally they call the overloaded version, passing it the same name for both the parameters. The following code snippet shows the implementation of the CropImage method that calls an overload:

```
Public Shared Sub CropImage(ByVal fileNameIn As String,
        ByVal theRectangle As Rectangle)
  CropImage(fileNameIn, fileNameIn, theRectangle)
End Sub
```

With this method, external code needs to pass the filename only once and the method ensures that the source file is overwritten automatically with the new and cropped image.

The UploadHandler Class

The UploadHandler class is a simple yet very powerful class used to make uploading files in an ASP.NET application a lot easier.

Usually, when you upload a file, you perform all kinds of checks on the uploaded file. For example, you may try to find out if the user uploaded a file at all, and whether it has the required extension. The UploadHandler class can handle this for you. All you need to do in the code-behind of a page is create a new instance of the UploadHandler, set a few properties (most of them have sensible defaults), and call

UploadFile and pass it an instance of an <asp:FileUpload> control. Figure 11-7 lists all the methods and properties of this class.

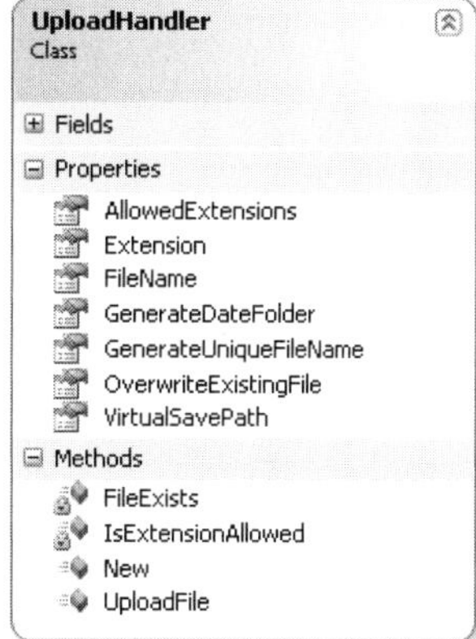

Figure 11-7

Before you can work with the UploadHandler class, you need to create an instance of it. That's why it has a public default constructor. Once you have an instance of the class you have to set at least the VirtualSavePath property; all the other properties are optional. The following table describes the seven properties of the UploadHandler class:

Property Name	Type	Default Value	Description
AllowedExtensions	String	String.Empty	Gets or sets a regular expression to use when checking file extensions. For example, ^.jpg|.gif$ allows only JPG or GIF files. If this property is not set, all extensions are allowed.
Extension	String	String.Empty	This read-only property returns the extension of the uploaded file.
FileName	String	String.Empty	Gets or sets the name of the file (without extension) as it should be saved.

Table continued on following page

Property Name	Type	Default Value	Description
GenerateDateFolder	Boolean	False	Determines whether subfolders are created for the current year and month to store the file in. This is useful when you have a lot of uploaded files and want to store them in logical folders.
GenerateUniqueFileName	Boolean	False	Determines whether the file gets a unique name. When set to True, the property FileName is ignored and the file is saved with a GUID as its name.
OverwriteExistingFile	Boolean	False	Determines whether existing files should be overwritten when they already exist.
VirtualSavePath	String	n/a	Gets or sets the virtual path to the folder where the uploaded files should be saved. This property is updated when GenerateDateFolder is True.

Once these properties have been set, your code should call the class's only public method UploadFile and pass it an instance of an <asp:FileUpload> control. This method carries out some checks using the private FileExists and IsExtensionAllowed methods and then either saves the uploaded file to disk or throws an exception. The following table describes the three methods (other than its constructor) of the UploadHandler class:

Method	Return Type	Description
FileExists	Boolean	Returns True when a file with the same name already exists.
IsExtensionAllowed	Boolean	Returns True when the extension of the uploaded file meets the criteria set in the AllowedExtensions property.
UploadFile	n/a	This method is the workhorse of the UploadHandler class. It performs a number of checks on extensions, paths, and so on, and then saves the file to disk or throws an exception.

You see a lot more of the inner workings of this class in the section "Code and Code Explanation."

In addition to the Toolkit folder, the App_Code folder contains two helper classes, which are discussed next.

Helper Classes

The two helper classes for the Greeting Cards application, called `FileHandlingEventArgs` and `AppConfiguration`, have been put in the App_Code folder directly. The reason for this is that they are used by the web application, and not by the code in the Toolkit. The design of these classes is discussed next. You see how and where they are used in the section "Code and Code Explanation."

The FileHandlingEventArgs Class

The four user controls that make up the largest part of the user interface of the application are all capable of firing an event called `ImageFinalized` to signal to the application that they're done with their work. When they fire this event, they pass up an instance of the `FileHandlingEventArgs` class that inherits from the standard `System.EventArgs` class. The `FileHandlingEventArgs` has the same behavior as this `EventArgs` class, but adds an additional property called `FileName`, as you can see in Figure 11-8.

Figure 11-8

This `FileName` property holds the name of the image that the user control has been working with. The constructor for this class accepts this filename and stores it in a private backing variable that is made accessible through the public `FileName` property. You see how this works later when the code for the user controls is discussed.

The final class in the App_Code folder is `AppConfiguration`, the configuration class you also saw in previous chapters.

AppConfiguration

The `AppConfiguration` class is a simple wrapper with five public properties around application settings keys in the Web.config file. This class is used in some of the user controls in the site to determine the maximum height or width of an image, the path where the uploaded images should be saved, and the name and e-mail address used to send out e-mails. Figure 11-9 shows these five properties.

The two `Email` properties hold the e-mail address and name of the sender of the e-mails that are sent by the application.

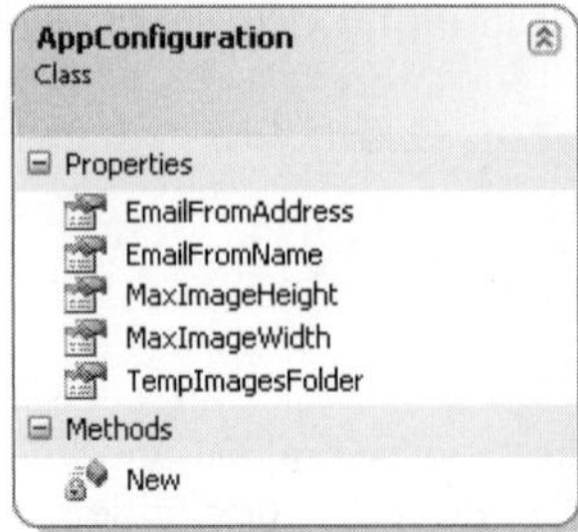

Figure 11-9

The `MaxImageHeight` and `MaxImageWidth` properties work together and determine the new maximum height or width of the image that is uploaded. The user control that uploads and saves the image in the first step of the Greeting Card generator automatically resizes the image so its dimensions fit between these two maximum properties. You see how the image is resized later.

The `TempImagesFolder` property holds the virtual path to a folder in your site where temporary images are stored. The Web.config file for the application sets this value to `~/Images/Temp`, but you can change that so it points to a different folder.

Now that you have seen the design of the classes in the Toolkit and their methods, it's time to look at the actual implementation of these classes and the user interface of the web site. The next section explains how the web site is set up using a single web page and four user controls and how these controls and the page interact.

Code and Code Explanation

Although the code in the Toolkit is already very reusable, the entire application has been made even more generic and reusable by implementing the various actions on the image inside four user controls. Each of these controls can be used separately in a different application and has no dependencies on the host page or any of the other user controls.

In the case of the Greeting Cards application, these four controls have been added to a host page located in the root of the site. This page serves as a controller to orchestrate the actions of the various user controls. In the next section, you see how this host page is able to communicate with the four user controls. After that, each of the four controls is discussed in more detail separately.

The Host Page

The host page, called Default.aspx, contains a reference to each of these four controls in an `<asp:MultiView>` control. The host page is responsible for displaying the right user control at the right time, allowing the user to sequentially progress through the Greeting Cards application. The code in the code-behind file takes the user through the following five steps:

1. Select an image and upload it to the server.
2. Optionally rotate or flip the image.
3. Optionally crop the image to a user-defined region of the image.
4. Add text to the image at a user-defined location.
5. Send an e-mail with the image as an embedded object.

The first four steps are carried out by user controls, whereas step 5 takes place in the code-behind of the host page itself. Figure 11-10 shows these five steps. The outer rectangle represents the host page, and the smaller inner rectangles represent the four user controls.

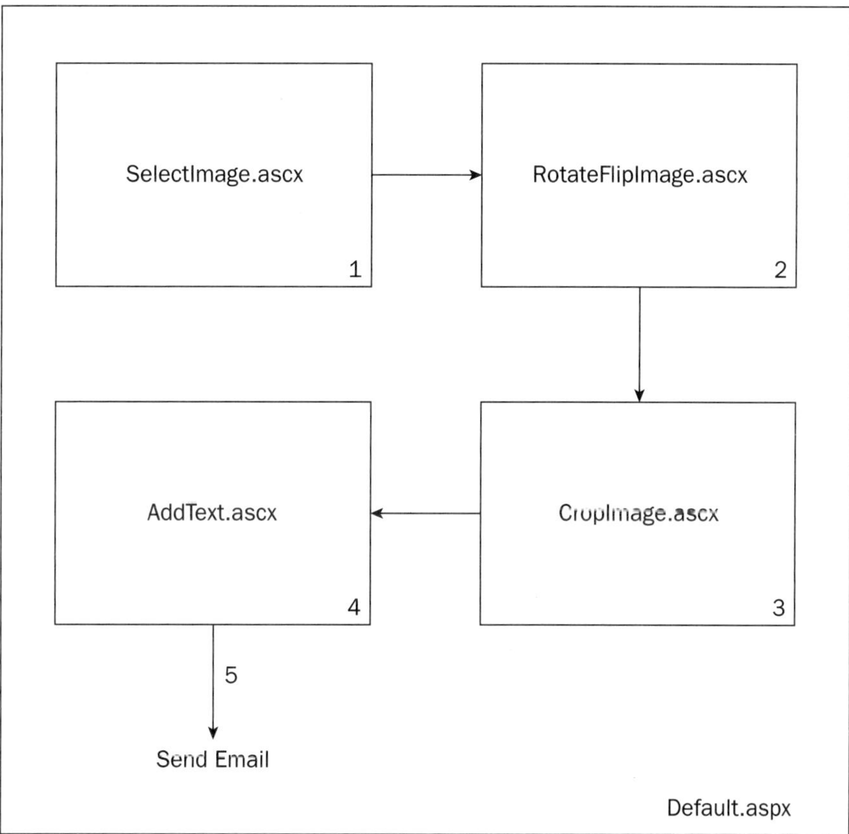

Figure 11-10

Inside the Controls folder in the root of the web site you find the four user controls mentioned in Figure 11-10. The following table lists each of these controls and describes their purpose:

Control Name	Description
SelectImage.ascx	Allows a user to select an image from the local hard drive and upload it to the server where it is stored on disk. The uploaded image is resized automatically to meet the maximum height and width rules set in the Web.config file.
RotateFlipImage.ascx	This control allows a user to rotate or flip an image. Rotating and flipping is optional.
PictureCropper.ascx	With this control a user can select a portion of an image by cropping the original image. Cropping is optional.
AddText.ascx	This control allows a user to add text to the image at an arbitrary location. The user is free to choose from a list of font families and sizes and specify the color of the text.

Inside the host page, these four controls have been added to a `View` control inside a `MultiView` like this:

```
<asp:MultiView ID="MultiView1" runat="server" ActiveViewIndex="0">
  <!-- Other views go here -->
  <asp:View ID="View2" runat="server">
    <!-- View specific markup goes here -->
    <Wrox:SelectImage ID="SelectImage1" runat="server" />
  </asp:View>
  <asp:View ID="View3" runat="server">
    <!-- View specific markup goes here -->
    <Wrox:RotateFlipImage ID="RotateFlipImage1" runat="server" />
  </asp:View>
  <!-- Other views go here -->
</asp:MultiView>
```

This code snippet shows two of the user controls in the highlighted lines; the one used to select and upload an image and the one to rotate or flip the image. Because with a `MultiView` control only one view can be active and thus visible at any given time, the host page shows only one user control at a time.

Because the host page is responsible for displaying the user controls in the right order, it has to know when to load which user control at which time. Because there are no dependencies between the user controls or between a user control and the host page, the Greeting Cards application uses an event-driven mechanism to determine when a specific control is done with its work. Each of the controls defines an event called `ImageFinalized` of type `ImageFinalizedEventHandler`:

```
Public Delegate Sub ImageFinalizedEventHandler(ByVal sender As System.Object, _
        ByVal e As FileHandlingEventArgs)
Public Event ImageFinalized As ImageFinalizedEventHandler
```

Whenever a control is ready, it raises the event by calling `RaiseEvent` and passing it an instance of the `FileHandlingEventArgs` class you saw earlier. This `EventArgs` class exposes a property called `FileName` that holds the location of the image that has been processed by the control.

To see how this works, look in the code-behind for the `SelectImage` control that you find in the Controls folder in the root of the site. Near the end of the file, you'll see the following code, which gets triggered when the user clicks the Finish button on the control:

```
Protected Sub btnFinish_Click(ByVal sender As Object, _
        ByVal e As System.EventArgs) Handles btnFinish.Click
  RaiseEvent ImageFinalized(Me, New FileHandlingEventArgs(FileName))
End Sub
```

This raises the event `ImageFinalized` and passes it a reference to itself using the `Me` keyword. It also passes the name of the file that has been uploaded using the public `FileName` property. Inside the code-behind for the host page, this event is caught and handled with the following code:

```
Protected Sub SelectImage1_ImageFinalized(ByVal sender As Object, _
       ByVal e As FileHandlingEventArgs) Handles SelectImage1.ImageFinalized
  MultiView1.ActiveViewIndex = 2
  RotateFlipImage1.FinishButtonText = "Next"
  RotateFlipImage1.FileName = e.FileName
End Sub
```

The first thing this code does is change the `ActiveViewIndex` of the `MultiView` control so it displays the next user control — `RotateFlipImage1` in this example. It then sets the `FinishButtonText` property of that control to `Next`. This determines the text that is displayed on the Finish button of the `RotateFlip` user control. This is useful if you want to reuse only a few of the user controls in your application or want to reorder them. All but the last control can then be set up to display Next, and the last control could have the text Finish on the button. If you only reuse a single user control, you could set the button text to the action it's performing, such as Crop or Rotate Image.

The final step in this code is to set the `FileName` property of the `RotateFlipImage1` control equal to the `FileName` property of the `e` argument. As stated earlier, when a control is finished with its work (the user clicked the Finish button) it raises an event and passes an instance of the `FileHandlingEventArgs` class with it. This `EventArgs` class holds the filename of the finalized image. In the case of the `SelectImage` control, the filename is the virtual path to the image that has just been uploaded. This image will then be the source of the next control so it has an image to work with. By setting the `FileName` property of the `RotateFlipImage` control, that control knows with which image it should start working.

Although this example shows the code for the `SelectImage1_ImageFinalized` only, all four controls implement the same mechanism. The code-behind for Default.aspx has handlers for the `ImageFinalized` event, which run similar code to pass the filename from control to control and display the next step in the process.

In addition to the `ImageFinalized` event, all four user controls have the following properties and method in common:

Method or Property Name	Type	Data Type	Purpose
`FileName`	Property	`String`	Determines the name and location of the source file that each control works with. The source file of a control is usually retrieved from the previous control.
`TempFileName`	Property	`String`	A filename to store temporary versions of the images. Because the `SelectImage` control doesn't need a temporary image to work with, it doesn't have this property.
`FinishButtonText`	Property	`String`	The text displayed on the Finish button for each control. To create a wizard-style application, the text for most buttons is set to Next.
`btnFinish_Click`	Method	n/a	Fires when the Finish button gets clicked. Inside this event handler, the final image is updated and an `ImageFinalized` event is raised.

You see how these properties and the method operate when each of the four individual controls are discussed.

In addition to the `ImageFinalized` handlers, you'll find two more methods in the code-behind of Default.aspx. The first is `btnStart_Click`, which fires when the user clicks the Start button on the homepage. The code for this method sets the `ActiveViewIndex` property of the `MultiView` to `1` to display the `SelectImage` control so a user can select and upload a file.

The second method is fired when the user clicks the `btnSendEmail` button. The code for this method sends an e-mail with the image as an embedded object in the message. You see how this works near the end of this chapter, after the four user controls have been discussed.

Uploading and Resizing Images

In the Greeting Card application, the user control `SelectImage.ascx` is the first step in the whole process, because it allows a user to select an image from the local hard drive and upload it to the web server. In addition to a number of `Label` controls that display various error messages and two placeholders that determine what part of the control is visible, it contains a few important controls that are listed in the following table:

Control Name	Control Type	Purpose
`FileUpload1`	`FileUpload`	Allows a user to select a local image.
`btnUpload`	`Button`	Uploads the selected image to the server.
`RequiredFieldValidator1`	`RequiredFieldValidator`	Checks whether a file has been selected when the Upload button is clicked.
`litFinishButtonText`	`Literal`	A placeholder in the instructive text that is updated with the same text the Finish button has.
`imgUploaded`	`Image`	Displays the image that the user uploaded.
`btnNewImage`	`Button`	Allows a user to select a new image and ignore the previously uploaded file.
`btnFinish`	`Button`	Moves the user to the next step of the Greeting Card application.

You saw earlier that the control has a `FinishButtonText` property that determines the text on the Finish button. In the `Page_Load` event of the user control, this text is also applied to the `Literal` `litFinishButtonText` to synchronize the user instructions (click Next to continue) with the button's text.

When a file has been selected and the Upload button has been clicked, the code in `btnUpload_Click` fires. This method is responsible for handling the uploaded file and displaying an error message in case of an exception. The method consists of two parts; the first half of the code uploads the file and saves it to disk. The other half resizes the image to the maximum dimensions specified by the `MaxImageHeight` and `MaxImageWidth` in the `AppConfiguration` class. Both of these parts are now discussed.

Uploading Files

The following code snippet shows the code that uploads and saves the file:

```
myUploadHandler = New Toolkit.UploadHandler()
myUploadHandler.GenerateUniqueFileName = True
myUploadHandler.AllowedExtensions = "^.jpg|.gif|.png|.jpeg$"
myUploadHandler.VirtualSavePath = AppConfiguration.TempImagesFolder
Try
  myUploadHandler.UploadFile(FileUpload1)
Catch aex As ArgumentException
  Select Case aex.ParamName.ToLower()
    Case "extension"
      lblIllegalExtension.Visible = True
    Case "filename"
```

```
        lblFileName.Visible = True
      Case "myfileupload"
        lblNoFile.Visible = True
    End Select
  Catch Ex As Exception
    lblErrorMessageUnknownError.Visible = False
  End Try
```

The first thing this code does is create an instance of the `UploadHandler` class. Notice how the class name is prefixed with `Toolkit` — the namespace that the `UploadHandler` class lives in. As you recall from earlier in this chapter, this class is responsible for saving an uploaded file to disk. Next, three properties are set on the `UploadHandler` object. The first dictates that the uploaded file should get a unique filename in the form of a GUID. This ensures that the uploaded file isn't accidentally overwritten by another file with the same name. Then the `AllowedExtensions` property is set. This property can contain a regular expression that dictates the allowed extensions for the uploaded file. In the preceding example, only JPG and GIF files are allowed. The final property determines the path where the uploaded images are saved, which is retrieved from the `AppConfiguration` class again.

Next, `UploadFile` is called, which gets a reference to the `FileUpload` control defined in the markup of the `SelectImage` control. The `UploadFile` method throws `ArgumentException` objects when one or more of the criteria aren't met, so the code in the `Catch` block handles these errors and displays a label with an error message that describes the problem. The `UploadFile` method is the workhorse of the `UploadHandler` class, because it carries out a number of checks, builds up the path and filename where the file must be saved, and finally saves the uploaded file to disk. It's a bit too much code to repeat here completely, but the following code block shows the first part of the method that determines the filename, extension, and the path where the uploaded file is saved:

```
If myFileUpload.HasFile Then
  If _GenerateUniqueFileName Then
    _FileName = Guid.NewGuid().ToString()
  Else
    If _FileName IsNot String.Empty Then
      _FileName = Path.GetFileNameWithoutExtension(myFileUpload.FileName)
    End If
  End If

  _Extension = System.IO.Path.GetExtension(myFileUpload.PostedFile.FileName)

  If _VirtualSavePath = String.Empty Then
    Throw New ArgumentException("Cannot save the file without a " & _
          "VirtualSavePath.", "VirtualSavePath")
  End If
  If _GenerateDateFolder Then
    _VirtualSavePath &= DateTime.Now.Year.ToString() & _
          "/" & DateTime.Now.Month.ToString().PadLeft(2, "0"c)
  End If

  ' Other checks go here

  ' File is saved here

End If
```

It starts off with checking whether a unique ID must be generated for the uploaded filename. The calling code set this property to `True`, so in the Greeting Card example the code in the first `If` block runs and then `_FileName` is filled with a GUID. In situations where no external filename has been set and the class doesn't need to create a unique filename, the filename is retrieved from the file the user has uploaded. Then the extension is retrieved from the uploaded filename. The last part of this code block builds up the virtual path to the upload folder. When no folder has been specified, the code throws an exception and ends. Otherwise, the path is extended with the current year and month as separate folders when `_GenerateDateFolder` is `True`. This creates a path like 2006\03 under the `_VirtualSavePath` folder. This can be useful to segment the uploaded files by year and month.

The `UploadFile` method repeats similar checks to see if the image can be overwritten and if the extension of the file is valid. It does the latter with the private function `IsExtensionAllowed`, which uses a regular expression to validate the extension:

```
Private Function IsExtensionAllowed() As Boolean
  Dim tempResult As Boolean = True
  If _AllowedExtensions IsNot String.Empty Then
    Try
      tempResult = Regex.IsMatch(_Extension.ToLower, _AllowedExtensions, _
          RegexOptions.IgnoreCase)
    Catch
      tempResult = False
    End Try
  End If
  Return tempResult
End Function
```

Only when the `AllowedExtensions` property has been set does the code validate the extension. It uses the `Regex.IsMatch` method to check whether the uploaded file matches the extension pattern stored in `_AllowedExtensions`.

The remainder of the `UploadFile` method (not shown here) creates the requested folder and finally saves the file using the `SaveAs` method of the ASP.NET `FileUpload` control. Because these operations can result in exceptions, the code is wrapped in a `Try Catch` block. In case an exception occurs, it's caught and handled by the code in the `SelectImage` control that you saw earlier.

Once the file has been uploaded and saved successfully, the second half of the code in `btnUpload_Click` inside the `SelectImage` control fires. This code resizes the image to the maximum size defined in the Web.confg file.

Resizing Images

Because the Toolkit shields you from the complexity of the code to resize an image, the code in the `SelectImage` control is really simple:

```
FileName = Path.Combine(myUploadHandler.VirtualSavePath, _
     myUploadHandler.FileName) & myUploadHandler.Extension
Toolkit.Imaging.ResizeImage(Server.MapPath(FileName), _
          AppConfiguration.MaxImageWidth, AppConfiguration.MaxImageHeight)
imgUploaded.ImageUrl = FileName
plcUpload.Visible = False
plcImage.Visible = True
```

The first line of the code block builds up the full filename by combining the path, the filename, and the file extension. The second line calls the `ResizeImage` method of the `Imaging` class in the `Toolkit` namespace. This overloaded version of `ResizeImage` expects a physical path to the image (that's why `Server.MapPath` is used) and the maximum width and height of the image. After the image has been resized successfully, the last few lines update the `Image` control with the new image and switch the visibility of the `plcUpload` and `plcImage` placeholder controls. This effectively displays the uploaded and resized image on the page, and hides the `FileUpload` control.

To understand how the `ResizeImage` method works, you need to open the Imaging.vb file from the Toolkit folder and locate the method with the following signature:

```
Public Shared Sub ResizeImage(ByVal fileNameIn As String, _
          ByVal maxWidth As Integer, ByVal maxHeight As Integer)
```

This method does nothing more than call another overload that has almost the same signature but accepts additional `fileNameOut` and `ImageFormat` parameters. If you locate that method (to navigate to it, right-click the method's name and choose Go To Definition), you'll find the following code:

```
Public Shared Sub ResizeImage(ByVal fileNameIn As String, _
         ByVal fileNameOut As String, ByVal maxWidth As Integer, _
         ByVal maxHeight As Integer, ByVal theImageFormat As ImageFormat)

  Dim originalSize As Size = GetImageSize(fileNameIn)
  Dim newSize As Size = New Size(0, 0)

  Dim resizeFactor As Decimal = System.Math.Max( _
         Convert.ToDecimal(Decimal.Divide(originalSize.Height, maxWidth)), _
         Convert.ToDecimal(Decimal.Divide(originalSize.Width, maxWidth)))

  newSize.Height = Convert.ToInt32(originalSize.Height / resizeFactor)
  newSize.Width = Convert.ToInt32(originalSize.Width / resizeFactor)

  ResizeImage(fileNameIn, fileNameOut, newSize, theImageFormat)
End Sub
```

The first thing you may notice is that this method doesn't actually resize the image; all it does is calculate the new dimensions of the image. First it gets the dimensions of the original image by calling the helper method `GetImageSize`. With these dimensions, the `resizeFactor` is calculated. This is done by taking the maximum value of the required resize factor for the height and for the width. To understand how this works, consider the following example. Imagine you upload a file that's 1000 pixels wide and 600 pixels high. Also imagine that the maximum dimensions for the image in the Web.config file have been set to 640×480. With these numbers, the factor by which this image should be resized is 1.5625 (1000 divided by 640) for the width and 1.25 (600 divided by 480) for the height. The highest value of these two factors is 1.562, which means the image should be resized by that factor. To calculate the new dimensions of the image (stored in the variable `newSize`) both the height and the width are divided by `resizeFactor`. In the end, the `newSize` will have a width of 640 and a height of 384 pixels.

Once the dimensions are known, the code calls yet another overloaded version of `ResizeImage` and passes it the source and target filenames, the `newSize` variable, and an image type. This version of the `ResizeImage` does all the hard work by resizing the image:

```
Public Shared Sub ResizeImage(ByVal fileNameIn As String, _
      ByVal fileNameOut As String, ByVal theSize As Size, _
      ByVal theImageFormat As ImageFormat)

  Dim mySourceBitmap As Bitmap = Nothing
  Dim myTargetBitmap As Bitmap = Nothing
  Dim myGraphics As Graphics = Nothing

  Try
    mySourceBitmap = New Bitmap(fileNameIn)

    Dim newWidth As Integer = theSize.Width
    Dim newHeight As Integer = theSize.Height

    myTargetBitmap = New Bitmap(newWidth, newHeight)

    myGraphics = Graphics.FromImage(myTargetBitmap)

    myGraphics.InterpolationMode = _
          System.Drawing.Drawing2D.InterpolationMode.HighQualityBicubic

    myGraphics.DrawImage(mySourceBitmap, New Rectangle(0, 0, newWidth, newHeight))
    mySourceBitmap.Dispose()

    myTargetBitmap.Save(fileNameOut, theImageFormat)
  Catch
    Throw
  Finally
    ' Clean up objects. Not shown here.
  End Try
End Sub
```

After the variable declaration, the code creates a new bitmap object based on the source image. Then a new bitmap called `myTargetBitmap` is created, which gets the dimensions of the `Size` object that was passed to this method. On this target bitmap the resized version of the original image will be drawn. Then a new `Graphics` object is created. You can see the `Graphics` object as a virtual canvas and a virtual painter at the same time. The new `Graphics` object is created with the `FromImage` method and is passed the new and empty bitmap. This bitmap serves as the canvas to paint on. Then the `InterpolationMode` of the `Graphics` object is set. This enumeration defines the algorithm that is used when images are scaled or rotated. This enumeration has quite a few members, each resulting in a different image quality. In the preceding code, `HighQualityBicubic` is chosen because it ensures the best quality of the image.

Then `DrawImage` is called to paint the original image (stored in `mySourceBitmap`) at the specified location and size on the target bitmap. For this location and size it expects a `Rectangle` object, which is created on the fly in the method call. The `Top` and `Left` of the rectangle are set to `0`, and the `Height` and the `Width` come from the `Size` object passed to the `ResizeImage` method. When `DrawImage` draws the bitmap from `mySourceBitmap` onto its internal bitmap object (`myTargetBitmap`) it resizes and positions the source bitmap. In this code example, it places the new bitmap at 0, 0 (the upper-left corner) but when you have other drawing needs you can choose a different location. For example, when you want to draw a border around an image, you could specify 10, 10 as the upper-left location. If you also specify the target bitmap to be 20 pixels higher and wider than the original, you get a nice border of 10 pixels on all four sides of the image.

The final step is to save the new bitmap using its `Save` method. However, before that is done, the original bitmap is disposed first. When .NET creates a new bitmap based on a file location, it holds on a lock to that file. So, until you release that lock by calling `Dispose`, the original file cannot be overwritten. To ensure that calling code can resize an image that is saved under the original name (effectively overwriting the original) the source bitmap is disposed before `Save` is called.

The `Finally` block eventually cleans up any object that has been created in the `Try` block.

Back in the SelectImage.ascx control, there is one event you need to look at; the `Click` event for the Finalize button:

```
Protected Sub btnFinish_Click(ByVal sender As Object, _
          ByVal e As System.EventArgs) Handles btnFinish.Click
  RaiseEvent ImageFinalized(Me, New FileHandlingEventArgs(FileName))
End Sub
```

This code raises the event called `ImageFinalized` and passes the `FileName` of the image that has just been uploaded and resized. As soon as the event is raised, the code in Default.aspx catches it with the following code:

```
Protected Sub SelectImage1_ImageFinalized(ByVal sender As Object, _
             ByVal e As FileHandlingEventArgs) Handles SelectImage1.ImageFinalized
  MultiView1.ActiveViewIndex = 2
  RotateFlipImage1.FinishButtonText = "Next"
  RotateFlipImage1.FileName = e.FileName
End Sub
```

This code sets up the next user control called `RotateFlipImage1`, which allows a user to rotate and flip an image. It sets the `FinishButtonText` of that control to `Next`, and it sets the `FileName` property to the filename retrieved from the `e` argument. The `FileName` property of the `RotateFlipImage1` is the source file this control will work with.

Rotating and Flipping Images

When the `FileName` property is set by the host page, the `RotateFlipImage` control (called RotateFlipImage.ascx in the Controls folder) calls a private method called `InitializeControl` (in bold text in the following code), but only the very first time this property is set. This is done to avoid calling `InitializeControl` more than once:

```
Public Property FileName() As String
  ' Get accessor goes here (not shown)

  If ViewState("FileName") Is Nothing Then
    ViewState("FileName") = value
    InitializeControl()
  Else
    ViewState("FileName") = value
  End If
End Property
```

`InitializeControl` in turn calls a helper method called `GetRotateTypes` in the `Imaging` class of the Toolkit to get a string array of all the available rotation types:

```
Public Shared Function GetRotateTypes() As String()
  Dim tempResult As String() = [Enum].GetNames(GetType(RotateFlipType))
  Array.Sort(tempResult)
  Return (tempResult)
End Function
```

It does this by calling `GetNames` on the `Enum` class and passing it the type of `RotateFlipType`, which is defined in the .NET `System.Drawing` namespace. The `RotateFlipType` enumeration defines rotating and flip types like `Rotate180FlipNone`, which rotates an image 180 degrees; `RotateNoneFlipX`, which mirrors the image horizontally; and so on. The array that `GetNames` returns is sorted and then used as the `DataSource` for the `DropDownList` control called `lstRotateFlipTypes`. When the user chooses one of the types from the drop-down list and clicks the Rotate button, the code in the code-behind fires:

```
Dim myRotateFlipType As RotateFlipType = [Enum].Parse(GetType(RotateFlipType), _
           lstRotateFlipTypes.SelectedValue)
  Imaging.RotateImage(Server.MapPath(FileName), Server.MapPath(TempFileName), _
           myRotateFlipType)
HasBeenRotated = True
plcRotate.Visible = False
btnUndo.Visible = True
UpdateImageControl(TempFileName)
```

This code first parses the chosen `RotateFlipType` from the `SelectedValue` of the `DropDownList`. It then uses `Server.MapPath` to translate the virtual path of the `FileName` property (retrieved from the `SelectImage` control and set by Default.aspx) and of the `TempFileName` property, which is generated by the code automatically:

```
Private ReadOnly Property TempFileName() As String
  Get
    If ViewState("TempFileName") Is Nothing Then
      ViewState("TempFileName") = AppConfiguration.TempImagesFolder & "/" & _
             Guid.NewGuid.ToString() & ".jpg"
    End If
    Return ViewState("TempFileName").ToString()
  End Get
End Property
```

Only the very first time this property is accessed, a filename is built up by combining the temp path for the images, a GUID, and the extension .jpg. On subsequent calls to this property, its value is retrieved from `ViewState`. This ensures that the control has the same unique filename available during the control's lifetime.

When the paths have been translated to physical paths correctly, they are passed into `RotateImage`, which is defined in the `Imaging` class in the Toolkit and looks like this:

```
Using myBitmap As New Bitmap(fileNameIn)
  myBitmap.RotateFlip(theRotateFlipType)
  myBitmap.Save(fileNameOut, ImageFormat.Jpeg)
End Using
```

This method simply calls the `RotateFlip` method of the `Bitmap` class and passes it the specified `RotateFlipType`. It then calls `Save` on the same object to save the changes to disk.

Once the user is done with rotating and flipping the image, she can click the Finish button. When that button is clicked, the control updates the `FileName` property with the value from `TempFileName` (that now holds the rotated image) but only when the image has actually been rotated. Otherwise, the `FileName` property is left as is and passed to the event handler in the calling code. The final line of code in the method raises the event `ImageFinalized`:

```
If HasBeenRotated Then
  FileName = TempFileName
End If
RaiseEvent ImageFinalized(Me, New FileHandlingEventArgs(FileName))
```

The host page has an event handler for this event. Inside this handler, called `RotateFlipImage1_ImageFinalized`, the host page now passes the filename up from the `RotateFlip` control to the `CropImage` control, which is discussed next.

Cropping Images

Recall from the introduction of this chapter that the cropping page displays a rectangle that the user can move around and resize. When the correct portion of the image is selected, the image is cropped with the click of a button. The rectangle that is drawn on top of the image is a visual cue to the user. When the actual crop operation is performed, the image is cropped to the area that is visible inside the selection rectangle.

The entire cropping is handled by the `CropImage` control, saved as CropImage.ascx in the Controls folder. The left side of the control displays the image that has been set by the previous `RotateFlip` control. At the right side, you see a drop-down list that allows you to change the color of the selection area. It's useful to change the color when you have uploaded a dark image, which makes the default color of black hard to spot. The items in the drop-down list are set in the `InitializeControl` method that is called when the `FileName` property is set for the first time, similar to the code you saw for the `RotateFlip` control. Just as with the `RotateFlip` types, the `Imaging` class has a useful method that returns an array of `Color` objects:

```
Public Shared Function GetColors(ByVal includeSystemColors As Boolean) As Color()
  Dim tempColors As KnownColor() = _
          CType([Enum].GetValues(GetType(KnownColor)), KnownColor())
  Dim colors As New ArrayList

  For loopCount As Integer = 0 To tempColors.Length - 1
    If (Not Color.FromKnownColor(tempColors(loopCount)).IsSystemColor _
           Or includeSystemColors) And Not _
           Color.FromKnownColor(tempColors(loopCount)).Name = "Transparent" Then
      colors.Add(Color.FromKnownColor(tempColors(loopCount)))
    End If
  Next
  Return CType(colors.ToArray(GetType(Color)), Color())
End Function
```

This method uses `Enum.GetValues` to get an array of `KnownColor` objects. This array also includes system colors like ActiveBorder and ButtonFace. Because these colors are defined by the system settings of the server and the end user has no way to find out what color they represent, they are removed from the list when the Boolean parameter `includeSystemColors` is `False`. This is done by looping though the array with colors, and adding each valid color to a new ArrayList. At the end of the method, the ArrayList is converted to an array of `Color` objects and returned to the calling code where it is used as the DataSource for the color drop-down.

Below the color drop-down, you see two sets with four button controls each. The first set, displayed in Figure 11-11, is used to change the location of the cropping area on the image.

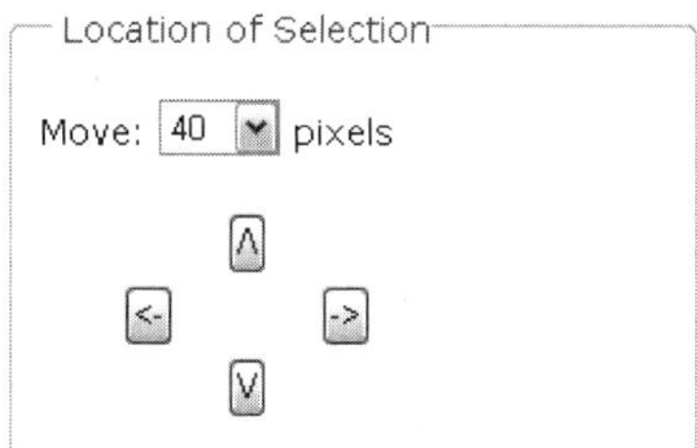

Figure 11-11

With the pixels drop-down control you can determine how many pixels the selection area is moved when one of the buttons is clicked. When you click one of the buttons, the code in the code-behind for the control recalculates the location of the selection area and then draws a new rectangle on top of the image. This is done with the following code, which is fired when you click the upward-facing arrow:

```
Protected Sub btnLocationUp_Click(ByVal sender As Object, _
          ByVal e As System.EventArgs) Handles btnLocationUp.Click
  Top -= MoveIncrease
  If Top < 0 Then
    Top = 0
  End If
  DrawRectangle()
End Sub
```

The `MoveIncrease` property is a simple wrapper around the `SelectedValue` of the pixel drop-down list you saw in Figure 11-11. The code then subtracts this increase size from the `Top` location of the control. This property is stored in ViewState, just like its counterparts `Left`, `Width`, and `Height`. The code also checks if the `Top` property doesn't exceed the image's boundaries. In this case, when `Top` is less than 0, it is set to zero, so the rectangle is displayed at the very top of the image.

The code for the three other buttons for navigation work pretty much the same way in that they increase or decrease the values for the `Top` or `Left` properties.

At the end of the code, `DrawRectangle` is called. This method is discussed in full detail after the Resize buttons for the selection area have been discussed.

Figure 11-12 displays the four buttons that are used to control the size of the selection area. The code in the code-behind is almost identical to that for the navigation buttons, but the size buttons operate on `Width` and `Height`, rather than on the `Top` and `Left` properties.

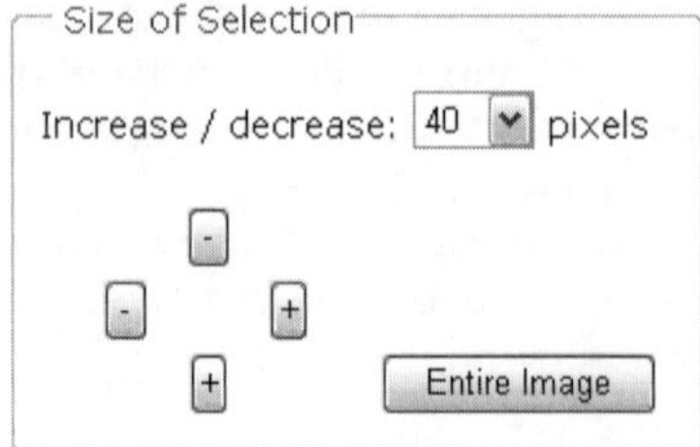

Figure 11-12

Each of the eight event handlers for the navigation and size buttons calls `DrawRectangle`. This method creates a new rectangle based on the `Top`, `Left`, `Height`, and `Width` properties and creates a new color based on the `SelectedValue` of the `lstPenColor` control. These values are then passed to `DrawRectangle` in the `Imaging` class of the Toolkit, which draws a rectangle on top of the image:

```
Public Shared Sub DrawRectangle(ByVal fileNameIn As String, _
      ByVal fileNameOut As String, ByVal theRectangle As Rectangle, _
      ByVal myColor As Color)

  Dim myGraphics As Graphics = Nothing
  Dim myBitmap As Bitmap = Nothing

  Try
    myBitmap = new Bitmap(fileNameIn)
    myGraphics = Graphics.FromImage(myBitmap)

    Dim myPen As New Pen(myColor, 1)
    myGraphics.SmoothingMode = Drawing2D.SmoothingMode.None
    myGraphics.DrawRectangle(myPen, theRectangle)
    myPen.Dispose()

    myBitmap.Save(fileNameOut, ImageFormat.Jpeg)

  Catch ex As Exception
    Throw
  Finally
    If myBitmap IsNot Nothing Then
      myBitmap.Dispose()
    End If
    If myGraphics IsNot Nothing Then
      myGraphics.Dispose()
    End If
  End Try
End Sub
```

Similar to the resize code you saw earlier, this code creates a new `Bitmap` and a new `Graphics` instance. This `Graphics` instance stores the `Bitmap` as its drawing canvas. Then .NET's `DrawRectangle` draws the actual rectangle on top of the image. The size and color of the rectangle are determined by the `Pen` object that is passed to `DrawRectangle`. To keep the rectangle from getting blurred, the `SmoothingMode` of the `Graphics` object is set to `SmoothingMode.None`, which ensures that the line isn't anti-aliased. After the rectangle has been drawn, the `Pen` object is disposed and the image is saved.

As you can see, the `DrawRectangle` isn't performing the cropping. All it does is draw a rectangle on top of the image. However, the same location and size used to draw the rectangle are used when the user clicks the Preview button to do the actual cropping:

```
Protected Sub btnPreview_Click(ByVal sender As Object, _
                 ByVal e As System.EventArgs) Handles btnPreview.Click
  Toolkit.Imaging.CropImage(Server.MapPath(FileName), _
        Server.MapPath(TempFileName), New Rectangle(Left, Top, Width, Height))

  ' Rest of the code is shown later
End Sub
```

This code calls `CropImage`, another method defined in the `Imaging` class. As parameters it gets the filename of the original image, the filename of the target image (`TempFileName`), and a `Rectangle` object that is constructed on the fly using the `Left`, `Top`, `Width`, and `Height` properties. The code for `CropImage` in the Toolkit looks like this:

```
Public Shared Sub CropImage(ByVal fileNameIn As String, _
        ByVal fileNameOut As String, ByVal theRectangle As Rectangle)
  Dim myBitmap As Bitmap = Nothing
  Dim myBitmapCropped As Bitmap = Nothing
  Dim myGraphics As Graphics = Nothing

  Try
    myBitmap = New Bitmap(fileNameIn)
    myBitmapCropped = New Bitmap(theRectangle.Width, theRectangle.Height)
    myGraphics = Graphics.FromImage(myBitmapCropped)

    myGraphics.DrawImage(myBitmap, New Rectangle(0, 0, myBitmapCropped.Width, _
          myBitmapCropped.Height), theRectangle.Left, theRectangle.Top, _
          theRectangle.Width, theRectangle.Height, GraphicsUnit.Pixel)

    myBitmap.Dispose()
    myBitmapCropped.Save(fileNameOut, ImageFormat.Jpeg)

  Catch ex As Exception
    Throw
  Finally
    If myBitmap IsNot Nothing Then
      myBitmap.Dispose()
    End If
    If myBitmapCropped IsNot Nothing Then
      myBitmapCropped.Dispose()
    End If
    If myGraphics IsNot Nothing Then
      myGraphics.Dispose()
    End If
  End Try
End Sub
```

This code uses the `Graphics` object to draw the image from the source onto the target. It does this with .NET's `DrawImage` method, which accepts the following parameters:

Parameter Name	Parameter Type	Description
image	Image	This parameter contains the source bitmap that holds the original image. The Bitmap class used in the code example inherits from Image, so this method happily accepts it for its image parameter.
destRect	Rectangle	The rectangle determines where the cropped source image should be drawn on the new bitmap that was created. Since the entire new image should be filled, the Rectangle control is set to be as large as the target image.
srcX	Integer	This parameter determines the X coordinate of the original image from where the image should be copied to the target image.
srcY	Integer	This parameter determines the Y coordinate of the original image from where the image should be copied to the target image.
srcWidth	Integer	This parameter determines the width of the area of the original image that should be copied to the target image.
srcHeight	Integer	This parameter determines the height of the area of the original image that should be copied to the target image.
srcUnit	GraphicsUnit	Determines the units of measurement that DrawImage takes into account. Because the image's width and height are specified in pixels, GraphicsUnit.Pixel is passed.

Because of the large number of parameters, you may have trouble understanding how this all works. To clarify things, consider Figure 11-13.

Imagine that the source image is 1000 pixels wide and has a height of 700. The outer rectangle in Figure 11-13 depicts that image. The inner rectangle represents the crop area the user has chosen. As you can see, the crop area is 600×400 pixels, while it has a Left of 180 pixels and a Top of 150. When CropImage is called, this is what gets passed:

```
myGraphics.DrawImage(SourceBitmap, New Rectangle(0, 0, 600,400), 180, 150, _
          600, 400, GraphicsUnit.Pixel)
```

What this does is copy a part of the bitmap held in SourceBitmap onto its internal Bitmap (created off the myBitmapCropped object). With this paint operation, the copied part is placed at 0, 0 and has a width of 600 and a height of 400 pixels (the dimensions of the target image). The four integer parameters determine the location and dimensions of the part of the source image that should be copied, which is the cropping area that the user has selected. The final parameter instructs the DrawImage method to use pixels for all dimensions and location calculations.

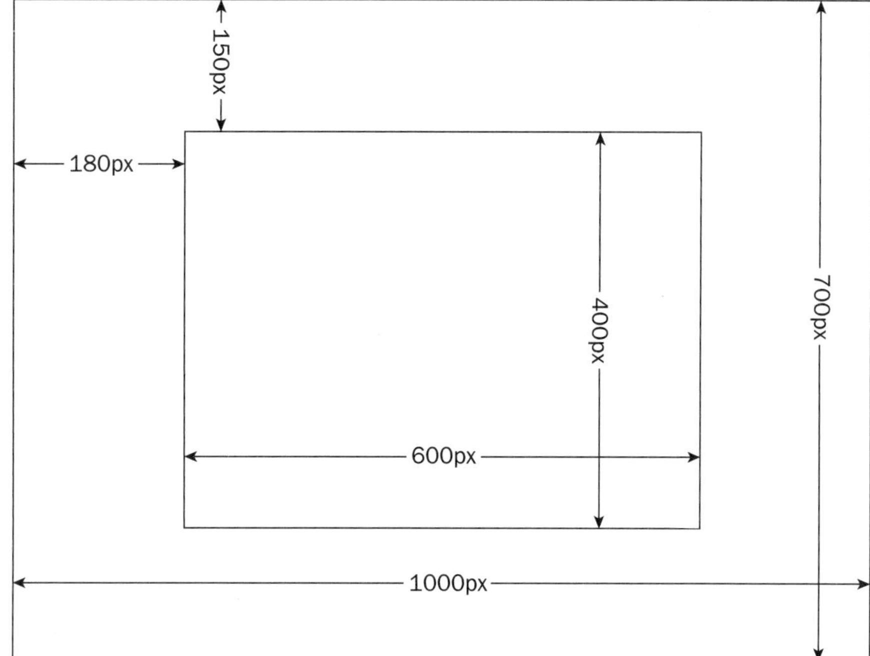

Figure 11-13

When `CropImage` has completed successfully, control is returned to the `CropImage` user control where the `<asp:Image>` control that displays the cropped image is updated and the visibility of two panels is switched:

```
    Toolkit.Imaging.CropImage(Server.MapPath(FileName), _
           Server.MapPath(TempFileName), New Rectangle(Left, Top, Width, Height))
    UpdateImageControl(TempFileName)
    plcPreviewImage.Visible = False
    plcFinalizeImage.Visible = True
  End Sub
```

This then shows the Finish button for the control (with the text Next) that allows users to continue, and an Undo button that enables them to restore the original image. The Undo button simply switches back the visibility of the two placeholders, so the original image with the selection area is shown again.

The Finish button fires the same code as the `RotateFlip` control does. It assigns `FileName` the value of `TempFileName` (which holds the cropped image) and then uses `RaiseEvent` again to signal the host page that it is done with its work. The host page then changes the `ActiveViewIndex` of the `MultiView`, which causes the `AddText` control to become visible. This control is discussed next.

Adding Text to Images

The AddText.ascx control is responsible for adding the text that the user typed on top of the image. The user can select a font family and size and a color to style the text that is displayed on the control.

As you probably guessed by now, this control follows the same pattern as the other controls. It has the same properties and method — such as `FileName` and `FinishButtonText` — as the controls used for cropping, rotating, and uploading. Because the implementation for these properties and method is almost identical to that of the other controls, it isn't discussed here.

However, a number of significant methods and properties are worth looking at. First of all, there's the `InitializeControl` method that fills two `DropDownList` controls with font families and colors. You already saw the code that lists the colors in the code for the `CropImage` control, so the following code block lists the code for the `GetFontFamilies` method in the `Imaging` class in the Toolkit only:

```
Public Shared Function GetFontFamilies() As FontFamily()
  Dim fonts As New ArrayList

  For loopCount As Integer = 0 To FontFamily.Families.Length - 1
    fonts.Add(FontFamily.Families(loopCount))
  Next
  Return CType(fonts.ToArray(GetType(FontFamily)), FontFamily())
End Function
```

The .NET Framework has a very convenient `FontFamily` class, hosted in the `System.Drawing` namespace that exposes a shared (and read-only) property called `Families`. This `Families` property returns an array of all the `FontFamily` objects that are present on the computer where the code runs. It's important to understand this code depends on the machine where it is run, because it could mean a big difference between your local development machine and the final production server. On your local machine you may have a lot of fonts that are installed by Microsoft Office or by drawing packages such as Adobe PhotoShop or Corel Draw. However, on a production server, you often find only the default fonts installed by Windows, which is somewhere around 20 to 30 fonts.

The code loops through this array and adds each `FontFamily` to an `ArrayList` because this class has a very convenient `Add` method that allows you to add objects to it. At the end, the `ArrayList` is casted back to an array of `FontFamily` objects. Without the `ArrayList`, you'd need to define a new array of type `FontFamily`, and then manually resize and add the elements to it. The `ArrayList` class shields you from this hassle so it's a lot easier to use. It's a bit slower than working with regular arrays, but its added usefulness is well worth the performance hit.

The array of `FontFamily` objects is returned from the method and then set as the `DataSource` for the font drop-down list:

```
lstFontNames.DataSource = Toolkit.Imaging.GetFontFamilies()
lstFontNames.DataTextField = "Name"
lstFontNames.DataValueField = "Name"
lstFontNames.DataBind()
```

The `FontFamily` object has a `Name` property that is used for both `DataTextField` and `DataValueField`.

When the user selects a new font from the `lstFontNames` control, it fires its `SelectedIndexChanged` event. Inside the event handler for that event, a drop-down list with font styles is created. The code that builds up the list looks like this:

```
    lstFontStyles.Items.Clear()
    lstFontStyles.Visible = True
    Dim styles As FontStyle() = New FontStyle(3) {FontStyle.Regular, _
           FontStyle.Bold, FontStyle.Italic, FontStyle.Bold Or FontStyle.Italic}
    Dim family As FontFamily = New FontFamily(lstFontNames.SelectedValue)
    For Each style As FontStyle In styles
      If family.IsStyleAvailable(style) Then
        lstFontStyles.Items.Add(style.ToString())
      End If
    Next
```

This code creates a new array of `FontStyle` objects and adds four new `Style` items to it in its initializer code. Notice the use of `FontStyle.Bold Or FontStyle.Italic` to indicate a font style that has both a bold and an italic typeface at the same time. The code then checks if the selected font supports each of the four font styles by calling `IsStyleAvailable`. If the style is available it's added to the drop-down list. Otherwise, it's simply ignored.

The next important thing to look at is how the control keeps track of where the user has clicked so it knows where to place the text. This consists of two parts. First, two private properties called `X` and `Y` store their value in ViewState so it's persisted across postbacks. These properties get a value when the user clicks the image with the following code:

```
  Protected Sub ImageButton1_Click(ByVal sender As Object, ByVal e As _
              System.Web.UI.ImageClickEventArgs) Handles ImageButton1.Click
    X = e.X
    Y = e.Y
    AddText()
    cellControls.Visible = True
    plcAddText.Visible = True
  End Sub
```

The `ImageClickEventArgs` instance exposes an `X` and a `Y` property that hold the location where the user clicked the image at the client. This is standard behavior implemented in the `ImageButton` class. When these properties have been set, `AddText` is called (discussed next) and the visibility of the placeholder and the table cell with the server controls is switched. This then displays the drop-downs with the font-style, size, and color.

The first time the user clicks the image no text is added to the image, because the text box doesn't contain any text yet. However, on subsequent clicks on the image, the page reloads and the text is moved to the location where the user clicked last. To see how the text is added to the image, look at the `AddText` method in the user control first:

```
  Private Sub AddText()
    If txtTextToAdd.Text.Length > 0 AndAlso lstFontNames.SelectedIndex > 0 Then
      Dim aFont As Font = New Font(lstFontNames.SelectedValue, _
             Convert.ToSingle(lstFontSizes.SelectedValue), _
             CType(FontStyle.Parse(GetType(FontStyle), _
             lstFontStyles.SelectedValue), FontStyle))

      Dim myColor As Color = Color.FromName(lstKnownColors.SelectedValue)
      Dim textLocation As Point = New Point(X, Y)

      Toolkit.Imaging.AddTextToImage(Server.MapPath(FileName), _
```

```
            Server.MapPath(TempFileName), aFont, myColor, _
            textLocation, txtTextToAdd.Text)

        ' Rest of the code is shown later
      End If
    End Sub
```

The first thing this code does is create a new `Font` instance. The `FamilyName` that is passed to the `Font` constructor is retrieved from the drop-down `lstFontNames`, the size from `lstFontSize`, and the style is retrieved by casting the `SelectedValue` of the `lstFontStyles` list back to a `Style` object. Effectively, this creates a font with the user-specified font family and size, which is then used to draw on the image.

Next, a new `Color` object is created, using `Color.FromName`, which accepts the name of a known color. The final object that is created is a `Point` object to which the `X` and `Y` values are passed in its constructor. This `Point` object determines the upper-left corner of the text that is about to be added.

Then `AddTextToImage` in the Toolkit is called to add the text to the image. The `Font`, `Color`, and `Point` objects that have been created are passed to it, together with the filename and the text that should be added:

```
  Public Shared Sub AddTextToImage(ByVal fileNameIn As String, _
      ByVal fileNameOut As String, ByVal myFont As Font, ByVal fontColor As Color, _
      ByVal textLocation As Point, ByVal textToAdd As String)

    Dim myGraphics As Graphics = Nothing
    Dim myBitmap As Bitmap = Nothing

    Try
      myBitmap = new Bitmap(fileNameIn)

      myGraphics = Graphics.FromImage(myBitmap)

      Dim myStringFormat As StringFormat = New StringFormat
      myStringFormat.Alignment = StringAlignment.Near

      myGraphics.TextRenderingHint = Drawing.Text.TextRenderingHint.AntiAlias

      Dim myBrush As SolidBrush = New SolidBrush(fontColor)
      myGraphics.DrawString(textToAdd, myFont, myBrush, _
                  New Point(textLocation.X, textLocation.Y), myStringFormat)
      myBitmap.Save(fileNameOut, ImageFormat.Jpeg)
    Catch ex As Exception
      Throw
    Finally
      If myGraphics IsNot Nothing Then
        myGraphics.Dispose()
      End If
      If myBitmap IsNot Nothing Then
        myBitmap.Dispose()
      End If
    End Try
```

The first part of the code should look very similar, because it's the same code used by the other imaging methods. It creates a new `Bitmap` object from the filename passed to this method and then creates a new `Graphics` object based on that bitmap.

Next, a new `StringFormat` object is created and its `Alignment` property is set. This property determines in what direction the text is aligned. The enumeration has three options: `Near`, `Center`, and `Far`. In a Left to Right (LTR) language (most Western languages), `Near` equals left, whereas in Right to Left languages, such as Arabic, `Near` equals right. With the `Near` setting in a LTR language, the `Point` object passed to this method determines the upper-left corner of the text. With a setting of `Far`, it defines the upper-right corner of the text, so the text is placed to the left of the point chosen. Because the entire site is in English, it's safe to assume that `Near` is a sensible default. When users click the image to determine the location of the text, they'll most likely expect they have to indicate the upper-left corner of the text.

The next line of code sets the `TextRenderingHint` to `AntiAlias`. This causes the text placed on the image to be slightly anti-aliased, causing a smoother transition to the background. Whether you like the effect of this setting depends largely on personal preferences. If you don't like the result of the `AntiAlias` setting, try one of the other options such as `ClearTypeGridFit` or `SingleBitPerPixel`. Look at the `TextRenderingHint` enumeration in the MSDN documentation for more information.

Then a new `Brush` object is created. In the code example, a new `SolidBrush` is created that fills the letters drawn on the image with a solid color. However, you're not limited to solid colors. Instead of a `SolidBrush`, you could create a `HatchBrush` or a `LinearGradientBrush` or another brush that inherits from `System.Drawing.Brush`. For example, the following `Brush` draws the letters on the image with a light gray background and a black brick pattern:

```
Dim myBrush As Drawing2D.HatchBrush = New Drawing2D.HatchBrush( _
           Drawing2D.HatchStyle.DiagonalBrick, Color.Black, Color.LightGray)
```

This results in the text on the image shown in Figure 11-14.

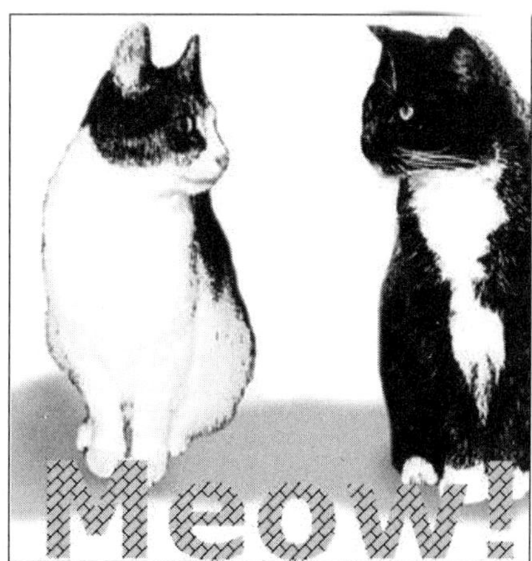

Figure 11-14

A lot more is possible with brushes and text in GDI+ than you have just seen here. For more information about brushes, look up the `System.Drawing.Brush` class in the MSDN documentation to see what classes inherit from it that you can use. Look at the `HatchStyle` enumeration for more information about the 54 available hatch patterns.

With the `Graphics`, the `StringFormat`, and the `Brush` set up, the final step is to call `DrawString` to draw the text on top of the image:

```
myGraphics.DrawString(textToAdd, myFont, myBrush, _
            New Point(textLocation.X, textLocation.Y), myStringFormat)
```

With the previous description, this should now be easy to understand. The parameter `textToAdd` holds the text that must be added to the image, and the other parameters determine the font, the brush used to draw the text, the `X` and `Y` coordinates of the text relative to the image, and the text alignment, respectively.

The final line in the `Try` block saves the image to disk, the code in the `Finally` block cleans up the objects created in the `Try` block, and then control is returned to the calling code.

Back in the AddText.ascx user control, the final code that runs in the `AddText` method updates the image held in the `ImageButton1` control and then enables the Finish button:

```
UpdateImageControl(TempFileName)
btnFinish.Visible = True
```

Just as with the `RotateFlip` control, the Undo button simply assigns the `ImageButton1` control the original image. This way, the old image is restored and the temporary image is overwritten automatically next time the `AddText` button or the image itself gets clicked.

The `AddText` control concludes the discussion of the four user controls that make up the Greeting Card application. In this section, you saw how to upload and resize images, how to rotate and crop them, and how to add text to images.

The final step performed by the Greeting Card application is to send out the generated image together with a personal message from the user as an e-mail. This is done by the host page itself with code that is discussed next.

Sending E-Mail with Embedded Images

The controls and the code that allow users to send the image together with a personal message to their friends have been placed in the host page, Default.aspx. The last `View` in the `MultiView` control holds a simple `Image` control, and three text boxes for the user's name, the recipient's e-mail address, and the personal greeting message. When all three have been filled in, a button called `btnSendEmail` is responsible for sending the image and the message as an e-mail.

When sending images through e-mail, you basically have two options. You can send an HTML-formatted message that holds a normal HTML `<img>` tag. This `<img>` tag should point back to an image that is stored somewhere on your web server and that is accessible over the Internet. A disadvantage of this method is that modern e-mail programs like Microsoft Outlook often block these images to protect the privacy of the user. Although for an end-user it's very easy to unblock them so the images can be viewed, the message doesn't look as intended when the user first receives it. There's also the chance that the user doesn't even unblock the images, because he doesn't fully trust the message or the sender.

With the second option, you can embed the image inside the HTML body of the message, so it gets sent to the user together with the actual e-mail message. This ensures the user is able to see the images without a need to download them from a web server after the message has arrived.

The Greeting Card application sends the image that has been uploaded and altered as an embedded image through e-mail with the following code:

```
Protected Sub btnSendEmail_Click(ByVal sender As Object, _
        ByVal e As System.EventArgs) _
        Handles btnSendEmail.Click
  Dim emailFromAddress As String = AppConfiguration.EmailFromAddress
  Dim emailFromName As String = AppConfiguration.EmailFromName
  Dim emailToAddress As String = txtEmailAddress.Text
  Dim theSubject As String = txtYourName.Text & " sent you a Greeting Card"

  Dim theMailBody As String = String.Format("{0} sent you a " & _
        "greeting card.<br /><br /><img src=""cid:imgGreetingCard""/>" & _
        "<br /><br /><h3>Personal message from {0}</h3>{1}", _
        txtYourName.Text, txtYourMessage.Text)

  Dim myMailMessage As New MailMessage()
  myMailMessage.To.Add(emailToAddress)
  myMailMessage.From = New MailAddress(emailFromAddress, emailFromName)
  myMailMessage.Subject = theSubject

  Dim myAlternateView As AlternateView = _
        AlternateView.CreateAlternateViewFromString(theMailBody, _
        System.Text.Encoding.ASCII, MediaTypeNames.Text.Html)

  Dim myLinkedResource As LinkedResource = _
        New LinkedResource(Server.MapPath(AddText1.FileName))
  myLinkedResource.ContentId = theContentId
  myLinkedResource.ContentType.Name = Server.MapPath(AddText1.FileName)

  myAlternateView.LinkedResources.Add(myLinkedResource)
  myMailMessage.AlternateViews.Add(myAlternateView)
  myMailMessage.IsBodyHtml = True
  Try
    Dim mySmtpClient As New SmtpClient()
    mySmtpClient.Send(myMailMessage)
    plcMailSent.Visible = True
    plcSendMail.Visible = False
  Catch ex As Exception
    lblErrorMessage.Visible = True
    plcMailSent.Visible = True
    plcSendMail.Visible = False
  End Try
End Sub
```

First a number of variables are declared and assigned a value. These variables hold the To and From address information (retrieved from the `AppConfiguration` class) and the subject. Then the mail body is built using `String.Format`, which replaces the placeholders in the text (`{0}`, `{1}`, and so on) with the actual values passed in the parameter list. Notice the use of the embedded `<img>` tag. It has a `src` attribute that points to `cid:imgGreetingCard`. This ID, `imgGreetingCard`, is used later in the code again when the `ContentId` of the `LinkedResource` is set.

Then a new MailMessage is created and the To and From addresses and the Subject are set. In .NET 1.x, these addresses were simple String properties so you could assign to them directly. However, in .NET 2.0 the To address is now a collection of MailAddresses, so you should use the Add method to add a new MailAddress. The From address property can hold a single MailAddress object, which is set with New MailAddress(emailFromAddress, emailFromName).

The next two blocks of code create an AlternateView and a LinkedResource object. The AlternateView is normally used to send an alternate version of an e-mail message. For example, when you send out an HTML-formatted mailing, it's a good idea to send the plain text version of that message as an AlternateView. Users with e-mail programs that are not capable of displaying formatted HTML e-mails can then still see the plain text version. In the preceding code, the AlternateView is used to create an HTML body with an embedded image. This AlternateView takes precedence over the normal Body property of the message on e-mail packages that can display HTML. The AlternateView is created by calling CreateAlternateViewFromString, which accepts the message body as a string.

The LinkedResource class is then used to embed the image in the mail body. The constructor of this class expects a filename that points to a file on local disk, so Server.MapPath is used to translate the virtual path held in AddText1.FileName to a physical path. The next line of code sets the unique ContentId of the myLinkedResource object. This ContentId has a direct mapping to the cid:imgGreetingCard construct that was used as the src attribute for the image. When the e-mail message is viewed, the e-mail application replaces the src attribute with the path to the image. Where this path points to depends on the e-mail application you're using.

Once the LinkedResource object is ready, it's added to the LinkedResources property of the AlternateView using the Add method. The AlternateView is then added to the AlternateViews property of the MailMessage.

The final piece of the code sends the mail message using a new SmtpClient instance. This is identical to the other e-mail code you have seen in previous chapters.

When an error occurs while sending the message, the code in the Catch block displays an error message describing a possible cause for the problem.

The discussion of sending e-mail with an embedded image concludes the "Code and Code Explanation" section. Not every bit of code in the entire application has been discussed, but instead you have seen the most important concepts, classes, and methods. The remainder of the code in the application is either very straightforward or very similar to the code you have seen so far, so you should be able to apply the knowledge gained in this chapter to that code.

Now that you have seen how to use the Greeting Card application and how it works, you're ready to install the application so you can play around with the code. The next section guides you through the process of installing the application.

Setting up the Greeting Card Application

Setting up the Greeting Card application is even easier than some of the applications you saw in the previous chapters. Because the Greeting Card application doesn't use a database, there is no need to configure or change connection strings.

However, you need to change the security settings of your hard drive so the web application can write the temporary images to a folder under the web root. These settings are discussed after the next two sections that describe installing the application using the supplied installer or through a manual process.

Using the Installer

The companion CD and the code download come with an automatic installation application in the form of a Microsoft MSI package. To install the application using this MSI file, open the folder Chapter 11 - Greeting Cards\Installer on the CD-ROM or from the downloaded zip file.

Next, double-click setup.exe and keep clicking Next until the application is installed completely. Finally, click Close to dismiss the installation wizard.

Now that the application is installed, you need to tweak some security settings. Refer to the section "Configuring the Application" that follows directly after the next section that describes manual installation.

Manual Installation

Manual installation is probably just as easy as installing the application with the supplied installer. For a manual installation, all you need to do is extract the contents of the supplied zip file to a folder on your hard drive. To do this, open the folder Chapter 11 - Greeting Cards\Source on the CD-ROM or from the zip file you downloaded from `www.wrox.com`. Next, open the zip file Chapter 11 - Greeting Cards.zip and extract its contents to any folder you want (for example, `C:\Projects`). Make sure you extract the file while maintaining the directory structure. How this option is called depends on your extracting utility, but you should look for a feature called Use Folder Names or something similar to that. In the end, you should end up with a folder like `C:\Projects\GreetingCards` that in turn contains a few files and folders.

To view and test the code, open Visual Studio Web Developer Express edition and choose File⇨Open⇨Web Site. Make sure that File System is selected in the left-hand pane and then browse to the folder where you just extracted the contents of the zip file. Select the folder and then choose Open. Visual Web Developer will load the files and folders in the folder you selected, so you can look at the source for the Greeting Cards application.

With the extraction done, the final step is to configure the security settings for the application. This step is discussed next.

Configuring the Application

Configuring the Greeting Cards application is straightforward and easy. All you need to do is change security settings so the application can write to the temporary folder and configure the mail server. The security settings are discussed first, followed by the mail server.

Configuring Security Settings

The Greeting Cards application needs a place to store the temporary files that are uploaded, created, and saved by the various methods in the Toolkit. To make it easy to change where these files are stored, the application uses a single application setting to denote this temporary path. By default, this folder is a

Temp folder inside the Images folder of the application as is shown by the following code from the Web.config file:

```
    <add key="MaxImageHeight" value="480"/>
    <add key="TempImagesFolder" value="~/Images/Temp"/>
  </appSettings>
```

To allow the application to write to this folder, you'll need to change the security settings for the account that the web server uses. If you're using the integrated Developer Web Server that comes with Visual Web Developer, this account is your own account that you use to log on to your machine. If you're running the site under IIS, the account is called ASPNET on Windows 2000 and Windows XP or Network Service on Windows Server 2003. To change the security settings, follow these steps:

1. Open a Windows Explorer and locate the Images folder of your application. If you used the installer, this path is `C:\Inetpub\wwwroot\GreetingCards\Images` by default. If you did a manual install and followed the instructions, the path is `C:\Projects\GreetingCards\Images`.
2. Inside the Images folder, right-click the Temp folder (if you don't see the folder, you can create a new folder called Temp first), choose Properties, and click the Security tab. The dialog in Figure 11-15 appears.
    - If you don't see a Security tab, close the dialog and then choose Tools➪Folder Options in Windows Explorer. Then switch to the View tab and scroll all the way to the bottom of the Advanced settings list (see Figure 11-16). Make sure that Use Simple File Sharing (Recommended) is not checked.
    - Click OK to close the dialog and open the Properties for the Temp folder again.

Figure 11-15

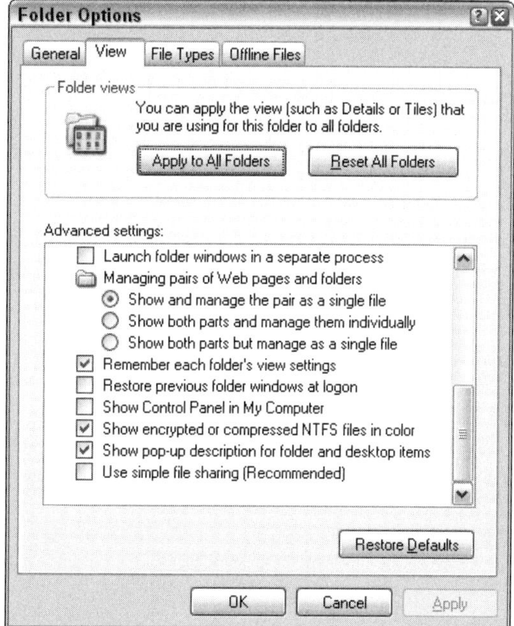

Figure 11-16

3. Depending on your system and configuration, you may have more or fewer users listed in the Group or User Names list. Click the Add button to add the user account described in the introduction of this section. You should either add your own account or the ASPNET or Network Service account. When you have typed the account name, click OK to add it to the list. It should now be visible in the list with Group or User Names that you saw in Figure 11-15.

4. Next, in the Group or User Names list, click the account you just added and then in the Permissions list at the bottom half of the screen, make sure that at least Modify, Read, and Write are selected. As soon as you click Modify, some of the other options are automatically selected for you.

5. Click OK to dismiss the Security dialog. You should now be able to run your application and create images with the Greeting Card application. If you get an error, make sure you added the right account for the right folder, and that you selected the right permissions.

Configuring the Mail Server

Because the application sends out e-mail, you need to configure the name of your outgoing mail server in the Web.config file. To change that setting now, open that file and scroll all the way down to the bottom. You'll see the following `<mailSettings>` node:

```
<system.net>
  <mailSettings>
    <smtp deliveryMethod="Network">
      <network host="smtp.YourProvider.Com" port="25"/>
    </smtp>
```

```
      </mailSettings>
    </system.net>
  </configuration>
```

Change the `host` attribute of the `<network>` node to the name of the server you use for outgoing mail. If your mail server supports authentication, you can set the `userName` and `password` properties of this node as well.

With this last modification, the application is ready to run. Either browse to `http://localhost/GreetingCards` when you installed the application with the supplied installer or press F5 in Visual Web Developer to start the application.

If you're feeling adventurous, head to this book's download page at `www.wrox.com` to find a list of possible enhancements to the Greeting Cards application and the Toolkit. You'll learn how to extend the Toolkit by adding support for drop shadows on the text on the images. You'll also learn how to add one image to another so you can display your company's logo on each image that gets uploaded in the Greeting Cards application.

Summary

This chapter covered a lot of ground on working with images through the GDI+ library. Although GDI+ is a very large subject, you have seen how to perform basic imaging tasks, such as resizing, rotating, cropping, and adding text to images. These basic tasks should create a solid basis on which you can build to increase your imaging skills in .NET applications. To recap, you have seen how to do the following:

- Use the Greeting Card application to upload and alter a custom image that can be sent by e-mail.
- Use the `UploadHandler` class to allow a user to upload files from a local computer to the web server. This `UploadHandler` is not limited to images alone; it can also handle other kinds of documents.
- Use the .NET `System.Drawing` namespace to perform operations on images, such as rotating, cropping, and resizing.
- Create a reusable framework of user controls that split up a more complex application into smaller pieces that can be reused in other applications separately.
- Create a reusable toolkit with code that can be used in many applications. By creating a DLL from the code in the Toolkit folder, you can create a reusable binary file that can be incorporated in other applications very easily.

Toward the end of the chapter, you saw how to install the Greeting Cards application, either with an automated installer or manually. The automated procedure is useful if you want to get the application up and running on a production server in no time. The manual process is useful if you want to look at the code and make modifications to it.

The Bug Base

If you have ever done any web or other software development before, it's likely that the applications you wrote contained bugs. No matter how good a programmer you are, it's almost impossible to write an application that does not contain a single bug. Some bugs are caused by logic or coding errors and some are the result of a difference between the expectations of the project's client and the programmer. Yet other bugs may not be discovered until you actually start using the application. For example, usability or performance issues are often discovered only once the end-users get hold of the web site or application. Somehow, you need to keep track of those bugs, so they can be fixed in a next release or service update.

If you're a one-man development shop, you might be doing all your bug-tracking using sticky notes on your monitor with text such as "Fix security bug in login module; don't allow access to just anyone." But once your application starts to grow, or you work in a team of developers, this is no longer a viable solution. If you're working for a large software development company, you may be working with advanced bug tracking tools like the Work Item Tracking feature from the new Microsoft Visual Studio 2005 Team System Edition (`http://msdn.microsoft.com/vstudio/teamsystem`), or tools like Bugzilla (`www.bugzilla.org`) or SourceGear's Dragnet (`www.sourcegear.com/dragnet`). However, these types of applications often cost a lot of money, or may require considerable amounts of time, knowledge, and resources to set up and maintain.

The Bug Base introduced in this chapter is positioned right in between the sticky notes on your monitor and an advanced bug tracking application. The Bug Base allows you and your team members to collaboratively file, change, and report on bugs through a web interface. The Bug Base can be installed on a server connected to the local network or the Internet, so it can be reached from any convenient location. It uses a role-based security mechanism, allowing you to determine who in your team can perform which operation. The member accounts and role settings and all other application settings are configurable within the web application itself so you can change them anywhere, anytime.

The first section of this chapter briefly guides you though the application, showing you the main screens and functionality. The section that follows digs into the design of the Bug Base. It describes the classes used in the application and how they interact. The section "Code and Code Explanation" analyzes all of the important files used in the application. If you want to know how to set up and use the Bug Base, you'll find installation instructions in the section "Setting up the Bug Base" later in this chapter.

Using the Bug Base

The Bug Base application allows you to carry out four important tasks: filing bugs, changing bugs, reporting about bugs, and application maintenance. The role-based security mechanism implemented in the Bug Base grants access to each of these features to the roles defined in the system. Each user should be assigned to at least one role so they can log in and perform one of these tasks.

The database that comes with this chapter's code (available for download at `www.wrox.com`) has five member accounts already defined, one for each of the four roles in the application and a super user:

Username	Password (case sensitive)	Description
Tester	Tester123#	A tester can only file new bugs, change his or her own bugs, or add comments to existing bugs.
Developer	Developer123#	A developer can perform the same actions as a tester, but in addition a developer can also change existing bugs and change their status.
Manager	Manager123#	A manager has the same rights as a developer, but can also use the reporting functionality.
Administrator	Administrator123#	An administrator has the same permissions a tester has. However, an administrator can also access the maintenance section to manage applications, features, and members.
SuperUser	SuperUser123#	The super user has been assigned to each of the four roles. This allows you to view the functionality for all roles without constantly having to log in and out. In normal operations, you wouldn't use this account.

Once you're logged in, you see the homepage appear (shown in Figure 12-1), which displays a welcome message and the main menu that appears at the top of each page.

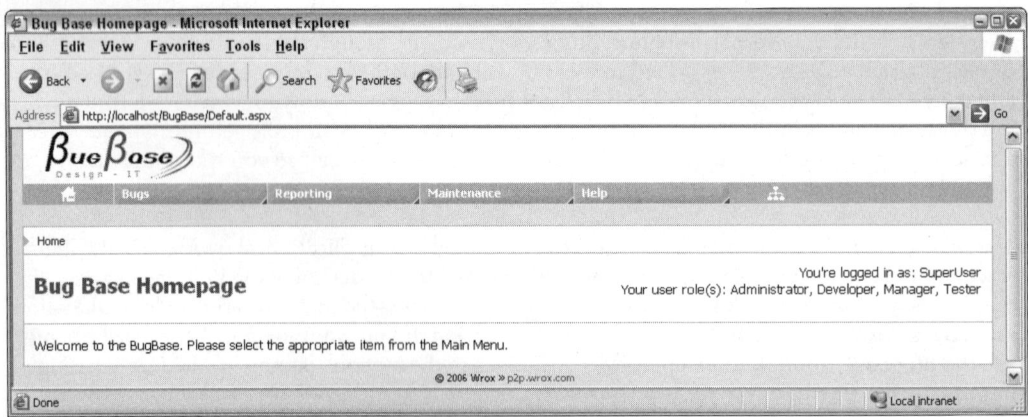

Figure 12-1

On this screen you see the main menu, right below the logo. This menu has four menu items: Bugs, Reporting, Maintenance, and Help. It also has two icons on the sides that take you back to the homepage (the home icon on the left) and that display the sitemap (the icon on the right). Depending on the roles you are assigned to, some menu items are invisible.

To file a new bug, choose File New Bug from the main Bugs menu as shown in Figure 12-2.

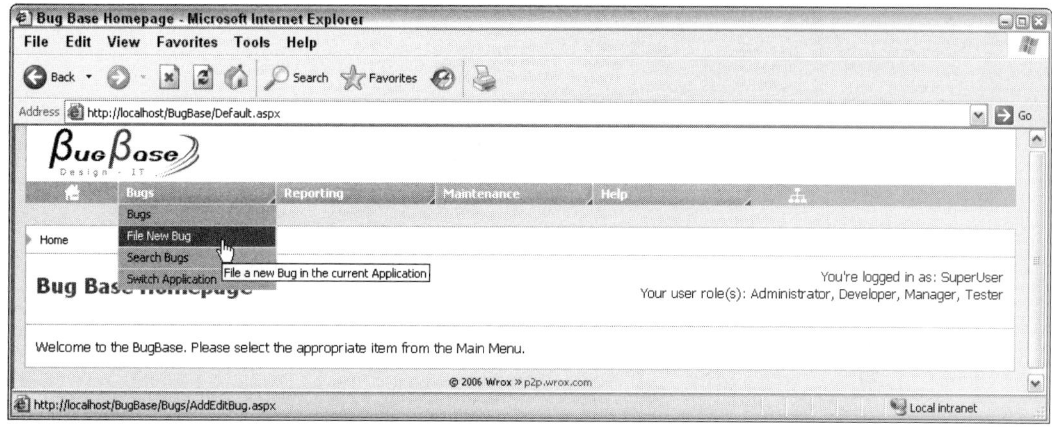

Figure 12-2

Before you can file a bug, you need to select an active application to work with, so you're taken to the SwitchApplication.aspx page first. This page shows a simple drop-down list with the available applications and an Apply button. Choose any application from the drop-down list and click the button. The page depicted in Figure 12-3 appears.

At the upper-right corner of the page in Figure 12-3 you see how you're logged in (as a Tester in this example), which roles you're assigned to (Tester), and which application you're working with (Instant Results - BugBase). The rest of the page allows you to enter information about a bug. The Feature of a bug describes the section of the application in which the bug occurs. Features are application-specific and are manageable in the Maintenance section described later. The Reproducibility of the bug indicates if and how often the bug is reproducible. This can be important for developers to know when they try to reproduce the bug and find the problem. The Frequency describes the scope of the bug by asking how many users will encounter the bug. With the Severity drop-down the bug filer can indicate the impact of the bug, ranging from a simple spelling mistake to loss of data and application crashes.

After you make valid selections in each of the drop-downs, you need to type a title and a description of the bug. The text area has been filled with a short template for the bug report, making it easier for users to describe the problem in a detailed manner.

Once you click the Insert bug button you see the Bug List page, as shown in Figure 12-4.

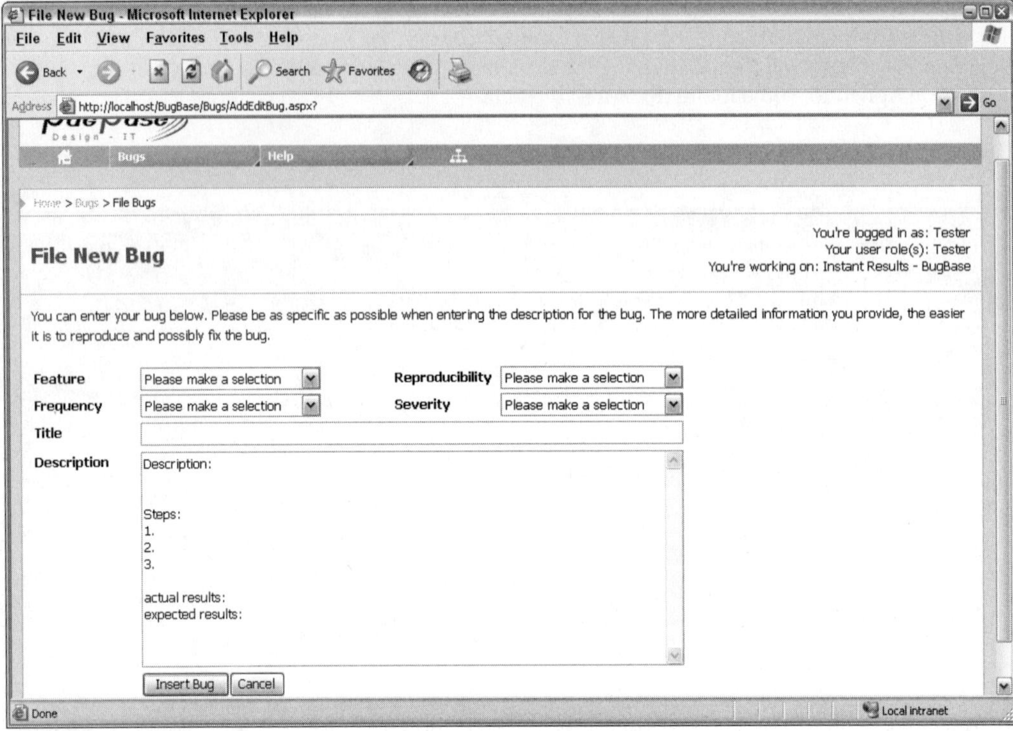

Figure 12-3

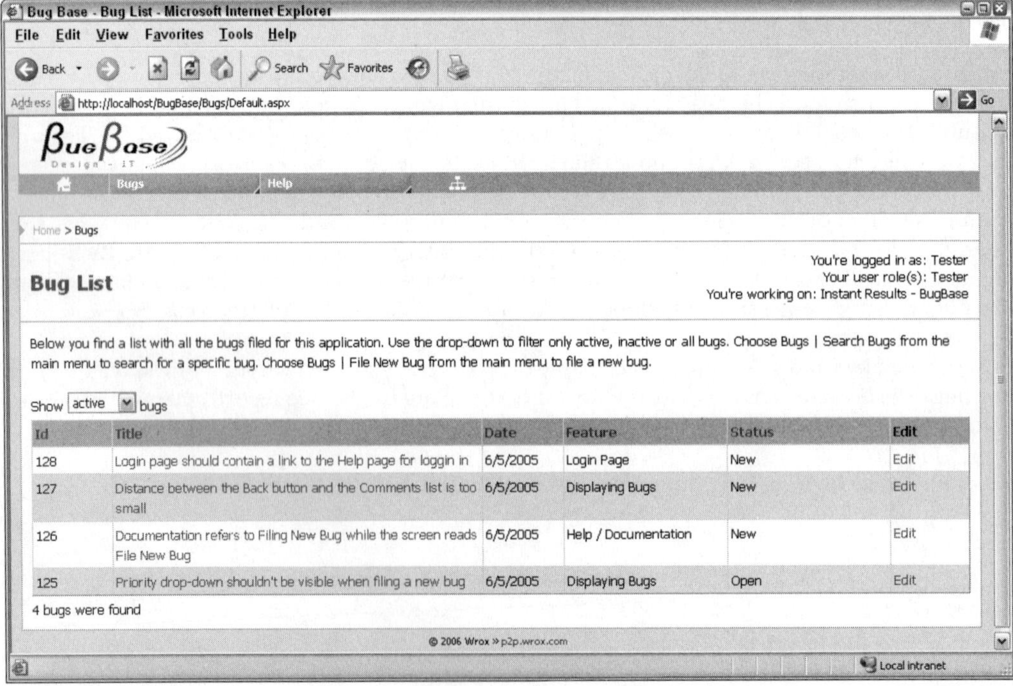

Figure 12-4

You can limit the list to Active or Inactive bugs using the drop-down menu to the top-left of the bug list. Inactive bugs are bugs that no longer need attention or work, such as Fixed and Deferred bugs. The Reporting and Search pages that are discussed later allow you to refine the list with bugs even further, by searching for only Deferred or Fixed bugs, for example. In the Maintenance section you can select which status items of a bug determine whether or not the bug gets closed.

If you click the Edit button for a bug you get a screen similar to the File New Bug window (see Figure 12-5). This time two new drop-downs have appeared, allowing you to change the current status for the bug from New to another appropriate status and to change the bug's priority. The Priority drop-down list displays the numbers 1 through 5, where 1 means a bug that needs to be fixed right away, and 5 indicates a less important bug. The Status drop-down holds items like Open, Fixed, and Deferred.

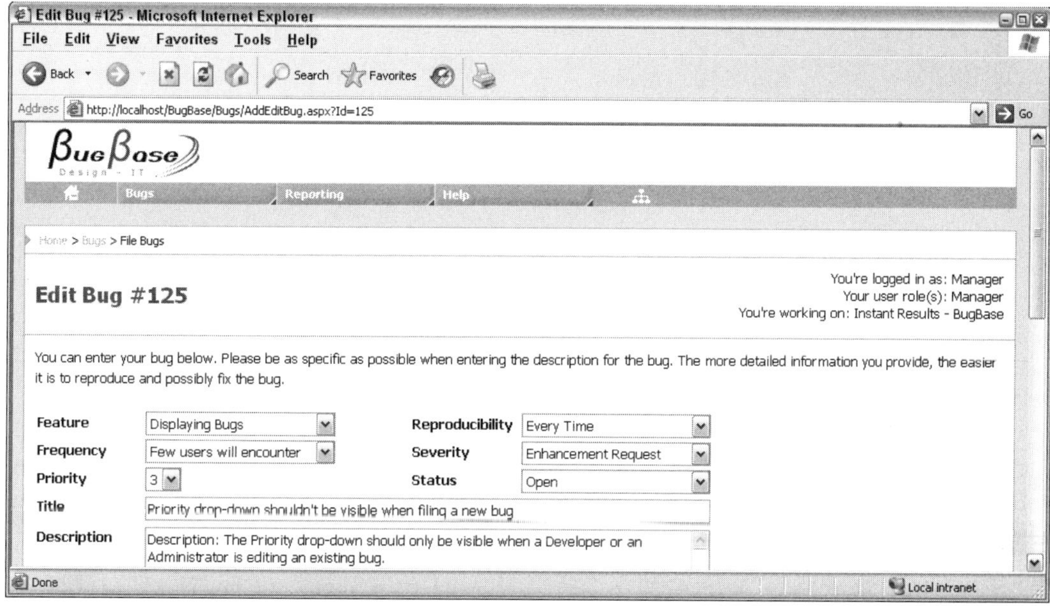

Figure 12-5

When you select Search Bugs from the ever-present main Bugs menu (shown in Figure 12-2) you can search for specific bugs in the currently selected application. With the item Switch Application on that same menu you can select another application to work with.

The Reports item under the main menu item Reporting allows you to generate reports about all bugs in the application regardless their status or application they are filed against. This menu is available only to members in the Manager role.

Under the main menu item Maintenance you'll find various menu items that allow you to change application settings. You can change and create applications and features for those applications. You can also change the items that appear in the drop-downs for Status, Frequency, Reproducibility, and Severity. You'll find the latter three under the Other Bug Properties menu, which is also a sub-menu item of the main Maintenance menu, shown in Figure 12-2. Figure 12-6 shows a list of all the Frequency Items in the system with the first one being edited:

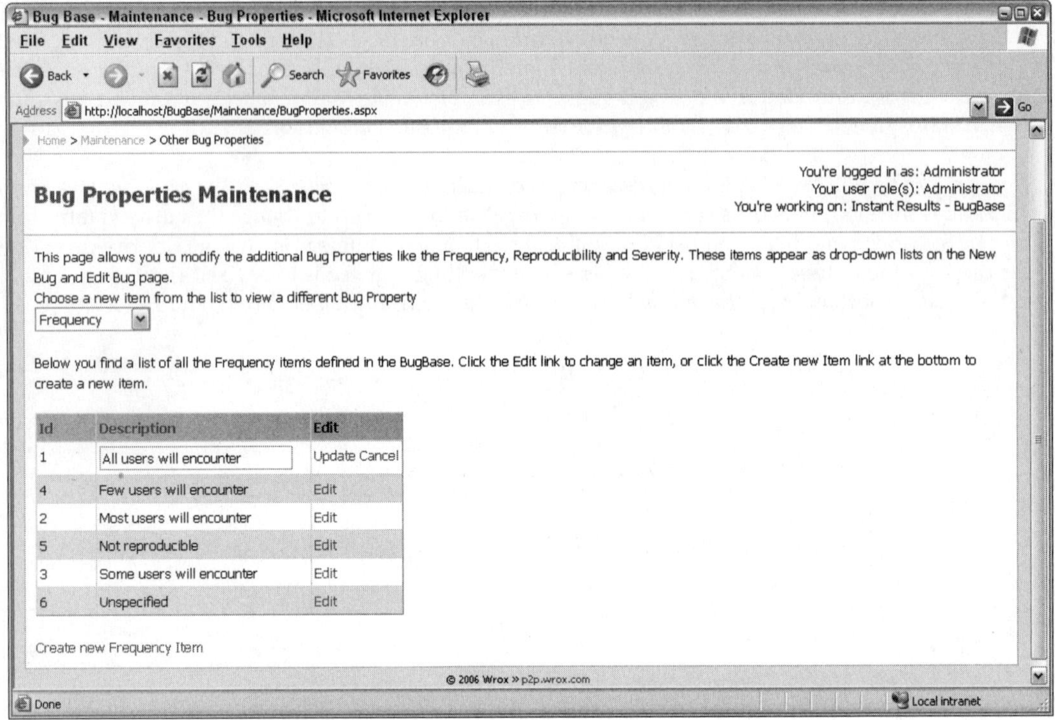

Figure 12-6

To change the Reproducibility and Severity, choose the appropriate item from the drop-down list on the Bug Properties Maintenance page shown in Figure 12-6.

The final page in the Maintenance section allows you to assign Members to roles and applications. This way, you have fine control over which member is allowed to do what in the Bug Base.

At the very right of the main menu you'll see the Help menu and a site map icon. The site map icon takes you to the site map page, and you can get help about the Bug Base with the Help menu.

Design of the Bug Base

The Bug Base is designed as a three-layered architecture, which means that presentation, business logic, and data access are each placed in different layers or *tiers*. As is often the case with ASP.NET applications, the presentation layer consists of a number of .aspx pages and .ascx user controls that use ASP.NET server controls. These pages talk to classes defined in the business layer that in turn talk to the data access layer to get information in and from the database.

The new code model of ASP.NET 2.0 makes it easy to separate the business and data access logic from the presentation tier with the introduction of the App_Code folder. Any code placed in this folder is automatically compiled and available to all your other files in your application, including .aspx pages and other code files. If you're using the full version of Visual Studio 2005 (for example, the Standard or Team System edition) you can move this code to a separate Class Library project, which you can then include in your web project. This allows for even further abstraction of the code and promotes reuse. However, for many applications this new code folder is all you need to create well-designed applications.

The remainder of this section discusses the business layer and the data access layer. The presentation layer is discussed in the section "Code and Code Explanation."

The Business Layer

The business layer of the Bug Base is located in the BusinessLogic folder inside the App_Code folder in the root of the application. It consists of eight classes and one enumeration, each of which is discussed in detail in the next section.

Bug

The `Bug` class, shown in Figure 12-7 and located in Bug.vb in the BusinessLogic folder, is the main entity in the application. It represents the bug that is filed through the web interface and stored in the database.

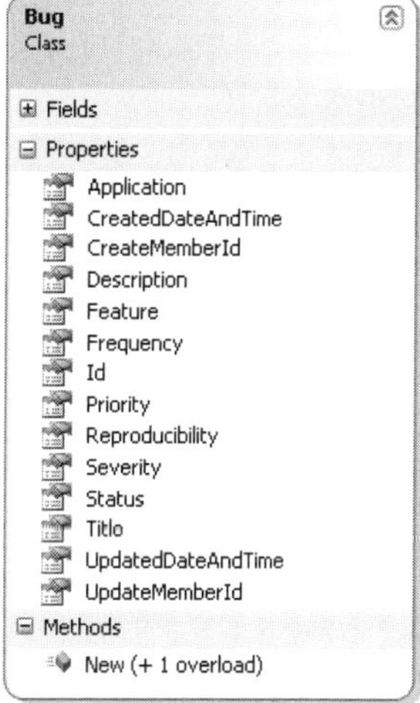

Figure 12-7

The `Bug` class exposes only properties; it has no behavior in terms of methods, other than two constructors. All actions you can perform on a bug, such as filing, changing, and searching lists of bugs, are carried out by the `BugManager` class.

The `Bug` class has the following properties:

Property	Type	Description
`Application`	`NameValue`	A NameValue object holding the `Id` and the `Description` for the application the bug is filed against.
`CreatedDateAndTime`	`DateTime`	The date and time the bug was filed.

Property	Type	Description
CreateMemberId	Guid	The unique ID of the user who filed the bug.
Title	String	A short description of the bug, used to quickly identify bugs.
Description	String	The full description of the bug, possibly including a detailed set of instructions to reproduce the behavior and describe the problem.
Feature	NameValue	A NameValue object holding the `Id` and the `Description` for the feature of the application the bug is filed against.
Frequency	NameValue	The `Frequency` describes how often a bug occurs and how many users are likely to run into it.
Id	Integer	Each bug is represented by a unique ID. The ID is automatically generated by the Bug table in the database whenever a new bug is inserted.
Priority	Integer	The `Priority` of a bug often determines the order in which bugs should be fixed.
Reproducibility	NameValue	The `Reproducibility` describes if and how often the bug can be reproduced.
Severity	NameValue	The `Severity` describes the impact of a bug, ranging from usability issues to loss of data and application crashes.
Status	NameValue	The `Status` indicates the current state of the bug. A status in turn can determine if the bug should be treated as closed. Refer to the Status table in the database for a full list of all the `Status` items.
UpdatedDateAndTime	DateTime	The date and time the bug was last updated.
UpdateMemberId	Guid	The unique ID of the user who last updated the bug.

The `Bug` class also has two constructors:

Property	Description
New ()	Creates a new `Bug` object with all properties set to their default values.
New (ByVal id As Integer)	Creates a new `Bug` object with most properties set to their default values. The `id` that is passed to the constructor is set as the `Id` of the bug.

Because the `Bug` class has only properties, it cannot perform any actions, such as saving itself in the database. Instead, these actions are carried out by the `BugManager` class.

BugManager

The `BugManager` class (see Figure 12-8) is responsible for all actions on bugs. It has methods to insert new and change existing bugs and to retrieve lists of bugs that match specific search criteria. The `BugManager` class exposes two read-only properties called `Count` and `MemberId`. The `Count` property returns the number of bugs currently held by the `BugManager` in the private field `_theBugList`. The `MemberId` property contains the current member's ID and is used to check access rights in the business and data access layers.

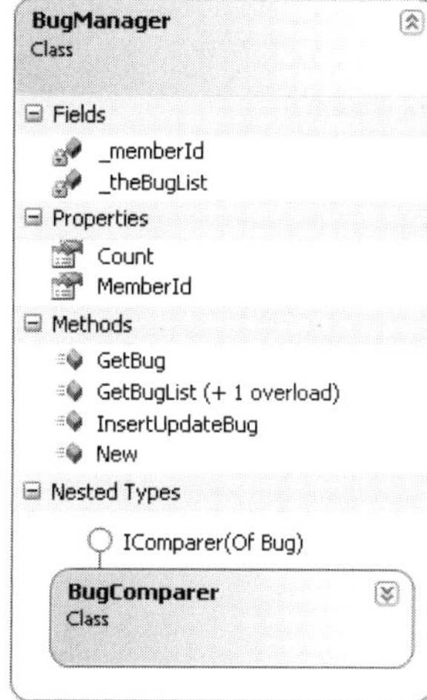

Figure 12-8

The `BugManager` class also has the following methods:

Method	Return Type	Description
`InsertUpdateBug (ByVal theBug As Bug)`	Integer	Saves a fully populated `Bug` object. It does this by calling `InsertUpdateBug` on the `BugManagerDB` class and passing it the instance of the bug. The Integer returned from this method is the new or current ID of the bug in the database.
`GetBug (ByVal id As Integer)`	Bug	Retrieves a bug based on the ID passed to this method. Returns `Nothing` when the bug could not be found or the user doesn't have permission to view it.
`GetBugList` (+ one additional overload)	List(Of Bug)	Retrieves a list of bugs optionally based on search criteria and sorted on one of the bug's properties. The list that is returned is actually a strongly typed list of bugs, using the new generics feature of the .NET Framework. Each of the two overloads is discussed in greater detail in the section "Code and Code Explanation."

Almost all of the methods in the `BugManager` class do nothing more than delegate their responsibility to a method with the same name in the `BugMagagerDB` class. The only exception is the `GetBugList` method that also sorts the list of bugs by using the `BugComparer` class, which is discussed in the next section.

BugComparer

The `BugComparer` class implements the `IComparer(Of Bug)` interface, which enables sorting of objects in a list that uses generics. It implements the only required method, `Compare`, and has a constructor that accepts the name of a `Bug` property to sort on as a parameter. The `Compare` method compares the two `Bug` objects passed to it and returns an integer indicating whether the first `Bug` object is less than, equal to, or greater than the second `Bug` object. Because of its tight relation with sorting bugs in the `BugManager`, the `BugComparer` is implemented as a nested class in the `BugManager` class, visible in Figure 12-8.

CommentManager

When users update an existing bug, they can add a comment to provide additional information. These comments are handled by the `CommentManager` class, which is shown in Figure 12-9.

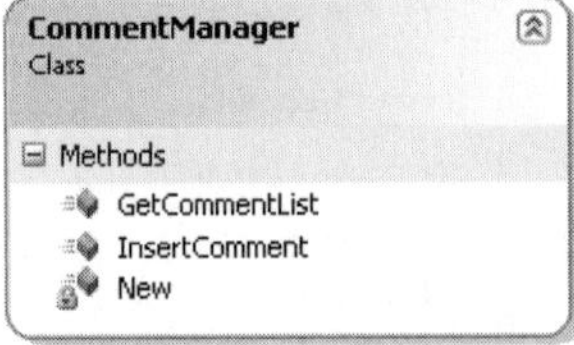

Figure 12-9

This is a very simple class to insert and retrieve comments and has only two methods:

Method	Return Type	Description
`GetCommentList (ByVal bugId As Integer)`	DataSet	Returns a list of comments for the requested bug by calling into the `CommentManagerDB` class.
`InsertComment (ByVal bugId As Integer, ByVal theBody As String, ByVal theMemberId As Guid)`	n/a	Inserts a new comment in the Comment table in the database and associates it with the `bugId` passed to this method.

To get the various lists, such as Frequency and Severity in the presentation layer, the business layer has a `ListManager` class, which is discussed next.

ListManager

The `ListManager` class is responsible for retrieving lists that are displayed on the web site. It has nine public shared methods (see Figure 12-10) to retrieve applications, features, and lists of other bug properties, such as the Severity, Reproducibility, Status, and Frequency. These lists are used in the presentation layer to fill drop-down menus. Because it has only shared methods, the constructor of the class is hidden by marking it Private. This prevents you from accidentally creating instances of the `ListManager` class. To use the methods in the class, you can simply call them on the class name.

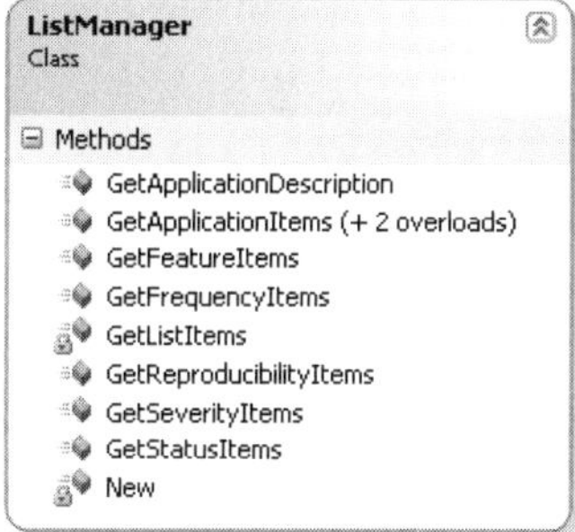

Figure 12-10

The `ListManager` class caches most of these lists in the ASP.NET cache using a `SqlCacheDependency`, so there is no need to hit the database every time they are needed. Because these lists are used quite often, this greatly increases the application's performance. You see later how this works. The following table lists the public methods that are used for working with Applications and Features:

Property	Return Type	Description
`GetApplicationItems`	DataSet	Returns a list with Applications as a DataSet (+ two additional overloads). The DataSet contains two columns: the ID and the Description of the item in the database. The overloads are used to limit the list to active applications, or to applications to which a user has access.
`GetApplicationDescription (ByVal applicationId As Integer)`	String	Returns the user-friendly name of an application.
`GetFeatureItems`	DataSet	Returns a list with Feature items as a DataSet. The DataSet contains two columns: the ID and the Description of the item in the database.

The methods that return the lists for Frequency, Reproducibility, Severity, and Status all follow the same pattern. They return the requested items as a DataSet that has an ID and a Description column. Under the hood, they call the private method `GetListItems` and pass it a custom `ListType` enumeration (defined in the BusinessLogic folder in the file called ListType.vb) to indicate the type of list to retrieve. The `GetListItems` method then calls into the data access layer to get the items from the database.

MemberManager

The `MemberManager` class (see Figure 12-11) is responsible for changing the user's access rights in the database. Because the ASP.NET 2.0 Framework already provides a lot of ready-to-use classes to work with users and security settings in your application, the implementation of the `MemberManager` is very simple.

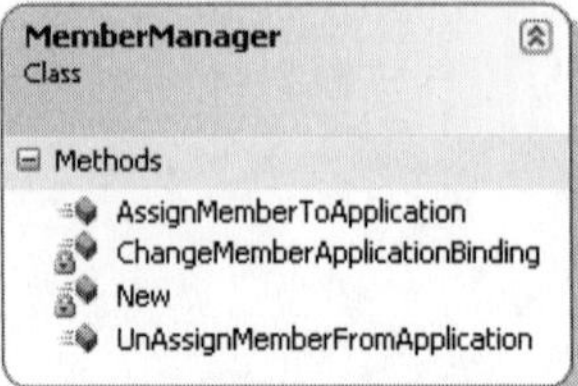

Figure 12-11

The `MemberManager` class has two public subs that allow you to assign and unassign a user to a specific application:

Property	Description
`AssignMemberToApplication (ByVal memberId As Guid, ByVal applicationId As Integer)`	Assigns a member indicated by `memberId` to the requested application.
`UnAssignMemberFromApplication (ByVal memberId As Guid, ByVal applicationId As Integer)`	Removes a member from the requested application.

Both these methods call a private member in the `MemberManager` class called `ChangeMemberApplicationBinding` and pass it either `True` or `False` to indicate whether the user should be added to or removed from the application.

NameValue

Many of the properties of a bug in the database, such as the Severity and the Reproducibility, are actually foreign keys to other tables in the BugBase database. These tables are often referred to as *domain tables*. This means that only the ID is stored with the bug. To the end-user of the application, these IDs are meaningless. To display the friendly name of these properties in the user interface, the `Bug` class exposes these properties as `NameValue` objects. The `NameValue` class (see Figure 12-12) has a `Value` property that holds the underlying ID in the database. The `Name` property exposes the friendly name.

You can create a new `NameValue` by calling the default constructor and then set the `Name` and `Value` properties individually. Alternatively, you can call the overloaded constructor that accepts values for the `Name` and `Value` properties as arguments.

SearchCriteria

The `SearchCriteria` class (see Figure 12-13) is used by the `BugManager` in the `GetBugList` methods. The `GetBugList` allows you to search for bugs that match a comprehensive list of search criteria.

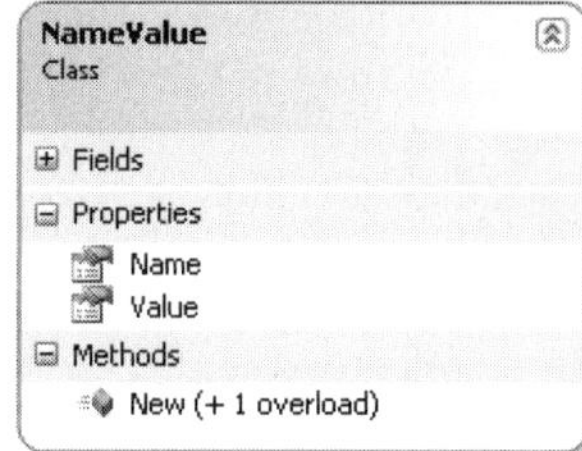

Figure 12-12

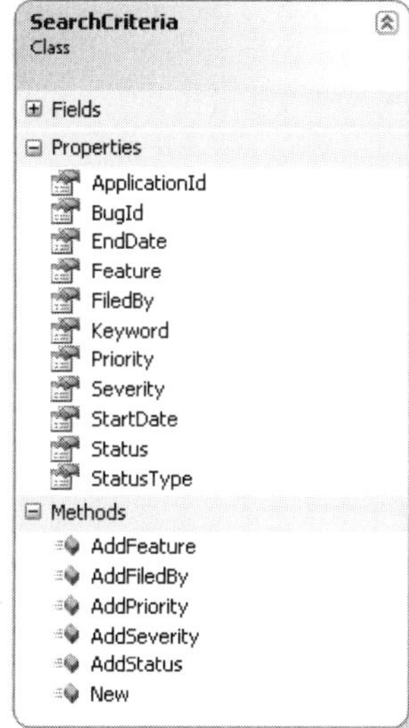

Figure 12-13

Instead of passing each of these criteria separately to this method, you can pass a single `SearchCriteria` object that exposes public properties for each of the criteria. The `GetBugList` method examines each of these properties and builds up the criteria parameters that are passed to the database. This is explained in more detail when the `BugManagerDB` class is examined in the next section.

The Data Access Layer

The data access layer in the Bug Base is designed to work with SQL Server only, because it uses types you find in the `System.Data.SqlClient` namespace, like the `SqlConnection` and `SqlCommand` objects. However, to make it easier to switch databases later in the lifetime of the application, none of the methods in the layer returns data provider–specific types. Instead, each of these methods returns standard types like a DataSet, or custom generics lists, like the bug list. If you decide to change the database you're using, all you need to change is the methods in the data access layer. As an alternative to changing the data access layer each time you want to target a different database, you can also recode the data access layer using the provider factories pattern that you saw in Chapter 6.

The only exception to this rule is the `GetList` method in the `ListManager` class. This method uses `SqlCacheDependency` classes to cache data from the database. The cache is invalidated whenever the underlying table in the database changes. SQL cache invalidation only works with SQL Server, so if you decide to switch databases, you'll need to modify the `GetList` method by either removing the code responsible for caching altogether or by implementing a different caching strategy.

The use of DataSets in the data access layer causes some overhead when compared to lightweight objects like the `DataReader`. However, this overhead can be minimized by implementing a thorough caching strategy, as is done by the methods in the `ListManager` class. By creating a `SqlCacheDependency` on the relevant tables in the database, you can in fact increase performance. All of the domain list tables, such as Severity and Reproducibility, are cached as DataSets in memory, so there is no need to hit the database each time you need them. Only when the table is changed — something that won't happen very often — is the item removed from the cache and needs to be reconstructed. This greatly reduces the number of calls made to the database, something that cannot be accomplished using `DataReader` objects.

Before discussing the data access layer, you should take a look at the design of the database first. Because each of the methods in the data access layer talks directly to the SQL Server 2005 database, it's important to understand how the database is designed. Figure 12-14 displays the database diagram for the Bug Base, showing most of its tables and relations.

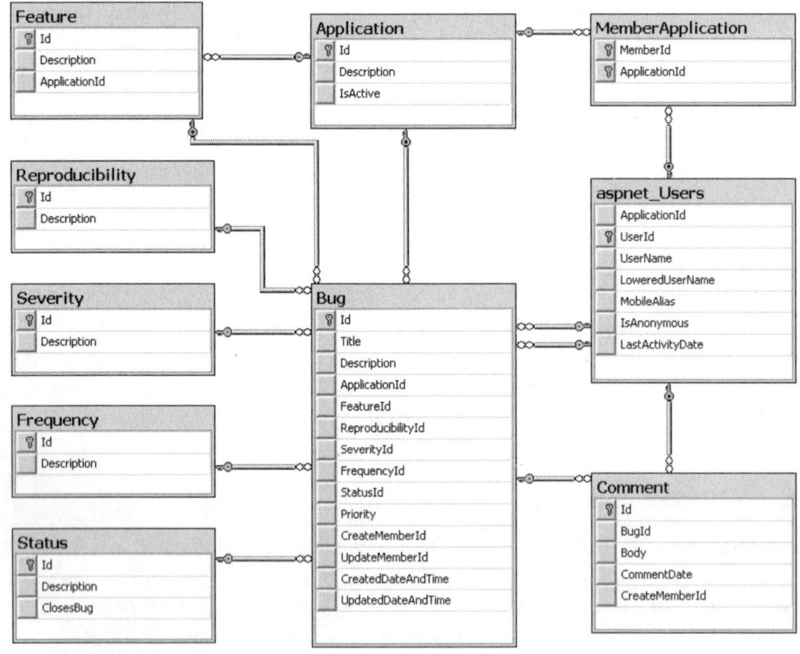

Figure 12-14

Figure 12-14 does not show the tables that have been added for the ASP.NET 2.0 Membership and Role providers, except for the aspnet_Users table that has relations with other tables in the Bug Base. The following table discusses each table in the database and its intended purpose:

Table Name	Description
Application	Holds a list with all the applications you can file bugs against. The column IsActive determines whether the application is still in use.
aspnet_Users	This table is added by the aspnet_regsql.exe tool when you enable the database for Membership and Roles. It holds the user accounts for the Bug Base application. The UserId, a GUID, is used to link other tables to this table.
Bug	The logged bugs are stored in this table. Besides a Title, a Description, and the date the bug was created and updated, this table largely consists of foreign keys pointing to *domain list* tables.
Comment	Holds comments that users can add to existing bugs. The CreateMemberId has a link to the aspnet_Users table to keep track of who added the comment.
Feature	Features are the main parts that make up your application. A bug should be logged against a specific feature, to make it clearer where the bug occurs and who's responsible for it. A feature is always tied to an application, so the Feature table has an ApplicationId column that points back to the Application table.
Frequency	The frequency of a bug defines how often, or by how many users, a bug will be encountered. This table holds a list with possible options that the user can choose from.
MemberApplication	Users should not be able to log bugs against any arbitrary application. An Administrator can assign members to a specific application through the web application. This assignment is stored in the junction table Member-Application.
Reproducibility	The reproducibility of a bug defines whether a bug is reproducible at all, and if so, how often. Just as the Frequency and Feature tables, this is a domain list table that stores the description for each item with a primary key. This key is then used as a foreign key in the Bug table.
Severity	The severity describes the impact of the bug. This domain list table holds the various options for this bug property.
Status	This table holds a list with possible status options for a bug. The ClosesBug column determines whether the bug becomes inactive with a specific status. This is the case for a status such as Deferred, Closed, or Not a Bug.

In addition to these 10 tables, the database also contains a number of stored procedures. Many of these procedures follow a strict naming pattern:

- `sproc`*`TableName`*`SelectSingleItem`
- `sproc`*`TableName`*`SelectList`
- `sproc`*`TableName`*`InsertUpdateSingleItem`

The first procedure selects a single record from a table referred to by *TableName*. The `WHERE` clause always uses at least the primary key of the table to limit the number of records to a maximum of 1, as in the following procedure that queries a feature from the database:

```
CREATE PROCEDURE sprocFeatureSelectSingleItem

@id int

AS

SELECT
  Id,
  Description,
  ApplicationId
FROM
  Feature
WHERE
  Id = @id
```

The `*SelectList` procedures query a list of related items from the database, such as a list of features, bugs, applications, and so on. They often look very similar to the `SelectSingleItem` bugs in terms of the columns they return, but they don't use the primary key of the table in the `WHERE` clause, and they often sort the result set using an `ORDER BY` clause.

All the `*InsertUpdate` procedures are capable of both inserting new and updating existing items in the database. They do that by looking at the `@Id` parameter passed to this procedure. If that parameter— which represents the primary key of the record in the table—is null, a new record is inserted. Otherwise, an existing record is updated where the `@id` parameter is used in the `WHERE` clause as demonstrated in the following code:

```
CREATE PROCEDURE sprocFrequencyInsertUpdateSingleItem

  @id int = null,
  @description nvarchar (100)

AS

  DECLARE @returnValue int

  IF (@id IS NULL) -- New Item
  BEGIN
      -- Insert the item here and return its new Id
      -- Insert code is left out of the example
      SELECT @returnValue = Scope_Identity()
  END
  ELSE
  BEGIN
      -- Update the item here and return the existing Id
      -- Update code is left out of the example
      SELECT @returnValue = @id
  END

  - Return the new or existing Id to the calling code
  RETURN @returnValue
```

Most of the items in the tables should have unique values. For example, there is no point in having two identical "Not reproducible" items in the Frequency table, because you wouldn't be able to distinguish between the two. Most of the `*InsertUpdate` procedures use the following code to check for duplicates:

```
IF (@id IS NULL) -- New Item
BEGIN
  IF NOT EXISTS (SELECT 1 FROM Frequency WHERE Description = @description)
  BEGIN
    -- Insert the item here and return its new Id
    -- Insert code is left out of the example
  END
  ELSE
  BEGIN
    -- There is already an item with the same description, so return -1
    SELECT @returnValue = -1 -- Item already exists
  END
END
ELSE
BEGIN
  IF NOT EXISTS (SELECT 1 FROM Frequency WHERE
         Description = @description AND Id <> @id)
  BEGIN
    -- Update the item here and return the existing Id
    -- Update code is left out of the example
  END
  ELSE
  BEGIN
    -- There is already an item with the same description, so return -1
    SELECT @returnValue = -1 -- Item already exists
  END
END

RETURN @returnValue
```

With this general pattern in mind it should be easy to understand how most of the procedures work. Not all procedures follow this strict pattern, so the few exceptions are explained during the discussion of the data access layer methods that use them.

These stored procedures are called from, and only called from, the methods in the four classes in the data access layer, which are discussed next.

BugManagerDB

Just as the `BugManager` class in the business layer, the `BugManagerDB` class (shown in Figure 12-15) is responsible for creating, changing, and getting bugs. Methods in this class talk directly to the database, using objects like the `SqlConnection` and `SqlCommand`. None of the methods contain SQL statements — all data access is done through the use of stored procedures. Most of the methods in this class accept a Guid that holds the current member's ID. This ID is used in all stored procedures to determine if the member has sufficient rights to access the data.

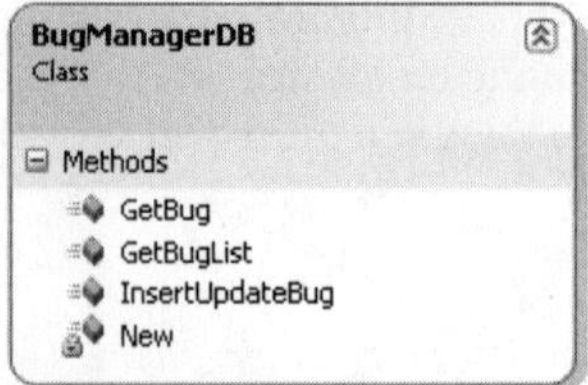

Figure 12-15

Similar to other classes you have seen in this book, the `BugManagerDB` class has only shared methods, so its constructor is marked as Private. The three other methods of the `BugManagerDB` class are listed in the following table:

Method	Return Type	Description
`GetBug (ByVal id As Integer, ByVal memberId As Guid)`	Bug	Retrieves a bug from the database, based on the ID passed to this method. Returns Nothing when the bug could not be found or the user doesn't have permission to view it.
`GetBugList ()`	List(Of Bug)	Retrieves a list of bugs from the database based on search criteria.
`InsertUpdateBug (ByVal theBug As Bug)`	Integer	Saves a fully populated `Bug` object in the database. The Integer returned from this method is the new or current ID of the bug in the database.

CommentManagerDB

The `CommentManagerDB` class, shown in Figure 12-16, performs the data access for the two methods defined in the `CommentManager` class.

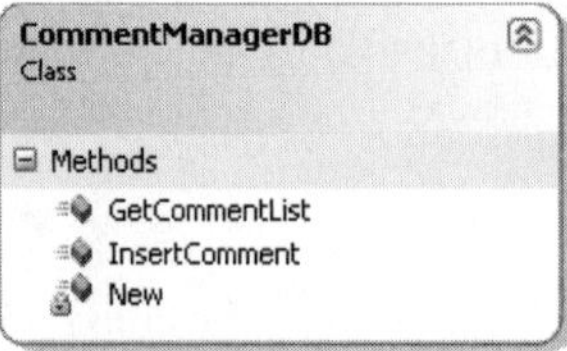

Figure 12-16

Just as the `CommentManager` class, the `CommentManagerDB` class has only two methods (besides its hidden constructor): one for getting a list of comments that belong to a certain bug, and one to create a new comment, as explained in the following table:

Method	Return Type	Description
`GetCommentList (ByVal bugId As Integer)`	DataSet	Returns a list of comments sorted by date in descending order for the requested bug.
`InsertComment (ByVal bugId As Integer, ByVal theBody As String, ByVal theMemberId As Guid)`	n/a	Inserts a new comment in the Comment table and associates it with the bug designated by `bugId`.

To get lists of items, such as Frequency and Severity, from the database, the application has a `ListManagerDB` class.

ListManagerDB

The `ListManagerDB` class has fewer methods than the `ListManager` class in the business layer because four of the methods in the `ListManager` class use the same `GetListItems` method. In addition to the `GetListItems` method, the `ListManagerDB` class has three other methods that map to the ones in the business layer (see Figure 12-17).

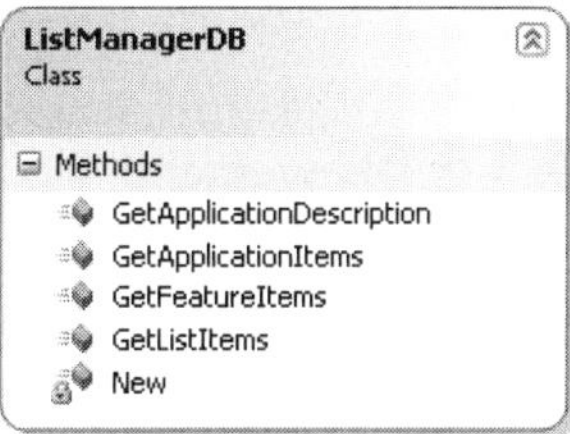

Figure 12-17

The following table gives a description of the entire `ListManagerDB` class:

Method	Return Type	Description
`GetApplicationDescription (ByVal applicationId As Integer`	String	Returns the full description of an application based on its ID passed to this method.
`GetApplicationItems (ByVal activeOnly As Boolean, ByVal memberId As Guid)`	DataSet	Gets a list of Applications from the and returns it as a DataSet. The `activeOnly` parameter is used to limit the list to active applications. The `memberId` can be used to limit the list to applications to which the member has access.
`GetFeatureItems (ByVal applicationId As Integer)`	DataSet	Gets a list of Feature items from the database and returns it as a DataSet.
`GetListItems (ByVal theListType As ListType)`	DataSet	Returns a list with the requested items as a DataSet. The `ListType` parameter determines the type of list to return.

The `Member` class in the business layer also has a counterpart in the data access layer: the `MemberManagerDB` class.

MemberManagerDB

The `MemberManagerDB` class has a single sub that can assign or remove a member from a specific application:

Method	Description
`ChangeMemberApplicationBinding (ByVal memberId As Guid, ByVal applicationId As Integer, ByVal mustAssign As Boolean)`	Assigns or removes a member from an application. When `mustAssign` is set to `True`, the member is assigned to the requested application; otherwise the member is removed.

In addition to the files in the BusinessLogic and DataAccess folders, two other files located in the App_Code folder are used throughout the site. The file AppConfiguration.vb contains a class with read-only properties that are essentially wrappers around the various `<appSettings>` keys in the Web.config file. Instead of typing `ConfigurationManager.ConnectionStrings("BugBase").ConnectionString` each time you need the connection string, you can now simply type `AppConfiguration.ConnectionString`.

The Helpers.vb file contains a few helper methods that are used in various pages in the site. The following section, "Code and Code Explanation," discusses some of the methods defined in the file, such as `SetMemberId` and `CheckApplicationState`. The `FormatGridViewPagerBar` method is used to format the pager bar that is displayed on each of `GridView` controls used in the application. That method isn't explained any further, but it has enough inline comments for you to understand how it works.

Now that you've seen the design of the Bug Base and all of its important classes, it's time to examine the .aspx pages, their code-behind files, and the implementation of the classes in the business logic and data access layers.

Code and Code Explanation

This section digs into each of the important pages and shows you how they interact with each other and use the classes in the business layer. Instead of listing each page separately, this section takes a more usage-oriented approach by examining typical workflows for the Bug Base and discusses each page you're visiting in the process. But before starting the tour, a few files need to be discussed first.

Root Files

In the root of the site you'll find a number of files that are critical for the Bug Base application. Not each file is explained completely, but instead the focus is on the most important areas.

Web.config

The Web.config file is the central place for storing application settings and configuration information. For the Bug Base, there are a few important bits in this file.

First of all, there is the connection string that is used throughout the site:

```
<add name="BugBase"
connectionString="server=(local)\SqlExpress;AttachDbFileName=|DataDirectory|BugBase
.mdf;Integrated Security=true;User Instance=true" />
```

This connection string points to a local name instance of SQL Server called SqlExpress and uses a database called BugBase. The `|DataDirectory|` token in the `AttachDbFileName` attribute tells SQL Server to try to automatically attach the database located in the App_Data folder of the web site.

The next important piece in the Web.config file is the setup for the Membership and Roles providers that are used in the Bug Base. These providers allow you to implement security on your site with little to no coding. By default, when you enable the Membership on a site, ASP.NET creates a default database called aspnetdb.mdf for you. For the Bug Base, a different database was created that, in addition to the tables and procedures for membership and roles, also holds the objects required for the Bug Base. To tell the ASP.NET run time where to look for that database, the `<providers>` section of the `<membership>` node in the Web.config file must be configured correctly:

```
<membership>
  <providers>
    <clear />
    <add name="AspNetSqlMembershipProvider"
      type="System.Web.Security.SqlMembershipProvider, System.Web,
           Version=2.0.0.0, Culture=neutral,
           PublicKeyToken=b03f5f7f11d50a3a"
      connectionStringName="BugBase"
      enablePasswordRetrieval="false"
      enablePasswordReset="true"
      requiresQuestionAndAnswer="false"
      applicationName="/"
      requiresUniqueEmail="true"
      passwordFormat="Hashed"
      maxInvalidPasswordAttempts="5"
      passwordAttemptWindow="10"
      passwordStrengthRegularExpression=""
    />
  </providers>
</membership>
```

The `<clear />` element removes the `AspNetSqlMembershipProvider` that is set up by default in the Machine.config file that applies to all sites on your server. The default setup points to the aspnetdb.mdf database mentioned earlier. Without removing this element, it's not possible to override the settings and have the `MembershipProvider` use the custom database instead. With the original element removed, you can add your own and then indicate you want to use the BugBase database by setting the `connectionString` attribute that in turn points to the connection string defined earlier. The other attributes have to do with security settings for the provider. Refer to the MSDN documentation for their usage.

The Bug Base uses a role-based security mechanism to determine which actions a user is allowed to perform. Just as with the `MembershipProvider`, ASP.NET 2.0 has a ready-made provider for this, called the `RoleProvider`. The section that sets up this provider in the Web.config file looks like this:

```
<roleManager defaultProvider="SqlProvider"
  enabled="true"
  cacheRolesInCookie="true"
  cookieName=".ASPROLES"
  cookieTimeout="30"
  cookiePath="/"
  cookieRequireSSL="false"
  cookieSlidingExpiration="true"
  cookieProtection="All"
>
  <providers>
    <add
      name="SqlProvider"
      type="System.Web.Security.SqlRoleProvider"
      connectionStringName="BugBase"
    />
  </providers>
</roleManager>
```

To show you the different options, the `<roleManager>` takes a different approach. Instead of using the `<clear />` element to clear a previously defined role manager (called `AspNetSqlRoleProvider` in the Machine.config file), this code block sets up an entirely new provider with the name of `SqlProvider`. Because there is no conflict with an existing provider on the system, you don't need to use `<clear />` first.

This is all that's required to configure the application so it uses the built-in Membership and Role providers.

The Web.config file also contains settings that determine if and to what e-mail address errors that occur should be e-mailed by code in the Global.asax file. The usage of these keys is further explained when the Global.asax file is discussed.

At the bottom of the Web.config file you find a number of `<location>` nodes. These nodes override the default `<authorization>` element to block or allow access to some files and folders for specific roles.

MasterPage.master

The master page defines the look and feel for all the pages in the site. This ensures a consistent layout throughout the site and makes it very easy to apply site-wide changes. The file consists largely of static HTML for the layout of the site, but a few sections are worth examining in greater detail.

The main menu that appears at the top of every page is made up of nested `<ul>` and `<li>` tags. The CSS file for the menu, Menu.css, is responsible for hiding or displaying the menus when you hover over them. Inside the menu a `LoginView` control is used to determine which menu items a user has access to, based on the current user's role. The following code snippet demonstrates this:

```
<asp:LoginView runat="server" ID="lvReporting">
<RoleGroups>
  <asp:RoleGroup Roles="Manager">
    <ContentTemplate>
     <li>
       <div>
         <a href="~/Reporting/Default.aspx" runat="server">Reporting</a>
       </div>
```

```
          <ul>
            <li>
              <a href="~/Reporting/Default.aspx" runat="server">Reports</a>
            </li>
          </ul>
        </li>
      </ContentTemplate>
    </asp:RoleGroup>
  </RoleGroups>
</asp:LoginView>
```

The content defined in the `ContentTemplate` is only accessible to users that are in the roles defined on the `RoleGroup` element, in this case the Manager role only.

The second important piece in the Master file is the use of `ContentPlaceHolder` controls. A `Content PlaceHolder` defines a region that can be overridden by pages that use the master page. The master page has two placeholders — one for the page title and one for content section of the page. The page title looks like this:

```
<h1>
  <asp:ContentPlaceHolder ID="plcTitle" runat="server"></asp:ContentPlaceHolder>
</h1>
```

The placeholder is put inside an `<h1>` tag so the content is always rendered as a heading. The placeholder for the main content section of each page looks very similar to the one for the heading.

Global.asax

The Global.asax file contains code for only one of the events, namely `Application_Error`. Whenever an unhandled exception occurs in the application, this event is fired. The code for this event builds up a string with the error details and sends it as an e-mail to the address configured in the Web.config. Before you enable this feature by setting `SendMailOnErrors` to `True`, make sure you also set valid e-mail addresses and an SMTP server in the Web.config file.

Web.sitemap

The final file in need of discussion is Web.sitemap. This file contains a lot of `siteMapNode` elements that define a conceptual map of the web site. This file is used as the data source for the `SiteMapPath` control in the BreadCrumb section of the master page. It's also used to feed the `TreeView` control used in the SiteMap.aspx page in the Help folder.

Now that you've seen some of the framework files, it's time to look at the files that are used in a typical workflow.

Filing a Bug

The central action of a Bug Base application is of course filing a bug, so it's a logical choice to look at that first. This section walks you through filing a new bug, explaining each of the important parts of the files you visit in the process. This section assumes that the Bug Base is installed at `http://localhost/BugBase`. Refer to the section called "Setting up the Bug Base" for more details about installing the application.

When you open the homepage of the Bug Base at http://localhost/BugBase the first time, you're presented with a Login screen instead. The <authorization> section in the Web.config file blocks access to each of the pages in the site to unauthorized users. When an unauthorized request is made, you're redirected to the Login page instead. This Login page contains very little code because most of the functionality required to log in a user is available out of the box. The markup section of the page contains just a Login control:

```
<asp:Login ID="Login1" runat="server" InstructionText="Before you can
    work with the Bug Base, you need to login.<br />Please type your user name and
    password and click the Log In button."
  TitleText="" DestinationPageUrl="~/Bugs/SwitchApplication.aspx"
  DisplayRememberMe="False">
</asp:Login>
```

The DestinationPageUrl attribute is set to SwitchApplication.aspx, the page the user is redirected to after a successful login. As a security measure, the Remember Me checkbox is disabled so users are required to log in each time they visit the bug base. If you get tired of entering your name and password every time, simply set the DisplayRememberMe attribute to True. This will display an additional Remember Me checkbox allowing you to automatically log in each time you return to the site.

There is no code in the code-behind file for this page — the authentication is completely carried out by the ASP.NET Framework.

When you supply a valid username and password (you can log in with the accounts listed at the beginning of this chapter) and click the Log In button you're automatically logged in. ASP.NET validates the user against the database, and when the login details are correct the roles for the user are retrieved and stored in an encrypted cookie.

After you log in you're redirected to SwitchApplication.aspx. Before you can work with most of the pages in the Bug Base you need to select an active application to work with. The SwitchApplication page allows you to select that application. In the Page_Load event of this page, the following code fires:

```
    Helpers.SetMemberId()
```

The SetMemberId method, which you'll find in the Helpers.vb file in the App_Code folder, tries to retrieve the current user's ProviderUserKey, which is the unique ID for the user. This key is stored in a session variable so it's available to all pages in the site. When the retrieval fails, the user is redirected back to Login.aspx.

The drop-down on the SwitchApplication page lists all the applications to which the user has access. The drop-down is filled by an ObjectDataSource control that calls an overloaded version of the method GetApplicationItems in the business layer:

```
<asp:ObjectDataSource ID="ObjectDataSource1" runat="server"
     SelectMethod="GetApplicationItems" TypeName="ListManager">
  <SelectParameters>
    <asp:SessionParameter Name="memberId" SessionField="MemberId" />
  </SelectParameters>
</asp:ObjectDataSource>
```

This method expects the current user's ID, which is passed to this method using a SessionParameter that retrieves the ID from a session variable called MemberId set earlier by the SetMemberId method.

The GetApplicationItems method in turn calls another overloaded version that delegates the call to a method with the same name in the data access layer. This method is responsible for retrieving the applications from the database. The code in this method is typical for many of the data access methods in the data access layer:

```
Public Shared Function GetApplicationItems( _
      ByVal activeOnly As Boolean, ByVal memberId As Guid) As DataSet

  Dim dataSet As DataSet = New DataSet()
  Dim sql As String = "sprocApplicationSelectList"

  Try
    Using myConnection As New SqlConnection(AppConfiguration.ConnectionString)
      Dim myCommand As SqlCommand = New SqlCommand(sql, myConnection)
      myCommand.CommandType = CommandType.StoredProcedure

      myCommand.Parameters.AddWithValue("@activeOnly", activeOnly)
      If Not memberId = Guid.Empty Then
        myCommand.Parameters.AddWithValue("@memberId", memberId)
      End If

      Dim myDataAdapter As SqlDataAdapter = New SqlDataAdapter()
      myDataAdapter.SelectCommand = myCommand
      myDataAdapter.Fill(dataSet)

      myConnection.Close()

      Return dataSet
    End Using
  Catch ex As Exception
    Throw
  End Try
End Function
```

First, the name of the stored procedure in the database is set. Then a new SqlConnection is created. The connection string comes from the custom class AppConfiguration that you saw earlier.

Then a SqlCommand is set up by assigning important properties such as the CommandText, CommandType, and Connection. The activeOnly parameter of the stored procedure determines whether all or only the active applications are to be retrieved from the database. As a second parameter, the ID of the member is passed. This ensures that you only get applications back that are assigned to the current user.

Finally, a SqlDataAdapter is created, which is then used to fill the DataSet with the results from the database using the SqlDataAdapter's Fill method.

The stored procedure that gets the items from the database looks like this:

```
CREATE PROCEDURE sprocApplicationSelectList
  @activeOnly bit = null,
  @memberId uniqueidentifier = null

  AS

  SELECT DISTINCT
```

```
    Id,
    Description,
    IsActive
  FROM
    Application
    LEFT OUTER JOIN MemberApplication
       ON Application.Id = MemberApplication.ApplicationId
  WHERE
    (IsActive = @activeOnly OR @activeOnly IS NULL)
    AND (MemberApplication.MemberId = @memberId OR @memberId IS NULL)
  ORDER BY
    Descriptionn
```

This stored procedure retrieves a list of all the applications that are assigned to the current member. You'll recall from the discussion of the data model that members are linked to applications with the junction table called MemberApplication. The code in the stored procedure uses that junction with the `LEFT OUTER JOIN` to limit the list of applications to those that the member has access to. The `LEFT OUTER JOIN` as opposed to an `INNER JOIN` is used to allow the procedure to return all applications regardless of the member's access rights when the parameter `@memberId` is null. This is used in the Management section that you see later.

When the `ObjectDataSource` in the .aspx page is done with the `GetApplicationItems` method, having retrieved the data, it fires its `Selected` event. In this event you can check if any data was returned from the database by looking at the `ReturnValue` property of the `e` argument. If the DataSet is empty — which it will be when the current member has no applications assigned — the drop-down is hidden and the user is presented with an error message:

```
Protected Sub ObjectDataSource1_Selected(ByVal sender As Object, _
      ByVal e As System.Web.UI.WebControls.ObjectDataSourceStatusEventArgs) _
      Handles ObjectDataSource1.Selected
  If CType(e.ReturnValue, DataSet).Tables.Count > 0 _
       AndAlso CType(e.ReturnValue, DataSet).Tables(0).Rows.Count = 0 Then
    lblErrorMessage.Visible = True
    lstApplication.Visible = False
    btnApply.Visible = False
  End If
End Sub
```

When the user has chosen an application from the drop-down and clicked the Apply button, the following code is executed:

```
Helpers.SetApplication (Convert.ToInt32( _
      lstApplication.SelectedValue), lstApplication.SelectedItem.Text)

Dim redirectUrl As String = "~/Bugs/"
If Request.QueryString.Get("OriginalPage") IsNot Nothing Then
  redirectUrl = Request.QueryString.Get("OriginalPage")
End If
Response.Redirect(redirectUrl)
```

This code sets the active application by calling `Helpers.SetApplication`, which stores the application ID in a session variable and then redirects the user to the previous page or to the default page in the Bugs folder when there was no previous page.

With all the required variables set up, it's time to file an actual bug. If you choose File New Bug from the main Bugs menu, the AddEditBug.aspx page located in the Bugs folder appears. This page is shown in Figure 12-3 at the beginning of this chapter.

Theoretically, the form on that page would have been an ideal candidate for the new `<asp:FormView>` control that allows you to quickly set up an Insert and Edit page. All you need to do is bind the `FormView` control to a few methods in your business layer, and Visual Web Developer will create the necessary insert and edit templates for you. However, the way the Bug class is designed proves to be problematic for the `FormView`. By design, the `FormView` can only work with direct properties such as the Bug's Title or Description. However, some of the Bug's properties are actually `NameValue` objects of which the `FormView` has no knowledge. Because of this lack of knowledge, the `FormView` isn't able to correctly bind to the data stored in the `Bug` object. Future versions of the .NET Framework may bring direct support for more complex properties like the `NameValue` object, but until that time you need to work around these limitations. Although there are ways to make the `FormView` work with the `NameValue` objects, the amount of code required to make that work isn't worth the benefit of the `FormView` in the first place. That's why the Insert and Update forms were built as a regular form with text boxes and drop-down controls nested in an HTML table. If you do decide to implement a `FormView` to bind to objects with complex custom properties, the trick is to use `Eval` in your binding syntax in the .aspx portion of the page instead of `Bind`. Then in the code-behind you can write code for the `FormView` control's `ItemInserting` and `ItemUpdating` events and create and assign new instances of your custom objects to the `e.Values` or `e.NewValues` properties of the arguments of the Inserting and Updating methods.

The AddEditBug.aspx page can be viewed in two different ways—one where each of the controls like the drop-downs are editable, and one where most of the controls have been replaced with static labels. The first view is used when any user is filing a new bug or when a developer or manager is editing a bug. The second view is used when a tester is editing a bug. Once a bug has been filed, a tester can no longer change the properties of a bug, so all controls are replaced with static text, showing the underlying values.

Determining which controls to show and which to hide takes place in the `LoadData` method, which is discussed after the exploration of `Page_Load`.

The first thing that the AddEditBug.aspx page does when it loads is execute the following code in the `Page_Load` event:

```
If Request.QueryString.Get("ApplicationId") IsNot Nothing Then
  Dim applicationId As Integer = _
          Convert.ToInt32(Request.QueryString.Get("ApplicationId"))
  Dim applicationDescription As String = _
          ListManager.GetApplicationDescription(applicationId)
  Helpers.SetApplicationSession(applicationId, applicationDescription)
End If

Helpers.CheckApplicationState ( _
    Server.UrlEncode(Page.AppRelativeVirtualPath & "?" & _
    Request.QueryString.ToString()))

If Request.QueryString.Get("Id") IsNot Nothing Then
  bugId = Convert.ToInt32(Request.QueryString.Get("Id"))
End If

If Not Page.IsPostBack Then
  LoadData()
End If
```

The first seven lines of code check if there is an `ApplicationId` on the query string. If there is one it switches to that application automatically. This is used in the Reporting page, described later in this chapter.

Then the application is validated. The AddEditBug page requires an active application stored in a session variable. If the variable isn't present, the `CheckApplicationState` method redirects the user to the SwitchApplication page and passes along the URL of the current page so the user can be redirected back after an application has been chosen.

If there is also an `Id` on the query string, it's converted to an Integer and stored in the private variable `bugId`. This `bugId` variable is later used in the code to determine the bug that must be retrieved from and stored in the database.

Finally, when the page is loading for the first time, all the controls are data-bound by calling `LoadData()`.

The `LoadData()` method starts off with binding the four drop-downs (lstFeature, lstFrequency, lstReproducibility, and lstSeverity) to their data sources. Each of these controls is bound to an `Object DataSource` control. These `ObjectDataSource` controls get their data by calling static methods in the `ListManager` class. Take a look at how the Frequency drop-down is bound to understand how this works. First, the page contains the following `DataSource` declaration:

```
<asp:ObjectDataSource ID="odsFrequency" runat="server"
       SelectMethod="GetFrequencyItems" TypeName="ListManager">
</asp:ObjectDataSource>
```

The page also contains the following declaration for a drop-down:

```
<asp:DropDownList ID="lstFrequency" runat="server"
     AppendDataBoundItems="True" DataSourceID="odsFrequency"
     DataTextField="Description" DataValueField="Id" Width="180px">
  <asp:ListItem Value="">Please make a selection</asp:ListItem>
</asp:DropDownList>
```

The drop-down is bound to the `DataSource` by setting its `DataSourceID` attribute. To ensure that the static "Please make a selection" list item remains present, `AppendDataBoundItems` is set to `True`.

When the drop-down is data-bound in the code-behind, the `ObjectDataSource` control's `DataBind` method is invoked. The control then calls the `GetFrequencyItems` method located in the `ListManager` class. This method calls a private method called `GetListItem` and passes it an enumeration of `ListType .Frequency`. The `GetListItem` method then gets the requested items from the database and stores them in the cache with a `SqlCacheDependency` attached to it. This ensures that the cached item is invalidated when the table used for the dependency is changed. The `GetListItem` method looks like this:

```
Private Shared Function GetListItems( _
    ByVal myListType As ListType) As DataSet

  Dim listItems As DataSet
    Dim cacheKey As String = myListType.ToString() + "DataSet"
    Dim tableName As String = myListType.ToString()

    Dim SqlDep As SqlCacheDependency = Nothing

    If HttpContext.Current.Cache(myListType.ToString() _
```

```
        + "DataSet") IsNot Nothing Then
      listItems = CType(HttpContext.Current.Cache(cacheKey), DataSet)
    Else
      ' (Re)create the data and store it in the cache
      listItems = ListManagerDB.GetListItems(myListType)

      Try
        ' Create a new SqlCacheDependency.
        SqlDep = New SqlCacheDependency( _
            AppConfiguration.DatabaseName, tableName)

      Catch exDNEFNE As DatabaseNotEnabledForNotificationException
        ' Handle DatabaseNotEnabledForNotificationException
        Throw
      Catch exTNEFNE As TableNotEnabledForNotificationException
        Throw
      Finally
        HttpContext.Current.Cache.Insert(cacheKey, listItems, SqlDep)
      End Try
    End If

    Return listItems

  End Function
```

This method first tries to get the requested item from the cache. If it exists, it's cast to a DataSet so it can be returned to the calling code. If the item no longer exists, it's created by calling `GetListItems` in the `ListManagerDB` class and passing it the requested `ListType`. That method returns a DataSet that is stored in the cache using a `SqlCacheDependency`.

Before you can use `SqlCacheDependencies` in your application, you need to set up your database to support them. The database that comes with the Bug Base has already been set up for SQL cache invalidation, but if you're using your own database, or need to enable caching on an existing database, use the following command from your ASP.NET 2.0 installation folder (located under `%WinDir%\Microsoft.NET\Framework`):

```
aspnet_regsql.exe -S (local)\InstanceName -E -ed -d DatabaseName -et -t TableName
```

This registers the table you specify with *TableName* in the database *DatabaseName*. You can type `aspnet_regsql.exe /?` to get a help screen for this application.

The constructor for the `SqlCacheDependency` expects the name of the database you're setting up the dependency against. Instead of hard-coding *BugBase* in the constructor method, there is a shared and public property in the `AppConfiguration` class that returns the name of the database. With that property, you can simply pass `AppConfiguration.DatabaseName` as the first argument to the constructor.

The constructor for the `SqlCacheDependency` class throws errors when either the database or the requested table hasn't been set up for SQL caching. When an error is thrown, you simply rethrow it using the `Throw` keyword, so it will bubble up in the application to eventually cause an error that is caught by the `Application_Error` handler in the Global.asax file. If you don't want to use SQL caching because you're using a different database, you can simply remove the caching code from the `GetListItems` method. Alternatively, you can decide to store the data in the cache for a limited amount of time. This way you still have the benefits of caching, but you run the risk of working with stale data.

The code for the GetListItems method in the ListManagerDB class is very similar to the code you saw earlier for the GetApplicationItems. The only thing that's different is the way the name of the stored procedure is determined by looking at the ListType argument that is passed to this method:

```
Dim sql As String = ""
Select Case theListType
  Case ListType.Frequency
    sql = "sprocFrequencySelectList"
  Case ListType.Reproducibility
    sql = "sprocReproducibilitySelectList"
  Case ListType.Severity
    sql = "sprocSeveritySelectList"
  Case ListType.Status
    sql = "sprocStatusSelectList"
  Case Else
    Throw New ArgumentException("ListType must be a valid " & _
      "ListType enum. Current value is " + theListType.ToString)
End Select
```

This process is repeated for each of the four drop-downs at the top of the page: lstFeature, lstReproducibility, lstFrequency, and lstSeverity.

With the four drop-downs bound to their data source the next step is to retrieve the bug from the database, but only when AddEditBug.aspx is in edit mode. Retrieval of a bug is done with the BugManager class:

```
Dim myBugManager As BugManager = New BugManager(Helpers.GetMemberId)
```

A new instance of the BugManager is created and the current member's ID is passed to the constructor by calling Helpers.GetMemberId, which simply returns the session variable MemberId as a Guid. The MemberId is used for access rights checks in each of the BugManagerDB methods.

```
Dim myBug As Bug = myBugManager.GetBug(bugId)
```

The Bug object is retrieved by calling GetBug and passing it the ID of the requested bug. The GetBug method checks if a valid member ID has been passed and then delegates the responsibility of retrieving the bug from the database to the GetBug method in the BugManagerDB class. This method is similar to other methods in the data access layer when it comes to setting and opening the SQL connection. What's different is that a SqlDataReader is used to hold the data instead of a DataSet. This DataReader is then used to fill the properties of the Bug object like this:

```
Using myReader As SqlDataReader = _
    myCommand.ExecuteReader(CommandBehavior.CloseConnection)
  If myReader.Read Then
    theBug = New Bug(myReader.GetInt32(myReader.GetOrdinal("Id")))
    theBug.Title = myReader.GetString(myReader.GetOrdinal("Title"))
    ' ... other properties are set here
  Else
    theBug = Nothing
  End If
  myReader.Close()
End Using
```

If the bug was found in the database, a new `Bug` object is created and then all of its public properties are set. Notice that `GetOrdinal` is used to retrieve a column's index in the `DataReader`. This is because each of the `Get*` methods expects an Integer with the column's position and not a string with the column name. Using `GetOrdinal` might make this code just a little slower, but it also makes it a lot more readable and flexible. Instead of knowing the exact location of a column in the result set, all you need to remember is the column's name.

You pass the enumeration `CommandBehavior.CloseConnection` to the `ExecuteReader` method to ensure that the connection is closed when the reader is closed at the end of the `Using` block. This is good programming practice, because it explicitly closes the connection object, freeing up valuable resources.

Six of the properties of the `Bug` class are `NameValue` objects to expose both their internal ID and the user-friendly description. The `NameValue` objects are retrieved from the `DataReader` like this:

```
theBug.Status = New NameValue(myReader.GetInt32( _
    myReader.GetOrdinal("StatusId")), _
    myReader.GetString(myReader.GetOrdinal("StatusDescription")))
```

This code creates a new `NameValue` object, passes the ID and Name to the constructor of that class, and then assigns the object to the `Bug` object's `Status` property. This allows you to access the property in your code like this, for example:

```
lblStatus.Text = theBug.Status.Name
```

When the bug is not found in the database, or the user doesn't have enough rights to view it, `Nothing` is returned. Therefore, in the calling code back in AddEditBug.aspx you need to check if the object equals `Nothing`. If the bug is not `Nothing`, the bug's properties are bound to the form controls:

```
If myBug IsNot Nothing Then
  If User.IsInRole("Developer") OrElse User.IsInRole("Manager") Then
    If lstFeature.Items.FindByValue( _
            myBug.Feature.Value.ToString()) IsNot Nothing Then
      lstFeature.Items.FindByValue(myBug.Feature.Value.ToString()).Selected = True
    End If
    ' ... other controls are set here
```

This code executes only when the current user is in one of the required roles. If the user is a not a developer or a manager, she is not allowed to change any of the existing fields; static labels are shown instead, as in Figure 12-18.

Feature	Login Module	**Reproducibility**	Once
Frequency	Few users will encounter	**Severity**	Enhancement Request
Priority	3	**Status**	Open

Figure 12-18

Whereas a developer or a manager sees Figure 12-19.

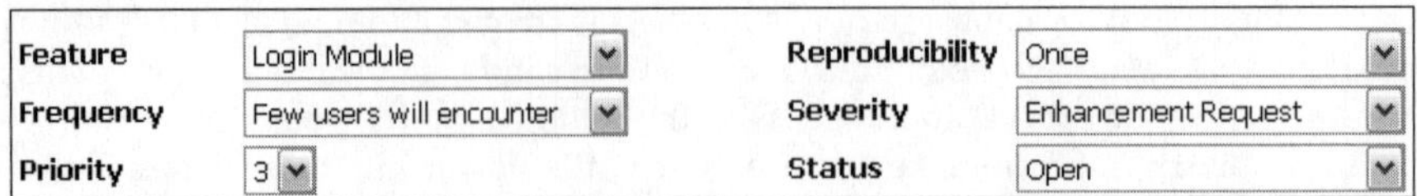
Feature	Login Module	Reproducibility	Once
Frequency	Few users will encounter	Severity	Enhancement Request
Priority	3	Status	Open

Figure 12-19

The rest of the code in this method is responsible for hiding or displaying the relevant controls on the page.

When the Save button is clicked, `btnSave_Click` is called and the page is validated by calling `Page.Validate()`. When the page is completely valid, a new `Bug` object is created or an existing one is retrieved from the database using an instance of the `BugManager`:

```
Dim memberId As Guid = Helpers.GetMemberId()
Dim myBugManager As BugManager = New BugManager(memberId)
Dim myBug As Bug
If bugId > 0 Then
  myBug = myBugManager.GetBug(bugId)
Else
  myBug = New Bug()
  myBug.Application.Value = Helpers.GetApplicationId()
  myBug.CreateMemberId = memberId
End If
```

Next, each of the bug's properties is retrieved from the form controls:

```
myBug.Title = txtTitle.Text
myBug.Feature.Value = Convert.ToInt32(lstFeature.SelectedValue)
myBug.Frequency.Value = Convert.ToInt32(lstFrequency.SelectedValue)
myBug.Priority = Convert.ToInt32(lstPriority.SelectedValue)
' ... other properties are set here

If bugId > 0 Then
  ' Only when we're editing the bug, update the status field.
  myBug.Status.Value = Convert.ToInt32(lstStatus.SelectedValue)
End If
```

Notice that you only need to set the `Value` of each of the `NameValue` properties. The database only works with the internal IDs and doesn't care about the "friendly descriptions" of these objects.

Once all the public properties have been set, the bug is saved by calling `myBugManager.InsertUpdateBug(myBug)` on the `BugManager` class. The `InsertUpdateBug` method passes the bug to a method with the same name in the data access layer that saves the bug in the database:

```
Public Shared Function InsertUpdateBug(ByVal theBug As Bug) As Integer
  Dim sql As String = "sprocBugInsertUpdateSingleItem"

  Try
    Using myConnection As New SqlConnection(AppConfiguration.ConnectionString)

      Dim myCommand As SqlCommand = New SqlCommand(sql, myConnection)
      myCommand.CommandType = CommandType.StoredProcedure

      If theBug.Id > 0 Then
```

```
          myCommand.Parameters.AddWithValue("@id", theBug.Id)
        End If
        myCommand.Parameters.AddWithValue("@title", theBug.Title)
        myCommand.Parameters.AddWithValue("@description", theBug.Description)
        ' ... other properties are set here
        myCommand.Parameters.AddWithValue("@frequencyId", theBug.Frequency.Value)

        Dim myParam As SqlParameter = New SqlParameter
        myParam.Direction = ParameterDirection.ReturnValue
        myCommand.Parameters.Insert(0, myParam)

        myConnection.Open()
        myCommand.ExecuteNonQuery()
        theBug.Id = CType(myParam.Value, Integer)
        myConnection.Close()

        Return theBug.Id
      End Using
    Catch ex As Exception
      Throw
    End Try
  End Function
```

When the `Bug.Id` is greater than zero, it is passed to the stored procedure by the `AddWithValue` method that creates a new parameter and sets the ID of the bug. Otherwise, the parameter remains null. The stored procedure knows that when the `@id` parameter is null it should insert a new bug item or update the item otherwise. Just as with the `Id` property, the code adds parameters for each of the public properties of the bug. At the end, an additional `ReturnValue` parameter is set up that retrieves the ID of the bug once it has been inserted or updated. With all the parameters set up, `ExecuteNonQuery` is called to save the bug in the database.

After the bug has been saved, the user is redirected back to the Bug List page, where the new bug appears at the top of the list. From this list, you can click the bug's title to open the ViewBug page. This page displays a read-only version of the bug that is easy to print. The concepts used in this page are very similar to those in the AddEditBug page, without the additional complexity of hiding and displaying the relevant controls.

This concludes the process of inserting and updating bugs. The next step is to look at how you can retrieve bugs that have been filed from the database.

Searching and Viewing Bugs

When the number of bugs you have logged in the Bug Base grows, it becomes harder to manage them. The Bug List page for an application allows you to select active or inactive bugs, allowing you to focus on the open bugs. However, even that list of open bugs may grow quite long. And what if you wanted to find an older bug you know exists that has similar characteristics as a new bug you have found? With just the bug list pages, you'd be browsing through the list of bugs forever.

So to make it easier to find bugs, you need a good search tool. Fortunately, the Bug Base comes with a useful search tool. In fact, it comes with two search tools! On the main Bugs menu you find the Search Bugs item, which allows you to search for bugs in the current application. Under Reporting you find the

Reports menu item that also allows you to search for bugs. Both search pages have a lot in common, but there are some important differences.

First of all, the Reports page is only accessible by members of the Manager group. If you're not in that group, the menu item Reporting is not even visible. On the reporting page, you can search for bugs in all applications at the same time, whereas on the Search page your search is limited to the current application. This distinction is necessary to prevent testers or developers on one application from seeing bugs logged in an application they don't have access to. Another difference is the possibility to search for a bug by its ID or a keyword on the search page. When searching for a bug, this is very useful because bugs are often referred to by their ID. On the reporting page, this option makes less sense. Usually, the purpose of the reporting page in a bug tracking tool is to get a list of bugs of a certain status, such as all open bugs. This allows a manager to quickly view the progress made in an application, or get a list of all bugs that still need work.

Despite the differences in functionality from a user's point of view, these two pages work pretty much the same in terms of code. The next section dissects the Reports page and shows you how it works. Once you understand the Reports page you should have no trouble finding out what goes on in the Search page.

When you open the Reports page from the Reporting menu, you get the screen displayed in Figure 12-20.

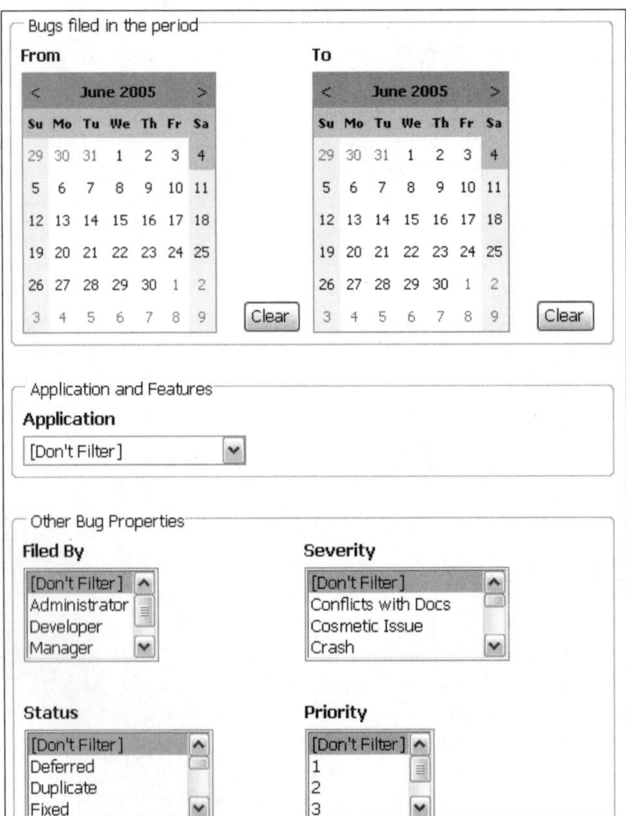

Figure 12-20

This form allows a user to set up a list of search criteria including the period the bug was filed, the application and its features, the person who filed the bug, and the severity, the status, and the priority. Once you choose an application from the Application drop-down, the page reloads to show you a list of features for the selected application. Except for the Application drop-down, you can select multiple options for all the other lists. Once you click the Report button, you get a list with the bugs that match your criteria, as shown in Figure 12-21.

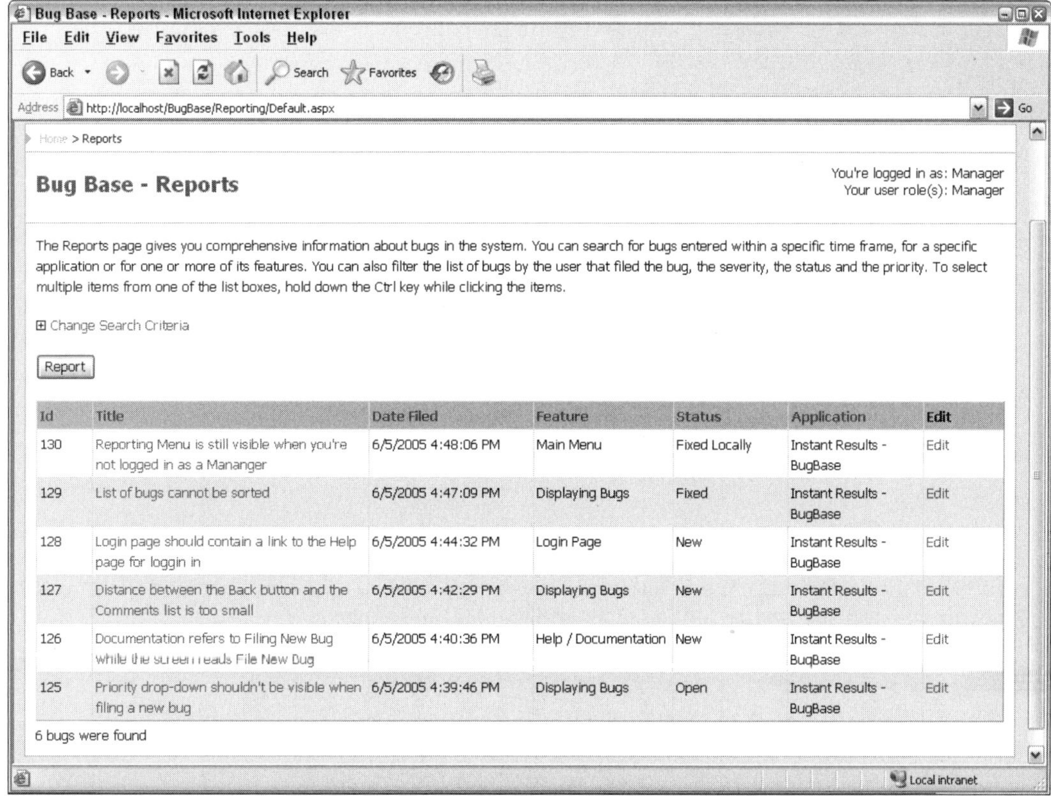

Figure 12-21

If you want to change your search criteria, click the Change Search Criteria link at the top of the page. This reveals the form controls from Figure 12-20 again.

Take a look at the markup of Default.aspx in the Reports folder to see how this page works. Most of the concepts used in this page have already been used in other pages, such as AddEditBug. The page consists largely of controls that are bound to `ObjectDataSource` controls, which in turn are bound to methods in the business layer. A few things are different, though, and worth examining more closely. First of all, there's the `ObjectDataSource` called `odsMembers` created with the following code:

```
<asp:ObjectDataSource ID="odsMembers" runat="server"
      SelectMethod="GetAllUsers"
      TypeName="System.Web.Security.Membership"
>
```

Instead of calling a method in the business layer of the Bug Base, this control is hooked up to the Membership provider and calls its `GetAllUsers` method. This method then returns a collection of `MembershipUser` objects. A `MemberhipUser` has a `ProviderKey` and a `UserName`, the two fields that are used as the `DataKeyField` and `DataValueField` of the drop-down that displays the users:

```
<asp:ListBox ID="lstMember" runat="server" DataSourceID="odsMembers"
     DataTextField="UserName" DataValueField="ProviderUserKey"
     AppendDataBoundItems="True" SelectionMode="Multiple">
  <asp:ListItem Value="" Selected="True">[Don't Filter]</asp:ListItem>
</asp:ListBox>
```

Getting a list of users in a web page doesn't get any easier than this!

The next piece of code you should look at is the code for the drop-down that displays the applications. The drop-down has its `AutoPostBack` property set to `True`, which means the page is posted back to the server whenever a new item is chosen in the drop-down. In the code-behind for the page you'll find a method that fires whenever a postback occurs:

```
Protected Sub lstApplications_SelectedIndexChanged( _
     ByVal sender As Object, ByVal e As System.EventArgs) _
     Handles lstApplications.SelectedIndexChanged
  lstFeature.Visible = True
  lstFeature.Items.Clear()
  lstFeature.Items.Insert(0, New ListItem("[Don't Filter]", ""))
  lstFeature.Items(0).Selected = True
End Sub
```

Inside this method, the `Visible` property of the Feature drop-down is set to `True`, and a new, static item is added to the list. By making the control visible, the ASP.NET run time knows that it now has to bind the control to its associated `ObjectDataSource` that looks like this:

```
<asp:ObjectDataSource ID="odsFeature" runat="server"
     SelectMethod="GetFeatureItems" TypeName="ListManager">
  <SelectParameters>
    <asp:ControlParameter ControlID="lstApplications"
         DefaultValue="-1" Name="applicationId"
         PropertyName="SelectedValue" Type="Int32" />
    </SelectParameters>
</asp:ObjectDataSource>
```

This `ObjectDataSource` control has a `SelectParameter` of type `ControlParameter` that looks at the `SelectedValue` property of the Applications drop-down and passes it to the `GetFeatureItems` method. This method, placed in the business layer, only returns the features for the requested application.

The `ObjectDataSource` for the feature then fires its `Selected` event when it's done retrieving the data. Inside this method for this event, the Feature drop-down is hidden when there are no items returned from the database:

```
Protected Sub odsFeature_Selected(ByVal sender As Object, ByVal e _
      As System.Web.UI.WebControls.ObjectDataSourceStatusEventArgs) _
      Handles odsFeature.Selected
  Dim featureListVisible As Boolean = _
```

```
        (CType(e.ReturnValue, DataSet)).Tables(0).Rows.Count > 0
    lstFeature.Visible = featureListVisible
    lblFeature.Visible = featureListVisible
  End Sub
```

The first line of code in this method looks at the number of rows in the table in the DataSet, exposed by the `ReturnValue` property of the `e` argument. When the number is greater than zero, `featureListVisible` is `True` and the list is visible. Otherwise, the list is made invisible.

All the other drop-down controls don't need additional code to function. Because they are always visible, the ASP.NET Framework binds them when the page loads. And with their `EnableViewState` property set to `True` (the default), they automatically maintain their state so there is no need to bind them again on postback.

There is, however, one control that must be bound manually and that's the `GridView`. There is no need to bind that control on every page load or postback, because you should be able to make a detailed selection first. Once the selection is complete, you should click the Report button to get the selected bugs from the database. The `Click` event of the Report button causes the following chain of events to fire.

First, the `LoadData` method is called:

```
  Private Sub LoadData()
    GridView1.Visible = True
    GridView1.DataSourceID = "odsBugList"
    GridView1.DataBind()
  End Sub
```

In this method the `GridView` is made visible and then its `DataSourceID` is set to the ID of the `odsBugList` that is defined in the markup of the page. Finally, by calling `DataBind()` on the `GridView` control, `odsBugList` gets the data from the database so it can be displayed on the page. Easy as that last sentence sounds, it's actually quite a complicated process. You need to look at a few sections in more detail to understand how this works.

First, there is the `ObjectDataSource` control in the markup that is set up to call `GetBugList` in the business layer:

```
  <asp:ObjectDataSource ID="odsBugList" runat="server"
          SelectMethod="GetBugList" SortParameterName="sortExpression"
          TypeName="BugManager" EnableViewState="False">
    <SelectParameters>
      <asp:Parameter Name="sortExpression" Type="String" />
      <asp:Parameter Name="searchCriteria" />
    </SelectParameters>
  </asp:ObjectDataSource>
```

In the discussion of the `BugManager` class you learned that the `GetBugList` has two overloads. The `ObjectDataSource` is targeting the overload with two parameters: the first is a string holding the name of a property the bug list should be sorted on, and the other is a `SearchCriteria` object that holds a range of criteria that the list should be filtered on:

```
  Public Function GetBugList(ByVal sortExpression As String, _
              ByVal searchCriteria As SearchCriteria) As List(Of Bug)
```

How is ASP.NET able to pass the correct parameters to this method? If you look at the definition for the `ObjectDataSource` you see two `<asp:Parameter>` attributes defined in the `<SelectParameters>` section. The first one holds the name of the argument of the `SelectMethod` that is used when sorting. Here the `GridView` and the `DataSource` play nice together. Whenever you click one of the column headings of the `GridView`, the `SortExpression` of the `GridView`'s column is passed into the `SelectMethod` defined on the `DataSource`. Eventually, this `sortExpression` ends up in the `GetBugList` method where it's used to sort the list of bugs. This is examined in more detail later.

The second `<SelectParameter>`—called `searchCriteria`—is set up in the code-behind for the page. To see how that object is created and passed to the `GetBugList`, you first need to understand how the `ObjectDataSource` sets up the `BugManager` it's going to use. Whenever the `ObjectDataSource` tries to bind itself to its `DataSource` (triggered by calling `DataBind` on the `GridView` in the `LoadData()` method), the `DataSource` fires its `ObjectCreating` event. Inside this event, you can assign the `BugManager` to the `DataSource` object:

```
Protected Sub odsBugList_ObjectCreating(ByVal sender As Object, _
      ByVal e As System.Web.UI.WebControls.ObjectDataSourceEventArgs) _
      Handles odsBugList.ObjectCreating
  e.ObjectInstance = myBugManager
End Sub
```

The `myBugManager` object is defined as a private variable at the top of the code-behind for the Reports page and instantiated in `Page_Load`. In other circumstances there is often no need for this additional code; the `ObjectDataSource` itself is able to figure out how to create a new instance of the object it's bound to. However, in the Reports page you need access to an instance of the `BugManager` class to get the total number of bugs it's holding, using the `Count` property.

Once the `ObjectDataSource` is done with the `Creating` method, it fires its `Selecting` event. This event fires right before the data is retrieved, so it's a perfect location to set up the values for the arguments that are going to be passed to `GetBugList`. In the case of the Reports page, a `searchCriteria` object is passed:

```
Protected Sub odsBugList_Selecting(ByVal sender As Object, _
        ByVal e As System.Web.UI.WebControls.ObjectDataSourceSelectingEventArgs) _
        Handles odsBugList.Selecting

  ' Build up a SearchCriteria object and set its properties
  Dim searchCriteria As SearchCriteria = New SearchCriteria()

  ' Set the Application when selected
  If Not lstApplications.SelectedValue = "" Then
    searchCriteria.ApplicationId = Convert.ToInt32(lstApplications.SelectedValue)
  End If

  ' Set the Feature when selected
  For Each myItem As ListItem In lstFeature.Items
    If myItem.Selected = True Then
      searchCriteria.AddFeature(myItem.Value)
    End If
  Next

  ' ... other properties are set here

  ' Set Start Date
```

```
    If Not calStartDate.SelectedDate = DateTime.MinValue Then
      searchCriteria.StartDate = calStartDate.SelectedDate
    End If

    ' ... other properties are set here

    ' Assign the SearchCriteria object to the InputParameters
    ' collection of the DataSource
    e.InputParameters.Item(1) = searchCriteria
  End Sub
```

In this method a new `SearchCriteria` object is instantiated. Then the values of each of the controls on the page used for filtering are added to the `SearchCriteria` object. You'll notice that for some properties a method is used that starts with `Add`. This method adds the value passed to it to an internal comma-separated list. So, if you selected the features 1, 4, and 16 in the list, the internal variable would hold 1,4,16. When the stored procedure for the `GetBugList` method is explained, you discover how this list is used.

Once the properties for the `ObjectDataSource` are set up, the object is assigned to the `InputParameters` collection of the `ObjectDataSourceSelectingEventArgs` object, using `e.InputParameters.Item(1) = searchCriteria`.

The next step in the process is the actual call to `GetBugList` in the business layer. This method simply checks if the internal`_memberId` field is valid, and then calls into the `BugManagerDB` class, passing up the `memberId` and the `searchCriteria` object:

```
  _theBugList = BugManagerDB.GetBugList(searchCriteria, _memberId)
```

The `GetBugList` method in the data access layer and its associated stored procedure are probably the most complicated pieces of code in the application, so again they are explained in great detail. First take a look at the beginning of the function:

```
  Public Shared Function GetBugList(ByVal searchCriteria As SearchCriteria, _
            ByVal memberId As Guid) As List(Of Bug)
    Dim sql As String = "sprocBugSelectList"
    Dim theBugList As New List(Of Bug) ' BugList to hold all the bugs
    Try
      Using myConnection As New SqlConnection(AppConfiguration.ConnectionString)
        Dim myCommand As SqlCommand = New SqlCommand(sql, myConnection)
        myCommand.CommandType = CommandType.StoredProcedure
```

The syntax `As New List(Of Bug)` creates a new strongly typed list that can hold `Bug` objects. This is part of the new generics feature in .NET 2.0 languages that allow you to quickly create custom strongly typed lists and collections without the need to write a lot of code. This code simply creates a new `List`, which is basically an array that can hold only `Bug` items and whose size automatically changes when you add new items to it.

Next, the properties of the `searchCriteria` object are added as parameters on the `SqlCommand` object:

```
    If searchCriteria IsNot Nothing Then
      ' Add the Application Id
      If searchCriteria.ApplicationId <> -1 Then
```

```
        myCommand.Parameters.AddWithValue("@applicationId", _
             searchCriteria.ApplicationId)
      End If
```

This code creates a new parameter called `@applicationId` and assigns it the value held in the `ApplicationId` property of the `searchCriteria` if it has been set. This process is repeated for each of the properties of the `SearchCriteria` class. Notice that the comma-separated list of values for properties like `Status` and `Severity` are simply passed as strings to the stored procedure:

```
        ' Add the severity, which can be a comma separated list
        If Not searchCriteria.Severity = String.Empty Then
          myCommand.Parameters.AddWithValue("@severity", searchCriteria.Severity)
        End If
```

Then a temporary bug is declared and the connection is opened:

```
Dim theBug As Bug  'Temp bug to add to the BugList

myConnection.Open()
```

The bugs are retrieved from the database using a `SqlDataReader` that is executed with the following code:

```
Using myReader As SqlDataReader = _
                myCommand.ExecuteReader(CommandBehavior.CloseConnection)
  While myReader.Read()

    ' Add bugs retrieved from the database to the list here.
    ' This is shown later

  End While
  myReader.Close()
End Using
```

The code for the stored procedure that is used to feed this `SqlDataReader` is quite lengthy, so it doesn't appear here; rather, this section focuses on the important bits. The complete code for the BugBase application is available on the companion CD-ROM and can also be downloaded from `www.wrox.com`. The first important thing you'll notice in the procedure is the use of the `dbo.fnSplit` function in some of the `JOIN`s:

```
LEFT OUTER JOIN dbo.fnSplit(@feature, ',') joinFeature ON Bug.FeatureId LIKE
     joinFeature.[value]
```

Remember that some of the `SearchCriteria` properties were actually comma-separated strings with values? This is where those come into play. Here you'll discover how it works for the Bug's feature, but the principle applies to each of the other properties that use the `fnSplit` function.

To select the bugs that are filed for one or more features, you would normally use a SQL `IN` statement like this:

```
SELECT Bug.Id FROM Bugs WHERE Bug.FeatureId IN (1, 4, 16)
```

This selects all the bugs that are filed for either feature 1, 4, or 16. This `IN` statement cannot be used in a stored procedure directly because SQL Server does not support parameterized `IN` filters. One way to work around that is to create your SQL statement dynamically in the stored procedure and then use `EXEC` to execute it. However, in addition to the messy code this creates, it also opens up SQL Server to all kinds of SQL injection attacks if no additional security measures are taken.

Instead, you should use a function that accepts the comma-separated list of IDs and returns it as a table object that can be used in a `JOIN`. If you think of the result of the `fnSplit` function as a table that has one column called `value` that holds three rows with 1, 4, and 16, the `JOIN` becomes a lot easier to understand:

```
LEFT OUTER JOIN FeatureTempTable ON Bug.FeatureId LIKE
FeatureTempTable.[value]
```

This `JOIN` links the list of bugs to the Features in the temp table returned by the function.

You'll find the `dbo.fnSplit` function — taken directly from Microsoft's MSDN web site — under the Functions node of the Database Explorer in Visual Web Developer. The function has inline comments describing how it works.

The `WHERE` clause in the procedure eventually filters the bugs that match the items in the temp tables:

```
AND ((Bug.FeatureId LIKE joinFeature.[value]) OR (@feature IS NULL))
```

This statement filters the bug list to those that have a direct match to a record in the temp for Features. If the parameter `@feature` is null, no filtering takes place and all records are returned.

This process is repeated for the other bug properties such as the `Severity` and `Status`, resulting in a sophisticated filter on the bug list.

Once the procedure is done selecting the right bugs from the Bug table, it returns a result set back to the `SqlDataReader` in the `GetBugList` method. The code then loops through each of the items in the `SqlDataReader`, creates a new instance of a `Bug` object, sets all of its properties by filling them with data from the database, and then adds the new `Bug` object to the `BugList`, as illustrated by the following highlighted code:

```
Using myReader As SqlDataReader = _
      myCommand.ExecuteReader(CommandBehavior.CloseConnection)
  While myReader.Read()
    theBug = New Bug(myReader.GetInt32(myReader.GetOrdinal("Id")))
    theBug.Title = myReader.GetString(myReader.GetOrdinal("Title"))
    theBug.Description = myReader.GetString(myReader.GetOrdinal("Description"))
    ' ... other properties are set here
    theBug.Application = New NameValue(myReader.GetInt32( _
           myReader.GetOrdinal("ApplicationId")), myReader.GetString( _
           myReader.GetOrdinal("ApplicationDescription")))
    theBug.UpdatedDateAndTime = _
           myReader.GetDateTime(myReader.GetOrdinal("UpdatedDateAndTime"))

    theBugList.Add(theBug)
  End While
  myReader.Close()
End Using
Return theBugList
```

This code is very similar to the code that retrieved a single bug from the database. The only difference here is that the bug itself is not returned, but that it is added to the `BugList` first, which is then returned at the end of the function.

As soon as the `BugList` is returned from the data access layer back to the business layer, the remainder of the code in the `GetBugList` method fires:

```
_theBugList = BugManagerDB.GetBugList(searchCriteria, _memberId)
```

```
  ' If there is more than 1 item in the list , sort it.
  If _theBugList.Count > 1 Then
    _theBugList.Sort(New BugComparer(sortExpression))
  End If
Return _theBugList
```

The `Sort` method of the generics `List` class expects a generic class that implements `IComparer`. The `BugComparer` class is such a class and implements `Compare`, the only method in the interface. This method should return an Integer indicating whether an object is less than, equal to, or greater than another object. The `Compare` method contains the following code:

```
Public Function Compare(ByVal a As Bug, _
           ByVal b As Bug) As Integer Implements IComparer(Of Bug).Compare
  Dim retVal As Integer = 0
  Select Case _sortColumn.ToLower()
    Case "id", ""
      retVal = a.Id.CompareTo(b.Id)
    Case "title"
      retVal = String.Compare(a.Title, b.Title, _
                StringComparison.InvariantCultureIgnoreCase)
    Case "feature"
      retVal = String.Compare(a.Feature.Name, b.Feature.Name, _
                StringComparison.InvariantCultureIgnoreCase)

    ' ... other properties are compared here

    Case "updateddateandtime"
      retVal = DateTime.Compare(a.CreatedDateAndTime, b.CreatedDateAndTime)
  End Select

  Dim _reverseInt As Integer = 1
  If (_reverse) Then
    _reverseInt = -1
  End If

  Return (retVal * _reverseInt)

End Function
```

The method is designed to accept two instances of a bug object, `Bug a` and `Bug b`, which are passed to this method. The private variable`_sortColumn` holds the name of the property that the bugs should be compared on. This takes place in the `Select Case` block where each of the comparable properties of a bug has its own `Case` block. Instead of trying to figure out which property is larger than the other with custom code, this code uses the `Compare` method of the underlying data types. Note that when `NameValue` objects are compared, the `Name` property is used and not the `Value`. The user is expecting the list to be sorted alphabetically on the name of the properties and not on the underlying value.

Finally, when all retrieving and sorting is done, the `BugList` is returned to the presentation layer where it is displayed in the `GridView`. Displaying of the `Bug` objects and paging through the list is all handled by the `GridView` and works similarly to other `GridView`s you have seen before. The only thing that might be different is the way that the `GridView` displays the information for the `NameValue` objects:

```
<asp:TemplateField HeaderText="Feature" SortExpression="Feature">
  <ItemTemplate>
    <asp:Label ID="Label1" runat="server" Text='<%# Eval("Feature.Name") %>' />
  </ItemTemplate>
  <ItemStyle Width="130px" />
</asp:TemplateField>
```

The `ItemTemplate` holds a label with its `Text` property bound to the `Name` property of the `Feature` item so the end user sees the friendly name and not just a number.

With the Reports page done, you have come full circle. Testers and developers can file new bugs in the system. Developers can then change the bugs in the Bug Base, marking them as Closed, Fixed, or Deferred, for example. Members of the Manager group can get detailed lists about bugs in the system on the criteria they specify.

This also concludes the detailed explanation of the pages that make up the Bug Base. The final section of "Code and Code Explanation" lists the other files that are used in the application and describes their purpose.

Other Files and Folders

You have seen many of the concepts used in these files in the previous chapters, so how the files work isn't explained in detail here. They come with extensive inline documentation where possible, so you're encouraged to open the files and see how they work.

- **GridView.skin:** This file, located in the BugBase skins folder (under App_Themes), defines the look and feel of the many `GridView` controls used throughout the site. Instead of defining their looks and behavior in each of the files, a simple skin file was created so you need to define the layout only once. If you want to change any of the colors, CssClasses, PageSize, and padding of the `GridView`, you should change it right here in the .skin file. The design was abstracted even one step further by not setting fonts and colors in the skin file directly. Instead, various styles, such as the HeaderStyle and AlternatingRowStyle, were defined and their CssClass was set to a class defined in the file Styles.css, discussed later.
- **Controls:** This folder contains a single user control named MemberDetails.ascx that displays information about the current member, and the application she has chosen to work with. This user control is added in the master page, so each page in the site is displaying its content.
- **Css:** To increase the maintainability of the site, almost all presentation details are put in separate CSS files. This allows you to quickly change the look and feel of the site by modifying a few properties in these files. The folder contains four files (outlined in the following table), each serving a distinct purpose:

Filename	Purpose
Core.css	Contains the behavior for standard HTML elements, such as images and links. It also defines the general layout of the site, such as the location of the menu, the page header, the breadcrumb, and the content section. Refer to the discussion of the master page to see where these classes are used.
Menu.css	Defines the look and feel for the main menu of the application.
PrintStyles.css	The styles in this file are applied when printing pages in the Bug Base. This allows you to hide screen elements that don't make sense on a printed sheet of paper, such as the main menu.
Styles.css	This CSS file contains all the custom classes used in the site. The selectors in this file change the look and feel of form controls, error messages, and data that is displayed in repeating controls.

- **Help:** This folder contains the Help index file, accessed by choosing Help⇨Overview from the main menu. This page provides help for the various tasks in the Bug Base. The About page displays general information about the Bug Base.
- **SiteMap.aspx:** Displays a hierarchical view of the site, using a `SiteMapDataSource` control that in turn uses the file Web.sitemap, located in the root of the site. You can open the SiteMap page by clicking the little Site Map icon on the main menu of the Bug Base.
- **Images:** This folder contains a few images that are used throughout the site, such as the Logo and the background image for the main menu.
- **JavaScripts:** This folder contains a single file called ClientScripts.js that holds various JavaScript functions used at the client.
- **Maintenance:** This folder allows you to make changes to the configuration of the Bug Base. You can add new applications and features; modify the items that appear in the drop-downs for Severity, Reproducibility, and so on; and manage Members. The following table lists each of the pages in the Maintenance folder:

Filename	Purpose
AddMember.aspx	Allows you to create a new Member. By default, this member will be put in the Tester role.
Applications.aspx	Allows you to create new and change existing applications.
BugProperties.aspx	Allows you to change the items for Severity, Reproducibility, and Frequency.
Default.aspx	This is the homepage for the Maintenance section and provides links to the other pages.
Features.aspx	Allows you to manage the features that belong to an application.
Members.aspx	Displays a list with the Members in the system and allows you to assign members to roles and applications.
Status.aspx	This page allows you to manage the Status items in the system.

With the discussion of the entire Bug Base application done, including the Management section and all the additional files in the site, it's time to find out how you can install the Bug Base so you can start using it.

Setting up the Bug Base

Setting up the Bug Base is a pretty straightforward process. You can choose between the installer that comes with this book or manually unzip the application's files to a folder of your choice. Using the installer is ideal when you have IIS running on your machine and want to use it for the Bug Base. If you plan on using the Bug Base with Visual Web Developer's web server, the manual deployment is a better choice.

The next two sections describe how to use to the installer and how to manually set up the application. For both methods it's assumed that the .NET Framework, which is an installation required for Visual Web Developer, has already been installed. It's also assumed that you have installed SQL Server 2005 Express edition with an instance name of SqlExpress. If you chose a different instance name, make sure you use that name in the set up of the Bug Base.

Using the Installer

On the CD-ROM that comes with this book or from the code download for this chapter that you can get from `www.wrox.com`, locate the folder Chapter 12 - Bug Base and then open the Installer folder. Inside that folder you'll find two files: setup.exe and BugBaseInstaller.msi. Double-click setup.exe to start the installation. Keep clicking Next until you get a confirmation dialog that the Bug Base has been installed. Then click Close to dismiss the installer.

On a default installation of Windows, the files that make up the web site are now available in the folder `C:\Inetpub\wwwroot\BugBase`.

Before you can browse to the Bug Base, there is one more change to make. By default, if you have earlier versions of the .NET Framework installed, new web sites created in IIS will run against that older version. To tell IIS to use ASP.NET 2.0 instead, you need to change the settings for the virtual folder BugBase so it runs against the .NET 2.0 Framework. Refer to Chapter 5 for detailed instructions about changing these settings.

The Bug Base is now set up to be run under IIS. However, before you can use it there may be a few others settings you need to configure before you can run the Bug Base application. Refer to the section "Browsing to the Bug Base" for the next steps.

Manual Installation

Another way to set up the Bug Base is by manually copying the file from the accompanying zip file to your local hard drive. To install manually, locate the folder Chapter 12 - Bug Base on the CD-ROM or from the code download and then open the Source folder. In that folder you'll find a zip file called Chapter 12 - Bug Base.zip. Extract the contents of the zip file to a location on your hard drive (for example, `C:\Projects`). You should end up with a folder similar to `C:\Projects\BugBase`. If you want to open the web site in Visual Web Developer, choose File➪Open Web Site and browse to the folder where you extracted the files.

Browsing to the Bug Base

If you used the installer, the Bug Base is now available at `http://localhost/BugBase`. If you chose the manual installation, you can open the web site in Visual Web Developer and then press F5 to open the site in your browser. The first time the site loads in your browser you may get a time-out error first. The Web.config file for the Bug Base instructs the ASP.NET run time to attach the database for the Bug Base automatically. This happens only the first time you run the application. Attaching the database takes some time, so you could get the time-out error. Whenever that happens, just refresh the browser window and the error will go away.

If your version of SQL Server Express has a different instance name than the default of `(local)\SqlExpress`, you'll need to modify the connection string in the Web.config file located in the root of the Bug Base folder. Search the file for `(local)\SqlExpress` and replace that with the name of your database server and instance name.

The final thing you need to do is make sure that the necessary users are available in the database. The application comes with the five users you have seen before, but you may want to add your own users. To add a user, follow these steps:

1. Start Visual Web Developer and choose File⇨Open Web Site.
2. Browse to the location where you installed the Bug Base. The default location is `C:\Inetpub\wwwroot\BugBase`. Click Open. Visual Web Developer opens the project at the specified location. You should see the files that make up the Bug Base listed in the Solution Explorer.
3. Choose Website⇨ASP.NET Configuration. A new browser window starts, showing you the Web Site Administration Tool.
4. Click the Security tab and then click the Create User link. Type in a new username, password, and e-mail address and assign this user to one or more roles.
5. Repeat step 4 for all the users you want to add. When you've added all the required users, you can close the Web Site Administration Tool.

Now that you know all about the Bug Base, head to this book's download page at `www.wrox.com` to learn about some extensions to the application.

Summary

This chapter covered a lot of ground in working with ASP.NET 2.0 and Visual Web Developer. The Bug Base application presented in this chapter is the most versatile and extensive application in this entire book. In its current state, it's ready to be used in a production environment so you and your team members can use it to keep track of the bugs that you find in the applications you built. The introduction of this chapter showed you how to use the Bug Base, including its role-based security features that allow you to make a distinction in functionality between users in the different roles.

In addition to building on the knowledge you gained in previous chapters, this chapter taught you how to do the following:

- Work with `ObjectDataSource` controls to connect your ASPX pages with the business layer. With these controls, you can create a flexible yet easy-to-maintain design based on a three-tier architecture.
- Use SQL Server caching with the `SqlCacheDependency` class and the ASP.NET 2.0 cache to cache data that doesn't change often. Using this caching mechanism greatly increases the performance of your application.
- Use the new Generics feature of the .NET 2.0 languages. With Generics, you can create reusable code that works on different types you can develop yourself. By passing around a strongly typed list of Bug instances from the business layer to the presentation layer instead of a weakly typed DataSet, you get design-time support in Visual Web Developer. You also get improved IntelliSense and type checking as additional benefits.
- Create classes that implement the IComparer interface so you can easily sort custom classes based on the rules you can define yourself.
- Build complex reporting pages with custom search criteria to allow users to get exactly the data from the system that they are looking for and present it in an easy-to-use report page.
- Build custom Management pages on top of the Membership and Role providers. ASP.NET comes with its own Web Site Administration Tool that allows you to manage users, roles, and other application settings. However, this tool does not provide access to all the features that the Membership and Role providers have. By building pages on top of these providers, you get the best of both worlds: pages that are very easy to build yet have all the advanced features that your application requires.

In addition to these coding techniques, you learned how to install and configure the Bug Base application so you can use it for your own bug tracking needs.

With the Bug Base application, you have also come to the end of this book. In the past twelve chapters you have seen many of the new features that ASP.NET 2.0 offers out of the box. Some of those features differ only marginally from the way that ASP.NET 1.x handled it. Others will radically change the way you design and build your applications. The best example of this is probably the inclusion of the Membership, Role, and Profile providers. In ASP.NET 1.x, implementing these kinds of features meant writing (and testing) a lot of code and a fair amount of database design. In ASP.NET 2.0, using these features can now be as simple as dragging a control on the design surface of the page.

With the applications that come on the companion CD-ROM, and the knowledge you gained from this book, you are ready to use these applications as-is, or reuse parts of them in new applications you are going to build yourself.

No matter how you use these applications, they'll give you a head start in any future project. Have fun on your ASP.NET 2.0 journey!

Index

SYMBOLS

A

B

E

F

Wiley Publishing, Inc.
End-User License Agreement

READ THIS. You should carefully read these terms and conditions before opening the software packet(s) included with this book "Book". This is a license agreement "Agreement" between you and Wiley Publishing, Inc. "WPI". By opening the accompanying software packet(s), you acknowledge that you have read and accept the following terms and conditions. If you do not agree and do not want to be bound by such terms and conditions, promptly return the Book and the unopened software packet(s) to the place you obtained them for a full refund.

1. **License Grant.** WPI grants to you (either an individual or entity) a nonexclusive license to use one copy of the enclosed software program(s) (collectively, the "Software") solely for your own personal or business purposes on a single computer (whether a standard computer or a workstation component of a multi-user network). The Software is in use on a computer when it is loaded into temporary memory (RAM) or installed into permanent memory (hard disk, CD-ROM, or other storage device). WPI reserves all rights not expressly granted herein.
2. **Ownership.** WPI is the owner of all right, title, and interest, including copyright, in and to the compilation of the Software recorded on the disk(s) or CD-ROM "Software Media". Copyright to the individual programs recorded on the Software Media is owned by the author or other authorized copyright owner of each program. Ownership of the Software and all proprietary rights relating thereto remain with WPI and its licensers.
3. **Restrictions on Use and Transfer.**
   - **(a)** You may only (i) make one copy of the Software for backup or archival purposes, or (ii) transfer the Software to a single hard disk, provided that you keep the original for backup or archival purposes. You may not (i) rent or lease the Software, (ii) copy or reproduce the Software through a LAN or other network system or through any computer subscriber system or bulletin-board system, or (iii) modify, adapt, or create derivative works based on the Software.
   - **(b)** You may not reverse engineer, decompile, or disassemble the Software. You may transfer the Software and user documentation on a permanent basis, provided that the transferee agrees to accept the terms and conditions of this Agreement and you retain no copies. If the Software is an update or has been updated, any transfer must include the most recent update and all prior versions.
4. **Restrictions on Use of Individual Programs.** You must follow the individual requirements and restrictions detailed for each individual program in the About the CD-ROM appendix of this Book. These limitations are also contained in the individual license agreements recorded on the Software Media. These limitations may include a requirement that after using the program for a specified period of time, the user must pay a registration fee or discontinue use. By opening the Software packet(s), you will be agreeing to abide by the licenses and restrictions for these individual programs that are detailed in the About the CD-ROM appendix and on the Software Media. None of the material on this Software Media or listed in this Book may ever be redistributed, in original or modified form, for commercial purposes.

5. **Limited Warranty.**

   (a) WPI warrants that the Software and Software Media are free from defects in materials and workmanship under normal use for a period of sixty (60) days from the date of purchase of this Book. If WPI receives notification within the warranty period of defects in materials or workmanship, WPI will replace the defective Software Media.

   (b) WPI AND THE AUTHOR(S) OF THE BOOK DISCLAIM ALL OTHER WARRANTIES, EXPRESS OR IMPLIED, INCLUDING WITHOUT LIMITATION IMPLIED WARRANTIES OF MERCHANTABILITY AND FITNESS FOR A PARTICULAR PURPOSE, WITH RESPECT TO THE SOFTWARE, THE PROGRAMS, THE SOURCE CODE CONTAINED THEREIN, AND/OR THE TECHNIQUES DESCRIBED IN THIS BOOK. WPI DOES NOT WARRANT THAT THE FUNCTIONS CONTAINED IN THE SOFTWARE WILL MEET YOUR REQUIREMENTS OR THAT THE OPERATION OF THE SOFTWARE WILL BE ERROR FREE.

   (c) This limited warranty gives you specific legal rights, and you may have other rights that vary from jurisdiction to jurisdiction.

6. **Remedies.**

   (a) WPI's entire liability and your exclusive remedy for defects in materials and workmanship shall be limited to replacement of the Software Media, which may be returned to WPI with a copy of your receipt at the following address: Software Media Fulfillment Department, Attn.: ASP.NET 2.0 Instant Results, Wiley Publishing, Inc., 10475 Crosspoint Blvd., Indianapolis, IN 46256, or call 1-800-762-2974. Please allow four to six weeks for delivery. This Limited Warranty is void if failure of the Software Media has resulted from accident, abuse, or misapplication. Any replacement Software Media will be warranted for the remainder of the original warranty period or thirty (30) days, whichever is longer.

   (b) In no event shall WPI or the author be liable for any damages whatsoever (including without limitation damages for loss of business profits, business interruption, loss of business information, or any other pecuniary loss) arising from the use of or inability to use the Book or the Software, even if WPI has been advised of the possibility of such damages.

   (c) Because some jurisdictions do not allow the exclusion or limitation of liability for consequential or incidental damages, the above limitation or exclusion may not apply to you.

7. **U.S. Government Restricted Rights.** Use, duplication, or disclosure of the Software for or on behalf of the United States of America, its agencies and/or instrumentalities "U.S. Government" is subject to restrictions as stated in paragraph (c)(1)(ii) of the Rights in Technical Data and Computer Software clause of DFARS 252.227-7013, or subparagraphs (c) (1) and (2) of the Commercial Computer Software - Restricted Rights clause at FAR 52.227-19, and in similar clauses in the NASA FAR supplement, as applicable.

8. **General.** This Agreement constitutes the entire understanding of the parties and revokes and supersedes all prior agreements, oral or written, between them and may not be modified or amended except in a writing signed by both parties hereto that specifically refers to this Agreement. This Agreement shall take precedence over any other documents that may be in conflict herewith. If any one or more provisions contained in this Agreement are held by any court or tribunal to be invalid, illegal, or otherwise unenforceable, each and every other provision shall remain in full force and effect.